MW01672425

Pride, training, esprit de corps, tough as nails screaming boot camp Drill Instructors who mold undisciplined young men into an elite fighting force to be reckoned with...all goes into the make-up of a U.S. Marine, also called Leatherneck, Jarhead, Gyrene and Uncle Sam's Misguided Children. All Marines—enlisted and officers--are first and foremost "03" infantrymen no matter what their designated military occupational specialty is. Fighting is the cornerstone of what the U.S. Marine Corps is all about. Marines are not burdened with civilian politics or society's waffling indecision of whether their commitment to war is right or wrong. Given a mission or objective, Marines have but one goal and that is to be the point of the spear and overcome by force with the weapons at their disposal, if it's required. "No better friend, no worst enemy" is their mantra.

*Book II* picks up where *Book I* left off with fighting in Vietnam. Author Michael Dan Kellum, who served in Vietnam in 1970 as an infantry Marine lieutenant, cites 529 Marines and 16 Navy Corpsmen in *Book II* in telling of their combat activities, 1965, '69-'70. This is the Vietnam War as seen by Pilots and their crewmen who flew combat, medevac and insertion/extraction missions as well as Grunts and their "Docs" who trudged through the rice paddies, sandy lowlands, jungles and mountains of Vietnam. The war tested the very fiber of each and every Marine who served a 6-month, 13-month or longer tour. The VC/NVA were a formidable enemy we reluctantly admired for their tenacity and discipline to continue fighting in the face of our overwhelming firepower. Like us, they policed the battlefield of their dead and wounded and collected their casualties' weapons for use against us another day. Marines and their Navy Corpsmen went toe-to-toe with the VC/NVA and acquitted themselves with the same fighting spirit as those who went before them in previous wars. Our enemy found out much to their demise, that Marines knew how to fight as well. *Book II* is about those magnificent Marine warriors in the air and ground-pounding Grunts and Recon. This is how we remember and honor them...by telling their stories. AARUGHA!

Book II

# American Heroes

# Grunts, Pilots & "Docs"

Leathernecks Find 'em, Fix 'em, Destroy 'em,
Vietnam Combat Stories, 1965, '69-'70

Michael Dan Kellum

Semper Fi,
Michael Dan Kellum

Navarro-Hill Publishing Group
2011

The opinions expressed in this manuscript are solely the opinions of the author and do not represent the opinions or thoughts of the publisher. The author has represented and warranted full ownership and/or legal right to publish all the materials in this book.

Disclaimer: "All views, opinions or stories cited in those books are solely the views, opinions or stories generated by the author or the Marines and Navy Corpsmen interviewed and in no way reflect the views, opinions or official stories generated by the United States Marine Corps."

Dorothy Fall has graciously given the author permission to use excerpts from her books and her husband's, Dr. Bernard B. Fall, books in *American Heroes: Grunts, Pilots & "Docs"* on a limited self-published basis. The author thanks Dorothy Fall and the late Dr. Fall for allowing him to reprint some of their insightful writings on the French Indochina and Vietnam Wars to better explain the conflicts.

*The Associated Press* granted the author permission to use the March 1965 combat photo of USMC Maj. Bill Leftwich Jr. that appears on the front cover of this book. The Leftwich family also provided their concurring permission. The author thanks both the *AP* and the Leftwich family for allowing his use of this dramatic image which photographically defines what a hero is and what these books are about.

Book II, American Heroes: Grunts, Pilots & "Docs"
Leathernecks Find 'em, Fix 'em, Destroy 'em, Vietnam Combat Stories, 1965, '69-'70

v2.0



FRONT COVER PHOTO: Maj. William G. "Bill" Leftwich Jr., Marine advisor to the Vietnamese Marine Brigade, stays in contact with overhead air cover calling in airstrikes on enemy troops after being shot in the face by the Viet Cong from upper lip to ear March 2, 1965 at Hoai An in Binh Dinh Province. Gen. William C. Westmoreland, Military Assistance Command, Vietnam, Commanding General, would call him "the best advisor in Vietnam" months later at Duc Co. For this action he would earn the Navy Cross. (Photo courtesy of *The Associated Press* and William G. Leftwich Jr. family; front cover design by Michael Dan Kellum and Vinnie Burdziuk)

BACK COVER: Unit insignias of many of the various air and ground outfits covered in Book II, are, bottom left, clockwise: 3/4, 1/7, HMM-262, 2/26, 2/5, 1/5, HMM-263, 1/1, 2/1, HMM-364, HML/A-167, 3/5, 1st Recon Battalion, HML/A-367, U.S. Navy Medical Corps, 1/9, VNMC, VMO-2, 1st Tank Battalion and HMM-163. Bottom photo: 1st Recon Battalion Marines held a Memorial Service March 26, 1970 for two of its MIA officers, 2ndLt. David Skibbe and Capt. LaVoy Don "Mac" McVey, at Camp Reasoner, RVN. (Photo appeared in the *SEA TIGER*, a publication of the Public Affairs Officer of III Marine Amphibious Force, RVN; permission to use unit insignias granted by Marine Corps Trademark Licensing Office; back cover design by Michael Dan Kellum and Vinnie Burdziuk)



Paperback ISBN: 978-0-9845132-2-2
Hardback ISBN: 978-0-9845132-3-9

Library of Congress Control Number: 2010940532

PRINTED IN THE UNITED STATES OF AMERICA

Navarro-Hill
Publishing Group

# Dedication

*Book II, American Heroes: Grunts, Pilots & "Docs"* is dedicated to the Marines, Navy Corpsmen and other U.S. military servicemen and women whose names appear on The Wall in Washington, D.C. but whose spirits and smiling faces will forever be frozen in time in all returning Vietnam veterans' memories. AARUGHA!

I would also like to single out in my dedication for *Book II* (all ranks listed are as they were when these gentlemen served in Vietnam): Lt.Col. William G. "Bill" Leftwich Jr.[+], Cpl. John F. Stockman[+], 2ndLt. David W. Skibbe[++], SSgt. Joseph E. "Joe" Strausbaugh, 2ndLt. Anthony E. "Tony" Kupka[+], 2ndLt. Phillip N. "Nick" Huth[+], 1stLt. Cleveland R. "Butch" Harvey[+], 2ndLt. John H. Lakin[+], 1stLt. John I. Lassitter[+], 2ndLt. William G. "Garry" Schanck Jr.[+], 2ndLt. Theodore R. "Vivi" Vivilacqua[+], 2ndLt. Albert D. "Al" Benson[+], 2ndLt. Albert O. "Al" Nelson Jr.[+], Capt. LaVoy D. "Mac" McVey[++], 2ndLt. Robert J. "Bob" Fawcett, Gy.Sgt. Terrence L. "Terry" Moore[w], SSgt. John F. Hare[w], 1stLt. L.K. "Les" Williams, 1stLt. Paul E. Wilson, Capt. Bill Woidyla, 1stLt. Jim Martin, 1stLt. James H. "Jim" Webb Jr.[w], 2ndLt. Gilford G. "Gil" Robinson[w], 1stLt. Michael O. "Mike" Fallon, Cpl. Edward A. "Ed" West[w], HM3 Frank P. "Doc" Doronzo[+], Lt.Col. Walter R. "Walt" Ledbetter Jr., PFC Raymond M. "Mike" Clausen Jr.[w], Lt.Col. William C. "Wild Bill" Drumright, Cpl. Larry M. Feldman[w], 2ndLt. Joseph A. "Joe" Silvoso[w], Sgt. Larry K. "Giff" Gifford[w], Dr. Bernard B. Fall[+], 1stLt. Thomas H. "Tom" Marino, Maj. John S. Grinalds, HM3 Thurman G. "Doc" Mullins and 1st Reconnaissance Battalion's Team Rush Act[+].

[+]Killed-in-Action
[++]Missing-in-Action, presumed dead
[w]Wounded-in-action

# Introduction

In *Book II, American Heroes: Grunts, Pilots & "Docs,"* I relate the stories of Marines and Navy Corpsmen in combat in Vietnam and, as in *Book I*, their uncommon heroism. The following personal narratives tell a unique history of the Vietnam War period. It was a time when idealistic young men served in the Marines in a war between two countries half the land mass of Texas on the other side of the earth to stop the spread of Communism.

*Book I* dealt with the training of Marine enlisted and officers leading up to Vietnam and the ensuing combat stories from my unique viewpoint of having been an enlisted man and commissioned as an officer through the Enlisted Commissioning Program. Many other Marines and Docs added their insights of being personally involved in fighting the Viet Cong and North Vietnamese as well. *Book II* goes to the heart of both books by relating the stories of Leathernecks and their medical personnel, in the air and on the ground, involved in the Vietnam War from the get-go. This is a book about the bleeding side of WAR.

A perfect example is the opening chapter which tells of a Marine mobile heliborne force codenamed Kingfisher consisting of men from Alpha Co., 1st Battalion, 1st Marine Regiment who are dropped into various landing zones by Sea Knights to cut off the escape of an enemy platoon. Two squads of 3rd Platoon, Alpha Co. Leathernecks chase the fleeing Viet Cong troops into an extensive minefield above Hill 55 either in or near the Da Nang Anti-Infiltration System barrier where they are pinned down by enemy fire and trip numerous devastating mines. The title of the book comes into play as *American Heroes: Grunts, Pilots & "Docs"* all work together on the ground and in the air to defend, treat and extract the battered squads with their dead and wounded from the battlefield...and annihilate the enemy.

I put my heart and soul into a chapter tracking down the stories of nine Marine officers from my officer training class at The Basic School (TBS) at Quantico, Virginia in Charlie- or 3-69 graduating on February 5, 1969, who were killed in Vietnam in 1969-70. Five of the nine officers killed-in-action, KIA, from my class of 238 second lieutenants came from my 3rd Platoon at TBS---Tony Kupka, John Lakin, Nick Huth, Butch Harvey and John Lassitter. Three other TBS platoons suffered the losses of Garry Schanck Jr., Al Nelson Jr., Al Benson and Ted Vivilacqua. Eight of the nine were either in grunt platoons of the 5th Marine Regiment or 1st Reconnaissance Battalion while the ninth KIA was a Cobra gunship pilot as part of Scarface HML-367. It truly was a labor of love to tell these brave young men's brief histories and how their loved ones and friends felt a void in their lives at their passing. I wanted to give depth and a life lived to the fullest and humanize their loss rather than leave their mark in passing in the Vietnam War as just a name chiseled on the Vietnam Veterans Memorial "The Wall" in Washington, D.C.

All the research and time I lavishly allotted over 20 years to tracking down each story allowed me to solve a mystery of a newfound friend I had made in Vietnam. He ended up missing-in-action, MIA, while on his very first 1st Recon patrol deep in enemy controlled territory. After a firefight with VC soldiers, a wounded 2ndLt. David Skibbe was accidentally left behind in the darkening shadows of the Que Son Mountains, southwest of Da Nang, South Vietnam, as night fell March 2, 1970. A cable line he was attached to and being hoisted up to a Sea Knight transport helicopter snapped sending him plummeting to the ground unseen by his Recon team. His commanding officer, Capt. LaVoy Don "Mac" McVey, would also be declared MIA as he met the same fate as Skibbe in trying to reach the ground by cable hoist to search for the missing lieutenant later that same night. I finally solved the nagging question as to whether the Illinois native survived his approximately 50-foot fall in a surprising revelation by a Viet Cong deputy commander 21 years after he went missing.

Visiting with 1st Recon Marines from Col. Bill Drumright's unit from 1970 at his Tennessee farm in 2003, I had the good fortune of meeting MSgt. John F. Hare. He told an intriguing war story about his good friend Gy.Sgt. Terry Moore whom he served three tours in Vietnam with beginning in 1961.

While on a daring rescue mission the night of September 1, 1970, Moore repelled down a rope hanging from a hovering Sea Knight helicopter without his Swedish-K submachine gun to be with three of his 1st Recon Marines who had repelled to the ground before him unbeknownst to them into the middle of a large North Vietnamese force, either a battalion or a regiment! Seems the Recon officer on board wanted to point out green tracer ground fire to Moore and accidentally dislodged the gunny's weapon from his shoulder sending it off into the darkness to the ground. Rather than take time to grab another automatic weapon from someone aboard the helicopter, he never wavered leaping on the rope to rappel to his waiting men below as the helicopter came under fire and had to abandon the four Marines to their fate and prevented the remainder of the team from joining them. Heroism like Moore's or any enlisted man is rarely awarded medals for such actions. Their reward is the respect of their men and an inner feeling of having done the right thing...to live and should it come to it...die with their Marines with honor. It is tough men like Moore...and Hare, that the Marine Corps turns out year after year and takes its mystical tradition and Semper Fidelis, Always Faithful, to heart.

For some strange reason through the years nothing beyond a few paragraphs in books here and there has been written about Lt.Col. Bill Leftwich Jr. of Germantown, Tennessee. He was my CO at 2nd Battalion, 1st Marine Regiment from May-September 1970, otherwise he might have escaped my notice as well had I not briefly served under him in Vietnam. At 2/1 he managed to earn a Silver Star with his heliborne strategy that wiped out a significant chunk of the Viet Cong leadership south of Da Nang August 4, 1970. Before that he served with the Vietnamese Marine Brigade in 1965 for 11 months as an advisor and earned a Navy Cross as well as a chest full of medals to go along with the Marine Corps' second highest medal.

In *Book I* Leftwich was praised as an outstanding officer who made some major changes at 2/1 as CO upon assuming command without going into his impressive background. In *Book II* exactly six chapters attempt to tell this Tennessean's story and his untimely death in a helicopter crash in 1970. Texas billionaire Ross Perot, who graduated with Leftwich from the U.S. Naval Academy in 1953, awards a *Leftwich Trophy* to the most outstanding Marine captain in combat each year (since 1979). The Commandant of the Marine Corps with Perot in attendance generally makes the presentation. Having personally observed Leftwich in Vietnam, I already had a high opinion of his leadership methods and was impressed he listened to subordinates down to the enlisted ranks. Actually, on several occasions the colonel implemented their suggestions. He had a leadership characteristic that, in my opinion, many great officers have that inspires men in combat and had he lived beyond 1970 would have seen him eventually reach the top position in the USMC, Commandant of the Marine Corps. He led from the front and it ended up getting him killed.

Col. "Wild Bill" Drumright was another tough combat Marine I was honored to interview before his death in December 2003. I write about Drumright's war exploits from taped conversations during a Memorial Weekend in 2003, over the phone prior to that and comments made in the *U.S. Marines in Vietnam, Vietnamization, 1970-71* publication. The 1st Recon colonel's gravelly voice at 75 was strong as he related war stories and no bullshit truisms about Marines in combat from the Korean and Vietnam Wars.

As was the case in *Book I*, I have included a special feature of this book that entails some of the maps we used in Vietnam with all the grid lines depicting specific points where Marine activities occurred (Dai Loc map of the famed Arizona Territory and Dodge City areas southwest of Da Nang, South Vietnam and Da Nang map located at the back of the book after "Perspectives on the Vietnam War--Part II").

The actual map coordinates of most the activities are shown by a footnote numeral followed by a letter of the alphabet and referred to in the Footnote section under the respective chapter. Not all the activities are depicted on the maps but a fair amount are referenced in that section, i.e., Hill 848.[1A] Map Reading 101 is simple. Basically the two numbers at the front end of a six-number map coordinate, i.e., (1. Dai Loc map, Sheet 6640 IV: A. AT907507), AT90 are the numbers marked on the map left to right. The fourth and fifth numbers, 50, are the numbers running up and down the map. Where AT90 and 50 intersect on the map will be the 1,000 meter grid square you're working with. Each of the numbers in the third and sixth slots equal 100 meters or 1/10th of a 1,000 meter grid line. AT907 would be 700 meters from the left corner of the intersecting map coordinates moving to the right on the 90 grid line. The 7 or sixth number in my example represents how many meters north or up you go, 700 meters on the 50 grid line, after moving to the right 700 meters, hence, AT907507. Those coordinates put you on the (3) of Phu Nhuan (3) which is roughly 100 meters west of a loose surface all-weather road.

As was the case in *Book I*, an additional visual dimension and stories relating to this book includes color combat maps, color photos, research background information, U.S. military, RVN and enemy units, a listing of individuals, excerpts from the book and biographical backgrounds of some of the interviewees on the website **www.MichaelDanKellum.com** which will bring these brave young warriors to the attention of a worldwide audience through the Internet.

"Perspectives on the Vietnam War" at the beginning and end of this book gives a forum to 21 individuals, mostly Marines and Navy Corpsmen, to say what's on their mind relating to their combat experiences fighting in Vietnam. Some of the quotes came from excerpts in interviews I had with these men looking over their shoulder in hindsight at the war while others were a direct request for a heartfelt comment on combat in retrospect almost four decades later. I tried to include a representative response from enlisted and officers, grunts/Recon and Navy Corpsmen, pilots and a crew chief, two ladies one of which lost her brother and the other her fiancé, an *Associated Press* war correspondent as well as a Pulitzer Prize winning *Associated Press* photographer.

For instance, Col. Drumright talks about how he managed the fear he felt when extracting his Recon Marines from a hot landing zone and praying to God for his Marines safe return. LCpl. Howard Ball, 2nd Battalion, 5th Marines

Forward Observer, says he was the luckiest Marine in Vietnam after his foot crashed through a small well-camouflaged hole almost tripping a wire attached to a large bomb. Sgt. J.D. Barber, HMM-263 Peachbush crew chief, explains his reason for joining the Marine Corps was to be a part of the world's greatest fighting force and more importantly, because he felt that he owed a debt to his country. Lt.Gen. Wallace C. "Chip" Gregson, a 1st Recon lieutenant in 1970, felt his Marines would never get the credit they deserve for serving in Vietnam.

Also, from the beginning I use military time in this book. For those unfamiliar with military time, we operate off a 24-hour time period. For instance, 0100 is 1 a.m.; 1000 is 10 a.m.; 1200 is high noon; 1300 is 1 p.m.; 1600 is 4 p.m.; 2000 is 8 p.m.; and 2400 is midnight. In a war zone a Marine needs to differentiate hours night from day when issuing orders calling for a specific time as he's on call 24/7.

My intentions initially were to write about my time in the Marine Corps, a core of 21 Marines and Navy Corpsmen as well as Dr. Bernard Fall, who wrote extensively about the French Indochina and Vietnam Wars, and was killed among Marines. As my research found other combat stories needing to be told, *Book I* grew into *Book II*. The final tally on individuals covered in *Book II* alone came to roughly 529 Marines (392 grunts/Recon/attachments and 137 Marine Air Wing pretty well evenly split between officers and enlisted men), 16 U.S. Navy Corpsmen called "Docs" in the bush, two U.S. Navy doctors in battalion-level medical facilities, 22 U.S. Army, 15 U.S. Navy, seven U.S. Air Force and one state department personnel. So an interesting little book centered around Marines and Docs in the Vietnam War grew into an historical epic with a cast of thousands...okay, make that roughly 592 men in this book alone.

In the 2-book series, I wanted the reader to feel what the Marines and Navy Corpsmen experienced during their tours in Vietnam through their personal recollections corroborated in many instances by official Marine Operations Journals, After Action Reports and USMC publications. I think the only way to understand what went on in a war, whether it be World War II, Korea, Vietnam, Gulf War I or II or the wars still being waged in Iraq and Afghanistan (as of 2011), is to read what the men have to say who have been and understand their sacrifices of life, trauma and loss of civilian innocence. War is not a place for the weak of heart or will. It hardens young men into old men and that 1,000-yard stare combat veterans lapse into occasionally is not a myth or an "act" but of horrors seen at war too terrible for them to recount.

Maybe *Books I* and *II, American Heroes: Grunts, Pilots & "Docs"* in some way will help those who have loved ones who have been to war understand them better. The other hope is that the men named in these books are remembered and honored for their service. We who shared combat with them as part of the Marine/Navy Corpsmen brotherhood will never forget our comrades-in-arms.

Semper Fi,
Michael Dan Kellum
PFC/1stLt., USMCR

# Perspectives on the Vietnam War—Part I

Col. William C. "Wild Bill" Drumright, USMC (Ret.), CO, 1st Recon, 2/26

"I wanted to be in the fight with my boys. I told Gen. (Edwin B.) Wheeler I'm going to be with them as long as you let me command that battalion (1st Recon Battalion). Every time an extract helicopter went out, I went out with it. (With my extract team,) I would pick up Big Fella's (6-foot-6 1stLt. John R. Hoff Jr., Echo Co., 1st Recon and '68 Boston College graduate) team and others. I enjoyed it. It was trigger time. My guys had trigger time...I wanted trigger time as well. It was the excitement (I liked to go for).

"A pastor asked me down here (in Tennessee) if I was ever afraid in combat. I said when I first jumped on an extract helicopter for an emergency extract, I was very much afraid. It went away as soon as the chopper wound up--*Whop, Whop, Whop*--and as soon as it did all my fear that had come from me went back to (my men) I was going to pick up. I was afraid for them. I was afraid I would fail. I was afraid they were going to get hurt. I was afraid what I wanted to happen wouldn't.

"I never said one prayer for myself. As soon as the helicopter was airborne and started west out of Camp Reasoner, I said a little prayer, 'God, give me the strength to bring them home.' That's all I ever said. I was never afraid. It was because of my boys. I was afraid for them that I forgot about dying because dying never entered my mind. I told the pastor that."[1] Col. Drumright served in Vietnam in 1969-70 as a 41-year-old lieutenant colonel who was CO of 2nd Battalion, 26th Marine Regiment then 1st Reconnaissance Battalion, 1st Marine Division; also served in the Korean War (Silver Star, Bronze Star, Purple Heart, Combat Action Ribbon, Korean Presidential Unit Citation).

Sgt. Larry K. "Giff" Gifford, team leader, 1st Recon

"We are all heroes. We showed up and did our jobs in Vietnam regardless of what it was...in the bush or in the Rear. We did what was asked of us (by our government). And that was what it was all about (the Recon Marine was shot three times by a Viet Cong point element on a patrol in the Que Son Mountains to end his tour on March 2, 1970---MDK)."[2] Sgt. Gifford served in Vietnam in 1969-70 as a 20-year-old Team Thin Man patrol leader, Bravo Co., 1st Reconnaissance Battalion, 1st Marine Division (Bronze Star, Purple Heart).

Richard Pyle, *AP* war correspondent/bureau chief

"You might not realize this, but the USMC had a special place in the hearts of the real media, those who actually covered combat operations in Vietnam. Marines had better leadership, fewer helicopters and less bullshit in dealing with the press. They wanted somebody to tell their story, and they'd do almost anything to get us into the field...sometimes against our better judgment!"[3] Richard Pyle was an *Associated Press* war correspondent in Vietnam from 1968-73; Saigon bureau chief, 1970-73; co-author with *AP*'s 1965 and 1972 Pulitzer Prize winning photographer Horst Faas, *Lost Over Laos*.

MCHC David L. "Doc" Snider, USN (Ret.), 1st Recon, 1st Medical Bn.

"Serving with 1st Recon was a heady experience. My teammates became my family and I loved each and every one. We were bad asses. Ran 20 Recon patrols, hid from Charlie, got chased a few times...cornered once when five of our 8-member team were WIA in the Dodge City area near the Arizona Territory (dangerous ground highly trafficked by the VC/NVA). After I left Recon, I realized I hadn't seen anything.

"I spent 4 months triage at 1st Medical Battalion Hospital in Da Nang. I was working when they brought in my best friend, (HM3 Walter Joseph) "Wally" Junger (21 years old from Tulsa, Oklahoma) killed April 15, 1969 (in-country less than a month while, ironically, on *Operation Oklahoma Hills*). On June 21, 1969 they brought in my former Recon team, fortunately, due to rotations only two of the KIAs were my brothers--LCpl. Frank Bosco, 19, of Providence, Rhode Island, and PFC Jim Hall, 20, of Vista, California. All but two of 8-man Team Grade Level were killed when their Sea Knight helicopter was shot down in Elephant Valley (six Recon Marines, the pilot and crew chief died in the ensuing fire and ordnance detonation).

"I saw every piece of human anatomy during my tour in Vietnam particularly remembering the 19 grunts KIAs on the medevac CH-46 stacked like cordwood taken off some hill. I witnessed some pretty horrible sights coming through 1st Med of KIA Marines and realized when I came home I *had* seen the worst of what Vietnam had to offer. If I had to do it over again, I would have stayed in the bush with those wonderful brothers. I trusted them."[4] Master Chief Hospital Corpsman, MCHC, Snider, U.S. Navy (Ret.), served in Vietnam 1968-69 as a 20-year-old HM3 Navy Corpsman with 1st Reconnaissance Battalion from July 1968-February 1969; HM2 Triage Supervisor at 1st Medical Battalion Hospital from February-June 1969, 1st Marine Division; 3 years active duty, 27 years Reserve, recalled for *Operation Desert Storm* (Purple Heart, Navy Commendation Medal with Valor, Navy

Achievement Medal with Valor, Combat Action Ribbon).

H. Ross Perot Sr., multi-billionaire businessman, former U.S. Navy officer

"(Lt.Col. Bill Leftwich Jr.) could've been CEO of any company in the country, a U.S. Senator, a Congressman or even President of the United States but he chose to go to Vietnam and fight and die for us...I talked to any number of Marine colonels and generals over him who said, 'Ross, that guy would've been Commandant of the Marine Corps'...He was just one of the finest men I've ever known and America should never forget people like that...great man, big loss. (Lt.Col. Leftwich 39, of Germantown, Tennessee, was CO of 1st Reconnaissance Battalion, died along with 14 other men in a Sea Knight helicopter crash November 18, 1970 in the Que Son Mountains of South Vietnam while attempting an emergency extract of 7-man Team Rush Act)."[5] Ross Perot, a 1953 U.S. Naval Academy honor graduate with Leftwich; sponsor of the annual *Leftwich Trophy* awarded to the most outstanding captain in the Marine Corps; Texas multi-billionaire businessman (Perot received the Medal for Distinguished Public Service by the Defense Department for focusing the world's attention on POWs treatment by North Vietnam during the Vietnam War).

MSgt. John F. Hare, USMC (Ret.), SOG, 1st, 3rd Recon

"They called us 'Super Grunts' in Recon. We had emotions but we tried to hold them in. In Recon there are men closer to me than my own son. While I was in Vietnam, they made sure I returned whether dead or alive. And that means a lot to me.

"I knew that Recon Marines like Larry Feldman, for instance, would have come to get my body if I died or got hurt or if I was lost. Never doubted it. Any man in that Recon Battalion, anytime we had a team in trouble we had to fight people to get them off the helicopter that was going out to rescue the team. Everybody wanted to go. The whole battalion would go but you could only send so many.

"There are Recon Marines who I've served with to this day who I know I can depend on in time of need."[6] MSgt. Hare served in Vietnam 1961-63, '66-'67, '69-'70. He was a 33-year-old staff sergeant who was part of Team Mission Impossible in 1969-70 tasked with going after teams in trouble or downed pilots in the bush in Vietnam, 1st Reconnaissance Battalion, 1st Marine Division; Studies and Observation Group; 3rd Reconnaissance Battalion; retired after 25 years in the Marine Corps (Navy Commendation Medal with Combat "V" and one gold star; Navy Achievement Medal with Combat "V" and one gold star,

Presidential Unit Citation w/gold star, Vietnamese Cross of Gallantry with gold star, Vietnamese Service Medal with 8 stars).

Cpl. Larry M. Feldman, Echo Co., S-3 radioman, 1st Recon

"Going out on a patrol as a 1st Recon team (with alternating call signs that included Flakey Snow Delta, Trailer Park, Vesper Bells, Grim Reaper, Clay Pipe, Donnybrook, Terrapin, Puppet Show, Thin Man or War Cloud to name a few) involved a set pattern that involved a frag order, S-2 (Intelligence section) brief to the team leader and possibly an overflight of the target area by the team leader and his radioman followed by a formal brief of the team the night before the insert. The day of the patrol we took all our gear to the LZ (helicopter landing zone) while the team leader and his assistant attended the pilot brief where the S-2 or S-3 (Operations section) officer explained the mission.

"At our team brief we decided who was to carry what equipment, set primary and secondary radio frequencies and established the chain of command as to who would take over the team in the event of incapacitating injuries affecting the officer, sergeant or corporal team leader on down to the lowest ranking PFCs. On the ground the point man led out followed by the team leader, primary radioman and Navy Corpsman while the secondary radioman and assistant team leader walked tailend Charlie bringing up the rear. That allowed the 6- to 7-man team to smoothly reverse direction should the point make contact or stumble across an overwhelming enemy force.

"As the helicopters fired up on LZ 401 at Camp Reasoner, everybody's stomach would begin to quiver in nervous anticipation as to what awaited us in the bush. We put cigarette filters in our ears as earplugs to save our hearing from the ear-piercing high whine of the Sea Knight's engines. At the insert LZ we removed the cigarette filters and stuffed them in our pockets. If we discarded them on the LZ, the enemy would know where we were put in and be able to track us down.

"En route to the insert site we'd sometimes sing some gallows humor songs to relieve tension like: 'You're going home in a body bag, do-da, do-da' or a Beatles' song about Maxwell's silver hammer coming down to make sure a guy was dead. Most of the time the Sea Knight's crew looked at us like we were crazy.

"When we got over the insertion point and the helicopter began spiraling down, you could see everybody's eyes get as big as saucers. No matter if you were a Navy Cross winner or first time newbie in the bush, mouths got dry, nostrils flared and everybody tried to hide the fear they were experiencing to concentrate on the mission. The bottom line was that we were confident each team member would do their job when the time came. The crew chief would give us a thumbs up that we were approaching the insert LZ. The team leader would yell, 'STAND UP! LOCK AND LOAD!'

"The helicopter flared for landing and we could smell the jungle and feel the oppressive heat coming off it. All of us were generally wondering if we were going to beat the odds again...or not. Is the LZ going to be hot (occupied by enemy troops firing us up)? The hydraulic motor kicked in and the helicopter's back ramp began to lower as the ground rushed up towards us. You felt as if your asshole was coming through your throat.

"The team leader and primary radioman would run down the ramp first, followed by the rest of the team and set up in a perimeter around the helicopter. The chopper lifted off leaving us to patrol dangerous ground. We pull the plugs from our ears and began humping out of the LZ for a half-hour and corkscrew (take off in one direction and loop around to see if anyone was following us). Satisfied nobody was onto us, we would head off at a pace they couldn't possibly keep up with.

"Being the primary radio operator on a Marine Recon team in contact gave me an unreal feeling of power with my handset. I had the Marines, Air Force and Navy at my fingertips that would give me anything I asked for in the way of ordnance. When they screwed with one of our Recon teams, they didn't live to tell about it. We killed a mess of them and we all lived to talk about it. WE WON.

"We requested an emergency extraction while in contact with the enemy on Charlie Ridge southwest of Da Nang on one occasion and our CO War Cloud 6, Lt.Col. Drumright came back with this admonition in a radio transmission, 'Flakey Snow Delta, this is War Cloud 6. You spread some hate and discontent in that area then I'll give you an extract.' I think the teams in 1st Recon Battalion lived up to our battalion's logo and motto, skull and crossed bones with the words, 'Swift, Silent, Deadly' underscoring it."[7] Cpl. Feldman served in Vietnam 1969-70 as a 20-year-old radioman with Echo Co. then S-3 (Operations section), 1st Reconnaissance Battalion, 1st Marine Division; testified before the U.S. Senate Select Committee on POWs/MIAs in Vietnam in 1990 and 1991 (2 Purple Hearts).

Capt. John Patrick "Pat" Kenny, HMM-364 pilot

"One of the reasons I became a Marine aviator versus Navy or Air Force, was the mission of Marine aviation. We existed for one thing and one thing only...to support the Marine Ground Unit. I am proud to this day that I was part of Marine aviation in Vietnam and especially a HMM-364 Purple Fox (Sea

Knight helicopter pilot). I love tradition and in 2008 we saw the CH-46 Sea Knight still working in Iraq and Afghanistan and other places in the world. The Purple Foxes are alive and well in theater in Iraq and still supporting the Marine Ground Unit. Amen."[8] Capt. Kenny served in Vietnam 1970-71 as a 26-year-old first lieutenant HMM-364 Purple Fox pilot, Marine Air Group-16, 1st Marine Air Wing (29 Air Medals).

LCDR. John H. "Doc" Erceg, Navy Corpsman, USN (Ret.), Hotel, 2/1

"I was one of many Hospital Corpsmen who was fortunate to receive extensive training with the Marines at Camp Pendleton (18 months in a line company) before deployment to Vietnam. This led to an easy transition to the grunts. My unit, Hotel 2/1's radio call sign for Corpsman was 'mother.' Radio traffic for the senior mother, 3rd Platoon mother, etc. was common. This call sign was an example of the relationship between the 'Docs' and their Marines. The Docs felt a special relationship to care for the Marines from Band-Aids to battle dressings. The Docs' presence was always welcomed. The most pressing need was to ensure a Doc was with every patrol. The thought of immediate medical response by the Doc and our ability to get helicopter medevacs greatly helped morale. There was an underlying respect between professionals for each other expressed by the Marines when a Corpsman was called 'Doc.'"[9] LCDR. Erceg served in Vietnam 1969-70 as a 22-year-old HM2 Navy Corpsman with Hotel Co., 2nd Battalion, 1st Marine Regiment, 1st Marine Division.

Lt.Col. G.G. "Gil" Robinson, USMC (Ret.), G-3, 1stMarDiv; S-2, 2/1

"I had the privilege to serve with some extraordinary people in Vietnam. For instance, Sgt. Rod Rodriguez, Scout Platoon sergeant and team leader of Spooky Trip, and Sgt. Tom Burke, team leader of Woodstock, worked for me in the S-2 Intelligence section at 2/1 and were both seriously injured tripping boobytraps in October and December 1970. Rodriguez would actually apologize for losing his foot to a toepopper boobytrap (a boobytrap containing a small amount of C-4 plastique explosive or a shotgun shell designed to blow a foot off) and leaving us. This is what they each had to say in letters written to me after they were medevacked:"

*'October 21, 1970. Hi LT., greetings to all my buddies back there...My leg still hurts, but now I'm sure I won't lose it. All I lost was my foot. I'm now in Guam, but I was told I would probably leave for the states in about six days...I got here okay and I haven't had any problems at all. I also had no problems leaving Nam. Thanks to all of you for helping me out.*

*'Sir, I'm so sorry I let you guys down the way I did. I never expected to*

*trip a boobytrap at the time that I did. I guess I just couldn't help it. I'm glad nobody else was hurt. All the VC can rest easy now. They probably know that I will never return to Vietnam. Tell the guys to give the VC/NVA Hell for me...All of you take care of yourselves. Rod Rodriguez.'*

"And from Sgt. Tom Burke:" *'December 1970. Dear Sir, Hi, how's things at good ol' 2/1 S-2? I'm pretty good now. I was hurting pretty badly a little while ago. I got hit in both legs, my back (very superficial) and my right arm. I lost the use of my right leg and I have to wear a brace for the rest of my life, so they say but I hope to work out and get the muscles back in shape. I don't know whether Doc Baker knows it or not but he saved me from bleeding to death and Rienow (the radioman from Louisiana) was real fast with that medevac. I really appreciate what the guys did for me.*

*'By the way, I'm home now and I'll be getting out in February. I'd just like to say Sir that it was real great having you as a CO and that as I'm sure all the guys do, have the greatest respect for you. Take care Sir and I pray that no one else has the same fate as me. The place isn't worth the pain. Sincerely, Sgt. Tom Burke. Merry Christmas?'*

"I held onto those letters the entire time I was in the Marine Corps and showed them to my Marines when they thought the going was tough for them and to illustrate the true meaning of Semper Fi (Always Faithful).

"I requested a bush battalion after working in the G-3 (Operations) at 1st Marine Division in Da Nang from March 30 to the end of July 1970. Upon arriving at 2/1, I had a talk with the battalion commander, Lt.Col. Bill Leftwich. I knew I didn't want to be 'the black officer' at 2/1. I wanted to be 'a Marine officer.' The one thing he got over to me was that I was going to be treated the same as any officer in the battalion. I asked the CO how I could make a good officer in the battalion. He gave me a copy of the first volume of *Lee's Lieutenants* by Douglas Southall Freeman to read while I was attending the one week Mine and Boobytrap School. Later he asked me what I had learned from the book and I told him that Lee had maximized the officers' strengths under him and minimized their weaknesses to get the best out of his people. He learned to deal with different personalities in different ways. Leftwich said that was exactly right.

"Like Lee, Leftwich was the quiet leader. For instance, when Confederate cavalry Gen. Jeb Stuart apologized to Lee after Gettysburg for failing to be his eyes and ears to give him intell on the Northern Army, Lee said there was no time for apologies (that was something in the past and they had to move on). I served 26 years in the Marine Corps. I had the lieutenants under me read from the first volume of *Lee's Lieutenants* so they would know what leadership was all about. And that came from the genius of Leftwich.

"I remember sitting in the 2/1 Command Operations Center bunker as the S-3 Operations chief Maj. John Grinalds (a 1959 U.S. Military Academy honor graduate and Rhodes Scholar) and Lt.Col. Leftwich (a 1953 U.S. Naval Academy honor graduate and Spring '53 Brigade Commander), pondered, 'Where did we go wrong in the Vietnam War?' They agreed that Lt.Gen. Victor H. Krulak got it right pushing the Combined Action Platoons to win the hearts and minds of the people and going after the VC leadership rather than the search and destroy missions we were running (that alienated the peasants).

"Leftwich gave me some sage advice as to how to succeed in my assigned job wherever the Marine Corps posted me. Here I was a second lieutenant and I'll never forget what he told me, 'Do your job better than the reporting senior officer ever thought you were capable of doing it and you'll always succeed.' That has stuck with me and been my motto."[10] Lt.Col. Robinson was in Vietnam 1970-71 as a 21-year-old second lieutenant briefer and liaison with the Vietnamese forces in the G-3 at 1st Marine Division then S-2 officer at 2nd Battalion, 1st Marine Regiment, 1st Marine Division (Bronze Star with Valor, Vietnamese Cross of Gallantry, Purple Heart, Combat Action Ribbon).

# Chapter 1

**Marines from 3rd Platoon, Alpha Co., 1st Battalion, 1st Marine Regiment were drawn into a minefield pursuing NVA troops January 31, 1970 south of Da Nang, South Vietnam. Exploding mines and enemy fire resulted in 12 WIAs and 3 KIAs. Marines and a Navy Corpsman initially unhurt tended to the wounded and dying, returned the enemy's fire and performed numerous acts of heroism this day. PFC Mike Clausen Jr., an HMM-263 Peachbush Sea Knight crew chief, entered the minefield from the safety of his helicopter to save many of them while his pilot, Lt.Col. Walt Ledbetter Jr., maneuvered their aircraft around the killing field picking up the dead and injured Marines/Navy Corpsman. What happened next may be viewed by some as a waste of humanity. It would be recognized by others as representative of a Marine's commitment to his fellow Marines and would answer two questions: How many Marines does it take to save a Marine? As many as it takes. How many times do they try? As many as it takes.[1]**

**LCpl. Edward A. "Ed" West, TACP radioman with Alpha 3, 1/1**
***"Gopher Broke: The Story of 'Blood, Sweat & Tears' And the Marines of 3rd Platoon, Alpha Co., 1/1"***

## Grunts, Pilots & "Docs"
## Kingfisher: Find 'em, Fix 'em, Kill 'em

During the Vietnam War, the 1st Marine Division conducted a new system of heliborne combat patrols codenamed Kingfisher beginning December 26, 1969 which supplemented the usual ground patrols and ambushes. In January and February Marines from the 1st and 26th Marine Regiments participated in the operations. The Marines had been experimenting with the quick-reaction heliborne assaults since 1965.[2]

"This is an offensive weapon that goes out and hunts them...They actually invite trouble," said Col. Herbert L. Wilkerson, the G-3 (Operations) III Marine Amphibious Force deputy chief of staff.[3]

"In my job there were always people eagerly waiting for me. They waited hidden, heavily armed and ready to kill," noted retired Col. Walter R. "Walt" Ledbetter Jr., 40 in 1970 from Dallas, Texas. He was a lieutenant colonel serving as the pilot flight leader and CO of HMM-263 Peachbush, whose Sea Knight transport helicopters carried the Marines into battle. "Like every

**Lt.Col. Walt Ledbetter Jr. (Photo courtesy of Walt Ledbetter)**

other day of the month, I got up about 0400 in the morning, dressed, tried to hold down my breakfast and act calm in front of the other pilots.

"For January and the next month, my HMM-263 Peachbush squadron had been assigned a mission codenamed Kingfisher. We worked with the 1st Marine Regiment as an airborne roving assault force against the NVA (North Vietnamese Army) forces. The air portion of the force consisted of a lead Huey (HML-167 Comprise), my three assault Sea Knights (HMM-263 Peachbush), four Cobra gunships (HML-367 Scarface) and an OV-10 (Bronco) observation aircraft (VMO-2 Hostage). The ground element (for many of the operations) was 1stLt. William R. Purdy's Alpha Co., 1st Battalion, 1st Marine Regiment (Alpha 1/1)." (Purdy was in my officers' Basic School, TBS, company graduation class, February 5, 1969, Charlie- or 3-69, at Quantico, Virginia---MDK).

From January 2 until mid-February, 1970 Alpha Co., 1/1 ran 13 Kingfisher packages while Delta Co., 1/1 was involved in five. The helicopters would fly out of Marble Mountain Air Facility in Da Nang before dawn occasionally with the initial ground assault force aboard and sometimes the Sea Knight transports would pick a platoon up at Hill 55 (Nui Dat Son),[4A] which was a large joint U.S. Army, U.S. Marine and ARVN base southwest of Da Nang about 13 clicks (kilometers). The Huey would scout out a designated area to look for anything out of the ordinary or people who should not be there.

Lt.Col. Kermit W. "Andy" Andrus, Marine Air Group-16 S-3 (Operations officer), set up the Kingfisher operations. "When we actually saw enemy troops, I would call Walt who was airborne with a platoon on board with two reserve platoons waiting to be called. I set up every Kingfisher operation. No briefings on the operations were needed. We sort of operated on not very good intelligence sent in from that huge free fire zone. What it boiled down to was that I went hunting for gooners. When I saw enemy troops, I would guide Walt and his wingman into where I wanted him to land by placing a smoke exactly where I thought best. Many of the landings incurred a firefight."

"My flight (of three helicopters) would follow 2 or 3 miles behind carrying a reinforced platoon. We flew low down on the deck to limit the enemy's observation. When something unusual was spotted, the Huey would call on the radio and tell me what had been sighted and we would speed up coming toward him. After he marked the objective area with a smoke grenade, we would land right on top of whatever was there. Every landing was a shit sandwich," recalled Col. Ledbetter.

Lt.Col. Andrus noted that the Cobras would shoot up the LZs and they would never let the troops chase the enemy troops very far, but would pick them up and move them in front of the Viet Cong/NVA soldiers therefore not running into hastily set boobytraps. Or they would drop a reserve platoon right on top of them. "The troops loved it. We never lost a Marine that way. Word had it that the troops would pay somebody to take their place being in the first platoon (where all the action was)."

Alpha Co., 1/1 ran its first Kingfisher mission January 2, 1970. Unfortunately, the lead Huey mistook a large green field for what it really was…a rice paddy with water up to waist deep. A second landing that day would yield no enemy but lessons were being learned about the heliborne operation.[5]

On January 6 Alpha Co. CO Lt. Purdy's 2nd Platoon was dropped on top of a Viet Cong company having breakfast. His Marines killed two VC coming off the Sea Knight in a running firefight.

"We landed directly on top of people and…they were running right beside the windows of the choppers, and we got a couple of kills right out of the choppers. We were almost within distance to bayonet them as they were running along the windows of the choppers," enthused 2ndLt. Jon C. Swenson, Alpha Co.'s 2nd Platoon (Alpha 2) commander, in a taped interview with the 1st Marine Division Historical Team.[6]

In that same action, Ledbetter's aircraft sustained hydraulic system damage from a hail of small arms fire (AK-47 rifles) from the sizeable group of departing VC. He made an emergency landing next to a hut.

"Six enemy soldiers came out of that hut firing AK-47 rifles and throwing grenades. (My aircraft took) 57 hits...before my gunner took them out with his .50 caliber machine gun. I was able to isolate the remaining hydraulic fluid into the control system and air taxied back to Marble Mountain Air Facility to get another aircraft. A Marine Air Wing staff lieutenant colonel was my copilot and he told me he was sorry but that he couldn't go back out with me because he had very important work at headquarters he had just remembered he had to get back to. I grabbed a lieutenant walking down the flight line as a replacement copilot," said Col. Ledbetter.

For the day, between 0730 and 0855, Alpha Co. grunts and Cobra gunships accounted for 15 VC dead. This was the goal of the Kingfisher program---hit quick from above and put Marines on the deck before the enemy had a chance to escape and annihilate him.[7]

At 0810 Friday, January 16, Alpha 2 was again deployed by Sea Knights near Tuy La (2)[8A] northwest of the Song (River) Thu Bon approximately 9 clicks south of their home base on Hill 55. The Kingfisher platoon was inserted amidst a heavy volume of automatic weapons fire from approximately six enemy troops in a tree line. The Marines answered with M-60 machine gun fire, M-79 grenade launcher and rifle fire silencing the enemy fire.

2nd Platoon assaulted the tree line killing seven enemy and taking two POWs while capturing numerous weapons, mines, ammo, medical bags and located a brick reinforced bunker. The platoon's luck held this day as they again escaped without sustaining any injuries, according to the 1/1 Spot Report. Alpha Co.'s casualty figures would jump just 15 days later.

**Information Oversight on Minefield Locations**

In January, 1970 there was an information oversight on the part of 1st Marine Division and the Marine Air Wing to assure its pilots and ground troops knew where "friendly" minefields were as part of the partially constructed Da Nang Anti-Infiltration System barrier that surrounded the Da Nang Vital Area. (Before going to the bush in March 1970 at 2nd Battalion, 1st Marines, I copied down underneath my laminated Dai Loc/Hoi An maps where all the notable land features were as well as the location of two "friendly" minefields that were part of the incomplete barrier around Da Nang. 1/26 followed by 3/26 oversaw security for the construction of the barrier in 1969 that began in June 1968. 1/1 then 2/1 would inherit the minefield in their Tactical Area of Responsibility's southern boundary upon the 26th Marines departure from Vietnam in March 1970. The minefield in question in this story was 1800 meters north of Hill 55 running 100-200 meters wide west to east from the Song Yen and 3 clicks long to roughly 200 meters short of what appears to be the Song Bau Xau. (See map on page 11). No other maps or Marines could confirm what I had marked on my old bush map but I did get a "looks about right" as to where the ARVN/American minefield was from 2/1's former S-2, 2ndLt. Gilford G. "Gil" Robinson---MDK).

"I flew over the remnants of the barrier a couple of times (around August 1970), but never operated close to it on the ground so (I don't have an exact location of the minefield) for you. I just recollect that when I saw it from the air, there were numerous paths through it and the wire barrier on either side seemed to be in disrepair. Probably all it ever did was provide a source of mines and explosives that the VC could use against us," noted retired Col. Robert J. "Bob" Fawcett, a lieutenant in 1970 and Echo 1, 2/1 platoon commander. (Fawcett would lose eight Marines to numerous boobytraps--toepoppers and a fragmentation grenade...a dud bouncing betty mine scared the bejesus out of his men--in the An Trach (2) and An Trach (3) as well as An Trach (1) areas August 5-21, 1970 in virtually the same locations in some instances as Alpha Co., 1/1 sustained devastating casualties January 31, 1970 as recorded in this chapter. He did not consider those boobytraps as being near the Da Nang Barrier minefield. See *Book I*, Epilogue---MDK).

"Apparently, G-2 and S-2 (1st Marine Division or MAG-16 S-2) did not deem it necessary to pass this data (exactly where 'friendly' minefields were located around Da Nang) down to the individual helicopter squadrons," said former Capt. Walter R. "Walt" or "Worm" Wise, HMM-364 Purple Fox pilot. "On most of our missions, we were only briefed on the day of the mission and we were never given a whole lot of data. This included the CCN missions where we were flying individuals dressed in NVA-style black pajamas, across the border into Cambodia and Laos. The NVA and VC always had better intell than we did."

### ***Blood, Sweat & Tears*, January 31, 1970**

Ledbetter was matched with a crew headed by crew chief, PFC Raymond Michael "Mike" Clausen Jr., 22, of Hammond, Louisiana on Saturday, January 31, 1970. Clausen joined the Marines in May 1966 after graduating from Hammond High School and 6 months at Southeastern Louisiana University in Hammond.

"Mike was a great combat Marine, but he could not stay out of trouble on the ground. He was still a PFC after nearly 3 years serving in Vietnam," said the colonel. Other crew members on this history-making mission were copilot, 1stLt. Paul D. Parker II of Arlington, Virginia; gunner, Cpl. Steve M. Marinkonic; and moonlighting gunner, Sgt.Maj. Morton S. Landy. Clausen would prove just how "great" a combat Marine he really was January 31st, 1970 despite his failure to attain and maintain higher enlisted rank.

"PFC Clausen had come to me a month before and had asked if he could name his aircraft and paint the name on the side of the helicopter. I told him okay as long as he didn't paint a big target on the side of the aircraft. He named it after his favorite rock band, *Blood, Sweat & Tears*," said Ledbetter. The Sea Knight, better known as the "Guardian Angel" of injured Marines, that Clausen named would live up to its moniker as would the symbol painted on the CH-46's tail representing the squadron: a little gopher with its tail twirling like a rotor with the motto "Gopher Broke" written there as well.

Clausen, who was on his third tour in Vietnam with over 1,900 combat missions, was tardy in arriving at *Blood, Sweat & Tears* for the day's operation and was chewed out by Sgt.Maj. Landy. Ledbetter noted Clausen's stripes should've been put on with Velcro and that he definitely marched to the beat of his own drum. Cpl. Doug Woods, USMC Combat Correspondent/ photographer, agreed by noting, "I flew medevac and Recon insert/extract missions with Clausen and was not aware of what he'd done (January 31). He was an excellent crew chief, but wasn't your classic Marine. He danced to his own drummer...literally. Flying back to MMAF, he would tune-in Armed Forces Vietnam-Da Nang radio and dance in the 46. He made rank and then was always busted. I've always thought his exploits would make a great movie."

At 0635 Saturday the Kingfisher operation kicked off involving Swenson's reinforced 2nd Platoon, Alpha Co. with its CO, 1stLt. Purdy aboard the Command and Control, C&C, Huey piloted by Maj. Dan Sharr, 36, of Ashland, Ohio. The mission started off like any other day in search of the enemy. Nothing hinted at what a tragic turn of events the day's fortunes would hold for Purdy's Marines as they lifted off from the Marble Mountain Air Facility in Da Nang. Maj. Sharr would have as his copilot Lt.Col. Andrus; crew chief Howard P. "Paul" Lineberger of Herndon, Virginia; and the doorgunner was Earl T. "Tom" Sines of Clifton, Virginia.

Flying 100 feet off the deck, the Huey crew's first contact was east of the Song Vinh Dien near Tu Cau (3).[8B] They directed a reactionary company to check out a suspicious gathering of about 30 people and discovered only women and children at the site and resumed their aerial patrol.

"We had searched the area and hadn't found one gooner. We were actually on the way back home and were passing over Hill 55 when we got word that a U.S. Army Loach (Hughes OH-6A light helicopter) working with Marine artillery had taken fire from three NVA. We went there and there were about 20 or 30 NVA so we had the first platoon set in and routed them. A second platoon was brought in and was set in ahead of them and it all worked as advertised," recalled Andrus. Sharr's After Action Report, AAR, shows the initial contact in the Le Son (4) area near the Song Yen 400 meters north of the Da Nang Barrier.

The Da Nang Anti-Infiltration System, also called Da Nang Barrier, surrounds the city and contains heat sensors, motion detectors...and mines. The Loach spotted 3 NVA troops altogether and took fire from them.[8C] The Huey investigated the sighting and took fire as well. Marine Cobra AH-1G gunships from the Scarface squadron worked the area over flushing 20-30 NVA troops. The reinforced reactionary platoon was alerted aboard the three Sea Knights following in trace and were dropped all around the enemy troops to prevent their disappearing into the surrounding countryside, tunnels or populated villes.

Ledbetter offloaded 17 of Lt. Swenson's men from 2nd Platoon over 700 meters northeast of the original sighting in a open area 300 meters west of

An Trach (2) in the middle of some rice paddies and 700 meters east of the Song Yen to block the NVA force's escape in that direction into the nearby villes.[8D] Alpha 2 Marines encountered a sizeable enemy force trying to break out of the aerial cordon. The other pilots, Lt.s Carroll L. Wright with copilot Peter A. Maznrak dropped off 16 men at the same location and Lt.s Robert W. Watkins of California, Maryland with copilot Thomas E. Heifner of Panama City, Florida dropped 19 men roughly a click northeast of Ledbetter and Wright's inserts.[8E]

The three HMM-263 Peachbush Sea Knights were directed to ferry Marines from the 3rd Platoon followed by the 1st Platoon of Alpha Co. into the fray from Hill 55, which was only 4 clicks to the south. The transport helicopters set them down in blocking positions to keep the NVA troops bottled up. The Marines and Navy Corpsmen of Alpha Co., 1/1 were about to step off the aircrafts' ramps into their own private Hell.

**LCpl. Edward A. "Ed" West's Firsthand Account**

"As a survivor of that mission, it is my responsibility to share the unbelievable courage and bravery I witnessed that day. I was surrounded by heroes,"[9] recalled LCpl. Ed West, an 18-year-old radioman for the Tactical Air Control Party (TACP) with only 45 days in-country. He accompanied 1stLt. Bruce Cruickshank, a 24-year-old A-4 Skyhawk pilot calling in air support for Alpha Co., 1/1. (Most of the narrative of the battle from the ground perspective comes from Ed West's "*Gopher Broke: A Tribute to the Crew of 'Blood, Sweat & Tears' and the Marines of 3rd Platoon, Alpha Company, 1st Battalion, 1st Marine Regiment, 1st Marine Division*."[10] He has graciously allowed me to use his research and personal observations contained in this article, in part, to tell of the selfless acts of heroism performed by all those involved in the battle January 31, 1970---MDK).

LCpl. West (whose call sign was Delivery Boy 1-4) and Lt. Cruickshank received a heads up alert at the Hill 55 command bunker and ran down to the lower landing zone to accompany 2ndLt. Joseph A. "Joe" Silvoso's 3rd Platoon, Alpha Co. (Alpha 3), 1/1 on yet another Kingfisher mission. So far the Kingfisher operations had been highly successful with the Marines killing or capturing the VC/NVA in the targeted areas. This day would be a bad one for two squads of 3rd Platoon. As LCpl. West points out, "Most of them would never see Hill 55 again."[11]

3rd and 1st Platoons helilifted into the fight in short order to serve as a blocking force to cut off the enemy's retreat. The idea was to decimate the NVA between the three Alpha Co. platoons with support from the overhead gunships and Sea Knight gunners. Lt. Cruickshank and LCpl. West were on the ground to orchestrate the air support in the killing field.

West indicated this was his first combat mission. As he looked around at the committed faces of the 14 Marines and their Navy Corpsman (a squad) boarding the Sea Knight on Hill 55, he felt he was in the presence of seasoned warriors. He realized that many of them were his own age. The first thought that crossed his mind was to not look scared.[12]

"Jon Swenson and I graduated out of the same platoon at The Basic School at Quantico, India-69. We were roommates," said Lt. Silvoso, 23 in 1970 from Columbia, Missouri and a 1968 graduate of the University of Missouri in Columbia. "We had been in-country since around October while the 1st Platoon commander was a new guy (2ndLt. Raymond W. "Ray" Tripp, who would later change his last name back to his birth name, Tripicchio). I had the headset on during our flight so the colonel could let me know what was going on on the ground and the terrain we were going into...like the river was on the other side of some trees to the west."

"We had to bring the third Alpha Co. platoon from Hill 55 as well due to the heavy fighting encountered by the first two platoons already on the ground," said Col. Ledbetter.

The colonel noted that all their platoon inserts were into heavy fire. He got his first call for an emergency medevac after dropping off the last Alpha Co. platoon. He had his wingman orbit the battlefield while he picked his first wounded Marine up just north of a drainage ditch (actually the Song Yen Ne) near a trail about 500 meters east of the river.[13A] He flew him back to Charlie Med in Da Nang.

Silvoso didn't recall that many rounds directed at them upon landing at their LZ. The gunner in the Sea Knight hosed down the nearby tree line. Only two squads were set in at their insertion point which was exactly where 2nd Platoon was dropped in. The third squad of Alpha 3 with 17 Marines including platoon sergeant SSgt. Slocum was set down far from Silvoso's two squads and would not catch up to them until much later into the fight.

Andrus said that a single NVA who bolted out and got into a ditch area was one of the bravest men he'd ever encountered. The enemy soldier had the bearing of an officer and he saw him actually throw his AK-47 rifle away before he disappeared in a ditch. "I thought it possible to capture him and moved in close where he was. He had another AK-47 and started to hose us. I rolled left and got away from the fire. In a few minutes he either went around the minefield or through it on a safe path. He again dropped his weapon and started a marathon run down the dirt road along the minefield. Both Cobras hosed him down and rockets went between his legs even, but he kept on running. At the east end of the minefield he left the road and ran into a significant batch of banana trees."

Exiting the Sea Knight, West noted, "I could not believe it. Right there in front of us was Charlie wearing black pj's, running diagonally across the rice paddy dike in a southwesterly direction. I raised my weapon to my shoulder and squeezed off about four rounds when I felt Lt. Cruickshank's hand on my shoulder. He gave me a stern, 'That's not what we're here for,' and then was back on the radio." West couldn't believe he had missed the running enemy soldier but he wasn't alone. About 14 3rd Platoon Marines had also zeroed in on the soldier and they had all missed him as well![14]

A Marine Scarface HML-367 Cobra gunship glided in at treetop level on the heels of the running soldier and let loose with its automatic grenade launcher pods to finish off what the bush Marines had failed to do. "Charlie disappeared in a circle of explosions only to emerge looking as if he was running a 50 meter dash. He had picked up the tempo and now disappeared into the jungle at the far right corner of the rice paddy. He was one dedicated individual, who was now full of holes and must've dropped dead in the jungle,"[15] surmised West.

The Alpha 3 Marines, probably totaling 31 men or two squads, got on line to West's right and moved down a paddy dike with Cruickshank and West in trace. Shortly, there came the repeated warning, "Boobytrap."[16]

"That's why Charlie was so set on his direction across the rice paddy, not zigging or zagging to escape our fire. He was leading us to a place of death even as we were killing him. We didn't know it yet, but his buddies were doing the same thing (with the other Alpha platoons),"[17] said West.

The Marines skirted the boobytrap and were on the move turning east and reached a clearing. They crossed a drainage ditch that had a narrow tree line running parallel to it. The lead elements of 3rd Platoon were already across the drainage ditch and into the tree line when West heard sporadic firing in the distance.[18] (The drainage ditch/Song Yen Ne[19A] is roughly 900 meters north of where I was told at 2/1 to mark the Da Nang Anti-Infiltration System minefield on my old Dai Loc combat map. Alpha 1/1 Marines would walk off into a minefield between 200-400 meters south of and right at the drainage ditch. 2/1's S-2 Lt. Robinson notes that the VC had a habit of digging up the Allied minefield and moving the mines to a new location more to their liking and to our great surprise. Either this was the case or my topographical and aerial maps are in error. Regardless, the VC knew precisely where the minefield was as they lured the Marines directly into it---MDK).

Meanwhile, Lt.Col. Ledbetter returned from delivering his first medevac to Charlie Med to answer another call for an emergency medevac. "This time I picked up five Marines in the middle of a fight who apparently had been wounded by a boobytrap and automatic weapons fire." He medevacked the wounded from just past the drainage ditch/irrigation canal south of the insertion LZ in the vicinity of An Trach (3)[19B] and headed back to the Da Nang trauma hospital. He didn't know it at the time but his day was far from over and picking up casualties on the ground was only going to get dicier for *Blood, Sweat & Tears*.

Andrus felt they could capture the NVA soldier who had run down the road and directed Lt. Purdy to order 3rd Platoon to go down the same road and into the banana trees where he was last seen. His Huey was running on fumes so he flew back to Hill 55 to refuel after telling 2ndLt. Silvoso to pursue the man.

Upon crossing the drainage ditch/irrigation canal, Silvoso got the order from Alpha's CO to "close on the enemy." Swenson's 2nd Platoon was on the other side of a tree line. "We pivoted to our right (west) to try and catch the enemy in a double envelopment between us. Two enemy soldiers ran parallel to us to our front as we turned," recalled Silvoso. 1/1's Spot Report would note: "Patrol landed, spotting approximately 20 NVA. Enemy fled toward Da Nang Barrier with (1) platoon of Alpha Co. in pursuit..." The Marines were being drawn into a lethal hailstorm prepared by the enemy.

As Cruickshank, West and two trailing Marines crossed the drainage ditch and entered a high, scattered brushy area, they lost sight of the rest of the column (probably due to the two squads' pivot to the west---MDK). "It just seemed to be the four of us there at the end of the column," said West. The Marine wielding the M-79 grenade launcher accompanying them apparently saw something move in the tree line to their front and squeezed off a 40mm high explosive round in that direction. In answer a bush in front of them erupted in an explosion from what West said he thought was a grenade.[20]

"We both cringed and dropped to the ground. I'm sure the expression on my face said, 'Don't do that again.' Then we heard that first deafening explosion. It came from our 8 o'clock, behind us in a northwesterly direction approximately 50 yards away behind a group of small trees and brush. The words 'boobytrap' still echoed in my head,"[21] said West.

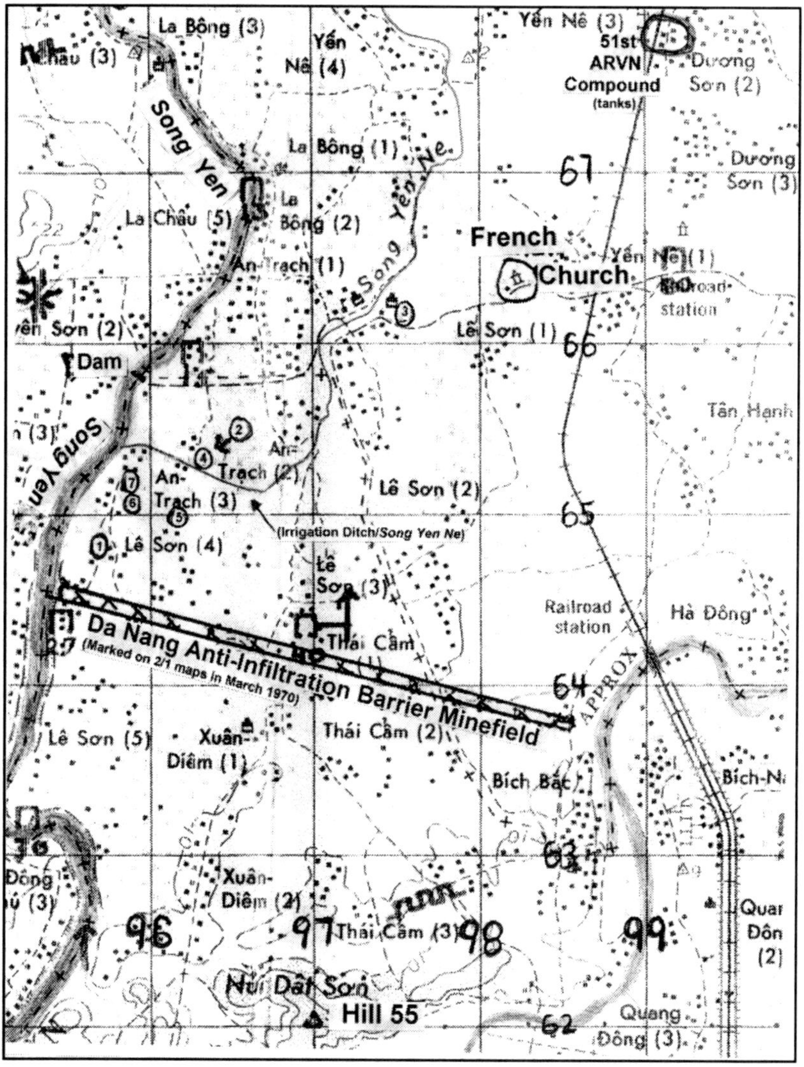


**Alpha Co., 1/1 was lured into a minefield by enemy troops January 31, 1970. The Da Nang Anti-Infiltration Barrier Minefield and the location of the Sea Knight medevacs indicate the Marines were injured in a newly constructed enemy minefield. The circled numbered sequence of events marked on the map are: 1. Enemy troops spotted by gunships and taken under fire in this grid square; 2. Two Alpha 2 squads followed by two Alpha 3 squads inserted by helicopters; 3. An Alpha 2 squad inserted and, most likely, an Alpha 3 squad also inserted in this grid square; 4. A Marine WIA is medevacked; 5. 5 Marines WIA by automatic rifle fire and boobytraps; 6. 7 Marines downed by boobytraps and snipers; 7. 4 men downed by boobytraps and snipers. (Dai Loc map, Sheet 6640 IV, Map courtesy of National Imagery and Mapping Agency, Illustration by Dan Kellum)**

The four Marines turned and ran towards an opening in the brush just to the left of a small clump of trees. It was there they hit barbed wire and as fast as they could go, went through it towards the explosion they had heard. They moved into a large open area with a tree line in the distance. They caught up with the Marines who had been wounded by the first mine explosion.[22] (Barbed wire was strung around the perimeter of the Da Nang Barrier minefield with triangular signs denoting "MIN" for mines in Vietnamese printed on them every few feet to keep the peasants from accidentally wandering off into them. West does not mention seeing those signs in his commentary. Ledbetter states that some of the barbed wire fencing had been taken down by the VC---MDK).

Marines were huddled around their wounded on the ground as if they were in a football huddle, according to West. He looked around Lt. Cruickshank into the face of a young Navy Corpsman. They made eye contact.[23]

"I will never forget the look of sheer terror on his face as he looked up at me. His blood-soaked hand held an IV needle and was shaking uncontrollably. In those brief seconds something changed in his eyes. His face relaxed and his mask of terror was replaced with a blank stare. He had conquered whatever fear and trauma had gripped him. He looked back down and his now steady hand disappeared in search of the intended target of the IV,"[24] said West.

LCpl. Steve Bish was an H&S Co. radio operator assigned to Alpha Co. moving with elements of the 2nd Platoon en route to link up with 3rd Platoon in order to assault the tree line full of NVA. He had seen the five Marines get blown up that Ledbetter had medevacked to Charlie Med. He called for "Corpsman up!" and was moving towards West and Cruickshank's position to help out his fellow Marines wounded and under fire when he stopped to call Ledbetter in the medevac bird to explain the situation on the ground in preparation for a medevac.[25]

*Blood, Sweat & Tears* was coming into the zone as Ledbetter asked for a smoke grenade to mark friendlies and those in need of a medevac. LCpl. Bish repeated over the radio, "Popping smoke." Some men ran past Bish towards the first group of wounded Marines when another mine was detonated killing the Corpsman with them.[26] Lt. Silvoso said that after the first explosion he also recalled a Navy Corpsman running towards the injured men when someone yelled, "Incoming," and a second explosion killed the Doc. It was thought two mines went off simultaneously and that Bish's smoke grenade had actually set one of those charges off. (Only one Navy Corpsman was killed and none wounded this day so there is some disagreement as to when HM3 Frank Paul "Doc" Doronzo of Denver, Colorado who was with Alpha Co. was hit and killed---MDK).

"The Marines in front of us cringed as dirt and shrapnel from that second explosion brought home the realization we were in a minefield. It had come from behind the first group of wounded Marines, further down the tree line and a bit further into the clearing," said West. He was hit by a tiny piece of shrapnel from that explosion that had made it past the Marines in front of him and Lt. Cruickshank and embedded in his right knee. "It was nothing but it had gotten my attention as if someone had stuck a lit cigarette to my flesh."[27]

Andrus said upon his return 20 or 30 minutes later he was only 50 yards out when he saw a Marine disappear in a cloud of blood and was cut in half by an exploding mine. "That's when all went to hell."

Cruickshank was busy on the radio calling for a medevac as a sergeant and Doc Doronzo shifted positions to help the second group of Marines hit nearby. Three Marines about 60 yards away (West felt they might've been from 1st Platoon) were in a bad place laying down a base of fire into the tree line full of NVA troops sporadically firing at all the Marines in the open field. The three men's fire was somewhat taking the heat off the two groups of wounded Marines being targeted by the NVA. They must've realized they, too, were in a minefield but continued to give covering fire and knew as they all did at this point…to move was to die,[28] according to West.

The Cobra gunships overhead rolled in on the tree line and emptied their ordnance into the enemy troops making them think twice about holding their position.[29] 1stLt. L.K. "Les" Williams, 25, Peachbush pilot from Lakewood, Colorado, recalled being a copilot fairly new in-country on that operation and received a request from the Marines on the ground to hose down that same tree line with his on board .50 caliber machine guns to suppress the enemy fire.

"For the three Marines to stay where they were was asking for a sniper to end their dilemma. The Marine on point appeared to kneel and reached down as if to probe the ground. Then they were gone. They had disappeared in an eruption of earth filled with searing metal and with the blood, sweat & tears of young Marines," noted West. The third explosion created another group destined for medevac from the minefield.[30]

West figured he and Lt. Cruickshank were going to be okay. The lieutenant was on the radio giving someone a situation report (sitrep). He recalled the two Marines still with him and the lieutenant had a look on their faces that they understood their situation as well.[31]

"Our world filled with the sound of the larger CH-46 as it came in from behind us, seemingly skimming the treetops. They must've seen those three Marines disappear (in the third explosion) as it had just happened,"[32] said West.

Andrus watched helplessly as Marines set mine after mine off and was wondering how the hell they could rescue them from the minefield. "I didn't know there was a minefield there until (Purdy) said over the intercom when the first Marine died, 'Oh, my God, they're in the minefield!' Just about that time Walt came in and landed (where a mine had exploded moments before)."

Ledbetter's "shit sandwich" only got worse as the day wore on, "Upon my return from taking the wounded to the hospital, I was informed that a part of the 3rd Platoon in pursuit of the enemy had inadvertently walked into a minefield. It was a U.S. minefield (Da Nang Barrier). The South Vietnamese Army was supposed to tend it. Of course, they didn't and the NVA had taken down one side of the fence and led the platoon into the field and trapped them."

"A number were badly wounded and the rest could not move. To move was to die. To compound the problem they were under fire. There was really no choice. I had to land and get them out of the minefield. I told my crew what we were going to do and what might happen. I told them to take off their flak vests and stand on them. In case we landed on a mine that would render some protection from shrapnel coming up through the floor. I also told them to stay in the helicopter because I didn't want them to get blown up and become part of the problem."

The two Marines with West and Cruickshank were told to go to the safety of the wire where the three Marines had been blown up earlier. They made it to the wire without incident. Lt. Cruickshank and West started off in that direction to join them when they saw Ledbetter's *Blood, Sweat & Tears* arrive to take on its first load of Marines in the minefield.[33]

"I noticed a crew member (PFC Mike Clausen disobeying Lt.Col. Ledbetter's order for the crew to stay inside the aircraft and let the Marines come to them) run down the ramp and into the minefield (to retrieve his first group of wounded Marines)," said West. "They had worked together to place the main wheel mounts on craters left by detonated mines. They would repeat this process three times in the minefield."[34]

LCpl. Bish saw Clausen as well and yelled across to him a warning, "You dumb son-of-a-bitch, you're in a minefield!" Clausen was well aware of what he was doing and at the time was trying to locate the body of a Marine hit in the third explosion.[35]

"Clausen directed me into the minefield to a landing close to a number of Marines that were wounded. He guided me to put the main landing gear in a crater caused by an earlier explosion of a mine. I was a little concerned because that meant that the nose gear that was right under my feet was either going to hit a mine or just dirt. You pay your money and take your chances. I won. There was no explosion. Thank God for dirt," said a relieved Ledbetter.

"I lowered the ramp and Clausen went to the back of the aircraft and just walked out into the minefield to pick up the wounded. He did it knowing full well he could die at any step. After we picked the wounded up at that spot, we had to move forward about 10 yards because we had landed right over one of the dead Marines. We played the same game of Russian roulette with the nose gear and once again out went Clausen to pick up the body." Clausen would later say that he tried to stay in the same footsteps he made going out to pick the wounded up in returning to *Blood, Sweat & Tears* knowing that was safe ground to walk on. Lt.Col. Andrus watched as Clausen exited the aircraft to make two trips to recover the body of the Marine cut in half.

As Lt. Cruickshank and West stepped off in the direction of the two Marines across the field, one of them stepped on a mine that had been between them the whole time. Cruickshank was talking on the handset connected by a 3-foot cord to the radio West was carrying when both men took the full brunt of the explosion.[36]

"Defying the laws of gravity, I was flying in slow motion through the air. It seemed an eternity before I felt the earth bring my flight to an end. Stunned and confused, I realized my rifle was gone and noticed the blood at my right elbow. I felt as if I had been hit by a Mack truck. There was a strange numbness accompanied by an intense burning sensation,"[37] recalled West.

"I looked behind me for Lt. Cruickshank and saw him lying on his back with a large smoking hole between us. Through the ringing in my ears, I heard this loud hissing noise. The large column of yellow smoke coming from the radio strapped to my back told me it was from the smoke grenades I had attached there earlier.

"I put my hands on the ground and attempted to get up to go to Lt. Cruickshank's side when a new reality confronted me. My right pants leg dangled in the air and my right leg was gone! I looked at my left leg to find it severely mangled with my left foot lying at some unnatural angle barely attached. Suddenly one of the two Marines that had made it to the wire (and safety) was in front of me knocking me back to the ground. He began applying tourniquets to my legs. The other Marine (had also crossed over dangerous ground a second time to come to their aid...Marines unknown to West whose heroics went unrecognized in the confusion of the disastrous, stressful day) was now on top of me as well. He was busy slipping the radio off my back and then knelt there with his hands on my shoulders as if to hold me down.

"I looked down at the Marine working on my legs and asked, 'How are my legs?' to which he replied, 'Don't worry about them...they're gone.'" West told the Marine on top of him to go check on the lieutenant and he was gone before he could finish his sentence.[38]

"There were two Marines KIA that morning, LCpl. Edward Arnold Rozell (18, of West Seneca, New York) and Cpl. Raymond Dale Harrell (19, of Fries, Virginia). I couldn't' tell you who was killed where and by which mine. I can tell you that they both died trying to get to and help wounded Marines,"[39] said West.

"Cpl. Harrell was my radioman. He stepped in front of me and took a sniper's bullet dead center in the heart," lamented Silvoso. "If he had not stepped around me, that bullet would've hit me. The round went right through Harrell and hit the PRC-25 radio on his back taking it out as well. I think I must've gotten a ricochet off that same bullet as something hit me in the head and the next thing I remember was that I was on the ground. I checked my family jewels to make sure they were okay then realized I somehow had gotten water all over me. It turned out to be my blood from a head wound. Not a day goes by I don't say a prayer for my radioman for saving my life with his."

Meanwhile, SSgt. Slocum came upon the carnage from the edge of the minefield with the remaining Alpha 3 squad. Silvoso yelled at them to stay where they were. Slocum assessed the situation and told his men not to move. He proceeded to get down on his knees and slowly made a path into the minefield with his bayonet probing for mines. Silvoso noted that for his actions this day he wrote SSgt. Slocum, an Indiana native who was in his 20s, up for a Silver Star. (Apparently the Silver Star was either downgraded to a Bronze Star at Division, as was typically the case, or the paperwork was never acted upon as SSgt. Slocum was not on any list I could find for Marines receiving a Silver Star in Vietnam---MDK).

"Here I was trying to get my Marines to stay out of the minefield so they wouldn't set anymore off, Slocum is making his way to us very carefully and here's this crazy guy (PFC Clausen) running down the ramp of a medevac helicopter to pick people up! I figured he was either crazy or had balls bigger than whatever. He must've had his Guardian Angel with him this day," surmised Silvoso.

Ledbetter noted the last group of Marines (which included Cruickshank and West) was 50 yards away from their last pickup and they flew over to them.

"Clausen was all over that minefield. Six times he got out of the aircraft to pick up the wounded and dead. On his last trip out another mine detonated and knocked him down. He just got up and continued to carry a wounded man into the aircraft. The explosion damaged our rotor system and put a few holes in the fuselage but the aircraft was still flyable," said Ledbetter.

West recalled that he was pretty much out of it as far as knowing who was injured in what location after he went down. "Lt. Cruickshank and I watched as they formed that huddle over the wounded. A Marine placed a stretcher on the ground next to me. It may have been PFC Clausen. I just don't know. I could feel the torn muscle and broken bones for the first time. There is no gentle way to quickly move a mangled limb. The pain had become excruciating as the Marines carrying my stretcher ran to the ramp of *Blood, Sweat & Tears* and deposited me on the deck,"[40] said West.

"As bad as things had been, nothing could compare with what happened next. When they dropped into the minefield, Lt.Col. Ledbetter had directed his flight crew to take off their flak jackets and place them on the deck. It was a wise decision. Again, there are no words to describe that last detonation. PFC Clausen was returning from the left front of the aircraft with a wounded man. Lt. Cruickshank was just steps from the ramp of the aircraft being treated by a Corpsman, possibly by the one I had made eye contact with earlier. Two Marines were preparing to move him into the chopper (when there was a horrific explosion)."[41]

Metal and debris smacked into the rear rotor and left rear of the aircraft as West rolled on his right side and covered his head with an arm all the time thinking, "God, please don't blow me up again." He held on tightly to the stretcher as he heard the sound of metal hitting metal.[42] Andrus said the mine explosion could have been disastrous but no damage was sustained by Ledbetter's Sea Knight.

Clausen finished helping the wounded Marines into the Sea Knight and returned a fifth time to the minefield to retrieve the body of Doc Doronzo. West indicated this was when he thought the Navy Corpsman was killed while treating Lt. Cruickshank.[43]

"I didn't know that Doc yet I can never forget him, the courage he displayed that day saved so many lives,"[44] said West.

Lt. Cruickshank was blown into some tall grass nearby. Clausen came to the end of *Blood, Sweat & Tears'* ramp and motioned to the lieutenant to get to the aircraft 30 yards away. Having just regained consciousness after being blown up a second time, Cruickshank indicated he couldn't walk on his own after the explosion and needed assistance. The crew chief threw his arms up in the air as if to say, "You gotta be kidding me. I have to go out there again?"[45]

Clausen stepped off into the minefield for the sixth and final time. He grabbed Cruickshank under the armpits and dragged him to the chopper.[46] *Blood, Sweat & Tears* was finally able to depart the minefield.

LCpl. Bish walked out of the minefield without incident to return to the fight. He cringed with every agonizing step he took to escape the killing field. A sergeant (possibly SSgt. Slocum) walked point and managed to get them to safety. "It had turned into just another bad day in Vietnam," philosophized Bish when he last talked to LCpl. West about January 31, 1970.[47]

Ledbetter's aircraft picked up seven men about 250 meters east of An Trach (3)[48A] and four men 100 meters north of the previous position[48B] in the minefield. "This continued until every dead, wounded and unharmed Marine was in the bird. You had to be there to be able to describe the scene. On the south side, a group of Marines had gathered. There were prisoners and wounded gooners. It was finally over, "said Lt.Col Andrus. The medevac helicopter aptly named *Blood, Sweat & Tears* made a beeline to Charlie Med with its cargo of dead and wounded Marines and the Navy Corpsman.

West was shivering from the cold lying on his stretcher and told a passing crewman, "I'm cold." The crewman, West figures it was PFC Clausen, retrieved some flak jackets and put them over him as if tucking him in for the night. West indicated he made eye contact with Sgt.Maj. Landy who looked upon the massive carnage in the helicopter and turned back to stare down the barrel of his .50 caliber machine gun with the expression of wanting the son-of-a-bitches who caused this to die.[49]

"It was a horrible incident that is forever etched in my mind," said Ray Tripicchio.

At Charlie Med, West remembers being carried into the ICU on a stretcher that with every running step jarred his broken bones causing him immediate and unbearable pain. "I tried to rise to my elbows and was yelling at them to stop. All I could do was hold on."[50]

He was taken into a room full of sawhorses with stretchers put between two of them. Five men jumped in cutting his clothes off while others worked on his legs and took his pulse. One of them knelt at his head with a clipboard and kept asking him for his name, rank and serial number.[51]

"Whatever they were doing to my legs hurt. I moaned in agony. It felt as if they had just closed bear traps on them. A voice came from behind him saying, 'Hang in there West.'" He noticed Lt. Cruickshank on a stretcher nearby and made eye contact with him. The lieutenant closed his eyes and passed out.[52]

At one point West said he tried to get up and leave by rising up on his elbows but made it halfway and fell back to the stretcher drained by the effort. A doctor pushed his way between the people standing around him, rubbed something on his chest and pushed a long needle between his ribs and into his heart. "It may as well have been his fist. The sensation was that of a crushing pressure as if he was trying to push my heart out of my back. He never spoke a word and then he was gone."[53]

After X-rays, West was taken to the Operating Room where through the blinding bright light above him, he saw the face of a kindly older man with short, graying hair bordering his head cap like a halo. "He reached down placing his right hand on my forehead and said, 'It's OK son, you're going to sleep now.'"[54]

Due to the severity of their wounds, both Lt. Cruickshank and LCpl. West would lose both their legs.

Ledbetter medevacked 12 wounded-in-action, WIAs, and 2 killed-in-action, KIAs, Marines and a KIA Navy Corpsman off the battlefield to Charlie Med. Four additional Marines were either unhurt or lightly wounded and itching to get back to their platoon. Col. Ledbetter said that 2ndLt. Silvoso refused treatment for his head wound at Charlie Med and reboarded his helicopter to go back into the action.

"I cannot imagine the courage it took to go back after the horror they had been a part of," marveled Col. Ledbetter. Silvoso commented that he didn't want to stay at Charlie Med while his men were still engaged in the fight and said he just wanted to be taken back to the field. He received a Purple Heart for his wound.

Silvoso wasn't sure if the NVA soldiers were deliberately leading them into the minefield. Unlike West, he said he never saw any barbed wire and wasn't aware of exactly where the Da Nang Barrier minefield was. The 1/1 Marines did not have the minefield marked on their maps. "After January 31, 1970, every Marine coming into 1/1 was made aware of where the Da Nang Barrier was and that it was a 'no go' area."

Ledbetter noted that the day wasn't over until the fight was finished. Another Marine company was flown into the fray with Alpha Co. to destroy the NVA. He and his Sea Knight flight of three logged in 6 hours in the air apiece.

The *Blood, Sweat & Tears* pilot said February was far better than January for him as he had only seven or eight Kingfisher missions to fly before he was transferred up to Marine Air Wing headquarters in Da Nang to become the new Operations officer. "In my 6 months with the squadron, I flew over 400 missions for a total of 515 missions. I was shot down three times and flew home numerous badly damaged aircraft. That kind of work plays games with your mind.

"In early December, I had gone on R&R to Hawaii. I went to say goodbye to my wife and children because I knew I could not survive the next 2 months. You cannot imagine how hard it was to get on that aircraft and go back to Vietnam.

"It was a bad office to work in, but the other employees were unbelievable. That was 36 years ago and I still miss them. Would I do it again? Certainly. We all fought for each other."

The Alpha 1/1 Marines and another company inserted to overcome the NVA force managed to take 9 POWs and kill 10 NVA. Weapons captured were six AK-47 rifles, a 7.62mm pistol, two satchel charges and numerous grenades.

Marine casualties for the day were officially listed in 1/1's Spot Report from four mine explosions in the minefield as 12 Marines WIA (8 emergency medevacs), 2 Marines KIA and 1 U.S. Navy Corpsman KIA. The KIAs were LCpl. Edward Arnold Rozell, a relatively new Marine in Alpha 3-1, Cpl. Harrell, Alpha 3 CP radioman and Doc Doronzo who had turned 23 a little over 3 weeks earlier.[55] Rozell's squad mate Roger Rosdahl noted that he had introduced Rozell by mail to a friend of his, Sandy, in North Dakota and they had written each other daily. Rosdahl said she was devastated when Ed Rozell was killed.

The Marine WIAs that West and Ledbetter were able to come up with were J.E. Chill of St. Louis, Missouri; A.L. Forbes of Dade County, Florida; W.A. Gillin of Maryland; L.E. Lasater of Cook County, Illinois; F.G. McKeever of San Francisco County, California; Chris Nick of Broward County, Florida; E.W. Sanderson of Mobile County, Alabama; J.K. Singleton of Montgomery County, Arkansas; Arthur "Indian" Trujillo of San Antonio, Texas (received 37 shrapnel wounds from the explosion that hit him); L. Wynn of Washington County, Minnesota; and 2ndLt. Joe Silvoso of Boone County, Missouri.[56] (One other unknown WIA was listed on the 1/1 Spot Report---MDK).

### *Blood, Sweat & Tears* Crew Honored

For their heroic actions on January 31, 1970, the crew of *Blood, Sweat & Tears* became one of the most decorated in the Vietnam War. PFC Mike Clausen Jr., crew chief, was awarded the Medal of Honor; Lt.Col. Walt Ledbetter Jr., pilot, received the Navy Cross (also the Legion of Merit for being part of 32 Kingfisher missions from January 1 until February 11 which the citation noted had stopped the NVA's intention to have a Tet Offensive in 1970).

Also, receiving medals were 1stLt. Paul D. Parker II, copilot, Silver Star; Sgt.Maj. Morton S. Landy, gunner, Bronze Star; and Cpl. Steve M. Marinkonic, gunner, Bronze Star.

**PFC Mike Clausen Medal of Honor (USMC Photo)**

Clausen was the only enlisted Air Wing Marine to receive the Medal of Honor. Pres. Richard M. Nixon presented him with the MOH at the White House on June 15, 1971. A parade was held in his honor through downtown Hammond, Louisiana welcoming the Medal of Honor recipient home from the Vietnam War on July 31, 1971.

At some point after his return home and getting out of the Marine Corps, the MOH winner survived a car crash that left him in a coma for several months and impaired his ability to work. Upon his recovery he found work as an inspector for Boeing at its aircraft plant in Lake Charles, Louisiana. He and his wife, Lois, called Ponchatoula, Louisiana home. He spoke often to veterans' organizations.[57]

## Monument Erected to Honor Clausen in Ponchatoula

In 2004 Clausen suffered from liver failure and, through the efforts of Texas billionaire businessman Ross Perot, who sent his private jet and took care of his medical expenses, he was rushed to Baylor University Medical Center in Dallas for treatment. The disease was too far advanced and he died on May 30, 2004, Memorial Weekend, at 56.[58]

Preceding him in death were his parents Raymond and Mary M. Clausen Sr. and a brother, Jerry Clausen. Funeral services were held at the St. Joseph Catholic Church in Ponchatoula. He was buried in Ponchatoula Cemetery. He was survived by his wife of 28 years, Lois of Ponchatoula; two brothers, Gy.Sgt. Carl Clausen, USMC (Ret.) of Hammond, Louisiana, and Marine Erdwin Clausen of Manila, Philippine Islands; and a sister, Christine Clausen Ballard of Albany, Louisiana. Initially, Clausen's grave was marked with a small plaque on a stake due to his wife being unable to afford a proper headstone for him. She wanted him buried close to home rather than Arlington National Cemetery.[59]

And that's where Marine Sgt. Greg Davis, Philip Monteleone, a Louisiana State Trooper, and HMM-263 Peachbush pilot Ron "Hawk" Cornetta, took it upon themselves with the help of local Ponchatoula residents to raise money for an appropriate grave marker befitting a Marine MOH recipient through the Mike Clausen Foundation. Over $19,000 was raised with the help of the USMC Combat Helicopter Association (Popasmoke.org) and on January 27, 2007 a 7-foot-6 black granite monument weighing 2,000 lbs. as well as a smaller granite gravestone were dedicated in a ceremony. The large monument has a picture of Clausen and a scene from that rescue mission etched on it while on the other side is the engraved MOH along with the citation that depicts his heroics.[60]

In attendance for the unveiling of the monument were 200 visitors from all over the United States and many local townspeople and Louisiana dignitaries. West, who owed his life to Clausen, and Col. Ledbetter, USMC (Ret.) were there along with some Green Berets, paratroopers, Marines from the USMC Combat Helicopters Association, Louisiana State Rep. Henry Powell, Ponchatoula Mayor Bob Zabbia and others. Ledbetter noted that not only was Clausen a hero January 31, 1970 but also many others including the Navy Corpsman Doronzo who was aware of the danger he faced but was still running to the aid of the fallen Marines when he was blown up by a mine. A Celtic bagpipe band was on hand as was a Navy bugler playing "Taps."[61]

### Dedication of Sea Knight *Blood, Sweat & Tears*

In 2004 *Blood, Sweat & Tears* was still involved in combat in Iraq 34 years after its amazing rescue of the Alpha Co., 1/1 Marines in Vietnam. The Marine Corps is well-known for squeezing every ounce of productivity out of its military equipment and it's not surprising to see such equipment in use well beyond its posted expiration date...unlike the other military services.

The "pedigreed" Sea Knight made a hard landing in March 2004 (roughly 3 months before Clausen died) causing some damage and had to be loaded onto an Army flatbed truck and transported to a repair depot to be fixed. En route the truck driver misjudged the height of a bridge he was going under and slammed the Sea Knight's tail section into the unforgiving concrete bridge. The estimate to repair the new damages to the tail and fuselage was in the prohibited vicinity of $4.5 million.[62]

Someone with a sense of history realized *Blood, Sweat & Tears* was still an important helicopter in terms of Marine Corps legends. As a result, it was loaded into a C-5 Galaxy cargo plane and flown back to the Marine Corps Air Station in Cherry Point, North Carolina. It sat at the air station for a year before a curator for the National Museum of the Marine Corps in Quantico, Virginia and officials with the Carolinas Aviation Museum in Charlotte, North Carolina arranged a permanent temporary loan of *Blood, Sweat & Tears*.[63]

Gy.Sgt. Steve Fresina, a former production control chief with Marine Aviation Logistics Squadron 29 at Marine Corps Air Station New River, North Carolina, along with several volunteers went to work on the famous helicopter. After hundreds of hours of work, they made *Blood, Sweat & Tears* presentable to the public but, of course, it would never fly again even after all the repairs were made on it.[64]

A dedication ceremony was held Saturday, October 14, 2007 attended by approximately 150 people. Among those attending the much anticipated event were Lois Clausen and family as well as six of the rescued Marines and three of the helicopter's crew. Some of those listed as attending were Peachbush crew members: Col. Ledbetter (and his daughter Melissa), Lt. Parker, Sgt.Maj. Landy and Col. Williams; TACP Marines: Cpl. West and Lt. Cruickshank; and Alpha 1/1 Marines: Trujillo and Chris Nick (two other unnamed Marines were in attendance from that January 31, 1970 day).[65]

Retired Col. Williams commented from the standpoint of being a pilot meeting the Marine survivors for the first time from that terrible day, "Our reunion with the Marines of Alpha 3, 1/1 in North Carolina helped us all better understand what happened in that minefield and how the wounded handled the loss of limbs. The camaraderie among the Marines who didn't know each other that day was a bond that was never broken. We hugged each other like the brothers we are and the mental anguish of all those preceding years melted away. We talked about Mike Clausen and we all celebrated the lives lost that day and the ones who made it home."

"(Clausen) had done this over and over," said Ledbetter, who had attended his crew chief's funeral 3 years earlier. "How can you be surprised at what he did? God called him home. He needed a crew chief.[66]

"He was a Marine you wanted with you when you were really in trouble," noted Ledbetter.[67] As for the restoration and display of the dependable Sea Knight *Blood, Sweat & Tears* at the museum in Charlotte, he said, "We're looking at a thing bigger than me or Mike. It's a symbol of the sacrifice of Vietnam. A lot of people feel they were not respected...This is a final sort of closure."[68]

"If not for Mike Clausen and these guys, I would have been another name on The Wall in Washington (D.C.)," said Cruickshank. "I've had to live my life without my legs, but my life's been a whole lot better than the guys who didn't make it back."[69]

# Chapter 2

**"...Visions haunt me every day, not of the nightmares of war but of the steady consistency with which my Marines faced their responsibilities, and of how uncomplaining most of them were in the face of constant danger...The quick certainty when a fellow Marine was wounded and needed help. Their willingness to risk their lives to save other Marines in peril. To this day it stuns me that their own countrymen have so completely missed the story of their service, lost in the bitter confusion of the war itself."[1]**

**James H. "Jim" Webb Jr.**
**Delta Co., 1st Battalion, 5th Marines**
**U.S. Senator, Former SecNav**

## Enlisted Man to Marine Officer

In *Book I, American Heroes: Grunts, Pilots & "Docs,"* I explained the different enlisted and officer training levels involved in my going from PFC to second lieutenant in the Marine Corps (as well as 86 other enlisted men in my officers' class at Quantico, Virginia). It was a cultural shock to go from being yelled at on the enlisted boot camp parade ground, known as The Grinder, in San Diego, California to being the person over the drill instructor doing the yelling.

I thought I had a unique perspective in writing about Marine Corps training since I was chosen from the enlisted ranks to attend Officer Candidate School (OCS) and The Basic School (TBS) at Quantico after completion of enlisted boot camp followed by Infantry Training Regiment at Camp Pendleton.

The Marine Corps, in a bind to fill its officers ranks, anointed a large number of us enlisted Marines, Enlisted Commissioning Program (ECPs), along with young college men as second lieutenants in our OCS class in August 1969. In our Charlie Co.-1969 (C- or 3-69) class of 238 second lieutenants graduating from TBS following OCS, 31 of 65 men assigned the military occupational specialty, MOS, of infantry officers, 0301s, were ECPs. We learned how to efficiently and with a great amount of pyrotechnic noise and small/automatic arms fire to completely destroy America's enemies...in particular, our Viet Cong/North Vietnamese counterparts in Southeast Asia.

## Nine C-69 Officers KIA, 15 Infantry Officers WIA

Of the 65 C-69 second lieutenants designated 0301s graduating February 5, 1969, eight would die in Vietnam. Four grunt lieutenants were killed serving with 1st Recon (three in 1969 and one in 1970) while the remaining four were in the 5th Marine Regiment when they were killed in 1969 alongside hundreds of Marine KIAs/WIAs in the meat grinder known as the Arizona Territory or Dodge City area southwest of Da Nang, RVN. In addition, a Cobra pilot from C-69 (and specifically my 3rd Platoon) was also KIA in 1970.

Fifteen C-69 grunt officers were wounded-in-action as well, according to 1stLt. Jim Webb Jr., a fellow member of my C-69 class. His recollection of the WIAs was a cursory count and by no means the final tally of all the wounded C-69 infantry officers. I was unable to track down a complete listing of all our 1969-70 casualties from the 1st, 5th, 7th or 26th Marine Regiments, 1st or 3rd Recon Battalions, 1st Force Recon or other units' figures unknown to me at this time. Webb was in-country in 1969 with Delta, 1/5 when most of our C-69 class was there, thus, had firsthand knowledge of many of the WIAs/KIAs. I didn't arrive in Vietnam until 1970 after almost all of C-69 had rotated to Okinawa or stateside.

Roughly 28 percent or 23 of C-69's 65 infantry officers were either KIA or WIA in Vietnam 1969-70. The 65 figure is also arbitrary considering some officers might have washed out or dropped out of their respective MOS schools and ended up in Vietnam as 0301s.

Taking into account that so many infantry officers from C-69 were wounded primarily in the 5th Marines by Webb's recollection, a similar attrition rate was highly possible in the other units as well in 1969-70. This could make the percentage of KIA/WIA well over 50 percent for our brother officers.

A $15,000 life insurance settlement went to the KIA officers' beneficiaries. Free white marble headstones (measuring 24 inches high, 13 inches wide and 4 inches thick) provided through the Veterans Administration were also available to the Marines' families and all servicemen dying before September 11, 2001. Five of those nine C-69 officers KIA were well known to me as they were in my 3rd Platoon at TBS. In Webb's 5th Platoon two officers were KIA while the 1st and 4th Platoons each lost one.

The average Government Comprehensive Test (GCT or Intelligence Quotient) score for 64 C-69 grunt officers was 139.17 (one officer's GCT score was not available), which was not too shabby. At Camp Pendleton as enlisted Marines, we exchanged information on various officers' record books passing through our offices and especially talked about the brilliant officers with 150 or higher IQs. The running joke was that they were so intelligent that something as mundane as tying their bootlaces was too simple for them to figure out. Surprisingly, 14 of our 65 infantry officers were "bootlace challenged."

Unfortunately, of those 14 "super intelligent" infantry officers five would be confirmed killed and three wounded in Vietnam. We were quite simply losing our best and brightest in Southeast Asia.

Of the 65 grunt officers graduating February 5, 1969, 50 would receive orders to report directly to WestPac (Western Pacific: Vietnam/Okinawa). Drawing orders for Vietnam upon graduation from TBS included 22 of the 31 ECPs, three of the four U.S. Naval Academy graduates, two of the five Naval Reserve Officers' Training Corps (NROTC) program college students and 23 of the 25 Platoon Leader Class college students.

Those newly minted "03" infantry C-69 second lieutenants receiving orders for WestPac to go into harm's way included (Webb recalled 15 WIAs of which four were wounded twice and one officer lost a leg while another lost both legs): G.D. Acker Jr. (WIA), G.C. Allord, D.J. Andrea, Gerald J. Ayers (WIA), C.J. Barnhart, Albert Du Ward Benson (KIA), S.R. Bland, G.A. Blass, J.D. Bowen, C.F. Caldwell, H.D. Chapin, J.L. Clark Jr., G.B. Davis, D.Z. Deats (WIA), A.A. Desantis Jr., M.T. Donahoe, E.J. Doyle, J.D. Farmer, M.P. Gillespie, W. Harley (WIA), P.J. Hayes, James K. Heatherman, Raymond J. Helmick, Cloyce A. Kelly (my TBS roommate), Anthony Edward Kupka (KIA), (since he wound up in 1st Recon in Vietnam, his orders were most likely changed to Recon School stateside---MDK).

Also, A.K. Law, D.M. Lohr, J.D. Majchrzak, J.N. McIntosh (WIA twice), P.N. Meier (WIA), Albert Oscar Nelson Jr. (KIA), J.E. Nickel, Don G. Owens III, W.J. Peters Jr., R.L. Pugh (WIA), William R. Purdy (See Chapter 1, CO, Alpha Co., 1/1), J.B. Reeside IV, K.J. "Ken" Rosser, William Garrett Schanck Jr. (KIA), William J. "Bill" Schuler (WIA), Henry Sokol, G. Solhan (WIA), R.W. "Wayne" Spruell (WIA), T.W. Summers, J.R. Thomas (WIA), G.G. Todd (WIA twice), Theodore Russell Vivilacqua (KIA), James H. Webb Jr. (WIA twice), P.T. Williams (WIA twice) and R.A. Wood.

Headed off to Recon Replacement School at Camp Pendleton then, most likely, onto Vietnam were J.J. Bonsee Jr., Philip Nicholas Huth II (KIA), John Hayes Lakin (KIA) and T.I. Leach. Assigned to the U.S. Army's Ranger School at Fort Benning, Georgia were S.N. Allen, D.A. Andriacco, and Robert B. Haseman. Filling billets at Camp Lejeune, North Carolina were P.N. Ellis, S.D. Greene, Cleveland R. Harvey (KIA) (he was another one of those officers who would end up in 3rd Recon then 1st Recon in Vietnam and probably attended Recon School before going over as well---MDK), Michael Dan Kellum (author, who would be delayed almost a year until January 1970, before beginning a tour in Vietnam) and William G. Nichols. Headed off to Camp Pendleton in California were L.T. Roberts (WIA) and P.H. Reed Jr. while L. Nugent's destination was not available in the records from Quantico.

(In researching the backgrounds of 9 KIA C-69 officers, I was fortunate to find friends and family willing to talk about many of them after 30-plus years. I regret not being able to find out more from some of the officers' families and eyewitnesses concerning the combat that took their lives. The lengthy passage of time since their deaths in Vietnam has resulted in some aspects of their stories being lost, in part, to this recounting. All eight C-69 infantry officers were killed in and around the Arizona Territory, which is southwest of Da Nang, South Vietnam---MDK).

I honor those nine TBS C-69 Marine officers' memories here by recalling their personal stories, their units' combat activity during the brief time they were in-country and the circumstances behind their being killed in Vietnam. What follows is the precise order in which they were cut down in Vietnam. (In telling of the demise of the lieutenants in the 1st Recon units and the men involved on their patrols, I was unable to locate the first names, ages or hometowns of many of the Recon Marines as rosters and Patrol Debriefs detailing the patrols only give their rank and last names---MDK).

## 2ndLt. Anthony E. Kupka, KIA, April 16, 1969, boobytrap

Buddy (also called "Kups" by his friends, although he preferred we call him Tony at TBS) Kupka spent 9 years (grades 4-12) matriculating through the exclusive, non-sectarian all-boys Landon School before graduating in 1964. Landon is located outside Bethesda, Maryland, a few miles northwest of Washington, D.C. The school allows its students to return home each evening and in Buddy's case it was to Kensington, Maryland (population approximately 2,322).

**2ndLt. Tony Kupka (Photo courtesy of Frank Porpotage II)**

He was described by former classmate, John Hanks, as "....the leader, the golden boy, but he didn't swagger. He was a workingman's hero."[2]

Buddy came from "good stock." He was the only child of parents who were as strict as they were loving. His mother was a (physical education) teacher and his dad, also named Anthony, was a legendary coach and mentor of young people at Woodrow Wilson High School in the District of Columbia, according to Knight Kiplinger, a '65 Landon graduate. He went on to say that Buddy was motivated by simple, rock-solid values---duty, hard work, loyalty to family, friends, school and country.[3]

"Buddy was one of the finest all-around athletes who ever attended Landon: 10 varsity letters in three sports. He was All-Interstate Athletic Conference (IAC) and All-Prep in football. Landon's quarterback (in 1964) was a true superstar, Joe Bailey, but it was (co-captain) Buddy Kupka who was voted MVP," recalled Kiplinger. "In his senior year at Landon, he was elected (senior class) president (vice-president 10th and 11th grades) and named 'Most Popular' and 'Most Respected.'"[4]

In the IAC, which in 1964 included Sidwell Friends, Georgetown Prep, St. Albans, St. Stephens and St. James, Buddy was on the baseball team that won the championship in his 9th, 10th and 12th grades; participated in basketball his 10th-12th grades; and won the football championship his 11th grade having participated 10th-12th grades.

"(Buddy Kupka) won the Headmaster's Award in Middle School and again as a senior. The award recipient personified the type of person Landon encouraged each student to be," said Tom W. O'Bryon II who graduated from Landon in '64. "When we graduated, there were only 39 seniors so we were a close-knit group. In high school when Buddy was dating his future wife, Jeanne, her parents thought they were seeing too much of each other. I don't think her parents ever knew this but half a dozen of us would rotate going to her house to pick her up for a date and drop her off with Buddy around the corner."

"I was with Buddy when he met Jeanne for the first time. He loved her immediately," said William Bertalan "Bill" Walsh Jr. who graduated with him from Landon as well.

"I was always impressed with his determination as an athlete and a student. He was special," said Maclear "Mac" Jacoby Jr., Landon Middle School principal for 20 years and teacher/coach who was honored in May 2005 for 50 years of teaching at Landon. He recalled a photo that appeared in *The Saturday Evening Post* of Buddy's best friend, Joe Bailey, as quarterback about to hand the football off to him in an IAC game against St. Albans and captioning it "The Perfect Play." Jacoby helped Buddy work up the required forms to attend his old alma mater Trinity College in Hartford, Connecticut.

### ...Trinity College, 1964-68

In the 4 years he attended Trinity College, Buddy participated in football (varsity end), baseball (hit .312 his junior year) and rowing.[5] His major was engineering, one of the hardest schools at Trinity. "Buddy wasn't a math whiz but he applied himself and kept plugging away. He was disciplined and navigated through the good, the bad and the ugly of college life with considerable maturity compared to the rest of us," said Walsh, who also attended Trinity with Buddy.

Walsh went on to say, "Buddy was an honorable guy who stood by his principles and his friends, respected others regardless of their status...rich or poor; dumb or smart; quiet or gregarious; anti-war or not...and treated everybody the same. He was well-liked and well-respected."

He graduated from Trinity in June 1968. In rapid succession following graduation, he married his high school sweetheart, Jeanne, and went off to the Marine Corps' officer training facility at Quantico to prepare himself for war.[6] He entered the Marine Corps Officer Reserve program at Trinity and received his second lieutenant's bars the day before he graduated.[7]

"He joined the Marines because he thought this was the most honorable way to serve his country. I never talked to him about it. You just expected Buddy to go with the best, those having the hardest assignments in Vietnam," said Walsh.

**...TBS's Boobytrap Lane Problem, Quantico, Virginia, November 1968**

At TBS 22-year-old Tony claimed Falmouth, Massachusetts (population 14,444 in 1969) as his home residence since his parents retired there in 1967. He was my boobytrap lane partner and platoon comrade at Quantico as we carefully disarmed several simulated boobytraps late into a drizzly November '68 evening until we were the only ones left not "killed" in Charlie Co. We made a pact not to "die" that night. And we didn't until the soaking wet range personnel ordered us to yank our respective landmines up that were both rigged with "mousetrap" boobytraps underneath.

*"POP! POP!"* We lifted the mines simultaneously and "died" under duress.

C-69 got together at Quantico's Base Theatre for some type of ceremony (probably the base chaplain wishing us all Godspeed) at the end of training. I ran into Tony and his wife, Jeanne (E. Sullivan) Kupka, outside the theatre and noted that she was pretty far along in her pregnancy so I asked when the baby was due. Tony said she'd give birth to their firstborn child sometime after he was to arrive in-country. Wherever his next duty station was after TBS (I'm not sure if he had gotten orders for Recon Replacement School at that time---MDK), it would put him in Vietnam before the birth.

Since my orders put me stateside at Camp Lejeune, I told him I wished I could somehow trade assignments with him if it were possible allowing him to be present for his child's birth. I could tell that Tony was not happy about the prospect of missing his baby's arrival or being with Jeanne for this momentous event in their young marriage.

**... 1st Recon Battalion, Camp Reasoner, RVN, March 16, 1969**

Tony arrived in Vietnam Sunday, March 16, 1969 and reported to 1st Reconnaissance Battalion, 1st Marine Division, at Camp Reasoner in Da Nang.

After a period of required acclimatization to the extreme weather conditions... hot, humid weather...and taking Recon refresher course training, Tony was assigned as 2nd Platoon commander of Echo Co.

"Lt. Kupka was new to 1st Recon," said PFC David A. "Bozo" Rivard of White Bear, Minnesota in 1969, one of Echo Co.'s 2nd Platoon radiomen, "but he was one of those lieutenants who tried hard to be one of us and he was well-liked and trusted. You could tell he also listened to the veterans and in no way could be categorized as the 'stereotypical second lieutenant.' I also recall that in his Recon patrol with us everyone was impressed with his natural abilities, which we thought superseded ours, but he wisely heeded the advice of everyone on the patrol. In fact, of any officer with 1st Recon, I believe he would have been our first choice to go on patrol with. Lt. Kupka achieved a lot of trust within 1st Recon in a short period of time."

"He came into the EM Club and had a few beers with us. First time any officer had ever done that. He just wanted to learn a lot of things as quickly as possible," said PFC Thomas M. "Tom" Rudd, 20 in 1969 from Gurnee, Illinois. Rudd recalled Lt. Kupka going on a patrol prior to April 2 in which he said he showed good instincts for bush work. (No doubt Tony went out on patrols prior to April 2-16 but I was unable to find those reports in 1st Recon's records---MDK).

**...Team Nail Brush, Hill 146 (Nui Tu Duong), April 2-15, 1969**

Sea Knight helicopters inserted Team Nail Brush, which consisted of three teams totaling 25 men including a scout dog and his handler, on top of Hill 146, Nui (Mountain) Tu Duong in the Que Son Mountains on Wednesday, April 2 to observe enemy troop movement and conduct patrols off the hill.[8A] The teams were scheduled to remain there until April 23.

Hill 146 was a lightly fortified observation post (OP) just 5 clicks northwest of Antenna Valley overlooking the infamous Arizona Territory and river traffic on the Song (River) Tinh Yen. A Dai Loc map dated December 1968 showed previous enemy activity and positions overlaid in red blanketing the Arizona for as far as the eye could see from Hill 146. Hill 642 towered over the OP just 2½ kilometers to the south. It was so bad in this area that the enemy had overrun this particular OP on previous occasions. Enemy ambushes and boobytraps were commonplace. This was exceptionally dangerous ground.

In 1970, 1st Recon Marine Cpl. Larry M. Feldman of Dover, Delaware said he heard that it got so bad around Hill 146 that an arc light (bombers from either Guam or Thailand each carrying a payload capable of 96 500-lb. HE bombs) was called in to pulverize the area. "The old joke (after the airstrike) soon became that Hill 146 was now redesignated Hill 127."

The team's first reported sighting was at 1141 Friday, April 4 when a rocket was launched 8 clicks away and passed right over Hill 146 headed for the An Hoa Combat Base. Team Nail Brush directed an artillery mission in the general vicinity of the rocket launch.

At 1040 Monday, April 7 Lt. Kupka's OP used binoculars to observe two VC carrying packs and rifles moving in the vicinity of An Bang (2) about 1900 meters to the northeast. The VC entered the ville. An artillery fire mission was called and rejected as friendlies were moving in that area. Later in the day at 1500 six VC/NVA in green utilities, wearing bush covers, carrying new gear and rifles were spotted 800 meters northeast of Hill 146. An artillery fire mission was called down on them. And to close out the day's activities at 1620 two more VC wearing black silk pajamas (typical peasant clothing) and coolie hats with rifles and packs were spotted walking on a levee 1800 meters northeast of Hill 146. Lt. Kupka called in an aircraft strafing mission.

Team Nail Brush must've been getting bored with the lack of sightings over the next 6-day period. Five Vietnamese were stopped and their IDs checked at noon on April 13, a Palm Sunday patrol. They reported excessive movement of enemy troops through their ville.

PFC Robert "Bob" Hungate, 18 in 1969 from Sidney, Ohio recalled Lt. Kupka taking another patrol out Tuesday, April 15. They captured a prisoner but instead of bringing him in, they let him go for some reason. He added that a patrol was scheduled for the next morning using the same trail, which didn't set well with some old salts, according to Hungate, who had been in Nam 30 days.

### ...500 meters north of Hill 146, April 16, 1969

On Wednesday, April 16 Kupka and six other Marines ran a patrol off Hill 146 before dawn to check out the reported sightings of VC/NVA troops below them. They departed the perimeter in complete darkness as a new moon on the rise April 16 meant their movement would go unseen but, conversely, it meant any boobytraps set along their path would be harder to detect. Short, stocky PFC Steve Karrels was on point; Lt. Kupka was next; Sgt. Williams; tall, skinny, blond-headed LCpl. Randall T. Johnson on radio; LCpl. McGuire; LCpl. Walter E. Gierman II, 21, of Lake Worth, Florida; and Hungate said he walked tailend Charlie. Gierman and Hungate were both first-timers to the bush.

At 0530 the 7-man Nail Brush "B" patrol was moving down the main trail off Hill 146 approximately 500 meters due north of the OP when a devastating explosive boobytrap was tripped at the front of the column.[8B] Nail Brush's Patrol Debrief would later identify the explosive as a chicom grenade and, indeed, Hungate would initially say he thought it was a couple of grenades but would admit that in the dark he had no earthly idea what type of boobytrap exploded. The lethal blast killed Kupka and Gierman while seriously injuring Karrels, Johnson and Williams. McGuire and Hungate were the only two Marines untouched by the shrapnel storm.

Rivard said some of the uninjured team members returned to Hill 146 later and felt bouncing betty boobytraps were tripped by Nail Brush "B" as well as by a relief team. (A typical enemy boobytrap that would have to be taken into consideration for both explosions was an artillery round rigged in a tree detonated by a tripwire as it had the same widespread airburst-like effect and both teams were either entering or on the periphery of the same tree line when they were struck down---MDK).

A bouncing betty is composed of a booster charge that blows the main mine into the air at waist level where it explodes over a wide kill zone. Regardless of the powerful mine's composition, it was situated on the downhill path so that it had a coverage radius of most the patrol. Hungate ran forward and began helping those critically wounded in the darkness that still enveloped them.

Sgt. Williams took bad hits in his foot and leg. He called for help back at Hill 146. Gierman was killed instantly with a piece of shrapnel the size of a BB piercing his heart. "He was cold stone dead by the time we got there," said Rudd, who would see the carnage as part of a relief team.

Gierman was originally assigned to office duty and had wanted to go on the hill with Team Nail Brush, according to Rivard. Oddly enough, Hungate said Gierman had been saying all the time he was on the hill that he was going to get killed.

"Lt. Kupka was pretty well messed up," said Hungate. "The lieutenant had a gas grenade on him that had detonated and set his chest on fire. I beat that out. They all got knocked off the trail. I dragged Lt. Kupka back up on the trail and was gagging with snot coming out of my nose from the tear gas. I felt around his head in the dark and could tell that he had multiple injuries."

Rudd said that whoever came up on the radio was almost incoherent in his call for help. "We didn't know what was going on."

The second team that came down to help them consisted of Sgt. Roger Cleland, 23 from Eugene, Oregon and on his third Vietnam tour, team leader; LCpl. Karl Howard Culp, 18 and PFC Clayton Tidwell, both from Fort Worth, Texas, alternating point men; PFC Willard Slusher; HM3 Bill "Doc" Lancaster, a Minnesotan; PFC Ron "Gap" Halvorsen from Katy, Texas; and PFC Rudd at tailend Charlie, according to Cleland and Hungate.

The 7-man team detached from Hill 146 and moved to Lt. Kupka's location as a medevac helicopter package was in-bound. Rudd said that as soon as the forward elements of the team reached the tree line where the casualties were, he turned back 180 degrees for rear security.

Hungate recalled that Culp and Tidwell asked if there was anybody providing security further down the hill when they came by him working to patch up Johnson on the path. They could hear gunshots in the valley and worried the enemy was about to come up to finish the job the boobytrap had started. He told them there wasn't anyone forward. The two Marines walked about 10 more yards down the trail where they tripped another powerful high explosive boobytrap. Culp was mortally wounded while Tidwell was critical. Cleland miraculously escaped getting hit. Halvorsen, a transfer from the grunts, caught a big piece of shrapnel in his upper thigh while Hungate took shrapnel in his left finger, left shoulder and left thigh.

The Marine next to Rudd on rear security was blown onto the tailend Charlie's back. Rudd escaped injury. Also, uninjured was the man most crucial to treating those remaining alive...Doc Lancaster. He came through the huge explosion unscathed and went to work with an urgency.

Having lost 2 KIAs before his arrival, Doc had his job cut out for him taking care of 7 WIA Marines on that dark mountainside but did his medical magic endearing himself to those who survived. And that's why Marines have a special place in their hearts for Navy Corpsmen. The four uninjured Marines provided security and helped the Doc with the wounded.

Rivard said that Tidwell recalled Culp taking his hand as they were being loaded on the medevac helicopter and saying, "Don't you worry homebrew, we'll make it through this one."

Culp's dad had signed papers to allow him to join the Marine Corps at 17 as "it seemed a good idea to join the service" after he'd gotten a girl pregnant back home in Texas, according to Rudd. Culp had been writing to the girl from Vietnam trying to take responsibility for his part in the pregnancy.

"I helped carry Lt. Kupka onto the medevac helicopter. When I turned him over, he let out a breath and I yelled over to Doc Lancaster that I thought the lieutenant was still alive. Doc said that was only because he still had air in his lungs and that was just a death rattle," said Rudd.

"At 1st Med, Culp went into a spasm on the stretcher and fell onto the floor where he died of his wounds. The medical personnel turned to work on Tidwell saying that Culp was too far gone," said Rivard. Tidwell would spend over a year in the hospital and in rehab.

PFC Duane W. Bourdo, Nail Brush's chief radioman, was at Freedom Hill awaiting a flight out for a week's R&R when he got word of his friends being hit on Hill 146. He was close to Culp most of all. Bourdo canceled his R&R and rushed to 1st Med to be with them, according to Rivard.

Cleland noted that later on his men were upset to have to stay on Hill 146 for seven more days without replacements for all the Marines medevacked. They also missed a memorial service for Kupka, Gierman and Culp at Camp Reasoner.

Kupka's death came exactly one month after his arrival in-country and gave him the unfortunate distinction of being the first KIA from our C-69 class. Kupka, Culp and Gierman were among 12 Marines and 28 from all U.S. military services killed in Vietnam on April 16, 1969.

**...Team Nail Brush Welcomes Tony Kupka's Baby Girl Into The World**

Jeanne gave birth to a daughter, Christine, on April 13 while Tony was on Hill 146. Since he was on patrol from April 2 until his death April 16, it was bantered about by some of his TBS platoon mates that he may not have been told of her birth. It saddened us all to think that he might have died without ever knowing of his daughter being born.

1stLt. Frank M. Porpotage II, a 24-year-old from Fairfax, Virginia and executive officer (XO) of Echo Co., 1st Recon in April 1970, was charged with going down to 1st Med to identify the bodies of Kupka, Gierman and Culp April 16. He contacted me in June 2003 after I questioned Tony being notified of his child's birth before his death on a Vietnam Veterans Memorial Fund website posting on vvmf.org on the Internet.

Porpotage said the American Red Cross notified 1st Recon Battalion of the news of a brand-spanking new Kupka and he immediately radioed "an ecstatic" Tony about his baby girl's arrival back home just a few hours before he was killed.

The Recon officer wrote that he was also able to sit down with Jeanne upon his return from Vietnam and personally tell her that he notified Tony of Christine's birth. A letter was sent to his parents as well letting them know Tony was informed. He indicated that in the short time he got to know Tony they became best friends.

PFCs Rudd and Hungate also confirmed that Tony had received word of his daughter's birth prior to his last patrol. In celebration of the event Team Nail Brush had a "Mad Minute" by firing off their M-16s in a stream of red tracer rounds, lit up the night with multi-colored pop flares and threw grenades off Hill 146 from their perimeter bunker positions. Tony's Marines knew how to make the arrival of his firstborn reverberate in the Que Son Mountains to friend and foe alike.

## ...The Aftermath

An ironic twist to Tony even being in combat in Nam was that he was the last Kupka in his generation and really didn't have to be in this war, according to his childhood and lifelong friend, Richard W. Besley, who finished a year's tour in the Air Force in Vietnam as of September 1968. It was also said that his grandparents were quite wealthy but Tony never alluded to it or took advantage of the situation to avoid the war zone or his military service.

"We were all devastated when we heard of Buddy's death. The athletic coach had a friend of his, professional football player and a pretty good artist, Tommy McDonald of the Philadelphia Eagles, paint a portrait of Buddy from old photos we had of him. It hung in the Landon Middle School hallway for awhile until it got scratched up. We had it restored and it's now in the Banfield Alumni Room where the teachers go on break," said Mac Jacoby.

So that he may not be forgotten, an annual *Kupka Distinguished Alumnus Award* is presented each year (since 1981) at the Landon School. O'Bryon noted that fellow Landon classmate and 7-69 TBS graduate, former 1stLt. John Curtis "Curt" Bradley, was the driving force to get the award named in his honor.

Bradley said it was a collective effort on the part of several Landon classmates working through Mac Jacoby at the school. "I'm not sure that we would have made the effort for anyone other than Buddy which says a lot about him."

Kiplinger received the award in December 1998. He said he was surprised and honored to be recognized by his fellow alumni for his alma mater's prestigious award.[9]

"But the strongest feeling that came over me was humility. I felt humbled--indeed, almost unworthy--to be linked, through this award, to the memory of Buddy Kupka." He went on to say he admired him enormously for his personality, leadership style, role model attitude towards underclassmen and athletic prowess.[10]

"Buddy was not an intellectual, and I repeat, this is not a put-down. Intellectuals fret too much over moral ambiguity, and in the 1960s the chief moral dilemma was one's personal stance towards the Vietnam War.

"Many of us were tormented by the tough choices it presented, almost paralyzed with ambivalence and indecision. Most Landon graduates in that era, myself included, ended up not serving in the military--whether out of fear, sincere moral objection, self-centeredness or some combination of these sentiments.

"But Buddy Kupka saw things more simply, more clearly. He saw a duty to serve his nation...Eight months after graduating from college, he arrived in Vietnam, a second lieutenant. Buddy had been there just one month when he was killed...The date was April 16, 1969. A few (hours before his death), he had received wonderful news from the states, news that his wife had given birth to a baby girl (Christine). His daughter would never have the privilege of knowing a fine man who would have been a wonderful father, Buddy Kupka. We at Landon were far more fortunate," concluded Kiplinger at his awards ceremony.[11]

Tony not only brought his athleticism to Quantico in 1968 but also an impressive IQ of 152. He, like many of the officers killed from C-69, was a highly intelligent young man. His untimely death as well as the 58,277 other KIAs in Vietnam would silently impact the future of this country. Of the 10 infantry officers who either attended the Army Ranger School at Fort Benning or the Marines' Recon Replacement School, five would die in Vietnam.

"Buddy was one of the greatest losses of the Vietnam War," said John Sherman Jr., a Landon School classmate. "We used to stretch out on a field at night to look at the stars and proclaim we would be buddies until the end. He was an outstanding athlete with a wonderful sense of humor and not a mean bone in his body. He loved Jeannie very much and was just an incredible human being. I don't say that because he died in 1969. I say that because of his parents, his Catholic upbringing, his love of family and country. Buddy will always live on in my heart. I have seen his name on The Wall. We will be buddies until the end." (Buddy wrote "buddies to the end" in Sherman's '64 yearbook---MDK).

Sherman said he got his Army draft notice the day he was notified he was accepted to Naval OCS. He would serve as a U.S. Navy communications officer aboard the destroyer *USS Rupertus* off South Vietnam's coast in gunfire support of IV Corps for 2 years beginning in 1969.

"My attitude towards Vietnam changed dramatically when he died. I remember coming home from Quantico to McLean, Virginia one weekend in April 1969 and my mother meeting me on the front step to tell me Buddy had been killed. I went up to my room, sat in the closet and cried for a long while. It was 6 weeks before I was to get out of TBS and (my fiancée) Maristeve and I were to be married. I began to lose any patriotic ideas I had about Vietnam at that point and probably adopted a survival mode," recalled Bradley, who spent most of his Western Pacific (WestPac) tour on standby in ships offshore with 2nd Battalion, 4th Marines. That was the Marine unit he was with during the *Cambodian Incursion* in April 1970.

O'Bryon, who made a career out of the Navy retiring as a commander after

*Operation Desert Storm,* summed up his friend's desire to join the Marines and ending up in Vietnam, "It was just a part of his image. If there was to be a fight, he would fight with the good guys because that was where he wanted to be."

"I did go to his funeral but do not remember the funeral service itself. I remember crying and feeling a deep sense of loss and despair that the world had lost one of its truly outstanding people who made a difference in the lives of all he touched. He had come to see me before he left for Vietnam. We just talked about our times together in high school and college. I hope there's a Hereafter. I would sure like to see him again," said his good friend Walsh.

Services were held for Tony at the Fort Myers Chapel in Arlington, Virginia Monday, April 28, 1969 with burial following in Arlington National Cemetery at Grave 298, Section 53 (located at the entrance to ANC next to Memorial Drive) across the Potomac River from Washington, D.C. His final resting placc is not far from Landon School or where he fell in love with Jeanne upon seeing her his junior year in high school and dated with the help of his buddies.

It's a fine tribute to Tony/Buddy that the Landon School and its alumni are keeping his memory alive for future generations through their annual award in his name. Good men like Kups should be elevated as an outstanding example to others to strive for and never be forgotten.

### 2ndLt. Theodore R. Vivilacqua, KIA, May 13, 1969, RPG

The only USNA (Class of '68) graduate in our TBS C-69 class to die in Vietnam was 2ndLt. Theodore Russell "Ted" or "Vivi" Vivilacqua, 22, of Long Beach, California (Thomas Victor "Tom" Parry, Lt., USN, (Ret.), of Needles, California who knew him back home and was a '68 USNA graduate as well, said he was actually from nearby Maywood, population roughly 20,000 in 1969). With a 153 IQ, he was another bright 03 officer.

**2ndLt. Ted "Vivi" Vivilacqua (Photo courtesy of USNA)**

"We attended Boys State, sponsored by the American Legion, our junior and senior years of high school in Sacramento, California. That's how I got to know him through the leadership program at the state capitol. Vivi attended Pius X High School (a Catholic school from which he graduated as valedictorian in 1964) in the Long Beach area. He was named to the All-Catholic Football Team as an offensive lineman his senior year at 5-foot-8, 185 lbs. (The *Huntington Park Daily Signal* in Huntington Park, California also selected him to its All-Southeast Team).[12] We visited each other's homes, but never talked about what we were going to do beyond high school," said Parry.

### ...Vivilacqua, Parry USNA Bound

"I was selected from among several applicants by my Congressman to attend the Naval Academy and called Vivi with the good news. He was also excited because his Congressman hadn't been able to get him a California slot for the Naval Academy but had gone the extra mile by picking up an unused appointment from an Illinois Congressman (according to USNA records).[13] We were going to be midshipmen together," recalled Parry.

Vivi, an Italian-American, majored in German at Annapolis. His twin brother as well as his father were named John Vivilacqua. Vivi's dad was born in Locicero, Italy before immigrating to America. His mother's name was Mary Steele. Parry thought Vivi would go to surface warfare aboard ships with him as part of the U.S. Navy at the end of 4 years but was surprised to discover his friend had chosen the Marines out of USNA.

To get an idea of what kind of special person Vivi was, his roommate for their last 2 years at the USNA, Edward Bennett "Ed" Powell Jr., Lt., USN (Ret.), related this story: "One weekend when we were Firsties (seniors), I had a date with this girl that I was very interested in but didn't have enough cash to take her out. I was going to cancel the date and said something to Vivi. He said he had some money he would loan me until payday so I borrowed the money and had a great time.

"After I got back to school, I found out that he had given me money that he would have used on a date that he had, and canceled his date. He was that type of friend."

Vivi graduated 277th out of 842 graduates in his '68 class with a Bachelor of Science degree. His senior photo in the USNA's yearbook, *The Lucky Bag*, had these remarks under it, "Ted was born in New York and moved to L.A. where he discovered contact sports. Here at the Naval Academy, Ted, better known as 'Vivi,' excelled in football, rugby, German and friendliness. Everyone, except plebes, always got a friendly 'Yo' when passing him in the hall. As a German major, Vivi spent much of his time in the 'last room on the top deck' of the foreign language building. With his excellent mastery of the German language, his short haircut and his determination, Vivi will make a very fine addition to the Marine Corps."

### ...Marine Training at TBS, Orders for WestPac: Vietnam

2ndLt. Vivilacqua matriculated through TBS for roughly 6 months graduating in February 1969. He received orders for "WestPac: Vietnam" and began his tour the next month on Tuesday, March 18. He was a platoon commander in Hotel Co., 2nd Battalion, 5th Marine Regiment (Hotel, 2/5) and probably didn't get assigned to his platoon until near the end of March after orientation/acclimatization.

**...S-3 Operations Journal for Hotel, 2/5, March 25-May 12, 1969**

(Four of C-69's officers served in the 2nd and 3rd Battalions of the 5th Marine Regiment. What follows are strictly highlights of the general combat activities experienced by those officers' companies as their specific platoons are rarely designated in the S-3's Operations Journal reports. These glimpses of each officer's respective company's combat record will give the reader an idea of what these young officers and their enlisted men saw day-in and day-out on the ground in the always dangerous Arizona Territory/Dodge City battlefields---MDK).

April Fool's Day fell on a Tuesday and was most likely the first day Lt. Vivilacqua received shots fired in anger at him in Nam. Two NVA soldiers in a tree line at Phu Binh (1) opened up with automatic fire on Hotel 2/5 at 0830.[14A] Hotel called in an artillery mission followed by 200 rounds from a fixed wing Bronco OV-10 overhead. As a rule bush Marines generally spared no expense or delay in destroying even the smallest number of enemy troops.

Vivi's company sustained casualties coming off Hill 29 at the beginning of a sweep when the enemy took them under fire with small arms (rifles), automatic fire and M-79 40mm grenade rounds at 1630 Friday, April 4.[14B] The company moved to the reverse slope and called in high explosive 60mm, 81mm and artillery rounds on the VC/NVA's position outside Phu Loi (2).[14C] Three Hotel Marines were WIAE and 2 WIANE.

Hotel joined Golf, Fox and Echo 2/5 in participating in *Operation Muskogee Meadow* April 7-20. Working in the notorious Arizona Territory, the companies were involved in providing security for Vietnamese farmers and rice denial to the enemy at harvest time. The area being saturated by Marines was the breadbasket for the VC/NVA's supply needs.

The operation started off ominously for Hotel as one of its Marines tripped a grenade boobytrap at 1200 Monday, April 7 east of Phu Loi (2) near a trail through a tree line.[14D] Luckily the two Marines hit by the shrapnel didn't need evacuating.

At 0900 Thursday, April 10, seven enemy troops took Hotel Co. under fire with small arms and M-79 fire from a tree line in the vicinity of Phu Loi (4).[14E] The Marines responded with a hail of 60mm and 81mm mortar rounds and 106mm recoilless rifle fire, then assaulted the enemy position due north 300 meters across flooded lowland rice paddies to a slight hillock about 10-20 feet high.[14F] Two Marines were WIANE in the firefight. Later that day at 1645, two VC/NVA had had enough and turned themselves in as Chieu Hoi (Open Arms

Program) handing over their AK-47 and M-16 rifles.

Hotel walked off into a heavily mined area on Saturday, April 12. A Marine detonated an M-26 grenade boobytrap northwest of Phu Long (2) in a rice paddy at 0900, 1 wounded-in-action-evacuated, WIAE, 1 wounded-in-action-not-evacuated, WIANE;[14G] while awaiting a medevac at 1100, a Marine detonated an M-26 grenade boobytrap approaching a wooded area near Phu An (1), 1 KIA;[14H] and at 1410 during a sweep in the rice paddy area still northwest of Phu Long (2) an 81mm boobytrap round was detonated, 1 WIAE.[14I]

Vivi's Hotel Co.'s results alone for *Operation Muskogee Meadow* were Marines—2 KIA, 9 WIAE, 10 WIANE; while the enemy had 6 NVA KIA, 1 NVA POW; 1 VC KIA; and 1 VC/NVA KIA. (The casualties wrought on the enemy were always askew as they were phenomenal at evacuating their dead and wounded as well as most their weapons from the field as a psychological ploy to make it look as if they escaped unhurt---MDK).

Three Marines from Hotel were injured and evacuated due to an M-26 grenade boobytrap at 0730 Monday, April 21 on a trail running through Ben Dau (3) about 450 meters northwest of the Song Tinh Yen.[14J]

A Hotel squad sprang a nighttime ambush on four enemy troops at 0320 Friday, April 25 on a trail west of Ben Dau (3).[14K] One Marine was KIA and 3 WIAE. A VC was killed at 1100 in another clash at Dai Khuong (2) near a tributary running off the Song Tinh Yen.

VC/NVA sought to wreak retribution on Hotel's nighttime perimeter at 0400 Saturday, April 26 as the Marines set up on what appears on the map to be a levee outside An Bang (1).[14L] The enemy launched a coordinated ground attack by 30-40 troops firing small arms and detonating 20-25 chicom grenades and 20-25 60mm mortar rounds in their position. Hotel held its own by returning fire and calling in mortars and artillery to break up the onslaught. As a result, the Marines had 7 WIAE, 5 WIANE while the enemy left 2 VC KIA and 4 NVA KIA on the battlefield.

Still operating in the Arizona in May, Hotel Marines tripped an 81/82mm mortar round, a 105mm artillery round and an M-26 grenade boobytrap, respectively on May 6 in the Dai Khuong (3) area,[14M] May 8 in Dai Khuong (2)[14N] and May 10 in the Loc Hoa area,[14O] resulting in 3 WIAE altogether.

On May 9 Hotel discovered an NVA's body in the My Binh area and received fire from two NVA which they promptly assaulted and killed.[14P] One Marine was WIAE in the process.

Fifteen NVA troops took a Hotel Co. platoon under fire at 0958 Sunday, May 11 east of My Binh near a cluster of isolated huts surrounded by rice paddies.[14Q] The Marines' firepower and supporting arms forced them to break contact and flee to the southwest into a wooded area. Two Marines were WIAE while 3 NVA were KIA. Lt. Vivilacqua was awarded the Silver Star for his "courage, aggressive fighting spirit and steadfast devotion to duty in the face of extreme personal danger" this day. A Bronco OV-10 spotted one of the fleeing NVA troops and dispatched him.

Later that same day at 1740, Hotel Co. encountered four bunkers in Trang Dien (1) occupied by NVA with automatic weapons.[14R] A fierce battle ensued before Hotel could secure the bunkers. Hotel Marines lost 3 KIA, 9 WIAE, 11 WIANE while killing 19 NVA and capturing 2 POWs. On Monday, May 12 Hotel Co. was checking out a bunker complex roughly 200 meters south-southwest of the previous day's location on a trail when they discovered an additional 3 NVA KIA.[14S]

**...Trang Dien (1) vicinity, May 13, 1969**

Vivi had seen a lot of scattered combat since joining Hotel Co. on March 18. It all came to an end in the vicinity of Trang Dien (1) on Tuesday, May 13.

Hotel Co. was on a sweep 400 meters due west of the previous day's activity at 0900 when it received small arms and automatic weapons fire, 60mm mortar rounds and accurate B-40 (RPG) rounds from a tree line on the west side of Trang Dien (1).[14T] The enemy was situated astride a footpath crossing about 300 meters away at what appears to be flooded rice paddies between Trang Dien (1) and Quang Hue where there was a small cluster of huts. The Hotel Marines were confident they could overrun the enemy's position as they assaulted it with small arms, automatic weapons and M-79 grenade rounds with tanks in support.

The company overwhelmed the NVA troops killing three and routing the rest from their tree line ambush site. In the process Hotel lost Vivi and two others KIA, 4 WIAE and 3 WIANE. The NVA left behind one RPD machine gun, one RPG-2 rocket launcher, two B-40 rounds, two AK-47 magazines and 80 AK-47 rounds in their haste to depart. The enemy undoubtedly evacuated a larger number of their dead and wounded from the field.

"Vivi caught an RPG to the face in the Arizona (southwest of Da Nang). (Delta, 1/5) was on the same operation at the time," said former 2ndLt. Webb, who was a fellow TBS 5th Platoon mate in C-69 with Vivilacqua as well as a 1968 classmate at the USNA.

During his short time with Hotel Co., 2/5 March 18-May 13, Vivi's company sustained 11 KIA, 46 WIAE, 42 WIANE, while the enemy's confirmed casualties were 43 NVA KIA, 3 NVA POW; 4 VC KIA; 2 VC/NVA KIA and 2 VC/NVA POW.

## ...1stLt. John Walling's Tribute to Vivilacqua

A touching tribute to Vivi was made on the Vietnam Veterans Memorial Fund website, vvmf.org, by his TBS roommate John Walling, an ECP in C-69. "Dear Vivi, We shared many memories while at The Basic School in Quantico. I couldn't have wished for a better roommate during those 6 months. God, did we have some good times. I'll never forget the day of our graduation, when we were having a beer at Major Spooner's Pub (a well-known Marine establishment owned by retired USMC Maj. Richard T. Spooner called The Globe & Laurel Restaurant in the Town of Quantico, restaurant burned in 1972, reopened in Triangle in 1975, relocated to Stafford, Virginia in 2008, south of the National Museum of the Marine Corp outside Quantico. Maj. Spooner served in the Marine Corps for 29 years seeing combat in World War II at Saipan, Tinian and Okinawa, and in Vietnam. Marine memorabilia adorn the walls of the establishment.) and you gave me your St. Christopher (medal) to keep me safe while in Vietnam. I told you at the time that you better keep it, that you needed it more than I did, but you wouldn't listen. It turns out that I should have made you keep it.

"Two years ago, in October of 1998, I found your final resting place in Los Angeles at a site that I had driven by at least 50 times without knowing that you were there. When I went to visit you, I left (the St. Christopher medal) there for you. God you were a great friend. May your courage, never-ending smile and love be the joy and memory to all your friends and family. Rest in peace buddy, I'll see you again someday. Your Viet Nam and Marine brother, John."[15]

## ...He Saw His Own Death

Vivi might have accepted his inevitable demise as to why he gave his St. Christopher to his best friend. "Ted could see his own death in Vietnam while still at TBS. Either some of his friends told me or he himself told me. I don't recall, but I know when I graduated the platoon, the memory of his feeling that death was imminent was firmly fixed in my brain housing," said 1stLt. Tom Saal of Akron, Ohio, Vivi's platoon commander at TBS. Saal had served with the 5th Marines in Vietnam in 1967.

A Rosary was recited for Vivi at the St. Rose of Lima Catholic Church in Maywood Wednesday evening, May 28, 1969 with a Requiem Mass offered at 9 a.m. Thursday morning, May 29 by the Rt. Rev. Monsignor Maurice J. Ryan. He was buried in Calvary Cemetery. His father preceded him in death. Besides his mother, Vivi was survived by his brother John of Azusa, California who was in the National Guard, and his grandmother, Leona Owicz of Glendora.[16]

Vivi and 102 other Long Beach, California Vietnam War KIAs are honored on a memorial plaque in Houghton Park by the Vietnam Veterans of America

Chapter 756. A Huey helicopter is an eye-catching addition suspended in the air on steel poles above the memorial.

### 2ndLt. Albert O. Nelson Jr., KIA, May 21, 1969, boobytrap

2ndLt. Albert Oscar "Al" Nelson Jr., son of Marine Col. Al and Gloria Nelson Sr., could rightfully claim a hometown wherever his dad was posted for duty. He went to high school while his dad was stationed at MCB Quantico, Virginia but didn't finish there as his father took courses to complete his college degree at Syracuse University in Syracuse, New York. Upon graduation from high school at Syracuse, Al enlisted in the Marines at 19 on the Delayed Enlistment Program.

**2ndLt. Al Nelson Jr. (Photo courtesy of Gloria C. Nelson)**

His dad was posted to Okinawa in 1968-69, in the meantime, and his mother and sister, Linda, were uprooted to Oceanside, California to await his return. Lt.Col. Nelson took his golf clubs and anticipated a year of easy duty off the coast of Vietnam in nonhostile Okinawa. When he arrived in Okinawa, the officer he reported to was flummoxed as to why he would bring golf clubs to go in-country. The colonel was surprised to be sent on to the Force Logistics Command as Operations officer in Vietnam for his year's tour.

### ...Enlisted "Hollywood" Marine, Chosen for ECP Program

Meanwhile, Al entered the Marines on the West Coast to be close to his family, thus becoming a "Hollywood" Marine rather than head off to Parris Island in South Carolina. He was chosen for the ECP Program during boot camp and while awaiting orders to Quantico at Camp Pendleton was promoted to lance corporal in April 1968.

Col. Nelson, who would later retire from the Marines in 1981 after 36 years of service, said he had also joined the Marines out of high school but before finishing his senior year in 1945. He lamented the fact that he missed his son's commissioning at the Combined Platoon Leaders Class in August 1968 as he was still in Vietnam. Al was less than 2 months beyond his 20th birthday when he was anointed a second lieutenant in the United States Marine Corps. He had to have been one of our youngest officers.

After the C-69 class graduated from TBS in February, Al surprised a 4th Platoon buddy, 2ndLt. Ed Mattingly Jr., by showing up at his wedding in New Orleans, Louisiana February 8, 1969. He attended his friend's wedding in all his dress blues splendor sporting his flashy Marine Corps Mameluke sword in its sterling silver scabbard by his side impressing all the wide-eyed children, according to Mattingly's posted tribute on the Vietnam Veterans Memorial Fund website, vvmf.org, dated July 19, 2000.[17]

Col. Nelson said he wasn't aware of Al going to that wedding. He added that his son didn't purchase the required officer's sword at TBS but rather sported his dad's sword saving a bundle of money on the expensive piece of sterling silver. "ALBERT OSCAR NELSON" was beautifully etched on one side of the sword which covered both son and father's name.

At some point while Al was learning the fine art of war at TBS, his dad was transferred out of Vietnam and posted to South Korea.

"Al flew to Korea on leave to see me before going to Vietnam. We talked about (the rules of engagement he would face as an infantry officer). I told him, 'Don't kill a man who can't kill you.' And that was my advice before he reported for duty in-country," said Col. Nelson.

2ndLt. Nelson was the first of the 9 KIA C-69 officers to arrive in Vietnam on Thursday, March 6, 1969. He became the platoon commander for 1st Platoon, India Co., 3rd Battalion, 5th Marine Regiment (India 1, 3/5) on March 20th. His troops in India 1 said he often talked glowingly about his dad who was a Marine colonel and was quite proud of him.

**...S-3 Operations Journal for India, 3/5, March 13-May 20, 1969**

India Co., 3/5 appears to have been on perimeter duty at An Hoa Combat Base or Liberty Bridge duty and road sweeps in March as activities involving them don't show up on the S-3 Operations Journal. The company seemed to encounter very little action in April and May compared to other Marine units in the area. Occasional boobytraps and harassing fire by the enemy highlighted April. (Line companies whose activities looked to be nonexistent for several weeks or a month may very well have been put under operational control, Opcon, to other battalions in the 1stMarDiv and therefore are lost to this recounting---MDK).

As of Wednesday, April 2, India received small arms fire and 8-10 60mm rounds in the vicinity of a road northwest of Phu Nhuan (9) resulting in 1 WIAE.[18A]

At 1845 Thursday, April 3, India Co. was sniped at by seven NVA soldiers who ran into a tree line north of Phu Nhuan (6).[18B] Fast-movers (fixed wing) were called in to level the area. At 2015 in a night position in the Phu Nhuan (8) area, the unit received three incoming chicom grenades. India pulled back as artillery prepped the tree line with negative results.[18C]

Friday, April 4 was highlighted by a 4-round barrage of 60mm round fire at 1955 in its nighttime position northwest of Phu Nhuan (9) on a road.[18D] Neither small arms return fire nor enemy mortar rounds resulted in casualties.

India Marines ambushed three VC at 2000 Saturday, April 5 100 meters south of their previous night's ambush site killing one enemy soldier and taking 3 WIAE Marines from six chicom grenades thrown into their position.[18E]

3/5's S-3 Journal notes that India Co. was held back for guard duty at Liberty Bridge as well as patrols and sweeps around that area of the Arizona Territory in May while the remainder of the regiment was participating in *Operation Pipestone Canyon* on treacherous Go Noi Island.

The month started badly for India as four Marines were WIAE after tripping a 60mm boobytrap at 0905 Thursday, May 1 outside Thu Bon (2) 400 meters southwest of the Song Tinh Yen on a small tributary.[18F]

India Co. engaged 15 VC crossing the Song Thu Bon north of Thu Bon (1) killing three and taking a POW on Monday, May 5 at 0710.[18G] At 0920 they fired upon a lone VC crossing the same stream 600 meters away from the original contact with negative results. At 1930 the VC/NVA pumped M-79 rounds into the India Co. position and raked it with small arms fire south of Phu Nhuan (6) resulting in 1 WIAE and 2 WIANE.[18H]

Two 60mm mortar round boobytraps were found on a path in Phu Nhuan (6) at 0745 Wednesday, May 7 and destroyed in place.[18I] Boat traffic was heavy Thursday, May 15 on the Song Tinh Yen where a path intersected the river coming down off Nui Nhu as India's Marines had three sightings.[18J]

Two Vietnamese children approached India Co.'s perimeter on Hill 196, Nui Loi Giang,[18K] on Friday, May 16 to report that the VC had killed their parents in the nearby ville (apparently Phuong Ranh (2) at the Song Tinh Yen ferry crossing 800 meters away). They were turned over to the S-2 (Intelligence section).

In five incidences Sunday, May 18, India Co. killed 3 VC and sustained 1 WIA and 2 WIANE. Three boobytraps were found and destroyed on Monday, May 19. Two VC were picked off by small arms fire and two India Marines were WIAE due to a 81mm boobytrap in the vicinity of the road passing through Thu Bon (3) on Tuesday, May 20.[18L]

### ...Phu Nhuan (3), May 21, 1969

Three to four VC/NVA started India Co.'s day off at 0630 Wednesday, May 21 by pumping six M-79 rounds and small arms fire into its nighttime perimeter on the western edge of Phu Nhuan (9).[18M] At 0700 the enemy blooped six more M-79 ordnance and 100 rounds of AK-47 fire at an India Co. platoon 300 meters south of Phu Nhuan (9) resulting in 1 WIA.[18N]

A warning of how the day was to go came as a fire started by Mike Co., 3/5 in a tree line roughly 250 meters due east of the India Co.'s nighttime perimeter detonated a 105mm artillery boobytrap at 0815.[18O] The 3/5 companies were moving in an area south of the Song Thu Bon about 4 clicks northeast of the An Hoa Combat Base.

"We were told we were coming into a friendly village, and it was not. They must have known where the boobytrap was (that we hit but didn't tell us)," said PFC Edward A. "Ed" Mason, India 1, 1st squad's radioman for 8 months who was from Covington, Kentucky.

At 0930, Nelson's platoon approached Phu Nhuan (3) ville. "On the edge of the village, Lt. Nelson tripped a 105mm boobytrap. He was killed instantly. His radioman was wounded very badly as well and medevacked," recalled PFC Mason, a 19-year-old at the time. He would replace the platoon's radioman who never returned to the unit. 2ndLt. Nelson tripped the 105mm boobytrap in what looks like on the map as a woodland, brushy area.[18P]

Although the S-3 Operations Journal lists two Marines as WIA, Mason and others on the ground disputed this entry by saying the artillery round took his life as soon as he detonated it. Both men were transported to 1st Medical Battalion Hospital by helicopter. Nelson's death was attributed to "multiple fragmentation wounds." Al died just over a month short of his 21st birthday.

Later that afternoon at 1635 India Co. lost another Marine to a chicom grenade boobytrap. One other Marine was lightly wounded but was not evacuated from the field.

During Al's time at India Co., 3/5 March 6-May 21, the company would have 2 KIA, 14 WIAE, 7 WIANE, while enemy casualties were 1 NVA KIA, 8 VC KIA, 1 VC POW and 3 VC/NVA KIA.

Of the 51 men who died from all U.S. military services in Vietnam on May 21, 1969, five, including 2ndLt. Nelson, came from the Marine Corps.

### ...Letters From CO of India Co., 3/5 and the Commandant

The Nelsons received a condolence letter dated May 31, 1969 from India Co. CO Capt. Robert A. Beeler. "Albert was assigned as a platoon commander in India Co. During the morning of May 21, 1969, India Co. was conducting a search and clear operation in an area approximately 2 miles northeast of our combat base at An Hoa when contact was made with an enemy force of undetermined size. During the initial contact with the enemy, an enemy surprise-firing device exploded causing Albert to receive multiple fragmentation wounds to his entire body. Although medical aid was immediately administered by the platoon's Corpsman, Albert succumbed instantly to his wounds at approximately 9:35 a.m.

"It may comfort you to know that Albert received the ministrations of his faith from Lt. W.E. Ebarb, chaplain, U.S. Navy." Capt. Beeler went on to say that

Al's actions reflected "the qualities of an outstanding Marine officer" and that his "excellent performance of duty was constant and earned him the respect of his superiors and men alike."[19]

2ndLt. Nelson was awarded the Bronze Star with Combat "V" in a letter from USMC Commandant Gen. Leonard F. Chapman Jr. His letter dated April 1, 1970 noted, "The Bronze Star Medal with Combat "V" awarded your son, the late 2nd Lieutenant Albert O. Nelson Jr., USMCR, for meritorious service in the Republic of Vietnam from 20 March to 21 May 1969, has been presented to you on behalf of the Secretary of the Navy..."[20]

### ...Funeral Service, Pendleton Names "Nelson Drive"

A funeral service was held in the Lutheran Church in Annandale, Virginia with interment in Arlington National Cemetery at Grave 1266, Section 46, between Memorial Drive and Sigsbee Drive and just south of Farragut Drive. "They buried him near the mast of the *USS Maine* behind the Memorial Amphitheater. I think a lot of Marine officers are buried there," noted Col. Nelson.

In Al's honor, Nelson Drive was named at the 1st Tank Battalion's Camp Los Flores on the sprawling Camp Pendleton military reservation in California Tuesday, November 25, 1986 with the Nelson family in attendance about 17½ years after Al's passing. Also on hand for the ceremony was Maj.Gen. Robert E. Haebel, commanding general, MCB Camp Pendleton; 3/5 CO Lt.Col. Jack W. Klimp (Golf Co., 2/1 CO in 1970 and a '68 USNA graduate); and the 1st Marine Division Band.[21]

Col. Nelson remarked at the street naming ceremony how difficult the Vietnam War was compared to others before it, making it harder for veterans and families to adjust. He indicated that returning veterans came home to a hostile society but that after 20 years it was finally getting better.[22] Al's sister, Linda, recalled that Arlington National Cemetery had open spaces of grass at one time but now after 17½ years those areas are filled with headstones.[23]

### 2ndLt. John H. Lakin, KIA, May 24, 1969, mishandled grenade

Col. John W. Lakin, USAF (Ret.) noted that as a reward for being a good boy he would often take his young son, John, to watch Retreat involving the crisp movements of the fancy uniformed cadets lowering of the flag and ceremonial gunfire at West Point, New York when he taught at the U.S. Military Academy. Near the end of each day, the little boy would implore his dad to take him to where they "shoot the flag down."

Coming to C-69 from the Naval Reserve Officers' Training Corps (NROTC) college ranks at Auburn University in Auburn, Alabama, the 6-foot-2, redheaded 2ndLt. John Hayes Lakin, 22, of Fort Walton Beach, Florida (population

2ndLt. John Lakin
(USMC Photo)

approximately 88,187 in 1969) was someone who had been patriotic and eager to serve his country since he was a child old enough to be stirred by the Stars and Stripes blowing in the wind.

The colonel and all three of his brothers served in the military in World War II so there was a tradition involved in serving in the U.S. armed forces in the Lakin family. Neither John's brother nor his sisters elected to follow in their dad's career choice footsteps.

John was in the Top 10 percent of his high school class and would earn himself a NROTC Scholarship to attend Auburn University. He went through the U.S. Army jump school at Fort Benning, Georgia, during the summer before graduating from Auburn. He completed his studies at AU with a degree in aeronautical engineering, according to Col. Lakin, who retired to Fort Walton Beach. John chose the Marines over the Army and Navy.

### ...Lakin Ranks Among Top 10 at Quantico

With an IQ rating at 157, John scored among the top five lieutenants intelligence-wise in our class of 238 and among the "Top 10" in a combined score of academic, leadership and military skills at graduation. He chose Recon Replacement School out of TBS.

John's dad served in Vietnam 1962-63 with the USAF. His job involved a research and development study working with U.S. Special Forces and Montagnard tribesmen. The war that early in the campaign had not widened into what it would become just a few years later.

Col. Lakin posted on the Vietnam Veterans Memorial website: "John was a patriot from the day he was able to stand at attention across from the parade ground while they 'shoot the flag down.' He was born on Flag Day and was proud to join the Marines the day he graduated from Auburn University. He was soon sent to South Vietnam as a new lieutenant in the 1st Marine Division. After a short time (2 months) at Division Headquarters, he volunteered for duty in the field."[24]

### ... 1st Recon Battalion, Team Date Palm, April 23-May 7, 1969

At 1st Recon, 2ndLt. Lakin was assigned a platoon in Echo Co. His first patrol was with the 22-man Team Date Palm sent to replace Lt. Kupka's ill-fated Team Nail Brush on Hill 146 for the duration of April 23-May 7.

On Thursday, April 24 at 0630 the VC/NVA sent Lt. Lakin's team a welcome aboard gift of eight 122mm rockets fired from the northeast about 2500 meters away. Two of the rockets exploded in their wire while the other six were way off their mark. At 1235 the same day a VC/NVA was spotted on a trail several clicks to the north wearing a cartridge belt and pack. A Team Date Palm M-60 machine gunner took the enemy soldier under fire causing him to drop his gear and run like hell to avoid being shot.

At 1900 Saturday, April 26 the team observed four 122mm rockets 3400 meters to the northeast near An Bang (3) fired at the An Hoa Combat Base and called in a fire mission.

In the next 16 days they spotted seven VC/NVA and called two fire missions with negative results. Like Nail Brush, Lakin's Team Date Palm tripped a boobytrap on May 2 losing six Marines WIA.[25A] The boobytrap was only 100 meters away from Nail Brush's two devastating detonations of April 16 apparently along the same trail that descended from Hill 146.

On Saturday, May 3, five VC/NVA were spotted running out of An Bang (2) to the east wearing black and white pajamas and carrying bundles. On-call aircraft worked the area over but as soon as they left four VC moved back into the ville. Lt. Lakin called a fire mission on the ville.

A VC wearing black pajamas was spotted outside the Hill 146 wire at 0315 Monday, May 5. The Date Palm perimeter watch popped illumination and took the intruder under small arms fire. The area was swept with negative results.

### ...Team Offspring, Dong Den, May 14-18, 1969

From May 14-18 John worked the infiltration route south of Dong Den with 8-man Team Offspring.[25B] The upshot of the patrol was finding a 10-man harbor site that was 5-6 days old.

### ...Team Grey Prince, Hill 425 (Nui Hon Coc), May 22-June 5, 1969

His third and last patrol scheduled to run 15 days came with 15-man Team Grey Prince in the vicinity of Hill 425, Nui Hon Coc.[25C] Special equipment for the lofty hilltop position in addition to their M-16s was an M-14 rifle, three M-79s (40mm grenade launchers), 44 claymore mines, three M-60 machine guns, one VC scope and four Starlight Night Vision scopes. The two teams were inserted at 1000 Thursday, May 22. Lakin's SNCO assistant, SSgt. Crouch, would later cite at the conclusion of the patrol that the Hill 425 OP needed 20 rather than 15 Marines to adequately defend the perimeter.

At 1645 Friday, May 23 they spotted smoke coming from a nearby towering ridgeline on the side of Hill 845 2900 meters to the southwest indicating enemy troops in the process of cooking their chow. An artillery fire mission was called on the probable area of the smoke. A light 400 meters to the north at the base of their hill was taken under fire by M-79 followed by an illumination round with negative results at 2055.

Action continued this night as Lakin logged in six mortar flashes and automatic weapons fire aimed at a ridgeline to the northeast at 2105 roughly 5 kilometers away. Two lights at the base of the ridgeline moved off to the east. He called in an artillery fire mission on the target. Another target of opportunity presented itself as lights believed to be campfires 1400 meters to the south on a mountainside were engaged by small arms fire at 2110 but the lights remained on. An enemy harbor site was found at 2225 and at the same time three fires and a steady light on a ridgeline were spotted. Another fire mission was called.

### ...Lakin Mortally Wounded, Hill 425, May 24, 1969

At 0940 Saturday, May 24, 2ndLt. Lakin's team found a possible underground bunker complex with air vents a bare 150 meters east of their hilltop position.[25D] Team Grey Prince must have suspected their enemy was as close as being underfoot a few meters on Hill 425, Nui Hon Coc, OP position in a worst case scenario. The team threw smoke grenades into the vents in an attempt to uncover the tunnel entrances with negative results. An M-26 baseball grenade was inserted into one of the air vents to enlarge the hole.

Following the explosion, John pulled the pin on a second M-26 baseball grenade and was in the process of putting it in an air vent and letting the spoon fly when he fumbled the compact explosive. He tried to retrieve the grenade from where it had fallen on the ground and place it in the vent before it could explode injuring his Marines around him but it detonated before he could do so. The C-69 3rd Platoon mate was listed as an emergency medevac by HN Doc Shoemaker. Another Marine was said to be a routine WIA as a result of the blast.

The 1st Recon's Team Grey Prince patrol debrief sadly notes, "*Emergency medevac* (John Lakin) *died en route to USS Sanctuary*."

Prior to leaving Hill 425, the Recon team with SSgt. Crouch taking over for Lt. Lakin spotted 401 VC/NVA over a 2-week period and called in 12 fire missions down on their heads killing a confirmed 17 enemy soldiers before their extraction June 5. Lt. Lakin's Team Grey Prince accomplished its mission by disrupting and killing the VC/NVA within their surveillance area.

At Camp Pendleton while I was an enlisted Marine going through ITR training, the bush-savvy Vietnam vets hammered a point into our heads during the live grenade throw. Having thrown many grenades in their Vietnam tours and heard stories of others who had done so as well, the consensus was that the manufacturer's claim that a grenade had a 3- to 5-second delay was an arbitrary number. They warned us to never pull the pin on a grenade, let the spoon fly and hold it to throw for, say, 1 or 2 seconds like in a John Wayne flick so the bad guys couldn't throw it back.

Not to confirm that John got a "short-fused" grenade but Nam veteran instructors at Pendleton warned us in the most colorful obscenity-laced wording that it did occur on occasion in combat.

2ndLt. John Hayes Lakin's funeral was held in the First Presbyterian Church of Fort Walton Beach followed by graveside services at the Barranza National Cemetery in Pensacola, Florida.

For John, the "shooting down of the flag" by the Marine Honor Guard with its 21-gun salute one last time was apropos. Rather than lowering of the Stars and Stripes at Retreat like he'd begged his parents to let him go see as a child at West Point, the flag was removed from his casket by the Marines, folded expertly 13 times with tight tri-corners, stars out, and presented to his parents from a grateful nation in recognition of his sacrifice in Vietnam.

## 2ndLt. William G. Schanck Jr., KIA, June 21, 1969, CH-46 crash

2ndLt. William Garrett "Garry" Schanck Jr., from the small village of Chepachet within the Town of Glocester (population around 5,140 in 1969), Rhode Island, was a 1966 graduate of Ponagansett High School in Scituate, R.I. He briefly attended the University of Rhode Island in Kingston before dropping out. His URI friends still recall the outgoing Garry's memorable freshman year and all the good times they had.

**2ndLt. Garry Schanck Jr. (Photo courtesy of Mary Schanck-Wasilewski)**

### ...Chooses Marines, Selected for ECP Program at Parris Island

"Garry had a low lottery number for the draft so he decided to enlist in the Marines rather than be drafted into some other military service," indicated his sister, Mary Arvaline Schanck-Wasilewski. He went to boot camp at Parris Island where he was chosen for the ECP program.

The Schancks made a tradition of serving in the military through the generations: grandfather, dad, uncles and a brother. "He was the oldest of five, four boys (Garry, Clint, Jeff and John) and me. Within minutes of knowing him, you knew about the rest of us. He was groomed to be the oldest and was wonderful at it. I was the only girl and he made me feel special," recalled Mary, who was 11 (Clint, 19; Jeff, 17; and John, 7) when her brother was killed.

### ...Camp Reasoner, RVN, March, 17, 1969

Schanck arrived at 1st Recon's Camp Reasoner in Vietnam on St. Patrick's Day, Monday, March 17, 1969 and took over a Delta Co. platoon in the 1st Recon Battalion.

### ...Team Aunt Mable, March 25-28, 1969

He ran his first mission March 25-28 as patrol leader of Team Aunt Mable. The patrol located an enemy's company-sized base camp that had been completely destroyed by artillery.

### ...Team Hanover Sue, near Hill 119, April 8, 1969

The Rhode Island lieutenant's next foray into the bush was short-lived as patrol leader of 23-man Team Hanover Sue. The team was inserted on top of Hill 148 in the Tra Sons at 1215 Tuesday, April 8.[26A] A huge lake was 600 meters due south.

As Lt. Schanck's team moved to check out an enemy corpse at 1410, the Marine behind him accidentally detonated a surprise firing device near the dead body. The result was one emergency and two routine medevacs. The lieutenant was peppered in his back with shrapnel from the blast earning him a Purple Heart and a trip out of the bush after only an hour and 55 minutes on the ground. His slight injuries didn't keep him out of the fight for long.

### ...Team Prime Cut, Hill 119, April 25-May 13, 1969

He returned to the field as patrol leader April 25-May 13 as 7-man Team Prime Cut spent 18 days gathering intelligence on enemy movement near Hill 119, also called Doi Chiem Son, which is about a click northeast of Hill 148.[26B] Lt. Schanck's team recorded 72 sightings of 527 VC/NVA, five .50 caliber machine gun positions, 17 civilians, one bunker complex and tripped an M-26 grenade boobytrap resulting in negative injuries. He called in 51 artillery fire missions and 11 aircraft sorties that accounted for one confirmed enemy KIA.

### ...Team Segment, Hill 119, May 13-27, 1969

When Team Prime Cut was extracted from Hill 119, Lt. Schanck remained behind to take over as patrol leader of its replacement, Team Segment, consisting of 21 Marines May 13-27. This go around his team had 44 sightings of 285 VC/NVA resulting in 32 artillery fire missions and one airstrike which netted five confirmed enemy KIAs.

### ...Team Pony Boy, June 2-6, 1969

From June 2-6 Lt. Schanck took 7-man Team Pony Boy out on patrol and was inserted by Sea Knight.[27A] Their only notable sighting was a partially built hooch on stakes. One Marine was injured by flying debris by a Sea Knight's tornadic burst of wind upon extraction. His final trip to the bush would be June 21 aboard a HMM-165 helicopter.

### ...Teams Grade Level, June 18-20, 1969

1st Recon's records show that Lt. Schanck's 8-man Team Grade Level and Cpl. Bill Evans' 8-man Team May Fly were scheduled to make inserts 2 kilometers apart from separate Sea Knights Wednesday, June 18 in preliminary planning. Schanck's team consisted of LCpl. Frank J. Bosco, PFC Arthur Coby "Art" Councill III, PFC Robert L. "Bob" Crites Jr., PFC James O. "Jim" Hall Jr., LCpl. Richard A. Weil Jr., PFC Albert Udo "Al" Herlicka and Navy Corpsman Doc Rucker.

Cpl. Evan's team included LCpl. Cole, LCpl. Steve Campbell, LCpl. James "Jim" Benedict, LCpl. Horton, PFC Nagel, PFC C. Cabreras and PFC S.D. Bunker.

May Fly was to be inserted at either "UL (upper left) of Bach Ma, Sheet 6541 II map grid quadrant ZC0487 or LR (lower right) of grid quadrant ZC0685" while Grade Level was to be dropped at either "UL ZC0287 or LR ZC0485" (Bach Ma map) on June 18 but the mission was canceled. It was rescheduled for Thursday, June 19, but was again canceled due to a lack of aircraft.

On Friday, June 20, the teams were en route to those same coordinates 22½ miles west-northwest of Da Nang when Grade Level's Sea Knight gunner engaged eight VC/NVA crossing a bridge, about 2700 meters west-northwest of Hill 606 (Dong Rong), near their projected LZs and received ground fire.[27B] The mission was aborted, as every VC/NVA in the area knew they were in their neighborhood.

"We met (the lieutenant) the night before we got shot down. He seemed like a pretty likeable guy. I remember he made a few comments on a tape I was making for my mother that night," recalled former PFC Al Herlicka who was from Los Angeles, California, and a Team Grade Level M-79 (grenadier) man. On the day Grade Level was to be inserted, Herlicka said he turned 20...in California time which was 9 hours behind Vietnam. God's birthday gift to him this day would be his life, he reflected.

LCpl. Bosco, 19, of Providence, Rhode Island had taken Team Good Luck out on his first stint as a patrol leader June 10-14 and had five members of the upcoming Team Grade Level's Marines in his command. He had also been on patrol with Lt. Schanck's Team Segment May 13-27 and wrote his parents, Carl and Amelia Bosco, about the upcoming June 21 patrol that he had volunteered to go out with him as he felt his fellow Rhode Islander needed his help. Ironically, "Good Luck" would not follow him or most his compatriots on that patrol as they flew to their insert point aboard a HMM-165 Lady Ace Sea Knight.

### ...Lady Ace Sea Knight, Team Grade Level Shot Down, June 21, 1969

The teams' mission on Saturday, June 21 was to conduct reconnaissance and surveillance operations to detect possible enemy troop movements or arms infiltration with special emphasis to locate and monitor enemy transit routes.

Herlicka was more specific, "The other Recon team that went out with us were guys who lived in our hooch and the hooch next to ours. We all knew each other. We were supposed to run through this area for a week and just do hit and run tactics. We knew it was going to be a hot patrol."

The two teams returned to the same general area (1200 meters from where the gunner opened up on the enemy troops crossing a bridge June 20) believed to be a VC training center June 21 accompanied by a fixed wing aircraft and two Cobra gunship escorts. The fixed wing prepped the LZ (1700 meters northwest of Dong Rong) by bombing it thus clearing the area but inadvertently announcing the Recon teams' insertion point.[27C] The Cobras circled menacingly overhead drawing further attention to the insertion LZ as well. The LZ was on a flat area at the 220-meter level between two blue lines (rivers) with the mountains rising to over 1,000 meters to the north and south.

At 1100 the first HMM-165 Lady Ace Sea Knight approached the insert location and hovered over the vines, thick shrubs and elephant grass as Cpl. Evan's Team May Fly leaped 15 feet to the deck below. The aircraft and Evans' team took incoming from three VC/NVA letting loose with a steady stream of small arms fire from a riverbed to the south approximately 50-75 meters away. No injuries resulted as Team May Fly moved into the safety of the surrounding jungle and the Sea Knight departed unharmed.

Five minutes later Sea Knight pilot 1stLt. William Lee Peters Jr. and his copilot 1stLt. Stan Jorgensen maneuvered their aircraft into that same LZ, according to LCpl. Benedict, with Lt. Schanck's Team Grade Level aboard when all hell broke loose. Enemy troops zeroed in on the LZ as the second Lady Ace Sea Knight approached the insertion point. The CH-46 took a heavy volume of small arms and automatic weapons fire from a towering ridgeline to the south as it hovered.

"We got just below the treetops in a roughly opened up area when I heard what sounded like the blades hitting some small tree limbs or something. As we hovered, a machine gun opened up on us. Some rounds went through the copter's skin. We all returned fire. It seemed like the VC had very good cover since they were still there after the jet dropped its bombs," noted Herlicka.

"My buddy, PFC Art Councill, and I were firing out the same window. He was using an M-16 (rifle) and I was firing my M-79 grenade launcher. Art got hit and fell backwards. When I turned to him, I saw the gunner get hit as well (most likely the crew chief, LCpl. Paul Edward Petroline, took a round as neither gunner was listed as hit by incoming fire). This all happened pretty fast but as I remember it, it went by (in slow motion). I felt the bird hit something hard and it jolted me to one side."

1stLt. Peters' aircraft attempted to leave the hot zone and abort Team Grade Level's insert but was hit by some large explosive ordinance shutting down the engines.

"(Jorgensen) thinks that they lost boost pressure. It is suspected that the aircraft was hit in the control closet area by a rocket-propelled grenade (RPG)," wrote John Dullighan, Boeing Tech representative to HMM-165. He noted the area was too hot to go back to inspect the destroyed helicopter to determine for sure what brought it down.[28]

"During the climb (out of the zone), a loud explosion occurred aft of the cockpit area as we cleared the treetops. The aircraft pitched extreme nose up and rolled slowly right to a somewhat inverted position with no control input," noted Jorgensen.[29]

"I remember my M-79 floating in the air. As I grabbed the seat, my glasses fell off. I was thinking I would pick them up after we get out of this mess. I don't recall seeing anything after that but instead heard glass breaking, metal twisting and trees breaking," said Herlicka.

The aircraft came to rest in a tree line 125 meters east of the LZ and burst into flames. Most of the Recon Marines probably fell to the back of the Sea Knight into the burning inferno of the fuel tanks when it went nose up before crashing.

"It got real quiet. I was thrown from the front of the bird to the rear. I was in a sitting position. Seemed like a dream sort of. I saw a light from the front of the bird. Then two figures of people moving things around. It appeared they were looking for something. I guess that's when I started to come around from my dazed state. I heard a crackling behind me. I turned to see a huge flame. My senses came to and I realized I was getting burned. The pain hit me and I let out a scream.

"When I looked to the front where I saw these two figures, they stopped, looked startled and disappeared. The light also went away. Today, I believe these were the angels of death looking for souls to take," said Herlicka. He was having a hard time getting up to escape the flames consuming him and prayed to God to take him quickly as the pain was beginning to be unbearable.

"God spared my life by getting the Corpsman, Doc Rucker, to wake up and give me the push I needed to reach the ribs of the bird and pull myself up. Whatever or whoever was on top of me rolled off and I was standing up."

The two men ran for the side door at the front of the aircraft. Herlicka became momentarily hung up on some jagged metal until Doc Rucker pulled him loose. They joined the copilot Jorgensen and the HMM-165 crew's two gunners outside the aircraft.

LCpl. W.T. Gibson, gunner, received a contusion to the right arm and a laceration to his right knee; Cpl. J.E. Gauvin, gunner, fractured the right portion of his jaw and dislocated his shoulder; and copilot 1stLt. Jorgensen received a laceration to his nose, according to USMC researcher John Lane.[30]

Jorgensen said he received a concussion, torn muscles in his lower back, his left knee had a torn and severed ACL and MCL and his helmet visor broke and lacerated his nose.[31]

Herlicka and Doc Rucker were fortunate as the Corpsman threw bandoleers of ammo off his lap before they cooked off in the fire aboard the helicopter and likewise Herlicka's pack containing 20 40mm M-79 HE (grenade) rounds failed to explode. The Recon Marine sustained 2nd and 3rd degree burns over 17 percent of his body…the burns stopped at the base of his backpack containing the high explosives!

Shortly after their exit from the helicopter, some of the Recon Marines' explosives aboard blew up. Two men still alive inside the burning aircraft began screaming as the flames consumed them. In rapid succession the rest of the ammunition/explosives---.50 caliber rounds from the onboard machine guns, M-26 baseball grenades, rifle rounds and two claymores---cooked off inside the conflagration. After all the pyrotechnics stopped detonating, it became very quiet, according to Herlicka.

Someone yelled out to them, "HEY! HEY!" A crew member yelled in response. "WE ARE OVER HERE!" That's when the VC/NVA calling out to them opened up with their AK-47 rifles.

"We had no weapons except for a .38 (caliber pistol) one of the crew members had. God was with us that morning. The two Cobras opened up and were firing their rockets and miniguns at the VC. Shrapnel was flying everywhere. The noise was deafening," said Herlicka.

At 1130 Team May Fly reached the crash site to look for survivors. The wreckage was still on fire and the team couldn't get close to it. They searched the surrounding area and found the five survivors who had escaped the burning aircraft. A medevac was requested and completed for the injured Marines and Navy Corpsman. They were flown out to the hospital ship, *USS Repose*, anchored in Da Nang Harbor.

Team Serviceman, a reaction force consisting of 42 Marines, arrived to secure the crash site at 1257. A Graves Registration Team was also brought in to retrieve the bodies. The Marines on the ground were all helilifted out by 1800.

1st Recon's Teams May Fly/Grade Level Patrol Debrief indicated that the two 8-man Recon teams were put down in a "probable enemy base camp." A Recon team was reinserted into the same general location after the June 21st patrol attempt, according to Herlicka, and found that the area was still "very hot" with enemy activity.

LCpl. Benedict, who was Cpl. Evan's radioman on the June 21 insert, noted that a few weeks before that last operation Lt. Schanck had approached him and asked that he be his primary radioman on a patrol. "His team had been shot out of a couple of LZs and I told him no thanks that he was jinxed, not knowing that was the last time I would talk to him. I didn't mean to be hurtful. Superstition has deep roots. On the ground that day (when Lt. Schanck and most of his team were killed), I saw people with rocket-propelled grenades and was wondering if we (Team May Fly) were even going to get out of that mess alive. The brothers that lost their lives that day still visit me to this day."

Besides Lt. Schanck, others killed in the air crash were: pilot, 1stLt. William Lee Peters Jr., 26, Fort Dodge, Iowa (Navy Cross, April 12, 1969; Silver Star, June 21, 1969); crew chief, LCpl. Paul Edward Petroline, 22, Lincoln Park, Michigan; Team Grade Level Marines: LCpl. Frank Joseph Bosco, 19, Providence, Rhode Island; PFC Arthur Coby Councill III, 20, Hawthorne, California; PFC Robert Lincoln Crites Jr., 19, Colton, California; PFC James Oscar Hall Jr., 20, Vista, California; and LCpl. Richard Anthony Weil Jr., 20, Anaheim, California.

Forty-five U.S. servicemen died in Vietnam June 21, 1969. Lt. Schanck and seven other Marines aboard the HMM-165 helicopter would account for most of the 10 Marines KIA of those 45 American servicemen killed across the country.

### ...Fourth of July Wake

In a fitting tribute to Garry Schanck, his wake was held on the Fourth of July in the living room of his parents William G. and Arvaline Jo (Lambert) Schanck Sr.'s Chepachet residence, according to his sister Mary. The whole town turned out for Garry's funeral at the Chepachet Union Church and the graveside burial service at Acotes Hill Cemetery in Chepachet on July 5th. She also noted that *Born Free* was sung at his funeral. His mother and brother, Clint, (who was 10 months younger than Garry and died in 1973), were later buried next to him. Mary indicated that the loss of the oldest son greatly impacted and changed the course of her family's lives.

So that the citizens of Chepachet may not forget him, a bridge in the center of town was named for 2ndLt. Garry Schanck and a plaque was erected on the site. Also, beginning in 1999 at the annual University of Rhode Island's ROTC Cadet Awards ceremony, the *2ndLt. William Garrett Schanck Jr. Award,* that includes a plaque, a photo of Garry, a synopsis of his military service and Army dress blues, is presented to an outstanding URI ROTC graduate thanks to Lt.Col. Paul Helweg, USA (Ret.), URI ROTC Alumni Association president, and his wife, Kathy (Fahey) Helweg. Kathy and her friends got to know Garry their freshman year, 1966-67, at URI.

Also, U.S. Army Spec. 4 Richard N. "Dick" Smith, former Military Policeman in the 11th Air Assault Division, raised $80,000 collecting aluminum cans to erect two rappelling towers at the Narragansett Council of the Boy Scouts of America's Camp Yawgoog Scout Reservation at Rockville, Rhode Island. The towers are named for the two former scouts who spent their summers there as young boys, 2ndLt. Schanck and Marine 1stLt. Carl William Myllymaki III, 25, of Westerly, Rhode Island, who served with Echo Co., 3rd Recon, 3rd Marine Division and was KIA on October 2, 1968.

At the dedication ceremony of the towers July 15, 2000, a bronze plaque bearing Schanck's name was unveiled by David and Priscilla (Greene) Feeney, who were freshman classmates of Garry's at the University of Rhode Island in 1966.

LCpl. Ken Andróes, a Delta Co., 1st Recon Marine who accompanied PFC Bosco on his first patrol March 19-23 and again when LCpl. Bosco was the patrol leader of Team Good Luck June 10-14, sent two USMC flags that were hung on the two towers until the end of the ceremony when they were presented to the honorees' mothers. In addition, Smith helped raise funds to set up a scholarship named for Myllymaki for an outstanding Westerly High School graduate each year to attend URI. Smith and Myllymaki were former teammates playing left and right offensive and defensive tackles on the Westerly football team 1960-61 back in high school.

Smith also spearheaded a fund drive to erect three granite benches outside URI's Mackal Fieldhouse as a Vietnam Memorial honoring all 18 URI students and employees killed in the war.

"I don't remember a lot of the particulars about why Garry left school and went off to war. What I do remember and very vividly is 'who' he was and 'what' he 'meant' to us as his community and as friends. His death was something the small community of Chepachet, Rhode Island and the school, Ponagansett High, will never forget, especially the class of 1966," said Maureen Delfarno, a longtime family friend who babysat some of the younger Schanck siblings.

And in the Schanck/Arvaline family line, the tradition continues with young men sent off to war. Mary and Michael F. Wasilewski's (U.S. Air Force in Vietnam) youngest son, Pvt. Zekiel Garrett "Zeke" Wasilewski of the U.S. Army's 1st Armored Division, returned from a tour in the Iraq war zone in March 2005. Mary noted her son drove a gasoline truck in Iraq. She said Zeke's middle name Garrett is in honor of her brother's memory.

**2ndLt. Albert D. Benson, KIA, July 6, 1969, boobytrap**

2ndLt. Albert Du Ward "Al" Benson, 23, of Sidney, Iowa (pop. 1,000) was an outstanding track and cross-country athlete before joining the Marine Corps.

In 1964 he set the mile run record, 4:33.3, in his Iowa high school's Corner Conference that stood for 40 years...surpassed at long last in 2004. His brother, Lynn, noted he was also active in the 4-H Club for 9 years in Sidney.

**2ndLt. Al "A.D." Benson (Photo courtesy of Lynn Benson)**

**...Wayne State College: All-American Honors for NAIA Cross-Country**

Al or A.D., as his siblings and friends back home in Iowa called him, attended Wayne State College in Wayne, Nebraska. He lettered in spring track and cross-country each of the 4 years he was at WSC. As a distance runner, he was the champion for 2 years in both the Nebraska College Conference Cross-Country and the NAIA District Cross-Country. In national competition, A.D. placed 14th in the NAIA Nationals and won NAIA All-American status in 1967 as a college junior. Consequently, in college and high school, his strong legs had never failed him, helped define his existence and brought him recognition and fame far beyond his corner of the country.

In 1967 he was awarded the Fred Dale Athlete-Scholar Award at Wayne State. He graduated in 1968 with a bachelor's degree in speech with the prospect of coaching someday, according to Lynn, who is the county extension agent and 4-H youth leader in Sidney.

**...Marine Officer Training, Vietnam**

With an eye for serving his country as a Marine, Al attended 6-week USMC Platoon Leader Class summer sessions at Quantico in 1967 and 1968. He was commissioned a Marine officer in August 1968. I'm sure the long forced marches and runs at Quantico were a piece of cake for Al.

After TBS, Al trained as an elite Force Recon Marine. He departed Omaha, Nebraska for his Vietnam tour March 7, 1969. He arrived in Vietnam Saturday, March 15. He was assigned as platoon commander of 3rd Platoon, Fox Co.,

2nd Battalion, 5th Marines (Fox 3, 2/5). The Iowan was another one of those Marines with an impressive IQ, 150, who ended up in a bush unit.

### ...2/5's S-3 Operations Journal for March 23-July 5, 1969

Fox Co. is highlighted in the 2/5's S-3 Operations Journal for March-April for tripping four M-26 grenade boobytraps resulting in 4 WIAE and 1 WIANE. The company also had a Marine wounded by small arms fire on Saturday, April 19 at Tan Phouc (1).[32A] Airstrikes directed by Fox had a probable KIA VC/NVA on Wednesday, April 30.

May 1-11 Fox Co. Marines accidentally set off five boobytraps, two of which were 105mm rounds that resulted in 2 KIA and 2 WIAE.

The VC/NVA attacked Fox Co. at Phu Bac (2)[32B] at 1230 Monday, May 12 with 60mm and 82mm mortar fire.[32C] Fox called in its own heavy metal with 60mm, 81mm, artillery and two flights of fixed wing. The Marines sustained 22 WIAE and 8 WIANE.

At 1715 Tuesday, May 13 Fox Marines were sitting in a defensive position on a little hillock outside Dai Khuong (2) when they were surprised by two VC/NVA point guides who accidentally walked into their position and were captured.[32D] Before they could be subdued, they shouted a warning to 15 more enemy troops just emerging from a tree line 50 meters back. Their compatriots escaped except for one NVA soldier that Fox Co. Marines managed to kill.

Fox Co. spent time at Liberty Bridge and the An Hoa Combat Base the latter part of May and the first of June as the fighting slacked off in their sector. The road sweeps became more worrisome as 250-lb. and 500-lb. HE boobytraps (probably altered dud bombs from our aircraft) were found and destroyed in place. The 2/5 Narrative Summary for June cited the majority of what few casualties the battalion received for the month was due to surprise firing devices.

Fox Marines discovered two boobytraps, an M-26 grenade and a 5-lb. satchel charge at 1430 in the La Thap (4) area on Saturday, June 14.[32E] At 1420 Saturday, June 21, a Fox Co. patrol found a pressure-detonation boobytrapped 155mm artillery shell in Hoa Tay on a major trail through the ville.[32F] They destroyed it in place.

I can only assume that Al Benson's platoon must've had some action with the varied encounters Fox Co. had with enemy troops at the end of June and the beginning of July.

### ...Cu Ban (2), July 6, 1969

At 1250 Sunday, July 6, Fox Co. was moving through tall grass to its night position in the Arizona, according to 2/5's S-3 Operations Journal.

"We were working out of Liberty Bridge (2 kilometers east-southeast of the bridge) which spans the Song Thu Bon. We were on a search and clear platoon-sized patrol. I was radio operator for 3rd squad, Fox 3 which was on point and found a dead indigenous who had hit a boobytrap (the Vietnamese male had destroyed his legs stepping on a surprise firing device and bled out)," said LCpl. Dave Fuller, 19 years old in 1969 from La Puente, California.

He continued, "The body was several days old. I notified Lt. Benson (by radio). He wanted to link up with our squad to view the scene. I advised against this since our AO was known to be heavily boobytrapped, but he insisted. Lt. Benson moved to our position with the platoon CP (command post) leapfrogging my squad when the incident occurred. He stepped on a large mine." The 2/5's S-3 Operations Journal reported it as being a pressure type 60mm mortar round. The boobytrap was detonated in the Cu Ban (2) area.[32G]

"Both his legs were shattered to above the knees. The Doc and I immediately applied tourniquets to his legs. I used my web belt. The lieutenant raised up and looked at his legs. I understand he was a long distance runner. I truly believe that if Lt. Benson hadn't been a long distance runner he would have been able to survive. But after he looked at his legs he was gone. He immediately went into shock.

"The Doc administered CPR but to no avail. He never regained consciousness. He was KIA when the medevac arrived. Lt. Benson was a good man and a strong leader but did not take advice from subordinates. I wish he had," lamented LCpl. Fuller.

The explosion occurred in a rice paddy/scrub grass area and also killed another Marine and wounded three others who required medevacking. Two additional Marines were so slightly wounded they didn't require medical attention at 1st Med. Lt. Benson and one of his enlisted Marines would join eight other Marines to die in Vietnam on this date. Twenty-eight from all services would lose their lives July 6, 1969.

Five minutes later while waiting for the medevac bird two additional Marines were wounded by an M-26 grenade boobytrap requiring their medevac from the bush. Another 60mm mortar round pressure detonation boobytrap was found 600 meters away at 1450 and blown in place.

In Benson's time with Fox Co., 2/5 between March 15-July 6, the company had 4 KIA, 40 WIAE, 21 WIANE, while inflicting on the enemy 7 NVA KIA, 7 VC KIA and 5 VC/NVA KIA, 2 VC/NVA POW.

"The Arizona Territory, Goi Noi Island and Phu Nhuans were known as 'Boobytrap Triangle' in our AO. I can remember a 3-month period when I lost over half my platoon due to the damn things," recalled Fuller.

"(Lt. Benson) wouldn't ask anyone to do something he wasn't willing to do himself...even walking point," commented former LCpl. Howard Ball, 19 in 1969 from Council Bluffs, Iowa. He was attached to Fox Co. as an artillery forward observer, FO, and had become acquainted with the fellow Iowan. "At one point Secretary of Defense Robert McNamara made the comment that the Arizona Territory was the hottest place in Vietnam for detonating boobytraps. I think we lost more Marines to boobytraps than to other injuries."

Ball would spend 19 months in Vietnam serving as an FO before returning stateside. One of his duty stations was at Marine Barracks 8th and I in Washington, D.C. where he was a member of the Parade Platoon and served on the Burial Detail Firing Squad.

When he returned to Iowa, Ball said he and his girlfriend double-dated with a girl who turned out to have Al Benson's USMC photos on her wall. When he recognized the photos and asked her how she knew Lt. Benson, she said she was his cousin...small world. The H&S Co. FO for artillery and mortar tubes for Fox Co., 2/5 said he met with Benson's family and identified the Marines in the photos their son had sent home from Vietnam shortly before he was killed.

**...Benson Honored, Buried in Sidney**

The *Sidney Argus-Herald,* Al's hometown weekly newspaper, reported his death on Thursday, July 10, 1969 in a front page story with the headline at the top of the page, "Lt. A.D. Benson Was Killed In Vietnam Battle July 6." The article indicated two Marine officers from Lincoln, Nebraska had arrived to notify Al's parents, Mr. and Mrs. Gilbert Benson of Sidney, on Monday following his being killed on Sunday. They said his death was due to "a fragmentation bomb." The official telegram from the Defense Department of Al's KIA status didn't arrive until Tuesday, July 8.

Al's body was delayed in returning to Sidney thus his funeral wasn't until July 22. The service was held in the Sidney United Methodist Church with the former church's pastor, the Rev. James Dendler of Knoxville giving the sermon. Casket bearers and Color Guard came from the Marine Air Reserve Training Detachment in Lincoln. Burial was in the Sidney Cemetery. Besides his parents and brother, Lynn, Al was survived by two sisters, Kaye and Linda.

Lynn noted that poet Robert Frost's "A Road Less Traveled" was included in the funeral memorial folder. "A.D. referred to it in a letter home not too long before he was killed," said Lynn.

As part of the funeral service, Melvin Taylor sang *The Impossible Dream* accompanied by organist Mrs. Harry Davis.

In C-69's *Mess Night* class graduation book, 2nd, 3rd, 4th and 5th

Platoons' lieutenants were pictured involved in TBS field problems with silly brief captions under them concluding with the whole platoon shown stiffly standing on bleachers in a mock-up Vietnamese ville.

In Al Benson's 1st Platoon, they thought outside the box as all the photos were underscored by lyrics from the song, *The Impossible Dream (The Quest)* from the musical *Man of LaMancha*...Don Quixote, no less. The idealistic wording, of course, reminded me of what the French Army's Col. Wainwright was quoted as saying (in Chapter 1, *Book I* of *American Heroes: Grunts, Pilots & "Docs"* ) in Howard (Washington, D.C.) University's professor Dr. Bernard B. Fall's famous book *Street Without Joy* about there needing to be someone willing to tilt at windmills in a materialistic world. What an absolutely perfect choice of songs for this outstanding Marine's funeral.

*The Impossible Dream* lyrics tell of fighting a tenacious foe to one's last ounce of courage no matter how hopeless the cause. As in the story of Don Quixote, our hero might not triumph in the end but he would pass through this world knowing that he had given it his best shot.[33]

So that he may not be forgotten, Al's high school friends, Chuck Offenburger and Steve Strong of Sidney, furnished a travelling trophy inscribed, "The A.D. Benson Memorial Mile," that is awarded each spring with the winner's name of the mile run at the Corner Conference track meet. Each new winner joins a long line of top milers from previous years...that includes A.D. Benson.

On October 11, 1980, A.D. was posthumously inducted into the Wayne State College Hall of Fame for his outstanding achievements in track and cross-country from 1964-68. Also, family and friends endowed over 50 track scholarships worth $100 each in A.D.'s name over a 25-year period following his death. The balance remaining in the scholarship fund was given as a memorial to the family's church.

"A.D. was a member of a record-setting mile medley relay team at Sidney High School in addition to his distance running. Three of the four relay team members died during the Vietnam War--A.D. as a Marine; John Hein as a Green Beret; and Bob Harris in an Army unit stationed in Korea. Kind of a big loss for a small rural Iowa community of about 1,000 people," lamented Lynn.

### 2ndLt. Philip N. Huth II, KIA, July 12, 1969, boobytrap

2ndLt. Philip Nicholas "Nick" Huth, 23, of Corpus Christi, Texas (population approximately 284,832 in 1969) got his nickname "General" from his 3rd Platoon mates at TBS for being so doggone smart. He attended Southwestern University in Georgetown, Texas and Del Mar Junior College (2-year community college) in Corpus Christi, Texas before moving onto the University of Texas at Austin where he completed his junior year.

## ...Enlisted in Marines, ECP, Vietnam

**2ndLt. Nick Huth (USMC Photo)**

Nick dropped out of UT to join the Marine Corps. He attended boot camp in San Diego where his test scores made him a candidate for the Enlisted Commissioning Program.

He was an ECP like me but that's as far as the comparisons go. His IQ was an impressive 151. Upon completion of TBS, the General got his pick of a MOS out of TBS due to his outstanding academic standing in the company and chose Recon Replacement School.

He arrived in Vietnam on Sunday, March 30, 1969. After orientation/acclimatization, he became the platoon commander of 3rd Platoon, Golf Co., 2nd Battalion, 5th Marines (Golf 3, 2/5) while it was involved in *Operation Muskogee Meadow* April 7-20.

## ...S-3 Operations Journal for Golf, 2/5, April 6-July 11, 1969

Something Nick would see or be within the vicinity of was the frequent devastating detonation of boobytraps...some large--some small. While in a squad size ambush site at 2010 Friday, April 18, a Golf Co. Marine detonated an 81mm mortar shell boobytrap killing two Marines and wounding three others in the Loc Thanh area in what appears on the map to be a stand of trees near some hooches northwest of the Song Tinh Yen.[34A]

During *Operation Muskogee Meadow*, Golf Co. alone sustained 4 KIAs, 26 WIAE and 5 WIANE while the VC/NVA had 7 KIAs.

At 0500 Monday, April 28 an enemy force of undetermined size attacked Golf's nighttime defensive position in the Huu Chanh (1) area off a major trail and a built up levee.[34B] The company was providing security for the Battalion Command Group at the time. The enemy opened up with B-40 rockets, 60mm mortar rounds, small arms and chicom grenades from three different directions—300 meters from the north,[34C] 400 meters from the east[34D] and 400 meters from the west.[34E]

A reinforced Golf Co. threw everything it had at the enemy--small arms fire, 106mm recoilless rifle shells, 60mm, 81mm, artillery missions and 90mm. The battle resulted in 3 Marines WIAE versus 4 NVA KIA and the capture of two AK-50 and two AK-47 rifles and three chicom grenades.

During May Golf Co. was regularly engaging NVA troops along with the rest of the 2/5 companies in the Arizona. The enemy was estimated to be in battalion strength. 2/5's S-3 Operations Journal entries for Golf Co. shows no activities the first week or last week of May but in-between those dates the company made up for the rest of the month.

On Monday, May 12 at 1700 Golf Co. discovered an NVA soldier who had been buried that was killed 3 hours earlier by artillery due west of Tan Phuoc (2) located on a tributary just off the Song Tinh Yen.[34F] At 1730 a Golf Co. platoon approaching Tan Phuoc (1) to the southwest of the previous position spotted two NVA with packs running from near where the soldier was buried and killed them. At 1830 a Golf Co. Marine walked into a tripwire detonating a C-4 type boobytrap resulting in 4 WIAE just north of Dai Khuong (7) in an open rice paddy.[34G]

Next day, Tuesday, May 13, Golf captured 2 NVA POWs at 0745 south of Khe Bac Tie (large tributary off the Song Tinh Yen) outside My Le (1)[34H] and two more NVA POWs 1200 meters due east near the Khe Da Mai (tributary) northwest of Hanh Tay (2) at 1145.[34I]

May 13 was topped off with Golf Co. uncovering a partially buried enemy 75mm recoilless rifle on the southern edge of Hanh Tay (1) next to the Song Tinh Yen at 1600. An enemy force 20 meters away opened up on them as they were digging up the weapon. The Marines immediately assaulted the position and found themselves being fired upon from across the river about 600 meters away and from another unknown location by 60mm mortar fire.

The result was 1 Marine KIA, 6 WIAE, 1 Kit Carson Scout WIAE and 7 WIANE while only 1 NVA soldier's body was recovered. (Eleven NVA bodies were uncovered by Lt. Huth's Golf 3 and Golf 2 400 meters west of the May 13 firefight on May 23 adding to the enemy's losses). The day's activities ended as six 82mm mortar rounds pounded Golf and Hotel companies' nighttime perimeters next to the river in Hanh Tay (1) at 2000 resulting in 2 WIAE.[34J]

On Thursday, May 15 the NVA took a special interest in Golf Co. and engaged them in four separate firefights culminating with trying to infiltrate their company perimeter at day's end to inflict more casualties. At 0100 in the Ben Dau (3) ville just off the Song Tinh Yen, Golf Co. received B-40, 60mm, automatic and small arms fire from the NVA resulting in 5 WIAE and 4 WIANE.[34K] At 0615, the enemy troops resumed the attack on Golf and left 3 NVA KIAs on the battlefield, one RPG-2, an AK-47 rifle, six B-40 rockets, eight chicom grenades and other sundry items in their hasty departure.

At 1600 that same day, Golf Co. swept north 500 meters finding four additional NVA KIAs, an NVA map case, eight 82mm rounds, 20 chicom grenades and AK-47 magazines.[34L]

Thirty minutes later while aggressively sweeping the battlefield 800 meters west of where they found the NVA bodies, Nick's company was sucked into an ambush on the edge of My Le (3) next to an open rice paddy area.[34M] The company received small arms and automatic fire from the northeast. As it assaulted the position, an estimated 80 enemy troops in well-entrenched positions opened up from the northwest and southwest. Golf Co. sustained so many injuries in the huge firefight that it withdrew as fixed wing Bronco OV-10s and helicopter gunships pounded the enemy with suppressive fire during the maneuver. Golf Co. pulled back and called for Sea Knight medevacs but the intensity of the enemy's small arms and B-40 fire hadn't lessened.

The medevacs weren't able to get into the hot zone until after dark. Later that night an estimated eight NVA attempted to infiltrate Golf Co.'s lines but were driven back by small arms fire, air support and artillery, as contact was broken at 2330. Nick's company took a hard hit of 8 KIAs, 12 WIAE, 5 WIANE while 3 KIA NVA soldiers were left behind and I suspect many others were carried off KIA and WIA.

Echo Co. operating about 600 meters away from Golf Co. at 1630 Thursday, May 15 was also ambushed by an NVA force which rendered the two tanks accompanying them inoperable with B-40 rockets and rained 60mm rounds on top of the Marines as well as intense small arms and automatic fire. Echo Co. sustained 6 KIAs, 16 WIAE and 18 WIANE. No enemy bodies were found.

Golf Co. rotated out of the bush with another 2/5 company for Liberty Bridge duty and Liberty Road sweeps as a break on occasion from the treacherous Arizona Territory operations over unsafe ground. Late May into June the company took a breather with bridge duty.

On Thursday, June 12 a Golf Co. platoon came across a 250-lb. command-detonated mine on Liberty Road near Phu Loc (3) with wires running off into the bush.[34N] A Vietnamese was spotted running away. About 2 hours after the mine was blown in place, a Golf Co. Marine detonated an M-26 grenade boobytrap 400 meters to the west of where the large mine was discovered resulting in 2 WIANE.

Five Golf Co. Marines fell victim to a command-detonated boobytrap on a trail Sunday, June 15 while pursuing a fleeing VC in Thu Bon (3).[34O] The ensuing firefight resulted in 3 VC KIA while the five Marines were WIAE.

The enemy boobytrap-setters began to upgrade their typical M-26 grenade boobytraps to the more lethal 60mm, 81mm, 105mm, 155mm and box mines on a regular basis to bring down more 2/5 Marines in the Arizona. In July, the VC/NVA set 27 boobytraps with the more lethal ordnance with nine being unintentionally detonated. Grenades accounted for 28 additional boobytraps with nine being tripped as well.

On Thursday, July 10 a Golf squad was credited with thwarting a possible sapper team headed towards Liberty Bridge. On a trail running through the Phu Lac (5) ville, the squad set up an ambush on a slight rise in the terrain in a wooded area at 2225.[34P] An enemy force somewhat larger than a platoon, outnumbering the Marines by an estimated 4 to 1 ratio, attacked them astride that trail with B-40 rockets, claymore mines, chicom grenades and automatic weapons. The Marines returned fire and as the enemy broke contact the squad called in artillery missions on the VC/NVA's suspected routes of withdrawal. The Golf Co. Marines lost 2 KIA, 1 WIANE while the enemy policed the field of their dead and wounded.

### ...East of Phu Nhuan (3), July 12, 1969

At approximately 1010 on Saturday, July 12, 1969, Golf's 3rd Platoon was in the middle of a heavily mined area trying to tiptoe through without detonating any surprise firing devices. The mines were located southwest of Da Nang in an area between Liberty Bridge and An Hoa. Golf Co. was conducting a "hammer and anvil" sweep coordinating with Fox Co. in the notorious Phu Nhuans.

Golf 3's Navy Corpsman Jeff "Doc Jeff" Lippincott of Wilmington, Delaware picks up the story from there, "We'd been finding boobytraps and homemade box mines all day. As we swept near the 'hammer' unit, we approached a heavy tree line and slight grade. Lt. Huth halted us and passed the word for all to stand fast, keep our gear on and plant ourselves. He told us not to mill around since we were in a heavily mined spot.

"He grabbed a squad leader and cut across in front of me and turned left. He headed straight for a break in the tree line to eyeball the area. As he made his cut, he touched off what was reported to be a 200- to 250-lb. box mine east of Phu Nhuan (3) and 400 meters west of Liberty Road.[34Q] It literally happened before my eyes. The NCO was blown back off the edge of the blast cone and though stunned, not too seriously injured." The 2/5's S-3 Operations Journal showed the Marines suffered 1 KIA, 1 WIAE and 1 WIANE.

Doc Lippincott picked up his principle med "Unit 1" bag and ran to check on the squad leader briefly and after passing the lightly wounded man to others he moved on to try and locate Lt. Huth out of sight beyond the blast crater. In doing so he would later find out he had passed over a second "kicker" boobytrap twice, coming and going, that for some reason failed to detonate. "That's when you get the 'shakes' and never forget the 'news.'

"He wasn't in plain sight. He'd been blown into a stand of bamboo and was hanging there. He made sounds for me to locate him. I got him out onto my chest and started my job in earnest. The blast had blown off everything he wore except his web belt and a few loops. One leg had been blown away with the heat searing major blood vessels. I applied a tourniquet to his leg and started an IV into collapsed veins from the extreme blood volume loss.

"I got him stabilized as best I could with what I had to work with and brought him out to a point for an incoming Priority 1 medevac. He was barely conscious and in bad shape. I offered last rites and prayed as hard as I knew how. I talked to him and begged him to hang on. He was in really rough shape. He fought hard. As the CH-46 swept in to evacuate him, he looked at me and faintly smiled and died." Their return to Liberty Bridge that day was "long and painful."

Doc said Lt. Huth was his first KIA in Vietnam. Nick's military ID card one of the Marines came across was turned over to Lippincott who in turn passed it along to the Battalion Rear. He noted that "his face as I knew it and on that card stays with me clearly even to this day."

He recovered Nick's Camillus Pilot Survival Knife from the web gear he had dropped before heading off towards the tree line. "My Marines urged me to carry it. 'Willing' one's gear was a custom in those days. It was done after someone's death or upon their rotation home. I carried his knife the rest of my tour. It served me well and was 'willed' to a fellow Corpsman upon my rotation home." He went on to say that Lt. Huth was "a good man" and "I'm sure God has held him close."

During Nick's time with Golf Co. March 30-July 12, the casualties for his company alone were 17 KIA, 61 WIAE, 24 WIANE while accounting for 48 NVA KIA, 5 NVA POW; 8 VC KIA, 5 VC POW, 2 VC Chieu Hoi (changed sides) and 22 VC/NVA KIA, 2 VC/NVA POW. On July 12, 1969, 28 U.S. servicemen were killed in Vietnam...three of those 28 were Marines...all from Texas like Nick Huth.

Nick's military funeral was held at the Christ the King Catholic Church in Corpus Christi, Texas with burial in Seaside Memorial Park. The *Corpus Christi Caller* (Texas) newspaper noted in Nick's obituary that he was the 102nd Nueces County man to be killed in the Vietnam War as of July 12, 1969.[35]

Years ago Doc Lippincott called 2ndLt. Huth's family in Corpus Christi. "I was told they might want to know he didn't die alone. It was hard on them... not easy on me."

He paid "General" Huth the highest compliment any platoon commander could hope to get calling him "first class" and, "Honestly, the best of all (the platoon commanders) we had."

### 1stLt. Cleveland R. Harvey, KIA, November 18, 1970, helicopter crash

1stLt. Cleveland Ray "Butch" Harvey's dad, Leon D. Harvey, set the standard for his seven sons when he fought in World War II. He had the distinction of serving as a second lieutenant in the 29th Infantry Division, 116th Regiment, H Co. in the Heavy Machine Gun Platoon during the landing at Omaha Beach on D-Day, according to Richard James "Jim" Harvey, Butch's brother.

1stLt. Butch Harvey (USMC Photo)

2ndLt. Harvey was wounded several times and sent home in early April 1945 to train officers back in the states. He passed away in 1966 before Butch joined the Marines. His mom, Ruth Ann, was also part of the WW II war effort having worked at the Pentagon in Washington, D.C.

Of the seven boys in the Harvey family growing up in Alexandria, Virginia (population 110,938 in 1970), Butch was the oldest and kept the bar raised for the others to match or beat...becoming a Marine officer was a good start and would've made his dad very proud if he had lived to see it.

**...North Carolina Wesleyan College, Rocky Mount, North Carolina**

After completing high school where he played on the varsity football team, Butch attended North Carolina Wesleyan College in Rocky Mount, North Carolina from 1965-67 majoring in business and psychology. He was the goalie on the NCWC soccer team during the 1965-66 seasons, an avid scuba diver and a member of the Universal International Skindivers Association. Butch was at peace driving around the countryside on his Triumph 650cc motorcycle.

He dropped out of college to enlist in the Marine Corps in August 1967. He graduated from enlisted boot camp at Parris Island, South Carolina in October. While stationed at Camp Lejeune in Jacksonville, North Carolina, he was selected for OCS as an ECP. He graduated as a member of my 3rd Platoon at TBS.

**...3rd Recon Battalion, South Vietnam, July 13, 1970**

Butch spent time at Camp Lejeune outside Jacksonville, North Carolina before getting orders to report to Vietnam. 1stLt. Mike Fallon would later become acquainted with him at 1st Recon Battalion. He noted that Butch was initially assigned to the 3rd Recon Battalion. He was reassigned to 1st Recon when 3rd Recon rotated out of Vietnam.

(3rd Recon is not "research friendly" as no individual "Patrol Debriefs" nor listed patrol members exist in their unit's records as of 1970 therefore there's no way of knowing Butch's combat record in that outfit...unlike the 1st Recon Battalion---MDK).

**...Team Clay Pipe, 1st Recon Battalion, October 8-11, 1970**

One of Butch's patrols with 1st Recon to the bush was accompanying 1stLt. Stephen A. "Steve" Zrenda Jr. with 7-man Team Clay Pipe (Bravo Co.) October 8-11, 1970. The team was inserted at 0900 Wednesday, October 8 in a draw south of Hill 224 and north of the ville An Son (1) in the Que Son Mountains.[36A]

The team had some anxious moments as they observed a flashlight 200 meters to the west at 1925 searching for the team's insert LZ. After 30 minutes, the light was extinguished. At 2100 the team was in its harbor site for the night when it heard four rifle shots followed by impacting artillery rounds 30 seconds later. Lt. Zrenda's team figured out that enemy troops on Hill 218 about 1400 meters to the northeast could observe the flash of the distant firebase's artillery and would fire four shots to warn their comrades to take cover. The Recon team called a fire mission on the suspected lookout position and never heard another rifle fired after that.

At 0300 Thursday, October 9 Clay Pipe estimated 30-40 enemy mortar rounds passed overhead impacting 2 clicks northwest of them. They called in a fire mission on the suspected mortar site. The next 2 days were uneventful and the team was extracted.

### ...Team Saddle Bag, October 17-20, 1970

Lt. Harvey took out 8-man Team Saddle Bag Friday, October 17 and was inserted at 0931 about 300 meters below the summit of Hill 405.[36B] The team broke brush for about 15-20 meters to the north and halted when they heard movement and breaking brush 10-15 meters further to the north. After a 25-30 minute security halt, the team proceeded north with negative findings.

Saddle Bag moved about 600 meters west and set up shop on the steep mountain Saturday, October 18 and struck pay dirt. The team observed five VC/NVA carrying rifles and large packs. The troops were moving in and out of a tree line gathering wood for a fire. Harvey called in a fire mission at 1145 with the first round impacting at 1230 followed by an adjustment on target at 1310. The enemy soldiers scrambled up the draw out of sight before the second salvo landed.

At 1245 the team observed two VC/NVA come out of a tree line approximately 2 clicks away to the northwest. The two men walked south 200 meters and began digging. Harvey called in a fire mission with a white phosphorous (willie peter) spotting round at 1530. Thirty minutes later the WP round impacted near the two men, which inspired them to dig faster. The patrol leader made his adjustments and 15 minutes later dropped HE rounds right on top of the two men killing them both and causing two secondary explosions.

When he returned to Camp Reasoner Monday, October 20th, Lt. Harvey told his debriefer that he felt there might be two base camps/OPs in the general area where they were patrolling.

### ...Team Icebound, October 23, 1970

On Thursday, October 23 at 0930 6-man Team Icebound under Harvey's command was inserted 4 clicks due east of Team Saddle Bag's previous insert. At 1030 Friday, October 24, the team was headed up Hill 953, Hon Nui Tau, when the point man accidentally shot his tailend Charlie as the team came back on itself on a U-shaped trail 300 meters from the summit.[36C] The point saw a bush shaking and emptied 10 rounds into it. Walking trace, LCpl. Urbach was wounded in the left shoulder resulting in the whole team being extracted.

### ...Helicopter Crash Claims 1stLt. Harvey's Life, November 18, 1970

The lieutenant would go on a much deserved R&R to Hawaii around November 5-12 to meet his wife, Catherine. This would be the last time she would see her husband alive. Butch Harvey would die in an aircraft mishap 6 days later aboard a Sea Knight in his capacity as extract officer trying to remove his Bravo Co. Marines off the side of Hill 848 in the Que Son Mountains in miserable monsoon conditions. (See Chapters 14 and 15 for the helicopter crash that killed 1stLt. Butch Harvey, 23, of Alexandria, Virginia.).

Butch would receive a posthumous Purple Heart and Bronze Star with Combat "V". He is honored at the Humbert Rocque "Rocky" Versace Memorial in Alexandria, Virginia with other Alexandrians who lost their lives in Vietnam. (U.S. Special Forces Capt. Versace was a POW when he was murdered by his VC captors in Cambodia in 1965).[37] The memorial contains a beautiful bronze statue of Rocky Versace, a USMA graduate, in the center and a semi-circle of granite benches on each side with names of the fallen etched with a gold star on them.

Butch's widow, Catherine "Cathe," received a letter from a 1st Recon lieutenant noting, "Butch had such a tenacious enthusiasm for life. What a loss for all of us."

"He was special and we all remember his energy, his joy of life and his love for his family. He fit a lifetime into his short 23 years," said Cathe (Harvey) Nitti. Butch would also leave behind a 2-year-old son, Matthew "Matt." The Virginia lieutenant was buried in Grave 9050-1, Section 7 at Arlington National Cemetery between Grant and Roosevelt Drives ironically on his son's second birthday, November 27, 1970, according to Cathe.[38]

### 1stLt. John I.. Lassitter, KIA, December 4, 1970, Cobra pilot, air crash

On New Year's Eve 1968 four of us 3rd Platoon, C-69 lieutenants decked out in our spiffy eye-catching dress blues drove a few miles up the road from Quantico to the Fort Belvoir Army Officers Club looking for young available women and finding none did the next best thing. We challenged the Army

**1stLt. John Lassitter (USMC Photo)**

officers there to an old-fashioned fisticuffs and getting no takers, we crashed John and Peggy Lassitters' couples-only party a short distance outside Quantico's front entrance. Since we were platoon mates, John and his pretty wife, both Alabamans, waived the couples' rule.

I remember sitting around negatively discussing with John the former Alabama Gov. George C. Wallace's presidential run that year. I was impressed that he appeared to agree with me by dissing the racial views of the old governor. We exchanged stories and laughed at old jokes while Bob Manes and I intermittently threw back straight shots of Wild Turkey in a drinking contest, which I won when he rushed outside to throw up. We were all Marine officers...confident and cocky enough to believe we were indestructible and would live forever.

John, as designated driver, had to run several couples back to the Holiday Inn off Interstate 95 nearby as the New Year bore down on us. His wife fretted that John wouldn't return before midnight. She wanted to be with him when we passed into 1969 so she could plant the traditional New Year's Eve kiss on her husband's lips. It's one of those "Suthun'" things like eating black-eyed peas for good luck and something green on New Year's Day to generate better chances of making more money in the upcoming year.

With Peggy in tow, my three mates and I hurriedly piled into my car. We finally tracked John down after a brief moment of getting lost and having to ask a gas station attendant for directions to the Holiday Inn off the interstate. Lord knows what must've been going through his mind. It was a moment permanently frozen in time that was full of laughter and not a little champagne drank out of cheap plastic cups to ring in 1969. We cut it close but managed to make sure the Lassitters were together for their New Year's Eve kiss. Even as inebriated as we were, me and the boys were suckers for a happy ending in those days.

### ...TBS Grad Becomes a "Snake Driver"

John Irving Lassitter of Summerdale, Alabama (population approximately 250 in 1970) graduated from William Carey College (a small Baptist college) in Hattiesburg, Mississippi. He entered the Marines through the Platoon Leaders Class at Quantico. After TBS, he went to flight school where he received his wings and became an AH-1G Cobra gunship pilot (with the cool moniker of "snake driver") for HML-367 Scarface in Vietnam. Their insignia is a coiled Cobra about to strike.

The sleek, heavily-armed Cobras were manned by a pilot and copilot one behind the other. They were the flashy gunfighters in the war zone feared by our adversaries with good reason and a welcome sight by bush Marines pinned down on the ground.

**...South China Sea Offshore From MMAF, December 4, 1970**

(No After Action Reports were available for HML-367 pilots' activities in the Marine Corps Archives for 1970 so I have no way of reconstructing John Lassitter's combat missions in Vietnam. I relied on eyewitnesses to fill in the blanks for his last flight in-country. He arrived in Vietnam on July 30, 1970 so he saw plenty of action over a 4-month period---MDK).

John, 24, helicopter aircraft commander, HAC, and his copilot 1stLt. Walter E. "Walt" Pinkerton Jr. of Ramona, California were returning to the Marble Mountain Air Facility, MMAF, from gunship escort for a medevac around 0900 Thursday, December 4 when they were told to check out some boats in the harbor in a restricted area too close to the air facility's beach.

Pinkerton recalled making a pass then getting ready to execute a gun run when their Cobra was hit by small arms fire in the engine compartment and the engine quit. The canopy shattered as they crashed into Da Nang Harbor 3500 meters northeast of MMAF (in about 15 meters/49.28 feet of water).[39A] After some struggling, the copilot was finally able to release his harness and get to the surface.[40]

John as the pilot was sitting behind the copilot in the Cobra and was wearing a vest in addition to his "bullet bouncer" (a ceramic upper body protection weighing approximately 35 lbs.). Pinkerton indicated he saw John on the surface and after his rescue was surprised to learn he had not been recovered as well.[41]

"I was the copilot in the other bird (Cobra) the day John Lassitter crashed," recalled 1stLt. Neil Whitehurst, 24 at the time from Bethel, North Carolina. "We had already made two passes at the sampans. I don't know why John made that last pass. We were not taking fire. I saw him all the way to impact. The aircraft just disintegrated into a thousand pieces. There was a tremendous oil slick and a huge amount of debris in the spot where both John and Walt surfaced. I couldn't believe that either of them could have remained intact much less survived the crash.

"I jettisoned my canopy into the South China Sea as an emergency egress maneuver (pilot and copilot each have their own canopies on the Cobras). I tried to get my pilot to hover over them so I could jump (in the water). Our bird was full of ammo and fuel and the pilot (he was fairly certain that 1stLt. Tom

Summers was his HAC) was having a hard time deciding what to do (taking away the weight of the copilot in the front seat of a fully loaded Cobra made it difficult to hold in a hover)." The pilot decided against it and they threw their life jackets to the two men.

"John was there then he was gone…just like that. A CH-53 (Sea Stallion) was the first transport to the scene and almost blew Walt away. Later the 46 (Sea Knight) arrived and sat down in a partial water landing just enough to pluck Walt out. He was hanging onto some small pieces of debris," said Whitehurst.

Tasked with rescuing any survivors was Peachbush HMM-263 Sea Knight pilot Maj. T.J. "Ted" Toben Jr., 35, and his copilot Maj. Royall "Goose" Geis, 33, of Riverside, Connecticut and a VMI graduate, with wing pilot 1stLt. John C. Muir and 1stLt. James V. "Jim" Porto of Carrboro, North Carolina as his copilot.

"Allegedly, they didn't pull up quick enough. Nobody fired at us and I don't remember the flight having been briefed about any firing. It all happened so fast. Ted and I were on the scene within 10 minutes after receiving the call. The boats were still there but not in as close as prior to the crash," recalled Geis, who would retire a lieutenant colonel in 1982 with 23½ years in the Corps. "We actually landed in the water and taxied over to pick Pinkerton up. It was the first and only time I've been in a CH-46 on the water and wondering if a wave or swell would knock us over."

What remained of the Cobra had sunk out of sight by the time the two Sea Knights arrived. Lassitter's aircraft was never recovered from the depths of the harbor so no physical evidence existed to determine the cause of the crash. Toben and Muir's helicopters spent 3½ hours crisscrossing the bay on a Search and Rescue (SAR) mission. Apparently John's body armor weighed him down and caused him to drown. "Lassitter's body was not visible. He resurfaced about 3-5 miles south of MMAF on the beach a day or two later," stated Geis.[42]

Several years after Geis returned from Vietnam, he was in a donut shop in Kailua, Hawaii, when a former pilot recognized him. Geis said he failed to identify himself but said, "You saved my life," and recounted being pulled out of Da Nang Harbor when his Cobra crashed. Since he was the only Cobra pilot Geis had pulled from the drink, he figured it must have been Pinkerton.

All total, 11 Marine HML-367 Scarface pilots would lose their lives during their deployment in the Vietnam War between June 8, 1967 and December 4, 1970 (HML-367 transitioned from Hueys to Cobras in December 1969, according to Cobra pilot, Capt. Herb Silva). John Lassitter would be the last Marine "snake driver" to be killed in Vietnam.[43] Twelve U.S. servicemen would be killed in Vietnam on December 4, 1970, John and one other Marine would be a part of that total.

John left behind his wife, Peggy, a daughter, Terri, and parents, Mr. and Mrs. Daniel J. Lassitter of Summerdale. He is buried in Pine Crest Cemetery in Mobile, Alabama.

**A Tribute**

The tragic deaths of Kupka, Vivilacqua, Benson, Schanck, Nelson, Lakin, Huth, Harvey and Lassitter seem a terrible price to pay for them and their loved ones back home. I honestly believe that those nine young men would not have wanted someone else to take their place on the frontlines. The C-69 officers all stood up to be counted like their forefathers before them when their country needed brave men to fight its wars. They were not alone as Marines in Vietnam sustained 1,051 killed and 9,286 wounded in 1969 while in 1970 the figures dropped precipitously with 403 killed and 3,625 wounded, according to the 1stMarDiv Command Information Notebook figures.[44] As a sign of respect this is where most Old Corps Marines would give them all a heartfelt, "AARUGHA!"[45]

# Chapter 3

**On offensive tactics: "In the attack people will get killed and wounded. Some wounded will scream. Don't let the screamers slow your assault." Also, general observation: "Today I saw a Marine guard on a bridge. He had taken the (plastic) plates out of his flak jacket to make it lighter. He had a *Playboy* magazine in one pocket and a bottle of ketchup in the other pocket. This man was saying to the world, 'My leaders are fools, and that's why I'm dressed like this.'"**

**Lt.Col. William C. "Wild Bill" Drumright**
**2/26 CO, 1st Recon CO, 1969-70**

## Grunt Stories: 2/1 and Others

Following six somewhat uneventful weeks as the executive officer, XO, then briefly CO of H&S Co., 2nd Battalion, 26th Marines, nicknamed "The Nomads," in South Vietnam, January 23-March 6, 1970, the combat part of my (1stLt. Michael Dan Kellum) serving in-country picked up with my joining The Professionals of 2nd Battalion, 1st Marine Regiment south of Da Nang. What follows are some of the scattered stories from Vietnam I did not include in *Book I*.

I spent 2 months in the bush with Echo Co., 2/1 under the command of Capt. Vincent "Vince" O'Neill, a 1964 U.S. Naval Academy graduate, followed by Capt. M.T. "Ted" Hopgood Jr., 26, from Williston, North Dakota, a 1965 Texas A&M graduate. I can honestly say I never experienced a dull moment while platoon commander of 1st Platoon, Echo Co. (Echo 1), 2/1, quite the contrary. The remaining 8 months of my 11 months, 26 days tour involved being the XO of Echo Co. with a brief stint as the CO at the end of my time in-country.

## The Perfect Platoon

Sometime after I took over command of Echo 1 on April 1, 1970, my platoon sergeant, SSgt. Joseph E. "Joe" Strausbaugh, 30, of Chillicothe, Ohio, and I got into a philosophical argument over what I considered would be the "perfect platoon." I had given an order to some of my Echo 1 Marines that they had somewhat misinterpreted and I had to carefully explain what I meant for them to do. I was perturbed they had not grasped my order from the get-go and worried that at a crucial moment, i.e., firefight, a similar situation might arise.

**1stLt. Michael D. "Dan" Kellum, Echo 1 actual, left, and SSgt. Joseph E. "Joe" Strausbaugh, platoon sergeant, pause to read *The Longview* (Texas) *Daily News* from the platoon commander's hometown in April 1970. The headline splashed across the front page dated April 7, 1970 reads "Vietnam Battle Situation Said Critical" involving a Special Forces camp at Dak Seang attacked by the NVA. The three men's photos on the front page are the original Apollo 13 astronauts preparing for their ill-fated trip to the moon April 11. (At the time we were shaking our heads to think we had the know-how to put men on the moon but we couldn't seem to find a way to defeat a Third World country---MDK). (Photo courtesy of Dan Kellum)**

Thinking about that misunderstanding of my orders, I opined to Strausbaugh that it would be nice to have the "perfect platoon" consisting of all college-educated Marines of high intelligence who would comprehend my orders faster and carry them out without foul-ups. I hadn't been in the bush long as Echo 1's platoon commander at that point and was a little frustrated at some of the men's mental processing of the orders I was giving them.

My much wiser platoon sergeant who was on his second Vietnam tour looked me in the eye as if I'd lost my mind and proceeded to eat my lunch with his better thought out argument debunking an over-educated platoon as the "perfect platoon." (A competent, 2-tour experienced platoon sergeant like Strausbaugh had the tactful ability to let you think you were in charge when he was actually the quiet spoken older mentor and you were the student. He was so good that Capt. Hopgood, Echo Co. CO, at one point moved him to another platoon to straighten them out after I had assumed the XO's post and 2ndLt. Robert J. "Bob" Fawcett, a 1969 U.S. Naval Academy graduate and in the Bravo- or 2-70 TBS class, took over Echo 1---MDK).

"Lieutenant, your 'perfect platoon' made up of college boys would ask so many questions about the orders you give--questioning the validity of the order and its finite parameters--that nothing would ever get done (Okay, so Strausbaugh didn't exactly put it like that but that was the essence of his argument minus the interspersed profanity---MDK).

"These so-called 'non-college-educated' or high school kids tend to ask fewer questions, readily accept authority after going through a harsh boot camp environment, follow orders without hesitation and live longer as a result. You may not realize it, lieutenant, but they *are* the 'perfect platoon.' (Strausbaugh, as he usually did when making a profound comment, punctuated his final remark by passing gas---MDK)."

Rethinking my hypothesis while holding my nose, I realized he was right. I saw the logic in what he was saying and ate some crow by agreeing with him. I already had the "perfect platoon" and just didn't have the patience or bush sense to realize that. The imperfection in the platoon was me and in the future I would just have to make my orders crystal clear and if a Marine chose not to follow my orders to the letter I would have to make a believer out of him as to my unquestioned authority if it was just a case of selective comprehension.

The few short weeks that I held the platoon commander's post in the bush in Nam was the most rewarding job I have ever held in my life. To have the life of someone's son, husband, brother, grandson, best friend or fiancé in your hands was an awesome responsibility and I was honored to be their Echo 1 actual.

### Freedom Bird, Freedom Bird

A huge commercial jet departed the Da Nang Airport one afternoon and seemed to come right over the top of us while we were in our platoon patrol base, PPB, in The Cemetery south of Marble Mountain climbing steeply for altitude. It slowly turned due east as we sat in the sand with our eyes glued on the aircraft taking Marines back to The World after completing their Vietnam tours. Everyone was wishing they were on that jet. It was an intense moment of homesickness that overwhelmed us as the sound of the powerful jet engines receded in the distance taking our hopes and dreams with it. I would bet a few of my Marines were teary-eyed wondering if they would ever get to make that ride home in one piece.

An anonymous voice came over the PRC-25 company radio net on our squawk box for the whole perimeter to hear breaking our sad introspection,

"Freedom Bird, Freedom Bird, be advised I'm to your sierra so drop on down and pick me up. I'm ready to go home." Several "Roger, that," and "Me, too," from other anonymous radio operators in the other platoon positions from several kilometers away as well as my radioman seconded the caller's request.

We all had a good laugh and watched the jet become a small dot in the sky headed outbound for home. You could just imagine hearing the military personnel on board cheering as they left Vietnam's airspace and a year's worth of war behind. They were the lucky ones leaving Vietnam physically intact.

## DEROS

In the bush we all lost track of the day of the week and date to some extent. What did it matter if it was a Monday or a Friday? Every day we sent out a morning and an afternoon patrol and one all-night ambush. Days began to merge after awhile. Although past days in a month were remembered only because someone the bush Marines knew was either killed or severely wounded or a specific patrol area was recalled.

Sometimes we knew it was Sunday only because the resupply helicopter might deliver better food. But, most likely, we generally just didn't have a clue.

About the only date that counted was each Marine's Date Eligible to Return from Overseas (DEROS). Every Marine eventually learned what his DEROS was as that was the day of deliverance from Hell. It was meticulously kept up with by a countdown for the number of days left on their short-timer's calendars. The camouflage cloth helmet cover usually kept everyone updated, as the Marine would mark off the days left in-country in ink on it.

Large messages would also start to appear on the short-timer's helmet as his DEROS grew nearer. "Don't Shoot ME, I'm Short!" or "I'm so short, I'm gone!" or "My feet don't touch the ground I'm so short!" or "I'm shorter than the instep of a centipede's foot!"

## Chicken Man Was Everywhere in Vietnam

When I was first assigned as platoon commander over Echo 1 in the bush, I quickly discovered I was required to turn my personal battery-operated radio up to full volume just after daybreak in order to catch the continuing saga of my Marines' favorite U.S. Armed Forces Radio program. We had a weird stereophonic sound thing going on as a result.

"BUCK! BUCK! BUCK! BUUUUUUUUUUUUUUUCK! It's Chicken Man. It's Chicken Man! He's everywhere! He's everywhere!" It was the continuing nonsensical adventures of Chicken Man and my Marines loved him and his goofy, funny stories. The program started everyone's day off with a chuckle and a smile.

All my Marines knew the opening lines so they'd all yell them out in unison. Poor Vietnamese peasants and our enemy hidden among them must've been mystified about our excitement over some "Chicken Man" character as they trudged off to tend their rice paddies or went about their daily chores or prepared to do us harm during our morning patrols.

And I'd be remiss in not giving U.S. Armed Forces Radio credit for playing some of the best songs of that era from the Rolling Stones, Jefferson Airplane, Beatles, Jimi Hendrix, Beach Boys, Janis Joplin, Mamas and Poppas, Bob Dylan, Crosby, Stills & Nash, Righteous Brothers, Chuck Berry, Elvis Presley, Diana Ross and the Supremes, James Brown, etc. Their music reminded us there was a civilized world we'd be returning to someday…God willing.

## Fast Movers Drop Napalm

Capt. O'Neill got approved for a napalm airstrike not far from the deserted Cau Ha Combat Base where Echo Co. had settled in at some point in April 1970. I think it was a couple of Marine F-4E Phantom jets that came on station late that night to drop the huge napalm cigar-shaped bombs, a flammable jelly substance.

It was an awesome sight to watch as the jets flew a few hundred feet off the deck under the glow of the illumination rounds we had fired from our 81mm mortar tube. Spectacular fiery explosions erupted just under a click away to the east in a free fire zone. All the villagers, approximately 1,700 of them from all the surrounding villes, were required to leave the area and stay in the Xuan Tra Peace New Life Hamlet just to the west of us each night. That way we avoided injury to any innocent civilians...in theory.

Our mortars kept up the illumination fire after the jets finished making their runs and possibly so they or a patrol in the area could make a bomb assessment of any VC they might have killed or injured. A middle-aged Vietnamese man ran out of the targeted area towards the Cau Ha Combat Base in pain and moaning having been caught in the napalm conflagration.

I seem to recall he had burns on his back, as well as bruises or red welts on either shoulder from possible backpack strap marks (this generally gave enemy soldiers away to us), and knew we would medevac him to the hospital if he ran towards our company's position making enough noise in order not to be shot as a VC. He wasn't supposed to be in that area and was probably VC or someone providing aid or safe passage through our ambush sites to the VC. I think he was tagged possibly VC due to the backpack markings on his shoulders and medevacked aboard a Marine helicopter to a hospital in Da Nang.

He was one very lucky individual not to have gotten shot by us and to get almost immediate medical attention at a proper hospital. If he had elected to be treated by the VC or NVA, he would've died of infection before finding any medical help which was generally way off in the distant mountains and been too little, too late. Marine Air Wing pilots recalled an East German ship docked in Da Nang that treated injured or sick Vietnamese that included our enemy. The problem for the VC/NVA was getting there through a loose cordon of ARVN, RFs or local Vietnamese police without being arrested.

## True Meaning of Marine Brotherhood

We were notified in Echo 2/1's company office one morning of a Marine wounded in the field from a boobytrap explosion. I was, by then, Echo's XO and as best as I remember, his name was LCpl. Osia Cabingabang. An unusual name like that sticks in your memory, plus I think he was of Philippine descent. A Sea Knight whisked him away to 1st Medical Battalion Hospital in Da Nang along with an emergency medevac.

Back at the Echo company office, we were still awaiting word on the medical conditions and disposition of the Marines at 1st Med when the same Echo Co. platoon called in another emergency medevac later that afternoon. The Marine's last name's first initial and four numbers from the back end of his service number sounded familiar. It was Cabingabang, again. I got on the PRC-25 radio and asked the platoon's radioman what was going on since Cabingabang was supposed to still be at 1st Med undergoing medical treatment.

He explained that it *was* Cabingabang again and that, unbeknownst to us in the company office, the Marine had hitched a ride from the hospital back to his platoon in the bush in time to make the afternoon patrol with his squad...and be injured once more. In the span of one day, he had accounted for two Purple Hearts. My memory is that the radioman said he would not be hitching a ride back out to the field like before as his boobytrap-inflicted injuries were serious.

At the time I recall being touched by the Marine's loyalty to his buddies in the bush and not wanting to be dawdling at 1st Med or the Battalion Rear with a slight injury when he could be in Indian Territory with his brothers keeping them from harm's way. Grunts are crazy loyal like that to men they have bonded with. It's one of those Marine things.

I'm not sure if Cabingabang was a U.S. citizen of Philippine ancestry or if he had joined the Marines in the Philippines in which case he would have had to serve somewhere between 3 to 6 years in the Marine Corps in order to become a naturalized U.S. citizen. When I was stationed in Guantanamo Bay, Cuba, prior to coming to Vietnam, two of our Filipino U.S. Navy cooks explained the naturalization process they were going through to become

American citizens. My fervent hope at the time was that if Cabingabang was involved in that naturalization process and did receive an early out due to a medical discharge that that would not adversely affect his becoming an American citizen. He earned his papers the hard way fighting and bleeding for the country he wanted to be a part of so much that he was willing to make that sacrifice.

Regardless, Cabingabang's return to the field in short order made me realize the essence of the Marine Corps' Latin motto, Semper Fidelis—Always Faithful. His desire to be with his squad rather than temporarily somewhere safe and sound represented the true meaning of the Marine brotherhood.

**Kodak Moment**

An Echo Co. Marine was wounded by either a boobytrap or a sniper one day as the unit was on the move to a new area of operation. Relying on my memory, the first scenario that comes to mind was that it was a sniper from a tree line that put a round into the Marine that was not life-threatening. A hail of return fire chased the sniper off. But to be on the safe side in telling this story, it could just as easily have been a boobytrap that felled him.

Regardless, the platoon's Doc went right to work plugging up the leaking hole while the radioman got on the horn and called for an emergency helicopter medevac. The Marine wanted something from his gear and it was brought over to him. I'm sure everyone must have thought he didn't want to leave a valuable keepsake behind and wanted to get it out of his pack or flak jacket. He pulled a small camera out of his personal gear and asked someone to take a picture of the Doc working on him.

Turns out his dad had been a Marine in either World War II or the Korean War and did quite well in the hero medal department...but he never was wounded so the Purple Heart was one medal he didn't have. The wounded Marine was excited to be wounded and wanted photographic proof of his one-upmanship over his dad. "This will chafe my dad's butt that I have a Purple Heart and he doesn't," he allegedly bragged to his compadres.

This story would have escaped my notice if it hadn't been for one of the Marine's buddies getting a letter from him still in the hospital somewhere recuperating. He was showing the copies of photos the wounded Marine had developed to the Echo Co.'s office staff. I overheard the laughter and comments and asked them what was so funny. He showed me the photos they had taken. One was the Doc with the wounded Marine and another looked like the whole squad mugging for the camera around him and flashing peace signs and laughing while waiting for the medevac. I had never seen someone so happy about getting dinged and the photos cracked me up as well. Shock was not an option for this happy, bleeding Marine.

And who would have thought getting wounded would result in a Kodak Moment?

## The Reason Light Vehicles Stick to Hardtop Roads

Capt. D.G. "Dave" Pound (Echo Co., 2/1 CO, August 25-December 3, 1970) was an excellent combat officer but, on at least two occasions, he chose not to listen to advice and as a consequence bad things happened.

On October 15, 1970 he called me, his company XO, over the PRC-25 radio in the Echo Co. office for additional supplies over and above the regular morning helicopter resupply. The list was so long I had to direct my driver to check out a small truck from Motor Transport to take it to the bush far out in the western AO.

I noticed on my Dai Loc map that the captain's command post with Echo 2 was about 2½ clicks or so off the hardtop road down a dirt/sandy road in the vicinity of Le Son (1).[1A] I warned the captain the truck wouldn't be able to leave the hardtop because of the dirt/sandy road being so easy to set mines along and he needed to send a big working party to haul the supplies the 2 clicks-plus back to the platoon's patrol base.

The captain didn't sound too enthusiastic with my suggestion so I reinforced it with a reminder of a Division Order saying light vehicles were not to leave the hardtop. I gave it my best shot.

My company driver and an Echo supply Marine made the trip with the requested items and met the captain on the hardtop. I impressed upon my driver he was to refuse an order to leave the hardtop and I would back him up. Then I explained the Division Order to him and that he was signed out for the truck and was responsible for it.

We received a call from Echo 6 (Capt. Pound) later that day after the vehicle had been gone quite awhile to drop off the supplies. He said simply that I was right. I asked about what, and he said about not taking the vehicle down that dirt/sandy road. My first thought was that the truck had gotten stuck in the soft sandy portion of the road en route to the PPB otherwise we'd have heard them calling for a medevac had they run over a mine.

Pound had accompanied the working party to retrieve the supplies off the hardtop. I'm not sure if they figured it would take two too many trips to get all the supplies back to the PPB or just figured this would be the easiest route to go to have the vehicle make the trip onto the dirt/sandy road and save them from lugging the supplies a long, long way. Regardless, the captain directed the company driver to go down that road. The driver was not about to argue with a captain when he was only backed up by a mere lieutenant's word in support of refusing the order. I'm not sure if the working party piled in the back of the truck or were walking outside it on the way to their PPB.

Shortly into the trip around 1545 the truck rolled over a bouncing betty mine. The booster charge fired the main charge into the air. The mine hit the edge of the vehicle and must've gotten damaged as a result as it came at eye level to Capt. Pound riding shotgun looking out the passenger's side and did not explode. Seeing his mortality in the main charge of that mine just a foot or so from where he sat must've scared the bejesus out of Pound. I know I would've had one of my "Oh, shit," profane moments.

Approximately 45 minutes later the truck rolled over another bouncing betty mine on the dirt road. It also failed to explode (I think Capt. Pound was still riding shotgun in this vehicle when he had his brush with death a second time. Regardless he came within a hairsbreadth of buying it---MDK). My understanding was that the mine disabled the truck when its initial booster charge sent the explosive into the truck's axle damaging it.

Capt. Pound said he was waiting for a wrecker from Motor Transport to haul the crippled truck back to Camp Lauer. They were fortunate no one was hurt. Marine Guardian Angels were working overtime this day. The captain said my driver told him what I'd advised him to say about refusing an order to go down that road…after the near death experience. With the circumstances being what they were after hitting faulty high explosive mines damaging the truck and almost killing the captain, he wasn't in a position to be angry with me…and I knew better than to rub it in by saying, "I told you so."

One good thing that came out of the incident was that Capt. Pound listened to my counsel with a more open mind in the future…before going ahead and doing it his way, of course.

### Navy SEALs Are Really Good

I had the pleasure to make liaison with the U.S. Navy SEALs on one occasion in coordination with an Echo squad for one of their many operations working the waterways in 2/1's area of operation. I drove up to their river base in Da Nang a day or two before the scheduled operation to pass along map coordinates where they were to come ashore, call signs, radio frequencies and the lake we wanted them to set their floating ambush in, etc.

I recall being directed to see someone working on a PT boat (a 1970 version of John F. Kennedy's PT-109) to give all my information to. None of the Navy personnel I saw had any rank on that I could see and caught one of the guys in the middle of a recounting, perhaps an impromptu briefing, of a recent run up the South China Sea coast to or near North Vietnam. I was a little impatient at having to wait out the story but gradually got caught up in the

SEAL's descriptive blow-by-blow accounting and stood enthralled by the "John Wayneness" of the combat tale. Finally, he finished and I was able to impart my information and departed with a little more respect for the Navy SEALs than when I arrived.

### ...Vietnamese SEALs Work With Golf to Ambush VC

A SEAL team consisting of 12 South Vietnamese Navy personnel dressed in black pajamas like the enemy wore and carrying Kalashnikov AK-47 rifles with U.S. Navy SEAL personnel acting as advisors joined forces with a Golf, 2/1 squad to work the lake area south of Marble Mountain and Camp Lauer Sunday, November 15, 1970. The SEALs carried green tracer rounds in their banana clip magazines making them indistinguishable from the bad guys in a firefight. It was always important for us to know where these guys were in our AO and avoid running into them otherwise there would be one huge friendly on friendly.

On Sunday, 2/1 reacted to a report from one of 3rd Counterintelligence chief 1stLt. Thomas H. "Tom" Marino's informants that the VC were going to hold a political meeting that night in An Tru (1)[2A] below Camp Lauer on the east side of the Song Can Bien. Lt.Col. Donald Norris, 2/1's CO, and Maj. John S. Grinalds, 2/1's S-3, contacted the SEALs and worked out a plan involving a Golf Co. squad flushing the VC into a trap on the Song Can Bien flooded basin.

It was customary for the VC to approach An Tru (1) by boat along the shallow lake south of the hamlet and flee by the same route if infantry approached from Camp Lauer. My recollection was that one of the SEALs' PT boats dropped the Vietnamese SEAL team and its advisors offshore and they either swam in or used a rubber boat. A Golf Co. squad led them to the Song Can Bien and they entered the water swimming to the west side buoyed by individual floatation devices. They got in position with their "floating ambush."

At approximately 2220 Sunday the Golf Co.'s 1st squad, 2nd Platoon came charging in from the east of An Tru (1) with a great deal of noise flushing five VC into two sampans to effect their escape on the waterway. The VC paddled their sampans 400 meters south of An Tru (1) near the west side of the flooded plain and probably thought they were home free. They weren't by a long shot.

Fifteen minutes after the enemy was flushed from the ville the Vietnamese SEALs sprang their ambush and blew the VC out of their sampans from a range of 10 meters with their AK-47s stitching the night with green tracer rounds.[2B] It was a turkey shoot. Four of the bodies and their weapons sank to the bottom of the 5- to 7-foot deep flooded portion of the river.

The SEALs used the enemy's commonly used weapons to confuse the

VC and one enemy soldier who had survived the initial ambush was really flummoxed. We were told he was in the water and blurted out something like, "Hey, what the hell do you think you're doing? We're on your side! We're VC, too!" The SEALs followed the sound of the VC survivor's voice and shot him again mortally wounding him.

The wounded VC was brought back to Camp Lauer's Battalion Aid Station where U.S. Navy surgeon Lt. R.D. Cox attempted to save his life. The Vietnamese interrogators tried to take the dying prisoner with them to get some information from him before he expired from his mortal wounds. Dr. Cox refused to release him into their custody. A staff officer tried to use his clout to break the man loose but Dr. Cox insisted he was the lord and master when it came to the BAS and ordered the man to leave his domain. It was a gutsy thing to do. The prisoner soon died of his injuries despite Dr. Cox's best efforts. I seem to recall one of the AK-47 rounds had lodged in the man's brain through his nasal passages.

Next day, most of us had a new respect for the Navy doctor for standing up to the staff officer and the interrogators. It was refreshing to have a man of principle in our midst.

The SEAL team's bountiful take on the night from the ambush was 5 VC KIA, two sampans, two M-26 grenades, two ammo cans containing 2 lbs. of documents, assorted clothing and food. 2/1's Recon Squad recovered a second body the next day and a reward was posted in the ville for information leading to the other bodies or their weapons. The two VC bodies were turned over to the Hoa Long village chief for exploitation in Nui Kim Son. All the documents were sent to the Naval Advisory Detachment for deciphering.

**When is an 11-year-old, not an 11-year-old?**

Answer: When the 11-year-old is the enemy, and the child is classified a VC. American children at 11 are given protection from certain judicial punishments due to their age and assumed innocence since it is deemed they are unaware of the consequences of their youthful indiscretion. Of course, "offenses" don't reach the intensity involved in wars in Third World countries.

Echo Co.'s 3rd Platoon was working with the 593rd RF Company in Yen Ne[3A] at 1230 Thursday, August 20, 1970 to discover who had thrown two grenades that exploded in the ville the previous night.

An 11-year-old boy admitted to throwing the grenades during questioning. He led the Marines and RFs to seven other accomplices who also worked with the VC...ages 9 to 11. The 2/1 Operations Journal noted the children were being held for interrogation.

In that same ville at 1500 Echo 3 reported a Vietnamese man had taken an overdose of drugs. The Marines requested a medevac. The medevac was cancelled when the man expired. Pondering scenarios of why the man overdosed on drugs, one wonders if he was about to be uncovered as a VC or if one of the children taken into custody was his child and he was so distraught he committed suicide.

A day later just 2 clicks south-southwest of Yen Ne on Friday, August 21, Echo 1, 2/1's platoon commander 2ndLt. Bob Fawcett sent his 2nd squad ambush patrol (Echo 1-2) out around dusk. The patrol came across an M-26 grenade boobytrap on a rice paddy dike outside An Trach (1)[3B] 500 meters from their PPB.

"(The squad leader and I) talked about it," recalled Col. Fawcett, USMC, (Ret.) "It was a place we knew people were working regularly during the day so we knew (the boobytrap) had to have gone in after the villagers finished working in their rice paddies during the day. They'd already gone in for the night. I told them to pull back to a tree line about 50-75 meters away and watch and see what happens to the boobytrap in the morning (when the villagers return to work in their rice paddies)."

Their all night vigil paid off when, according to the 2/1 Operations Journal, at 0640 two 11-year-old Vietnamese boys came out of the ville to check on the boobytrap. "In the morning out comes a (11-year-old) kid right to the boobytrap. He starts to pick it up and it's just as clear as can be to the squad leader that the kid knew right where the boobytrap was as he was about to pick it up (to dismantle it) for the day."

Echo 1-2 Marines leapt from cover and yelled for the boys to halt. "Dung lai! Dung lai!" The two boys began running and Fawcett recalled that one of them was shot right through the thigh by one of the Marines. Apparently the other boy was captured unharmed.

Fawcett heard the gunfire and grabbed his radio operator and two Marines back at the PPB and took off at a dead run to Echo 1-2's position. "By the time I got there I mean we have his mom and dad, grandma and granddad, really old Vietnamese, on the scene. They're wailing and throwing themselves on the deck and getting back up. 'Ooooohhhh!' then they'd all wail and throw themselves on the deck again. 'Oh, babysan, babysan, he no do it! He no do it! He not set boobytrap!'"

"I told (papasan), "Okay, then, you walk down the paddy dike and show us there's no boobytrap.' He said, 'Oh, no way.' It was a righteous shooting. I bet the guy is walking around Vietnam today with a limp." Echo 1-2 called a medevac for the wounded boy. The boobytrap was destroyed with C-4 plastique explosives.

Later that morning at 1030, a Tango CUPP platoon got involved in the incident with its Marine/Vietnamese troops and apparently the unharmed 11-year-old was joined by a 35-year-old male and three 35-year-old females as VC suspects. I'm guessing the youngster gave up the individuals who provided he and his friend with the boobytrap material. They were all sent back to 2/1's Battalion Rear for interrogation by the 3rd Interrogation/Translator Team, (3rd ITT).

We never could quite get used to seeing Vietnamese children set against us by the VC. Marines wondered if the children they befriended and slipped some extra C-rations to during the day might be the ones setting boobytraps that would kill or maim them for life that night. And if Echo 1-2 had not apprehended those two kids, they would have continued setting boobytraps to take down Marines. It infuriated us that the VC felt a need to put innocent children in jeopardy to avoid putting their own lives on the line.

**Strange Weapon Fire Spooks Marines**

A Marine in one of Echo Co.'s bush platoons made an interesting purchase one day of a World War II Thompson machine gun off some ARVN soldier.

The exceedingly heavy weapon with its clip of .45 caliber ammo is not only unique to the weaponry we and our enemy counterparts carried but also had an altogether different report when fired in the automatic mode.

Few other Marines outside his squad knew he'd gotten himself the Thompson. While on perimeter watch late that night, he either opened up automatic on a suspicious noise outside his position or else he just wanted to see how it fired.

*"POW!POW!POW!POW!POW"*

Ears perked up all around the Echo perimeter as this was not a sound a Marine weapon made nor anything anyone had heard to date. The only assumption was that if it ain't ours…it must be theirs.

Everyone on the perimeter joined the ensuing brouhaha of small arms gunfire sending red tracers flying off into the darkness at whatever was firing at them from out there. They had a Mad Moment on the lines and had quite a one-sided firefight, I was told.

When things quieted down, Echo 6, the platoon commander and platoon sergeant investigated who initiated the firefight and discovered the new exotic WW II weapon in their midst. The Marine was given until the end of the next day to sell or get rid of the weapon to someone way outside our company and preferably an ARVN or U.S. Army soldier.

I was impressed with the Kalashnikov AK-47 rifle and would really have preferred to carry the more durable Russian/Czechoslovakian/Chinese-made weapon over our standard issued flakey M-16. It was pointed out to me that like the Thompson machine gun, the AK-47 had a distinctive sound compared to our M-16 and in a firefight it would draw the attention of those Marines carrying M-16s. It would, therefore, be unhealthy to carry the enemy's weapon in combat.

**Do Not Piss Off a Vietnamese Woman**

Crowsnest, a Marine Observation Post and 106mm recoilless rifle position on top of one of the Marble Mountain outcrops south of Da Nang, observed an interesting drama playing itself out on a road near Binh Ky at 1120 Thursday, April 30. They took note of an irate Vietnamese woman running like hell after a Vietnamese man east on the road[4A] below them throwing grenades at him that exploded behind him. The first thought that came to mind was "must've been something he said."

The explosions hurried the man's steps as he ran out of range of the lethal grenades. The woman stopped throwing grenades and retraced her steps picking up a bag she had dropped on the road and disappeared from sight moving to the northwest. The Vietnamese man was picked up by a buddy on a motorbike and mistakenly thought he had escaped the enraged woman as they putt-putted away. A shot rang out and the man fell off the back of the motorbike. This guy was just full of bad luck.

His buddy helped him back on the motorbike and they made a beeline to Camp Lauer's Battalion Aid Station for first aid. Fox Co. sent a patrol into the area with negative results. The 3rd Counterintelligence Team (3rd CIT) and Combined Action Platoon (CAP) 275 investigated and discovered the two men were policemen coming from Binh Ky. They claimed to have escaped five VC/NVA, one of which was a female, who had tried to assassinate them by throwing grenades and setting off a claymore mine. (That face-saving story sounds a whole lot better than to say a lone female routed them into flight---MDK).

Four VC suspects--three males and a female--were detained for questioning in the incident. The injured policeman apparently survived his injuries after being medevacked from 2/1's BAS to the 95th Army Evacuation Hospital. I imagine he steered clear of Binh Ky and its pissed VC female cadre after that.

**Do Not Piss Off a Vietnamese Woman, Part II**

(This is a story I recall either came from my research of four of the eight TBS KIAs in the 5th Marines or 2/1's activities---MDK). A Vietnamese woman approached a Marine position and said she knew where they could find four VC hiding in a tunnel nearby. The Marines must have been beside themselves with joy over the golden intelligence tidbit the woman was providing. They asked her how she knew they were there, probably suspecting a VC ambush.

She explained that she had an agreement to provide them with sexual favors in exchange for a set amount of money for each of the four VC to take turns with her. After she met her side of the bargain satiating their sexual needs, she asked to be recompensed as agreed upon. They told her to get lost and probably that she should be honored to have provided sexual relief to the people's liberators.

Freebies as a patriotic act towards Communist troops was not the agreed upon deal so she set about getting her revenge for their stiffing her out of her well-earned money. There's truth in the old saying: "Heaven has no rage like love to hatred turned, Nor hell a fury like a woman scorned."[5] The Marines found the men harbored up in their cleverly hidden tunnel just as the woman said. They killed them all.

The woman got her revenge and probably some piasters (money) from our VIP Rewards Program in return for turning the VC soldiers in. The lesson learned was that you should not piss off a Vietnamese woman or payback could very well be your life.

### "Tactical" *Holy Bibles*

When I was finally tapped to take over the XO's billet in the Battalion Rear for Echo Co., I pushed a lot of paper and only made it back to the field on special occasions. That would include paying the troops in the bush once a month, playing hooky from Camp Lauer by running something to the field for my CO or periodically going to all our bush units to collect their Military Pay Currency, MPC or "funny money" as we called it, to change it over to differently printed bills to thwart black marketers by leaving them with worthless script.

Headed out to pay the troops August 2, the S-1 Administration chief, Capt. D.D. "Don" Johnson called me over to his office to pick something up. Our new Methodist Navy chaplain had dropped off about 40 small pocket-sized *Holy Bibles* (the *Bibles* might have been *Gideon Bibles* but after so much time I don't really remember---MDK) to be distributed to the troops. Each company's paymaster was tasked with carrying this extra pack with the *Bibles* inside to pass them along to the Marines or Navy Corpsmen who wanted them.

As mentioned in *Book I*, I didn't exactly get along with our new chaplain and was irritated he didn't distribute the *Bibles* himself. Doing his work for him didn't set well with me and I asked Capt. Johnson why we were expected to distribute the *Bibles* seeing as how it was the chaplain's job to do God's work.

"Lt. Fuzz (Johnson's nickname for me from the *Beetle Bailey* cartoon from the day I reported in with my scraggly 2-week-old mustache), you know the chaplain expects the XOs to pass the *Bibles* out in the field to save him from having to go. Don't mess with a Sky Pilot's helper. He might put in a bad word with The Man then you're really going to be in trouble."

"You mean Maj. Henry, the battalion XO?"

"Aim a little higher, Fuzz. I'm talking about God."

I told him I'd hump the extra weight in the bush, but I wouldn't be happy about it. I hoisted the pack with the *Bibles* on my back and made a face as I headed for the door.

Capt. Johnson was laughing and made the observation that I looked like one of those circuit riding preachers back in the Old West who rode from town-to-town spreading The Word. I did not feel like a preacher and threatened to dump the *Bibles* at 3rd Platoon's position around Cam Ne...the first one I was to come to in the bush.

Echo Co.'s jeep dropped me and one of my office pogues off on the hardtop road near Cam Ne (2)[6A] where a 3rd Platoon squad was waiting to accompany us back down a dirt road a short distance to their PPB. This was the easy part. Lugging my combat gear, the payroll and the *Bibles* to the other two PPBs over suspect ground in that sweltering August heat was not going to be a picnic.

I set up in the shade of an overhead poncho at the platoon commander's CP and had the Marines line up outside to be paid. I'd run down the payroll list calling each man's name in alphabetical order, announce how much they were owed, count it out then have them count the money in front of me to verify the figure...then I'd offer them a *Holy Bible*. The Echo 3 platoon leader started kidding me about changing professions and joining the Navy Chaplaincy service when he heard me offer up the small *Bibles* to his troops. Not one Marine or Navy Corpsman wanted any of the *Bibles* but rather only brought laughter and jibes at my pushing *Bibles*. It was as if accepting a *Bible* was uncool to them and they'd be made fun of by their peers if they took one. I would have to make it cool to take one somehow.

It appeared as if it wasn't going to be a good day for Lt. Kellum, the *Bible* pusher, as 40 some odd men turned me down. One of my favorite black Marines, Washington*, chided me for finding Jesus and was trying to put the Navy chaplain out of business by doing God's work. He and I had some discussions in the Rear and he told me I reminded him of his dad or granddad with some of the folksy answers to questions he had asked me. He was a good kid whom I thought his family must have been very proud of.

I kidded right back about his not taking the *Bible* seriously or the true word of God contained therein. He patted his M-16 rifle and said the "True Word" in the bush was what came out of the end of his rifle. Four or five of the brothers gathered around to hear us jokingly banter back and forth.

"Washington, Washington, Washington, where have your family and I gone wrong in teaching you, my son?" Washington would come into the Rear on stand downs and poke his head in my office and refer to me as "dad," which drove the first sergeant across from me at his desk nuts. He started to launch into him about disrespecting officers when I held up my hand and told my first shirt it was okay, "He's my son, Top." I recall the Top getting totally upset and charging out of the office in a huff muttering about the Corps getting too loose for his taste.

On this hot August day in the bush, I explained to the few Marines gathered around me that the *Holy Bible* was not just for the meek at heart and actually was much better than the M-16 they carried as it was full of tactical combat information. "It's full of tactics beyond your wildest imagination. Why generals and kings kept a *Bible* by their sides throughout the ages not only for comfort but to give them a clue as to how to beat the hell, so to speak, out of their enemy."

A black Marine guffawed and suggested I had been in the heat too long and needed to splash some water on my face to bring me back to the Real World. A Chicano Marine indicated that sounded like so much bullshit...with all due respect.

Now this is where it gets really, really weird or to God-loving believers I guess you would have to call it Divine intervention. I personally think that God had a hand in what happened next as I tried to prove my case by flipping through the small *Holy Bible* randomly hoping to find an example to what I was talking about. Understand I only had a nodding acquaintance with the Good Book up to that point.

"You doubt what I'm saying, Hernandez*? Okay, for instance, let's open her up and I'll show you that no matter what page I turn to I can come up with some basic combat tactics out of the *Scripture*." I flipped the pages until I surprised myself by coming across an applicable passage.

In *Judges, Chapter 15,* I came across Sampson. "Sampson released 300 foxes with firebrands tied to their tails among his Philistine rulers' fields containing corn, vineyards and olives and burned them to a crisp...think crude arc light or, better still, napalm. The Philistine occupying force demanded satisfaction from the Judeans and the culprit be turned over to them so they could put him to death or there would be hell to pay. According to plan with Sampson as a willing 'prisoner,' the Judeans delivered him in the midst of his sworn Philistine enemy with his arms tied by his countrymen to appease the mighty Philistine rulers.

"Once surrounded by at least a thousand pissed and murderous Philistines,

Sampson threw off his bonds, took up the jawbone of an ass and killed every one of them," I explained to my growing audience of Marines. "What we have here are the North Koreans played by the Philistines at the Chosin Reservoir in the Korean War. No matter which direction old Chesty Puller's 1st Marines fired their weapons they hit Red Chinese. Old Chesty, like Sampson, had his enemy right where he wanted them."

A laughing Washington dared me to "Do that again."

I only had to flip a page to come across old Sampson again as a fine example of Marine firepower. "His eyes put out, hair sheared off by that cheating bitch Delilah to sap his strength and he was bound with brass this time. They let the dude's hair grow back thinking he was no threat to them anymore being blind and brought him out of the dungeon to one of their celebrations at their temple to be taunted and ridiculed. They let him lean on a pillar untied. He asked the Lord for strength and he was able to push two pillars apart bringing the temple down on 3,000 Philistine men and women killing them all as well as himself.

"That, gentlemen, is what we call either time-on-target arty strike or anytime the Viet Cong or North Vietnamese are overrunning us we have to button up in our foxholes or bunkers and call in airstrikes or arty on our own position. A lot of that was going on not that long ago up around the DMZ in those human wave attacks. That's just good old Marine tactics Sampson was showing us in the *Holy Bible*. He didn't do anything a good enlisted Marine with a PRC-25 radio wouldn't do in a crucial situation."

"I bet you can't do that again," dared another cluster of white Marines moving in to listen to my *Bible* "combat tactics." My initial crowd had grown as the guys listening to me had gotten into my stories and were yelling approval. I think I even got a few hearty *AARUGHAs*.

I thought I might be in trouble having run out of Sampson stories but the Lord was guiding my hand this day. "Okay, here's *Samuel, Chapter 17*. David took down the pride of the Philistine army, giant Goliath, with a rock striking and embedding in his forehead launched from a slingshot. Working alone, Marine sniper, SSgt. Carlos 'White Feather' Hathcock, is one of our modern day David's hitting a North Vietnamese general in the chest from 800 yards away killing him while he was in the middle of his army encampment. He smote over 100 'Goliaths,' Viet Cong/North Vietnamese, during his tours in Vietnam."

Washington was intrigued by now and asked for a *Bible* to see if he could do it. He did and impressed his compadres. More *Bibles* were handed out until my backpack was empty and everyone was reading passages and coming up with their own Marine combat tactics out of *Scripture*.

Okay, maybe it wasn't the most religiously correct way to get The Word out to the men in the bush but I figured the end justified the means as I headed off down the trail without my load of *Bibles*. The *Bibles* were in the Marines' hands and they were reading them and enjoying themselves in the process. The Lord works in mysterious ways and I figured this day I just might have been one of his instruments.

My feel good mission to put the *Bibles* in Marines' hands didn't last long as was the case too many times in Vietnam. About 30 minutes after I handed out the last *Bible* and was en route down a trail to pay troops at the next platoon patrol base, my point man stepped on a boobytrap losing the front end of his foot in the ensuing explosion. The reality of war came back into sharp focus...sometimes we were able to kill or injure a bunch of "Philistines" and sometimes the "Philistines" were able to kill or injure a few of us.

### The Media Comes to 2/1

From May 1970 until the first of January 1971, I recall only one media team coming to Camp Lauer below Marble Mountain. I never caught their names or whom they represented but they were a French documentary crew headed by a woman.

I'd have to say that the media was basically nonexistent beyond the hardtop below Da Nang during my time there. This French crew wanted to film our Combined Unit Pacification Program (CUPP) outfit out in the far western area of operation, AO. Around Hill 55 was like being in serious Indian Territory. Sgt. Rock's* CUPP unit composed of Marines and Vietnamese Popular Forces were making some interesting inroads in keeping the VC at bay and were a major thorn in their sides. As a result, they were hit more often than our Marine grunt units.

One day my company jeep driver and I ran out to just north of Hill 55 to collect the CUPP unit's military pay currency in order to later exchange it for new bills. Someone was supposed to meet me at the hardtop road on the way to Hill 55 to guide me back into the tree line but this was not the case. I knew we were in the right place as a freshly killed Viet Cong tied to two bamboo poles lashed into an "X" and propped up by a third pole marked the entrance to the trail to the ville they were occupying further back into the tree line. The shocking sight made me think of the Roman soldiers crucifying Jesus on the cross which did not set well with me.

I walked off down the trail into the tree line leaving my poor jeep driver to sit nervously holding his M-16 rifle on the road near the dead VC. The CUPP unit was a greater distance away than I figured. I did not have a leisurely stroll through the thick foliage on either side of the trail. I walked into the ville much to the surprise of the CUPP unit sitting down to a C-ration breakfast. They couldn't believe that I was walking the trail alone and explained that they had killed the VC I had seen near the road at daybreak at a little hut I had passed on the way to the ville.

I collected their MPC and for some reason pride kept me from asking for an escort to get back to my jeep. I told Sgt. Rock the VC out front needed to be cut down and buried by the time I drove back by from meeting with the Echo Co. CO on Hill 55. I explained that some important high-ranking officer or a civilian VIP on the way to Hill 55 might see the dead VC strapped to the poles from the road and it would not bode well for his unit. This order was not met with much enthusiasm. I really thought the CUPP NCO leader would make an offer to escort me safely, with their hard-earned money, back to my jeep.

Instead, he and his men with a mischievous glint in their eyes told me to be real careful in going back down that trail. I waited until I cleared the ville before making doubly sure a round was chambered in my M-16 rifle and switched it over to automatic fire. I don't think any VC or NVA was in danger of my itchy trigger finger this day but if a monkey had made a sudden move on or near that trail I'd have given him hell on rock 'n roll fire. I made it back to the jeep in one piece and was very happy, as was my jeep driver, to get the hell away from there and the VC corpse before we joined him. And the body was removed from sight of the road as we passed back by from visiting the CO.

As for the French lady war correspondent at 2/1, she had gotten her briefing from the 2/1 hierarchy and was sitting outside the battalion offices when I walked up and gave her and her crew some advice about seeing the "Real War." I suggested that they spend the night with Sgt. Rock's CUPP unit as they seemed to get sniped at or attacked often. She appeared to find this information quite interesting but made no commitment one way or the other.

I heard that evening the French crew made a point to shoot their documentary in short order and made damn sure they were back in Da Nang at their air-conditioned hotel several hours before sunset.

## Redheaded "Mad Blooper" Mystery Man

Sometime in the fall of 1970, 2/1's officers were alerted to a new danger to our Marines in the bush at the morning briefing in the Officers Club.

The S-2 passed the word that a redheaded Caucasian male who apparently was either a Russian with an excellent command of the English language or a turncoat American soldier was setting up various small units around Da Nang for nighttime VC attacks. He would show up at a Marine position in the bush and claim to be from another Marine unit located just out of their AO. It was thought he was a Marine as he talked like a Marine.

Lt.Col. Gilford G. "Gil" Robinson, USMC (Ret.), 21 in 1970, of Philadelphia, Pennsylvania who was a second lieutenant in charge of the S-2 at 2/1 from July 30, 1970-January 31, 1971, said the young man was called "The Mad Blooper." "The 5th Marines swore they'd seen him on occasion joining in on VC attacks of their positions with an M-79 (also nicknamed blooper). He worked the Hill 55 area and in the Arizona Territory."

The briefing I recall said that each night after every visit by this redheaded Marine the unit he had made contact with would be hit by a VC squad targeting the machine guns and their CP where the radios calling in support were located. It was thought this possible turncoat Marine was passing on these targets and any vulnerability he saw to the VC. It saddened and riled all of us to think a Marine might have gone over to the other side and provided intelligence to the VC that would result in brother Marines' deaths or injuries.

A 3-day quickie R&R to Saigon was announced as the reward for anyone capturing or killing this individual. I think the consensus was that he should fall in the latter category as his payback for betraying fellow Marines.

Shortly thereafter I had to run an errand somewhere in the far western part of our AO to meet up with my Echo 6, Capt. D.G. Pound at Nui Dat Son, Hill 55. Basically this was out in the Badlands where the VC/NVA didn't accept the fact we owned daylight movement and restricted them to skulking around after night fell.

Echo Co.'s jeep driver and I loaded up our M-16 rifles with inserted magazines as I stuffed a couple of baseball grenades in my flak jacket pockets… just in case. We drove north to Da Nang on the hardtop road crossing the Song Cau Do then looped around to head back south again crossing the same river headed towards our rendezvous with Echo 6. The roundabout route allowed us to stay on a hardtop road where there was generally plenty of traffic and lessened the chance we would meet up with any bad guys. There was safety in vehicular numbers.

After crossing the Song Cau Do and travelling a short distance, we came across the most unusual sight…about 20 Vietnamese Regional Forces or Popular Forces on patrol. Not only that, but they maintained good interval between men on either side of the road, were alert and no one was walking alongside a buddy or buddies, holding hands and grab-assing as RFs and PFs are wont to do. By golly they looked just like real soldiers!

Another thing, I was intrigued with the idea they were actually out on patrol. Hell, I'd never seen RFs or PFs on patrol on their own! I couldn't quite wrap my mind around what I was seeing. It just didn't compute in my brain-housing group. (First rule of combat: If something doesn't appear right, it probably isn't. Always listen to that little voice in your head that tells you something is wrong---MDK).

We encountered them as we passed through a ville. Light traffic was coming from the other direction and we were the only vehicle headed south.

Then it got stranger as we passed a Marine that looked about 19 or 20 accompanying them. He stood out being stockier built and about a foot taller. They were headed south like us and all I glimpsed of the Marine was a shock of red hair with his helmet hanging off his pack.

I knew this wasn't our CUPP unit (a mixture of Marines working with Vietnamese troops) as they were located way off to the south near Hill 55 and there would be many more Marines. I thought perhaps it was a Combined Action Platoon (also Marines working with Vietnamese troops) until I realized this couldn't be the case either. And that's when the alarm bells began going off in my head as I realized the redheaded Marine was the only "Marine" in the column. And we didn't send 19- to 20-year-olds out as lone military advisors.

On the far side of the ville I told my driver to slow down and either got a long look behind us through the side-mounted mirror or leaned out the jeep to get a really good look. The RF/PF unit with its redheaded Marine was nowhere to be seen. Not only were they gone but the villagers had gotten away from the road as well. The ville area around the road was absolutely deserted when only moments before it was teeming with people. It was about that time the hair stood up on the back of my neck and I realized what we had most likely just done...driven down the middle of a VC unit walking around boldly in broad daylight toting M-16 rifles, dressed as RFs/PFs and acting too professional to be our allies.

I turned to my driver and told him to get us the hell out of there. He asked me what was wrong as we picked up speed and he quickly shifted gears. I explained my suspicions about the VC unit and the redheaded Marine turncoat 2/1's S-2 had warned us about.

I was still shaking from the experience when we arrived at the captain's location. He thought I must be mistaken and was letting my imagination run away with what I perceived to have seen. I asked him if we had a single 19- or 20-year-old redheaded Marine advising RFs or PFs in our AO that he knew of. He assured me there must be a logical explanation. I just think he felt our enemy was not so bold to have pulled off something like that. And that is precisely how they got away with stunts like that...brass balls boldness. S-2 officer 2ndLt. Robinson noted that that area was the redheaded Mad Blooper's general area of operation and could have very well been him.

Upon leaving the CO, I broke out my trusty map and got my jeep driver's input on how to get back to 2/1's Battalion Rear at Camp Lauer by an alternate route. I was not about to go back the way we came on the off-chance those guys were still headed our way and were VC as I suspected. We drove back to base on some unfamiliar roads neither of us had gone down before but it was better than going back the way we came.

That night back at Camp Lauer as I lay my head down on my rack in my quarters and gathered my thoughts before falling into a restless sleep, I thanked God for sparing me and my driver if they were, indeed, VC. If you don't think each of us has a hard-working Guardian Angel keeping us out of harm's way, think again.

Retired Capt. Henry J. "Jim" Kyle, a 23-year-old second lieutenant who was the Echo 2, 2/1 platoon commander in 1970, noted, "I remember the redhead. He was a legend back then. Strange war, strange times."

Robinson noted that he knew of at least one set of remains sent to the lab at Hickam Air Force Base adjacent to Honolulu, Hawaii after the Vietnam War to be repatriated stateside was non-Asian and was never identified. Perhaps this was the legendary redheaded "Mad Blooper."

## Justice vs. the UCMJ

On occasion I found it necessary to weigh the preponderance of evidence that called for an offense to be waived in the interests of justice versus throwing the book at someone under the Uniform Code of Military Justice, UCMJ.

Around August or September 1970, 2/1's legal officer, 1stLt. J.W. Bates, came into Echo Co's office to request that I call a Mexican-American radioman from one of my platoons in the bush to come to the Rear to be punished for attempting to steal a PRC-25 radio from the Communication Shack. A comm sergeant apprehended him trying to run away with the radio a couple of nights earlier and only got a vague description, a squat-bodied Mexican-American, from a specific Echo platoon and no name.

The sergeant had laughingly told his comm officer, Lt. Jones, about the drunk Chicano Marine who boosted a PRC-25 radio from a pile of radios in the Comm Shack and was so drunk he couldn't run in the ankle deep sand and was easily apprehended. Jones, in turn, was laughing telling other officers about the encounter in the 2/1's Officers Club where the battalion XO, Maj. N.E. "The Rhino" Henry overhead the story and ordered him to file charges against the unknown Marine. Thievery would not go unpunished in 2/1 and the major was livid the officer hadn't already filed charges. The Marine would be made an example of once the comm sergeant positively identified him.

I called the platoon's lieutenant in the bush over the PRC-25 and he knew exactly whom I was talking about after a brief consultation with his primary radioman. It was his radioman, PFC Lopez*. I sent the company jeep out to the nearest road to his platoon's position and had him brought back to me to interview before going over to face the music at Battalion Legal.

PFC Lopez* and his best friend, PFC Gomez*, who was a radioman as well, sheepishly entered my office and I was able to talk to them alone. Lopez readily admitted to taking the radio. He explained that his new lieutenant had made an offhand remark about needing an extra PRC-25 radio for killer teams or listening post activities so he and Gomez had decided to take one from the Comm Shack as they had already put in a request for the additional radio and been refused. Each platoon had a set number of radios authorized in its table of equipment and this platoon had its complement, according to the comm personnel.

Echo Co. was in its 48-hour stand down at Stack Arms at Camp Lauer so Gomez and Lopez figured that was their best opportunity to go after the radio. They built up their courage to steal the radio by getting reasonably drunk at the EM Club. While Lopez entered the Comm Shack, which appeared deserted, Gomez stood watch in the shadows outside. Lopez didn't get far after grabbing a PRC-25. A sergeant came out of the back room of the Comm Shack and chased him down ricky-tick. Once caught, he handed the radio over without a struggle.

Gomez said since he was there and participated in the theft he would take the same punishment as his best friend, Lopez. They said everyone thought they were brothers since they resembled each other in body type and facial characteristics except for one small difference. Gomez had a mustache and Lopez didn't.

I knew Maj. Henry would push for the ultimate sentence for the fairly expensive radio. I was touched by Gomez's loyalty to his friend and the fact they were only "creatively acquiring" the PRC-25 radio outside the usual channels of supply to fulfill their platoon commander's wish list. Justice would not be served to bust these Marines to privates, loss of pay and, maybe, have them serve time in the brig and, worst case scenario, kicked out of the Marine Corps with a Bad Conduct Discharge. I told them what the ultimate possibility was as to punishment and got their full attention.

I made the decision to go out on a limb for these two Marines. I told them I understood the PRC-25 was only for the platoon's use and not something they were trying to sell to make a buck off of. I recognized the extenuating circumstances but I told them I didn't think the legal system would agree. The sergeant identifying Lopez was the key to their prosecution. I explained this to them and said there might be a way to get out of this but it had to be between the three of us. No one else could know or we would all be in trouble. Can you say obstruction of justice?

I instructed them to return to the bush and I would try to stall the legal officer as long as I could. "Gomez, you shave your mustache off. Lopez, you start growing a mustache. If the comm sergeant can't make a positive identification and you two don't admit to anything, I think you can beat this." They thanked me for trying to help them out of this jam and agreed to my plan.

A little over 2 weeks slipped by as the legal officer checked almost every day to see if I had gotten the two suspects that matched the comm sergeant's sketchy identification of the Mexican-Americans from that particular platoon. I had a different excuse every day, i.e., that platoon was involved in an operation, the jeep was not available to go get them, they missed the jeep since they were on a patrol, etc. It finally came down to Lt. Bates warning me that Maj. Henry was going to have me up on charges for interfering with the investigation. I called them to the Rear.

Lopez and Gomez came into the office before going over for the line-up at the legal office. The first sergeant was in the office so I took them outside to coach. I reminded them to admit to nothing. The amazing thing was that Lopez with his mustache now looked like Gomez while Gomez without his mustache looked exactly like the unshaven Lopez.

Later they came back by the office smiling widely. The comm sergeant couldn't positively identify the thief who took the radio from the two Mexican-American Marines he had to choose from. Lt. Bates had no choice but to let them go.

I lectured the two men about not trying to steal anything else in the Rear to help out their platoon commander and to leave "creative acquisitions" to the Echo supply people. I also took their lieutenant to task later about putting thoughts into their heads about coming to the Rear to steal for him. The two Marines came real close to being ground up and spit out by the indifferent UCMJ…real close. As a clincher and what probably made the story so funny in the Officers Club that the comm lieutenant had to repeat it was that the radio Lopez had "stolen" was one that was in a pile of hopelessly broken PRC-25 radios.

Lt. Bates later cornered me and asked what I had done to screw up the comm sergeant's identification of the culprit. He knew I had done something but he just couldn't figure it out. He said that Maj. Henry was spitting mad that the Echo Co. Marine had gotten away with the attempted theft. I took on airs of being hurt that he would think I would do anything to obstruct justice in the investigation.

"Bates, I had two men scared to death that your witness would inadvertently identify one of them for something neither one of them had done. Competent radiomen are an important integral part of a bush platoon and this bullshit has distracted them from their primary job the last 2 weeks or so. I'm just glad it's finally over with and my Marines can get back to concentrating on being radiomen." Sometimes I'm so full of bullshit I see brown. I don't think Bates believed me. Justice was served and I was able to put a rare one over on The Rhino.

## Flicks Shown in Vietnam

In the Battalion Rear we actually saw some oddly selected films considering we were in a war zone. It occurred to me that if you're trying to boost the men's morale a good theme would be films of Marines kicking some ass at war, i.e. *The Sands of Iwo Jima* or *Flyin' Leathernecks* starring the Duke, John Wayne; Western shoot 'em ups; or California surfing movies with bronze goddesses. Those films would be high on my list while anti-war and drug-based flicks would not. *Au contraire*.

*Easy Rider* with Peter Fonda, Dennis Hopper and Jack Nicholson was shown to the enlisted troops and at the Officers Club. Drugged out cross-country bikers headed to New Orleans from California to get stoned to a greater degree en route and upon arrival, sticking it to authority figures at every opportunity and end up getting killed by rednecks in Louisiana is not what I'd want my Marines to see especially with all the drug problems we were having in Nam.

At one point in the *Easy Rider* movie in the "O" Club, the Texas lawmen are shown throwing Fonda, dressed in his fancy red, white and blue biker duds, and Hopper in jail. The stoned Hopper tells the deputy he can't lock Fonda up due to the fact he's somebody important. When asked who he was that he couldn't be locked up, Hopper blurts out that he's Capt. America. Of course, I couldn't leave well enough alone and had to make a smart-ass remark from the junior officers' peanut gallery at the back of the darkened room.

"In some places, rank don't mean nuthin'." The lieutenants around me cracked up laughing at my cutting remark. The colonel and major at the front of the room wanted to know whoever said that should repeat it so we could all hear it. I thought they might not appreciate my "rank" humor so I kept mum. A captain was ordered to come back to where we were sitting to find out who said what. He lasered in on a newbie second lieutenant and demanded to know what was said and by whom. The cowed second lieutenant nervously pointed at me and repeated what I'd said. The captain was not amused.

He returned to the front of the room as I sarcastically thanked the second lieutenant for breaking under the pressure. The captain repeated the comment to the heavies on the front row and as I suspected no one laughed. Maj. Henry half turned in his chair on the front row and threw over his shoulder that he should've known it was Lt. Kellum and gave me a disgusted, "Humpf!" I stayed in the doghouse at 2/1.

Another movie I was surprised made it past the military censors was *Oh, What a Lovely War*, a British World War I era anti-war flick. It showed one incompetent general after another losing thousands of men in combat against the Germans in France in trench warfare.

It appeared that no tactical experience or military intelligence was needed to be a general in the British Army...just the right breeding and a collegiate background that included Eton or Cambridge or wherever bluebloods earn their diplomas appearing on their military resume. If ever there was a no-brainer anti-war flick, that was one.

In the movie, the British command decided to put a spin on the hundreds of thousands of British Tommies lost in France due to incompetent leadership by erecting a huge scoreboard and adding up the dead for both sides like at a football game. It got so screwy in the end that whoever had the most dead soldiers was thought to actually be "winning" the war.

I was incredulous we were watching this movie which I thought was a shot at officers in general (a pun of sorts) and war to achieve a goal that made no sense. The attrition contest we were involved with the VC/NVA seemed to parallel the movie's theme.

Then it dawned on me, "Have the enlisted Marines already seen the first reel of this movie in the EM Club?" I asked the enlisted projectionist. He assured me they had watched the first reel before us. If they hadn't seen it, I considered politicking with the colonel to have it squelched as it was a real morale downer in my estimation. It told of the hopelessness of war and dying for nothing. Escapism is a good thing in showing movies in Nam. A cinema propaganda theme that we were in Vietnam for no good reason except to add to the score sheets of some staff officers up on Division Ridge (1st Marine Division Headquarters) was a real bad message to send to the enlisted troops and young officers in the Battalion Rears.

I'm not sure who screened and approved those movies to show to the troops but I don't think they thought through the impact they would have on the men. Having said that, I'll have to admit that a bunch of us stuck around at the Officer's Club and watched *Easy Rider* a second time late into the night. I got some good-natured ribbing and horselaughs from some of my like-minded rebel contemporaries for my comment about Capt. America that got me in hot water with 2/1's staff officers.

## "Volunteered"

In October 1970 Quang Nam Province's monsoon season lived up to its billing as two tropical storms and two typhoons hit the region. Typhoon Iris hit on the 4th; the edge of Typhoon Joan struck Da Nang on the 15th; Tropical Storms Kate with 50 knot winds and torrential rain came through the 25th; and Louise on the 29th. More than 17 inches fell in 8 days with the last two storms flooding much of the province. The war ground to a temporary halt particularly during October 29-31 when the flooding was at its worst.

2/1's bush Marines had to be evacuated to high ground to either Hill 55 or Camp Lauer by helicopters to escape the rising waters. Over 200 people, most of them civilians, drowned; more than 240,000 temporarily or permanently lost their homes; and 55 percent of the season's rice crop was ruined.[7]

On October 30, 40 Marine MAG-16 helicopters, pilots and crews, braved the weather to perform search and rescue missions. The Marine helicopters spent 366 hours in the air flying 1,120 sorties in support of a humanitarian effort to help the Vietnamese people. The Marine crews rescued 11,057 civilians and transported 56.3 tons of food and clothing on October 31 as the floods began to recede and the winds died down.[8]

The typhoons and tropical storms hit Da Nang packing some pretty stout winds. We were directed to fill sandbags and put them on the tin roofs of our hooches to keep the roofs from being blown off. At one point towards the end of October it was feared Camp Lauer would go under several feet of water from either Kate or Louise.

2/1's XO called an emergency meeting of the battalion's company XOs and a few other officers as the wind howled outside to explain an evacuation plan in case a storm surge pushed the South China Sea ashore to flood the cantonment. Already the flooding was the worst Quang Nam Province had seen since 1964 and transformed most of the land into a vast shallow lake with small islands of high ground.

With all the flooding going on and the possibility it might get much worse, the Marines at Camp Lauer made contingency plans to evacuate the base to go to higher ground around Freedom Hill. A squad of volunteer Marines would ride out the floodwaters on top of 105-meter Marble Mountain about 300 meters to our west with the purpose of shooting any looters spotted trespassing onto Camp Lauer.

Okay, I'm sitting there feeling sorry for the squad of volunteer Marines who will have to ride out a possible 75-mile-per-hour-plus typhoon force wind and stinging rain squalls on top of the exposed mountaintop nearby. And I'm wondering how you keep the VC, NVA or Vietnamese peasants from trespassing while staring into those blow-you-off-the-mountain high winds exposed over 300 feet above the flat land. Also, taken into the troubles the squad of 12 or so Marines would face included the realization that Marble Mountain and the four smaller granite outcrops just to the south and southwest were the only high ground around in the flooded coastline. The mountains would draw all types of refugees, friendly and otherwise, escaping the floodwaters.

Then comes the kicker as 2/1's XO informs me I've been "volunteered" to head up the squad on the mountain, "Lt. Kellum, you will be in charge of the squad on Marble Mountain."

I tried hard to take it in stride and not make an audible swallow or say what was on the tip of my tongue, either *"HOLY SHIT!"* or "But, major, aren't you going to open this up to officer volunteers like the enlisted?"

Instead, I forced a smile back at him, gave him my best poker face and quietly said, "Yes, sir." I began to look at it as a lifetime adventure that I could tell my kids or grandkids about someday if the squad and I survived. As luck would have it, the tropical storm didn't turn into a typhoon around Da Nang nor did it slam us as hard as they expected and took a turn to the north at the last minute. The full force of it missed us. Camp Lauer did not have to evacuate and I breathed a huge sigh of relief.

### An Angry Marine Threatens to Shoot Me

Around October a Marine from my office came to get me at my Bachelor Officer's Quarters one evening. He said that Cpl. J.*, one of Echo Co.'s black Marines working in the Rear, had cold-cocked the black gunny running the mess hall and the battalion XO, Maj. Henry's replacement, wanted him standing tall before his desk as soon as I could get him there.

The Marine accompanied me to the enlisted men's living quarters where I found the drunk and/or high Cpl. J. with his black friend LCpl. D*. I had given Cpl. J. a few days off to get his head straight after his parents had written him that his younger siblings back home in Louisiana had been kicked out of school for the remainder of the year for joining a Civil Rights march against the principal's or school board's wishes. I found that damn severe but, then again, we're talking about Louisiana in 1970.

When he said he didn't know what the hell he was fighting for if his brothers and sisters were being denied an education back home, I simply told him I couldn't defend what the school officials had done in Louisiana and that he had a job to do as a Marine in Vietnam. Basically, there was nothing he could do for now for them from halfway around the world. He was terribly conflicted over the news in the letter they had sent him.

So the time off I had given him was spent getting wasted and slugging that "lifer" in the mess hall. When he saw me, a white officer, he said he was going to kick my "lifer" ass as well. I turned back to the Marine with me and told him to clear the room just in case he really was able kick my ass. I didn't want his hooch mates to witness whatever was about to transpire.

I was expecting this Marine to get everyone out of the hooch then return to help me subdue this other fellow but admittedly I wasn't exactly specific in my directions as I was interrupted by a very familiar sound I'd heard often in the bush before my Marines departed the perimeter to go on patrol. I turned around in response to the sound to see that Cpl. J. had inserted a full magazine in his M-16 rifle and pulled the bolt back letting it go home to chamber a round. I made a move towards him as he was flipping the weapon's selector from single fire to "rock 'n roll." This was one of those "Oh, shit!" moments I experienced on occasion.

I managed to quickly close to within 8 feet of him before he turned the rifle in my direction and aimed the muzzle at my midsection saying something like, "I just might shoot me a white officer today. Stay right where you are, lieutenant!" I froze in my tracks.

LCpl. D. tried to talk him into putting the weapon down but he adamantly refused. I kept up a line of conversation that this was not something he wanted to do and would not solve any of his brothers' and sisters' problems back home. There was some back and forth about his siblings then LCpl. D. suggested I leave and he would get him to put the rifle away. It crossed my mind that if I turned to leave and lost eye contact with him he would shoot me in the back. I did not want to die with bullets in my back like I was running away. If he was going to kill me, he would have to shoot me as I was looking at him. I figured that I had at least some control in this confrontation as long as I maintained eye contact with Cpl. J.

Each time I tried to reduce the space between us he would renew his threat to shoot me. I figured I could cross off crisis counseling as a job opportunity someday as I apparently sucked at it. Now I'm standing there unable to look behind me to see if the Marine accompanying me was there or if he was off somewhere getting help. I knew he had to have heard the loud sound of this angry black Marine pulling the rifle's bolt back and letting it go home apparently chambering a round in the M-16 as I had, so he had to be aware of my life and death predicament. I knew if I was going to get through this I needed to close the distance between us to grab the rifle barrel. I was looking for an opening at a point he might get distracted talking to his friend.

He was laughing at how he had cold-cocked that "honky" gunny in the mess hall. I corrected him and said he was a "black" gunny. LCpl. D. said,

"Man, you really are f**ked up if you think he was white. He was a black dude, man."

"No, shit? He was a brother?" He sluggishly turned to look askance at his friend. That was the opening I was looking for and quietly walked those last few feet and reached out to grasp the rifle barrel with one hand and gently redirected the muzzle to one side. I knew I couldn't yank it out of his hands as his finger was on the trigger and I would essentially cause him to accidentally open fire off to one side or, worst case scenario, shoot me. I also knew I had to keep my grip on the muzzle even if he opened fire and burned my hand from the hot barrel once rounds started coming out on automatic fire.

He felt the slight pressure on his rifle and looked down almost uncomprehendingly to see me holding the muzzle to one side. It took a few seconds for it to register that I now controlled my end of the rifle. "Leggo," he said slurring the words.

"I don't think so."

Visibly upset that I had a firm grip on the rifle's muzzle, he tried to pull it back. I held on for dear life, literally. We had a brief tug-of-war as he got more agitated. I told him he might as well let me have the rifle because I sure as hell wasn't going to let go of it. After a few more tense moments, damned if he just didn't turn loose of it! After all that high drama and the adrenaline rush from the fear of being shot for no damn good reason by an upset Marine, he let me have the weapon.

I flipped the rifle around and ejected the magazine and pulled the bolt back to take the live round out of the chamber. No 5.62mm round came flying out! Seems this Marine was so messed up he hadn't pulled the bolt back far enough to catch a round out of the magazine to chamber it. He had been threatening my life with an empty rifle...neither he nor I had known that.

I told him to hit the door as the major wanted to see him in his office. Afterwards I had all the best intentions of putting him under guard at the Officer-of-the-Day's duty hut at that late hour until I could get him up to the Da Nang Brig the next day. I was going to see to it Cpl J. got locked up, by God.

### ...Major Refuses to Allow Charges to be Filed

A runner from the major crossed our paths saying he wanted to see us at the Guard Mount rather than his office. LCpl. D. wanted to go with us so I let him tag along. I had no problem with LCpl. D. going with us. He had made an honest effort to disarm his buddy even though he was as polluted as he was.

Cpl. J. made a few threatening comments to me en route. Thinking he might turn on me to avoid seeing the major or going to the brig and make a break to go back to his quarters to retrieve his rifle and start this harrowing process all over again, I unsnapped the flap on my holster to my .45 caliber pistol. Cpl. J. saw me do this and asked sarcastically if I was going to shoot *him* now instead. I just told him to keep moving.

Over 100 Marines were in formation late that evening in front of the line of company offices as the OD and the major inspected them before they were to go on bunker and watchtower duty for the night around Camp Lauer's base perimeter. I tried to get the major's attention to tell him what all just transpired over and above the situation with the gunny in the mess hall getting knocked out. He waved me off and began addressing the Guard Mount in a loud voice.

At some point he referred to Cpl. J. saying that he understood he was having problems back home and that he was going to give him a pass for the incident at the mess hall everyone seemed to have been told about or seen in person. I tried to interrupt the major to go no further with this blanket pardon since he didn't know what I had just been through. He again abruptly waved me off and said, "I won't allow any charges being brought against him for anything he might've done this day."

He told Cpl. J. to go on back to his quarters and that he understood the pressures he was under and not to worry about it...loud enough for the men in the Guard Mount to hear his benevolence towards the black Marine. As the two Marines turned to leave, I yelled at them to plant themselves. Livid and in a barely controllable rage, I explained to the major in a low voice that I had spent the last 30 minutes in front of the muzzle of Cpl. J's M-16 rifle as he threatened to shoot me. I asked him if he wanted me to give him a walk on that...threatening to kill an officer? He said he had given his word and no charges whatsoever would be lodged. I opened my mouth to continue our discussion and he cut me off with a simple, "Drop it, Lt. Kellum."

I cannot describe the anger I had towards this major and considered going over his head to the battalion commander. As I stewed over what to do later in my BOQ quarters, I spent a fitful night tossing and turning in my rack trying to come up with a solution to my M-16 wielding/pugilist Marine. By the time I walked into the office the next morning, I had come up with an interesting "punishment" for this Marine that skirted the major's "no charges" edict.

I called Cpl. J. into the office and, now sober, he was embarrassed and very apologetic. I explained to him if I had my way he would be sitting in the brig as we speak but the major nixed that.

"Since you have such a predilection for wielding an M-16 rifle and you're looking for a good fight, I'm sending you to the bush. Go get your gear. The company jeep will take you to a platoon in the field in need of your services."

I was still fuming that the major gave this Marine a pass for threatening me with what he thought was a loaded rifle and punching the gunny out in the mess hall. What message did this send to the troops and boomed out to them at Guard Mount that they had carte blanche to do the same as long as they had extenuating circumstances that involved stressful situations out of their control on the other side of the world? I thought next time a rifle might actually be loaded and discharged or, perhaps, slugging a SNCO might result in his serious injury. I felt the major had made a huge error in judgment and put his officers, SNCOs and NCOs at a terrible disadvantage to discipline unruly individuals. He essentially threw the UCMJ manual out the window at 2/1. Lopez and Gomez's situation I could reconcile, but not this.

I got some satisfaction sending Cpl. J. to the bush from his cushy job in the Battalion Rear. I'm not sure if I could have held my temper if I was to deal with him every day. I still had sympathy for Cpl. J. and his frustration for what happened to his siblings back in Louisiana. I felt the offenses he committed the previous day in no way could be excused as "minor" excusable hiccups.

As for the Marine who hit the door in that crisis leaving me in the lurch, I never did ask him why he left me high and dry with a Marine threatening me with a loaded rifle. I don't think I wanted to know at the time as I had no choice but to work with him day in and day out.

Months earlier not long before he rotated home Echo Co. Gy.Sgt. Willie Williams, a 30ish black Marine, walked into one of our company transient hooches with me to face a reported white Marine sergeant strung out on drugs. He was said to be holding a live grenade in one hand against the head of a new in-country Marine he had taken a sudden dislike to in his altered state and a very sharp knife in the other hand against his throat. Fortunately for us a huge Marine awaiting a psyche evaluation to get out of the Marine Corps managed to disarm the sergeant before we arrived by grasping the knife and the grenade coming up from behind the sergeant and pulled them away from the scared shitless victim advising the sergeant to be very careful to release the weapons in his hands. Another Marine looking on found the cotter pin to the grenade on the deck and gingerly reinserted it to hold the grenade's spoon down.

Regardless, Gunny Williams shared my potentially dangerous "adventure" by entering the room beside me not knowing the danger had passed and spoiled me into thinking others would do the same. I recall on the way to confront the grenade-wielding sergeant I asked the gunny why I was the one called every time there was a shitty situation like this thinking, perhaps, SNCOs and NCOs could just as easily fill my boots. Gunny Williams laughed and made the point, "It's because they pay you the big bucks, lieutenant." I turned to him and said, "Guns, it ain't enough!"

I guess this other Marine in October didn't have the trust in me that the gunny had to end the standoff with Cpl. J. without having two white Marines lying on the floor bleeding and full of bullets at its conclusion.

Ah yes, and the sergeant with a penchant for sharp knives and live grenades did not get a walk like Cpl. J. He spent the night under arrest in the 2/1's OD duty hut after being checked out at the Battalion Aid Station by the Navy doctor and next morning I personally accompanied him to the Da Nang Brig. I remember watching as the now sober and distraught sergeant stood at attention in front of a tall desk like one you'd find a judge sitting behind in a courtroom. The SNCO or officer behind the desk yelled down at the sergeant to take all his clothes off. Four burly Military Policemen stood in near proximity to the sergeant to make sure he did as he was told. I had heard enough and left him in their charge. I seem to recall the sergeant was a good bush Marine. It was just coming to the Rear that was his downfall as it was most Marines who got in trouble.

### 1stLt. Kellum's Last Hurrah, December 3-12, 1970

Echo Co., 2/1 was chosen to be the assault company in a heliborne attack just south of Hill 55 Sunday, December 7. It was a large operation also involving 51st ARVN Regiment troops. The experienced Echo 6 Capt. Pound was to be at the center of this aerial operation while the Vietnamese units cordoned off La Huan (2),[9A] which was only about 1600 meters southeast of Hill 55[9B] in the always wild Dodge City area.

A huge meeting of all the participants including 2/1's S-3, 3rd Counterintelligence chief 1stLt. Tom Marino, 2/1's S-2 1stLt. Gil Robinson, 51st ARVN commanders, 1stMarDiv officers, Marine artillery Forward Observer (1stLt. Barry Post of Longview, Texas, someone who I knew from my hometown... small world), MMAF representatives and other interested onlookers joined Pound and other Echo Co. officers to coordinate the operation in 2/1's spacious Officers Club mess. I sat in on the meeting and other planning sessions running up to the target date knowing full well I would not participate and only had a little over a month left before rotating stateside. Let's say I was only half listening to the plans being made as a result. Physically I was in Vietnam but mentally I already had one foot on the Freedom Bird headed for home.

A month or so earlier I was required to stay behind to run the office while Echo Co. was involved in operations in the Que Son Mountains so this mission was not going to require an XO to participate as well. I had resigned myself to the boring task of pushing paper for the remainder of my tour.

Imagine my surprise when a new general coming in-country ordered Capt. Pound to report to 1st Marine Division Headquarters at Division Ridge to be his aide, at least that's the scenario I recall, 5 days before the operation! Capt. Pound told the 2/1 CO Lt.Col. Norris that "Kellum has been sitting in on all the planning sessions for this mission. He can step right in without missing a beat." And that's how I finally became Echo Co.'s CO for a sum total of 10 days.

**...Boobytraps Hit Echo 3**

Actually Capt. Pound departed on Tuesday, December 2 so I was at the helm that day when two tragedies befell Echo 3. Echo 1 and 3 platoons were still in the bush south of Camp Lauer, 2/1's Battalion Rear just east of Marble Mountain. Echo 2 was brought back to the base. Echo 1 was operating around Tra Khe (2)[10A] and (3)[10B] just over a click or two west of Echo 3. Since I was still getting up to speed on the fine points of the operation's plans, I remained at Camp Lauer and maintained a radio watch in a hooch next to mine and kept in contact with Echo 1 and 3. S-3 Operations ordered me to move Echo 3 into the An Tra area[10C] about 2 clicks below the 111th Regional Forces compound at Tan An[10D] and 400 meters from the South China Sea. Below Tan An was a hotbed of enemy activity in the past year and a favorite location to launch 82mm mortar attacks on Camp Lauer.

I passed the word along to Echo 3 to move into that area and once their platoon commander eyeballed the location he indicated they were either setting their PPB inside a tree line or too close for comfort to one and would be within throwing distance of enemy grenades. He asked to move further out into the dunes. I agreed. They walked off into a shit sandwich involving boobytraps in the high dune area.

An Echo 3 Marine stepped on a pressure-detonated M-26 grenade while the platoon was moving into its new PPB at 1215 Tuesday. He was hit with shrapnel from that grenade and was medevacked as an emergency to 1st Med by helicopter.

A short time later at 1320 Echo 3 uncovered an M-26 grenade boobytrap in a C-rat can at their PPB. After a tripwire was clipped, a Marine was instructed to put his flak jacket and helmet on, get behind a sand berm and throw the can containing the grenade away from the PPB site. (This is not how we dispose of no-delay grenades in cans...we blow them in place as experience has shown us that the heavier grenade will come out of the can within a short distance after being thrown. A Hotel 2 platoon sergeant was killed and three other Marines wounded September 11, 1970 when a grenade in a can was thrown---MDK).

LCpl. Francisco Vega, 19, of New York City, New York was directed to dispose of the grenade and in so doing was accidentally killed in the ensuing explosion and another Marine injured.

I was rattled with all the casualties Echo Co. was sustaining within only an hour or two of my taking command after going 6 weeks with Echo 1 before suffering my first casualty. Lt.Col. Norris called me into his office to ask what the hell was going on. I told him that Echo 3 was ordered to be in that area by S-3 for the night and it was apparently infested with an abundance of boobytraps. I honestly don't know the exact story of how Vega died as I was told a different version in Nam which I passed along to the colonel than what I read in 2/1's Operations Journal 30 years later. The constant in both stories was that a no-delay grenade exploded almost as soon as LCpl. Vega threw the can with the grenade in it. Grenade fragments hit the Marine in the throat, head, chest and arms. The Journal indicated he was not wearing a helmet or flak jacket at the time.

On either Friday afternoon or Saturday, December 5 or 6, I finally got all of Echo Co's platoons back to Camp Lauer to prepare for the heliborne mission. Actually, the first target date was scrubbed due to either bad weather or not enough CH-53 Sea Stallions being available from the HMH-463 Dimmer squadron. Thinking of leaks to the enemy with the ARVN involved in the operation, I had some dark scenarios of what awaited us below Hill 55. We had run a similar highly successful heliborne operation August 4 (See Chapter 12) and one of the reasons given for its success was due to excluding participation by our Vietnamese allies or forewarning them of our targeted area.

### ...The Heathens of Echo Co.

In the middle of bringing all my platoon commanders up to speed, our Navy chaplain informed me that he would hold a service in the chapel at 1400 Saturday, December 6 for Echo Co. I passed the word to the platoons indicating anyone who had a mind to get right with God before the operation could attend the chaplain's scheduled service. I was too busy to attend making last minute plans with all the units to be involved. Seems only five Marines including a Staff NCO took the time to attend the chaplain's Godspeed sermon.

The chaplain was furious with the turn-out and charged into the Echo Co. office as I was poring over maps concentrating on the attack scheduled the next day and a company briefing at 1600 followed by an inspection of the troops later that afternoon. He was giving me hell for not having my whole company at the service and that I should have been sitting on the front row with all my officers.

I told him I wasn't going to order anyone to go to church and that the choice was theirs. I indicated I'd never heard that attending a church service before a battle or operation was a requirement and I sure would have them there for the next operation...knowing full well I would be gone by then.

To be honest the chaplain and I didn't exactly get along and had a history. Basically, I had this dry, cutting sense of humor and he didn't. I think he took a personal affront once when I noticed he had strapped on a .45 caliber Colt pistol when he first came to 2/1 and chided him, "What's the pistol for, padre? If they don't come to Jesus, you gonna shoot 'em?" Now I did get a big laugh out of the other officers in the "O" Club but not him on that occasion.

For the major offense of my not ordering Echo Co. to attend his well-prepared service, the chaplain requested to see Lt.Col. Norris and complained bitterly and passionately to him. He wanted the colonel to tear me a new asshole. Next thing I knew I was standing tall before the battalion commander explaining my heathen ways as the angry chaplain waited outside in the major's office.

"Sir, I don't think I should have to order my men to attend a church service or pray to God. I left it up to them to attend the church service and only a handful turned out. Some of my men have just returned to the Rear today and I thought they should be allowed some time to get hot showers, a decent meal in them, clean their weapons and square away their gear in preparation for a company inspection after the briefing today. With the operation set for tomorrow, I decided not to order them to go to chapel if they chose not to."

Norris said he agreed with me but for the sake of being on the good side of the Lord and the Navy chaplain he asked that when I go past the outer office where the angry chaplain was waiting I should act as if he had chewed my butt out. I laughed and said that sounded good to me. We then discussed the operation plans and he wished me luck.

### ... La Huan (2) Heliborne Operation, December 7, 1970

We were trucked up to the Marble Mountain Air Facility the next day where three Sea Stallions CH-53Ds were waiting to load up my three platoons as well as engineer teams, 3rd CIT and 3rd ITT teams and scout dogs and their handlers for the heliborne operation. It almost appeared as if we were in the target area milliseconds after taking off just before 1200 Sunday, December 7. I watched out the doorway behind the cockpit as several Cobra gunships from squadron HML-367 prepped our landing zone with rockets down below. It all seemed so surreal that we were about to drop down into whatever was waiting for us knowing full well the VC had no doubt where we were headed by the exploding rockets in the LZ.

Suddenly the pilot chopped collective (changed the angle of the rotorblades) sending us spiraling into the landing zone. I think I left my stomach up around

2,000 feet. At one point it felt as if the aircraft was straining not to flip on its back out of control. We flared and landed with the back ramp already down by the time we got there. The platoon I was accompanying ran down the ramp and moved away from the Sea Stallion. All the helicopters offloaded without incident outside La Huan (2) in an open field. I breathed a sigh of relief with the first hurdle cleared.

I think we were all a little bit unsteady on our feet in the first few minutes of deplaning the helicopters. Also, the high whine of the Sea Stallions' engines had temporarily screwed up our hearing. It didn't take long to get our sea legs back and the platoons to head off to their assigned areas.

North of the ville was the Song (River) La Tho running east and west where tunnels were found on the north embankment. Smoke grenades were thrown into the tunnels to reveal any hidden exits but none were seen. I had the frustration of not being able to get that platoon's radioman to answer my calls. The other platoons were gathering up the villagers to be screened. 1stLt. Marino, 3rd CIT chief, and Lt.Col. Norris were in the Command and Control Huey informing me of any suspicious movement or areas they wanted me to check out.

In checking out the tunnels, the platoon was moving too far into the woods north of the river. On the other side of those woods was a 51st ARVN blocking force waiting for anyone to emerge to open fire on. With my entourage of radiomen, I walked over to their location and yelled for the platoon commander to blow the tunnels and get his platoon back across the river to help with the villagers screening process.

Once the situation was secure on the ground and we hadn't received any fire, Marino landed with a "source" to help screen the 80 villagers we had collected. The man identified one very upset VC female. Ten other Vietnamese suspects were detained for questioning as well. At the end of the day, we had destroyed three tunnel entrances at the river edge, found and destroyed one 8-inch dud mortar round, turned over various documents to CIT and a hypodermic needle was uncovered in a bunker. I was amazed we had found anything at all with the lead-in time heads up the VC must've had from their spies in the ARVN outfit.

Something else I recall we found was several large pots filled with rice. I was ordered to destroy them all to deny the VC a resupply haul of fresh rice. Also, when the helicopters came to extract us damned if the VC didn't come out of hiding to take the final helicopter leaving the LZ under fire...and missed. I was thankful that we had come through the operation without one single injury and had a few detainees to show for our effort.

## New Echo XO Sets Record Tripping Boobytraps

A brief period after the operation, December 13, Capt. C.H. "Charlie" Morrison III, assumed the reigns as the sixth Echo Co. CO since my arrival March 6. I returned to my role of being the soon to be departing XO. Shortly thereafter, a new lieutenant came to us who was to be my replacement. He went through the Mine and Boobytrap School put on by 2/1. The SNCO-in-charge of the school came to me complaining that this new officer had set some kind of record tripping the majority if not all the boobytraps in their boobytrap lane. When warned he needed to take the course more seriously, he laughed and said he wasn't going to the bush as he was the new Echo Co. XO and was going to push paper. I told the SNCO I would take care of the lieutenant.

I convinced Capt. Morrison that I had a couple of weeks left on my tour and could continue to handle the XO's duties...and we should put the new XO in the bush to see firsthand what the Marines need daily. I explained to the captain that the newbie lieutenant should experience the bush for the remainder of my time in-country so he could get a hands on feel of what support they required. Capt. Morrison thought that was a great idea.

I chewed the lieutenant out for not taking the Mine and Boobytrap School seriously but didn't get his full attention until I told him to go get his gear as he was joining the Echo 6 in the field by company jeep within the hour so he could learn up close and personal support the bush Marines needed. Hopefully, the experience made him a better XO. He returned to Camp Lauer the day before I departed Vietnam and seemed more seasoned and humbled to take on the XO's job. The bush will do that for you.

## HM3 Thurman G. "Doc" Mullins: A Marine Plan Gone Awry

HM3 Doc Mullins, 21 in 1969 from Murfreesboro, Tennessee, popped in to visit with us at former 1st Recon CO Col. "Wild Bill" Drumright's farm in Columbia, Tennessee Memorial Weekend 2003. He explained that he lived up the road and had watched an interview with three representatives, MSgt. John Hare, Cpl. Robert G. "Bob" Morris and Cpl. Larry Feldman, of the 1st Recon Battalion Marines gathered for a mini-reunion in Columbia on a Nashville TV newscast that afternoon. Mullins is the Ranch Manager for country singer Charlie Daniels' Twin Pines Ranch nearby. (Okay, I couldn't help but squeeze this story in as I still chuckle recalling Mullins giving the perfect example of the old adage from a Robert Burns' poem: The best laid schemes of mice and men oft go astray---MDK).

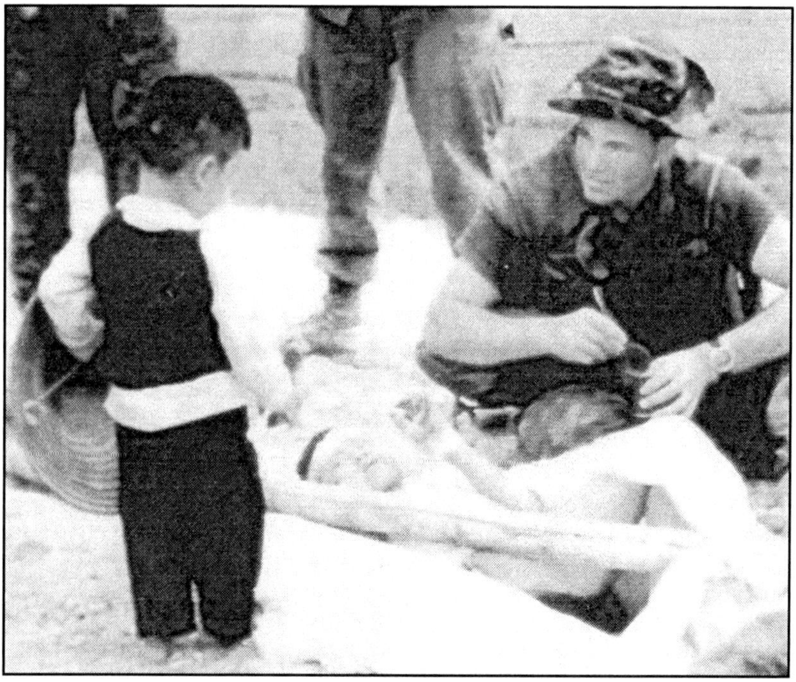

**1st Recon's HM3 Thurman G. "Doc" Mullins tends to a Vietnamese villager on Hill 119 as a young observer, conical straw hat in hand, looks on. (Photo courtesy of Thurman Mullins)**

The Navy Corpsman's Recon team was working with a grunt outfit off of Hill 119 between the Que Son Mountains and Go Noi Island. "We had grunts on the hill with us on at least two occasions when we were inserted there for OP duty. On this particular night the grunts' Corpsman's feet were in rough shape and I volunteered to go (in his place) with three Marines outside the wire as part of an early warning listening post," said Mullins. They were given a PRC-25 radio and were to notify the unit should they hear any movement headed in the direction of the Hill 119 position.

The three grunt Marines had hatched what they thought was a foolproof plan among themselves to return to the safety of the hill early and avoid staying up most the night in a hairy vulnerable position in the darkness. They approached Doc Mullins and wanted to know if they could count on him to go along with something they had already agreed to among themselves.

"I said, 'Now I ain't for no dope out here, boys. I'm not for no dope or nothing while on patrol.' They said, 'Naw, we're not talking about dope. We figure if we (fake getting hit) out there we can come in early and not get eaten up by mosquitoes on listening post. We can come back inside the wire and get a good night's sleep in those bunkers.''' Doc agreed that if they got hit they would have to return to the wire.

"He said a .45 caliber pistol going off sounded just like an enemy's AK-47 (rifle) and if they should crank off a few rounds and then fire their M-16 rifles in response...they could holler over the radio that they were under attack then go back up (to Hill 119) and sleep inside the wire. I said, 'I'm with you boys, whatever you want to do.'"

That night the four men exited the wire and crept into the darkness to a location that seemed like as good a place as any to settle in for awhile before putting their plan into motion. "In a little bit he takes that .45 and goes *'Pow!Pow!Pow!...Pow!Pow!Pow!'* We come back with our M-16 rifles *'Pop!Pop!Pop!...Pop!Pop!Pop!'* He's yelling into the radio that we're under fire.

"About that time, *'Pow!Pow!Pow!...Pow!Pow!Pow!...Pow!Pow!Pow!'* Green tracers start flying by our heads (from AK-47 rifles). We're saying among ourselves, 'OH, SHIT!' Then it's automatic fire, *'Clack!Clack!Clack!... Clack!Clack!Clack!'* And we found that we were in a nest of them (VC/NVA) sneaking up to attack the hill. They couldn't see us and we couldn't see them. We started running back to the wire when about that time the radioman catches a round through the radio and goes down. I helped him up the hill. It was dark and we didn't know who was or wasn't hit. It's pitch black and I can't see crap. Didn't find out until later he just had the breath knocked out of him and was a little scratched up.

"So we get back in the wire and the grunts have called artillery in and it sounds like World War III. Somebody asks what went on out there. I said, 'We walked into a nest of them little bastards. They opened up on us, man. They scared the hell out of us.' We sort of told a half truth because they did surprise the hell out of us when we opened up."

Doc Mullins said he heard a grunt lieutenant got panicked when the enemy opened fire and was going to box the hill in with artillery rounds while they were still out there trying to get back in. "If he had done that, he'd have blown us to hell. They said our Recon lieutenant ran over there when he heard what that grunt lieutenant was going to do and there was a 'heated exchange' and our Recon officer prevailed.

"You could've made a damn TV show out of this, you know? We lucked out on that Bad Boy," said Mullins, who would receive a Bronze Star with Combat Device in a later activity serving with 1st Recon.

## USMC Whopper of an Admin Glitch

1stLt. John P. Connolly Jr., platoon commander of 1st Platoon, Alpha Co., 1st Engineers attached to 2/1 in 1970, and I were exchanging Marine Corps screw-ups perpetrated by the paper pushers when he finally got the better of me with this story about one of his Marines.

"In February or March 1970 Sgt. Barry Cole extended for 6 months to get an extra 30 days leave, which he promptly used for a whirlwind tour of the Orient. He's not back out on Hill 55 for a day when I got a frantic radio call from our company office, 'Get Cole back here NOW!'

"Headquarters Marine Corps (HQMC) must've been updating Cole's leave records when they discovered that he's a Reservist, the kind that was meant to do no more than 180 days and go home to 'Jerkwater,' Arkansas or, maybe it was Alabama.

"I'll never forget his explanation, 'I kept tellin' 'em that I was in the Reserves, lieutenant, and all they kept saying, was, 'We're *all* 'in the Reserves,' Cole. *Get on the ship!'*

"Irony was that Cole had a kill. After leading a road sweep, he turned the corner in a ville and surprised an NVA swigging a soda. Cole yelled 'Chieu Hoi!' but the guy ran, but not far.

"My son's father-in-law says that HQMC lost enough of his records (on jump school, etc.) that they don't reflect that he qualified for Force Recon."

(And you have to wonder how Sgt. Cole made out when he reported to his Reserve unit back in Arkansas or wherever. You see, if you miss a certain number of meetings, the Marine Corps changes your status to Regular and sends you off to boot camp with the ultimate destination of Vietnam. When I went through Pendleton, we had one of those "Reservists" in his mid-20s whose status was changed to Regular for missing too many meetings. I'm sure 13 months of missed meetings had Cole's Reserve unit changing his status as well. Now that's one helluva Catch 22. He had one whopper of an explanation for them for missing those meetings---MDK).

### Bob Hope's USO Show

Being stuck in Vietnam for a whole year meant that at some point Bob Hope's Christmas USO Show would be coming to Da Nang. We had the rare honor of being a part of history by attending one of many shows he performed for the U.S. armed forces around the world over a 50-year span. The historical connection to our dad's and uncles and other relatives who served in prior wars or were stationed overseas or even in the states who had been entertained by Hope & Co. was just way cool.

Hope emceed the USO Shows and performed his soft-shoe routine and corny vaudeville jokes between 1941 and 1991, which is World War II to Desert Storm! Some of the performers the 67-year-old comedian showed up with in Da Nang in December 1970 were dancer Lola Falana, Cincinnati Reds catcher Johnny Bench, Les Brown and his Band of Renown, a Miss World and the Gold Diggers dancers. By the video I've seen of the show, the Outdoor Theater at Freedom Hill was jam-packed.

I say "by the video" only because I wasn't there. 2/1 officers in the Battalion Rear (and possibly the bush) were not allowed to attend the USO Show. I'm not really sure what the reasoning was except the show was aimed at bolstering the enlisted men's morale particularly those in the bush who didn't have the advantages we officers had in the Battalion Rear. Captain Johnson, the 2/1 S-1, gave me the bad news. I never missed Bob Hope's USO Christmas Show highlights from around the world on TV growing up and now I would be in the right place at the right time but forbidden from attending. Bummer.

"Whataya mean we can't go? Why do you think I came to Vietnam for? Fight a war? Hell, no. I came to see Bob Hope in December in a combat zone!" Well, I kind of overstated my desire to see old "Ski Nose" but my point was understood by Capt. Johnson. He just laughed and said that was the breaks and the order had come down from 1st Marine Division.

HMM-263 Peachbush pilot 1stLt. Les Williams had the distinct honor of delivering a portion of the USO troupe to Da Nang in his Sea Knight helicopter. He reminisced that a beautiful Gold Digger dancer sat between him and his copilot and gave him a peck on the cheek before departing.

A large convoy of 6-by trucks loaded with primarily bush Marines and I think a representation of Rear administrative Marines formed up behind Camp Lauer's company offices on the road in preparation to going to Bob Hope's USO Show. Weapons were permitted but no one was allowed to bring ammunition or grenades in order to avoid accidental discharges during the show.

I thought this was rather foolish to have a whole convoy of basically unarmed Marines travelling the hostile roads of Vietnam! An ambush would lead to a bloodbath if they couldn't return fire. Somebody in that place where they eat shrimp and lobster off generals' plates had forgotten a war was going on out in the boondocks.

Slightly skirting the order for the Marines to not have "loaded" weapons, I ordered my Echo Co. Marines in the convoy to take several cans full of ammo per truck...just in case. The other companies followed suit when they saw what the Echo Co. personnel were doing.

Camp Lauer looked like a ghost town when all the enlisted Marines departed. After the show, those who attended returned to Camp Lauer and just couldn't quit talking about how great it was.

I'm sure I'm not just speaking for myself but I think Bob Hope and his merry band of performers and beautiful women...sometimes we really did have to be reminded of what we left behind in The World...brought a little bit of home and a moment's respite from the war sacrificing their Christmas holidays away from their families. I salute all those entertainers and those who have kept up the tradition of entertaining troops around the world in time of peace and war.

Bob Hope passed away in 2003. Some of the recognition given him for entertaining the troops over 5 decades included: Pres. John F. Kennedy presented Hope the Congressional Gold Medal in 1963 for going to incredible lengths in four wars to get his show to the troops; awarded the Sylvanus Thayer Award by the United States Military Academy at West Point in 1968; the Presidential Medal of Freedom was bestowed upon Hope by Pres. Lyndon Baines Johnson; named an "Honorary Veteran" in 1997 by an act of Congress and presented by Pres. Bill Clinton; and a U.S. Navy cargo ship, the *USNS Bob Hope*, was named in his honor.

When he received the "Honorary Veteran" designation in 1997, Hope said, "I've been given many awards in my lifetime but to be numbered among the men and women I admire most is the greatest honor I have ever received." Actually, it was our honor to have known and be entertained by Bob Hope and his band of talented volunteers over the years.

# Chapter 4

**On March 2, 1970 in the desolate Que Son Mountains 29 miles southwest of Da Nang, two 1st Recon Marines literally fell off the face of the earth never to be heard from again. Their heroic actions before being declared MIA and eventually presumed KIA would earn one of them a Navy Cross and the other a Silver Star. They took their rightful place among the Marine Corps' revered warriors. Although the rugged Vietnamese landscape claimed their remains, their sacrifice will be remembered forever by the Marines whose lives they saved.**

**MDK**

## 26th Marines Regimental Headquarters, February 1970

The 26th Marine Regiment, which I spent all of approximately 6 weeks with, was standing down the first part of March 1970 as part of the incremental withdrawal of Marine units from Vietnam. Enlisted and officers with many months left on their "dance card" in-country were shuttled off to other Marine outfits designated to "turn out the lights" as the last to leave Vietnam.

At some point before leaving for my new in-country assignment I ran up to 26th Marines Regimental Headquarters where I was reunited with 2ndLt. David Skibbe, a 23-year-old Illinois native and newfound friend whom Col. Bill Drumright, 2nd Battalion 26th Marines CO who was reassigned as CO of 1st Reconnaissance Battalion, spoke highly of as an officer in 2/26. Skibbe was Fox Co.'s 3rd Platoon commander.

He had arrived in-country October 3, 1969. We first crossed paths when I came aboard in January. For some reason I kept running into him and found that the two of us shared a dry wit and I enjoyed his company. He was a former Boy Scout/Explorer as well as ran cross-country...both of which we vaguely had in common.

Lt. Skibbe was a 1969 University of Illinois at Urbana graduate with a Bachelor of Science degree in forestry. In college he was a member of Beta Sigma Psi fraternity, Alpha chapter; the Naval Reserve Officer Training Corps, 1964-68; NROTC Drill Team; and was named the NROTC Battalion Commander 1967-68. In other words, he was perfect Marine officer material.

As many young men were inclined to do during that period, he was following in the footsteps of his father, William C. Skibbe, and an uncle, Erwin W. Skibbe, who had proudly served in World War II in the U.S. Army. He dreamed someday of settling down with his fiancée, Georgine Tortorella, after

**David Skibbe and fiancée Georgine Tortorella at NROTC dance at the University of Illinois.**
**(Photo courtesy of Georgine Tortorella Hembrough)**

a stint in the Marines to become a U.S. Forest Service park ranger.

"David believed in discipline and duty and was proud to have been a Marine-option NROTC, even at a time when anti-government sentiment on campuses across the country didn't make it a popular choice. And he was very proud to serve his country," recalled his cousin Jeff Skibbe, a '71 University of Illinois graduate. Working his way through college as a bartender at Stan Wallace's Gridiron in Campustown, it was noted that many students would remember him as their confidant behind the bar.[1]

He was commissioned a Marine Corps officer on January 1, 1969 and as a graduate of TBS in India-69, he received the prestigious Superior Achievement Award. 2ndLt.s Joe Silvoso and Jon Swenson (serving in Nam with Alpha Co., 1/1 in 1970) and two other TBS officers ran with Skibbe during their 6 months at TBS. Silvoso called him a poster Marine so they nicknamed him "Jarhead" as a result. He said Skibbe's most prized possession at TBS was a copper-colored Corvette he had gotten after graduating from the University of Illinois.

## Chieu Hoi Demonstration

Col. James E. Harrell, CO of the 26th Marine Regiment, called a mandatory assemblage of officers and a smattering of enlisted Marines from the bush for a demonstration at headquarters sometime in February 1970.

A Chieu Hoi (Open Arms Program) VC/NVA, who deserts (maybe, maybe not) his comrades and comes over to our side for a cash bonus, better pay, food and housing, was about to give us a little demonstration. Working with Marines, we rechristened him a Kit Carson Scout.

He graphically showed us in absolute silence how he and his former friends breached several rows of razor-sharp German concertina wire avoiding trip flares as well as cans with pebbles in them hung from the wire. I closed my eyes and listened intently as he squirmed through the wire headed in our direction like a ghost. I heard nothing but the wind and distant road traffic.

It was about 1400 as Skibbe and I stood together visiting and watching this "sapper" slither and contort his body through coil after coil of concertina wire in the oppressively hot afternoon sun.

He disconnected trip flares along the way. It was akin to seeing how Houdini escaped chains and a sealed box. The Chieu Hoi wore a fake "satchel charge" backpack and carried a rocket-propelled grenade (RPG) launcher as I remember it.

Thirty, 45 minutes tops we looked on in awe and hushed conversation as he crawled through the last strands of wire, stood up, aimed the RPG our way and dropped the "explosive" at the regimental colonel's feet and grinned a nervous, crooked smile.

The Kit Carson Scout was exceptionally good, professionally better in his own way than any of us. What he did so soundlessly unnerved us all. You want to think your perimeter wire could slow the enemy down more than what he demonstrated and alert you to his presence.

A semi-loud anonymous voiced comment drifted over the heads of the gathered throng cracking us all up. "That bastard's good, too good. Somebody shoot him." We departed having learned a valuable lesson as to how stealthy our enemy could be.

That was the last time I saw David Skibbe alive.

### Skibbe Joins Drumright at 1st Recon

Skibbe and I transferred out to separate combat units the last of February and the first part of March 1970 as 2/26 stood down. He went up to 1st Recon Battalion to work for Lt.Col. Drumright.

"Lt. Skibbe and I had been in a lot of firefights together at 2/26. He was one of my best platoon commanders, a damn good one, too. He was a dadburn good fighting Marine. Skibbe was like my son. He and I were close," noted Col. Drumright. "Gen. (Edwin B.) Wheeler thought a lot of him, too.

"Back at 2/26 Skibbe and I were riding the train up north (Thursday, November 13 between Hue and Da Nang). Actually we were at the front of the engine on a steel reinforced flatbed car being pushed by the engine. The idea was that any explosive set off by the lead car on the railroad tracks wouldn't affect the engine and the cars it was pulling. Skibbe and I were riding along with our legs dangling off the front of that car...which was really dumb. The explosive was command detonated (on the railroad tracks) between the car and the train engine (derailing the engine). It tilted the engine over and I fell underneath the engine trying to get to the engineer. I don't recall if he survived the explosion or not. Skibbe pulled me out from under the engine saving my life."

On February 28, 1970 Drumright said he was walking down the street at Camp Reasoner where 1st Recon was situated when he saw Skibbe walking towards him. He thought he had come from 2/26 to visit him. When Skibbe told the colonel he had just come aboard at 1st Recon, Drumright's response was to the point.

"No, you're not. You're going home, son. You've had enough. I told Sgt.Maj. Charles Skinner that I wanted Skibbe out of there. Everything started hitting the fan about that time with a prediction of two enemy Divisions forming on the Laotian border preparing to attack Da Nang. I called back to (1st Recon's Command Operations Center) once I was airborne the next day to ask if we had another Recon team to send out and if we did to send 'em out. He put Skibbe in with the team. He was supposed to be going home." Two days after his arrival at 1st Recon on his first patrol Skibbe would be declared missing-in-action in the Que Son Mountains.

Col. Drumright initially thought Skibbe had extended his tour to stay in-country (actually Skibbe was beginning his sixth month in Vietnam and should've been rotating to Okinawa to train troops---MDK). "Did you know he had a 151 IQ? Skibbe was a very intelligent young man."

When Drumright assumed command January 27, 1970, he changed the scope of 1st Recon's overall mission with Maj.Gen. Wheeler's enthusiastic support to that of the old WW II Marine Raider Battalions. The 7-man Recon teams were to act as bait to search out the enemy--find 'em, fix 'em and kill 'em--with supporting arms at their disposal. Fixed wing, B-52 arc lights, Cobra gunships and 175mm artillery surrounded the teams with a curtain of steel upon request.

**Team Thin Man Sets Ambush on Razorback Above My Hiep**

Before I could depart for my new assignment, I heard that David had been left behind while on a patrol gone bad after his jungle penetrator's cable snapped as he was being hoisted aboard a Sea Knight as a WIA Monday, March 2, 1970. He was part of 7-man Team Thin Man of Charlie Co., 1st Recon. The same type of faulty cable line killed David's company commander later that same night when he tried to rescue him 32 miles from the Laotian border deep in enemy held territory.

"We were told that two NVA battalions were moving on Da Nang from the Charlie Ridge area and through the Song Cai mountain passes. I put a Recon team in those locations to track their movements. Approximately 600 enemy troops were in Thin Man's patrol AO," noted Drumright.

The VC/NVA referred to the series of high-speed trails running through that area as the People's Army of Vietnam (PAVN) Supply Corridor. The "corridor" was essential to their infiltration of men and materiel into the surrounding South Vietnamese provinces. In this part of the Que Son Mountains enemy forces had not been challenged by either the Americans or South Vietnamese military for several years. The local inhabitants were not only sympathetic to our enemy but also fought in their frontline VC cadre. They knew the terrain like the back of their hand and they had grown strong. This was their exclusive playground.

Lt. Skibbe was designated the patrol leader of Team Thin Man and Sgt. Larry K. "Giff" Gifford, 20, of Seattle, Washington the assistant. Capt. LaVoy Don "Mac" McVey, 32, of Lamar, Colorado, Charlie Co. CO, made it clear the more experienced Gifford was in charge of the patrol since it was Skibbe's first outing.

Other team members were Cpl. Michael S. "Steve" Plunkett, 20, of Fort Worth, Texas, point; LCpl. Gary D. Moreno, primary radioman; LCpl. Ezekiel "Zeke" Piere Jr., 2nd radioman; HM3 Larry W. "Doc" McLynn, Corpsman; and LCpl. Roy Lee Jones of Candler, North Carolina, tailend Charlie. Gifford and Plunkett were newly promoted to their ranks for this patrol. LCpl. J.H. "Mike" Simpson, 19, of Kansas City, Missouri, alternate point, was bumped from the patrol so Skibbe could get his feet wet.

Team Thin Man's mission was to patrol a series of low hills in relatively clear forests containing thick underbrush 10 miles southwest of An Hoa and roughly 17 clicks southwest of the 5th Special Forces Detachment A-109 Camp at Thuong Duc. The team's target area of observation was the Song Cai boat traffic to the west and south as well as My Hiep (4) along the meandering river to the west and My Hiep (2) over a click to the northwest next to the river. Highway 14 was a click to their northeast cutting through the mountains as a major road artery.

Drumright noted that the VC/NVA hated and feared the Marine "painted faces" and placed a high bounty on their heads, dead or alive. Recon Marines streaked their faces with black and shades of green grease paint to blend in with jungle scenery, hence, the term "painted faces."

"The pay-out was something like three lifetimes of salary for an average soldier to kill or capture one of our Recon Marines. They had killed or captured Special Forces, SOG (Studies and Observation Group), Army Recon and other special units except for 1st Recon. We had a record of bringing our boys home and doing them a lot of hurt," explained Col. Drumright with an air of obvious paternal pride in his Recon Marines.

As a historical perspective, American Indian tribes "painted their faces" to go to war and strike terror in their enemies. In the Seminole tribe down in Florida, for instance, each color had a special significance attached to it. Black streaks meant a "living color" worn on the face to prepare for war while green under the eyes was supposed to empower the wearer with night vision.[2] Team Thin Man was painted up for war.

On Monday, March 2, Skibbe/Gifford's team maintained a radio relay connection to Team Pony Boy (19-year-old Cpl. Feldman was on this team) in the mountains as their communications lifeline. All requests for "a ring of steel" or extraction passed through them.

The Sea Knight pilot put the team down on its alternate LZ at 0930 on the side of Hill 120 approximately 500 meters south of My Hiep (2) without a hitch.[3A] (In order to avoid confusion there are similar named My Hiep villages along the Song Vu Gia in the Arizona Territory---MDK). The CH-46D's back wheels settled onto the incline of the steep side of the ridgeline allowing Team Thin Man to run off the back ramp. Sgt. Gifford recalled the Song Cai approximately 700 meters to his west as a "raging gray dog" 30 feet wide, 8 feet deep racing towards a steep-walled canyon.

For 5 minutes the team stayed in place becoming familiar with their surroundings and listening for anything out of the ordinary that might spell trouble before moving out in a southerly direction. They intersected a trail they'd been told about in their briefing. Strands of barbed wire and old small fighting holes were found right off the LZ.

Plunkett broke bush for an exhausting 200 meters before stumbling across a well-used 3-foot wide speed trail along a razorback running towards the southeast in the direction of Hill 225. Rusted used C-rat cans were found at one harbor site off the trail leading the team to believe Popular Forces spent time there at some point. A U.S. Special Forces report later indicated that no friendly troops had been in this area for 2 years.

At another harbor site, barbed wire and flies buzzing around indicated humans had been there recently. "We figured we had gooks around and were in a world of shit," said Gifford.

After conferring with Lt. Skibbe and Sgt. Gifford, Plunkett headed off down what he now called a "high speed trail" to the southeast for approximately 400 meters. At that point the team dropped its gear and set up an observation post.[3B] The path widened to 4-feet with rudimentary "curbs" and made a turn to the left and began climbing upwards after 70 more feet in the direction of the summit of Hill 225. Two other smaller paths intersected the trail to their front along the razorback.

"I looked up the trail and turned to the lieutenant to tell him we couldn't go any further. 'They're up there,' I recall telling Lt. Skibbe," said Gifford, who was on his 12th long-range patrol. He would not see his 13th. The sergeant set his men in on either side of the trail splitting his force.

"I decided to be a decoy in the middle of the trail. At that point I just didn't give a shit. I mean we were young and gungy. It was my job as patrol leader to initiate contact and draw fire," recalled Gifford.

"That dumbass sat down out in the middle of the trail," said Plunkett assessing Giff's "strategy."

Gifford put Plunkett off the trail behind a large rock nearest the intersection to their front. Lt. Skibbe and the radioman, Moreno, sought cover on the opposite side of the path behind a tree and the other three men were behind rocks watching the rear off the well-traveled path…except for Gifford. He knelt down in the middle of the path like a staked out sacrificial lamb and waited.

Around 1625 three AK-47 rounds were heard to the west about 1,000 meters away. Since no sightings or movement crossed their location, Gifford decided to move the team to another area.

### VC Scouts Go Eye-to-Eye With Plunkett

At 1630 as Team Thin Man was preparing to move out, it found the elusive enemy the same time the enemy found them. The team's patrol report notes that the point man spotted two VC wearing black pajama tops, light colored shorts (khaki) and carrying their rifles at sling arms.

"I was sitting down getting a drink of water from my canteen when two dinks came around a corner on the trail from the high ground about 30 feet away. We went eye-to-eye. Nobody else saw them," recalled Plunkett. "I yelled, 'GOOKS!' and it started. All hell broke loose. I swear they aimed at me when they opened up fully automatic but the rounds went by me to my right rear and hit Gifford three times--in the head, left thigh and right hand."

Before being put out of commission, Gifford said he fired off a magazine at the two men who either had dirt or camouflage paint on their faces. As he was changing magazines, two rounds shattered the bolt assembly on his rifle blowing it out and hitting his thumb. He was also hit in the head and thigh at this time. "My right thumb was just dangling down. I was going to throw a grenade but my thumb was just too f**ked up. Suddenly, my vision narrowed into two tunnels of 3-inch pipes (no peripheral sight at all). My rifle didn't work and I'm blown to shit so I just laid right down on that trail."

"Because Gifford was out in the open, he saved my life by drawing fire from the two dinks," said Plunkett in reflecting how he came out of the initial enemy burst of fire without a scratch.

"I opened up fully automatic until my M-16 (rifle) locked up on me. I tried to eject the jammed round with my little finger and when that didn't work I grabbed Gifford's rifle and found the enemy rounds had messed it up as well. It was pretty wild and hairy up there," said Plunkett.

He complained that Lt.Col. Drumright made him turn in his old, reliable M-14 rifle before the patrol and put the newer, lighter M-16 in his hands insisting he use it. All the other team members carried the smaller, lightweight M-16 as well. The malfunctioning M-16 almost cost him his life.

"The M-16 was a piece of junk back then as far as I was concerned. Now they're a sophisticated, reliable weapon. We paid the price breaking them in," recalled Plunkett.

Piere, Doc McLynn and Jones found themselves pinned down behind some rocks further on down the trail as rounds aimed at Plunkett and Gifford were impacting the rocks all around them. Only Skibbe and Moreno were able to return fire as Plunkett and Gifford's weapons fell silent. Their fire forced the two enemy soldiers to retreat back up the trail.

Lt. Skibbe ran to Gifford and began treating his wounds. Plunkett said he yelled at Doc McLynn to help him get Gifford off the exposed trail. Gifford was playing possum (acting dead) to keep from drawing more fire when he said the lieutenant came to pull him off the trail.

"The lieutenant risked his life for me," lamented Gifford.

Either the radioman, Moreno or Skibbe called for a priority medevac through the radio relay, Team Pony Boy, at 1633. Communication was very poor. Pony Boy attempted to divert a fixed wing Bronco OV-10A from another Recon team, Cherry Jam, to Thin Man's location where they were pinned down. Due to all comm being lost between Pony Boy and Thin Man at 1653, the air support request was cancelled.

Piere, Jones and Doc McLynn ran forward having dropped their rigs (packs) behind some rocks to join in the fight. Since the enemy had chosen to disengage for the time being, Piere and Jones ran back to their former location to get their rigs and Doc's.

After briefly retreating, the previous two grew to four or five enemy soldiers who came charging back on their flank trying to overwhelm the Recon team but Skibbe and the remaining members held them off.

At one point, LCpl. Jones jumped up and single-handedly assaulted the enemy troops firing fully automatic driving them back up the hill so his team could recover and regroup. For this selfless act of heroism, Gifford later put him in for a Silver Star that was downgraded to a Bronze Star. Piere and Plunkett also earned Bronze Stars, Gifford said.

Within 5 minutes after the firefight started and a priority medevac for Gifford requested, Lt. Skibbe was hit with semi-automatic AK-47 fire in his ankle, according to Doc McLynn. The Navy Corpsman described Skibbe's injury as a "penetrating wound of the lower right leg, breaking the fibula 2 inches above the ankle leaving an open fracture, hemorrhage was moderate and ceased after a battle dressing was applied." He observed no exit wound. A splint constructed from a small tree limb immobilized his broken ankle.

"(Lt. Skibbe) took a round through the ankle and it was shattered. His foot was almost off," said Plunkett. He was the next senior man, thus assumed command. The point man said he would always remember the lieutenant's cool demeanor under fire and his encouragement to him even after being severely wounded. With 37 patrols behind him, he indicated that team leader was not a position he was familiar with and was undoubtedly more comfortable with walking point.

McLynn noted that the lieutenant was in command as well as in good spirits at all times and even provided security while he was applying first aid to his wound.

More enemy soldiers converged on the Marines fighting for their lives on the razorback.

**Extract Requested by Team Thin Man**

At 1654 Thin Man managed to reach Bronco OV-10A pilot Hostage 6, Lt.Col. James M. Moriarty, Marine Observation Squadron (VMO)-2 CO, who was in the air nearby, to request an extract. Four minutes later the team called for a ladder extract (3 to 4 flexible wire ladders sewn together, had lightweight aluminum as rungs, 120-feet long, about 6-feet wide, rolled up inside the Sea Knight and attached underneath the aircraft). Soon thereafter Gifford was upgraded to an emergency extract requiring the use of a hoist cable and a jungle penetrator. The hoist was installed on the low helo (extract Sea Knight) at the Marble Mountain Air Facility. 1st Recon's Command Operations Center (COC) at Camp Reasoner logged in another call at 1708 for two emergency extracts. Skibbe was also down by then.

Hostage Hotel Bronco pilot, 1stLt. George A. "Skip" Roberts, 26, from South Portland, Maine with his aerial observer, AO, 1stLt. Pete Flanagan (later made a career of the FBI), responded to Thin Man's request for assistance passed along from Moriarty. He came up on station within 15 minutes of the first call for help. The aerial observer in the Bronco directed fire on the enemy troops by 1717, according to message traffic from 1st Recon's COC log.

Within 25 minutes of Roberts' arrival, Hostage Igor, Capt. Charles E. "Chuck" Burin, 29, of Imperial, Pennsylvania (his logbook was a little vague but he thought his backseat AO was 1stLt. Bill Tobin, call sign Cowpoke 4) flew in with fixed wing air support and began making runs on the area around the stationary Recon team. Hostage Igor was marking targets with smoke as one of the airstrikes called in involved two F-4 Phantom jets with 250-lb.

"snake-eye" bombs that exploded 50-75 meters away from Team Thin Man in close air support. The ensuing explosions sent rocks, shrapnel, dirt and bits of trees raining down on Thin Man, which tried to merge with terra firma.

"When you have stuff like that falling into your position and you have to hold onto your (camouflage floppy hat) with both hands, you know it's close," said Gifford. Approximately 27 bomb runs from several fixed wing aircraft as well as strafing runs by Broncos and Cobras caused the enemy force to wisely break contact.

The Mission 80 (two HMM-263 Peachbush CH-46Ds and two HML-367 Scarface Cobra gunships) received word of the emergency extract mission at 1700 while on standby at MMAF. The CH-46Ds flew to Camp Reasoner's LZ 401 so the low helo, already rigged with the cable hoist, could also be rigged for a ladder and both aircraft could take on Recon Marines (Drumright and a tailgunner were in the high CH-46D while USN Lt. Charles F. Andras (surgeon) accompanied an extract team in the low aircraft). The Sea Knights departed there at 1742. They arrived on station with Cobra gunships over Thin Man at 1810.

With bombs falling all around Thin Man, the enemy pulled back. The Recon team notified their COC at 1745 that they hadn't received fire for 25 minutes. At 1757 the team changed its medevacs to priority since they were no longer under fire.

Communications with Thin Man and coordination between the Mission 80 Cobra, call sign Scarface 2, Capt. Ronald E. "Sand Dollar" Fix of Texas who was a pilot in five squadrons between 1966-70, lead pilot and OV-10A aircraft already on station, were not in sync and somewhat confusing, according to Capt. Burin. "FM (radio traffic) was very cluttered with helo to helo talk and the team was being left out." He pointed out that all the confusion and delay meant more time on station that consequently led to all aircraft running low on fuel.

1stLt. R.S. "Sam" Williams, Hostage Gringo (backseat AO to pilot 1stLt. Ketron "Kent" Ellison, Hostage Zebra), said some of the delay involved Hostage Igor being bypassed by the Mission 80 flight leader for a situation report (sitrep) from Team Thin Man directly. On the other hand, each Hostage crew coming on station that evening would pass on a sitrep to the relieving pilot.

Once the enemy had been beaten back and the decision was made to pick the team up, Scarface 2 asked Hostage aircraft to make a pass firing smoke rockets near Thin Man so the extraction helicopter's approach and hover would remain unseen by enemy gunners. Hostage Zebra began his run only to have Scarface 2 fire his own smoke rockets and interfere with his flight pattern causing him to abort. Coming around again, Ellison now encountered the extraction Sea Knight making a premature run into the zone complaining about running low on fuel.

HMM-263 Peachbush pilot Maj. B.L. "Bruce" Shapiro's Sea Knight with copilot 1stLt. Gerald W. "Jerry" Martin, 23, of Mesquite, Texas appeared in a hover overhead at 1906 hours for an emergency extract of the Marines off the razorback beginning with Gifford by hoist cable. The aircraft's gunner hosed the area down in front of them with .50 caliber machine gun fire, according to Gifford. The Peachbush crew was fighting the approaching darkness to remove all of Team Thin Man from the razorback.

Sgt. Gifford was for all practical purposes out of the fight after a grazing 7-inch wound to the head essentially scalped him and most likely gave him a concussion as well as limited his vision. Also, he was hit in the knuckle of his right thumb leaving it dangling with a blown out tendon and another round put a 3½-inch wound to the back of his leg. Apparently, Doc McLynn assessed Gifford's injuries as more incapacitating than the lieutenant's severely shot up foot and elected to evacuate him first. Plunkett felt that Gifford was in shock and not alert at all.

The lieutenant was in full command of his faculties--mental, physical and emotional, according to Doc McLynn. He could help defend the position in the event of a counterattack while Gifford's head wound and impaired vision drastically limited his ability to react to hostile fire. The Recon Marines feared the enemy was still out there preparing to attack in greater force as darkness fell.

1stLt. Martin had this take on the situation, "If Skibbe was the kind of officer I have heard he was, he naturally would have sent the other injured team member up first. I kind of doubt that the reason was to provide covering fire since the team was not in contact and nobody was shooting at anybody while we were there. It's simply the thing a good officer would do."

As Shapiro's aircraft hovered 75-100 feet above Skibbe's team, the helicopter's side door hoist cable, to which was attached a jungle penetrator, was lowered by crew chief Cpl. Roger L. Boyd, 20, of Waterloo, Iowa. The jungle penetrator is a 3-foot-long, 50 lb. cylindrical weight that holds two seats that pull-down to a 90 degree angle and can accommodate two men at a time in the sitting position,

It's a time-consuming tedious rescue maneuver to slowly lower the jungle penetrator on the end of a 150-foot, 7/32-inch in diameter, corrosive resistant, preformed, non-twist, flexible steel cable to the ground, strap in the wounded Marine and slowly hoist him through the canopy at what's specified as 100 feet per minute.

Although meant to haul up two people, the hoist mechanism actually could only handle one man at a time, as the maximum cable pull was 600 lbs. Skibbe weighed between 175-200 lbs. and with his heavy combat equipment the hoist would be pushed to its "advertised" limits to extract both men at the same time.

### Gifford Rides Jungle Penetrator to Shapiro's Aircraft

After Plunkett strapped the considerably smaller Gifford and his equipment onto the jungle penetrator, the hoist cable mechanism safely pulled him up to the helicopter's door with only a moment of excitement as the sergeant said he briefly got caught up in the canopy and his injured thumb was hung up in the brush before he broke loose. He was unbuckled from the cylinder and pulled aboard. Providing onboard medical help was Dr. Andras, 1st Recon Battalion's Navy doctor, who immediately went to work putting IV fluids into Gifford. The doctor thought Gifford was a priority medevac and wondered where the emergency medevac was.

"They tried to give me morphine but I didn't want any. I wanted to be conscious for the extraction of the rest of the team," said Gifford.

"I remember leaning over the control console to my right and looking back into the cabin when the crew chief brought in the first guy (Gifford) on the hoist," said Martin, a 1968 East Texas State College at Commerce, Texas grad, who was able to refresh his memory with a diary he kept the entire time he was in Vietnam. He wrote down his March 2 observations (against standing orders in Marine Air Group-16) on the extract/medevac mission within 24 hours after the incident.

### Skibbe's Jungle Penetrator Cable Snaps

Plunkett said the decision to extract Lt. Skibbe by jungle penetrator came from someone higher up than his team. He thought the lieutenant could've managed the ladder with the remainder of the team. The cable was dropped back down to pick Skibbe up. Again, Plunkett did the honors of strapping the team's second casualty onto the jungle penetrator seat on the end of the cable. He was slowly hoisted into the air "hitting several snags and branches while he was being lifted off the ground through heavy jungle canopy," according to a Navy/Marine Corps Headquarters' Casualty Message later sent to his parents.

"He got caught in the bushes twice but we got him untangled both times with no trouble," read McLynn's statement. Jones also noted that both Gifford and Skibbe got caught up in the foliage a couple of times before pulling free. The lieutenant brought out all his equipment except for his M-16 rifle. He broke loose from the dense canopy as Gifford had, clearing the tall trees, which were about 30-40 feet in height. Thin Man lost sight of Skibbe as the canopy and the failing light obscured him. Skibbe and Gifford's extraction point was off the high-speed trail east-southeast 200 meters from their encounter with the enemy soldiers below Hill 225 near a well-travelled footpath.[3C]

"Once the lieutenant cleared the canopy, I turned my attention back down the trail and waited for the ladder to be thrown out for the rest of us," said Plunkett. He and his stretched thin 4-man team redeployed in a wide 360 degree defensive perimeter and began preparing their harnesses for attachment via a "D" snap ring to the ladder, which would be thrown down from the helicopter once an open space in the tall canopy could be found. Shapiro notified Team Thin Man's radioman LCpl. Moreno when he was ready for them and where to go to hook up.

"When (Skibbe) was within 10-15 feet of the crew chief's door, the cable broke and he was dropped into the blackness below. Considering that when the cable snapped, Lt. Skibbe fell 100 feet or so, the equivalent of a 10-story building, it is highly unlikely that he survived the fall. Possible, but very unlikely," surmised Martin. The crew chief informed the pilots of the snapped cable and they contacted Moreno on the ground to make him aware of the situation so that Skibbe could be recovered.

"There are details of that mission which I remember quite vividly. Nobody mistakenly thought Lt. Skibbe was aboard our aircraft (Homecoming II Project and the POW Network computer websites carry a version of this story). The Recon team, at least the radioman, was aware that he had fallen and stated over the radio that he had probably been killed by the fall. He further requested that we get them (meaning the rest of the Recon team) out of there and come back at first light to search for him," said Martin.

On the other hand, Hostage River, Maj. B.C. "Butch" Miller, noted in his statement that the Recon team indicated the man who fell was okay and would be able to stay on the ladder.

HMM-263 crew chief Cpl. Boyd experienced his own near fatal close call in January when he asked a friend to take his place on the crew of his assigned Sea Knight so he could go on Rest & Relaxation (R&R) the next day. The helicopter subsequently crashed killing all but a gunner. Upon his return to the squadron, he spent time subbing on several aircraft before landing a job with the crew assigned to Shapiro's CH-46D which carried the side-mounted hoist cable March 2.

He was in the door running the hoist cable with a pistol grip control and watching as both men in turn were hoisted towards the helicopter. After the badly wounded sergeant was pulled aboard, the cable was dropped down for Skibbe. Plunkett strapped him in and, thus, began the slow rise towards the hovering Sea Knight.

"The cable somehow slipped off the pulley and started to unravel. It stopped unraveling after a few feet played out. The jungle penetrator was approximately halfway between the aircraft and the ground. I decided to continue the rescue and hadn't gone very far when the cable broke dropping (Skibbe) between 50-60 feet," said Boyd. Martin and his crew chief had different ideas of how far the officer fell. The Casualty Message informed Skibbe's parents he was MIA as of 1810 Monday, March 2, 1970.

Boyd immediately informed Maj. Shapiro and Lt. Martin about losing Skibbe. The pilot notified the team on the ground. "I heard (Maj. Shapiro) contact the Recon team that we had dropped him. I believe they replied that they had him and to send down the extraction ladder."

Again, Martin's recollection was that the Recon team's radio operator knew Skibbe was unaccounted for on the ground.

Maj. Shapiro called Scarface 2 to contact Thin Man to ask about the condition of the fallen man. Since he had no jungle penetrator or workable hoist cable and was quickly burning up his fuel, the major decided to proceed in picking up the remaining team members with the ladder.

"I contacted Thin Man and inquired as to the well-being of the man dropped. Thin Man replied he was all right and through further discussion said he would be strapped to the extract ladder. I informed the CH-46 of this and he dropped his ladder for the remaining portion of the pick-up," indicated Scarface 2's Capt. Fix in a statement taken shortly after the mission.

Capt. McVey was the senior extract officer aboard Maj. Shapiro's aircraft this day. 2ndLt. Tommie S. "Tom" Hodge, a member of the Recon extract team, yelled over to him from the hell hole when Lt. Skibbe fell to inform him of the accident. "Okay, I know," replied the captain grimly.

**Recon Team on Ladder Fails to See Skibbe Nearby**

Maj. Shapiro took the Sea Knight up and had Boyd tell him of any openings in the canopy so they could deploy the ladder. He found a spot and the major settled the CH-46D down among the treetops. Capt. McVey yelled at Lt. Hodge to kick the heavy wire ladder out the back ramp. The team struggled about 50 meters through underbrush to reach the dangling ladder.

"Cpl. Boyd then informed me that the man who had fallen was still lying inert about 15 feet from the men (who were by now snap linked to the wire) on the (flexible aluminum) ladder. I tried calling the people on the ladder, but they had already secured their radio," stated Maj. Shapiro.

1stLt. Martin recalls that after the Recon team gave a thumbs up from being securely hooked on the ladder, Cpl. Boyd notified them that one man was left behind and must be dead. "Maj. Shapiro asked how he knew he was dead to which he replied that the man was lying on the ground inert about 10-15 feet away from the others who had made no attempt to help or assist him, so he assumed that the man was dead.

"To this Maj. Shapiro replied that the man just couldn't be left there that someone had to get him out somehow. The major then called Scarface, informed him of the situation, then called our wingman, Peachbush 1-2, and asked if he had a jungle penetrator aboard. The wingman answered negative," Lt. Martin noted in his statement. The former pilot indicated that Shapiro was very angry at his wingman. Martin said that shortly after their return to MMAF that their March 2 wingman was sent down to the bush Marines as a forward air controller, FAC.

Dr. Andras wondered what happened to his other emergency patient and noticed the cable was gone from the hoist cable apparatus. He walked over to the hell hole, a roughly 3x3-foot hole in the aircraft's floor several feet beyond the gunners' positions, and was deeply disturbed by what he saw. "Lt. Skibbe was lying on his back with his left leg under him and the jungle penetrator laying off to the side. He wasn't moving. He was about 10 feet from where the team was mounting the ladder. The team evidently couldn't see him because of the (thick) foliage."

After kicking the ladder out the back ramp, Lt. Hodge returned to the hell hole where he was joined by McVey and Dr. Andras. "(We) observed Lt. Skibbe on his back some 10-15 meters from the team. From this position I could see both the team mounting the ladder and the lieutenant. At this time the team was on the ladder, I was yelling, 'PICK UP THE LIEUTENANT!' Naturally, the team couldn't hear me. After that, the bird just lifted up and flew away," stated Lt. Hodge.

Lt.Col. Drumright was aboard Peachbush 1-2 when Skibbe fell. 1st Recon Marine Sgt. Gerald R. Speakman recalled being the tailgunner on the orbit bird and asking the colonel if everything was all right with Thin Man, "He informed me that Lt. Skibbe had fallen from the penetrator and that the team hadn't seen his fall and that he was still out there."

Cobra pilot Scarface 17, 1stLt. David J. Cummings, 24, of Woburn, Massachusetts, was surprised to hear the Recon team abandoned one of their men on the ground. "Not believing my ears, I asked Scarface 2 if I could make a low pass. On the first pass (about 100 feet off the trees), both my front seat (copilot Maj. James W. "Jim" or "Rifle" Rider, 34, of West Seneca, New York) and I thought we saw movement in the zone. On the second pass, I was unable to pick anything out. We tried to make contact with the team on the ladder but were unsuccessful."

The Sea Knight copilot, Lt. Martin, said it came as disturbing news to him to hear that Skibbe might have survived his fall but was left to fend for himself on the ground. "It was a painful call to have to leave him there. Considering the terrain, the darkness and our fuel state, which was fast becoming critical. We really had no choice."

Martin explained that hovering in a helicopter out of ground effect (the air underneath the blades didn't reach the ground to add a cushion of air and additional lift to the Sea Knight to conserve fuel) as Shapiro was forced to do, is a maneuver that requires a great deal of power and consequently consumes fuel at a tremendous rate.

"We had been hovering for what seemed like an eternity and were down to 300 lbs. or less in each tank. In a CH-46, that's pretty close to running on empty. So by the time we had the rest of the team attached to the ladder and had lifted up to clear the foliage, we had no alternative but to head for An Hoa which was the nearest available fuel."

A near disaster was averted on lifting the team straight up 250 feet hanging from the ladder. The rotor rpm had dropped to 92 percent, according to Shapiro, and the helicopter began to lose altitude, sending the men on the ladder towards the canopy. "I ordered my copilot to jettison fuel, but no fuel was dumped because each tank was already too low. We regained our lost rpm's with an increase in airspeed and just managed to clear the trees."

At that point Shapiro turned the aircraft over to Martin to get them to An Hoa Combat Base. A direct route was out as gaining altitude to fly over the 1,000-meter (3,281-foot) high mountains required too much power and would have exhausted the remaining fuel in their tanks. He flew north-northeast along the Song Cai until it became the Song Vu Gia then onto the east out of the mountains. As this river merged into the Song Thu Bon, he dropped south and followed it into An Hoa.

Martin's worst nightmare en route was to run out of fuel and have to autorotate to the ground with the Recon Marines hanging off the 120-foot ladder in the darkness over the river or the hostile Arizona Territory. Shapiro was busy calling ahead to temporarily stop artillery missions across their flight path into An Hoa.

Meanwhile, back at Camp Reasoner 1st Recon's S-3 assistant 1stLt. Wallace C. "Chip" Gregson Jr. (a '68 USNA graduate who would retire a 3-star general after 37 years in 2005) received word around 1900 that "the extract had been unsuccessful in that one wounded Marine was still in the LZ." He notified the S-3 senior Operations officer, Maj. John M. Mattiace, who attempted to contact Shapiro to tell him to stop at Thuong Duc to offload the team on the ladder and put the two officers (McVey and Hodge) aboard at the bottom of the ladder "to personally secure the wounded Marine onto the ladder." Shapiro didn't receive the message as communications was apparently down with the Mission 80's four helicopters due to the mountainous terrain.

This was a moot point anyway, as Thuong Duc had no fuel, which they desperately needed, according to Martin. Maj. Mattiace figured the Mission 80 birds were already at An Hoa refueling and assumed they planned to go back after the Marine left behind.

Making sure they got his message, the major passed the information through his radio relay teams in the Que Sons, the OV-10A Hostage aircraft in the area and the 1st Marine Division's Direct Air Support Center (DASC). All attempts were unsuccessful, according to Lt. Gregson.

The CH-46Ds landed at An Hoa on fumes. Cpl. Boyd recalled the Recon team being surprised to find out Skibbe was not in the helicopter at An Hoa. Plunkett said the team thought both Gifford and Skibbe were on board the helicopter. Due to the deafening noise from the CH-46D hovering over the team on the razorback and the tremendous downward blast of wind from the rotor blades, none of the other team members saw or heard Skibbe fall in the fading light.

"If we'd known the lieutenant had fallen, we'd have stayed out there until we found him," stated Plunkett. At An Hoa Lt.Col. Drumright was visibly upset with the remnants of Team Thin Man for leaving their lieutenant behind and demanded to know why they didn't recover him. The only reasonable answer at the time was "a weak communication problem," according to Plunkett. He added, "We never got the word that Skibbe had fallen off the jungle penetrator. I guarantee you that word was never passed."

"I'd rather have died than lose the lieutenant. I wish they'd sent him up first rather than me," said Gifford, who's still deeply affected by the loss of Lt. Skibbe 38 some odd years later.

Scarface 17 copilot Maj. Rider seemed to think the radioman on the ground didn't absorb what the Sea Knight pilot had told him. Rider just came off duty the day before as air liaison officer (ALO) with the 1st Marines at Hill 55.

Moreno, Team Thin Man's primary radioman, only had this to say about the two emergency extracts March 2 in his short statement to an Informal Board of Investigation, IBI, "Cpl. Plunkett and PFC Piere put Cpl. (actually Sgt.) Gifford on the jungle penetrator, next was Lt. Skibbe. The last I saw of him was clearing the treetops. Then the remainder of the team set up a 360."

## VC Soldier's Account, The Razorback, March 2, 1970

(What follows comes from post-Vietnam War interviews conducted by the Joint Task Force-Full Accounting, JTF-FA, charged with locating American MIAs in past wars worldwide. Although falling into the category of "hearsay" as no Viet Cong directly involved in the fight that day would admit participation or bear witness to a VC soldier's story, the scenario that follows has a grain of truth to it due to a "war trophy" one of the soldiers held onto. Giang District Military Forces, GDMF, B1 (VC) Deputy Commander Zo Rum Au whose troops engaged Team Thin Man on the ground March 2, 1970 was interviewed in 1991, 1993 and 1998---MDK).

After the two CH-46Ds and two Scarface Cobras departed the area, a GDMF B-1 (1st Platoon) VC squad searched the razorback which the Marines fought so hard to defend. A danger existed for the VC as a Bronco OV-10A orbited their position overhead and a C-130 was dropping flares. Should the American planes spot their movement, high explosives could be expected to fall on them from distant artillery firebases or present air cover.

The squad combed the battleground possibly to retrieve their dead and wounded from the airstrikes supporting Team Thin Man earlier and to see if the Marines had left anyone behind as a flareship dropped illumination and aircraft buzzed overhead in the gathering darkness suggesting this might be the case. The VC cadre must surely have realized that if the "painted faces" had, indeed, left a comrade behind, they would return as they had always done in the past. It was only a matter of time before the Americans descended on the razorback trail once more.

Zo Rum Au, 30 in 1970, claimed he was not with the squad but received the report later. He related how he was told the firefight began just south of Khe Dienne Stream in early morning.[3D] (JTF-FA refers to him as Mr. Au, his first name, with his family name being Zo as is the custom in Vietnam, China, Korea and Japan which is the reverse of western style).[4] A helicopter arrived to rescue the Americans later that day but one American was left behind, according to Mr. Au, aka Chrumf Aaus (pronounced Chow Raam Aaus in the Katu language).

The deputy commander, an ethnic Trieng, told JTF-FA investigators that one of his soldiers, a Mr. Boh (also spelled Bowh), said he killed Skibbe. A second witness, Mr. Vu, stated that Mr. Boh told him he had found Skibbe crouched down on the trail and personally shot him in the chest before rolling him off the trail into a rocky area. The location is roughly 300 meters northwest of Hill 225 with an approximate 70-degree slope. A narrow trail runs along the ridge's slope. A virtually continuous limestone boulder outcrop is 5 meters below the trail. Additional limestone boulders are scattered across the site.[5A]

Mr. Vu said Mr. Boh told him the body was not buried but left out in the open in a forest off the trail. The VC force removed an M-79 grenade launcher, a pair of binoculars, a watch, a dagger and a radio from the Marine's body. All these items were turned into the B-1 squad commander, an ethnic Vietnamese Mr. Loc or Loocs, (Hooif Loocj) then given to the GDMF, who, in turn, passed them on to the Military Region 5 Headquarters. (No timeline is given for the shooting in the JTF-FA report. There's the possibility Lt. Skibbe could've been shot sometime after March 2. Only by extrapolating Dr. Andras' prediction that he might not have survived the night can it be suggested he was killed March 2---MDK).

Mr. Au was a retiree in Lang Dung Village, Thanh My Town, Giang District when a joint U.S./Socialist Republic of Vietnam field investigation team interviewed him between July 17 and August 12, 1991. He stated that a Mr. Boh held back a laminated in plastic color photograph as a war souvenir he took off the American's body. The photo that was in Mr. Au's possession showed a USMC second lieutenant in a short-sleeve khaki uniform standing beside a Caucasian female in front of a house, apparently located in the United States. A photographic laboratory stamp on the reverse side of the photo indicated "Nov 69." The eyewitness Mr. Boh later died in combat, noted Mr. Au. He also indicated a man called Koc (Kocs) also participated in the incident, but could not provide Koc's current address. The team made queries but could not locate a man by that name. Mr. Au said B-1 commander Mr. Loc may have been involved in the fight as well but attempts to find his whereabouts were also unsuccessful.

The JTF-FA team interviewed relatives of Mr. Boh who said he died in either September or October 1969 in Ba Vuong village. Skibbe's family positively identified the Marine officer in the photo as 2ndLt. Skibbe in 1993 giving credence to Mr. Boh's story despite the timeline discrepancies.[6] (No one has yet resolved Mr. Boh's participation in an event in which he supposedly died 4 or 5 months earlier. The timeline of the firefight Mr. Au related was askew as well. The VC deputy commander pinpointed Skibbe's location as 1 kilometer west up a steep trail and from there 3 kilometers north of Thanh My Town.[7A] The village is in mountainous terrain 80 kilometers southwest of Da Nang. Apparently someone other than Mr. Boh was involved in Skibbe's death on the razorback---MDK).

VC commander, Mr. Au, turned this photo of 2ndLt. David Skibbe and his fiancée, Georgine Tortorella, over to a Joint Task Force-Full Accounting team in 1991 saying another soldier took it off the Marine's body. The JTF-FA returned the photo to the Skibbe family. (Photo courtesy of William C. Skibbe)

# Chapter 5

**Stay with me God. The night is dark,**
**The night is cold: my little spark**
**Of courage dies. The night is long;**
**Be with me, God, and make me strong.[1]**
**"A Soldier--His Prayer"**
***Poems from the Desert (1944)***

## Camp Reasoner and MMAF, March 2, 1970

Skibbe's fate was unknown to the Marines returning to An Hoa and then onto Camp Reasoner and, consequently, to the Marine hierarchy which made the final decision as to whether or not to mount a rescue attempt to recover him later that night.

"Maj. Shapiro wanted to call out the night Mission 80 Bald Eagle and have them go out and look for the missing Marine officer. He contacted the Da Nang DASC to initiate the search," recalled Martin. He was informed that Lt.Col. Drumright radioed them from his wingman's helicopter to secure the mission until first light and advised the DASC of his decision. Having been told the mission was canceled, Shapiro and his wingman took Gifford to the hospital and the Recon team back to Camp Reasoner at about 2000. They arrived at the Marble Mountain Air Facility at 2010.

Before Thin Man returned to LZ 401, Gregson was called by the DASC helicopter director asking if Drumright had canceled the emergency recovery operation through 5th Marines' COC.

"I told him that was a definite 'negative.' We had not canceled it and we needed that package back as we still had a wounded Marine on the ground," noted Gregson's 1970 statement to the Informal Board of Investigation, IBI. He put in a call to 5th Marines' COC and they weren't even aware of the mission much less canceling it.

When the team and Drumright landed at Camp Reasoner, the mission was back on to retrieve Lt. Skibbe. Drumright and Mattiace put their heads together and began formulating a plan and requested aviation support at 2100.

"I considered at this time Lt. Skibbe's fall could have been 50 feet or less, and that with a possible broken leg. It was my decision we should go back on station," Drumright's statement to the IBI on March 8, 1970.

Broncos Hostage River, Maj. Miller, and Hostage Zebra, Lt. Ellison, were earlier replaced in the skies above Skibbe by Maj. Joe Roman's Hostage Romeo and 1stLt. Wayne A. Svenson's Hostage Zulu flareship. Scarface 2 notified them of the mission's cancellation. Aerial observer Capt. Paul Bloom, the AO in Maj. Roman's Bronco, wanted verification of that order. He called Vesper Bells (1st Recon) at 1952 before securing for the night. Svenson of Copper Canyon, Texas said that once Drumright and Mattiace were consulted it was learned the extract had not been canceled.

The mission was still on and they were to hold their position until the Mission 80 Bald Eagle package joined them. A basketball flareship arrived to provide continuous illumination. At 2036 they were informed the working birds were on the way and should be on station within 30 minutes. At no time did Skibbe lose his air cover or "night light" from alternating Hostage aircraft and the basketball flareship.

"When we got back to HMM-263's Ready Room, the place was abuzz with activity. We were told that (Skibbe) was 'like a son' to the Deputy CG of 1st Marine Division (Ground). Maj.Gen. (Edwin B.) Wheeler himself called (the S-3 duty officer) on the landline and personally ordered Maj. Shapiro to get back out there ASAP. By this time, the night Bald Eagle crews had arrived," said Martin.

Maj. Shapiro flew as copilot to Peachbush pilot 1stLt. Darcy A. Vernier, 25, of Great Falls, Montana on the Bald Eagle package. He explained why he took the second seat. "Since I'd been up 15 hours, had not eaten in 8½ hours and was physically tired and mentally depressed from (losing Skibbe), I did not feel that I was at that point safe to command an aircraft in the extremely dangerous flying conditions."

Martin said he remained in the Ready Room and later heard what happened next in the rescue attempt from Lt. Vernier. Cpl. Boyd again accompanied Maj. Shapiro as crew chief. A second helicopter was put into service to replace the CH-46D with the defective side hoist cable. A maintenance crew pored over the hoist cable to see why the cable failed.

Drumright said he remembered one reason Shapiro wanted to go back was, "He said he recalled a reference point of a tall tree where Skibbe had fallen. He wanted to go back out as he thought he could relocate the distinctive tree with the aid of the basketball illumination dropped over that area."

Cobra pilot Maj. Rider said he hitched a ride with one of the CH-46Ds en route to the Camp Reasoner LZ from MMAF. The major was on his second Vietnam tour (first tour was in 1965) and wanted to run an idea by Lt.Col. Drumright, whom he knew from TBS when he was newly commissioned. His plan was for him to go down on the hoist cable line to look for Lt. Skibbe.

Use of 1st Recon riggers' handmade ladder was no longer an option as

Drumright said he found one ladder cable that was frayed back at LZ 401 and, "In my decision, these conditions made the ladder unsafe." Due to there not being a back-up ladder, the hoist cable and/or rappelling ropes were the only means to get in or out of the heavily canopied area around Skibbe.

"I explained to Lt.Col. Drumright that I just finished serving as the 1st Marines Air Liaison Officer and had been a liaison officer with the Vietnamese for a few months in my first tour. I told him I was comfortable on the ground at night and having been at that location earlier in the day was familiar with the terrain. I explained that I wanted to go down the hoist by myself, see what I could find and that if I needed help I would call for it on my survival radio. Drumright slapped me on the shoulder and agreed (with my plan)," said Maj. Rider, whose first flight in-country on his second tour was May 12, 1969. After 33 years, Drumright said he honestly didn't recall how the rescue attempt was initially formulated in our 2003 interview.

At this time Charlie Co.'s CO Capt. McVey volunteered to go down on the hoist cable and look for one of his platoon commanders in the dark jungle below, according to Maj. Rider. Drumright acquiesced to McVey's request. And that's how close Rider came to being etched onto The Wall in the years ahead.

The night before, Capt. McVey briefed Sgt. Gifford and Lt. Skibbe on the mission putting the sergeant in charge because of the lieutenant's newness to the bush. And now Gifford was seriously injured and Skibbe was missing out in Indian Territory alone in the darkness.

McVey was a "mustanger" with 9 years in the enlisted ranks with much of that time spent in Force Recon. He previously attended Army Ranger School at Fort Benning, Georgia; Marine Corps Escape and Evasion School at Bridgeport, Connecticut; and Navy Scuba School at Pearl Harbor, Hawaii as well as completed 45 free fall and 55 static line parachute jumps from 1,250 to 5,000 feet. He also made a half-dozen jumps from A3D jet bombers as well as a jump into the Salton Sea, 80 miles northeast of San Diego, California, for the Navy Parachute Test Unit...all this before becoming a warrant officer in 1965.

Sgt. McVey was a Marine top to bottom. His fiancée, Karen Arrowsmith, received her USMC discharge on November 8, 1960 after 2 years of service. Their marriage ceremony 2 months later included all Marines--ushers, bridesmaids--except for one, the Navy chaplain, according to former 1stLt. William H. "Bill" Bond Jr., who was McVey's lieutenant at 1st Force Recon at Camp Pendleton (Maj. Bond would serve as the 1st Force Recon CO March 2-June 3, 1970 in Vietnam). Maj. R.G. Hunt Jr., McVey's company commander, gave the bride away.

He eventually reached the enlisted rank of gunnery sergeant before attending OCS and becoming a warrant officer (WO) in the Marine Corps.

On a 1966-67 tour of duty in Vietnam, WO McVey was tagged as the "food services officer" at the MAG-16 Officers Club facility. Serving in that same capacity at MCB Twentynine Palms in California, McVey was frustrated and threatened to leave the Corps if he was required to remain in food services. Generally, warrant officers were either in administration (food services in this case) or flew helicopters. He accepted a captaincy rank in order to change MOS classifications.

This he must have done in order to go back to his primary MOS and return to Nam to do what the Corps spent years training him to be...a behind-the-lines Force Recon scout. He got his wish.

**Sgt. LaVoy Don "Mac" McVey on his 100th parachute jump as an enlisted Marine. (Photo courtesy of Mildred McVey Holmes)**

In a letter to McVey's mother, Mildred, dated March 26, 1970, Lt.Col. Drumright says he concurred with a plan conceived by the captain involving himself and a 6-man Recon team. Following McVey's descent by hoist cable in the area where Skibbe had fallen, the Recon team would rappel down from ropes attached to the helicopter.

"It was imperative that operations commence immediately since delay until daylight of the following day would, in the estimation of medical authorities, seriously jeopardize (Skibbe's) chance for survival," stated Drumright in the letter. "Weighing these factors, I personally directed the commencement of recovery operations and placed myself aboard the same helicopter in which your son and the rescue team were being transported."

LCpl. Simpson said the sergeant major came into the EM Club at Camp Reasoner to ask for volunteers to go back after Skibbe. He turned to Simpson and said that since he was a member of Team Thin Man and didn't go out on the original patrol then he should be the first to volunteer. Put that way, Simpson said he volunteered along with several Recon Marines he wasn't familiar with. Plunkett and Simpson continually argued as to who would walk point for Thin Man…both Marines wanted the honor of leading their team in hostile territory, according to Gifford.

On March 2's mission, Simpson with 14 patrols behind him wanted to walk point for the third time in a row but Gifford pointed out that it was Plunkett's turn and he was ordered to take some downtime in the rear since Skibbe was taking his place on the team. Only seven men were designated to a patrol at that time.

The reactionary team consisted of Capt. McVey as patrol leader; 1stLt. Collin C. Roberts, assistant patrol leader; Sgt. John T. Gremillion; LCpl. Dudley K. Sparks, radioman; HMC Richard J. "Jim" Pearston, Corpsman; LCpl. James S. "Greek" Psaras; and Cpl. Richard H. Lappin, point man. Dr. Andras gave Doc Pearston six glass IV bottles with instructions to start two IV's on Skibbe when he found him presuming he would be in bad shape. Others on the CH-46D included Lt.Col. Drumright and Dr. Andras as well as the five crew members. LCpl. Simpson noted he was also on board Vernier's helicopter.

The idea for the recovery mission was for Capt. McVey to go down on the 150-foot hoist cable line with the radioman, LCpl. Sparks, to make sure the 120-foot rappelling ropes reached the ground. McVey's plan was to anchor the rope on the ground with the weight of his body for the others to rappel down while Sparks acted as security and communications with the helicopter.

"The team leader (Capt. McVey) was concerned about being left on the ground if we took fire and I assured him that we would not leave him there as long as the aircraft continued to fly, at which point we would all be there with him (having crashed)," recalled Lt. Vernier as he promised Capt. McVey that he wouldn't leave him behind. These words came back to haunt the Peachbush pilot in the years ahead even though the situation that cropped up was beyond his control.

McVey had just come off a long 99-hour patrol (0900 February 25 to 1200 March 1) as team leader of Team Texas Pete. The team consisted of Sgt. Speakman, Cpl. R.L. Snedeker, LCpl. DeLoach, LCpl. Sparks, LCpl. Thomas and HM3 White. Texas Pete worked a mountainous area[2A] north of Nui Nhu about 6 clicks southwest of the An Hoa Combat Base and west of the Song Tinh Yen. McVey reported six sightings of a total of 31 NVA on the trails around the team and heard voices and coughing in close proximity to them. He called in two fire missions. LCpl. Sparks, the primary radioman, and Capt McVey must've been worn out from the bush going out on aircraft a day after they returned.

### McVey Attempts Rescue Alone, March 2, 1970

1stLt. Svenson said Hostage Romeo briefed the incoming Scarface helicopters of their situation as they departed due to low fuel. He noted that Hostage Romeo had flown near the deck one last time to see if he could spot Skibbe on the ground before leaving but was unsuccessful. As they approached the Marble Mountain Air Facility, Hostage Turtle (pilot Maj. Bill Carroll) flew out to take Romeo's place orbiting above Peachbush 1-1 and 1-2 Sea Knights as well as Scarface 2 and Scarface 17 Cobra gunships. The "Thin Man Package" arrived above Skibbe's last known location at 2215.

"As we reached our destination and the penetrator was set up, approximately one minute from the captain getting on the penetrator, he informed me that he would go first and I would follow (later)," according to LCpl. Sparks' IBI statement of March 8, 1970.

Cpl. Lappin thought he was to be the first man down since he was walking point but Capt. McVey decided to take that responsibility on his own shoulders. He would descend alone.

The hoist cable was attached inside the replacement helicopter and the cable was dropped through the hell hole at approximately 2230. McVey was strapped to the jungle penetrator on the end of the cable.

The crew chief pointed out that besides the weight restrictions against pulling up two men on the jungle penetrator, two men wouldn't fit through the hell hole on a hoist cable. If McVey was fortunate enough to find Skibbe after his descent, the mission called for him to strap the lieutenant onto the jungle penetrator and remain on the ground waiting for a second lift.

Capt. McVey possessed an amazing amount of courage and an unflagging desire to retrieve Skibbe no matter what his condition was to go down into that enemy-infested formidable terrain by himself in the dark. Basketball flares would illuminate his descent making him a juicy target to any VC/NVA below.

I'm not sure if Mac McVey was a religious man but I know the biblical passage, "Ye though I walk through the valley of the Shadow of Death I shall fear no evil for Thou art with me," would have been running through my mind over and over as I was lowered towards that dark, foreboding razorback surrounded by towering mountains. "Evil" in this instance was the enemy soldiers waiting to shoot anyone foolish enough to return to their lair.

"Upon arriving at the objective area, basketball was on station and the area was well-illuminated. Gunbirds strafed low over the objective area firing 40mm," Drumright's statement to the IBI March 8, 1970.

In his statement to the IBI, Maj. Shapiro indicated he asked that basketball illuminations be dropped to the east out of the insert zone but somehow the flares ended up to the north. The huge hot-burning magnesium basketball flares blown by the wind floated on parachutes dangerously close to their stationary helicopter hovering into position.

Lt. Vernier settled the CH-46D into an opening in the trees that Cpl. Boyd and Maj. Shapiro remembered and put the nose bubble of the aircraft in the trees in a hover. As the captain was being lowered to the razorback below, the basketball flareship put out several large basketball flares behind a ridgeline to the north throwing Vernier's aircraft into darkness. With no reference point, vertigo became a distinct possibility although Vernier said he wasn't experiencing any problems at the time. Also, Boyd's lowering McVey on the cable became a dangerous proposition since he couldn't see what he was lowering him into. Both pilots also lost their night vision due to the sunshine bright illumination previously put down.

Doc Pearston, 23, from Fort Worth, Texas, noted in his statement that in addition to the basketball illuminations, the landing lights and interior lights of the helicopter were also extinguished. Lt. Vernier said he turned the lights out as it presented any enemy in the area an excellent lit stationary target to shoot at in the night sky.

"While the captain was going down on the penetrator, one or more basketball flares was a dud and everything went black. Without a hover reference, Vernier did just about the only thing he could do. He started to climb and directed Cpl. Boyd, the crew chief, to reel in the hoist cable. He planned to take it around and have another try at it when he got some more illumination from a basketball flare," according to Martin.

"The helicopter began to drop off down the hill to one side in the darkness. We had broken branches and the tops of the trees had come into the aircraft from the hell hole and back ramp...that's how close we were to the canopy. That pilot did an amazing job keeping us airborne," recalled Col. Drumright.

Boyd pushed the button on the hand-held hoist cable control to reel the captain up into the helicopter. He only descended about 20-30 feet below the aircraft when they aborted the insert.

"It was night when we arrived at the site. I was lowering the captain into the zone when the pilot stated that he was becoming vertigo (after a misdropped illume left the helicopter in total darkness) and to bring the captain back in," noted Cpl. Boyd's IBI statement.

"The crew chief tapped me on the head and told me to help him get Capt. McVey back into the bird," according to Sgt. Gremillion's March 7, 1970 statement.

LCpl. Sparks' written comment to the IBI was that the bird had doubled its altitude above the zone when he noticed that Capt. McVey wasn't coming any closer to the aircraft. He put his hand on the cable and realized it wasn't moving and informed the crew chief. Boyd felt of the cable, according to Sparks, and upon realizing it was not moving as well put continuous pressure with his finger on the hoist control switch. At that point, the captain began to approach the hell hole.

"I was standing in front of the hell hole with one hand guiding the cable aboard that supported Capt. McVey so that he would not hook on the bottom of the helicopter while operating the portable hoist control with the other hand," explained Boyd.

The corporal said the captain had slung his weapon over his shoulder so he could have both hands free to hold onto the cable. McVey was strapped onto the jungle penetrator by Boyd in a sitting position just as Skibbe was before his accident.

### Captain's Cable Snaps, Falls Equivalent of 60 Floors

"Capt. McVey's head and shoulders were inside the bird when he handed me his rifle. I placed the rifle in the bird and placed one hand on Capt. McVey's shoulder strap in order to stabilize him and also swing him over the edge of the hole when he was fully in the bird," noted Sgt. Gremillion.

Witnesses said there was a snapping sound as the captain was about to put his palms on the deck of the aircraft. McVey and the jungle penetrator dropped a foot in the hell hole and hung there. He yelled out to the men above just before a second snap separated the thin cable and he disappeared from sight.

"I had him within 3 feet of being entirely inside the aircraft when the cable broke. All I wanted to do was to get this man into that aircraft. I had just witnessed one Marine fall to his death just hours earlier. Never in my wildest dreams would I have thought this would happen again. He fell straight down. The captain was gone in an instant. My guess is he fell between 800 and 1,000 feet," explained Cpl. Boyd.

"The cable parted...I looked down and could see the yellow ends of the penetrator falling to the earth," recalled Sgt. Gremillion.

"The top of the penetrator was inside the aircraft and the captain had passed his rifle to Sgt. Gremillion when I heard the cable holding the penetrator come out of the pulley rig in the ceiling of the aircraft and then the sound of cable striking the side of the hatch. I witnessed the captain fall from the aircraft and hit the secondary growth," read Doc Pearston's 1970 statement. In a 2006 interview, the Doc indicated he had dove forward in an attempt to grab the captain before he disappeared from the hell hole but was unsuccessful. Someone grabbed his suspender straps from behind to prevent him from following McVey's plunge. Two Marines had to pull him and his 125 lb. combat rig back out of the hell hole into the Sea Knight, according to Pearston.

"Tears still show up when I think of the incredible loss for so many others. After getting back to Camp Reasoner that night, I sat and cried for a long time. Probably the best thing I could have done," said Pearston, a veterans counselor with the Texas Veterans Commission in 2006 at the VA Medical Center in Dallas, Texas.

Drumright stated to McVey's wife, Karen, in a letter dated April 17, 1970 that her husband fell about 600 feet, according to Maj. Shapiro's altimeter, about a quarter of a mile to a half mile from Skibbe's last known coordinates at approximately 2230.

"I turned to ask the pilot to cancel the mission if we couldn't get light. At that time, something snapped (the cable line), hit me in the shoulder and neck. I turned around to see what it was. When I looked back toward the hell hole, I heard a yell. I don't know who made it. After I had ascertained that Capt. McVey had fallen approximately 600 feet from the aircraft, I ordered the pilots to return to LZ 401," Drumright's statement to the IBI March 8, 1970. In the 2003 interview, he indicated he had permanent scars wrought by the cable line hitting him and that it "hurt like the dickens."

Former Capt. Bill Woidyla of Katy, Texas, a HMM-371 Flying Tiger Nam vet from 1967 who flew UH-34 Seahorse helicopters, said he and Mac McVey were close friends from their boot camp enlisted days through officer training at MCB Quantico, Virginia.

"We were platoon mates at San Diego boot camp in 1956. He was the left guide and I was the right guide. We met again at OCS in January 1965 and were commissioned warrant officers. I went to flight school and he went to the grunts."

Woidyla said Mac might not have been as afraid of falling into the dark void below as most men seeing as how he made well over a hundred parachute free falls since joining Recon in 1957.

"So falling wouldn't terrify him like it would you or me. Mac's body was never recovered because there was no precise location of it. It could have been anywhere in the valley," explained Woidyla. "The problem was the cable guide which allowed the cable to loop over another wind instead of next to it at the loop over point. The cable became weakened over time and eventually gave away. I think of him often." Lt. Martin said he heard the problem was traced to kinks in the hoist cables, which resulted in metal fatigue.

The Naval Aviation Training & Operations Procedures Standardization

(NATOPS) manual describes several ways the winch can be positioned. In four separate notes the manual states, "Warning...An improperly positioned winch assembly would create a sharp bend in the cable at the level-wind device and could result in excessive stresses leading to eventual cable failure," according to Lt. Martin.

Two Marine officers lost to two snapped cables was just too much in one night and it was decided to secure the mission until first light. Simpson said he never understood why the team on board was never allowed to rappel down to at least look for Skibbe or try to recover McVey's body since they were there.

Perhaps another consideration was the assumption both men sustained fatal injuries in their falls so their recovery efforts could wait until daylight. To reiterate the enemy situation, Drumright recalled that the area was "crawling with enemy troops" estimated to be "one to two battalions."

"Whenever my thoughts turn to that night, I think about how everything that could go wrong seemed to go wrong. But most of all, I think about Capt. McVey. He must have been an incredibly brave man to volunteer to ride a penetrator down into that black void to search for a comrade, who, in all probability, was already dead. We lost a great many good men in that God-forsaken part of the world," noted Martin.

Thuong Duc Special Forces "A" Team had been monitoring the situation on March 2 at their base and offered a small task force to be inserted around My Hiep (2) with one of the Marine Recon teams to go after the two Marine officers. 1st Recon's Maj. Mattiace said a plan was worked up over the sleepless night and a Mission 73 operation involving a Civilian Irregular Defense Group (CIDGs, pronounced CID-GEEs) platoon was approved for March 3 with Fox Co., 2/5 designated as a reaction company to render assistance if needed. No Recon team was authorized to accompany them.

# Chapter 6

**The fear of death is more to be dreaded than death itself...Valor grows by daring, fear by holding back.[1]** **Publilius Syrus**
***Maxim,* 1st Century BC**

## CIDGs Shot Out of My Hiep (2) LZ, March 3, 1970

Early Tuesday morning, March 3, the Sea Knight insertion package attempted to put a 29-man CIDGs force with U.S. Army Special Forces (Green Beret) advisors on the ground about 300 meters southeast of My Hiep (2) but were shot out of the zone by heavy small arms and automatic fire.[2A]

The Thuong Duc Special Forces unit wanted to make a second attempt March 3 but the 1st Recon Battalion advised against it and recommended they try again March 4 with a larger force. The CIDG/U.S. Special Forces commander agreed and offered to put 98 ground troops in the assault rescheduled for the next day. All the Marine air and ground participants which now included a 1st Recon team met at 1430 Tuesday, March 3 to hammer out the heliborne insert and support down to the last detail. Oddly, the U.S. Army's Special Forces representative missed the important "zipper" planning session. Lt. Gregson briefed the Special Forces commander later in the day. Maj. Mattiace wrote in his statement to the IBI that "according to the desires of the CG (commanding general), (the operation) was put back until March 6."

A letter dated March 5, 1970 from Maj. R.A. Splean to Mildred McVey stated, "A Reconnaissance team was inserted into the area on 3 March 1970 to search, however, the team was repulsed due to a heavy concentration of hostile small arms fire in the immediate and adjacent area." He was referring to the CIDGs and their Green Beret advisors. 1st Recon records show none of their teams going back into that area until March 6.

The Skibbe family (and, I'm sure, the McVeys and all POW/MIA next-of-kin) received information telling the circumstances behind their son, 2ndLt. Skibbe's MIA status as well as were issued a warning not to release information to people outside their immediate family or, by inference, the media. "...Since the possibility exists that your son is being held captive, it is suggested that you refrain from furnishing any persons outside of your immediate family with any background information regarding his personal history or military service. Release of such data could adversely affect his welfare since it may be used for coercion and propaganda purposes. I extend to you on behalf of the United States Marine Corps our sincere sympathy during this time of anxiety and uncertainty," 1stLt. F.C. Sinagra, Casualty Message, March 5, 1970.

**VC Clobber CIDGs, Helicopters Outside My Hiep (2), March 6**

Fixed wing was not available to hit the prospective LZ or provide covering fire for the mission March 6 therefore artillery prep was assigned to long-range 175mm guns from a distant U.S. Army firebase, according to retired Lt.Col. Wiley J. Sellers of Brooklyn, Mississippi, a major in 1970 who was the HMM-262 Operations chief and flight leader for the mission. "After pickup of the ground troops and en route to the LZ, I learned that only one gun was firing the LZ prep. The one tube, firing at the rate of about one HE round every 5 minutes, only tended to wake the gooks up and generally tee him off. Needless to say, when we arrived they were waiting for us."

At 0800 Friday, March 6 a flight of four HMM-262 Chatterbox helicopters with at least two gunship escorts began inserting 150 CIDG troops with four U.S. Army Special Forces advisors from Thuong Duc, a CIDG camp 30 miles southwest of Da Nang, and a few members of Team Thin Man now redesignated Team Turf Club commanded by 1stLt. Lawrence R. "Larry" Polster into the My Hiep (2) area to look for the two Marine officers. The primary LZ was one of two available in the area...something the enemy knew as well and set a trap. The "new" LZ was roughly 100 meters from the ill-fated CIDG's March 3 LZ.[2B]

Turf Club consisted of Lt. Polster, Cpl. Plunkett at point, LCpl. Simpson, HM3 McLynn, LCpl. Psaras and Kit Carson Scout (former VC/NVA soldier) Hao Phuk Troung. Polster, who was nearing the end of his tour, was unhappy returning to the Que Son Mountains to "go get the f**king bodies" on dangerous ground and felt it was "a f**king stupid idea to go back in there anyway," according to 1stLt. Michael C. Hodgins' account in his book, *Reluctant Warrior, A Marine's True Story of Duty and Heroism in Vietnam.*[3]

Detachment A-109 and A-153's U.S. Army Special Forces advisors in the assault element were Capt. James J. Duffy, 1stLt. Marion A. Baldwin, Sgt. John V. Norton and Sp/4 Timothy Harlan. MSgt. Gerald H. Adamski coordinated the action from A-109 headquarters while on radio relay was 1stLt. John N. Wiegnar and Sp/4 Kenneth W. Harmony. Before the operation could mercifully end March 11, three of the four Green Beret advisors with the CIDGs sustained wounds.

The CIDGs were primarily made up of Montagnard (pronounced mon-tun-yard and typically just called "Yards") tribesmen who are of Polynesian descent and generally occupy the mountainous regions of North and South Vietnam, Laos and Cambodia. By 1970 only about 600,000 to a million Montagnards were in Southeast Asia. Physically, they are taller than lowlander Vietnamese, heavier muscle, denser bone structure and darker features. More than 100 tribes, like that of the American Indians, are encompassed in the term "Montagnard." Thirty tribes are in South Vietnam alone and not all fought on America's side.

Vietnamese north and south distrusted the Montagnards as an inferior race and referred to them as "moi," savages. With the U.S. Special Forces soldiers as advisors, the Yards relished killing any Vietnamese. Plunkett indicated the Vietnamese and Montagnards were segregated to avoid potential problems. Chinese Nungs and other Asian mercenaries rounded out the CIDGs.

Drumright said he voiced the opinion that the CIDGs would not do well against a hardened NVA battalion and advised against inserting them into the My Hiep area. He noted the Army wanted a piece of the action to find the two missing Marine officers. "I said, 'General (Wheeler), all you're going to do is lose 'em. These are NVA, not VC. They're NVA and they've been trained well. They'll lose helicopters because CIDGs can't fight. He put 'em in there anyway and they wiped those CIDGs out."

Flying along the river route Shapiro-Martin then Shapiro-Vernier had taken, the four Sea Knights with their gunship escorts carried their first of two loads of CIDGs from Thuong Duc. Five villes are in the My Hiep chain along this portion of the river where the helicopters began insertion of the large force 300 meters east of My Hiep (2) next to Highway 14.[4A]

**Maj. Wiley J. Sellers (Photo courtesy of 1970 HMM-262 Chatterbox Cruise book)**

The first 4-helicopter lift was led by the 36-year-old Maj. Sellers. The insert went uncontested offloading 6-man Team Turf Club, half the CIDG force and some Green Berets in the My Hiep (2) area.

"The CIDGs didn't want to leave what they perceived as the relative safety of the helicopters and the crew chiefs had to threaten them with their sidearms," Martin related a Chatterbox pilot telling him.

Maj. Sellers flew the first Sea Knight into the same LZ on the second lift at 0820 without a problem. The second and third birds weren't so lucky.

"The insertion progressed without significant incident until the sixth sortie made its final approach to the landing zone," noted Special Forces Capt. Duffy.[4B]

The Chatterbox pilot went on to tell Martin that they took some heavy fire going into the LZ beside the Song Cai and one of the helicopters was shot down on its approach 50 feet off the ground. Enemy .51 and .30 caliber machine guns, AK-47s, mortar rounds and RPG rockets were zeroed in on the LZ and incoming helicopters. Duffy remarked that some of the bunkers the enemy was firing from were as close as 50 meters from their LZ. An estimated NVA company engaged the off-loading helicopters from the northeast. "The bad guys were waiting cocked and locked and everything went to worms in a hurry," recalled Martin.

1stLt.s C.W. "Chuck" Fleischer, pilot, from Santa Ana, California and John L. Kosinski, copilot, a 23-year-old from Gouldsboro, Pennsylvania, flew the unlucky Chatterbox Sea Knight that would be shot down while 1stLt.s Hugo T. Beck, pilot, of Brevard, North Carolina, and R.T. "Terry" Driskell, copilot, of Ojai, California, took several hits trying unsuccessfully to recover the downed crew and its injured CIDGs.

"One of the birds got shot down right out of the air and went down in the LZ," said Plunkett. Two crewmen in Fleischer's helicopter were injured. His three crewmen in the back of the aircraft included Cpl. D.L. Radish, crew chief, and aerial gunners, Cpl. J.L. Lindsey and LCpl. M.C. Billenbacher. Lt. Kosinski remembered Billenbacher as being badly wounded having been hit in the leg with a .51 caliber round upon crashing and later in the back as he was being evacuated.

HMM-262 Chatterbox pilot 1stLt. Norman F. "Pete" Hanner, 28, of Bloomington, Illinois, recalled Fleischer's bird (carrying 35 CIDGs) crashing after being hit by an RPG through the aft pylon containing the aft rotor. "Fleischer and his crew organized a defensive perimeter on the ground with the remaining troops and directed airstrikes from his position before we could get them out."

Kosinski said the Recon unit on the ground actually took the time to photograph his downed helicopter with the RPG hole in the aft pylon area while it was on the contested battlefield. "I remember that we took over 100 hits from small arms and .51 caliber fire. Everyone in the back was wounded of the CIDGs we were inserting. It seems higher than 50 feet that we fell...more like 200...but our memory sometimes makes the fish bigger.

"I crawled over Radish to go through Fleischer's emergency exit since mine was in the dirt, then helped him out. We started getting the dead and wounded out the side door. I remember bullets thwacking through the helo as I did this. The enemy was very close to us. We took fire for the 4 hours we were in the zone. A number of rescue attempts were aborted when the helos took heavy fire killing one of the medevac's crew chief."

Beck's aircraft took several hits and was shot out of the zone trying to pick up Fleischer's wounded. Three Marines were wounded aboard the medevac helicopter. One of the mortally injured was a relatively new crew chief LCpl. Jeffrey Lynn "Jeff" Wilson, 19, of Waterloo, Iowa who had arrived in-country December 21.

LCpl. Wilson, a Waterloo West High '68 graduate entered the Marines June 19, 1968 fresh out of high school, would die from his wounds although a gallant effort was made by U.S. Army Special Forces medics at Thuong Duc to revive him. Beck's After Action Report, AAR, didn't specify the other 2 WIAs but, most likely, were his gunners, Sgt. H.R. Rudersdorf and N. Carroll.

Simpson and Plunkett pulled a badly wounded Yard behind cover with them to protect him. He lost most of his face and lower jaw and took another round through the stomach by enemy .51 caliber rounds strafing the LZ force. He expired sometime during the battle.

"We waited for him to die while the Yards assaulted a machine gun nest and took it out," recounted Plunkett. Capt. Duffy confirmed in his IBI statement that the helicopter crash cost the insertion contingent 2 CIDGs KIA, 16 CIDGs WIA and 2 USMC WIA

A Purple Fox medevac helicopter removed the wounded at 1130. Lt. Kosinski said that as he was helping Billenbacher aboard the aircraft the gunner had the misfortune of taking his second wound that day in the back from an enemy bullet. The lieutenant would be shot down twice more before his tour ended, June 1 and October 9, and came away with two Purple Hearts.

Fixed wing airstrikes and Cobra gunships sought to silence the enemy located in well-hidden bunkers. After their casualties were finally cleared from the zone, the CIDGs attempted to overrun the enemy positions but met stiff resistance and were driven back by intense automatic fire.

At this time since the Special Forces were running the show, it was decided to call in two Mobile Strike Force (MSF) companies (200 additional troops of the same type ethnic make-up as the CIDGs) from Company C, 5th Special Forces at Thuong Duc. At 1530 they were helilifted in by 10 CH-46Ds escorted by four Cobra gunships and four fixed wing headed again by flight leader Maj. Sellers. He said the little resistance they received was quickly neutralized. After the reinforcements arrived, the enemy withdrew for the time being.

By their hit and fallback tactics, the enemy seemed to know where the CIDGs, Green Berets and Recon Marines were headed...the razorback to retrieve Lt. Skibbe whom "Mr. Boh" had allegedly killed. The enemy's tried and true tactic was to set up ambushes along a predetermined path to reach a destination such as a besieged town or a downed pilot or WIA/KIA SEATO personnel. VC/NVA knew Americans, and particularly, U.S. Marines generally went to extraordinary lengths to recover their compatriots from the battlefield thus ambushed them accordingly.

"It wasn't until later in the day that I went to the site with a reconstituted attempt to try a tactical recovery of the downed bird. The fire was still so intense we couldn't get the extract team into the LZ so the decision was made (the next day) to destroy the bird in the zone with bombs, rockets or whatever else the A-4s could hit it with. Fleischer was awarded the Silver Star for his efforts," said Hanner. Kosinski received a Bronze Star and both he and Fleischer, the squadron's Air Safety Officer, were awarded Purple Hearts. Maj. Sellers said he and Beck also received Silver Stars for their actions March 6.

The downed helicopter became a focal point of attention for the enemy 82mm mortars as eight rounds impacted around the bird at 2030. The Special Forces advisors were not happy about being stuck guarding the CH-46D all night while the Marines decided what to do about it.

During the night, a surveillance plane, Redeye, with infrared capabilities, informed the Special Forces captain that he had spotted "a large enemy force moving toward friendly positions from the north 2,000 meters out." Airstrikes were called in to destroy the gathering VC/NVA.

Maj. Rider returned to the My Hiep area as a Cobra pilot now that he was done with putting in his required time as a copilot and had flown the required three flights. He was also the S-3 Operations chief for Scarface by March 6.

"We used to have a Wednesday night Memorial Service at the MMAF and I remember that week we had a whole bunch of CH-46 crew members who had died or been wounded," lamented Rider. Meanwhile, the bloodied CIDG/MSF force on the My Hiep valley battlefield had to contend with a countryside crawling with enemy troops and the ink blackness of a new moon March 7.

"I was airborne and listening to Lt. Polster telling me about all the chaos out there. So the goddang NVA were just making mincemeat out of the CIDGs," recalled Drumright.

## Sea Knight Destroyed, March 7

Actually, the VC/NVA didn't withdraw from the field of battle. They just pulled back into the surrounding hills and mountains covered in forests and thick underbrush to await the large force to ambush on terrain of their choosing.

Turf Club didn't venture out of their perimeter formed near the downed helicopter until around 0800 Saturday, March 7. They accompanied 30 members of CIDG's Witch Doctor with two Special Forces men and linked up with the 20-member MSF's Booze Hound to search the valley floor for Capt. McVey. At the same time MSF's Royal King and the remaining men of Booze Hound covered the ridgeline where Lt. Skibbe was last seen.

Lt. Polster indicated in his Patrol Debrief that the entire area was searched for any trace of the two Marines. Nothing, not equipment or any sign, was found of the men. He suggested that the enemy might have hidden the two officers' bodies. Simpson noted that if the enemy found either Marine officer, they might have been buried like a previous Marine MIA, presumed dead. A Recon recovery team unearthed the Marine's body and brought him home.

At 1630 as the Recon team and its CIDGs returned to the harbor site near the helicopter, Lt. Polster spotted an NVA soldier carrying an AK-50 rifle and possibly a satchel charge 150 meters away running for all he was worth towards the crashed helicopter. He wrote in his patrol report that within 5 minutes they heard an explosion believed to have been the satchel charge thrown into Fleischer's CH-46D.

The decision was finally reached to destroy the helicopter at 1730 as fixed wing and Cobra gunships blasted it out of the LZ. Two NVA KIAs were found burned in the wreckage the next day.

## CIDGs Mortared, Bodies Mutilated in My Hiep Valley, March 8

Turf Club's day started off again at 0800 Sunday, March 8 in the company of the CIDG's Witch Doctor headed out towards a blocking position for CIDG's Tavern.

At 1245 the blocking force received seven incoming enemy 82mm mortar rounds resulting in the entire force leaving its blocking position in different directions. Lt. Polster yelled at his men to follow him through the barrage but LCpl. Simpson elected to go in another direction and the men chose to follow their enlisted compadre rather than the officer. Simpson would later lose a newly earned corporal's stripe back at Camp Reasoner after punching Lt. Polster for yelling at him in front of the team for not following him in that barrage.

CIDG Witch Doctor soldiers were trying to run out from under the mortar barrage to the northeast but ran into a well-planned NVA ambush losing 5 KIA and 3 WIA. To strike fear and payback in the CIDGs' hearts, NVA soldiers took time to dismember the bodies of three of the dead men.

As Cobra gunships rolled in on a strafing run to rout the NVA, the enemy soldiers pulled red and yellow smoke grenades off the dead CIDGs and threw the trailing smoke into the CIDG lines resulting in friendlies being attacked instead as they disengaged.

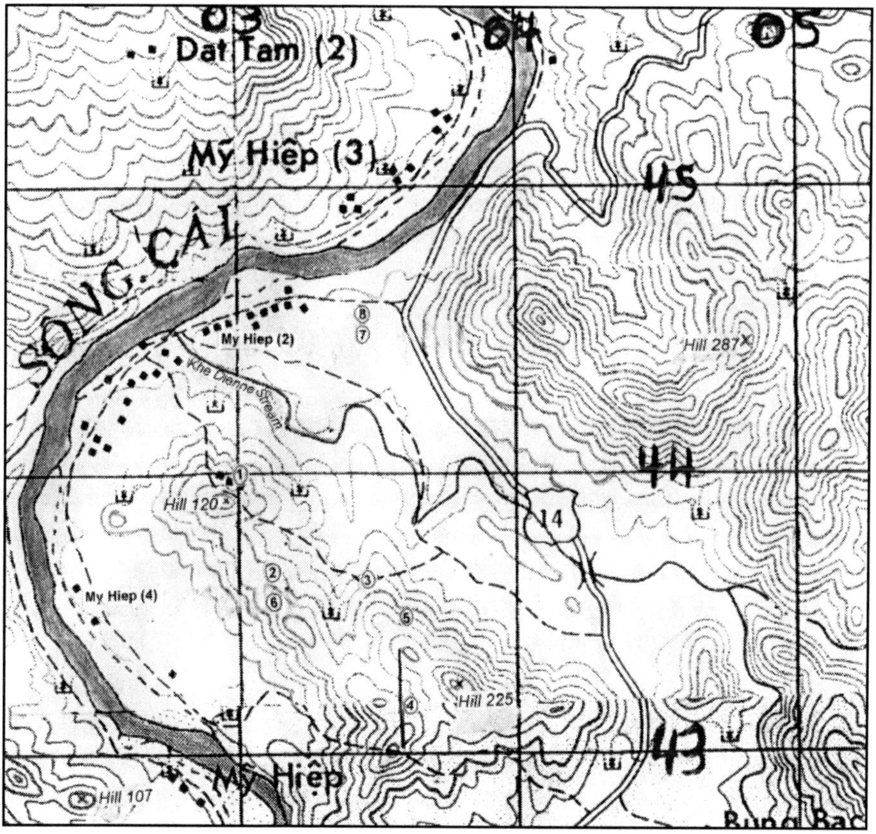


1. Team Thin Main inserted by Sea Knight in the vicinity of this location (later called Thanh My Town where Mr. Au lives) at 0930 Monday, March 2, 1970. 2. After connecting with high speed trail, Patrol Debrief shows team went another 350 meters and set up OP on razorback trail; enemy soldiers engaged; Broncos on station direct fixed wing bombing runs; Sgt. Larry Gifford followed by 2ndLt. David Skibbe, both WIA, extracted by jungle penetrator to Maj. Bruce Shapiro's Sea Knight; Skibbe falls approximately 50 feet due to snapped cable. 3. Shapiro's AAR has Recon team extracted by ladder at this location, Skibbe spotted on the ground. 4. Homecoming II Project cites this distant location that Skibbe was last seen. 5. VC soldier Mr. Vu says "Mr. Boh" claimed this is where Lt. Skibbe was located, shot and rolled off trail; 6. VC deputy commander Mr. Au claims this was the location Lt. Skibbe was killed and rolled off the trail. JTF-FA excavates this location June 20-July 3 without any luck; 7. CIDGs and U.S. Special Forces advisors shot out of hot LZ, Tuesday, March 3. 8. CIDGs, Special Forces advisors and Team Turf Club inserted just 100 meters from March 3 LZ and engaged large enemy force Friday, March 6, 1stLt. Fleischer's CH-46 shot down. (Thuong Duc map, Sheet 6540 I and Ben Giang map, Sheet 6540 II, Maps courtesy of National Imagery and Mapping Agency, Illustration by Dan Kellum)

After the CIDGs regrouped and assaulted the high ground, the enemy forces retired from the field leaving 3 KIAs of their own behind and an AK-47. The Special Forces report noted that one of the CIDG elements didn't participate as a blocking force leaving the NVA an avenue of escape from the trap. Avoiding contact by leaving an escape route for the enemy was a fairly common "live to fight another day strategy" of some less confrontational indigenous Vietnam allied forces.

Turf Club called in gunship fire onto a suspected bunker complex at 1530. Thirty minutes later three enemy 82mm mortar rounds landed 75 meters away in response. The Recon team linked up with Tavern and left the area posthaste.

## VC Fiery Boobytrap Demoralizes CIDGs, March 9

Tavern and Turf Club joined with MSF Royal King at 0800 Monday, March 9 on a sweep about a click to the east in the valley away from where Skibbe was last seen but in the vicinity of where it was thought Capt. McVey might've fallen. The location is near the confluence of two steams emptying out of the mountains into what VC Deputy Commander Mr. Au referred to as the Khe Dienne Stream that runs the length of the My Hiep valley.[4C] A bridge over the stream where Highway 14 crosses it is about 400 meters west of there.

The CIDGs and Turf Club walked smack into an enemy ambush anchored by automatic fire and two B40 rockets from an RPG launcher. "An MSF soldier took a direct hit from an RPG to the chest. There wasn't enough of him found to put into a body bag. We found the muzzle of his M-16 and that was about it," said Plunkett. The result was 1 MSF KIA and 11 MSFs WIA.

At 1130 the CIDGs and Marine Recon team were 200 meters south of where they had been ambushed earlier. With the CIDGs on point and Turf Club trailing, the troops walked down a path that entered a 2- to 3-foot deep creek bed for 200 meters before they exited the creek. The footpath led up towards the razorback where Skibbe was last seen.

"I was walking behind about 30 CIDGs so I was pretty relaxed," said Plunkett. His "relaxation" was short-lived. As they clambered up out of the creek onto a path,[4D] the enemy detonated two 82mm mortar rounds with a napalm canister attached. The area was covered with numerous toepoppers (a boobytrap consisting of a bullet or shotgun shell set off by a foot pushing it down onto a nail or perhaps a small amount of C-4 plastique explosive with a blasting cap embedded in it that explodes when a nail is stepped on driving it into the blasting cap) and homemade mines, which the CIDGs tripped trying to escape.

In the ensuing shrapnel-flavored conflagration, one CIDG was KIA, one

U.S. Army Special Forces WIA, one Marine (Plunkett) lightly WIANE and 16 CIDGs WIA.

The Special Forces report notes the uninjured CIDGs were not helping their comrades who were injured and it took a while to secure an LZ. Medevacs ran from 1430-1600 that afternoon.

## U.S. Special Forces/CIDGs Request Early Departure, March 10

Monday evening the Green Berets' Capt. Duffy requested that the Marine helicopters extract his CIDG and MSF early the morning of Tuesday, March 10. Nothing had been found of the two Marine officers and they were being ambushed piecemeal into an ineffective unit.

At one point during the operation, the captain said his CIDG counterpart was given several pounds of C-4 explosives flown in to clear trees to expand an LZ and instead parceled it out to his men to use as "heat tabs" for cooking their food.

Having suffered 14 KIA and 54 WIA in 4 days while reporting 5 confirmed enemy KIAs and an unknown number of WIA, the CIDGs, MSFs, Green Berets and Recon Marines for all practical purposes ended their search the afternoon of March 9. They blew a LZ among some trees at 0615 Tuesday.[4E] This was roughly 2 clicks northeast of Skibbe's last known location.

Trusting the Marines rather than the CIDGs to use C-4 to blow a LZ, Turf Club was given the job of preparing the pickup point.

"The Army was running the show. I remember standing at the extract LZ that we had to blow because we were getting the shit kicked out of us. They called for C-4 to blow a bunch of trees for an emergency extract but instead the helicopter brought us a pallet of beer! We had body bags stacked up and they brought us beer! I couldn't believe the Army. I'll never forget that for as long as I live," said Plunkett.

Capt. Duffy became irritated with the delay in re-routing Marine helicopters for the pickup of his unit until March 11, the original targeted extraction date. In his After Action Report, the captain complained of some of the MSFs as "ineffective as a maneuver element, lacked leadership, ineffective in its designated responsibilities and lack of action cost lives (failed to engage the enemy at a breakout point)." As a result, he suggested "drastic changes in the MSF" or "it be disbanded entirely and other means of reinforcement capabilities sought."

## Battered Units Depart My Hiep, Cobra Crashes, March 11

Turf Club and the remainder of the CIDGs, MSFs and Special Forces were extracted at 1059 Wednesday, March 11 from the LZ blown by the Marines. Their departure was not challenged by the enemy troops in the immediate area.

Drumright said the CIDGs were mauled as he said they would be by a more disciplined enemy force. No trace of either Skibbe or McVey was ever found in the attempted recovery operation.

As the CIDG/MSF ground force was extracted from the My Hiep area and flown back to its base at Thuong Duc, Maj. Rider flew gunship escort and said the rules of engagement this day were to only fire when fired upon. The Viet Cong were disguised as peasant farmers, according to Intelligence reports.

The Thuong Duc Special Forces camp was under siege much of the time along the Song Vu Gai at the base of the towering Que Son Mountains. "The Tennis Courts," a series of rising plateaus southeast of and across the river overlooking the camp, was held by the enemy and was an unusually hostile strategic location. "The macabre joke about the area was that you never had any trouble finding the Thuong Duc LZ because it would always be marked by a burning 46!" recalled 1stLt. Martin.

Lt.Col. Walt Ledbetter Jr., previously the HMM-263 CO became the MAG-16 helicopter Operations chief in February, was the mission's airborne commander March 11 in a Huey. "I directed the Cobras (Maj. Rider) to shoot along the left flank as we were going in and I had just sent the A-4s (Skyhawk jets) to shoot along the ridgeline to our right because we were receiving heavy fire from the ridge."

On Rider's second mission escorting the CH-46Ds full of CIDG troops back to Thuong Duc Special Forces camp from My Hiep along the Song Cai and Song Vu Gia, his Cobra slammed into a mountainside. The tail rotor either cut the tail pylon in the gusty mountain corridor as it had a tendency to do in such conditions and fell off or was blown away by an enemy airburst. The gunship was flying between 600-800 feet above the Que Son Mountains about 4 clicks north of Turf Club's extraction point when it crashed. Rider was the pilot with copilot 1stLt. Dennis Frederick "Denny" Grace, 26, of Niagara Falls, New York. The Cobra began to rotate wildly in tight right spirals heading for the ground.

The major cut power off so as to autorotate into the jungle-covered mountain below in a more controlled descent. "I got out a 'May Day.' As the ground came rushing up, I could see we were going to hit on a rocky, steep mountain slope. I flared and pulled collective as we went in, facing up the mountain." He told Lt. Grace to "secure fuel" as he shut the engines down.

The aircraft's nose was so high he couldn't see the looming mountainside to his front from his pilot's seat in the back of the Cobra due to his copilot blocking his view so he told Grace, "You've got it!" and turned the controls over to him. He took the controls with a kind of incredulous, "I've got it!" as they settled into the trees, according to Maj. Rider.

Rider figures his ceramic vest "bullet-bouncer" body armor protection was violently pushed up by the cyclic stick as they crashed into the mountainside and must have smacked him in the jaw knocking him unconscious. The violent impact tore the Cobra's canopies away. "I came to and could hear AK-47 fire very near us. I tried to call out to Denny but could hardly speak." He would fade in and out of consciousness.

At one point the major said he heard Vietnamese voices. He peeked out at them through a crack down the middle of his helmet as they stood nearby dressed in khaki uniforms and carrying AK-47 rifles.

"I was pinned in my seat by my bullet-bouncer. I think I broke my jaw, left arm, right ankle and tibia bones in my leg and cracked some ribs. I kept lapsing into unconsciousness. I had some green star cluster rounds in my .38 caliber pistol that Maj. Dan Sharr (who was circling above him at that moment) had given me. I managed to fire it through the jungle canopy to attract attention that somebody was still alive." By the time he fired the flare round, the VC/NVA had departed the area knowing a recovery team would soon be dropping in on the crashed Cobra.

Flying the difficult medevac on the side of Hill 487 near Hoa Hiep (1) about 400 meters west of the Song Cai this day was Chatterbox pilot 1stLt. Mike Ragin of Columbia, South Carolina with 1stLt. Hanner as his copilot.[4F] Crew chief LCpl. F.C. Pipich dropped Corpsman D.T. Sink (Hanner guessed that the Navy Corpsman was the man lowered to assess the pilots' injuries and strap them to the jungle penetrator) through the canopy to the crash site below.

Next thing Rider could remember was someone from the medevac helicopter shaking him awake and pulling him from the Cobra's cockpit. The rescuer was in such a hurry he didn't feel inclined to stop long enough to inject him with the morphine syrette from Rider's pocket or tie a tourniquet around his badly bleeding leg. The close proximity of the enemy troops made for a hasty extract. He was strapped on the jungle penetrator and hoisted in the air to the waiting medevac helicopter overhead under light sniper fire. Rider said he was hit by ground fire in the left wrist on the way up.

Lt. Grace died in either the crash landing or during the extraction. He was strapped onto a Stokes litter basket stretcher moments later and both officers were flown back to 1st Med in Da Nang after the brave enlisted man on the ground rejoined the aircraft. The irony is that the jungle penetrator/ Stokes litter basket stretcher and the hoist cable apparatus that failed to work two of three times March 2 and killed two officers, worked to perfection at least four times on March 11 saving one officer, recovering the body of the other and lowering and lifting a gutsy crewman/Navy Corpsman to safety as well.

"I asked the crew chief to roll the dead copilot over to see who he was. He did that and told me 'Denny Grace.' Denny and I had gone through flight training at the same time so it was a shock. The crew chief cut a dog tag out of Denny's bootlaces and brought it up to the cockpit on the way back to Da Nang," recalled Hanner.

"Embossed on it were these words, *'If you're the one who recovers my body--f**k you, you live son of a bitch.'*" Hanner indicated that Denny Grace had the last laugh on them all.

And the two enemy soldiers Rider saw on the ground managed at some point to strip both pilots of their watches, rings, cameras and other personal gear before leaving as Rider lay unconscious and Grace was dead or dying. Miraculously they failed to give the Scarface pilots coups de grace by putting a bullet in their heads, as they lay helpless and broken in their damaged Cobra.

The major was given last rites at the hospital, as was Grace. Rider was patched up and sent on to Japan. From there he went to the Bethesda Naval Hospital in Maryland where he recuperated.

"I remember Ledbetter kidding me years later about my high-pitched voice when I made the May Day radio transmission (as we were going down). I would like to buy the CH-46D pilot and especially that crew member a drink at the next reunion!" Rider said.

"I still have dreams about various parts of this incident. It was a shame that a young officer like Denny had to die. I sometimes feel a little guilty that he died so young and I lived on." He and Grace had attended rival Catholic colleges back in western New York and were getting to know one another when they crashed. He said Grace's brother, Ed, came to see him at Bethesda. The lieutenant's parents visited with he and his wife in Virginia before they passed on concerning the day their son died to give them some closure.

"I remember Denny and his family every week in my prayers."

In the end, the entire operation involved in attempting to recover Skibbe amounted to 3 USMC KIA, 7 USMC WIA; 12 CIDGs KIA, 44 CIDGs WIA; 3 U.S. Army Special Forces WIA; and 1 civilian WIA. One CH-46D was destroyed, Beck's aircraft was shot up and Maj. Sellers' CH-46D was vibrating badly from all the hits he took. A Cobra gunship could also be added to that total. All this massive effort and ensuing mayhem and the search failed to yield any evidence of either missing officer's body or any equipment associated with them.

## Drumright's Letter to the McVeys

Drumright's letters to the McVey family stated that Vietnamese troops numbering 300 men were inserted and sustained many casualties during the ground search.

He wrote McVey's wife that the area where both men were lost was "characterized by a dense undergrowth such as would cause one to lose sight of another at a distance of less than 10 feet. Movement through such heavy brush may quite typically be limited to 50-100 meters per hour.

"It is my carefully considered opinion, after weighing all the facts of this case that your husband was fatally injured as a result of his fall. I do not personally hold out hope for the recovery of his remains." He nailed this prediction on the head.

Lt.Col. Drumright said he flew into the area at a later date looking for any trace of either McVey or Skibbe's bodies or the distinctive orange jungle penetrators. He saw neither after a careful aerial survey of the target area. "We put out a sizeable amount of money for a reward to find their bodies and never found a trace of them. We went back in there several times. I made a personal trip back in there a month or so later and never found them."

Maj.Gen. Alan J. Armstrong, commanding general of 1st Marine Air Wing (1stMAW) and 3rd Marine Amphibious Brigade (3rdMAB), came down to Camp Reasoner to talk to the colonel about the loss of his two officers to faulty jungle penetrators that were the MAW's responsibility. "He threw his cover into my hooch and asked if it was okay to come in," said Drumright. "He was concerned the Recon Marines might not trust the jungle penetrators in the future and would blame the Air Wing for the fatalities. I took him down to talk to some of my Marines in the Briefing Room. I think it was three or four teams and the pilots in there getting ready to go out on patrols. Lt. Gregson introduced Gen. Armstrong after his briefing.

"(Armstrong) turned around and apologized for the jungle penetrator breaking because he knew that was (the Air Wing's responsibility). One of my big old patrol leaders from (either Kentucky or Texas) jumped up and said, 'General, without you or your pilots, we're nothing. It's an occupational hazard. We expect to die out there every once in awhile. We expect accidents. We live with it every day.' That answer your question, general?" asked Drumright.

In the official record Skibbe and McVey's deaths are listed as "Misadventure (possibly friendly fire) (Ground casualties)."

## Warrior's Code: Leave No Marine Behind on the Battlefield

After being reassigned from the departing stateside 2nd Battalion, 26th Marines in March to 2nd Battalion, 1st Marines, I first learned from a Marine grunt captain who was an aerial observer with the Hostage Broncos of VMO-2 that "someone had spotted Skibbe leaning up against a tree waving" during a flyover search mission in the area where he fell. I was terribly disturbed to hear this news which turned out to be an incorrect statement after reviewing the IBI statements. He indicated the second officer (McVey) was lost from a greater height in a rescue attempt and it was assumed he stood no chance of surviving his plunge.

The captain said that officers higher up the food chain decided neither Recon officer could have lived after their falls regardless of what was claimed to have been seen thus a search later that same night was discontinued. He knew of no other recovery missions (there was, indeed, two such missions March 3 and March 6-11).

At the time Skibbe and McVey's unrecovered bodies bothered me from the standpoint of not leaving Marines in the field while there was still a chance at least one of them was alive, especially someone I knew.

From the beginning of boot camp on into ITR training and hammered into us at OCS and TBS, Marines never leave their wounded or dead comrades in the field of combat. Of course there's always a common sense exception to every rule or understood obligation but, in this case, I felt there was a breach of trust, so much so I was having a hard time with it back in April 1970.

I think boot camp comments I made to OCS recruiter Capt. B.A. Meharg, Officer Selection Officer-Aviation, during his Officer Interview with me in December 1967 in San Diego posing a hypothetical question about a wounded Marine unable to make it to my medevac helicopter under fire...what would I do...came back to haunt me. I said that I would leave the Marine behind to save the passengers on board, my crew and aircraft. At that time I had not totally bought in to the Marine warrior code and was exhibiting my former civilian common sense approach to his question. Of course, the correct "Marine" answer would have been that Marines don't leave Marines/Navy Corpsmen behind and I would remain on the deck under fire until someone from the aircraft went back to retrieve him. I thought of Skibbe seeing Marines abandon him not once but possibly twice March 2, 1970 and it hurt my soul.

"I can appreciate how you must have felt thinking your friend was still alive when we left," said Martin. According to Mr. Au, whom the JTF-FA interviewed, this may sadly have been the case.

1stLt. Martin said that in the days following the March 2 loss of Skibbe and

McVey, 1stLt. Cummings, the Cobra pilot who claimed to have seen movement at the extract site, indicated to him that what he saw could just as well have been anything in the failing light of day...a shadow or even a monkey.

Martin's explanation of lack of fuel, darkness, the loss of McVey later that night searching for Skibbe and the massive casualties sustained by the CIDGs and MSFs accompanied by Green Beret and Team Turf Club helped assuage my hope over the intervening years that more was done to recover McVey and Skibbe.

# Chapter 7

**But the bravest are surely those who have the clearest vision of what is before them, glory and danger alike, and yet notwithstanding go out to meet it.[1]**

**Thucydides**
**"Funeral Oration of Pericles"**
***The History of the Peloponnesian War***

## Informal Board of Investigation Findings

An Informal Board of Investigation was convened to look into the circumstances surrounding the hoist cable failures of 2ndLt. Skibbe and Capt. McVey March 2, 1970 and the operations set in motion to recover them.

Forty-six enclosures involving 31 statements from key Marines—air and ground--as well as patrol reports from Thin Man, Turf Club and the U.S. Army Special Forces, photographs of the hoist cable mechanisms and a report from the Office of Naval Intelligence (ONI) were included.

Lt.Col. Drumright and Maj. Shapiro requested the investigation as the loss of two men the same night from the identical lift conveyance seemed highly suspicious. The board was to check for possible sabotage to the hoist cable system and its 150-foot cable line. Also to be considered was the feasibility of the recovery attempts of both men and their probable disposition.

The report issued on Sunday, April 5, 1970 concurred with both decisions to extract Team Thin Man at 1830 and McVey's attempt to recover Skibbe at 2230 Monday, March 2, 1970.

In the board's opinion, Skibbe's death was "probably not instantaneous." It was a hypothesis that turned out to be in accordance with the actual events.

This disturbing report listed the following to support its finding, a) Skibbe could have survived a fall of less than 50 feet (This portion of the report was later proved correct based on the JTF-FA's findings from the 1991, 1993 and 1998 interviews with B1 Deputy Commander Mr. Au---MDK), b) the jungle canopy could have cushioned his fall.

Also, c) injuries sustained prior to his fall were not of a grievous nature and had been expertly attended, d) two helicopter pilots had witnessed movement in the area after his fall, e) that neither he nor his apparatus were recovered, and f) that he may have been captured and received medical attention from the enemy force in the recovery area.

McVey's survival was "too remote to consider" after he fell from 400-700 feet. ONI examined the snapped cable ends and the two lift mechanisms. Physical and microscopic examinations of the frayed cable ends from Skibbe's extraction disclosed stretched areas at the ends of each wire near the separations reducing individual wire diameters at the breaks and irregular patterns at the breaks. Further examinations revealed multiple broken strands along each cable.

"It is the opinion of this examiner that the (cable wires) could have been damaged and considerably weakened by long periods of use through pulleys and cable guides or through improper alignment of equipment and separated under tension," according to the ONI examiner's report.

1st MAW conducted an investigation, which came out April 20, 1970. The report noted that cable inspections conducted in the four helicopter squadrons uncovered signs of fraying, kinks, broken strands and corrosion in 15 cables of three out of four squadrons.

The hoist rescue module (jungle penetrator mechanism) involved in Skibbe's fall was inspected for discrepancies and evidence of sabotage. There were indications that the cable in the module had been misrigged, as evidenced by grooves worn in the boom assembly and that subsequent wear was the probable primary cause of failure.

A survey of rescue modules in 1st MAW revealed "12 of the 14 showing signs of misrigging. Because of this large number of discrepancies and lack of adequate rigging and inspection instructions, this module has been removed from all 1st MAW aircraft (temporarily)."

In McVey's fall no definitive cause could be determined. Neither the cable nor the winch assembly showed any telltale signs of discrepancies, according to the 1st MAW report.

"I don't know how (the cable hoisting Capt. McVey snapped) because my father was an engineer and I had run a lot of heavy equipment and I never saw a cable in my life that didn't break because of a hang or a fault of some kind. That cable didn't appear to me to have any fault to it at all. In fact, it looked like a new cable," recalled Drumright in 2003.

The March 2 cable failures remained isolated incidents until April 12, 1970. On that day, an officer from the 1st Recon Battalion, 1stLt. Henry Porter "Hank" Rathmell, 23, of Muncy, Pennsylvania, team leader of Team Mission Impossible, rappelled to the ground on a rope from a hovering Sea Knight to check out the site of an A-4 Skyhawk fiery crash to recover the pilot's body when the Sea Knight pilot reported he was taking fire and attempted to abort the mission leaving Lt. Rathmell on the ground alone.

Gy.Sgt. Terrence L. "Terry" Moore, 31, of Wayne, Michigan, assistant team leader, told the pilot that that would be a bad idea and with Swedish-K weapon in hand convinced him to turn his aircraft back around to pick the lieutenant up. The aircraft received no small arms fire as a jungle penetrator was lowered to extract Rathmell. Upon reeling him back aboard the aircraft, the cable broke while he was 100 feet off the ground sending him plummeting earthward. The 10-story fall killed him. Gunny Moore and his Mission Impossible team rappelled to the ground and managed to recover and extract Rathmell's body (and most likely the pilot's remains as well---MDK).

No evidence of misrigging was found in the April 12 mishap. The failed cable revealed particles of wood embedded in it. An investigation concluded that the cable had snagged a tree (just like the Recon Marines said Skibbe and Gifford's had and most likely McVey's cable in the night rescue attempt) during extract thereby exceeding the cable's tensile strength pulling it free.

It was discovered the winch assembly had been improperly rigged and it was noted after an inspection of all CH-46D aircraft that this was again a common practice. All crew chiefs, maintenance personnel and pilots were ordered to check out their cables and become familiar with rigging procedures and inspection requirements. A new twist was that all winch assemblies were to be re-inspected with a one-time 600-lb. weight test.

### The Wall, Washington, D.C.

On The Wall in Washington, D.C., Skibbe and McVey are both listed as KIA even though their bodies were never recovered. Sadly, the second letter to next-of-kin, Mildred McVey, on March 12, 1970 misspells the captain's and mother's last name in informing her that his status had gone from "Missing-in-Action" to "Deceased."

### Skibbe's Parents Receive Navy Cross, October 7, 1970

Lt. Skibbe's family received the Navy Cross posthumously for his actions to pull Sgt. Gifford from harm's way and encourage his Recon Marines although severely wounded that March 2, 1970 afternoon. David's parents, William C. (assistant postmaster of Des Plaines, Illinois) and Ruth Skibbe, accepted the award October 7, 1970 in Des Plaines. His siblings on hand for the ceremony were Joan M. Tomoff, Janet R. Skibbe (later Preston) and William P. Skibbe. He was also awarded the Vietnamese Cross of Gallantry with Palm. His last letter home to his parents stated he was going on patrol and would tell them about it when he returned off it. That was David's first and last 1st Recon patrol.

Two 22-man platoon honor guards and the 4th Marine Aircraft Wing Drum and Bugle Team were on hand as Maj.Gen. Robert P. Keller, CG 4th Marine Air Reserve Training Command, made the presentation to Skibbe's parents.

Bill Skibbe had this to say of his son after the brief 15-minute ceremony,

"I'm very proud of Dave. I'm proud to know he was taking care of other people, as he always did."

**2ndLt. David Skibbe**
**(Photo courtesy of William C. Skibbe)**

Several hundred people attended a memorial service at St. Mark Lutheran Church in Mt. Prospect, Illinois Sunday afternoon, March 23, 1970. Three Marines from the Marine Air Reserve Training Detachment at the Naval Air Station at Glenview, Illinois were on hand to present the colors. Capt. Ralph Hundley, NAS, Glenview spoke of David's sacrifice in Vietnam. Lutheran Pastor David Quill's inspirational messages this day came from the *Holy Bible's 90th Psalm*, the *12th Chapter of Ecclesiastes* and the *23rd Psalm*. The gymnasium in the new youth center across the street from the church was named in David's honor. The Skibbes made the stipulation that if any other member from the congregation should fall in battle in Vietnam then his or her name should go up with David's.

At the University of Illinois, David's name, along with all the other UI KIAs in the Vietnam War, was placed on a plaque erected at Memorial Stadium next to the plaques listing the KIAs of previous wars, according to his cousin Jeff Skibbe.

The Illinois lieutenant was to be married upon his return from Vietnam. His family noted in a May 17, 1970 letter to the McVeys that David's fiancée, Georgine, was bravely struggling with the news of his death. She was the young woman standing beside David in the laminated photo Mr. Au's VC compadres recovered.

1st Recon Marines held a memorial service at Camp Reasoner for 2ndLt. Skibbe and Capt. McVey on March 26, 1970. An emotional Drumright gave the eulogy for both Marines as a photo of him that day clearly shows tears streaming down his face as he talked about them.

### McVey's Wife, Boys Receive Silver Star, October 9, 1970

Capt. McVey's wife, Karen, and her two young boys, Jeff, 8, and Shawn, under 2, were presented a Silver Star medal posthumously October 9, 1970 in Seattle, Washington by Maj. Dale R. Thibault, inspector-instructor of the 4th Shore Party Battalion. Her husband was cited for his bravery for going after Lt. Skibbe in the face of danger.

The captain's death compounded the family's grief having lost a third son, Devin, 5, the year before to a brain tumor.

Mac McVey's younger brother, Orin, carried on the family tradition by serving in the Marine Corps 30 years with two tours in Vietnam. He retired as a master gunnery sergeant in 1991.

## Memorial Service, March 1, 2003

On March 1, 2003, a memorial service was held for Capt. "Mac" McVey in Everett, Washington, through the efforts of retired Col. Bruce F. Meyers (1st Force Recon's first CO and author of the book, *Fortune Favors The Brave)* of Issaquah, Washington who organized the event. In attendance were McVey's sons, Shawn and Jeff, as well as Mildred, and Jeff's wife, Sally, and MGy.Sgt. Orin McVey. The former Karen McVey was also present for the service.

**Capt. LaVoy Don "Mac" McVey (Photo courtesy of Mildred McVey Holmes)**

Also at the service to honor and remember McVey and consequently 2ndLt. Skibbe were Col. Meyers; Capt. Woidyla; MSgt. Lawrence E. "Larry" Keen; Sgt. Gifford; Chaplain Schuppert; U.S. Marine Color Guard; and a host of friends, spouses and relatives. Col. Drumright was in poor health and was unable to make the trip. Touching moments were the playing of the bagpipes (Gy.Sgt. Bradley) and the haunting sound of taps played by a lone bugler. Capt. McVey was finally put to rest by those who loved and cared about him most back home.

Former Capt. Bill Woidyla was present for his old friend's memorial service and read the *23rd Psalm, "The Lord is my shepherd, I shall not be in want. He makes me lie down in green pastures, he leads me beside quiet waters, he restores my soul. He guides me in paths of righteousness for his name's sake.*

*"Even though I walk through the valley of the shadow of death, I will fear no evil, for you are with me; your rod and your staff, they comfort me.*

*"You prepare a table before me in the presence of my enemies. You anoint my head with oil; my cup overflows. Surely goodness and love will follow me all the days of my life, and I will dwell in the house of the LORD forever."*

Capt. Woidyla put off a trip to M.D. Anderson Cancer Hospital in Houston, Texas for throat cancer treatment to speak those words and others of comfort to the McVey family about Mac McVey. He was determined to not let a little thing like cancer get in the way of his attending the memorial service. It was something he felt an obligation to do for a fellow Marine and a close friend. I think he felt that Mac would have been there for him if the situation were reversed.

Capt. Woidyla succumbed to the disease 7 months later, September 21, 2003. "Two great men in God's hands now," wrote Sally McVey to inform me of his passing.

**Drumright's Farm in Columbia, Tennessee, May 22-28, 2003**

Jeff and Shawn McVey met with Col. Drumright and many of his Recon Marines from 1970 on his farm the latter part of May 2003 (Memorial Weekend) to hear about the legacy their father left behind as an outstanding Marine officer, enlisted man and Recon professional.

I also visited with the two young boys, now grown men, who Capt. McVey left behind March 2, 1970. The captain's sons finally got some closure and were able to know their father, whom they only retained childhood memories of, through other Marines' eyes.

In an emotional voice, 75-year-old Col. Drumright told Capt. McVey's sons and the assemblage of Recon Marines, "Mac McVey is still with us through the DNA carried by his boys. It's important this courageous Marine's seed never be extinguished. We need people like him in America today. Mac lives on through his sons."

Drumright said both McVey and Skibbe were good officers. "I hated to lose both those boys. Skibbe was a good kid. He was a gentleman, a fine young officer. A strange thing was we had only three officers killed (while I was the CO) and all were killed due to the penetrator."

**MIAs in Nam**

Total Americans MIA recovered post January 27, 1973 to January 19, 2010 was 926 while 1,720 are still unaccounted for from the Vietnam War. POWs dying in captivity and their remains not recovered was 34; 789 MIAs from all services are presumed to have a finding of death; and Skibbe and McVey fall into the latter category of 880 KIAs, bodies not recovered, according to the Department of Defense's Defense Prisoner of War/Missing Personnel Office's (DPMO) Personnel Missing-Southeast Asia (PMSEA) report.[2] Our South Vietnamese allies suffered an unknown number of MIA while the VC/NVA listed 300,000 of their troops missing.

The JTF-FA was formed in 1992 following up on previous U.S. government efforts by the Defense Intelligence Agency to account for Americans MIA in Southeast Asia as well as around the world from other wars. The DPMO listed

213 U.S. Marines still unaccounted for in Southeast Asia as of 2010. Skibbe and McVey join a total of 166 Marines and 835 for all U.S. military services unaccounted for in the confines of South Vietnam.[3]

Other U.S. military services still reporting MIAs from the Vietnam War as of January 19, 2010 were Army, 550; Navy, 369; Air Force, 556; and civilians, 32.[4]

"Four missions have been conducted to find Lt. Skibbe, Case #2051 (and Capt. McVey, Case #1565) occurring in 1991 and 1993 (investigative), and one in 1995.[5A] The excavation near Thanh My Town, Quang Nam/Da Nang Province recovered three C-ration cans (dated '5-68' on the bottom of the cans) and one Schick razor, but no remains. The site was closed after the excavation. A third investigative team mission in 1998 recovered no remains either," stated USAF 1stLt. Ken Hall, JTF-FA public affairs officer. To keep abreast of the unit's MIA/POW accounting efforts, Lt. Hall suggested visiting their website at www.jpac.pacom.mil/ that was still active in April 2011.

A 12-member American team headed by Capt. Nochefranca and a 13-member Socialist Republic of Vietnam team led by Tran Minh Tuan excavated 300 square meters to depths of 20-40 centimeters June 20-July 3, 1995. They closed the site July 4, 1995 after failing to find any trace of 2ndLt. Skibbe.

In August 1998, the JTF-FA team re-interviewed Mr. Au, at the time 58, VC B1 deputy commander who became commander in 1971 when a Mr. Ngan deserted, asking him why the excavation in 1995 failed to yield anything related to Lt. Skibbe. He speculated that because of the slash and burn farming in the area, it is possible someone moved or cremated the remains. This would have rendered the remains unidentifiable and therefore unrecoverable.

The second witness, Mr. Vu, corroborated Mr. Au's story. He said he was also in another squad during the firefight on the razorback March 2, 1970 but that Mr. Boh (Bowh) had later taken him to the location where he shot Lt. Skibbe[5B] and rolled him off the trail as well as pointed out the exact location where he said the firefight began[5C] with Team Thin Man. The JTF-FA team didn't find any indication of Skibbe's remains at either site.

After the Marine lieutenant in the laminated photo was identified as 2ndLt. Skibbe, the photo held by the former VC commander for roughly 23 years as a war souvenir was released through the Marine Corps to the 1st Recon officer's family as personal effects in 1993, according to T.A. "Ann" Hammers, head of the Casualty Section, HQMC.

James W. Wold, deputy assistant to the Secretary of Defense, contacted Skibbe's parents on June 17, 1997, citing the following in part, "Analysts of the Defense Prisoner Office and JTF-FA have worked together to carefully re-examine all of the information in this case. Regrettably, the circumstances of his loss and the results of the investigative efforts lead us to conclude that 2ndLt. Skibbe's remains were left on the surface, unburied and the effects of time and environment in the harsh and remote terrain (the steep slope was subject to heavy run-off during the rainy season) have made them unrecoverable."

The map coordinates the Vietnamese gave the JTF-FA team were 800 meters southeast of the razorback trail from where Plunkett and Doc McLynn last recalled seeing Skibbe going up on the jungle penetrator. This was the ridgeline that MSF Royal King and some of MSF Booze Hound soldiers said they swept on March 7, 1970 while Turf Club, CIDG Witch Doctor and a portion of MSF Booze Hound scoured the valley floor.

I was of the opinion then and have that same opinion today...Marines should look for Marines. Neither CIDGs nor MSFs felt the same urgency and personal interest that Marines might have held for finding other Marines and bringing them home. The VC/NVA overwhelmed the CIDGs/MSFs so much in 4-5 days of ambushes and overall harassment, I don't think they were able to do a thorough "beating of the bushes" on that ridgeline.

In addition, since the VC/NVA units had chosen to stand and fight the CIDGs/MSFs, it would seem to have been an ideal opportunity to bring in several elite Vietnamese VNMC or Airborne battalions or U.S. Marine combat units to annihilate them. Not only would that have been an apropos parting gift to the memories of 2ndLt. Skibbe and Capt. McVey but would have eliminated one helluva good enemy outfit from being around to fight the ARVN or CIDGs/MSFs upon our departure from Vietnam.

It must be acknowledged that the CIDG/MSF and accompanying Special Forces and Turf Club recovery force had a difficult time of it due to not knowing the exact locations of either the firefight or extract March 2, 1970. McVey, the extract officer, and Skibbe, the patrol leader, were not able to provide map coordinates for the day's activities having turned up missing. Sgt. Gifford was unsure of the map locations having been shot in the head and, most likely sustained a concussion and was somewhat confused about that day. Perhaps Plunkett and McLynn, the only members of Team Thin Man to be with Team Turf Club, might've been able to recognize the terrain features on the Razorback where they last saw Skibbe but they didn't make it to that ridgeline on the return trip.

Plunkett explained that he was never privy to the map portion of the mission and was just guessing at any coordinates. Several reports on the mission give conflicting map coordinates so perhaps Mr. Au and Mr. Vu were correct in the location they gave for Skibbe's demise.

What I do know is that the two Recon Marine officers will never be forgotten by their brothers-in-arms, nor will those Marines and CIDGs/MSFs who also lost their lives in attempts to find them.

As of November 2008, 2ndLt. Skibbe's Case #2051 remained categorized as "No Further Pursuit" (Capt. McVey's Case #1565 undoubtedly falls under the same ruling) along with 658 for all U.S. military services in Southeast Asia (351 of that total are in South Vietnam). The case is not closed, it just means that unless new information is received no further action will be taken.

"Those of us who have worked to account for your son and for our other brave Americans consider ourselves privileged to have done so. Even though his remains may never be recovered, 2ndLt. Skibbe's (*as well as Capt. McVey's*) name and memory will long be honored by this nation," Wold wrote to Skibbe's parents.

(On October 1, 2003, the JTF-FA assumed yet another name change to Joint POW/MIA Accounting Command, JPAC, headquartered at Hickam Air Force Base, adjacent to Honolulu, Hawaii. Three additional detachments are located at Bangkok, Thailand; Hanoi, Socialist Republic of Vietnam; and Vientiane, Laos. Annually 10 Joint Field Activities with the host countries are conducted in Southeast Asia—four in the Socialist Republic of Vietnam, five in Laos and one in Cambodia lasting approximately 35 days involving 30 to 95 personnel---MDK).

# Chapter 8

**"There's an unwritten (Recon) rule that if one man goes down a rappelling rope to the ground from a hovering Sea Knight...everyone goes."[1]**

**MSgt. John F. Hare**
**Team Mission Impossible**
**1st Recon Battalion**

## Team Chili Pepper, August 30-September 2, 1970

Small 6- and 7-man teams from the 1st Reconnaissance Battalion spent a lot of time reconning the mountainous areas surrounding Da Nang, South Vietnam in 1970 after being inserted by helicopter. These camouflaged descendants of World War II Marine Raiders served as an early warning and detection barrier.

Most of the time those patrols went off without a hitch as no enemy contact was made but on occasion they spotted concentrations of enemy troops and called in either artillery or airstrikes to annihilate them. Then there were those other times when unforeseen circumstances or accidents put the "painted faces," the Recon Marines, in some serious harm's way as occurred on September 1, 1970.

Team Chili Pepper, a team consisting of six Recon Marines and one Navy Corpsman, was inserted by Sea Knight helicopter on Hill 995 southwest of Da Nang at 0852 Sunday, August 30, 1970.[2A] Team members were Sgt. Rowley, team leader; HM3 McKinley, Navy Corpsman; LCpl. Timothy James "Tim" Luhrs, 18, of South St. Paul, Minnesota; LCpl. Jimmy Ray Holkem, 22, of Stevenson, Alabama; LCpl. Airaghi; LCpl. Dale Allen Pennington, 20, of Culver, Indiana; and LCpl. David V. "Dave" Delozier, 23, of Altoona, Pennsylvania. (Unfortunately, I was unable to locate the first names, ages or hometowns of Rowley, McKinley or Airaghi and only know their last names and rank thanks to the Chili Pepper Patrol Debrief---MDK).

LCpl. Luhrs, whose dad had served as a Marine sergeant in the Korean War, had joined the Marines with his parents' written permission at 17 and trained to be a Marine sniper at Camp Pendleton. Of the 15 Marine snipers he trained with, he had tied for the highest score. On the eve of his leaving for the combat zone with his fellow Sniper School graduates, a sergeant held him back as he was still only 17...too young to go to Vietnam.

Eventually he ended up on Okinawa in the S-2 (Intelligence section) of 2nd Battalion, 4th Marines. A staff sergeant informed him one day that the 1st

Recon Battalion in-country had a quota for two snipers...and he was to be one of those snipers now that he had turned 18.

A good portion of his tour with 1st Recon in 1970 was taken up by attending refresher courses as part of the Reconnaissance Indoctrination Program. For the Minnesotan this was his first exposure to the elite Recon Marines' training. Team Chili Pepper was Luhrs' third patrol after only a month and a half in Vietnam. He would not see a fourth patrol in his shortened Vietnam tour.

Inserted by Sea Knight, the terrain over which Team Chili Pepper was operating was steep mountains with 50- to 60-foot canopy of trees with a secondary growth of 8- to 10-foot tall vines, small bushes, bamboo, elephant grass, boulders, thorns and thick bushes. The team's progress through this patrol area was difficult averaging 30 to 50 meters per hour. An early problem developed as one of the team's two PRC-25 radios malfunctioned as soon as they were inserted on the ground leaving them with just one radio. This would prove crucial further into the patrol.

LCpl. Luhrs developed a high temperature, 103 degrees, 2 clicks[2B] and 3 days into their patrol. A routine medevac was called in at 1030 Tuesday, September 1. Their radio relay team in the distant hills passed along instructions from the 1st Recon Command Operations Center (COC) back at Camp Reasoner that they were to find a suitable LZ for a Sea Knight to set down to extract the whole team.

The situation went from bad to worse as they headed down a treacherously steep streambed with a 6- to 8-foot drop-off. LCpl. Holkem had the misfortune of falling and breaking his ankle. At 1230 Team Chili Pepper reported their new predicament and asked again for the extraction for Holkem as well only to be told to find a sit-down LZ for the Sea Knight.

At 1400 a fixed wing OV-10 Bronco came on station and directed the team to move another 100-200 meters up a hill and they would find a good LZ. Upon reaching the location and marking it for the aerial observer in the Bronco, they were told to move an additional 300 meters west then 200 meters south. Sgt. Rowley informed the AO they could not move that far with the two medevacs. They were told to retrace their steps and return to their former extract point back down the hill.[2C]

The team finally reached the designated location on the side of the hill at 1800 and a medevac helicopter arrived 30 minutes later. Luhrs recalled that LCpl. Airaghi had a pencil flare he shot into the air to direct the Sea Knight to their position. The Sea Knight's crew threw a 60-foot flexible ladder that was attached underneath the helicopter off its back ramp to the anxiously waiting Marines below. Unfortunately the ladder was too short to reach the ground through the opening in the hillside canopy.

The Sea Knight returned to Camp Reasoner to take on a 120-foot ladder to make up the distance needed to overcome the tall canopy. This was not a good situation for the small Recon team. Their position was now known to any enemy troops who might be in the vicinity. They stood a good chance of getting overrun by the VC/NVA as the enemy generally had superior numbers to the 7-man teams. Sgt. Rowley's team needed to be extracted quickly to avoid being discovered. With Holkem's broken ankle and Luhr's rising temperature they would not get far if they had to run.

To clear the way for the 120-foot ladder to reach them on the side of their steep hill, Team Chili Pepper attempted to blow a tree down with C-4 plastique explosives in their LZ at 1900. It either got hung up on another tree and did not fall down all the way or fell against another tree and made the other tree unstable on the way down. At least an open space was made in the canopy so the team would be able to quickly hook onto the ladder with the snap links on their Special Patrol Insertion/Extraction (SPIE) harnesses (a mountain climber's Swedish seat set up with a harness that extended behind their head that had a snap link attached to it) that they were already rigged with and they could clear their LZ before the enemy could track them down by the sight and sound of the hovering Sea Knights and circling Cobra gunships.

**A Sea Knight helicopter brings a Recon team back to An Hoa on a ladder. (Photo courtesy of George Curtis and the USMC Combat Helicopter Association)**

At 1915 the helicopter flight returned. The designated extract Sea Knight dropped the long 120-foot flexible ladder out its back ramp to the team below and hovered overhead waiting for the team to hook on. LCpl Luhrs, HM3 McKinley, LCpl. Pennington and LCpl. Delozier climbed up higher on the ladder while Sgt. Rowley and LCpl. Airaghi and LCpl. Holkem held it steady for them from the rocky ledge of the side of the steep hill.

Luhrs climbed up the ladder 15-20 feet and snap linked onto it as McKinley, Delozier and Pennington, who was lugging the PRC-25 radio, were still climbing up when the Sea Knight moved away from the cliff causing the three men at the bottom holding the ladder to let go else they would've been dragged over the side of the cliff to the rocks below.

The problem with the ladder was compounded by the downward thrust of tornadic wind from the helicopter's rotorblades causing an unstable tree to topple over hitting the ladder. The impact made the ladder jerk dislodging the three Marines still climbing upwards. It not only knocked McKinley, Delozier and Pennington off the ladder but also slammed into Holkem on the ground hitting him in the head and killing him instantly. Sgt. Rowley was knocked off his feet and rendered unconscious. Bouncing on the rocks the three men were standing on, the tree knocked Airaghi off his feet onto his back. He looked up to see only Luhrs dangling from the ladder by himself.

"I got rocked pretty good by that tree. I think I got a concussion from being hit by it. Airaghi was screaming at me, 'GET THE F**K OFF THE LADDER!' I looked down to see what he was screaming about. I had attached my M-16 rifle to the ladder and left it behind when I climbed down to the team. I think it was Pennington's rifle that was also still snapped onto the ladder," said Luhrs.

Airaghi quickly pulled his strobe light out to guide the helicopter back to the side of the hill with the ladder. Unhurt, Luhrs climbed down off the ladder and was sent to find Doc McKinley, Pennington and Delozier. At this point Airaghi waved the helos away and they departed the area.

Airaghi found that the tree had killed Holkem and that Sgt. Rowley had regained consciousness although he was complaining of back pain and seemed out of it. Luhrs said Delozier suffered a possible broken wrist further down the drop off. Airaghi, Luhrs and Delozier went looking for the other men with a flashlight as darkness now enveloped them. They heard Doc McKinley calling for help. When they got to him, they found he had a broken arm and his SPIE rig gear was caught in some tree limbs. They cut him loose.

Delozier stayed with the Doc while the other two men searched for the last remaining Marine unaccounted for, Pennington. They found him wedged between two large rocks with his gear torn off. His PRC-25 radio was also nowhere to be found. He had sustained mortal internal injuries. Airaghi and Luhrs pulled Pennington from the crevice and placed him on a flat rock. As Luhrs stayed with Pennington, Airaghi and Delozier went looking for Pennington's PRC-25 radio and Doc McKinley's unit one medical bag. They could find neither and realized they would have no radio communication to call in the medevac birds they knew would soon come back for them. They returned to where Doc McKinley was to ask him what they needed to do to help Pennington and by the time they returned to him he had expired.

"Dale expired in my lap. I tried to clear his throat (but was unsuccessful)," recalled Luhrs.

Without a radio and at least two rifles and an M-79 grenade launcher missing in the darkness, the three Marines hunkered down with their two KIAs, injured patrol leader and Navy Corpsman. They were not leaderless though as Airaghi, being the next senior man in the team, assumed the patrol leader's position. No help would come this night as Airaghi directed them to split their night watches with two men up and one sleeping. Luhrs remembered the night as being "just black."

Actually, "help" did make an attempt to come but the War Cloud Mission Impossible team sent out to recover Team Chili Pepper at 2130 that same night ran into problems of its own...major problems that prevented them from reaching their objective.

Cpl. Feldman from 1st Recon recalled the Sea Knight helicopter that had tried to extract Team Chili Pepper returned later that night to Camp Reasoner's LZ 401 with the ladder hit by the falling tree. As it approached the LZ, the aircraft turned its landing lights on to set the long ladder down on the LZ so it could be disengaged from underneath the Sea Knight. The Recon Marines at the LZ and on the hillside above the LZ, as was their habit, came out to see the team come in and to make sure they were okay. All they saw was the spooky sight of no Team Chili Pepper Marines snap linked onto the ladder but rather two M-16 rifles dangling from it spotlighted by the helicopter's landing lights in the darkness...an ominous sign that the team was in deep trouble out in the Que Son Mountains.

**War Cloud Mission Impossible: The Rescue Team**

The 1st Recon's reactionary team was alerted that a Recon team was down and needed help at approximately 2200. Gy.Sgt. Terrence L. "Terry" Moore was team leader of War Cloud Mission Impossible. He was on his third Vietnam tour having graced the shores '61-'64 with 3rd Recon, '66-'67 with the Military Assistance Command-Vietnam, Studies and Observation Group (MAC-V SOG) as an advisor with Team Vega Commando Command and Control North at Da Nang in I Corps and his final tour of '70-'71 with 1st Recon that began January 14, 1970. He would spend 32 years as a Marine from 1955 to 1987 and receive a battlefield commission in 1970, retiring as a lieutenant colonel in 1987.

Joining Moore would be SSgt. John F. Hare, 33, of Cayce, South Carolina, who served with him on all three of his tours; SSgt. D.M. Mushett; Cpl. R.J. Ravelo; a Navy Corpsman; and one other Marine (the Doc and the other Marine's name were unknown to Moore and Hare and would not show up on the Patrol Debrief after the operation---MDK). The team was made up of seasoned Marines from H&S Co. who were the first called anytime a team in the bush was in deep trouble and needed to be backed up. Hare noted the team was probably the most casualty prone as they were only called upon when things had gotten really hairy in Indian Territory.

**Sgt. Terrence L. "Terry" Moore, left, and Cpl. John F. Hare holding submachine guns called "grease guns" during their first tour in Southeast Asia in 1961. (USMC Photo)**

"Lt.Col. Drumright called Terry aside when he arrived at 1st Recon and told him he wanted to form an H&S Co. Team War Cloud Mission Impossible composed of the best experienced men in 1st Recon for going after downed pilots (and other tough, dangerous assignments outside regular patrolling in the boondocks)," said MSgt. Hare, USMC (Ret.). "He gave him a blank check to pick anybody he wanted. The first man he chose was me and pointed me out limping towards them. I had always limped and Drumright asked him, 'You mean you want a crippled Marine on your team?' He said he did and that's how I ended up on Team War Cloud Mission Impossible." Sgt. Gifford, who trained under SSgt. Hare stateside and served with him in Vietnam, noted, "He was the most outstanding Marine I served under all my time in the Marine Corps."

"We were in such a hurry to rescue the downed team that we didn't get maps for that area or take rations as we weren't expecting to be on the ground long. All we had with us was our combat load---weapons, ammo, basic 782 gear and water," said former Gy.Sgt. Moore.

A Sea Knight picked the team up from Camp Reasoner's LZ after being rigged with a SPIE rig (a 125-foot reinforced nylon strap with D-rings sewn into it every 8 feet for the Marines to snap onto with the SPIE rig harnesses) to extract the injured team.

Rappelling ropes were attached to the back ramp area, the helicopter's side door and the "hell hole" (a 3x3-foot square hatch in the middle of the aircraft) for the 6-man team to rappel down once they found the team should they need help. The only problem was that the Team Chili Pepper was not making radio contact with the aircraft in the area around them and no one knew exactly where they were located in the darkness. It could only be assumed their radios were not working...or the worst case scenario was they had already been overrun by the enemy.

"We just weren't sure where they were. We were flying along at about 3,000-4,000 feet approaching the area where the team was last seen in the mountains when someone saw a fire down below. The extract officer had the intelligent thought that the team (Chili Pepper) had lit a signal fire to direct us to them," recalled MSgt. Hare.

The Sea Knight turned its landing lights on as it spiraled down to hover over the "signal fire" which turned out to be roughly 4 clicks (4 kilometers) short of where the team actually was.[3A] The landing lights showed an area on the side of a hill below suitable for the team to rappel down their ropes to and the lines were thrown to the ground.

At 2225 Team War Cloud Mission Impossible moved to their rappelling ropes waiting for the team leader, Gy.Sgt. Moore, to move to make the descent to the ground.

"We couldn't see the troops below in the landing lights from the helicopter. Terry stepped out on the side door's steps (out of my line of sight) as I counted him walking down those four steps outside the aircraft (as I counted to myself)...1,000...2,000...3,000...4,000...then I began rappelling down my rope at the hell hole thinking he had already started down his rope. Shortly, I landed on the ground and immediately I could smell gooks all around me and a little fire about 30 or 40 feet away," said Hare. SSgt. Mushett and Cpl. Ravelo had done the same 4 second count at the back ramp before rappelling down their rope one after the other to the ground.

Meanwhile, Gy.Sgt. Moore was about to take off down his rappelling rope when the extract officer reached out and grabbed him from behind to pull him back aboard. The lieutenant dislodged Moore's submachine (grease) gun hanging from its strap off his shoulder and it disappeared falling into the foliage below. Moore stepped back into the helicopter. "He grabbed me and pointed to flashes from the far hillside thinking the flashes might be someone opening fire," said Moore. "When I realized that Hare had already repelled to the ground, I automatically broke away and rappelled to the ground thinking I could get a spare weapon from one of the men when I reached the ground. Once I got on the deck, Hare told me he'd heard gunfire but by then it had stopped."

Hare indicated he later heard that Moore had looked around the Sea Knight and when he didn't see me, asked, "'Where's Hare?' And upon being told I had already rappelled down, he turned around and rappelled down to join me." Both Moore and Hare agreed that it's a Recon rule that if one man goes down a rappelling rope everyone goes down.

Moore was only armed with his pistol and several golf ball-sized mini-fragmentation grenades (the V40 grenade was lethal up 5 meters and dangerous up to 300 meters, weighed 4.8 oz. with a 4 second delay, manufactured between 1960-84) as he leaped onto the rappelling rope in the door and joined his fellow Marines below. Unfortunately the next two men to go down their rope, the Navy Corpsman and the last Marine in the team, after Hare at the hell hole had a serious problem.

The Doc got hung up on his rappelling rope and was dangling from the hell hole under the aircraft about 120 feet off the ground as the helicopter took evasive action to avoid green tracers zeroed in on the Sea Knight's landing light, and, consequently the poor Navy Corpsman hanging below the aircraft. The other Marine team member could not go down in trace of the Doc as a result and before he could utilize one of the other rappelling ropes in the door or back ramp, the team and the helicopter crew discovered they had picked the wrong spot for an insertion. The pilot immediately turned off his landing light and gained altitude turning as he did so as to escape fire directed at him from below.

Moore figured the Doc's "D" ring must've gotten tangled with his clothing as the helicopter pulled away from the rappelling point.

"That poor Corpsman was hung up on that rappelling rope for 6 clicks before they could land and get him off it. He never went on patrol again after that and, frankly, nobody blamed him," said Hare.

After rappelling to the ground, Moore, Hare, Mushett and Ravelo knew they were in some serious trouble as movement was all around them. The radioman whispered into the handset of their SRC-70 radio for the Spooky flareship overhead to stop releasing their basketball illumination flares as it was only helping the large enemy force to locate them.

The team moved up the hill they were on to get away from their highly visible illuminated insertion point. Darkness descended on them after the last flare burned out. The men backed into a thick clump of bamboo on all fours to hide from the enemy troops now vigorously beating the bushes for them.

"We had birds I've never heard before singing in all directions around us. Of course, those 'birds' were the enemy troops signaling one another. One guy came so close to discovering us, I could've reached out and grabbed his ankle from our hiding place," noted Hare.

He continued, "We heard somebody tooting on a horn and it got deathly quiet. You know we figured those guys must've been trained by the Chinese as only they use horns like that. I wasn't sure I was breathing when it got so quiet. I was thinking I only had one more month left on my tour in-country and here I was in the middle of this deep shit."

The team wasn't about to open fire on the enemy in close proximity to them as that would give away their position and they were too few in number to take on such a large encampment of troops. It would've been suicide. Also, since they lacked a map of the area they couldn't radio in any map coordinates for artillery or airstrikes on the large troop concentration surrounding them. Any kind of pyrotechnic like a pencil flare or pop flare or even firing off tracer rounds to pinpoint their location to guide the overhead gunships in on Luke the Gook would be calling attention to their hiding place to the enemy as well. So they sat tight and prayed they wouldn't be discovered. One of the Marines handed his M-16 rifle over to Gy.Sgt. Moore and armed himself with the M-79 grenade launcher he was also carrying strapped to his pack.

After tooting the horn once more, the enemy troops around them began moving away from where they were to the north. The Recon team was able to maintain communications through their SRC-70 radio with a relay team all night (Moore thought the relay team was on Hill 119) to keep the 1st Recon COC back at Camp Reasoner apprised of their situation. During the night, they answered the relay team during radio checks by depressing the plunger on the handset rather than talking as that would've given their position away to enemy troops nearby.

Moore and Hare also each carried scrounged handheld search and rescue, SAR, PRC-90 survival radios as back-ups to their main source of communications. The PRC-90 didn't have much range but they could at least contact the overhead birds in a pinch. "We traded captured enemy SKS rifles, bogus NVA flags sewn together by our riggers then shot full of holes and bled on to pass as the real thing in trade for survival radios, additional ammo, beer for the troops and other items we needed down at Red Beach," said Moore, who like all good Marines knew how to circumvent the regular clogged up Marine supply system.

At 0110 the team reported hearing a loud crash in the valley below them as if a big stack of lumber had been knocked over.

The patrol record notes, "...There was some movement in the streambed 75-100 meters down a 75-degree slope southwest of the team and, in addition to breaking brush, they heard a metallic sound."

At 0500 the team reported what sounded like 122mm rockets being fired in the direction of Da Nang. As it became light, Hare spotted Moore's Swedish-K submachine gun lying nearby that the extract lieutenant had accidentally pulled off his shoulder. He reached out from their hiding place and retrieved it.

The dawn also revealed steps and handrails up the side of the hill they were on as well as classrooms and hooches in the valley. On an opposite hill on their level they spotted a possible anti-aircraft position for a .50 caliber machine gun. Several well-camouflaged bunkers were within their observation post. The area appeared to be abandoned by the enemy troops during the night.

Moore's team didn't enter the bivouac/training area as they figured the enemy had "left somebody behind to watch the store," according to Hare.

Team War Cloud Mission Impossible called for an extract but due to triple canopy their extract package couldn't locate them in the dense jungle. "They kept flying in wider circles asking, 'Can you hear us now?' (referring to the sound of their engines and rotorblades overhead).

"We heard this weird buzzing sound as we tried to talk our birds back to us. The buzzing didn't sound like any American helicopter we'd heard before. A U.S. Army Loach (Hughes OH-6A light helicopter) with two guys in it descended to where we were, saw us and gave us a thumbs up they knew where we were. They gave us a compass azimuth to where there was a bomb crater we could be lifted out of by SPIE rig. (Each of the Team War Cloud Mission Impossible Marines also wore the SPIE rig harnesses which could be snapped onto the rigging dropped down to them from the extract helicopter---MDK).

"The Army Loaches had directional finders our helicopters didn't have at the time and were able to lock onto our radio transmissions to locate us. They really saved our bacon," said Hare. The team was extracted at 1110[3B]...40 minutes after Team Chili Pepper would finally be located and extracted.

Fixed wing A-4 Skyraiders came in behind the extract package strafing and bombing the enemy camp resulting in secondary explosions from stockpiled munitions and explosives.

"The conclusion we (Moore and Hare) came to over the years as to what we dropped into was that it was an enemy regimental command post. Some colonel or general's snuffie had probably made a small fire to fix him some tea and that was what drew our attention (and to rappel down thinking we had found Team Chili Pepper).

"They probably thought we had balls bigger than bowling balls throwing ropes down from a helicopter and turning lights on to illuminate his CP. The colonel or general must've figured we were there to kill him and got brown stuff all in his skivvy drawers. I imagine he had 20 bodyguards huddled around him as he got out of there.

**CMC Gen. Leonard F. Chapman Jr. congratulates, L-R, SSgt. D.M Mushett, Cpl. R.J. Ravelo, SSgt. John Hare and Gy.Sgt. Terry Moore for a job well done as Team War Cloud Mission Impossible. Maj.Gen. Charles F. Widdecke, Commanding General 1stMarDiv looks on. (USMC Photo)**

"It's got to be in the back of their minds there's people out there like Marine sniper SSgt. Carlos Hathcock (Carlos Norman Hathcock II, of Geyer Springs, Arkansas, nicknamed 'White Feather') who once killed an NVA general in the middle of his encampment spending days to line up his shot to put a fatal round in the man's heart and escape. If you recall, Hathcock was said to have had several hundred kills--one shot, one kill--in Vietnam," said Hare. This fear of the famous Marine sniper or gung ho Marines like him might've saved the four Recon Marines' lives as the enemy unit quickly departed the "targeted" area.

"I think we landed at their regimental CP and other troops were off the finger depressions off from that area," said Moore. In Vietnam Gy.Sgt. Moore would be awarded two Purple Hearts to go along with his Bronze Star for combat action. Actually, he was slightly wounded two more times and basically could've claimed two more Purple Hearts but that would have sent him home (three Purple Hearts and you were on your way stateside).

"The pay overseas was good and I wanted to stay with the troops. We were like that *Band of Brothers* from World War II. Besides, (1st Recon's CO) Lt.Col. Drumright said that if you didn't spend overnight in sick bay or the hospital you didn't deserve the Purple Heart," laughed Moore.

"We were very lucky not to have been captured considering the number of enemy troops we rappelled into. Only our training and cool heads kept us safe," surmised Hare. (Imagine...four Recon Marines caused 500-1,000 or more enemy troops to take flight out of fear...*AARUGHA*---MDK).

**Team Chili Pepper's Recovery**

The surviving members of Team Chili Pepper had to have been disappointed a reactionary team, specifically a Team Mission Impossible--designated "Super Team"--had not come to their rescue overnight. They had no way of knowing the bad luck that had befallen that team as well just 4 clicks away.

Sgt. Rowley had caused some concern during the night as he had become delirious from his wounds and had made a lot of noise and repeatedly asked what had happened. By 2200 the sergeant had drifted off to a fitful sleep. Luhrs was in and out of consciousness all night and attributed that to having sustained a concussion on the ladder.

At first light the team members figured they had better locate the missing radio and other gear back down the hill. They recovered two rifles, one broken handset, the M-79 grenade launcher, 7x50 binoculars, but no radio. Doc's and Pennington's gear was moved to the top of the hill.

At 0830 Marine gunships were flying down in the valley away from them. The Marines attempted to get their attention by waving brightly colored air panels but with no success.

An Army Loach (God, bless 'em) came within 100 meters of their location but failed to spot them. A second pass by the Loach and he spotted the air panel. He circled their position and hovered as the team signaled the Loach that they had no comm, five Marines were still alive and two KIA. The pilot acknowledged their situation and left.

A few minutes later gunships and two CH-46 Sea Knights came on station and lowered a ladder for the team. Since the entire team was unable to use the ladder due to injuries and the KIAs that needed evacuating, the team tried to use hand signals to make them understand they couldn't use the ladder and needed a radio to explain their situation.

LCpl. Airaghi couldn't make them understand what they needed as the Sea Knight continued to hover over them dangling the ladder over their position. He got on the ladder to ride it back to somewhere he could explain what all they required to evacuate their wounded and dead. The helicopter continued to hover so he got back off it and joined his team.

The aircraft personnel must've realized the team's needs as they lowered a McGuire rig (a basket to strap in the wounded or dead in the prone position) by hoist cable. Sgt. Rowley was strapped in by the team and was hoisted back up to the helicopter.

1st Recon's extract officer aboard the helicopter, 1stLt. A.J. Pack, CO of Charlie Co., climbed down the ladder to help the team and passed Sgt. Rowley on the way up. (Cpl. Feldman noted that the ladder was attached underneath the Sea Knight and rolled up in the back of the helicopter before it was thrown out. For Pack to reach the ladder underneath the helicopter he would have had to exit by the hell hole and grab hold of the ladder which would have been one dicey move. The way the Patrol Debrief reads this is apparently what he did... down and back up the ladder---MDK). As the lieutenant got to the ground, Sgt. Rowley's basket got hung up on the ladder. Pack climbed back up the ladder and managed to get the sergeant untangled and into the aircraft with the crew chief's help.

Lt. Pack climbed back up and into the aircraft to retrieve a PRC-93 radio and rode the cable hoist's jungle penetrator back to the ground. By this time the Sea Knights were running low on fuel so they departed to refuel and take Sgt. Rowley to Charlie Med.

By 1030 the helicopters returned to extract Pennington, Holkem and Doc McKinley by jungle penetrator and Lt. Pack, Airaghi, Delozier and Luhrs by SPIE rig, the same type nylon strap that would be used to extract Team War Cloud Mission Impossible less than an hour later. Team Chili Pepper was finally extracted from the side of the hill and their ordeal was over.

Two nights after returning to Camp Reasoner LCpl. Luhrs was pulling guard duty near the LZ when he passed out. An officer came along and slapped him for falling asleep on duty. "The next day a gigantic abscess the size of an orange appeared on the back of my neck," said Luhrs. He was taken to the medical facility near the Air Wing and from there he was flown out to the U.S. Navy hospital ship in Da Nang harbor, the *USS Sanctuary,* where they performed major surgery and drew out 100cc's of green pus. (This was most likely the reason Luhrs was spiking a temperature of 103 degrees on the Chili Pepper patrol and had passed out on guard duty---MDK).

The Marine would spend 2 months on Okinawa recuperating and be sent home for an early release from the Marine Corps. He would not forget the Marines of Team Chili Pepper who lost their lives on September 1, 1970. In two postings on the Vietnam Veterans Memorial Fund website, vvmf.org, on March 28, 2007 Luhrs would note under Pennington's name: "It was I who tried to best comfort you that terrible night in Sherwood Forest. I'll never forget you man, never." And under Holkem's name: "I can hear that southern drawl as clear as a bell! I'll never forget you, never."[4]

**Team Movable Inserted/Extracted September 3**

At 0815 Thursday, September 3, Gy.Sgt. P.L. Hensley's Team Movable was dropped in the lowlands between two blue lines (steams)[5A] a little over a click away from where Team War Cloud Mission Impossible was extracted the day before. The area was still hot as the team soon found out. The patrol lasted all of 14 minutes!

Hensley, accompanied by Cpl. Hicks, Cpl. Davis, PFC Moreno, Cpl. Badger, PFC John Somers and HM3 Hunt, disembarked from a Sea Knight in high elephant grass and started to move out after the helicopter departed when they heard a rifle shot.

The team was unable to pinpoint the shooter's exact location but figured it came from the northeast about 20-30 meters away. The point man spotted six NVA wearing green uniforms carrying rifles approximately 30 meters away headed towards the team at a rapid pace.

Three minutes after being inserted the pointman dropped the first NVA dead in his tracks. The enemy soldiers disappeared in the tall elephant grass and opened fire on the team, which returned a heavy volume of small arms fire of their own. The enemy split its force and tried to encircle the team now that they knew where they were.

Team Movable spotted 4-5 additional NVA soldiers to their southwest approximately 30 meters away joining the fight. One of the enemy soldiers took cover behind a tree as his buddies assaulted the Recon team. The M-79 blooperman took the NVA at the tree under fire and scored a direct hit on his chest with a 40mm HE round killing him instantly. The entire team was now fiercely engaged from both the southwest and northeast.

At 0820 the enemy increased its small arms fire at the team and tossed two chicom grenades at them that landed about 15 meters away fortunately causing no injuries when they exploded. Hensley's men increased their volume of fire and threw grenades of their own at the enemy. They believed the enemy was working up to assault their position in one final push.

The primary radio operator (RTO) observed the elephant grass parting and an enemy soldier wearing a green uniform took aim at Hensley directing his troops. The radioman shouted a warning at his patrol leader and swung his rifle around to take out the shooter. Before the RTO could open up on the NVA soldier, he'd taken his best shot at the gunny and hit him in the left arm wounding him. The RTO emptied his magazine into the parted grass killing another NVA. Enemy soldiers continued to advance through the tall elephant grass attempting to overrun the team.

Marine gunships swooped in joining the fight tearing up the countryside surrounding the Recon team. A Sea Knight returned to the same LZ it had just inserted Team Movable and took them back aboard as the gunners on either side of the aircraft hosed down the area with .50 caliber machine guns. Fast movers came on station and blasted the entire area while 105mm artillery at a distant firebase expended 225 HE rounds after the airstrike was over. For those short 14 minutes on the ground, Team Movable claimed 3 NVA KIA, 1 probable NVA KIA and sustained 1 USMC WIA.

Just to make sure no stone was left unturned or enemy soldier was left alive where Moore and Hensley's teams encountered so many NVA, a B-52 arc light (B-52s flying out of Guam or Thailand saturated the area with 500-lb. high explosive bombs) was called in on the base camp and the surrounding terrain.

Gy.Sgt. Hensley made a tongue-in-cheek complaint to Hare after his team returned from its "adventure" and, again, years later made a comment to Moore about that September 3 day. "They got the shit shot out of them, Hensley was wounded and the birds had to turn right around and extract them. Hensley vowed never to follow up a Mission Impossible Team again," said Hare.

"Hensley hassles me at all the Recon unions for trying to get him killed. They ran into enemy troops wearing camouflage utilities," noted Moore.

**Ironic Twist**

Delozier would only come away with an injured wrist from his bad experience with the ladder extract attempt September 1. The SPIE rig he attached to the next day took him and the remainder of his team back to the safety of Camp Reasoner.

On November 18, roughly 2½ months later, another SPIE rig he was riding on after another emergency extract would take his life and his team's lives when they were dragged through trees and their helicopter crashed into a mountain killing all aboard (See Chapters 14 and 15).

## An Extraordinary Marine: Gy.Sgt. Terry Moore

In requesting some photos of both Moore and Hare from those multiple tour dates in Vietnam, MSgt. Hare included a Combat Summary of his friend submitted for consideration for the Combat Commissioning Program. His submission was accompanied by the endorsement of his two previous 1st Recon COs Lt.Col.s Leftwich and Drumright and approved by Lt.Gen. Lew Walt in 1970. Apparently the extraordinary combat record Moore compiled impressed a number of people as he was commissioned as a second lieutenant in December 1970. After a long successful career, he retired as a lieutenant colonel in 1987. He lives near Camp Lejeune in North Carolina where he has been known to keep his hand in the training process of young Marines.

I was impressed with Gunny Moore's unhesitating leap on the rappelling rope to follow his Team War Cloud Mission Impossible comrades into the darkness virtually weaponless. Hare let me know this was nothing new for his friend as he had done similar death-defying deeds disregarding his own life many times before.

## ...Laying His Life on the Line for Fellow Marines

Six days after returning to Vietnam for his third tour, Gy.Sgt. Moore was platoon sergeant of Delta Co., 1st Recon with Team Durham assigned to an observation post on Hill 119 in the Doi Chiem Son Tuesday, January 20, 1970. The battalion commander, Lt.Col. John J. Grace, flew in on a helicopter to inspect the position, according to Hare. Lt.Col. Grace, accompanied by two other men with at least one of them being another officer, was walking around the hill position at 1255 evaluating its defenses doing what officers do when one of them tripped an M-26 grenade boobytrap injuring all three men.[6A]

Without hesitation and disregarding the possibilities of other boobytraps, Gunny Moore ran to their aid and administered medical assistance. A medevac was called in for the emergency, priority and routine injuries. Hare noted that as the medevac package was inbound Moore spotted another boobytrap nearby. He was attempting to disarm it when the Sea Knight suddenly appeared overhead. The gunny put himself between the injured men and the boobytrap by covering the explosive device with his body so that the helicopter's rotor wash wouldn't cause a detonation further injuring the wounded men. In other words, Gunny Moore risked his life to save others. The casualties were medevacked without further incident thanks to Moore's brave deed.

Due to his injuries sustained by the boobytrap Lt.Col. Grace (October 8, 1969-January 20, 1970) would not return to 1st Recon as his XO Maj. Terry

Turner assumed temporary command until a lieutenant colonel could be named to fill the billet.

Hare heard the story of how his best friend, Moore, had laid down in front of that boobytrap as the helicopter medevacked the casualties and chewed him out, "Boy, are you crazy. That's the way people earn the Medal of Honor by getting killed. I knew you were dumb but not crazy."

**...Quick Action Saves Grunt**

On another occasion, the gunny and his 1st Recon team was involved in transporting an infantry company across the Song Vu Gia at 2330 Friday, April 3, 1970 during a night attack when one of the heavily laden men fell overboard. Hare said the Marine made the mistake of climbing out of the rubber boat on the backside away from the shore and began to disappear under the murky water from the weight of his combat gear. Moore reacted without hesitation by stepping across the boat and reached out to grab the grunt from under the water and pulled him back to the boat before the swift river current could pull him away from them. Moore earned a Navy and Marine Corps Medal for his quick action as well as a second medal for saving a drowning local man on Okinawa. (Also, see Chapter 7 about his fierce determination to retrieve his team leader Lt. Rathmell when a Sea Knight's pilot wanted to leave him behind alone on the ground thinking his aircraft was under fire).

**...Huey Gunbird Catches Fire and Crashes**

On July 19, 1970 Moore, Hare and Team War Cloud Mission Impossible were tasked with searching for and recovering the bodies of the crew of a HML-167 Comprise Huey UH-1E piloted by 1stLt. Richard William Dodd, 26 of Oglesby, Illinois which had crashed into triple-canopy jungle deep in enemy territory. Asked how far into enemy territory they had to go, Hare could only say, "Way out. We weren't told where we were."

Pilot Lynn L. Boyer III of Huntsville, Alabama noted that he and copilot Lawrence Rolstad of Mercer Island, Washington were on a three bird Sniffer Mission that included Dodd and his copilot 1stLt. Lewis Edgar Casner Jr., 25, copilot, of Potomac, Maryland flying at 700 feet above ground level and 1stLt. David Geaslin of Gonzales, Texas and 1stLt. Ralph Nelson Duemling, 25 of South Pasadena, California at 1,000 feet. (Duemling and his Huey crew would perish August 18 while on gunship escort for HMM-263 pilot Lt. Jerry Martin picking up four ROK KIAs in the Barrier Island area. Enemy gunners would bring his aircraft down in a fiery crash as he commenced a gun run to suppress their fire on the Sea Knight medevac birds). Boyer, in the Sniffer bird, flew at an altitude between them as the two gunbirds were in an overwatch flight formation covering him. "The gunbirds did not fly trail, but were in a combat spread so that they could immediately roll into a gun/rocket run if the Sniffer or low bird took fire."

A "Sniffer" is actually called an Airborne Personnel Detector, APD, developed by General Electric that is attached to the sides and skids of the Huey as two very large air scoops. It basically recognizes the chemical in human sweat, ammonium chloride, in the jungle below. The scoops lead to a special console positioned behind the radio console where an operator could stick his head in there and read what was being detected and he, in turn would alert the aircraft commander of any humans and fast movers would be called in to take over, according to Alan H. Barbour, VMO-2 pilot in Vietnam and Research Historian for the History and Archives Division, USMC Combat Helicopter Association in 2010.

Geaslin and Duemling indicated in their After Action Report that Dodd's aircraft, TV-21, crashed northwest of a razorback (the last map coordinates on Geaslin's AAR apparently shows the crash site as being just off lofty Hill 730).[7A] He indicates they had received no fire. Their flight was listed as a Mission 74 and it was, indeed, "way out" in the mountains not far from Laos.

"We had a routine hop, no contact and a good time low level snooping and pooping along the planned route. I don't remember how far into the flight we were, but heard 'Fire!' over the radio. We thought we were being called that we were 'taking ground fire' so I pulled up and climbed," said Boyer. "Then I heard Geaslin, I believe, calling to the low and forward gunbird, Dodd and Casner, that they were on fire. I turned toward the gun section and sure enough the lead gun was burning with flames engulfing the fuselage, the crew cabin.

"(We watched) as the flames spread forward toward the pilots and, I believe, aft and were burning fairly intensely. I don't remember how high they were, but it seems as though the tail boom separated from the aircraft and they started a slow rotation toward the deck. I believe there was enough control left of the aircraft the pilot was able to pull pitch at the bottom, because the aircraft hit fairly level, hard and collapsed. It didn't slide much from the impact point. I could see someone move in the crew compartment in the wreckage, but no one got out," said Boyer. Barbour indicated that Dodd's helicopter went down approximately 20 miles southwest of Da Nang at about the 2,600-foot elevation.

Boyer went on to say, "Geaslin, a good friend to the crashed crew, was extremely upset, as we all were, and was descending to try to hover over the wreckage to investigate. I told him to go high and cover us as he had a heavy gunbird. I told him we had the Sniffer bird and we would go down and check out the site and look for survivors. We descended and looked for survivors and a place to land." Boyer indicated he couldn't find any survivors as the fire continued to burn intensely as the ordnance aboard the gunbird began to cook off making it unsafe to land anywhere near the crash site.

"I don't remember any reasonable places near the site to set down either. The crash was reported and we stayed in the area as long as possible looking for possible survivors (someone might have gotten thrown out, a very slight chance, as we watched the burning aircraft throughout its descent) and hostiles, as fuel permitted. We were forced to return to base (as our fuel ran low). The crash as far as I could discern was not the result of hostile fire."

Boyer said he never saw an official accident report on Dodd's crash. The best hypothesis the pilots could come up with was that the main fuel interconnect line, which ran under or near the crew compartment (that is the 3- or 4-inch fuel line that ran between the main tank on the starboard side of the Huey and the auxiliary tank on the port side) probably failed in flight. This failure allowed fuel to run forward (reasonable since the Huey flies in a nose down attitude) and to pool under the crew compartment.

"As far as I know no one ever figured out what the ignition source might have been, but once the fire started there, it probably caused the rubber bladder type fuel cells to leak and then fail, which contributed to the intensity of the fire. Since the aircraft had forward airspeed, fire and burning fuel flowed both forward and was blown aft along the internal structure of the fuselage and tail boom (would be logical that an intense fire at the tail boom fuselage interface could cause the four tail boom attaching bolts to pull out of the fuselage or tail boom structure). I do not believe the aircraft had an engine failure, since it seemed to be powered until impact and the pilots seemed to slow the descent just before impact."

A Marine in the back of Boyer's aircraft never indicated he had seen ground fire either nor did the Sniffer equipment alert them as to the presence of enemy soldiers so the hypothesis of how the fire started seemed to be the most logical explanation.

### ...Recovering KIA Comprise Crew in Indian Territory

Moore's team arrived at the fiery crash site not long afterwards. Hare was first to rappel to the ground as point man. The tall triple canopy prevented the Sea Knight from descending very far towards the deck so the team had to depend on the rappelling rope to make up the difference. "The rope was about 20 feet short of the ground so we had to jump the rest of the way," said Hare.

Besides the possibility of confronting a hostile force that may have shot the Huey down, Moore's Recon team had to contend with the remnants of the fire still burning at the site of the helicopter crash and exploding ammunition. The Huey had crashed in the trees and the ensuing fire had burned the aircraft's metal structure down to only about 2 or 3 feet high by the time they got to it, according to Hare. Killed in the conflagration besides the pilots Dodd and Casner were Cpl. Johnny Michael Rodgers, 21, crew chief, of Fort Worth, Texas and LCpl. John Frank Barnett, 22, doorgunner, of Port Hueneme, California. Records show that three of the four men aboard the aircraft were married.

HML-167 pilot 1stLt. Jim Hunt had this comment to make about Lt. Casner, "Casner was like a mentor to me. He was a great guy to know and an excellent pilot and head work. I flew a bunch of missions with him as his copilot and/or wingman. He was what we tagged some pilots as a 'Magnet Ass.' He just seemed to attract lead. I think I took more fire when flying with him or as his wingman than I probably did with most all of my other missions put together. I understand he was written up for a DFC as the lead pilot for a March 15, 1970 mission in gunship support of HMM-263 pilot 1stLt. Darcy Vernier."

The Combat Summary report noted that burning fuel around Dodd's helicopter charred the Recon Marines' boots as they put the remains of the four crewmen's bodies in body bags and utilized a 150-foot jungle penetrator cable rig to hoist them up to the Sea Knight hovering above them. SSgt. Hare said he saluted each man out of honor for their sacrifice as they were reeled up to the transport helicopter by cable hoist.

Their ordeal wasn't quite over as the 125-foot Special Purpose Insertion and Extraction (SPIE) strap with rings sewn into it about every 8 feet was secured to the helicopter while the other end was weighted and dropped down to them from the Sea Knight to hook their harnesses onto. It was dangling several feet above them out of their reach. They had to boost each other into the air to reach the strap and climb up it a ways to snap on. Hare said he and Moore were the last two men on the ground and they had a time of it climbing up to reach the safety of the strap. Fortunately they all managed to snap onto the strap and were lifted out of the jungle having completed their mission to bring their dead Marine comrades home.

**...Attacking Radio Jamming Stations**

The summary of Moore's combat prowess noted that on two occasions in a 6-week period the gunny was called upon as team leader to lead his Recon Marines deep into enemy territory at night to destroy their radio jamming stations. His teams in each case were successful coming away with a minimum of casualties and brought back captured documents and a POW during one of those forays.

Lavishly recommending this outstanding Marine for a commission, the summary notes, "Gy.Sgt. Moore's professional experience, personal courage and tremendous leadership abilities tried time and again in the most crucial situations, in and out of enemy contact, are in accordance with the highest traditions and a credit to himself and his Corps."

Put into plain, less flowery English, I would have said, "You are looking for uncommonly brave men like this to anoint as officers. Warriors who would put their men before self and believe strongly in leaving no man behind. And if such a man were assigned the daunting task of attacking Hell, Marines who serve under him would surely follow him into battle with the Devil himself. That man would bc Gunny Moore."

## Etched on His Tombstone

"We were killing a lot of 'em (the enemy) in 1970 as well as 1961-62 and 1967 in SOG, 1st and 3rd Recon," said MSgt. Hare. "I felt guilty for those I left behind (when I rotated home). It hurts. It preys on your mind to leave your team behind in Vietnam. In 1970 I seriously thought about extending but I was married and realized that was bullshit because your luck only goes so far. If I had stayed, I probably would've been on that aircraft with Col. Bill Leftwich (a helicopter crash November 18, 1970 that killed nine Recon Marines, five Marine crewmen and one Navy Corpsman) and wouldn't be here today.

"My wife was in Japan while I served in Vietnam. In March (1970) I didn't think I'd make it home alive so I went to Japan and told her I wanted her to go back to the states. I didn't want her stuck far from home if I should get killed over there." His premonition of impending death turned out to be untrue much to his relief.

Hare, who spent 25 year in the Marines Corps--18 of those years in Recon units--retired in a location near his beloved Marines not far from his good friend, retired Lt.Col. Terry Moore, who would not leave Hare or his men alone in enemy territory in the darkness September 1, 1970. "We go back to 1960 and followed one another to duty stations for 15 years off and on. I was the best man at his wedding. He's the executor of my will should I die before him. Our kids call him uncle and his kids call me uncle. If I had to pick a family, I would want him to be a part of my family," said Hare. Friends and comrade-in-arms like Moore generally only come along once in a lifetime.

Probably as a result of that devotion to a fellow Marine, a comrade and lifelong friend, MSgt. Hare said he would have this abbreviated and somewhat altered portion of an old poem etched on his tombstone as his epitaph when the time comes for him to join the other Marines guarding Heavens Gates someday:

> Not the love of a beautiful maiden
> Or the staunch true love of a mother,
> Why they are nothing compared to the love
> Of an old Marine for another.
>
> (Author Unknown)

# Chapter 9

**"Enlisted men *own* the Marine Corps. They *are* the Marine Corps... The Marine Corps is the only outfit in the world that belongs to the enlisted men." Also, "Marines weren't made to fight from a hole... putting Marines in a big bowl like Khe Sanh was the dumbest idea I'd ever heard...They were made to fight in the open."**

**Col. William Covington "Wild Bill" Drumright**
**CO, 2/26, 1st Recon Battalion**

### Lt.Col. Bill Drumright: "Man of a Thousand Stories"

During a 1st Recon mini-reunion of "his boys" at his spacious 2-story Columbia, Tennessee country home Memorial Weekend 2003, Col. "Wild Bill" Drumright, USMC (Ret.), 75, was insistent that I interview him late into the night and into the wee hours of the next morning of my last day there. The outspoken colonel told me he didn't expect to see 2004 and wanted his Vietnam War recollections recorded for posterity as well as make some no bullshit comments about his beloved Marine Corps and some of the men who served under him. The colonel was apparently attuned to his time remaining as he did, indeed, die a little over 6 months later in December 2003.

**Lt.Col. William C. "Bill" Drumright is shown talking to Secretary of the Navy John H. Chafee, a former Marine officer who served in World War II and Korea, at Camp Reasoner. (Photo courtesy of Larry Feldman)**

(Before assuming command of 1st Reconnaissance Battalion, Lt.Col. Drumright had briefly been my CO at 2nd Battalion, 26th Marines in January 1970 when I first arrived in-country. At the time I interviewed Drumright in 2003, he was in deteriorating health and his memory was not as sharp as it would have been had I talked with him immediately after he had returned from Vietnam. Everything he told me was off the top of his head without referring to notes or official documents so some individuals he referred to and combat actions he recounted may be off or colorfully exaggerated to some degree as a result. Also, I should've gone back to double-check the spelling of names and the facts involved in selected combat stories covered in several hours of taped interviews but the colonel's untimely death prevented me from doing that. What follows are but a portion of the stories that Drumright could light up a room with---MDK).

The plain-spoken Tennessean could hold a crowd of Marines spellbound with his vibrant war reminisces ranging from the Korean War to Vietnam. As one of his Recon Marines noted, "He was the man of a thousand stories." In his Tennessee home the stories reverberated off the walls in his den that were covered with unique combat memorabilia and photos spanning his impressive Marine career and reinforcing what he had to say.

**Lost in a Snowstorm in the Korean War**

"I came into the Marine Corps in 1951 attending Officers Candidate School at Parris Island, South Carolina, after finishing college. I had set my sights on becoming a football coach someday but instead found myself joining the Marines during the Korean War. OCS consisted mostly of veterans back then.

"When I got to Korea in 1952, we were in a defensive line. I had 26 (infantrymen) in an advance anti-tank company Recon outfit that included five tanks and six recoilless rifles (mounted on jeeps). We crossed a bridge over the Han River north of Seoul at night in November. I was the second lieutenant platoon commander in charge and our objective was about 40 or 50 miles north of Seoul in a valley. I left the tanks and recoilless rifles behind to make a reconnaissance and 26 of us moved up to the valley and got lost in a snowstorm. The snow was coming down so heavy I didn't know where we were.

"The snow was coming from the north into our faces and we couldn't see crap. We found some burial mounds and decided to stay around there because it was getting too cold and we couldn't see nothing. We were about to freeze to death anyway. We got in our sleeping bags and all got together. Next morning when we got up we saw the Chinese just on the other side of our hill...north side of the hill. My platoon sergeant asked me what I was going to do. I told him we were going to walk out of there.

"So fast as we could we got everybody up and rolled up our sleeping bags. Some of the men were in such a hurry they dragged their unrolled sleeping bags behind them. We looked like shit! We took off down the valley back to the south towards the river. This wasn't an advance to the rear like Chesty Puller had (at the Chosin Reservoir). This was a goddamn run to the rear. There were

Chinese on our right so my men asked me if they should shoot at them and I said not until they shoot at us. There was Chinese also on our left and to our rear.

"I told my men not to start a fight until they started the fight. When they started the fight, I told my men we were going to take the hill to the left of us because there were fewer enemy troops holding it. Since there were only 26 of us, we couldn't take on too many." Drumright said his Recon unit spent 2 or 3 days on that hill which they managed to take and hold before a relief column came for them.

"We all got hit. Buck Hagh (or possibly Hague) of German descent from Minnesota and 'Bonnie' (I'm not sure if this was his actual last name or nickname---MDK) were on the machine gun when they hit us that night. They were as close as brothers. Buck and 'Bonnie' had two guys with them who fought and held their ground. None of them got medals for this action although Hagh would receive a Bronze Star with Valor later. When Bonnie was blinded by an explosion, Hagh did all the shooting and killed a pile of Chinese. Bonnie was only awarded the Purple Heart for his wounds." The Marines didn't plan to stay out long so hadn't carried provisions with them. They had to eat the Chinese soldiers' food they could scrounge off the dead bodies, according to Drumright.

"For the longest time I carried one of their canteens that had Chinese writing on it. By the time we were relieved, only 12 of us out of the original 26 were still alive. We brought our dead out with us. They were frozen by then. Hagh came to visit me (in 2003) and never said anything at all about serving in Korea."

Drumright recalled the interrogation techniques the Communist Chinese had used on some of the United Nations' prisoners they captured which probably made them fight harder not to be taken as a POW. "The way the Chinese made people talk (in the field) was to sit (their prisoners) down and have a conversation with them and ask the first man they came to for information. If he didn't tell them what they wanted to know, they would shoot him in the stomach (and it would take a long time for him to die an agonizing death). Then they'd turn to the next guy and ask him the same question and on down the line (killing each man the same way) until someone talked."

**Vietnam and The Nomads of 2/26**

"We had two bases for 2/26 (2nd Battalion, 26th Marine Regiment) when I arrived in Vietnam (in September 1969 at the Rockcrusher on the west side of Division Ridge and high up in the mountains at Hai Van Pass north of Da Nang). I really don't know why we had those two bases (rather than just one)," noted Drumright, CO of 2/26 from September 9, 1969 to January 25, 1970.

"I kept a jump CP with me consisting of a driver, a radioman and an S-3 officer, Ted Berryman, who had graduated from West Point (and chose the Marines over the Army to serve with) and was a right smart guy. Ted and I would get up every day and go east and west inspecting 2/26 outfits.

"(When I arrived at 2/26), those were the most terrible looking bunch of troops. They had no clothes. Had ropes for rifle slings. I gathered my S-4 together and told him what I wanted him to do. I gave him a blank checkbook with 20 blank requisitions signed for him to use to refit my Marines. I told him if you can't find what you need, steal it, do whatever, I want it. I wanted all new rifle slings, brand spanking new clothes (and boots most likely---MDK) for my troops. Get all the trucks you need and you go get them new gear. We were as ragged as hell." The Marines and Navy Corpsmen knew their new CO was looking after their welfare as a result.

"I had five of the finest company commanders you've ever seen in your life at 2/26. (Capt. Winkler then 1stLt. R. Macaskill, H&S Co.; 1stLt. Smith then Capt. J.G. Reynaud, Echo Co.; 1stLt. Duncan then 1stLt. L.P. Oakes, Fox Co.; Capt. G.V. Best then 1stLt. S.T. Waimey, Golf Co.; Capt. J.R. Wright then 1stLt. B.A. Ward, Hotel Co.). All of them were young except for Reno who was an old mustang. He wanted to be a rifle commander but I didn't have a place to put him. I had him start a training program in the Rear with the 60mm mortars that he called 'pact on impact.' He showed all my people how to shoot the 60mm mortars (with tricks of the trade precision). Lt. May, a graduate of Notre Dame, also trained troops in the Rear with machine guns and mortars.

## 2/26 Returns a Favor to 101st Airborne

U.S. Army's 101st Airborne operated just north of 2/26's AO. Occasionally, 2/26 would lend the 101st Airborne some help in return for helicopter assistance, according to Drumright. "Their table of organization strength per company was about 85 men. Foxhole strength per company was about 40 and they were stretched all over the place but had plenty of helicopters.

"We used their helicopters all the time. One day their commander came to me and asked, 'If I find out a heavy movement of North Vietnamese is coming into a village in our area to find food or rice, will you give me support with a company?' I said, 'Yeah.'

"So I gave one of my company commanders (I'm assuming either Wright or Ward, Hotel Co. CO---MDK) a heads up and told him to prepare to go to work in 101st Airborne's area. He studied the map (of the targeted area) and was ready (when the time came). The Army commander called up one day and said they're coming in that night or the next.

"I asked (my company commander) what his plan was. He said he was going to get in LVTs at Red Beach and come around on the ocean side to move into the village and stay in there until the next night. As it turned out, they ended up killing every one of those damn people (in that NVA outfit). 1stLt. Mike Hodgins (platoon commander in Hotel Co. who would end up at 1st Recon with Drumright) was in on that ambush."

Drumright said two Marines were wounded in the fight and were shipped up to the nearest hospital...an Army hospital. "The Army got all excited about Marines being in an Army hospital. Maj.Gen. (Ormond R.) Simpson (CG, 1stMarDiv) came up and asked if I knew I had two or three Marines up in an Army hospital. I said, 'No, but it doesn't surprise me.' I told him the boys wiped out a pretty sizeable outfit over in the 101st Airborne's AO."

Simpson figured out why Drumright was crossing over into the Army's domain when he asked him if he was using Army helicopters. "I said, 'Yes sir, they gave me anything I wanted when I helped them.'"

Drumright noted that the general came back with, "Boy, I gotta get onto you. Are you going to continue to use their helicopters?"

"I said, 'Yes,' and he said, 'I thought you would.'"

### Job Interview for 1st Recon

While Drumright was still CO of 2/26 he complained to a visiting Maj.Gen. Edwin B. Wheeler about a U.S. Army Brigade being helilifted to a mountain on the border with Laos. "It seemed we never learn our lesson. We can't shoot across the border but the NVA put their long range artillery and mortars there just across the border and shoot at us from Laos all day. I told him that Marines weren't made to fight from a hole. They were made to fight in the open. I thought putting a Brigade on the border like that or putting Marines in a big bowl like Khe Sanh was the dumbest idea I'd ever heard. He asked me what I would do.

"I told him I would attack the SOBs and he asked, 'With what?' I told him with the 1st Recon Battalion. We talked a little more and he flew off. I had no idea he was about to become the Commanding General of 1stMarDiv's Ground forces (taking over from Maj.Gen. Simpson December 15, 1969). A short time later here he comes again. 'What you told me (over a month earlier), can you still do it?'

"I said give me 1st Recon Battalion and you've got it. Give me support from the Marine Air Wing...Sea Knights, Cobras and F-4s and you've got it. Support of the 11th Marines (artillery) and you've got it. I'll kick their asses all the way back to the North. He asked me, 'When can you start?'" The "job opening" came about when Lt.Col. Grace, CO of 1st Recon Bn., was injured by a boobytrap January 20 on Hill 119 and Drumright took over from the interim acting CO, Maj. Turner on January 27 (See Chapter 8).

### Drumright "Fires" 29 1st Recon Officers

"The first day at 1st Recon I walked into the mess hall. The entire mess hall was full of goddamn lieutenants and we had a war going on! I asked Sgt.Maj. Charles Skinner why the hell the lieutenants aren't at war. The war is out there, not in here (in the mess hall)! I told him I wanted a list of all the lieutenants in the mess hall on my desk within the hour. I wanted to fire those sons of bitches!

"I fired 15 lieutenants (transferred them to other Marine units in Vietnam) the first day. Next day, I fired another 14 of those peckerwoods. I told them if you want to argue with me about it, come talk to me. You can't stay here 6 months and not go on patrol. Not on my watch! You're going to have your ass out there with your kids or you're not gonna be around. Not one damn lieutenant (that I fired) had the guts to come into my office. So I ended up bringing some goddamn lieutenants with me from 2/26.

"I had no use for junior officers who wouldn't go to the bush with their men so I fired 'em. Hell, PFCs, lance corporals, corporals and sergeants do most the fighting in the Marine Corps anyway. Who needs junior officers who won't fight?" asked Col. Drumright. The "firings" were significant considering 1st Recon only had 50 officers on its rolls in February, 1970. That would have been a huge turnover of officers.

### Recon Tactics in Vietnam

"...(Drumright) was an unparalleled troop leader in getting the most from his battalion and absolutely fearless," commented Maj. Bill Bond Jr., who was the 1st Force Recon's CO then 1st Recon Battalion's Operations assistant, S-3A in 1970 under Drumright.

"As far as I have been able to tell, you either respected him or you couldn't stand him. There was no in-between. I judged him the only way that mattered to me at the time. He never left a team high and dry. If you stepped in something you couldn't handle, he sent someone after you or he came and got you himself. I was proud as hell to be one of 'His Boys,'" said Cpl. Bob Morris, 20 in 1970, of St. Petersburg, Florida, Team Cayenne's patrol leader.

Drumright explained his Recon Marines tactics to me as his 1st Recon Marines listened in sitting around his large den/Marine paraphernalia decorated room on his farm in Columbia, Tennessee. The idea was for the teams to act like the old World War II Marine Raider Battalions who went out to draw fire from the enemy so that artillery, naval gunfire or airstrikes could annihilate them...find 'em, fix 'em and kill 'em.

"I had to explain to the 1st Force Recon guys that were attached to us that their job was not to 'observe' anyone while on patrol. Let's say you see three guys going east on a trail. Don't tell me you're observing them. You kill those three men. You see three more men, kill them, too. That's what our job was...to go out there and kill people. We were Raiders not Recon. I told them anybody who didn't want to be around there and do that should get the hell out. We don't need you. I'll find somebody who can do it. I found them in bars. I brought a bunch of them over with me from 2/26 when I left there as CO. I found them everywhere." Gy.Sgt. Terry Moore and SSgt. John Hare were assigned the job of re-training the new attachments into Raiders, according to Drumright. They taught the Recon Indoctrination Program, RIP, and re-introduced every Recon Marine, enlisted and officer, to what they were expected to do every day as members of the elite "painted faces."

"I'll tell you what (my work ethic was with my Marines). I didn't pat these guys on the ass one iota. I didn't walk around saying, 'Buddy, buddy, buddy.' My Marine Corps was the same as it has always been. When they worked for me, I kicked them in the ass every damn day," commented Col. Drumright.

"Recon was more a part of the Marine Air Wing than the 1st Marine Division because of all the inserts and extracts we depended on them for," noted the colonel.

In the *U.S. Marine Corps in Vietnam Vietnamization And Redeployment, 1970-71* publication, he graphically explained how the little 7-man Recon teams acted on the enemy as "a little bucket of honey" did on bees. "The bees, they'd swarm all around. And then you'd pull the bucket of honey out and you'd work it over, and then you get all the bees that don't run off…you get them out of their caves. They have to come out of their caves to fight."[1]

I asked the colonel if what the teams were doing was actually acting as bait rather than reconnaissance in the bush. He agreed that in many instances that was the case. One of his men listening in commented, "You mean *we* were the bait? I didn't know that."

After awhile the enemy caught on to the Recon teams' tactics, according to Drumright, and they would shadow the teams upon their insertion in their territory. They'd use dogs to track them which the Marines countered by spreading CS gas crystals along trails they were using and around their nighttime harbor sites to kill the dogs sense of smell. The enemy wouldn't approach the teams unless they came close to one of their base camps and would fire rifle shots to signal where they were.[2] (Team Thin Man in Chapter 4 put in their Patrol Debrief that they had heard rifle shots on the valley floor right before they were hit March 2, 1970. Gy.Sgt. Hensley's Team Moveable in the previous chapter was also hit after an enemy soldier fired off his rifle. In both cases the rifle fire was most likely enemy troops signaling one another of each of the Recon team's locations---MDK).

Rather than follow trails, the Recon teams would "break brush" in enemy territory staying clear of well-traveled trails. Occasionally they would hack through vegetation and find themselves stumbling into a well-concealed enemy base camp. They would immediately aggressively attack those in the camp throwing grenades into huts, bunkers and caches moving quickly through the camps.[3]

"Our guys could outshoot theirs. They could throw a hand grenade further. They could think a little faster. They used a technique of just going right through the camp throwing hand grenades into every hole and bunker you could find, usually about two or three going through the camp, and the other two or three covering...Then they'd move back out of the area and try to saturate the thing with artillery and air.[4]

"I wanted them to kill 'em. Find their hospitals. Find their supply dumps. Find their caches. Find their everything. Ambush every trail that leads in and out of Laos. The first month or two was a heyday. We killed everything that moved. They weren't expecting us back in there. Finally, they started tightening down their security a little bit. At one point they started putting women in their patrols (thinking Marines would not kill women). They decorated them up so there was no mistake that they were women. My men asked me what to do about them. I said we're going to kill every bit of them. Kill every damn thing that comes along. They played ruthless so we played a ruthless war."

The colonel didn't like how the U.S. Special Forces were used in Vietnam. "You should never put your troops in a position where you can't support them. You're dealing with people from West Point and they look at fighting differently than us. They seem to think their men are pawns to be moved around and do anything you want to with them."

### 1st Recon Patrols Predict Attack on Da Nang

Col. Drumright recalled all the Patrol Debrief sessions were broken down into something he called "Worm Diagrams" that lent itself to applicable Intelligence information they could use to predict enemy activities. When a patrol came back to Camp Reasoner, their intelligence information was marked down where they'd been, what they'd found, what they saw and that'd pretty well paint them a picture of whether future attacks were in the offering. (Drumright erroneously gave credit for the "Worm Diagrams" to 23-year-old S-3 assistant 1stLt. Chip Gregson. Maj.Gen. Gregson commented that he knew nothing about "Worm Diagrams" and that it was probably the work of Capt. Rodney Cooke, 1st Recon's S-2, who "made major improvements to the intelligence operation, both in the product we gave the Division HQ and in what we fed back to the patrol leaders. Cooke gets all the credit for that, not any of the rest of us."

Cpl. Feldman noted, "I remember the day Cooke reverted back to enlisted, I started to salute and he stopped me and I said I'm not saluting the rank I'm saluting you, sir." (That apparently is the respect Cooke had earned among the Recon Marines---MDK).

The reports breakdown showed the Recon teams were finding makeshift hospitals, food caches and ammo caches along Charlie Ridge and on down a corridor near An Hoa. Coupled with the teams finding a buildup of an NVA Division just on the other side of the Laotian border, Drumright said that in evaluating the information it was determined two or three enemy Divisions were massing to carry out attacks in the Da Nang area. He noted the "Worm Diagram" prediction had it down to within a week to 10 days.

"That's why we started patrolling heavily along the Laotian border. We only had 640 people in 1st Recon. We started spreading them out and moving them around." At one point Hare said 1st Recon saturated the area around Da Nang with 53 Recon patrols. As the 26th Marines then the 7th Marines departed, the 1st Recon Bn. would assume coverage of their vacated areas.

"We were a battalion taking on a Tactical Area of Responsibility that a whole Division had been patrolling," said MSgt. Hare. He added that some men preferred the "safe confines" of the bush to being at Camp Reasoner as they didn't want to hang around there and get fired by Drumright who didn't like to see his men dawdling in the Rear.

**Crossing Over into Laos**

In 1970 Intelligence estimates indicated that the North Vietnamese had three Divisions 4 clicks inside "neutral" Laos preparing to cross the border into South Vietnam and attack various targets, according to Drumright. At one point the Intelligence guys lost track of the 375th NVA Division and needed real time information on where they'd gotten off to otherwise they could slip in-country and do some major damage.

"I sent my men into Laos dozens of times. Our Recon teams changed their call signs frequently each time they crossed over the border so the enemy wouldn't catch on to which teams were in Laos. Three teams from other military units were sent to find (the 375th) and all three were killed. (The brass) was nervous from Saigon up to Da Nang.

"Gen. Creighton Abrams (CG of the U.S. Military Assistance Command

Vietnam, MAC-V) took over Gen. (William C.) Westmoreland's place in July 1968. I had briefed Abrams on what I knew from our teams' debriefs having been in Laos. There were these three squares on the map in Laos I was very familiar with and Gen. Abrams asked me how I knew about those locations. (American forces weren't supposed to be crossing over into either Laos or Cambodia to the west of South Vietnam). I said we had made a lot of mistakes...4 click mistakes (going into Laos). He said it looked like we were making a lot of 'mistakes' (to know that area so well).

"We used Cobras a lot (for support) when we went into Laos. It really is hard to tell where the boundary is between Laos and Vietnam. We'd sneak into Laos, find a base camp and call in an F-4 airstrike. Nobody ever said anything to us about it. The Marine Air Wing and Recon were the best thing that ever lived!"

Cpl. Larry Feldman crossed over into Laos a few times and said they never really knew where they were as the maps they were given didn't show any references to Laos on them. He recalled going a few minutes flight time north on an insertion helicopter then turning west for a longer period of time flying in the direction of Laos a mere 50 miles from Da Nang.

Drumright said that Maj.Gen. Wheeler (CG, 1stMarDiv Headquarters, Ground, January 1-April 26, 1970) got excited about locating the 375th NVA Division which was unaccounted for across the border in either Laos or Cambodia and impressed upon him his 1st Recon Marines had to find them. "My best team had just come out of the bush. 2ndLt. John Hoff was a crazy guy...a kind of wild guy. He was also a total gentleman. I never heard him say a curse word in his life. He would go on to earn two Navy Crosses (I could only confirm one Navy Cross, possibly he was put in for two and one was downgraded to another medal---MDK). I sent his team into Laos the next morning. Once they were in, they made contact early in the day and it took all day to get them out utilizing Cobra gunships, F-4 fixed wing and everything in the air we could make available to them. Our artillery couldn't reach them they were so far into Laos."

Cpl. Feldman, Hoff's team radioman, indicated their 7-man team found the 375th NVA Division at 0730 in the morning and spent the next 8 hours on the run from them. "It's a good story, enough to scare the holy shit out of me just thinking about it. The hair is standing up on the back of my neck talking about it." He recalled fixed wing coming to their rescue with roughly 16 bombing runs against the enemy troops trying to run them down and to part the thick jungle to help the Recon team escape and evade those pursuers.

**1st Recon's Team Flakey Snow Delta from Echo Co. poses in front of Cobra gunship at Camp Reasoner's LZ, L-R, PFC Andy Timmons, LCpl. Randy Robinson, LCpl. Robert J. Beagle, HM3 Kenneth D. "Doc" Toline and PFC Larry M. Feldman. Not pictured 1stLt. John R. Hoff, team leader, and Cpl. P.J. Hanley. (Photo courtesy of Larry Feldman)**

"I asked Col. Drumright how he was finally able to get us out of there and his story was that he had to give up a canteen full of scotch to a pilot he knew to come pull us out of Laos," said Feldman.

Gen. Wheeler, a large man at either 6-foot-4 or 6-foot-6, asked to meet the 6-foot-6 tall Lt. Hoff when his team returned safe and sound to Camp Reasoner. He asked him how they found the 375th NVA Division so quickly. "Hoff found them because we knew where they were to start with (having sent many patrols into Laos)," noted Drumright. In the vein of never letting the facts get in the way of telling a good war story, the colonel said he was told (perhaps by someone with typical Marine hyperbole) that once on the ground in Laos the Recon team fired their weapons in the air to let the enemy find them. When presented with Drumright's recollection of how the 375th NVA Division was discovered, Feldman laughed and said that was not how it happened.

"Wheeler said to give Hoff the Navy Cross for that action," said Drumright.

Feldman attended the 1st Recon mini-reunion of Drumright's "boys" at the colonel's farm in 2003. "I hadn't seen the colonel in 33 years and the first thing he said to me after I told him who I was, he said, 'You're lucky you're alive.' I asked him why he would say that and he came back with, 'I sent you out on missions (to Laos) and watched you get on helicopters and I knew you weren't coming back.'

"I introduced him to my wife and he told her, 'Honey, you're lucky you have a husband because he went out to die a couple of times.' Each of those times the colonel personally came out to get us in the extraction helicopter."

**Pilots Do Superb Job Supporting 1st Recon**

"The pilots did a great job for us at 1st Recon. We never had trouble with the 1st Marine Air Wing pilots because they were superb. For instance, the pilots involved in trying to retrieve Skibbe the night of March 2, 1970. They did the best flying that night you ever saw in your life. They worked their way into the top of the trees and were so low their props were hitting the trees. The pilots did a wonderful job of getting us out of there alive that night.

"The crews and the pilots were just outstanding...off the page. Without them we couldn't have done anything. They were the greatest bunch of guys and we had the greatest support from the Wing and their commanders. Maj. Gen. William G. Thrash followed by Maj.Gen. Alan Armstrong (CGs of the 1st Marine Air Wing) both gave us 100 percent support.

"I really liked one of the 46 squadrons, The Purple Foxes. They always landed differently than anybody else. They turned their tails straight up. Whenever we saw the Purple Fox, we knew we were flying with the best of the best. They were our favorite.

"We had a party at Camp Reasoner and invited the pilots (from all the squadrons) over so they could meet the team leaders. Best thing I ever did. A pilot would hear someone say, 'Thin Man' and he knew exactly who he was talking to as that was how he knew the Recon teams...by their team call signs. They met them eyeball-to-eyeball. We tried to keep the call signs the same with each team (operating in- country)."

Drumright went on to say that all the inspections they held were done with the Air Wing, not 1stMarDiv. We were part of the Air Wing. We loved those guys. Gregson would brief the pilots and Recon teams together. They were close. They'd fly us anyplace, anytime.

"Only time I had a problem with the Wing was when I shot some holes in a helicopter one time. I was trying to get an extract up and I was shooting out the back at a machine gun that was shooting at us. I was trying to tell the pilot what was going on. I went down to shoot out the hell hole (in the middle of the Sea Knight) and I shot some holes in the floor. I shot six of 'em (with my automatic weapon). I went to tell the squadron CO I had shot six rounds into one of his helicopters and he said if that was the biggest problem I had to tell him then he wasn't worried about it."

On another occasion, Drumright said he was pulling a Marine aboard an extract helicopter when he lost his balance and fell into a rice paddy. "The crew chief didn't know I'd fallen out of the helicopter so he had given the pilot the all clear signal and they lifted off leaving me there. I backed up against a dike and sat there all night. I really wasn't scared. I stayed awake. The enemy came close to me during the night. They walked across the dike but they didn't see me. I just backed into the grass.

"Gen. Wheeler and I were big buddies. He contacted my wife, Jean, to let her know (I was MIA) and that they would be back in there the next day. He told her, 'Don't worry about Bill. He's happy as can be. He's as happy as a duck out there. He's playing cowboys and Indians.' He said that to her." Drumright noted he was picked up the next day without a problem.

## Bounty Placed on Drumright's Head by Enemy

How well a commander or his men are hurting the enemy can sometimes be judged by how many men are assigned to kill him or how high a bounty is placed on 1st Recon's "painted faces." Drumright recalled Gen. Wheeler informing him that Intelligence informants learned that 12 enemy sappers had been trained to kill him and a nice reward would go to the man or woman who got him. The colonel said he was told he could only go from Camp Reasoner to the 1stMarDiv CP by jeep during this high threat period.

"We were hurting them bad. We were killing them. They had taken out three teams of SOGs, three teams of SEALS, CIA operatives and some long range Army Recon units, but they couldn't get our Marine Recon teams. The reward for killing or capturing a Recon Marine was something they could retire on for three lifetimes. What they wanted to do was to kill one of our whole teams. That was what they were really after," said Drumright.

## "Putting Fear Aside"

I asked Drumright a question about any personal fear he might have felt going into harm's way which he had touched on 2 days earlier while talking to "his boys" (See "Perspectives on the Vietnam War, Part I"). I guess I wanted to know if what he was saying to his Recon Marines was rhetoric or what he truly believed so I asked the question at 2 a.m. after he had consumed many Chivas Regal and Gatorade mixed drinks, which I can only assume was his new "man's drink" evolved from the double scotch on the rocks he consumed at 2/26 in 1970 when I first met him.

"Were you ever afraid to step foot on the extract helicopter knowing your people were in deep shit and this was going to be a really bad one?" I looked deep into his eyes and watched for a telltale flicker or a sudden glance away before answering. He held my stare without wavering, which 33 years earlier would have turned a junior officer, such as myself, into stuttering, incoherent mush.

"I was always afraid. It would have been unnatural not to be afraid. But you put the fear aside by concentrating on the mission at hand to bring those boys home safely. I overrode the fear by thinking of my boys as the helicopter lifted off from LZ 401 and not myself."

In admitting he was, indeed, afraid, which surprised me, but managed to put that fear aside to worry about others, I was convinced the crusty old colonel had honestly told me and his men earlier what was in his warrior's soul. I recognized the fire still burning in his eyes from when I first met him in January 1970. I still remember the first words he spoke to me when I tried to bail out on one of his rapid fire war stories in the 2/26 Officers Club, "Where do you think you're going, peckerwood?" He was able to freeze me in my tracks with just those few words.

MSgt. Hare said he thought Lt.Col. Drumright wanted to die in combat as he tended to be in the thick of the action on hot extracts. Hare noted that he took a lot of chances most lieutenant colonels would generally make a point to avoid.

**Finding the Enemy Within**

The colonel recalled when he and 2ndLt. David Skibbe were involved in the train wreck caused by an explosion on the railroad tracks while he was CO of 2/26 (See Chapter 4). They were on their way north between Hue and Da Nang when the train engine was blown off the tracks at 1030 Thursday, November 13 by a command detonated mine.[5A] Lt.Col. Drumright and three Vietnamese civilian passengers were slightly injured. Two VC/NVA soldiers were observed fleeing to the west. Fox, 2/26 sent out units to search the area with negative results. Three Vietnamese farmers were rounded up from the field adjacent to the wrecked engine. In the course of interrogating them Drumright found that they were too well-spoken and educated to be simple farmers. He took the interrogation to the next level and one of the men revealed who set the explosive charge and who among the locals were VC.

He also had invaluable inside knowledge that a local ARVN dai uy (captain) and a general were actually working for the VC. Dai uy Tap had 2/26 tied up on bridge, railroad and road duties preventing them from doing saturation patrolling which allowed the VC to have the run of the 2/26 AO. The ARVN general had access to all the operations and troop displacements in the region. Any planned operation was cleared through the general who turned around and informed his VC buddies.

The dai uy had little choice but to rally to the South Vietnamese side and served in many capacities under the ARVNs against the VC/NVA after he was confronted. At the end of the Vietnam War, Drumright said the man was relocated with his family to Los Angeles where he ran a small store. He got a call from him one day saying three North Vietnamese men had come into his store and shot him leaving him for dead without taking a penny from the cash register. He surmised some of his past history was catching up with him.

And the general? Before Drumright had a chance to talk to him, the general had an urgent need to be flown down to Saigon for an important meeting. He failed to land in Saigon and everyone assumed he had crossed the border to the west or north to avoid being captured, according to Drumright.

At 2/26 Drumright recalled that his unit gave their Vietnamese allies, including the covert VC/ARVN general everything they wanted. "(At 2/26) we gave them access to our bunkers, food, vehicles and most importantly we gave them information. Nothing moved until they knew about it. (This was not the case with 1st Recon). That was why 1st Recon was so successful. We didn't give anybody information in advance. We went out and did whatever we wanted to."

I made a point of griping to Drumright about Vietnamese workers inside 2/1's Battalion Rear at Camp Lauer and the possibility of any one of them being a VC spy. Drumright said when he got to 1st Recon there was only a Miss Han working at their Officers Club...and she was immediately fired. One Vietnamese man did the laundry for the Recon Marines at Camp Reasoner and he picked the dirty clothes up outside the front gate. "I allowed no Vietnamese inside our wire at Reasoner," stated Drumright.

"You want to know who spied on us and as a result we got shot out of about five landing zones? Gen. Wheeler called me up one day to say we must have a leak because somebody is telling the enemy where the Recon teams are being inserted and they're there waiting on them. Wheeler flew down to the U.S. Army's Special Forces camp at Thuong Duc in his Huey and walked into their Command Operations Center. He asked the Green Beret honcho there who all he allowed into his COC. He assured the Marine general only Americans had access to the COC...no Vietnamese. At the back of the COC was a Vietnamese worker sweeping the floor with a full view of the large map of the region on a board with a plastic overlay of where the Marine Recon teams were and where others were scheduled to be inserted the next day.

"Gen. Wheeler came back to tell me where the 'leak' was coming from. I advised Lt. Gregson to no longer provide the Special Forces at Thuong Duc overlays of where our teams were operating or about to go in." He indicated that stopped the Recon teams' insert LZs from being compromised.

## Messing with the "Boss"

"An Army helicopter pilot requested permission to land as I was about to lay out in the sun to take a nap one day. I didn't want to talk to anyone so I told my driver, Tiny, to tell them to go away. They left and came right back and requested to land again. I told Tiny to give me the damn radio and I told the pilot we had a fire mission called in and he was in the airspace where the artillery rounds were coming through.

"Tiny said, 'But, sir, we don't have a fire mission called.'

"I told him we do now. I just called one. Come to find out it was Gen. Wheeler in that Army helicopter. He landed down on the highway and, boy, did he chew me out for that one," chuckled Drumright.

## Medals: Officers Versus Enlisted Marines

In 1970 Drumright noted that Brig.Gen. Edwin H. Simmons (1st Marine Division Headquarters Assistant Division Commander, June 16, 1970 to April 14, 1971) came down to Camp Reasoner to chew him out for his 1st Recon Battalion having the least amount of decorations in the Division although they did the most fighting with 65-68 percent of their unit always in the bush on any given day. "The 1st Marine Division band is more decorated than your men," complained the general.

"He wanted every patrol leader who went on five patrols to get the Bronze Star. If he made contact, the patrol leader got a Silver Star. Everyone who made five patrols should get a Bronze Star. That was told to me by Brig.Gen. Simmons as coming from Maj.Gen. Charles F. Widdecke (Deputy Commanding General, Ground, III Marine Amphibious Force Headquarters, April 27, 1970-April 14, 1971).

Drumright said it was about that time he was being replaced at 1st Recon and he didn't act on the order. One of the major reasons he objected to signing off on medals was that officers tended to get more than their share of medals compared to the enlisted. "I gave them (my men) (very few) medals because I didn't believe in medals. Medals to me didn't mean anything. There was too much of this dadburn stuff in Nam of officers writing officers up for damn medals. It's still going on.

"The enlisted man didn't have a chance. Every time I wrote a letter to get a medal for my men, I couldn't get the medal through III MAF because I didn't cross a 't' or dot an 'i' correctly. I wasn't the world's greatest writer. We didn't have anybody able to write up the citations that would meet III MAF's approval. My enlisted men didn't get an end of tour medal for leaving Vietnam either. Medals that did go through got knocked down from the medal they were put in for because of III MAF." The colonel recalled the specific name of the officer who gave him trouble at headquarters after 33 years.

He said that Bobby Campbell had the wounds to prove his being eligible for three Purple Hearts and was pulled out of combat and sent up to III MAF to be a general's aide. The general was beside himself wanting to know why Campbell didn't have at least one medal to go along with his three Purple Hearts.

"I told him there was a logjam at III MAF and they were knocking down every damn medal recommendation he had sent over there. The general said he knew Lt.Gen. Keith B. McCutcheon (CG, III MAF Headquarters). I will undo the logjam. Twenty minutes later everything started going. He broke the logjam."

"I refused to take an award for an officer that wasn't initiated by an enlisted man. Enlisted men *own* the Marine Corps. They *are* the Marine Corps. Every medal I got came from the enlisted men. The Marine Corps is the only outfit in the world that belongs to the enlisted men.

"Maj.Gen. Wheeler put me in for the Navy Cross. I found it in my in-box basket and tore it up and threw it in my wastebasket. I just wanted to lead my troops. I didn't want medals. Wheeler came down to my office and asked me why I didn't want that Navy Cross. I said, 'General, don't do this to me. Don't embarrass me in front of my men. What they do every damn day of the week, I do every once and awhile. Put me out in front of them and put a stupid ribbon on my chest may give me a promotion but it'll cause my men to lose all respect they had for me. I would rather have their respect than any goddamn Navy Cross. I'm getting that respect right now with just you guys coming to visit me.'"

Drumright noted his Recon Marines were paid a high compliment by Gen. McCutcheon one day. "I had 1st Recon 6½ months and never had one troop inspection. Gen. McCutcheon visited one day and watched as our patrols readied themselves at Camp Reasoner's LZ 401 to go out on an insert. He said they looked like combat Marines ought to look. And they did. They did their job and did it well. When they returned off patrol, they'd go to the Debriefing Room to give their report then drink their beer or soda pop. From their information, the general was able to tell where any attack was coming from. After they cleaned up and had some chow, they looked like they'd just come from 8th and I (Marine Corps Barracks in Washington, D.C.)." Cpl. Feldman noted the Recon Marines had two pairs of boots, one well-worn pair they used in the bush and another shined to a high sheen they kept in the Rear for wearing there.

## Gen. Leonard F. Chapman Jr., CMC, Visits 1st Recon

Col. Drumright said either or both the S-2 and S-3 sections gave such brilliant briefings to a visiting USMC Commandant Leonard F. Chapman Jr., the 24th CMC, about what was happening in Vietnam (from the intelligence deduced from the various Recon teams' reports) that he cancelled his itinerary for the rest of the day so he could spend it with 1st Recon.

"I took him out to an OP (Observation Post in the mountains) and Sgt. Frank E. Diaz of Hephzibah, Georgia, an Echo Co., 1st Recon patrol leader, had captured a prisoner the night before and also gave the general a tremendous briefing. I got a photo of Gen. Chapman presenting Diaz a Silver Star (for a previous action June 14, 1970 as team leader of Team Flakey Snow involving 50 enemy soldiers, at least 18 of which the team killed, while sustaining one Marine mortally wounded, one Marine WIA and one South Korean WIA.[6] LCpl. Gary Wayne Ragsdale, 19, of Kerman, California would also receive a posthumous Silver Star for the action).[7] So the sun started going down and Chapman kept talking about how pretty it was out there (on that mountaintop). He said this was the most enjoyable day he'd had since becoming the Commandant of the Marine Corps. He remarked that since he had become the Commandant he had turned the Marine Corps over to his generals so he could spend time getting money from the U.S. Congress. That was the CMC's job...to get money." He noted that Chapman was a pretty good Commandant in his estimation.

Drumright said that too many Commandants and generals by the 1980s had never commanded a rifle platoon or was a CO of a combat company or battalion which did not bode well for the Marine Corps. He also complained, "Politicians are taking over the Marine Corps. Nice fellows don't win wars. You can't kiss asses and kill people."

The colonel said the Commandant couldn't go before Congress and tell them to go to hell. "You might not get too much money for the Marine Corps that way but you sure would get their respect. We haven't had a Commandant who has had enough balls to go to Congress and tell them (what he really thinks of them). That's what we need right now, a Commandant that's tough..."

He felt the Marine Corps had overlooked a good man in Gen. Ernie Cheatham Jr., a bona fide hero in the fight for Hue City during the Tet Offensive in 1968, in choosing its Commandants.

Hare said Drumright was an instructor at TBS for a lengthy period at a point in his career and got the respect of many Marine officers who went on to become generals. At Drumright's retirement from the Marine Corps, Hare recalled one of the high ranking officers offered this comment, "This is the kind of guy you put under glass and break that glass in time of war when you need him."

**Reclaiming Lives**

"(At some point after I retired to Columbia, Tennessee), a recruiter came to me with two young men (graduating from high school) who had been busted for possession of marijuana. The Marine Corps wouldn't take them with the marijuana conviction on their records. I called the judge and convinced him to wipe their records clean as I thought they would make damn good Marines after talking to them at length.

"As it turned out, one of them completed Parris Island number one in his platoon and the other one was recommended for OCS. I took them both down to see the judge when they returned home from boot camp and told the judge he had done a good job (giving them a second chance)."

**Drumright Honors Feldman, Passes in 2003**

Kurt Drumright, the colonel's son, told Cpl. Feldman that his father once said that he was his kid but that he wasn't his only "son" in referring to the corporal. "When I met Kurt, he told me his dad had talked about me all his life. I was adopted and Drumright was like a father to me. I respected him but some people were scared of him and would go the other way to avoid him when they saw him," said Feldman.

The former Recon corporal continued, "At Pendleton I went AWOL at staging not really worrying how much trouble I was going to get into. I asked myself, 'What are they gonna do? Shave my head and send me to Vietnam as punishment?' I was busted to private and frozen at that rank for 6 months. At 1st Recon in Vietnam I did my job in the bush for Lt.Col. Drumright so he promoted me meritoriously to PFC, then lance corporal during those 6 months. I heard he had an IQ above 160. He was well known as a very intelligent man. The last time we talked he told me, 'I love you, I love, I love you.' I'll never forget him."

The colonel's prediction he wouldn't live to see 2004 came true as he lapsed into a coma on Wednesday, December 3, 2003. He joined "his boys" guarding the gates of Heaven the next day.

Former LCpl. Mike Simpson, who had visited Drumright over the 2003 Memorial Weekend, notified several of us about the end of the colonel's long struggle with health problems by emailing, "Col. Bill Drumright passed away today. I feel like I lost my dad. Never a more unique person ever lived. He had a long, full life and was loved by many. We will miss him more than I can say. Semper Fi, Mike."

I didn't find out until he'd passed that the colonel had an impressive array of medals to his credit that stretched back to the Korean War. He was awarded the Silver Star, Bronze Star with Combat "V", Legion of Merit with Combat "V", Purple Heart and Vietnamese Cross of Gallantry with Palm and frame. Col. Drumright was laid to rest with full military honors in Williamson Memorial Gardens in Franklin, Tennessee, just north of his Columbia home. His pallbearers were Lt.Col. Terry Moore, MSgt. John Hare, Doc White, Cpl. Larry Feldman, 1stSgt. Larry Keen and MSgt. Dan Williams. Honorary pallbearers were members of the 1st Recon Battalion, 1stMarDiv, Da Nang, South Vietnam and members of the Round Table at Poplar House Restaurant.

I feel honored that Col. Drumright allowed me to interview him one last time even though I was only briefly one of "his boys." I was particularly touched by the colonel's words of comfort and heartfelt praise of Capt. McVey to his sons, Jeff and Shawn, during their long stay at his house that May 2003. He is definitely a rare breed of Old Corps Marine and I will always remember him answering my questions while wearing his coveted French Foreign Legion kepi cover he'd been presented as a Marine exchange officer with the world famous Legionnaires. "His boys" will never forget him.

Retired MSgt. Williams followed through on a request by Col. Drumright to present Cpl. Feldman with a Marine Raider's black Ka-Bar knife and sheath (the same type the colonel always carried in combat). I think this was the highest honor Drumright could bestow on any Recon Marine serving in his command. No better Marine could have been singled out than Drumright's "son."

As of 2011, Feldman was a defensive team coach for Wesley College, a private college in Dover, Delaware (12-1 in 2010; 13-1 in 2009; 9-2 in 2008; 11-2 in 2007; 13-1 in 2006; and 12-2 in 2005). Woverines made it to the NCAA Division III semi-finals 4 out of the last 5 years from a pool of 228 teams before losing. They were the champions of the Atlantic Central Football Conference all 5 years. I'm betting the former Recon Marine who impressed the likes of Col. Drumright made one helluva good defensive football coach as well.

**Drumright's View of the Vietnam War and Marines in Retrospect**

"I loved the Marine Corps. I ate it up. It was perfect for me. I commanded a rifle platoon, a rifle company, two Recon companies, a rifle battalion and two Force Recon companies (during my career). The best command was 1st Recon Battalion in 1970. I enjoyed those guys. I kicked their asses all the time. They said they were afraid of me.

"My guys could out walk their guys, could out-maneuver their guys and out shoot 'em. We got fire support, aviation and artillery when we needed it. Those Marines who stood out to me were big Lt. John Hoff, Cpl. Larry Feldman, Lt. Gary Allord and Sgt.s like Ed Gunkel (from Texas). I had the best teams you could ask for. I turned them loose. I let them carry the weapons they wanted to carry (M-16s, shotguns, AK-47s, M-14s, Swedish-K grease guns, etc.). Most teams liked to carry the M-14 for their long shots. I liked to carry an M-16 with the barrel reduced down to 6-inches and a sliding out stock on it I got from Larry Keen when he got leg shot. My guys didn't like the M-16 rifle." Drumright also spoke highly of Gy.Sgt. Terry Moore and SSgt. John Hare.

I asked Drumright what his overall view of the Vietnam War was in his final analysis?

"It was waste, a total waste. We wasted Skibbe. He could've been a senator. We needed these men to head this country. We need men to be Congressmen and President. We don't need any more weak-willed men to run this country...we've had enough of them. We need men who will stand up. George Washington once said there were two things that could destroy America. Don't ever send your boys out of country to fight and don't ever get your country in debt. We're doing both of them."

The colonel said he was terribly disappointed in *Desert Storm* when we had the Iraqis whipped the first time and didn't finish Saddam Hussein off. He figured that Saddam wasn't the real reason for our war with Iraq. "Everything in the Middle East is about oil. I think the Marines did great. But what did they accomplish? They did what Marines are supposed to do but did it make any difference since we didn't get Saddam (first time around)? There are people out there who can blow up anything because they have the money to protect themselves. My old Daddy once told me that greed will kill us all someday."

# Chapter 10

**The lure of Vietnam was more than an intellectual exercise for Dr. Bernard Fall. His wife, Dorothy, indicated he was returning to the excitement of war, to risk-taking and the camaraderie of soldiers in combat, which intoxicated him. She called Vietnam "his mistress" while he referred to it as "a bad love affair." He appeared to be reliving the death-defying moments of his youth fighting in the French Underground/Resistance (the Maquis) against the Germans in WW II as he flew combat missions in Vietnam on Marine helicopters in 1965. Also, later as he saw things "firsthand" and obtained "hard facts" while visiting 3/3 Marines at The Rockpile in December 1966. And again, by traversing dangerous ground one last time with 1/9 ("The Walking Dead") on the *Street Without Joy* in February 1967.[1]**

**Dorothy Fall, author**
***Bernard Fall, Memories of a Soldier-Scholar***

## Dr. Bernard Fall: French Indochina, Vietnam War Writer/Historian

Without a doubt, I have always felt I owed Dr. Bernard B. Fall a debt of gratitude for the two books he wrote that I read before embarking for Vietnam...*Street Without Joy* and *Hell in a Very Small Place: The Siege of Dien Bien Phu*. I'm sure other officers from all the U.S. military services had the same special feeling of having been prepared for what we were about to encounter in Vietnam through the vicarious exposure his writing gave us of the French Indochina War. All we had to do was substitute "American" and "VC/NVA" for "French" and "Viet Minh" and our war was strikingly similar to their war.

Dorothy Fall has written about her husband's death in Vietnam in two excellent books, *Bernard Fall, Memories of a Soldier-Scholar* and *Last Reflections on a War: Bernard B. Fall on Viet-Nam*. But, I wanted to tell the story of Dr. Fall from the viewpoint of the 1/9 Marines and Navy Corpsmen on the ground in the days leading up to his death and the day he was killed by a boobytrap. "Official" reports don't always tell the whole story and I've found "boots on the ground" and medevac pilots' view from the air generally give more clarity to what really happened as a result.

In my research I was pleasantly surprised to discover Lt.Col. Bill Leftwich Jr. had actually sat down with Dr. Fall for a brief interview before the professor left for Vietnam the last time. Dr. Fall's laser-like insights on war in Vietnam came out in Leftwich's article printed in the *Marine Corps Gazette*.

Dr. Fall was an amazingly inquisitive historian whose books saved many American lives in Vietnam by making us respect the tenacity of our VC/NVA foe...and that inquisitiveness is probably what killed him in the end. It only seemed right that when he died the former World War II French Maquis fighter should die among some of this country's most elite warriors...U.S. Marines.

## World War II

Life was tough for Bernard Fall growing up on the eve of World War II. He was born in Vienna, Austria in 1926 and by age 12 with his Jewish parents, Leo and Anna (Seligman) Fall, and sister, Lisette, fled Austria for France in 1938 when the Germans annexed it. The Nazis jailed many Jews and confiscated their businesses making it impossible for them to stay.[2]

By 16 Bernard was fighting in the French Underground/Resistance against the Germans, Italians and their French collaborators. His fight became personal with the cold-blooded murder of his parents—Leo was tortured to death by the Gestapo in 1943.[3] Anna was deported to the German death camp at Auschwitz outside Oswiecim, Poland in 1942[4] where she died along with 1.6 million other Jews (an estimated 5.6 to 6.25 million European Jews were murdered by the Nazis in WW II).[5] Bernard and Lisette managed to evade capture over the duration of the war.

## The Scholar

In the post-WW II Nuremberg War Crimes Tribunal, Fall served as a research analyst investigating the Krupp industrial giant. Exceptionally bright, he completed his undergraduate studies at the world-famous Sorbonne in Paris, France and the University of Munich in Germany.[6]

He came to Syracuse University in New York in 1951 on a Fulbright Scholarship to work on his masters' degree on the illegal re-arming of Germany. In 1952 after completing his masters, he was attending classes at Johns Hopkins School for Advanced International Studies in Washington, D.C. when his professor suggested he write his doctoral thesis on the French Indochina War and, thus, began his obsession with that part of the world.[7]

His fieldwork, May-December 1953, actually took him to Vietnam at his own expense while the French were still fighting the Viet Minh. The Frenchman exhibited the same "living on the edge" traits as he was thrown into during WW II with his research methodology in Vietnam by going into the jungle with French soldiers and flying on resupply and reconnaissance missions. He finished his 1,000-plus page doctoral work at Syracuse University in December 1954.[8]

The first book to come out of his doctoral paper was *The Viet-Minh Regime* in 1954. In 1956 he was hired as an associate professor to teach international relations at Howard University in Washington, D.C. He followed up his book with many articles and papers on Southeast Asia and two very well-written works, *Street Without Joy* (1961) and *Hell in a Very Small Place: The Siege of Dien Bien Phu* (1966). He researched extensively the decisive battle at Dien Bien Phu where the Viet Minh marshaled 49,500 combat troops with 55,000 in support and artillery to defeat the French Union Forces' 15,000-man garrison. A shaky cease-fire split the country into North and South Vietnam in 1954.

By 1962 the Frenchman was so respected as an impartial historian worldwide that he was granted interviews with French-speaking Ho Chi Minh and Pham Van Dong, North Vietnam's top leadership. Dr. Fall improved his standing with Ho Chi Minh by providing the introduction and editing a collection of his writings entitled, *Ho Chi Minh: On Revolution*.

Although he had been in America since 1951 and had married an American citizen, Dorothy Winer, February 20, 1954, Dr. Fall had retained his French citizenship and had not sought to become an American citizen. This probably allowed him to avoid the State Department's restrictions on Americans visiting places like North Vietnam and also opened doors that were otherwise closed to U.S. citizens by foreign countries at odds with us.

In his early writings, he didn't think the French would prevail over the Viet Minh and was critical of the United States for not supporting the French Army in Vietnam in 1954. He was equally negative on America's chances of winning the war when they took over from the French. He did not like the corrupt government of South Vietnam's Ngo Dinh Diem (Diem would be assassinated along with his brother in 1963 with the U.S. government's tacit approval). He warned that America had not learned from the French Indochina War and may very well be doomed to repeat the past. He gave this message in lectures at the Foreign Service Institute, National War College, the service academies and a multitude of other civilian venues.

The Federal Bureau of Investigation maintained surveillance on Dr. Fall due to his speaking out and writing that America couldn't win in Vietnam. Powers to be didn't want to hear his knowledgeable pessimistic outlook on the war...a pessimism that eventually became a reality.

In his book, *My American Journey*, (1995), Colin Powell made a poignant learned observation reflecting on the writings of Dr. Fall. "I recently reread Bernard Fall's book on Vietnam, *Street Without Joy*. Fall makes painfully clear that we had no understanding of what we had gotten ourselves into. I cannot help thinking that if President Kennedy or President Johnson had spent a quiet weekend at Camp David reading that perceptive book, they would have returned to the White House Monday morning and immediately started to figure out a way to extricate us from the quicksand of Vietnam."[9]

Powell's comment carried a lot of knowledgeable weight considering his background included serving two tours in Vietnam as a U.S. Army officer (1962-63, 1968-69), Deputy Secretary of Defense in Pres. Jimmy Carter's Administration (1977-81) and the National Security advisor under Pres. Ronald Reagan (1987-89). He was also chairman of the Joint Chiefs of Staff under Pres. George H.W. Bush (1989-1993) in the successful *Operation Desert Storm* in Gulf War I and was Secretary of State under Pres. George W. Bush (1999-2001).

**Leftwich Interviews Dr. Fall, December, 1966**

A year after his return from his first tour of duty in Vietnam (1965) Lt.Col. Bill Leftwich interviewed 40-year-old Dr. Fall, who was by then the acknowledged top expert on Vietnam, for a thesis research paper and later an article 2 days before the professor departed once more for the war zone to do additional research.

Dr. Fall was packing for the trip as they talked. He had just completed the final touches on *Hell in a Very Small Place: The Siege of Dien Bien Phu*, which would be published in January when he was in Vietnam. (Marine Maj. Bill Leftwich III recalled his dad receiving a copy of *Hell in a Very Small Place: The Siege of Dien Bien Phu* from his wife, Jane, for his birthday in April following its publication after he expressed to her what a great admirer he was of Dr. Fall---MDK).

In that December 1966 meeting, Dr. Fall said that he was continuing his studies on Vietnam thanks to a *John Simon Guggenheim Memorial Foundation Fellowship* grant. The scope of the grant involved a "socio-political study of the South Viet-Nam National Liberation Front (NFLSV)."[10]

To gain a perspective from the Viet Cong's point of view, Dr. Fall's winning proposal to the Guggenheim board was to conduct "interviews with hundreds of ex-members through the South Vietnam POW camps and procurement of documentation from Western sources in Vietnam and France. He also wrote that he would contact the NFLSV (in French, Nationale Front de Liberation South Viet-Nam or simply Viet Cong) representatives and interview American and South Vietnamese officials dealing with the Viet Cong problem."[11]

Gen. Wallace M. Greene, 23rd USMC Commandant (1964-1967), asked the impressive war historian to spend some time with his Marines in Vietnam (in I Corps) and he had agreed to do it.[12] From December 1966 to February 18, 1967 he would visit Saigon, Da Nang, The Rockpile, Camp J.J. Carroll and Dong Ha (the latter location was part of the highly volatile "Leatherneck

Square" that also included Cam Lo, Con Thien and Gio Linh) in Quang Tri Province abutting the DMZ.

Dr. Fall would also be embedded with 1st Battalion, 9th Marines (1/9), 3rdMarDiv in Thua Thien Province just below Quang Tri, February 19-21, 1967 during a portion of *Operation Chinook II*. This was Dr. Fall's sixth trip to Vietnam having graced its shores in 1953, 1957, 1962, 1965 and 1966-67. He would not survive his combat experience with the 1/9 Marines.

The commandant's purpose for asking Dr. Fall to visit with his Marines was that the USMC would receive free publicity and be a boost to its image to have him write about them.

*AP* Bureau chief Pyle's remark in the front of *Book II* in "Perspectives on the Vietnam War" comes to mind in that the Marine Corps would do anything to get the press, or in Dr. Fall's case, a famous French Indochina War/Vietnam War writer/historian, to cover them "against our better judgment" while engaged with the enemy on the battlefield.

The result of Bill Leftwich's interview became the article entitled, "An Afternoon With Bernard Fall" and wouldn't appear in the *Marine Corps Gazette* until 2 years later. The original research was for his thesis at the Marine Corps' Staff and Command College at Quantico.[13]

In the article Dr. Fall made some prophetic observations that not only applied to Vietnam but to future conflicts in Somalia, Afghanistan and Iraq, when Bill asked him about the magnitude of the enemies' losses. "Casualties don't mean anything to them; they do to us because we're round-eyes; we've got to quit thinking in terms of our own concepts of loss."[14]

Dr. Fall was not impressed with the U.S. Army's innovative air cavalry tactics because "...helicopters were simply too vulnerable to carry the total transportation load."[15]

When asked about what he thought of America's progress in the war, Dr. Fall stated, "We'll win when we ultimately get the 10 or 11 to 1 superiority that's needed. By that time American firepower will have destroyed everything in the country anyway; then what'll you have?"[16]

Dr. Fall based his figures on the anti-guerrilla warfare success of the Malaya/British forces of 50-1 versus the insurgents in Malaya; Cyprus/British forces of 110-1 versus insurgents on Cyprus; and French forces 10-1 in Algeria fighting insurgents.[17] Going by those numbers he predicted it would take over 1 million RVN troops (RVN barely had 500,000 in 1964) to overwhelm the estimated 125,000 VC guerrillas fighting them.[18]

The major's awe and admiration of Dr. Fall was evident throughout the *Marine Corps Gazette* piece. He even appeared embarrassed at one point that the professor had actually reviewed one of his many published articles on the advisor's role in Vietnam.[19]

In writing "...and a few Marines" in the *Proceedings of the United States Naval Institute* in August, 1968, Leftwich noted that there was a basic conflict between the energetic Westerner (Marine advisor, in this case) and the unhurried Oriental. The experienced counterinsurgent does not consider war a suspension of normal life as we do, but perhaps the only way of life he has known and is in it for the long haul compared to our impatience to get the job done quickly. Dr. Fall noted in their 1966 interview, "The American take-charge attitude is our own greatest enemy."[20]

"Bill was very impressed with Dr. Bernard Fall. He wished he could've spent more time talking with him. He was very interested in the French in Indochina and Dr. Fall certainly knew everything that had taken place during that war like Dien Bien Phu. Bill said he was a brilliant man and listened closely to what he had to say," said his wife, Jane.

In having read both men's thoughts and strategy concerns on Vietnam, a distinct similarity stands out in their writings. What Dr. Fall theorized on and suggested as a cure, Bill Leftwich had the opportunity to put into motion from a command position. They were a good fit and it was interesting they should meet and talk one last time.

**Fall Visits 3rdMarDiv Marines Near DMZ, December 1966**

Dr. Fall arrived at Tan Son Nhut Airport outside Saigon sometime in December after briefly stopping off to arrange housing for his family and schools for two of his three girls in Hong Kong. It wasn't long before he was off to I Corps to fulfill his promise to CMC Gen. Greene. He flew up to Da Nang and from there made his way to the highly contested area below the DMZ starting with Dong Ha.

At least one Marine officer attached to 1/9 would comment about the professor having a "death wish" when it came to walking through heavily mined areas in I Corps during a sweep on the *Street Without Joy* in February 1967. He complained that he wandered where he pleased on dangerous ground. His observation may not have been far off the mark.

In 1964 one of Dr. Fall's kidneys was removed and he was on medication to keep the other kidney functioning. His wife would note in her book, *Bernard Fall, Memories of a Soldier-Scholar* released in September 2006, that he seemed to be looking for that last hurrah, perhaps thinking that if he were to die soon anyway, why not go out in the thrill of battle?[21]

The 3rdMarDiv Informational Services Office (ISO) listed Dr. Fall as among 68 civilian news correspondents visiting Dong Ha as well as 23 newsmen at

Phu Bai in December. They would tread life-threatening terrain to gain inside information for their reports on the war.

### *Operations Hastings, Prairie*

Understand that three NVA regiments of the 324B Division--90th, 803rd and 812th--consisting of roughly 11,000 soldiers had fought 8,000 Marines and 3,000 ARVNs just 5 months before the professor's visit, July 26-August 3, 1966 in *Operation Hastings*. The fighting occurred between the DMZ and 6 miles (10 clicks) south to The Rockpile, a 750-foot "toothpick-type" mountain that stuck out in the middle of an open area that dominated the surrounding landscape where three river valleys converged. The Marines sustained 126 KIA and 448 WIA in pitched battles during the operation while the ARVNs had 21 KIA and 40 WIA compared to the enemy's 700 NVA KIA and 17 NVA POW.

*Operation Prairie* followed quickly on the heels of *Hastings* August 3-September 13, 1966 resulting in 200 Marines KIA and over 1,000 WIA. The enemy suffered over 1,000 NVA killed. The Marines established a base of operations at The Rockpile. It was 16 miles west of Dong Ha and a mere 7 miles to where the 324B NVA Division established its headquarters on Hill 208 just inside the DMZ during *Operations Hastings* and *Prairie*.

### Christmas '66 With 3/3 at The Rockpile

Both sides agreed to a cease-fire truce December 22-25. On Christmas Eve Dr. Fall wrote a brief letter to his wife Dorothy that he left behind in his personal effects to be opened only if he should die...which he did less than 2 months later. In the letter he would tell his wife and girls how much he loved them and was proud of them. He closed by saying he felt he had to be a witness to "this incredibly stupid and brutal war."[22]

Next day he flew out to The Rockpile to visit Marines from Lima Co., 3rd Battalion, 3rd Marine Regiment (Lima, 3/3) holding the position. 3rdMarDiv's Chronology notes that one of 3/3's units was mortared sometime Christmas Day and in all likelihood was The Rockpile. Dorothy doesn't mention her husband being involved in any mortaring incidents Christmas Day in the book she published a few years after his death. She pored over his notes and tape recorder that gave a day-by-day, play-by-play on the ground in her book.

The constricted top of The Rockpile consisted of a 6-square-foot platform good only for resting the right wheel of the UH-34D Seahorse helicopter on to offload supplies and troops or picking up same in the fall of 1966. By the summer of 1967 a platform had been built there of size and strength to land the UH-34D and was a definite improvement, according to Lt. Hugh Smith of Gilroy, California, Seahorse pilot with HMM-161 flying out of Phu Bai from August to October 1966 and with HMM-163 also at Phu Bai, from December

1966 to August 1967. (Lt. Smith said the unit was called "Evileyes" due to large eyes painted on the nose of the helicopters in deference to "Super Chief" others called the unit---MDK).

Dr. Fall visited Camp J.J. Carroll where Marine and U.S. Army artillery batteries were building up to give more support to the ground units below the DMZ. The base was named for Navy Cross winner Capt. James J. Carroll, 29, of Miami Beach, Florida who was killed after only one month in-country while leading Kilo Co., 3rd Battalion, 4th Marine Regiment (Kilo, 3/4) against entrenched NVA soldiers on Mutter Ridge, 3-4 miles due north of The Rockpile, October 5, 1966. Prof. Fall was on the cutting edge of combat to be in-country just under 3 months after a camp was named for a fallen Marine hero.

Also, the Marines had replaced a U.S. Army Special Forces team at Khe Sanh September 29, 1966, a little under 3 months before his arrival. For a war historian and a Type A personality when it came to wanting to be around combat when the bullets, mortars, RPGs, artillery and rockets were flying, Dr. Fall was pushing the envelope by being on the ground of a war evolving into widespread mayhem and, thus, was in his element with the Marines.

The color and action for Dr. Fall's research paper, funded by a Guggenheim grant and eventual book, would come from walking over a highly contested battlefield with 1/9 Marines during *Chinook II* February 19-21, 1967 on Highway 597 in an area better known as the infamous Street Without Joy. Over an 18-year period many bodies from opposing sides littered the bloodstained sand from both the French Indochina and present Vietnam Wars along this coast road. Dr. Fall had documented the most significant battles in numerous books over that same timeframe.

To get an idea of what danger awaited Dr. Fall and 1/9 during *Chinook II* in 1967, it's best to look at three previous operations in 1966-67 which encompassed the same general area. In all three operations, the Leathernecks would seek to destroy elements of the battle-hardened 802d VC Battalion.

### *Operation Oregon,* March 19-23, 1966

In *Operation Oregon,* March 19-23, 1966, 2nd Battalion, 1st Marines and the 3rd ARVN Regiment with support from six 155mm howitzers displaced to outside Phong Dien[23A] on Highway 1. They faced two companies of the 802d VC Battalion, 250 men, in the Ap Chinh An, Ap Phu An and Ap Tay Hoang area along Highway 597 above Phu Bai in I Corp's Thua Thien Province.

After waiting for a heavy fog to lift, Sea Knights landed two Marine companies from 2/1 in a LZ at 1255 Saturday, March 19 just 800 meters outside Ap Chinh An where, unbeknownst to the Marines, two VC companies and a heavy weapons company awaited them.[23B] The enemy opened up from bunkers and fighting holes within the fortified ville as the Marines drew near. A minefield surrounding Ap Chinh An added to the casualty count as 2/1 lost the equivalent of a platoon assaulting the ville. The VC pounded the Marines with 61mm mortars, 82mm mortars and heavy machine guns. The result was 9 USMC KIA and 41 USMC WIA.

The two USMC companies pulled back and clobbered Ap Chinh An with naval gunfire and awaited reinforcements the next day to overwhelm the enemy force. *Operation Oregon* concluded after 4 days with the enemy losing 48 VC KIA, 8 VC POW and an estimated 100 killed altogether with most of them removed from the battlefield by their compadres. The Marines had a final tally of 11 KIA and 45 WIA.

In analyzing the results of *Operation Oregon*, it was surmised that 2/1 was too lightly armed to take on the heavily-armed VC thus limiting their maneuverability. The Marine commanders grudgingly acknowledged that the VC they faced were seasoned and well-trained.

### *Operation Jay*, June 25-July 2, 1966

In *Operation Jay,* June 25-July 2, a major Marine force that included grunts from 2/4, 2/1 and 3/4 and 2/12 artillery, fixed wing and helicopter support from 1st MAW, U.S. Navy gunfire support from a ship in the Gulf of Tonkin along with two battalions from the 1st ARVN Division and 2nd Battalion of the Vietnamese Marine Brigade, VNMC. They were opposed by the VC's 802d, 806th and 812th Battalions. Future commandant, Lt.Col. Paul X. Kelley (1983-87), commanded 2/4 in the successful operation.

All the major fighting took place around Ap Chinh An, again, and Ap My Phu[23C] along Highway 597 and Phong Dien on Highway 1. These locations would be revisited by 1/9 and Dr. Fall during *Operation Chinook II*, February 19-21, 1967.

During the course of *Operation Jay*, Marines killed 475 enemy troops causing the 812th VC Battalion to cease to exist. 2/1 and 3/4 reported Marine casualties of 23 KIA and 48 WIA June 25-28 while the VNMC battalion lost 42 KIAs in a well-executed roadside ambush by the VC at Phong Dien.

A big difference between *Operation Jay* and the upcoming *Operation Chinook II* was that bad weather did not affect *Jay's* heliborne assault plans. Nineteen MAG-16 Sea Knights deposited Marines at several LZs along Highway 597 including the other side of a body of water separating Ap Trung Kieu (1)[23D] and the Ap Dong Ha (1)[23E] ville complex effectively stopping the 802d VC Battalion from using the water as a barrier to keep the Marines at bay, so to speak. The VC destroyed a bridge that had previously connected the two areas across a 100-meter wide river.

Rainy season in I Corps is from October to February. For the kick-off of *Operation Chinook II* February 19, 1/9 wouldn't have helicopters available to them due to inclement weather still hanging around from the monsoons. This changed the fighting dynamics of *Operation Chinook II* as compared to *Operations Oregon* and *Jay*.

3rdMarDiv's ISO indicated only 15 civilian news correspondents visited the Marines at Phu Bai and 50, including Dr. Fall, braved going into the Dong Ha area in February. By the summer of '67, the NVA would have 130 artillery pieces and long-range rockets situated north of the DMZ that could take all the Marine bases in Leatherneck Square under fire. Khe Sanh was targeted from mountainous locations in Laos. Compared to the 3rdMarDiv's TAOR, I'm sure less adventurous visiting reporters found Saigon a much safer location from which to gather information for their stories submitted to their publications stateside...not Dr. Fall.

### *Operation Chinook*, December 22, 1966-January 2, 1967

The active 802d VC Battalion attacked three South Vietnamese strongpoints around Phong Dien on December 10, 1966. The 3rd Battalion, 26th Marines (3/26) and Vietnamese units were supported by accompanying artillery which established a fighting position 3,000 meters south of Phong Dien and west of Highway 1 on December 19. During the Christmas truce December 22 and 23, the 802d VC Battalion launched two sizeable attacks against the Marines.

*Operation Chinook* began December 22 with 2nd and 3rd Battalions, 26th Marines and Recon troops from Phu Bai spearheading the sweep seeking to destroy the VC unit. Monsoons limited air support during the operation.

Taking advantage of the New Year's truce and stand down to slip away from the encroaching USMC units, Marine Recon patrols spotted 1,000 enemy troops moving north from Co Bi-Thanh Tan on the west side of Highway 1. They were amazed at what they saw.

"We heard they were marching at sling arms four abreast," said MSgt. John Hare, who was on his second tour in Vietnam serving as an advisor with MAC-V, SOG from 1966-67. "When the Recon team observing them reported this to their Recon unit, they reacted with disbelief and passed it along to MAC-V in Saigon. They found it hard to believe the NVA would do that (make themselves such a huge juicy target) and ordered a Bird Dog L-19 aircraft to overfly the reported formation. At first they didn't see anything below them then they realized all those 'bushes' (their typical camouflage) on the move were enemy troops. The Recon team was ordered to clear the area so artillery could bracket the whole formation."

Artillery was brought to bear on the large troop displacement. The running battle with the VC units ended on January 2, 1967 as *Operation Chinook* came to a close. Phase I of *Chinook II* began February 16 with the actual displacement of 1/9 and 1st ARVN Division units to the target area February 19. This coordinated force took the lead in chasing down enemy troops around Highway 597 east of Phong Dien and Highway 1.

### *Operation Chinook II*

### Dr. Fall Walks Dangerous Ground With 1/9

Dr. Fall was 1/9's VIP guest on its sweep from Phong Dien on Highway 1 to the northeast across a wide expanse of sand dunes and to what the 1st Marine Air Wing, MAW, referred to as the "Finger Lakes-Street Without Joy" area. 1/9 continued on down Highway 597 to the southeast during Phase 1 of *Operation Chinook II,* February 19-21, 1967.

Gy.Sgt. Byron Grant Highland, 33, of Detroit, Michigan, SSgt. Edward D. "Ed" Grantham and Cpl. Cal Guthrie accompanied Dr. Fall as 3rdMarDiv's USMC Combat Correspondents/photographers. Two other Marines who received photo credit during the operation and were probably ISO photographers embedded with 1/9 as well included LCpl. S.N. Leighty and LCpl. E.L. Cole.

The operation area was only 40 miles from the DMZ separating North from South Vietnam up always-dangerous Highway 1. A few miles to the south was a portion of the *Street Without Joy* area Dr. Fall wrote so much about as being the graveyard of French Union soldiers. 1/9 operated so far north in I Corps that at one point the battalion was 4 miles southwest of the Gulf of Tonkin (no longer called South China Sea on the area maps but the part of the sea that started America's participation in the Vietnam War at full throttle). To the west of Highway 1 from Phong Dien northward to the DMZ many small towns' and villes' names show up on the maps but were ominously underscored by the terms "(destroyed)" or "(abandoned)." Two wars back-to-back had devastated the area.

Dr. Fall was supposed to meet his wife and daughters in Hong Kong on February 19, a day before their 13th wedding anniversary, but the prospect of observing Marines in combat in real time during a rice denial/search and destroy mission was too enticing to walk away from. His "bad love affair" with Vietnam would come to an end. His "mistress" would lead to his demise, as Dorothy feared.

"Fall was in and out of Vietnam from Hong Kong. He would go visit different (military) units then write articles about them. He'd check out different theories and go out to places he'd been during the French Indochina War. In the end, he was just unlucky," recalled Peter Arnett, 30, of Invercargill, New Zealand, an *Associated Press, AP,* war correspondent.

## Phong Dien to Northeast of Highway 1, February 19, 1967

1/9 had departed Vietnam for Okinawa September 29, 1966 as part of the intratheater battalion rotation policy. The fresh battalion trained, refitted and was brought up to strength with replacement troops. 1/9 returned in-country at Phu Bai aboard ship on Sunday, February 5, 1967. They were thrown into battle with the VC just over 2 weeks later.

On Sunday, February 19, the battalion, minus one company, was transported by tactical truck convoy along Highway 1 about 25 miles from Phu Bai Airport to Phong Dien. From there they went by foot following Highway 599 10 clicks to the northeast and the targeted area along coastal Highway 597. This was the alternate plan as adverse weather grounded transport helicopters which would have inserted 1/9 at five LZs around their operation area.

1/9 and its company commanders were: Alpha Co.--Capt. Donald Festa of Stafford, Virginia; Charlie Co.--Capt. James H.R. Curd of Golden, Colorado; Delta Co.--Capt. William M. "Bill" Keys of Fredricktown, Pennsylvania; and H&S Co.--Capt. Frank Thomsen. Bravo Co. with Capt. Michael W. Sayers as CO was sent up to Khe Sanh. The battalion's CO was Maj. James L. Day (February 5-March 17, 1967). (Day would receive a belated Medal of Honor due to misplaced paperwork in 1998 for heroic actions above and beyond the call of duty with 2nd Battalion, 22nd Marines, 6th Marine Division on Okinawa, May 14-17, 1945 in WW II when he was a corporal---MDK).

"It was unnerving to go from Phu Bai to the jump off point in the dark (in a convoy)," stated PFC Fred Hillmann, 19 in 1967 from Mineola, New York, Forward Air Controller (FAC) radioman. "Quad .50s (four .50 caliber machine guns grouped together that fired in tandem and gained fire superiority over any incoming fire) were on vehicles at the front, middle and rear of the column. Snipers fired on us as we rode up Highway 1. The enemy was using tracer rounds in the darkness and it was like, 'Look, here we are. Shoot us,' as the quad .50s returned suppressing fire."

1/9's FAC officer (call sign Ruggles 14A), 1stLt. David A. "Dave" Marshall, 25, of Chelmsford, Massachusetts, had been loaned out to 1/9 by the O-1 (Birddog) Detachment, H&MS-16 flying out of Dong Ha and Marble Mountain Air Facility, MMAF, to coordinate airstrikes. Being a pilot, he could talk his fellow pilots' language better to put them on target. Previously, from May to December 1966, he had flown A-4 Skyhawks with VMA-223 Bulldogs out of Chu Lai. He would remain with 1/9 from January to June 1967 then get an extension on his tour to finish in January 1968 with the Birddogs...20 straight months in Vietnam!

Serving with 1/9 in and near the DMZ, Marshall noted, "That was the most interesting and rewarding experience of my 31-year active and reserve military career. Frankly, it was the best times of my life." He said he thought he might be the only FAC to be awarded the 0302 (infantry officer) MOS although he'd gone straight to aviation training and never been to The Basic School.

ARVNs from the 1st Division were also participating in the joint operation as part of *Chinook II*. Intelligence reports indicated that the enemy's 802d VC Battalion was in the area collecting rice.

The battalion advanced approximately 6 miles to the northeast of Phong Dien splitting up into three distinct groups once they cleared the Finger Lakes setting up in separate company-sized perimeters late the night of February 19th near Highway 597. Delta Co., H&S Co. and the battalion CP were in the vicinity of Ap Dai Phu;[23F] Alpha Co. was in sand dunes 500 meters due west of a huge cemetery;[23G] and Charlie Co was just off Highway 599 that intersects 597 south of Ap Trung Thanh.[23H]

A landmine and some punji pits were discovered (and destroyed in place) along the line of march. The Marines had to cross four blown-up bridges climbing over girders (spanning the Finger Lakes) with an occasional shot being fired, according to Dr. Fall's taped account.[24]

"I remember humping it for what seemed like several hours into darkness and ended up sleeping on or just off the trail. It was raining that night and it was really cold. All I had was a poncho, so I just crawled under it and tried to get some sleep while shivering the whole time," said Navy Corpsman HM3 Bob "Doc" Syler, 21, of Austin, Texas, who was with Alpha 1.

Each of the companies ran night ambush patrols out of their own perimeters with negative results.

### Professor Narrowly Avoids Punji Pit, February 20, 1967

Next morning, Monday, February 20, Alpha and Charlie companies moved to the northeast intersecting Highway 597, which was not much wider than a paddy dike with a well-worn path of packed dirt in the center. Once on the road, the two Marine companies commenced a deliberate coordinated search and destroy mission moving along the axis of Highway 597 (code-named Axis Green) to the southeast. The sweep continued into the next day until a 100-meter wide river held up forward movement.

1/9 reported finding thousands of punji traps, 3- to 8-man reinforced fighting holes, bunkers and well laid minefields. Occasional sniper fire kept the Marines on the alert.

A huge cemetery, 3 miles long and up to a half mile wide, occupied an area parallel to the dirt "highway" 400 meters off to the southwest and was fronted by a smaller "road" separating the cemetery from several highly populated villes in the area. Five pagodas, mainly to the southeast, were on the periphery of the gigantic cemetery. Alpha Co. swept along this area to the southeast receiving about six rounds from 12 VC rapidly departing Ap My Phu.

The Delta Co. perimeter was taken under fire by a sniper at 1250 resulting in no injuries.

Dr. Fall accompanied Charlie Co., which discovered 600 lbs. of rice earmarked for use by enemy troops at 0910. The company was involved in a brief firefight east of Ap Trung Thanh[25A] (15 rounds fired from a tree line) that broke off almost as soon as it started at 1130. Capt. Curd's 3rd platoon found two bunkers, 8x3 feet and 10x12 feet, at 1300.

At 1315 Dr. Fall was credited with finding a punji pit the hard way inside an old church alongside Highway 597 between Ap Trung Thanh and Ap Chinh An (the same ville Marines fought over tooth and nail with enemy troops during *Operations Oregon* and *Jay*). Vietnamese soldiers, a Marine point man and some other Marines preceded Dr. Fall into the old church that had an earthen floor. Dr. Fall walked out of the footsteps of the Marine in front of him and the ground gave way underneath his feet into a punji pit. He threw his weight forward and barely escaped impaling his feet on sharpened sticks.[26]

"Delta Co. CO Bill Keys introduced me to Dr. Fall a few days before he died. We listened to him over evening chow in the Delta Co. command area. Of course, at the time I was too stupid and provincial to appreciate the conversation," said 1stLt. Marshall.

Lt.Gen. Keys, USMC (Ret.), a 26-year-old captain in 1967 and a 1960 U.S. Naval Academy graduate, indicated that Maj. Day introduced him to Dr. Fall at the 1/9 Command Post. "I didn't even know who the hell he was to be honest with you. I had never read his books before coming to Vietnam. I would've if I could've. I know a lot of Marines did read his books. Anyway, afterwards I found out a little about the guy. He travelled with us for a couple days over there on the Street."

"The only thing I can remember in my talk with Dr. Fall was that he was happy to be with 1/9 and back on 'The Street,'" said Cpl. Joe Ferrante, 19 in 1967 of Newark, New Jersey, Maj. Day's field radio operator. "He talked about the difference in the way the French fought and how aggressive the Marines were. He told me about his book, *Street Without Joy*. I wrote a letter home that night and asked my mother to pick the book up for me. Well over 40 years later and I still can't bring myself to read it."

In conversations with 1/9 Marines in Vietnam, Dr. Fall confirmed remarks he had made to friends back home that upon his return to the United States from this Guggenheim-sponsored trip to Vietnam he would seek his American citizenship at long last. In Leftwich's "An Afternoon With Bernard Fall" article, he was constantly referring to the United States in terms of "we" and "us" so he was already subconsciously identifying himself with this country as a citizen.

At 1815 Alpha Co. captured two VC outside Ap Chinh An on Highway 597.[27A] Charlie Co. also captured two VC and detained seven others in the area. That night at 2225 Charlie Co. took 6-7 carbine rounds from four VC on a trail.

### 1/9 Uncovers VC Food Caches Off Highway 597, February 21, 1967

Fog and drizzle came with the dawn Tuesday, February 21. The enemy didn't have to worry about being spotted from the air during the morning since fixed wing and gunship helicopters were grounded until the weather cleared. Also, the Marines' lifeline, resupply and medevac helicopters out of Phu Bai, was intermittently grounded depending on the fluctuating weather conditions. This was not going to be a good day for 1/9, which was nicknamed "The Walking Dead" due to its high casualty rate, 620 KIA between June 1965 and July 1969 when the unit rotated stateside.

**1/9's Charlie Co. CO Capt. H.R. Curd shows Dr. Bernard Fall the battle plan for the day the morning of February 21. A mine explosion killed Dr. Fall later in the day on the Street Without Joy. (USMC Photo by SSgt. Ed Grantham, Information Services Office personnel, also injured in the blast)**

Capt. Curd was captured on film by ISO photographer SSgt. Grantham briefing Dr. Fall as to the company's mission this day in an early morning discussion in the ruins of a building in Ap Chinh An (probably the results of naval gunfire called in on the ville during 2/1's battle with three VC companies March 19, 1966). Marshall and his radio operators moved over to Charlie Co. He was able to observe and talk to Dr. Fall.

"I stayed with the point company that was engaged. As I remember it, we were going south on the 'Street Without Joy' with C Co. on the left and A Co. on the right," said Marshall. Keys noted that Delta Co. was moving in orchestration with Alpha Co.

At 0645 Alpha Co. captured two VC in a dwelling. At 0900 while moving across rice paddy dikes northeast of Ap My Phu a concussion mine was discovered and blown in place by Charlie Co.[27B] Dr. Fall saw his first casualty on the operation when a Marine tripped an M-26 grenade boobytrap near that same location.[27C] A second Marine was injured at 1220 detonating a mine. Three other mines were found within 500 meters of the previous detonation.[27D]

Charlie Co. located 1,000 eggs, over 4 tons of rice and 50 individual packaged rice rations wrapped in cloth at 1135. On the northwest side of Ap Lai Ha which was north of Highway 597, Curd's men uncovered 6-8 tons of rice at 1439 in their movement to the southeast.[27E] Numerous bunkers and fighting holes were also found. The 1/9 Marines were severely damaging the enemy's food pick-up operation.

As skies began to clear, an aerial observer spotted 10-15 VC carrying weapons leaping into sampans 1100 meters away and paddling out to sea. Charlie Co. Marines moved to intercept but the enemy managed to escape. The Marines were finding more minefields, boobytraps and heavy bunkers camouflaged by haystacks. Each hamlet was surrounded by 3-foot deep trenches with fighting holes staggered 20 yards apart on either side of the trench line.

Otters (amphibious tractors) were sent to resupply the two platoons at 1245 from 1/9's CP. They arrived at the forward positions at 1525.

## War Historian Given Latitude to Move Between Units

"Dr. Fall was kind of eager to get back and cover the ground where he had been before. Everybody told him, 'Hey, stay back. This area is mined and you're going to get in trouble.' He said, 'Naw, I know what I'm doing.' He went ahead of the company if I'm remembering correctly and they took small arms fire as he and his crew were running around...then he stepped on a mine," said Lt.Gen. Keys, who retired from the Marine Corps in 1994. He added that 1/9 was involved in numerous firefights and a lot of people were getting killed. In a 6-7 month period they lost 1,600-1,700 Marines and Navy Corpsmen WIA/KIA. The areas they fought in were generally heavily mined and the Marines knew to be extra alert as to where they put their next footstep.

"Dr. Fall was given much latitude to travel with any company. He was accompanied by a Marine ISO gunny (Gy.Sgt. Highland). That's the only person that I remember him having with him. Dr. Fall was with me in Charlie Co. most of the day," noted Marshall.

"'The Street' was one of the most heavily mined areas in Vietnam. The villages on 'The Street' were all pro-Viet Minh (the enemy's nom de plume during the French Indochina War). I had my troops off the paddy dikes and into the muck because the dikes were mined.

"Furthermore, when we came to a hedgerow, we picked the thickest place to push through. Dr. Fall would not do that. He continually walked on the dikes and made his way through the hedgerows anyway that he wanted." Marshall said he warned Dr. Fall on at least two occasions about his passage over dangerous ground. "I wondered at the time if he had a death wish for the way he was skipping around that mined area. If he had stepped on one, our folks were always out of range of a possible frag pattern so we didn't care. He definitely wasn't a distraction to us.

"(Dr. Fall) told me not to worry about it. I didn't. The timeline is hard to figure out but around early afternoon he told me he was going to cross 'The Street' and join A Company. We had a short conversation and I wished him luck. He was a hard guy to dislike," said Marshall.

Dr. Fall was carrying on a running commentary into his recorder as he walked along with Charlie Co. The Frenchman and his ISO contingent (Highland, Grantham and Guthrie escorted Dr. Fall although there may have been others---MDK) moved over to the left flank of Lt. Al Fagan's 2nd Platoon, Alpha Co. on Highway 597. Alpha had traversed the extensive cemetery and was moving forward three platoons abreast across varied terrain with Alpha 2 elements on the Axis Green "road" while the remainder of the two platoons were still in a portion of the cemetery approaching paddy dikes and a river. Up to that point they had not encountered any resistance. They would walk into a well-planned ambush that gave the enemy an opening salvo advantage but was short-lived as the Marines answered with a disciplined volume of fire.

### Huge Mine Explosion Kills Fall, 2 Marines

"We were finding mines--bouncing betties and toepoppers--all over the place. I even saw punji sticks," said PFC William J. "Weid" Weidenbacher, 25, of Scotch Plains, New Jersey, who was the Alpha Co. field clerk responsible for writing up the casualties. "We were approaching a wide stream when either Fall stepped on or someone command-detonated a bouncing betty (M16 type reported in the official reports) with extra explosives in it. The only reason I say it might have been command-detonated was that gooks were in holes inside our perimeter as part of an ambush."

"I watched as (Dr. Fall) and the gunny started down a major dike towards 'The Street.' I turned around and in about 2 minutes heard a loud explosion. I saw what I believed was Dr. Fall's body flying up in the air at the intersection of 'The Street' and the dike," stated the FAC officer.

"I believe I was the last person in 1/9 to talk to him before he died. The explosion was so large that most of us thought it was either an unexploded 250-lb. bomb or a large artillery shell. There was no medevac that I know of. Everyone who witnessed the explosion assumed all were KIA. I did not travel the 200 meters to the site," said Marshall.

Working as 1/9's S-3 Operations radio operator on *Chinook II*, PFC Ciro "Chick" Ciccarelli, 21 in 1967 from Brentwood, New York, recalled the device being more of a 105mm artillery shell in his estimation rather than an M16 bouncing betty from his vantage point 150 feet away. He seemed to think Dr. Fall got a little impatient and started to walk out on his own beyond the area being swept for mines.

"...Dr. Fall stepped on the mine at the junction of two paths. Although Fall was extremely careful staying in the footsteps of the Marine in front of him, this one time he apparently cut the corner of the intersection, trying to photograph something. He had been number six in the column," according to Cpl. Tom Evans, 19, of Simsbury, Connecticut serving as the squad leader of a 4-man 60mm mortar team in Alpha Co., 1/9 at the time.[28]

"I was a couple hundred yards away when it happened," recalled Lt.Gen. Keys. "We heard the mine explosion and was later told Dr. Fall was killed. I think it was a bouncing betty. When those things go off waist high, anybody close to it is going to get killed. It cut Fall to pieces and killed a Marine photographer. I think if Fall had stayed with the company he would never have gotten killed. When he ran ahead of everybody, that's when it happened."

A Leica camera around Dr. Fall's neck was torn apart in the explosion (the lens survived) and later returned to his wife among his personal effects as well as a tape recorder he was talking into at the time of death. A typewriter and new Polaroid camera were presumed stolen, according to Dorothy.[29]

The boobytrap detonation was in the vicinity of Ap Trung Kieu (1).[30A] A path came from around the southern and southeastern part of the cemetery and intersected with Highway 597 100 meters from a pagoda and 80 meters from a collapsed bridge over the 100-meter wide river. Moving immediately to treat the wounded was HM3 George J. "Doc" Carlucci.

Alpha Co. CO Captain Festa was on 2nd Platoon's right flank between 400-700 meters away with Lt. Phil Benedict's 1st Platoon when the powerful boobytrap explosion triggered an ambush.

**1/9's S-3 Operations Journal reads:**

*Dr. Bernard Fall moved in trace of Alpha 2 as it conducted its sweep along the Street Without Joy. He moved throughout Alpha 2's zone. At 211640H* (February 21, 4:40 p.m.) *an M16 type antipersonnel mine was detonated* (commonly called a bouncing betty). *The author, along with a Marine ISO representative* (Highland*), was killed instantly. Four other Marines were wounded in this detonation including two ISO Marines* (Grantham, Guthrie and two unnamed grunt Marines, according to a *SEA TIGER* article published after the incident).

**3rd Marine Division's official situation report reads:**

*211640--AP mine activated YD596398* (Hai Lang map, Sheet 6442 II). *4 Marines were in defilade. Two on each side of the road. Two correspondents (walked) up the center of the road and one tripped another mine injuring 4 Marines and killing two correspondents (a civilian, 1 Marine). The 1 Marine WIA subsequently died. Result 1 KIA (civilian), 2 KIA Marine and 3 WIA Marines.*

*Medevac helos YD596398 received ground fire from 3 directions (south, east and north) in addition to mortars; craft unable to evacuate.*

Dr. Fall's final words on his tape recorder as he was walking on "The Street" were, "...first in the afternoon about 4:30---shadows are lengthening and we've reached one of our phase lines after the firefight and it smells bad---meaning it's a little bit suspicious...Could be an amb...(end of tape)."[31] His comments were interrupted in mid-sentence by the tremendous blast.

An odd parallel exists between this ambush and one that occurred in 1965 as Dr. Fall accompanied American advisors with their ARVN infantry and tanks along Route 14. The professor was carrying a recorder then as well and recalled to Maj. Leftwich in "An Afternoon With Bernard Fall" article what his comments were spoken into the recorder at the time, "Watch out lieutenant. This is a probable ambush area," followed by the advisor's assurance, "There aren't any VC here." Then the rattle of gunfire caught on tape confirmed Dr. Fall's suspicions. The ARVN convoy immediately telescoped and the ARVN regimental commander was killed when he ran forward to spur the advance. He told Leftwich, "We never learn."[32]

"As soon as we hit the mines, the VC who were laying in ambush across the river opened up with a tremendous volume of fire forcing us to move for cover in the mined area. Dr. Fall was killed instantly by an M16 type mine," wrote Capt. Festa in a letter to Doc Syler's dad March 11, 1967.

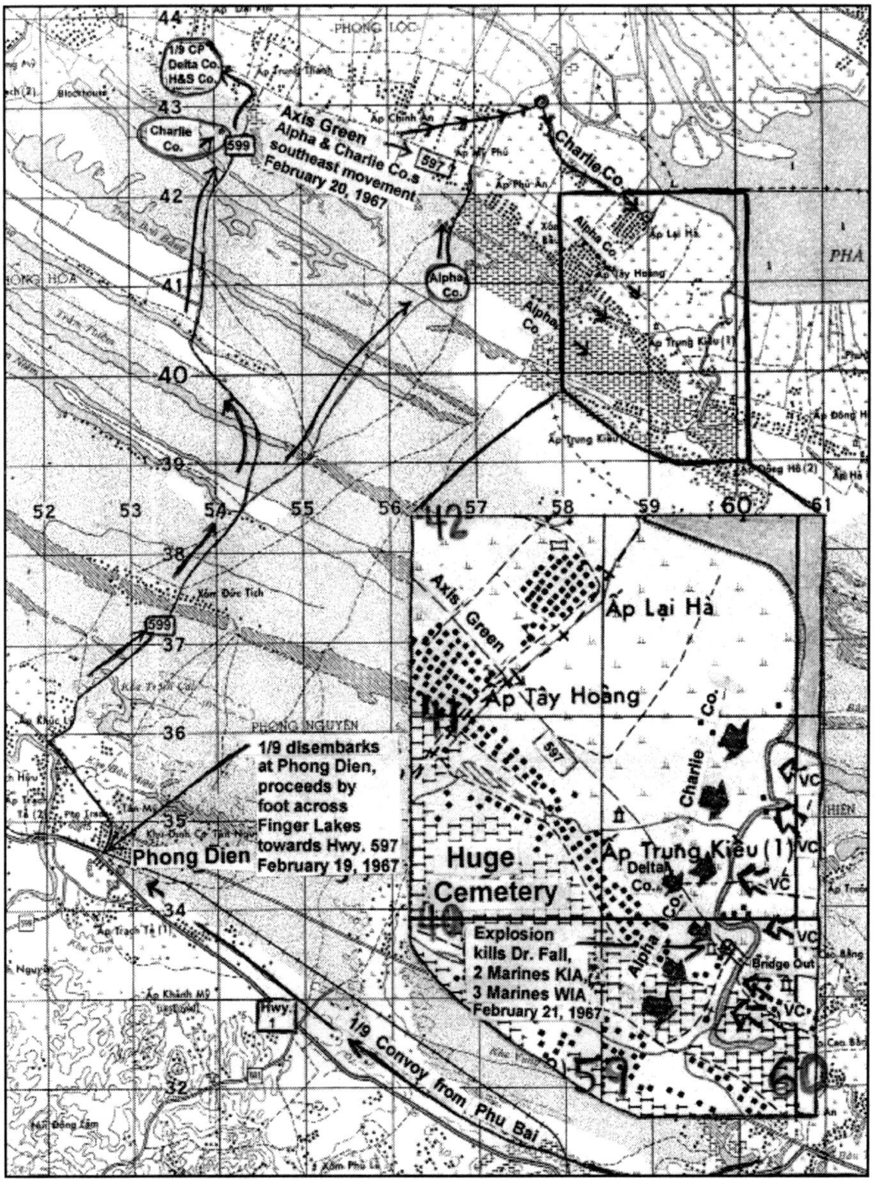


Map shows 1/9's movement February 19-21 during *Operation Chinook II.* Enlarged area, lower right, shows where 1/9 engaged VC across a wide river February 21. Dr. Bernard Fall was killed as was 1 Marine KIA, 1 Marine DOW and 3 Marines WIA by a large mine explosion on Highway 597 near a pagoda close to a destroyed bridge across that river. (Hai Lang map, Sheet 6442 II, 1968, Map courtesy of the National Imagery and Mapping Agency, National Geographic Service, Vietnam, Illustration by Dan Kellum)

## VC Fire Intensifies, Medevac of KIAs, WIAs Delayed

Flying out of Phu Bai, Maj. John E. Carroll, HMM-163 Super Chief UH-34D Seahorse pilot, with copilot 1stLt. S.Y. Fuentes attempted to land on the hot LZ where Dr. Fall had been struck down to pick up the dead and wounded at 1700. He had to abort the medevac mission due to the intense fire coming from three directions and exploding mortar rounds.

At 1705 Alpha 1's Cpl. Ron Bennett suffered a traumatic amputation of his foot when he stepped on a toepopper boobytrap east of Ap Trung Kieu (2),[33A] about 650 meters south of Dr. Fall's location. Doc Syler, ignored the heavy volume of fire now peppering the Marines' positions and ran to aid his close friend, Cpl. Bennett. He also stepped on a toepopper boobytrap injuring the heel of his foot. Both men were removed to some tall burial mounds from the area now being swept by fire from a tree line 300 meters to their front across the wide river.

"I remember a fierce firefight ensuing about the time we were wounded. Several of our guys were firing LAAWs (M72 Light Antitank Assault Weapon, a small disposable rocket launcher made of fiberglass and aluminum that fires a 66mm rocket) at a target that I couldn't see from where I was lying. Someone made a direct hit on a machine gun emplacement across the water obstacle and they celebrated with high fives all around when it was knocked out.

"Bennett and I were lying side-by-side cursing a couple of VC female prisoners that our guys had rounded up during the chaos. It took an unusually long time for them to get a helicopter to us. The helicopter could only handle six wounded and I was the seventh they loaded on the old UH-34. I think we took 13 casualties that day and six or seven KIAs," said Doc Syler.

Alpha Co.'s 60mm mortar team set up on the road about 25 yards away from the pagoda where Dr. Fall and Highland were killed and commenced firing, according to Evans. They were able to temporarily silence the VC fusillade in the distant woods across the river in their sector. 1/9's S-3 Operations Journal later stated they had tangled with an estimated VC company.

"Our mortar was called up to the front of the column not more than a couple of minutes after the mine exploded. We set up our gun very close to Fall's and Gunny Highland's bodies. Both were dead. I don't remember any corpsmen working on either of them," said Evans.

Boobytraps continued to plague the Marines of Alpha Co. as an anti-personnel mine was tripped at 1925 killing a Marine and wounding another. The cumulative losses for *Chinook II* through February 21 amounted to 5 Marines KIA and 26 WIA, according to the 3rdMarDiv report. Charlie Co. was also pinned down by heavy sniper fire from a nearby ville from 1730 to 1930.

"Because of a river, our elements could not cross. It was not possible to close with the enemy. Mines and boobytraps were the primary source of friendly casualties," the 1/9 S-3's Operations Journal noted. This was where *Operation Jay* with its use of heliborne forces over a wide area June 25, 1966 proved to have superior tactics by taking away natural barriers prohibiting the Marines from assaulting the VC ambushers.

"I remember seeing the black cloud of smoke and hearing the mine explode. I was 150 yards away from him when it happened," said Weidenbacher. "When the medevac helicopter came in, it received heavy fire and we couldn't get (our wounded) out. This touched off a battalion-wide firefight with all the companies involved."

Lt.Gen. Keys explained there was no way to know exactly how many VC troops had taken them under fire from across the river February 21. "You didn't know whether there was 10, 20 or 50 of them out there because they didn't have assaulting troops. They would ambush you and run. They had these mines planted. I don't know if they put them in but they sure knew where they were. I don't think the mine that killed Dr. Fall was command-detonated."

## Capt. B.S. Barnett Picks Up WIAs at Charlie Co.'s Location

Capt. B.S. Barnett, a HMM-163 Super Chief UH-34D Seahorse pilot, and 1stLt. Edward A. "Weasel" Weiss of Sierra Vista, Arizona as his copilot, attempted to make a night extract of the injured at 2100 in the Ap Trung Kieu (2) area.[33B] Charlie Co. reported green tracer rounds fired at the aircraft from the middle of a rice paddy 2 clicks away.[33C] The unit's 60mm mortars took the enemy under fire and the tracer rounds ceased. Capt. Barnett returned to evacuate the Alpha 1 Marines at Syler's location with the help of support aircraft and reinforcements from Delta Co. His helicopter took one hit with no injuries.

## Capt. Jack Maxwell Aborts Recovery of KIAs

Accompanied by gunship escorts, HMM-164 Sky Shadow (in the newer CH-46 Sea Knight) flight leader Capt. Jack C. Maxwell, 26, of Keota, Oklahoma and copilot Doug Manlief flew up from Phu Bai at 2015 Tuesday, February 21. They made an emergency resupply of a unit 3 clicks south of Phong Dien[33D] then flew on to the 1/9 units in contact 10 clicks to the northeast. The chase helicopter was piloted by J. Hodgson and G. Roberts as copilot.

In support of 1/9, their mission was twofold: emergency resupply of the Marines still in contact with the enemy forces and recovery of Dr. Fall and Gy.Sgt. Highland at Alpha 2's location on Highway 597. A casualty at that location was still alive since Alpha 2 had called for an emergency extract, according to Maxwell. He cautiously approached the disputed battleground.

According to HMM-164 S-2 chief Capt. Maxwell's AAR, the pilot succeeded in making a "night emergency resupply, received small arms fire from 1,000 meters east of zone (from across the river)." He made the resupply drop to Capt. Festa's Alpha 1 Marines in the cemetery around 2200 then proceeded onto his next assignment involving an emergency medevac at Alpha 2's position. Dr. Fall and Gy.Sgt. Highland were approximately 650 meters away.[33E]

Although Maxwell's AAR and 1/9's S-3 Operations Journal shows he picked up 2 KIAs, he stated on October 9, 2004, "We were on the way to pick up an emergency medevac (after the resupply) when it was changed to 'routine' so we aborted the pickup since both men were now KIA. We went back in the next day (February 22) and picked up Dr. Fall and the gunny's bodies." In the "Battle Evacs" part of Maxwell's AAR, he shows "2 KIA" being picked up but he only mentions making an emergency resupply in the narrative. The flight returned to Phu Bai at 2220. Maj. Day, call sign Ruggles 6, confirmed at 2330 in 1/9's S-3 Journal, "Death of BF confirmed by Rug 6 at 211640H."

Running short on water that February 21st night, Cpl. Evans exchanged his empty canteens for Fall's full ones. "He was the first American I saw get killed. When we couldn't medevac his body because of Viet Cong small arms fire, I traded my empty canteens for his full ones. I didn't ask anybody if it was all right to do that, because I was new in-country and was afraid it was taboo to drink a dead man's water."[34]

Capt. Festa included in his letter to Doc Syler's dad that Alpha Co. lost 7 KIA and 16 WIA by the end of *Operation Chinook II* February 26, 1967. WIAs were helilifted to Da Nang and from there to the hospital ship *USS Repose*. Lt. Gen. Lewis W. "Lew" Walt, Commanding General of III Marine Amphibious Force, would personally award Doc Syler his Purple Heart. He was sent to the Naval Hospital in Corpus Christi, Texas for rehabilitation and treatment.

### Future MOH Recipient Helps Load Dr. Fall on Helicopter

Sgt. Walter Keith Singleton, 22, of Memphis, Tennessee was the Alpha Co. supply sergeant and in charge of putting Dr. Fall's body on the chopper February 22, according to Weidenbacher. "They were cursing me for not being there (to help)."

Singleton would be posthumously awarded the Medal of Honor for heroic actions while knocking out an enemy machine gun with Marshall on Good Friday, March 24, 1967. Marshall said he heard that Singleton and his brother were on Okinawa together, both Marines, and were the sole surviving sons in their family. By USMC regulations only one of them could go into Vietnam. They flipped a coin to see who would go in-country. Walter "won" the coin toss. "He was a terrific Marine and a nice guy," said Marshall. He was with him assaulting an enemy position when shrapnel from an enemy soldier's grenade tore into his neck killing him. On November 7, 1971, Gen. Walt would be on hand to dedicate a Memphis park in Sgt. Singleton's honor.

The Alpha Co. field clerk took Dr. Fall's well-made rucksack to the battalion CP where Maj. Day told him to put it on the medevac helicopter with the author's body. He wondered at the time why the Corps couldn't come up with good equipment like that for its field troops.

**Street Without Joy: Poetic Symmetry**

Brig.Gen. Michael P. "Mike" Ryan, assistant 3rdMarDiv commander, arrived by helicopter Wednesday, February 22 and was quite perturbed with Alpha 2's Lt. Fagan who told him to be careful where he stepped. Boobytraps were reset inside the perimeter overnight in areas that had been swept by the Marine minesweepers. It was thought the enemy was popping up from hidden tunnels to set them in different locations of 1/9's position. Weidenbacher said there were some really upset field grade officers over Dr. Fall's death and that was why Brig.Gen. Ryan came to see for himself what happened.

He went on to say that the Alpha Co. commander caught some flack about not being able to find a way to extract Fall (or the gunny) until the following day. Evans concurred by saying Dr. Fall wasn't picked up until the next morning, February 22.

Cpl. Evans remembered Brig.Gen. Ryan coming out to view the spot where Dr. Fall was killed and surmised that he chewed Capt. Festa out for allowing the professor to be so near the front of the column. He indicated that Lt. Fagan was, in turn, chewed out over the matter and was still upset when they talked 30 years later. "As we both know, shit flows downhill in the Marine Corps," said Evans.

It was poetic symmetry that where Dr. Fall had earned his spurs by writing about such battlegrounds as *la rue sans joie* (*Street Without Joy),* he should shed his own blood and perish in that general area...just 8 clicks from where the French were mauled on coastal Highway 555. And the country he had tried through the years to influence over the conduct of the Vietnam War and made up his mind to finally apply for citizenship, he would find his final resting place on American soil...aptly enough, inside the Beltway in Washington, D.C.

In Maj. Leftwich's *Marine Corps Gazette* article he said he called Dr. Fall on the eve of his departure for Vietnam. "I concluded the call with a humorous rejoinder to 'stay away from Route 14,' the scene of his 1965 ambush. He laughed and said he would confine his activities to Route 1, which he knew better. This was sadly prophetic. On February 21, 1967, he was killed by a mine near his self-titled *Street Without Joy*."[35]

Dr. Fall joined the warring factions, French Union Forces versus Viet Minh and later VC/NVA versus RVN/SEATO forces, who had also bled and died, in and around those same rice paddies he had so eloquently described in book after book since 1954.

In closing out his impressive interview with Dr. Fall in "An Afternoon With Bernard Fall" in the December 1968 issue of the *Marine Corps Gazette,* Bill Leftwich wrote, "The nation thus lost a gifted writer with unique insight into a tortured area about which we still know too little. Often controversial, occasionally seeming outrageously biased, he was ever the probing scholar.

"More importantly to me, he retained an unflagging consideration for the trooper, be he French, American or Vietnamese. This appealing quality was amply demonstrated that December afternoon."[36]

*CBS*'s Morley Safer had run into Dr. Fall on his way out of Vietnam and noted that "Bernie" had mentioned he was headed up to Da Nang where the Marines were "tramping around" on operations in his country...the Street Without Joy. A few days after arriving back at the *CBS News* offices in New York he was informed Dr. Fall had been killed accompanying Marines and was asked to write "no more than a minute" for his airtime obituary. He noted the professor had gathered all the paperwork to apply for his American citizenship when he was killed.[37]

"...He was a restless man, full of ambition, a kind of scholarly Sammy Glick. He was contemptuous of academics and journalists who wrote about Vietnam from the intellectual and physical safety of Washington. His enormous ego hid, I suppose, a certain lack of self-confidence. He always said he wanted to be considered the most distinguished military writer of his generation. When he went out with the Marines that day, he'd already achieved it. Perhaps he was the only one who was not entirely certain," noted Safer in his book, *Flashbacks: On Returning to Vietnam.* [38]

### *Operation Chinook II* Phase 1 Casualties of War

1/9 cited the following casualties for Phase 1 of *Operation Chinook II*: 6 USMC KIA, 45 USMC WIA, 2 USMC DOW, 1 USN WIA, 1 U.S. Army WIA and 1 U.S. civilian KIA. On February 22, the 3rdMarDiv listed the VC dead as 12 KIA (confirmed), 36 KIA (probable), 14 VC POWs, 31 detainees, 16 innocent civilians and 6 captured weapons.

In the S-3 Operations Journal accounting for February 21, Capt. Festa inserted this comment, "As I personally observed (Dr. Fall) earlier in the afternoon, it was apparent he was a man who wanted to be up front." Alpha Co. would lose Capt. Festa in March 1967 from the concussion effects of an enemy HE mortar round landing in close proximity to him.

There had been some criticism about Dr. Fall being allowed so close to "the front" in the hotly contested combat zone. To tell the truth, all of Vietnam was "la guerre sans fronts"--a war without fronts--in 1967 and Dr. Fall knew full well the chances he was taking. Any writer or war correspondent that ventured beyond Saigon or Da Nang in Vietnam or Phnom Penh in Cambodia in the general direction of the Ho Chi Minh Trail on the border with Vietnam knew the mortality rates increased and accepted those dangers to get their story firsthand. And what I've read of his books and heard from others on the battlefield, Dr. Fall wanted to share in the danger we faced because he was one of us. He will always be remembered as a man with courage and keen intelligence.

In Richard Pyle and Horst Faas' book, *Lost Over Laos*, it is noted from April 5-16, 1970 that 10 journalists from half a dozen countries did not return from venturing outside Phnom Penh towards Cambodia's border with Vietnam. Actor Errol Flynn's son, Sean, working for *TIME* magazine accompanied by Dana Stone, a freelance cameraman for *CBS News*, were among those who were believed to be captured by either the VC or Khmer Rouge and died in captivity.[39]

3rdMarDiv's ISO report for March following Dr. Fall's death indicated 17 civilian news correspondents dropped in on Phu Bai and a jump from 50 the previous month to 133 newsmen descended on Dong Ha. I think those news correspondents had a fire lit under them to go get "hard facts" and were inspired to go see the Real War fought by the Marines up around the DMZ.

Pyle of the *AP* said "The real (hard core) press like *AP*, big newspapers and the TV networks had reporters in the field all the time."

He also pointed out that Dr. Fall was on a list of 72 war correspondents killed in combat situations in Indochina---34 in Vietnam, 34 in Cambodia and four in Laos---between 1965 and the war's end in 1975. The *AP* list includes all accredited journalists, freelancers and authors. Pyle explained that reporters' deaths could happen anytime, anywhere...not just in the field.

"Six were killed in air crashes, either shot down or accidental. At least eight were killed in Saigon, five during mini-Tet in May 1968. One guy was found shot to death, a Japanese reporter was killed in his own bed by a VC rocket and a French guy was mistakenly shot by Saigon police," said Pyle.

Some of the publications Dr. Fall's learned pieces appeared in included the *New Republic; Ramparts; Reporting Vietnam; The Nation; Pacific Affair,* a publication of the Institute of Public Affairs; *Wehrwissen-Chaftliche*

*Rundschau,* a German military publication; *Military Review,* U.S. Army's Command and General Staff College publication at Fort Leavenworth, Kansas; *Ost-Probleme,* a U.S. Information Agency publication in Germany; the *Far Eastern Survey;* and three articles for *The Washington Post* before his work was banned from that newspaper due to his views on Vietnam. He would win the George Polk Journalism Award for Interpretive Reporting in 1966.[40]

**Arlington National Cemetery, Interment Denied**

Dr. Fall was survived by his wife, Dorothy, and three daughters: Nicole, 9; Elisabeth, 6; and Patricia, 6 months. Dorothy indicated that Maj. Gen. Wood B. Kyle, Commanding General of the 3rdMarDiv (March 19, 1966-March 17, 1967), came to Hong Kong soon after her husband's death and explained to her that he had died from the detonation of a bouncing betty boobytrap while walking along a paddy dike. He told her that Dr. Fall was killed instantly.[41]

Dorothy returned to Washington, D.C. and approached the supervisor for the Arlington National Cemetery (ANC) in Arlington, Virginia. She requested that her husband be buried in that hallowed ground amongst warriors he had once been himself in WW II and written about since he began his doctoral work on the French Indochina War.

A Pentagon spokesman denied her request due to regulations put into effect just 4 days before his death. ANC was, quite frankly, running out of room for everyone who wanted to be buried within the boundaries of the present cemetery's restricted acreage with the tripling of burials from past wars veterans' deaths and the burden of the Vietnam War KIAs. The new guidelines indicated the burial at ANC was reserved for MOH recipients, servicemen who die while on active duty or who have served long enough for full retirement with honorable discharges, veterans who held Cabinet-level posts and the wives of all of those.[42]

An 18th century law extending the privilege of burial to "the fellow citizens of the Marquis de Lafayette" was taken under consideration and denied by the Defense Department.[43] (Lafayette was a wealthy 20-year-old Frenchman who joined Gen. George Washington's staff during the Revolutionary War against the British and rose to the rank of major general).

Funeral services were held Monday, March 6, 1967 in the Andrew Ranking Chapel at Howard University in Washington, D.C. with Dr. Evans E. Crawford, dean of the Chapel, officiating.[44]

Interment followed at Rock Creek Cemetery in Washington, D.C. 2 miles north of the nation's Capitol. The historical cemetery is noted for being the resting-place for many American politicians.[45]

## American Heroes

Altogether 12 Marines died in Vietnam on Tuesday, February 21, 1967. Alpha 2 Marines killed were Cpl. Harold Gomez, 20, a fire team leader from East Chicago, Indiana who was the recipient of the Silver Star for his conspicuous gallantry fighting against the VC February 21; LCpl. Walter Weiss, 20, of Middlesex, New Jersey; and LCpl. Glenn Alvin Harris, 19, of Chicago, Illinois. Six Marines appear on the Vietnam Veterans Memorial Fund website, vvmf.org, as dying this day in Thua Thien Province and are listed during the same timeframe as *Operation Chinook II*. (I can only confirm the three Marines listed above and ISO's Gy.Sgt. Highland were with 1/9 February 21, 1967---MDK).

Since two additional Marines were DOW later, their listed place of death may have been in another province at a Navy hospital or ship offshore thus the names are unknown to me for this accounting. Besides Dr. Fall, the two other Marines who died February 21, 1967 in Thua Thien Province were PFC James Richard Walker, 20, of Pittsburgh, Pennsylvania and PFC Thomas Edward Badavas, 20, of Garwood, New Jersey.

In *Last Reflections on a War: Bernard B. Fall on Viet-Nam,* which was published posthumously with Dorothy putting the book together from her husband's unpublished writings and recordings, she dedicates it to Marine Gy.Sgt. Byron G. Highland who died alongside Dr. Fall. She makes the poignant observation in the dedication that he was a "*...combat photographer, partner in death*."[46]

I think Dr. Fall left this life the way he had lived it...among brave men--U.S. Marines--in combat and on his much written about Street Without Joy that set the tone for his reputation as a great writer. He saved many American lives with his well-written books preparing us for the tenacious adversary we would face. For this, I tip my old camouflage helmet to the professor and offer him a heartfelt, *AARUGHA!*

# Chapter 11

**On or about August 12, 1965, Gen. William C. Westmoreland, CG, MAC-V, accompanied by military dignitaries and war correspondents, flew by helicopter to the U.S. Army's Special Forces camp at Duc Co on the Vietnam-Cambodian border to congratulate Marine Maj. Bill Leftwich Jr., Vietnamese Marine Brigade advisor, for routing an NVA regiment which had laid siege to the camp. Westmoreland stated that Leftwich was "the best advisor in Vietnam." His statement was also anchored on Maj. Leftwich's heroism on March 9, 1965 which earned him a Navy Cross at Hoai An with the VNMC as they lifted the siege of that district town as well.[1]**

**Gen. William C. Westmoreland**
**CG, MAC-V forces in RVN**

## Lt.Col. Leftwich Inspires "The Professionals" of 2/1

In this world there are those individuals that are special and seem to be anointed to lead a high profile life, spellbinding in their meteoric rise and equally as susceptible to a spectacular "fall." Their stories are like mythological Greek tragedies when the jealous gods bring the mortal to heel for unwittingly stealing their thunder.

William Groom "Bill" Leftwich Jr. was one of those rare people who was a born leader destined "to steal thunder from the gods." The humble colonel would vigorously disagree with this statement pointing out that it took hard work and constant attention to maintain being a leader of Marines. Whether his leadership skills came naturally or from renewed efforts every day to achieve the respect of his men, the colonel was praised and admired Marine Corps-wide as someone special and destined to achieve high rank over the course of his career.

When Lt.Col. Leftwich came to 2nd Battalion, 1st Marines May 16, 1970, he didn't sit back and let his battalion S-3 chief run the operations of the unit in a vacuum or the battalion's XO totally manage the Battalion Rear without some input. The new colonel, a 1953 United States Naval Academy, USNA, honor graduate, was a hands on type of commander.

Complementing Leftwich's aggressive tactical nature was Maj. John Southy Grinalds (a Rhode's Scholar--one of only 88 from the United States Military Academy, USMA, as of April 2009), 2/1's new S-3 chief on July 16. The 32-year-old major grew up in Macon, Georgia. He graduated with honors from the USMA at West Point, New York in 1959. Coincidentally, his parents moved to Memphis, Tennessee where Leftwich's parents still resided. Grinalds chose the Marine Corps as his preferred military branch upon graduating from the USMA.

Between the two "academy" men the fight was taken to the enemy, whereas previously it seemed like we waited for Charlie to make the first move before we reacted. 2/1 was energized with their enthusiasm and innovative methods of kicking the enemy's proverbial butt.

I ate some crow with the appearance of these two officers as I made the sarcastic irreverent statement more than once while throwing back stiff shots of cherry Cokes at the Officers Club that it seemed after an officer attained any rank above captain his brains had a tendency to turn to shit. Leftwich and Grinalds were decidedly exceptions to the rule.

Before their tours were up at 2/1, the Quang Nam Province's VC/NVA leadership was severely crippled, the enemy in our AO was in disarray and what was left of the local forces found themselves going on the defensive. The battalion's CO and S-3 chief each put their lives on the line on more than one occasion as neither man was adverse to sharing in their Marines' combat activities. 2/1's Marines responded with excitement to such "follow me" type leadership.

Maj. Grinalds directed the Command and Control Huey helicopter during a highly successful heliborne raid and firefight in August. He repeated this "out front" leadership tendency on other operations as well.

**Leftwich Wounded Early in Second Tour**

On July 21, 1970 Lt.Col. Leftwich was riding aboard a Huskie (LVTP-5) in the bush on a search and clear operation near the Republic of Korea Marine Corps', ROKMC, AO supporting the South Korean Marines with CAPs and Hotel Co., 2/1 Marines when the big tracked vehicle rolled over an 80-lb. command-detonated box mine on the driver's side of the vehicle. The resulting blast injured six Marines. Huskie driver, LCpl. Johnny Fred Scott, 20, of Americus, Georgia, with just 3 days left in-country before his tour ended was not about to let the new battalion commander go out without him, according to Lt.Col. Gil Robinson, a second lieutenant at the time who was initially slotted to assume command of a platoon in Hotel Co. when he arrived at 2/1.

"Lt. Larry Craig, Hotel Co. XO, said the company had contact and this would be a good opportunity for me to see the platoon in action that I was going to take over. I had been at 2/1 only about 2 days after begging for a transfer from Division. Riding at the front of the Huskie on the way down, the wind was blowing in my face and I couldn't light up my cigarette. On the way back I moved to the back of the vehicle to the jump seat so I could light up. That cigarette saved my life," said Robinson.

LCpl. Scott was sitting next to Leftwich at the front of the Huskie. They were the second or third vehicle to roll over the mine which led everyone to believe it was command-detonated. The ensuing blast blew Leftwich, Robinson and the Huskie's gunner out of the vehicle. LCpl. Scott was thrown backwards on the vehicle's radio hitting his head mortally wounding him. He expired later that same day at 1st Med.

"Leftwich motioned me over. Neither one of us could hear anything due to the blast f**king our ears up. We both had powder burns all over us," noted Robinson.

Lt.Col. Leftwich received fragmentation wounds to his face, injured his knee and suffered perforated eardrums. These injuries produced his second Purple Heart in two tours. This time around in his second Vietnam tour the colonel managed to go 3 months before he was wounded which was a better average than his initial tour in 1965. Two days later Leftwich was back in the field among his bush Marines.

"I recall when dad was wounded the second time because we heard about it after his death. Dad refused to allow the Corps to notify next-of-kin. In fact, he wrote a friend to do all that he could not to let mom know about the injury. He claimed that he never left the field despite the wound," said his son, Bill.

Golf Co.'s 2nd Platoon commander 1stLt. Michael J. "Mike" Cross, 24, of Mountain View, California, remembered his first meeting with Leftwich as occurring when he brought one of his Marines to the Battalion Rear for office hours for sleeping on watch in the bush. "In those days there was still a draft and a few judges allowed some criminals to go into the service instead of serving time. In my platoon I had one attempted murderer and one burglar. I don't remember why but we ended up in the Battalion CO's office rather than my company CO, Lt. Jack Klimp's. I told my burglar to get a haircut and he refused.

"When I went in, Leftwich was sitting at his desk with big balls of cotton sticking out of his ears. The day before he had been aboard an LVTP-5 that hit a mine and the noise of the explosion had damaged his ears. He was sitting there looking very CO-like, except for these big, white blobs coming out of his ears. It looked weird and somewhat un-Marine like. Luckily my burglar didn't laugh," recalled Col. Cross, who was a 1969 U.S. Naval Academy graduate and retired from the Marine Corps in 1999 after 30 years.

The former lieutenant said that he explained that he would be bringing the Marine back in for also refusing his order to get a haircut. Leftwich seemed to know about the outlaws the Marines were accepting and told him not to worry or get down about not being able to work with them. He gave Cross a pep talk without the lieutenant realizing that was really what he was doing. "Lt.Col. Leftwich really knew people."

2ndLt. Robinson did not get the Hotel Co.'s platoon commander's job but instead would be appointed to head 2/1's S-2 Intelligence section. Working in the S-2 shop, he recalled Leftwich not being satisfied with the 7th Air Force projected weather reports in Quang Nam Province for the upcoming monsoon season.

"The Vietnamese just seemed to know from instinct and centuries of experience when torrential downpours were coming and automatically moved to high ground before the rains began," noted Robinson. "Leftwich sent me to III MAF to see if there were any old Vietnamese or French maps showing what areas traditionally flooded and which areas didn't over the years. I found some old French maps that showed the flood plains during monsoon season and we were able to overlay those over our maps. When the rains began, we knew where to pull our people back to. A lot of other units were not prepared like us. Working for Leftwich was like going to Graduate School with lots of homework."

(To totally understand what kind of unique individual Lt.Col. Bill Leftwich was his story is best told from the beginning and work up to the point when I first met him in 1970. His past history and his influence on the Marine Corps is worth telling because it's about another true "American Hero"...and the part I like best is that he epitomized what being a Marine, an officer and a gentleman, meant in every sense of the word ---MDK).

## Growing Up in Germantown, Tennessee, April 27, 1931-June 1948

Bill Leftwich was grounded in all-around sports participation and military tradition thanks to his father, William Groom Leftwich Sr., who joined the U.S. Army's officer corps after graduating from the University of the South at Sewanee, Tennessee in 1917 at 21. The elder Leftwich served along the Texas-Mexico border during his military stint through 1920. This was during the time of the Mexican Revolution, 1910-1920. U.S. Army units patrolled the border to prevent raids from Mexican revolutionaries such as Pancho Villa.

After finishing his military service as a first lieutenant, the senior Leftwich became quite successful working his way up from a securities firm in New Orleans to being senior partner at Leftwich, Ross & Crisler, investment bankers, in Memphis, Tennessee. The son of a lawyer in Aberdeen, Mississippi he married the former Mattie Howard Scrape, from his hometown in 1925 and had but one child. They named the baby boy in the manner of all proud Southern parents at that time in his namesake, William Groom Leftwich Jr. "Groom" was Bill Sr.'s mother's maiden name.

Up until the youngster was 13 or 14 years old, he had a black nurse, Jenny, who watched after him, which was traditional among the well-to-do in the South. Following in Jenny's footsteps was Melton, an 18-year-old black companion, hired by his father. He watched out for the young Billy Leftwich until he went off to World War II. His leaving for war might have influenced Bill's thinking about his responsibility in time of conflict as well.

Bill Sr. brought the Springfield rifle he carried in the Army home with him and I'm sure this scratched up weapon fired up the imagination of Billy Leftwich in his early years. His dad expected perfection from his only son growing up while his mom greatly influenced him with a gentler approach.

Even as a young child he knew what he wanted from life...to be a United States Marine. He and his mother would tell his wife years later about drawings and scribbling as a youngster that would have as its theme someday becoming a Marine Corps combat soldier.

"From the very beginning, he wanted to be a Marine," said Chuck Bender, his lifelong friend beginning in kindergarten.

Bender, who lived just three houses down from him growing up in Germantown, said his pal would play with those metal toy-size British soldiers painted in exact replicas of their real-life counterparts. He threw them into battles against one another in reenactments of wars gone by. Bill knew some day he would be doing the real thing. It was his destiny.

The history of armed conflict was in his family's bloodline. Bill's great-grandfather, S.L. Sanders, enlisted in the Confederacy at 14 and due to his youth was the unit's standard bearer. Grape shot from Yankee artillery shattered his arm at the Battle of Murfreesboro.[2]

Bill at 5-foot-11, 185 lbs. with short legs and long torso proved to be quite an outstanding athlete at Central High School in Memphis and was always up for a competitive challenge. He excelled in tennis and was co-captain of the football team, lettering as well in basketball and baseball. The senior class of 1948 also saw his potential by making him their class president and as if his plate wasn't already full, he was the student commanding officer of the ROTC. He didn't neglect his studies either as he was in the Honor Society.

**Leftwich Earns Top Honors at U.S. Naval Academy**

While others were setting their sights on colleges and universities around the country looking for the freedom of an unchaperoned and discipline-free social and academic life, Bill was looking for something quite different.

He sought discipline and the hard life of a military man by accepting an appointment by Pres. Harry S. Truman to the United States Naval Academy at Annapolis, Maryland in 1949.

The young man's star shone brightly at the Naval Academy as he was at the top of his class in his studies there as well and all leadership billets. He also played football and tennis for the midshipmen. His innate abilities to lead men, something he later said that he worked hard at, saw him being appointed as the prestigious Brigade Commander on the Winter Brigade Staff in the graduating class of 1953. He had the honor of leading the midshipmen during Pres. Dwight D. Eisenhower's Inauguration Parade down Pennsylvania Avenue on January 20, 1953.

"Dad was very proud of that. The leadership positions were rotated to give more Midshipmen a chance to hold sets of key staff positions...Fall, Winter and Spring. After dad was Brigade Commander of the Winter set, he became 5th Company Commander for the Spring set," said Bill Leftwich III.

Of the 925 midshipmen graduating in June of 1953, Bill was selected as one of 15 outstanding officers of his class and received a Bachelor of Science degree in electrical engineering. Also honored in that elite group was future computer multi-billionaire Henry Ross Perot of Texarkana, Texas who would remain an admirer and good friend of Bill's for life.

"(Bill Leftwich) was the most outstanding man in our class by any measure. I don't even put myself in his league. He came from a very prominent family in Memphis. He didn't have to be in the Navy. He didn't have to be a Marine officer. He could have lived the life of a Southern gentleman but he wanted to serve his country," said Perot.

Although they had known each other for a long time, Bill didn't have his first date with his wife-to-be, Jane, daughter of Marvin E. and Vivian (Cisco) Ferrer from Memphis, until his USNA senior year. He asked her to accompany him to the very important Ring Dance, when seniors are presented their senior rings. Bill didn't meet Jane when she flew in to Annapolis for their date as he was tied up on several dance committees. She met him at the dance as his "drag" (date) and discovered he had been injured in a Navy football game and was on crutches.

"We never did get to dance on our first date because he was on crutches!" she recalled.

Her first impression of Bill Leftwich was that he was a calm person with a quiet sense of humor. Bill listened intently. He never said much but retained this photographic memory of people's names, hometowns and minute facts he would surprise them with by recalling them on subsequent meetings. Traits she liked about him was that he didn't drink or use profanity.

Jane remembered Bill's abiding interest in the Civil War even going so far as to writing his senior year thesis on the brilliant military tactics of Southern cavalry Gen. Nathan Bedford Forrest at Brice's Cross Roads in Mississippi on June 4, 1864. Gen. Forrest managed to convincingly defeat a superior Union Army cavalry force.

The fellow Tennessean enlisted as a private in June 1861 having no military education but was a lieutenant colonel by that October and ended his military career as a lieutenant general.

Bill probably liked the simple military axiom Forrest was alleged to have said citing the secret to his military victory at Brice's Cross Roads (Civil War historians dispute the "countrified" wording printed in a New York newspaper after the war), "To git thar fustest with the mostest men."[3] Bill would later join the Tennessee Historical Society, according to Jane.

A weekend getaway for the young couple saw them slipping off to New York City, Jane's first time in the Big Apple. "I was so excited, the clubs, the restaurants and all there was to see. The first night there Bill told me he had two tickets for Madison Square Garden and that's where we were going. The tickets were to a hockey game! Bill loved all sports," she said laughing.

**Lt. William Groom "Bill" Leftwich Jr. (Photo courtesy of Bill Leftwich III)**

They married in 1957 at the Second Presbyterian Church in Memphis. Bill's dad served as his best man for the ceremony. Instead of a Navy officer's wife, Jane became a Marine's wife. The USNA graduate had chosen the Marine Corps as his branch of service out of the United States Naval Academy...his childhood dream had come true.

The newly married couple spent almost 3 years, August 1957 to June 1960, at the USNA in Annapolis, Maryland. Bill was a company officer and also helped coach the Navy football team. At the conclusion of each game, he was off visiting gridiron-injured midshipmen at the hospital. Jane told him she would stick with him no matter what unless he got into coaching or politics.

Ensign Perot was so impressed with Bill he later stated that he could be anything he wanted to be--U.S. senator, CEO of a large company, Commandant of the Marine Corps or even President of the United States. Perot, of course, eventually made a fortune ($3.5 billion by September 2009, according to *Forbes* magazine) in the computer industry, investment and real estate. He also ran as a third party candidate for President of the United States in 1992 and again in 1996.

Perot still remembered what a charismatic and natural-born leader Bill was 13 years down the road after graduating from Annapolis and serving his required time in the U.S. Navy. Sometime after 1962, he sent his old USNA classmate information on his close-knit fledgling computer company, Electronic Data Systems, EDS, headquartered in Dallas, Texas, trying to woo him to work for him. Bill chose his first love, the Marine Corps, over a cushy civilian life and an 8 to 5 "noncombatant" existence.

### Lt.Gen. Frederick L. Wieseman Selects Leftwich as Aide

In 1960 Bill was appointed CO of a company of Marines at the U.S. Naval Base Guantanamo Bay, Cuba. Never one to sit still for long Bill reworked the Marine defenses at the base and drew high praise from his battalion CO. His hard work and innovative ideas came to the attention of not just one general but two.

2ndMarDiv Commanding General Lt.Gen. Frederick L. Wieseman heard of another general in his command, Maj.Gen. James P. Berkeley, considering Bill as an aide. Since he needed an aide as well, he talked the other general into graciously stepping aside so he could hire him.

Lt.Gen. Wieseman was appointed as the Commandant of the Marine Corps Schools at Quantico with Bill as his aide. The young Capt. Leftwich was able to see how things were done at the rarified air involved in the general's command position.

The general became so impressed with the young captain, Bill's oldest son recalls, that he favorably compared him to Gen. John A. Lejeune, the 13th USMC Commandant.[4]

Undoubtedly this is a high compliment from the general as Gen. John Archer Lejeune is most often referred to as "the greatest of all Leathernecks" having spent 40 years as a Marine 1890-1929 with 10 of those years as Commandant of the Marine Corps. Lejeune saw campaigns in Panama, Philippines, Cuba, Mexico and as Brigade then Division commander in WW I in France.

Lt.Gen. Wieseman became such a close friend and mentor to Leftwich that his two boys, Scott and Bill III, referred to him as "Uncle Fred."

## Cuban Missile Crisis, October 1962

During the Cuban Missile Crisis in October 1962, Jane and Bill were attending a Navy football game when the officers were called away by the stadium public address system by name one-by-one. Bill Leftwich's name was also announced.

Jane learned how it was to be a Marine officer's wife when she called the base later to ask to speak to him but the Marine on-duty said he wasn't there. She pressed and wanted to know when her husband would be able to call her back and let her know what was happening. The Marine told her, "Mam, Capt. Leftwich is not here. We're rear echelon. The captain has flown out." And that's how she found out he had been tactically deployed during the Cuban Missile Crisis.

## First Vietnam Tour, Bong Son, RVN, January 27, 1965

As Vietnam was heating up and advisors were being sought for the Vietnamese Marine Brigade, Bill volunteered for duty in Vietnam. The general reason for a Marine officer to train year after year for combat is that someday that officer will actually put all his learned knowledge, skill and leadership potential into a situation involving an armed foe of the United States. To test his mettle in the field of battle against an angry, determined enemy was the ultimate goal of men like Bill Leftwich, who was by then a Marine major.

Before going to Nam, he attended the Vietnamese Language Course put on by the Foreign Services Institute in Washington, D.C. from August 13-December 11, 1964. He could speak the Vietnamese language quite well before arriving in-country which put him a leg up on most of the American servicemen who came after him.

Records show Bill arrived in-country January 27, 1965 for a 11-month tour of duty. He reported to our counterpart South Vietnamese Marine Corps (VNMC) Brigade as part of the Marine Advisory Section of the Naval Advisory Group on February 11, 1965 operating in II Corps, the Central Highlands. When he came aboard, the VNMC was still reeling from having one of its four battalions, the 4th, ambushed and virtually destroyed as an effective fighting unit by two regiments of the 9th VC Division near Binh Gia, 40 miles east of Saigon, in December. A relief force was mauled by the enemy as well.[5]

He assumed the post of senior advisor and headed a 2-man headquarters team with four USMC battalion advisors under him. He would remain with that outfit for the next 11 months fighting alongside them every inch of the way. At that time America was involved with a token commitment of forces in Vietnam, approximately 500 Marines were in-country, used mainly as support and advisory.

## Maj. H. Norman Schwarzkopf, Airborne Advisor

U.S. Army Maj. H. Norman Schwarzkopf, 30, of East Orange, New Jersey, came in-country in June 1965. He would become known worldwide 26 years later as the successful Commanding General of the Coalition forces in the Gulf War in 1991. He noted that the Vietnamese Airborne Brigade to which he was attached as an advisor and the Vietnamese Marine Brigade were on "national reserve." That meant that whenever things went to hell in a hand basket in an important province in a battle involving the regular Vietnamese Army, the Airborne or Marines would be sent to the rescue...something that happened often, according to retired Gen. Schwarzkopf commenting in his book, *General H. Norman Schwarzkopf, The Autobiography, It Doesn't Take A Hero*.[6]

At the first of March 1965 there were approximately 23,000 U.S. personnel from all America's military services, mostly advisors and helicopter pilots, in-country. The Marines sent in an additional 3,500 troops March 9 to guard the air bases from increased instances of enemy attack.

By the end of 1965, the U.S. would deploy 180,000 U.S. troops to South Vietnam, 38,000 of them were Marines, according to Brig.Gen. Edwin H. Simmons.[7]

## Leftwich Shows His Mettle at Hoai An, March 9, 1965

On Tuesday, March 9, 1965 Maj. Bill Leftwich was with Task Force Alfa, four battalions of the Vietnamese Marine Brigade, as they left their garrison at Bong Son and marched 10 miles at mid-morning to the district post at Hoai An in Binh Dinh Province (not to be confused with Hoi An located just over a click from the South China Sea on the Song Hoi An---MDK). The district town is 10-15 miles inland of the South China Sea, about 290 miles north of Saigon. The ville and its defenders were engaged with three battalions of the 2nd VC Regiment. While one of the enemy battalions laid siege to Hoai An, the other two took up positions on the high ground as well as along Route 19 to ambush the anticipated relief force. The enemy was attempting a repeat of its annihilation of the 4th Battalion, VNMC and a relief force in December. Bill was about to face that aforementioned "angry enemy" and test what he was made of in the process.[8]

Peter Arnett, *AP* war correspondent and Huynh Cong La, also known as Huynh Thanh My (Mr. My), 27, *AP* photographer, caught up with the task force column en route to the Hoai An District headquarters. They requested and were granted permission to join them in anticipation of a big battle. They weren't disappointed.

The enemy regularly overwhelmed small ARVN garrisons in a 60-mile stretch along Highway 1, the north-south artery. The country was gradually being cut in two. The district town of Bong Son, with its small airstrip, became the last bastion on the northern frontier. Bill and his fellow Marine advisors accompanied 1,300 Vietnamese Marines sent into the breach to stop them.[9]

And worse news to the meagerly paid VNMC foot soldiers was that the price of Vietnamese beer, when it was available, spiked to 35 piasters in Bong Son compared to 8 in Saigon due to the anticipation of the roads being cut off thus stopping the supply of beer out of Saigon.[10]

The VC commander expected the Vietnamese Marines to blunder into a classic killing zone along the road. I believe by this time Bill had studied his enemy well enough to realize what was waiting on his unit if they walked in the "front door" of the town.

Any student of military history of the Viet Minh/French Indochina War in the 1950s would know how many times the French Union Forces were mauled or slaughtered time after time running these same roads in armored vehicles thinking themselves impervious to attack. And the Bill Leftwich I came to understand through others' eyes would be cognizant of his enemy's ambush tactics inside and out. He was prepared for all contingencies.

**Maj. Bill Leftwich Jr., VNMC advisor (Photo courtesy of Bill Leftwich III)**

Prior to setting out for Hoai An, Bill worked out a plan with the 22d Division Air Liaison Officer for supporting aircraft to deliver their ordnance in extra close proximity to the front lines. Also part of the plan was an ingenious innovation to continue simulated air attacks to keep Charlie's head down while the Vietnamese Marines assaulted the enemy positions[11]...a brilliant strategy.

Assistant commandant of the VNMC Lt.Col. Nguyen Thanh "Little Tiger" Yen, who had spent 15 years fighting Communists by 1965, received a key piece of intelligence on the way to Hoai An that pinpointed the enemy positions--two dominate hills outside the town and on the road. In response, three of the VNMC Marine battalions, accompanied by Bill and at least one other USMC advisor, marched several miles out of their way in a covered flanking movement to hit the two VC battalions from an unexpected direction to take the advantage away from them. The fourth VNMC battalion was held back in reserve.[12]

The tough Vietnamese Marines overran the immediate VC hillside positions only yards behind Bill's prearranged supporting air cover in the late afternoon. Bill and 1stLt. Dempsey H. Williams moved to the forward-most elements of Task Force Alfa with a radio so he could direct accurate aircraft bombing attacks on the VC troops who by now were engaging the hard-charging diminutive Marines with an ever-increasing volume of fire.[13]

The Navy Cross citation he was awarded this day reads in part: "By his own personal example of shooting point-blank and shouting, he led the attack which overran the immediate Viet Cong positions and carried the assault to within 40 meters of the crest of a hill overlooking Hoai An.

"Despite injuries by enemy machine gun bullets in the back, cheek and nose, he went to the aid of his mortally wounded comrade, 1stLt. Dempsey H. Williams, 25, of Fayetteville, North Carolina (an East Carolina University graduate in Greenville, North Carolina). Although bleeding profusely, he refused assistance and delayed his own evacuation until he could call for additional airstrikes and brief the Task Force Commander of the situation."[14] American advisors as a rule made easy targets as they generally stood a foot taller than the VNMC Marines they accompanied.

Bill put himself in the thick of the battle having thought out the strategic life-saving groundwork in advance. He came away with the knowledge he could handle himself when the bullets were flying. In the midst of the battle, the enemy was able to concentrate .51 caliber machine gun fire on the large Americans who were calling in air support on top of them.

The Germantown, Tennessee native turned to look at 1stLt. Williams beside him on the ground just as the VC's machine gun bullets found their mark striking the lieutenant multiple times. His wounds proved to be fatal. The large volume of fire hit Bill as well. The bullets creased his cheek, clipped his nose and struck him in the back as well. Eight .51 caliber rounds also tore through a map in his left hand riddling it with holes.[15]

One more inch or, perhaps, a mere half inch closer into his face and the machine gun bullet would have killed Bill as well. Although wounded, he continued to read off map coordinates pinpointing the enemy positions over the radio on the air tactical frequency to the overhead aircraft enabling them to make accurate strafing runs against the entrenched VC.

When Bill was struck in the face and back, it was the unflappable 5-foot-3, 100 lb. *AP* photographer Mr. My at his feet, according to Arnett. He calmly recorded the action snapping away with one of five 35mm cameras he carried, Nikon Fs or Leica M-2s, as a wounded and bleeding Bill pressed the PRC-25's handset against his ear calling in air support on the VC arrayed before him (See book cover photo). The dedicated photographer hunkered down doing his job and showed a lot of guts as bullets whizzed overhead. The air support and pressure from the Vietnamese Marines was too much for the VC force as it withdrew.

Mr. My's dramatic photos of Bill's close brush with death and Williams as a KIA were carried by *AP Wirephoto* worldwide and made the Marine major an instant recognizable hero. He would later say the photo showed him "bleeding like a stuck pig" and that it scared his family back home.[16]

Bill summed up the battle for Hoai An on March 9th by saying, "In the gathering darkness, the entire enemy force, outmaneuvered and inflexible, quit the battlefield. It was a classic demonstration of anti-ambush tactics, and the results changed the tenor of the entire campaign."[17] VC casualties were 63 KIA while the VNMC lost 4 KIA, 11 WIA (includes USMC 1 KIA, 1 WIA).[18]

And an added benefit of winning the battle at Hoai An was the plummeting price of beer back at Bong Son to 25 piasters now that the road to Saigon appeared to be unimpeded...and immediately shot back up to 30 piasters when the VNMC Marines were tactically redeployed away from Bong Son.[19]

**Huynh Cong La (aka, Huynh Thanh My), *AP* Photographer**

Huynh Cong La (or simply "My" as he was called by his *AP* associates) of Long An, South Vietnam, was later wounded by machine gun fire in May 1965 and after a few months of recuperation in the hospital he returned to the field creating unforgettable images of soldiers in combat like he did of Bill Leftwich. Horst Faas, *AP*'s Saigon bureau's photography chief (awarded the first Pulitzer Prize for photography in Vietnam in 1965), had hired My away from *CBS* where he was a camera crewman in 1963. Faas was sold on My when he saw how cool he was under fire in a muddy rice paddy on an operation covered by *CBS*.

On October 10, 1965, the Vietnamese photographer was wounded again in the chest and arm as he sought to be in the thick of the action with the ARVN's 44th Ranger Battalion (Tiger Lady's Battalion) in the Mekong Delta near Can Tho. While waiting for a medevac with the other wounded soldiers, 28-year-old My was killed when the aid station was overrun by the VC and everyone was shot in cold blood.

"They were overrun by a main force VC unit and killed to the last man," recalled Joseph L. "Joe" Galloway of Refugio, Texas, *United Press International* war correspondent. "*UPI* photographer Kyoichi Sawada (a Pulitzer Prize recipient for photography in 1966 was killed in an ambush in Cambodia in October 1970) and I accompanied Ed White (*AP* Saigon bureau chief) to the ARVN morgue in the delta. It was a charnel house, bodies everywhere. White finally found My's body. He had brought a folded up green body bag and zipped him up in it and flew back to Tan Son Nhut Air Base. His wife and family were there. His wife was wailing and screaming." (Galloway was the only civilian to be awarded a Bronze Star with Combat "V" for rescuing U.S. Army soldiers under fire in the Ia Drang Valley in November 1965. His wife, Karen, lost her father, U.S. Army Capt. Thomas C. Metsker, KIA at Ia Drang---MDK).

My's funeral was a major event attended by the entire close-knit Saigon press corps, which marched in a procession to the Mac Dinh Chi cemetery. He was survived by his 19-year-old wife, Arlette, and a 7-month-old daughter.

"My's brother, Nick (Huynh Cong "Nick" Ut), also became an *AP* photographer (under Faas' tutelage) and in 1972 shot the famous photo (Pulitzer Prize for photography in 1973) of the little girl (9-year-old Phan Thi Kim Phuc) running naked and burned from the napalm attack (by VNAF, South Vietnamese, pilots near Trang Bang). Nick now works in Los Angeles for the *AP*," said Galloway.

To get an idea what the photographers in Vietnam were paid for the photos they risked life and limb for, Galloway said that *UPI* paid him a base pay of $135 per week in 1965 and $10 for every photo they used. He carried a Nikonos 35mm underwater camera and two Nikon F bodies plus various lenses. "On a really 'bad' day I could make $150-$200 (over and above my base pay) so we all stuck our heads up and snapped off a roll or two even if our main job was reporting."

Nick Ut said he remembered the amazing action shots his brother took in his assignments for the *AP* working under Faas. He recalled the photos at Hoai An when My was with Peter Arnett and later the circumstances surrounding his death.

"I was 15 when my brother was killed. He was very handsome, a playboy and acted in at least two Vietnamese movies in love stories. He (and later Nick) never carried a weapon to the field because if the VC caught him armed they'd ask why he carried a gun and shoot him. Besides, the cameras were already too heavy a load for him. We were all gathered for a family dinner when we got word of his death. We all cried together. My's beautiful wife was able to get out of Vietnam and come to Los Angeles where she married an LAPD captain," said Nick. And the little Vietnamese girl in the photo that made them both famous now lives in Toronto, Canada. They talk occasionally…she calls him "uncle."

"My was killed before I got to Vietnam but Horst (Faas) and Peter (Arnett) spoke of him almost reverentially. The Vietnamese photographers were really incredible people," said Richard Pyle, Saigon *AP* bureau chief, 1970-73, and in-country since 1968.

## Leftwich Receives Navy Cross, Williams the Silver Star

For his actions at Hoai An, Bill received the Navy Cross. 1stLt. Williams was awarded the Silver Star posthumously.

Bill appeared to have all the criteria needed for a Medal of Honor...routed a vastly superior, well-entrenched enemy force while leading the charge and inspiring his troops; risked his own life in order to save a fellow advisor who had been shot; and was wounded himself but refused medical evacuation until the fight was won and the enemy vanquished from the field of battle. Also, despite his wounds he coolly called in life-saving ordnance on the VC positions and was able to brief the Vietnamese field commander before being evacuated.

Bender recounted a conversation with Bill upon his return to Memphis in which his old friend told him he had been put in for the Medal of Honor but it was downgraded to a Navy Cross.

Brig.Gen. Le Nguyen Khang, commanding general of the Vietnamese Marine Brigade, awarded his Brigade-saving senior advisor the Vietnamese Cross of Gallantry with Palm (equal to our Medal of Honor) for the March 9, 1965 Hoai An battle in a Saigon ceremony. This medal represented the highest decoration yet awarded by the Republic of Vietnam to a U.S. Marine Corps advisor.[20]

Bill's tour was just in its infancy at 6 weeks when he was wounded at Hoai An. He set his jaw and returned to the Vietnamese Marine Brigade after being patched up and spending 17 days at the 8th Army Field Hospital at Nha Trang 100 miles away from the battlefield and continued to kick the VC and NVA's butt until his rotation home after 11 months.

Upon his return to the states at the end of his tour, Jane saw the repair work the U.S. Army surgeons had done on his nose and cheek.

"You know he had his nose broken two or three times playing football. The nose looked so much better than it did before after the doctors worked on it to straighten out the damage the machine gun bullet had done. Bill was proud of the scar on his cheek and liked to call it his 'Heidelberg dueling scar,'" recalled Jane. Her oldest son, Bill, agreed with her comment. Mattie told a *Commercial Appeal* reporter interviewing her in 1965 that when Maj. Leftwich returned home she wouldn't let him go back (to war).[21]

## Fight for Survival at Phung Du, April 7-8, 1965

The major was again in the thick of it on April 7 at Phung Du as enemy mortars rained down on the 2nd VNMC Battalion and his fellow advisors at 2300. Three VC battalions--93rd, 95th and 97th of the 2nd VC Regiment--hurled themselves at the tough Vietnamese Marines in their fighting holes. The enemy made the mistake of thinking they were attacking one company rather than three. Ten consecutive attacks from three sides of their three companies were beaten back with the final thrust coming to within 75 yards of the battalion CP.[22]

At one point Bill noted his VNMC Marines became fatalistic as they were outnumbered 5 to 1 and felt they were about to be overrun and killed. He said he thought this was part of their Asian culture...reconciling the fact they were going to die. Jane remembered her husband telling her later, "There was no way I was going to die and I was going to do all I could do to stay alive."[23]

With devastating fire from the Brigade's 75mm pack howitzers and the sheer guts and firepower of what the Marines carried with them, they repelled the attackers. On April 8, the enemy retired from the field of battle leaving 59 VC dead near the perimeter and losing 70 more KIA carried off on litters and at least 200 WIA, of whom it was estimated half would die.[24] The 2nd VNMC Battalion had 4 KIAs and 22 WIAs and would later be awarded the U.S. Presidential Unit Citation for its heroic stand.[25]

The Vietnamese Marines claimed a 10 to 1 kill ratio operating out of Bong Son. Once the VNMC moved its base of operations out of the town, the VC filled the vacuum as the civil authority failed to reassert itself in the absence of the Marines.[26]

Bill dispelled the complaint that the Vietnamese wouldn't fight but rather if they had good leadership they could fight and fight well. One such outstanding commander was 5-foot, 90 lb. Lt.Col. Yen, 42 in 1965. He was the most decorated Vietnamese Marine in the VNMC.[27]

In the Vietnamese colonel's thick French-flavored English, Bill quoted Yen as telling him at the beginning of his tour, "Major Lakewich, I nevair weethdraw. Always I fight the Viet Cong. I nevair weethdraw. If eenyone weethdraws, I weel shoot him." Bill said he made a point of never "weethdrawing" in the presence of Yen. He said that the colonel was typical of the professional Vietnamese soldiers who fight on.[28]

## Battle for Duc Co Special Forces Camp, July 29-August 12, 1965

Another significant battle occurred August 9-11 involving the Vietnamese Marine Brigade, 15 M41 tanks, Vietnamese 21st Rangers, two ARVN 105mm artillery pieces, bridge repair engineers and 15 M113 armored personnel carriers (APCs), again designated Task Force Alfa. They faced off against at least one, possibly two, battle-hardened regular North Vietnamese regiments which included the 32nd Peoples Army of Vietnam (PAVN) Regiment.

For over 2 months the enemy laid siege to the U.S. Army's Special Forces/ Bahnar Montagnard tribesmen camp located in a basin at Duc Co (pronounced "due koh") on Route 19 just 5 miles from their sanctuary in Cambodia. They dominated the ridgelines surrounding the compound making resupply by air an adventure.[29]

The Special Forces camp at Duc Co would report losing two of its 12 American Green Berets killed and 60 other casualties involving the local tribesmen defending the town over 60 days.

Earlier on July 29th, 40 Huey helicopters transported a Vietnamese Airborne Brigade onto Duc Co's airstrip in two lifts expecting to rout what Intelligence sources thought to be "two VC battalions," an estimated 700 men, and discovered the overwhelming superior strength and make-up of "two NVA regiments" opposing them once on the ground, according to newly-promoted U.S. Army Maj. Schwarzkopf. The paratroopers were fortunate to have Schwarzkopf as one of their advisors calling in airstrikes to keep the two NVA regiments at bay.[30]

"This was the first time the NVA had come across the border in strength. Ia Drang, the first major battle involving helicopter-borne troops, occurred 4 months later about 15 miles south of Duc Co," according *AP*'s Richard Pyle.

There were approximately 300 indigenous tribesmen and their U.S. Army Special Forces A team defending Duc Co initially. Attrition and desertions reduced their numbers significantly by the time the paratroopers joined the fight. The camp, located in II Corps, was established to stop guerrilla infiltration from across the border and had essentially been under siege all summer.[31]

Schwarzkopf, with only a month and a half in-country at this point, said that *AP* correspondent Peter Arnett flew in aboard a Huey slick medevac helicopter and spent 3 days under siege with the airborne unit. Arnett took a memorable photo of the future Gulf War commanding general helping a Vietnamese paratrooper carry his wounded buddy to an aid station. In the first 2 days after arriving at Duc Co, the paratroopers lost 40 KIA and double that number wounded as the fighting intensified.[32] There was a growing concern the NVA might have the numbers and firepower to overrun Duc Co even with the reinforcements.

## Task Force Alfa Ambushed Outside Duc Co, August 9-10, 1965

In his book, *Street Without Joy*, Dr. Bernard Fall had well-documented the destruction of the French Army's tanks and armored vehicles as part of Groupement Mobile 100 going to the aid of Vietnamese Mobile Group 11 fighting for its life at Ankhe in May 1954. The beleaguered Vietnamese camp was along Route 19 east of Pleiku towards the coast. The French forces were clocked by the Viet Minh's well-laid ambush all along the route.

As Task Force Alfa (VNMC Brigade, 21st Rangers, engineers, APCs, tanks, artillery as well as USAF and VNAF overhead support aircraft) headed west from Pleiku along Route 19 Sunday, August 8, 1965 to Duc Co only 13 miles away, the NVA's tactical scheme had a familiar ring to it 11 years later. Leftwich differed with Schwarzkopf's estimate of the enemy's strength opposing Duc Co's defenders citing only the 32nd PAVN Regiment involved in the siege.[33]

An enemy battalion sat astride Route 19 waiting for the approaching Vietnamese Marines, Rangers and their accompanying tanks and artillery. They were determined to destroy them all. In one well-planned battle, the NVA could annihilate Saigon's premier battle-hardened "Praetorian Guard" units, thus breaking the fighting spirit of the other South Vietnamese units countrywide.

The enemy blew the bridges along Route 19 so the going was slow as the engineers made their repairs along the line of march to accommodate all the tracked vehicles. By the morning of Monday, August 9, the force was only 6 miles into its advance on Duc Co.[34]

The second relief force with Maj. Leftwich in the point element of the Vietnamese Marine Brigade reached the outskirts of Duc Co encountering the enemy's battalion-strength ambush at 1348 Monday along Route 19. A company of Vietnamese 21st Rangers rode the spearhead tanks while the remainder of their unit protected the artillery and engineers to the rear.[35]

NVA soldiers disabled the lead tank with 57mm recoilless rifle and P40 antitank weapon fire then swarmed it and stuffed grenades and automatic fire from machine guns into every opening. A trailing tank mowed the soldiers down in turn, thus began Task Force Alfa's battle for Duc Co.[36]

Enemy troops in a half moon ambush hosed down the front of the relief column with automatic machine gun fire and pounded them with 82mm mortar rounds. Maj. Leftwich swung into action with his fellow advisors calling in air cover and medevacs for the mounting casualties. Air cover unleashed a devastating hellfire of napalm (flame-thrower-like flammable jelly canisters authorized for use against enemy troops by LBJ in March) dropped from A-1E single prop Skyraiders, nicknamed "Spads." (The Skyraiders replaced the WW II Helldivers, armed with four M-3 20mm cannons on the wings and capable of carrying 8,000 lbs. of bombs at a maximum speed of 311 mph---MDK). The Vietnamese Marines' 5th Battalion rolled up the NVA's right flank followed quickly by the 2nd Battalion's overrunning of the enemy's left flank. In 3 hours the Marines owned the ridgeline overlooking their positions. Bodies and equipment littered the battleground. Victory was short-lived though.[37]

## USAF Pilot Shot Down, Executed by NVA

An F-100 Super Sabre jet from the 429th Tactical Fighter Squadron, 6251st Tactical Fighter Wing, 13th Air Force piloted by USAF Capt. Richard Lee Goudy, 27, of Sharon Springs, Kansas (population 800 in 1965) streaked through the battle area at approximately 600-mph. He pounded enemy targets with four M39 20mm cannons and 42, 2.75-inch rockets (5,000 lbs. of bombs) in close air support of the VNMC. NVA gunners zeroing in on the jet's flight path shot him down at approximately 1700. Goudy, who had only been in Vietnam 18 days, since July 23, managed to eject safely and parachute to the ground. He radioed the helicopters and fixed wing overhead for covering fire and an extraction.[38]

The captain had the misfortune to land closer to the enemy troops than the two VNMC battalions attacking the high ground. Leftwich noted that all the air support forces were diverted to recovering Capt. Goudy after he parachuted to safety within sight of the friendly troops about 3 miles south of the scene of the action. The loss of air cover at that crucial point in the battle changed the dynamics of the battle in favor of the enemy assault force.

Goudy evaded the NVA to make it to a tree line where the enemy managed to overtake him. "Despite gallant efforts, the rescue helicopters were driven off by ground fire, and the unfortunate pilot was later captured and executed on the spot by the North Vietnamese," according to Maj. Leftwich.[39]

Sadly, Capt. Goudy's body was not recovered after the Battle of Duc Co. He was listed as MIA until his remains were found in the area of his crashed F-100 3 months later at which time his status was changed to KIA. Goudy, a '61 Kansas State University graduate, was survived by his wife, Sarah; two children, Mark and Ann Margaret; parents, Mr. and Mrs. Glen Goudy; sister, Dolores Ward; and brother, Glen Eugene. After a memorial service at the Plains Baptist Church in Sharon Springs on Tuesday, November 23, interment was the next day in the Fort Leavenworth National Cemetery, Fort Leavenworth, Kansas with full military honors.[40]

In 2010 Sarah Goudy Walker of Bartlesville, Oklahoma had this memory of her husband, "He started flying as a child (a good friend's uncle had a plane). He loved to fly and it was his dream to fly jets. We met in college. He was in ROTC. He did enjoy being in the service. We both enjoyed our time he was in the Air Force, the separations were tough...it seemed longer than 18 days he was in Vietnam before he was killed." Sarah noted that on March 30 1966 Maj.Gen. Lucius Clay Jr., Commander of the Twelfth Air Force presented her Capt. Goudy's medals which included the Silver Star, Distinguished Flying Cross, Air Medal, Purple Heart and the Vietnamese

Cross of Gallantry w/Palms.

Mark S. Goudy, Capt. Goudy's son, was only 2 years old when his dad was shot down. "I was so young when we lost him and have learned about him from his friends over the years. I have even gone to KSU to his fraternity but couldn't find any information. I spoke with the CO of Richard's from Bien Hoa a few years back. He was living in Austin, Texas at the time and picked up a few more details, and just in the past year visited with a gentleman who is sure that he was the fixed-wing search aircraft pilot for that specific search." MM2 (Petty Officer 2nd Class) Mark Goudy served in the U.S. Navy's nuclear power program in the 1980s.

USAF Capt. Paul N. Erckman, 27, a flight surgeon from Atlanta, Georgia, made friends with Goudy and his wife Sarah when they were both stationed at Cannon AFB, just outside Clovis, New Mexico. He flew with him several times while at Cannon. Erckman recalled being informed by his squadron commander at Tan Son Nhut that his friend's body had been found and Sarah had requested he escort her husband back home for burial.

"I was honored to do it. It was my duty to accompany the casket at all times, be sure that it made all travel connections, oversee burial arrangements and ultimately to represent the country by presenting the flag to Sarah, and thanking her, and the family for his giving his life for our country."

"We flew from Tan Son Nhut to Anderson AFB in Guam than onto Hickam AFB in Hawaii to Travis AFB in California. I think there was a train ride in there somewhere before arriving at Leavenworth National Cemetery, Fort Leavenworth, Kansas. I'm not sure how in the world I did it, but I arranged a flyby from a nearby Air Force base, and I think I also arranged an honor guard. He had the standard military funeral with honors and taps, and I presented the United States flag to Sarah. 'On behalf of the President of the United States, the Department of the Air Force and a grateful nation, we offer this flag for Richard's faithful and dedicated service to the country...' or something close to that.

"It was a great honor, but presenting that flag to Sarah was one of the hardest things I've ever had to do...There were hundreds of people there and only me and the honor guard were wearing uniforms. I really felt out of place. It was like 'local boy goes to war and comes home dead.'" Erckman said he caught an empty commercial flight back to Cannon AFB after his emotionally draining experience bringing Capt. Goudy home and seeing to his funeral. He called his wife from the hangar to come get him and thought, "It was a very unceremonious way to 'come home from the war,' but at least there was no one there to jeer, or spit on me."

## Bird Dog Warns Leftwich

With air support otherwise occupied August 9, a USAF Bird Dog L19 (2-seater Cessna Model 170) pilot, acting as an overhead spotter for enemy activity on the ground, shouted an excited radio transmission to Leftwich, "Watch out, there's a whole gang of 'em coming up behind you!" An additional reinforced NVA battalion in two massed columns ran up two trails splitting off and blocking the road behind the Marines as well as attacking the medical evacuation point.[41]

This maneuver was the second phase of the classic VC meat grinder tactics. The attack managed to divide the Vietnamese Marines from their supporting artillery units and the rest of the Vietnamese 21st Rangers bringing up the rear. Trying to run the ambush site as per ordered and join the front half of the column, a 105mm artillery piece with accompanying infantry was lost in a hail of fire. It was going on 1800 and a new phase of the battle developed as the sun began to slip behind the mountains to the west. Again, 82mm HE mortar rounds began to fall on the Vietnamese Marines and Rangers and the artillery unit protected by the Rangers as each pulled into its own tight perimeter. Neither unit could contact the other by radio as a ridgeline blocked their transmissions and a 3-mile gap was created by the NVA attack. The two separate perimeters hunkered down to fight for their lives as darkness fell.[42]

A portion of the enemy battalion tried to overrun the evacuation point when it surged out of the elephant grass and put 20 bullet holes in a U.S. Army Huey UH1B medevac helicopter in the LZ before being driven off by Huey gunships at pointblank range. The gunships' defense of the medevac LZ gave the tanks and Marines time to consolidate their perimeter. Leftwich's 1,400 Marines and tanks were squeezed into a 200x800-meter perimeter with 50-odd vehicles lining the road. The NVA troops now held the ridgelines and fired down on them at will.[43]

The advisors spent a long sleepless night calling in air support from A-1 Skyraiders and directing tank fire each time they spotted the enemy massing for attack a mere 300 meters away. "Puff," a C-47 aircraft generally equipped with three Gatling-like machine guns on one side, arrived and periodically sowed illumination flares and blanketed the ridgelines with 7.62mm rounds at 6,000 rounds per minute with red tracers every fourth round as it circled overhead. (Puff's guns were capable of putting a round in every square foot of an area the size of a football field).[44]

Tank .50 caliber tracer rounds were able to pinpoint enemy targets for aircraft making bombing and strafing runs during the long night. As dawn broke, the NVA picked up the tempo of the fight firing 57mm and 60mm HE rounds into the tight perimeter and hurling at least two or more companies of NVA soldiers at the north edge of the perimeter before quitting the field. This attack was thought to be covering fire for the withdrawal of the main forces from the field of battle.[45]

The rest of the operation to relieve Duc Co was anticlimactic. The major battle had been won and the split perimeters each held their own. Final consensus of NVA losses, primarily due to airstrikes, were 155 enemy bodies counted on the ground (434 KIA estimated) with 71 weapons and one man captured. The VNMC lost 28 KIA, 60 WIA and 3 MIA. The talkative prisoner who had been a stretcher bearer and a letter found on a dead NVA officer's body to his battalion commander decrying the hardships of fighting in the South, (i.e., a shortage of drugs for the sick, bombing and strafing by airplanes, lack of soldiers and sour rice) were icing on the cake.[46]

## 173rd Airborne Brigade Moves into Blocking Position

As the battle for Duc Co intensified after midnight August 9 into Tuesday, August 10, the U.S. Army's II Corps Headquarters near Pleiku held a planning conference at 1900 that evening electing to send elements of the 173rd Airborne Brigade to Thanh Binh in Trung Phan Province to establish blocking positions to secure a route of withdrawal for the Green Berets' CIDGs, Vietnamese Rangers, VNMC and Vietnamese Airborne. Brig.Gen. Ellis W. Williamson was in command of Task Force 1/503 consisting of 1/503d Infantry, E/17th Cavalry, one battery 3/319th Artillery and elements of the Brigade command group. The task force left Holloway Field outside Pleiku at 0930 Wednesday, August 11 in a convoy down Route 19. The blocking force arrived several clicks short of the Duc Co battlefield around midnight. No resistance was cited in reports of the task force's movement to Thanh Binh.[47]

Task Force 1/503 set up positions to defend Thanh Binh Pass, established LZs for more of its troops from Camp Holloway, Pleiku and Bien Hoa to be flown in for extensive patrolling of the area, set up artillery firebases and found very little of the enemy to engage. The U.S. Army Task Force maintained their positions until August 18 when the Vietnamese forces passed through their lines over a 2-day period from Duc Co back to Pleiku.[48]

## Westy Ignores Schwarzkopf's Stand, Lauds Leftwich

In his autobiography, Gen. Schwarzkopf said that his paratroopers spent 10 days at Duc Co before the Vietnamese Marines and Rangers came down the road fighting off an ambush and sending the NVA troops back to their sanctuary across the Cambodian border. "Our daylight patrols stopped getting shot at and planes were able to fly low enough to air-drop supplies."[49]

Schwarzkopf, who would go on to earn three Silver Stars and three Bronze

Stars in two tours of Vietnam (again in 1969-70), lived to fight another day. He rose to the rank of 4-star general commanding 700,000 Coalition troops in the Gulf War in 1991. He not only soundly defeated but humiliated Saddam Hussein and his vaunted Iraqi military in a 6-week air bombardment and 100-hour ground campaign with few casualties during *Operation Desert Storm*.

Gen. Westmoreland, CG MAC-V, referred to the March 9 Hoai An battle when talking about Leftwich after the relief of Duc Co in August by saying he had distinguished himself again and was "the best advisor in Vietnam."[50]

Schwarzkopf later wrote that Gen. Westmoreland pulled him aside at Duc Co after arriving by helicopter with a load of VIPs, eager reporters and news cameras rolling. The general asked him out of earshot of the throng if he was receiving hot chow and if his mail was getting through to him regularly in the bush![51] (After tenaciously holding off a much larger NVA force, sustaining numerous KIAs and WIAs, fighting for their lives for 10 hellish days and having refused to remove himself from a Huey's skid until its pilot agreed to remove his dead Vietnamese Airborne soldiers from the battlefield once the siege was lifted...that was all the general could think to say or ask Schwarzkopf---MDK)!

## Fighting VC/NVA Begets Medals

Leftwich would participate in approximately 27 hardcore engagements with the enemy during his tour. Major medals awarded him by the VNMC Brigade, dates and locations of the battles were: Gallantry Cross w/Palm, 9March65, Hoai An; Gallantry Cross w/Silver Star, 7-8April65, Phung Du; Gallantry Cross w/Gold Star, 14-24July65, Dan Tien 109 (Route 19); Honor Medal, 1st Class, 9-10August65, Duc Co; and Navy Distinguished Service Order 2d Class, end of tour.

In plain English, the Vietnamese awards represent their Medal of Honor, Navy Cross, Legion of Merit (U.S. Army also awarded him that one) and three Bronze Stars. Most of the medals were for different battles and accomplishments during his entire tour.

In an article he authored in the *Proceedings of the United States Naval Institute* in August 1968 titled *"...and a few Marines,"* Bill summed up his duties as advisor to the Vietnamese Marine Brigade in part: "Advisors during the 1961-1965 period played out a colorful and demanding role. A (war news) correspondent depicted the advisory crusade as 'a wonderfully American invention, idealistic and romantic in the Lawrence of Arabia mold and basically unworkable.'

"Indeed, this period recaptured for a new generation a measure of appeal as the Lafayette Escadrille provided an earlier one. Theirs was a multi-faceted endeavor accentuated by a backdrop of increasing combat intensity. Vietnamese Marine battalions by 1964 were spending 83 percent of their time in combat operations."[52]

I asked Arnett if he was that "correspondent" and he responded by laughing heartily, "I guess that could've been me being my observant, critical self about the Vietnam War. We were much younger then, of course."

Bill pointed out that American advisors had no authority per se to tell the Vietnamese commanders who had more wartime experience what to do and were junior in rank to them. What it all came down to was "pure counseling, persuasion and marshalling the U.S. assets available to the advisor...air power and artillery in close support of the Vietnamese troops."

He became acquainted with several news correspondents and photographers during his first tour since he was on the cutting edge of all the action. Among Bill's media contacts besides Arnett (*AP*) were Hanson Baldwin (*The New York Times*) and Charlie Black (*The Columbus Enquirer*), according to his son, Bill. Maj. Leftwich later corresponded with all three men in order to get background information for "The Role of the Advisor in Counterinsurgency" thesis paper that he was writing at the Marine Corps' Staff and Command College at Quantico.

## Charlie Black, War Correspondent

Charlie Black wrote a story for *The Columbus* (Ohio) *Enquirer* on January 13, 1967 telling about following the Vietnamese Marine Brigade and, in particular, Lt.Col. Yen's battalion around advised by Marine Maj. Bill Leftwich, call sign "Leatherneck 6." Seems either the Vietnamese field rations he ate or a bug that attacked his intestinal tract had him doubled up in an immobile knot so bad that Leftwich had to carry him on his shoulders to load him onto a medevac helicopter east of Ban Me Thuot.[53]

Black indicated that Maj. Leftwich requested his 2 cents worth of observation on the advisors' role in Vietnam from his time spent there for a paper and kidded, "That's asking quite a bit of a guy just because you saved his life one day, Leftwich!"[54]

## Leftwich's Reputation Grows

Marines on the perimeters of Da Nang and Chu Lai often talked of "the hard charging advisor down south," having heard of Leftwich via that mysterious verbal communications channel which keeps men in combat aware of what's going on even hundreds of miles away.[55]

Reporters used to ask, "Where can we find Leftwich?" Though few of them did because it was difficult to tell which rice paddy the major was in at any given hour. Of the 11 months spent with the Vietnamese Marines in 1965, he would spend roughly 300 days of that in the bush.[56]

"I knew him well and admired him enormously," said Arnett. "I would go with the Vietnamese Marines a week or two at a time and Bill Leftwich was, of course, an advisor to them. They were in constant mini-ambushes and skirmishes with the VC. They'd go out in the woods after them and track them down."

The former *AP* reporter continued, "He was a superb officer and had the greatest respect of his Vietnamese associates. He was really very good to the reporters who joined him. He was unfailingly polite and was a very energetic and intelligent leader. I liked him a lot and I remember corresponding with him about the whole phenomenon about the war. He was a student of the war and really had a smart attitude. I don't think there was any doubt he was destined to becoming a general officer."

Arnett was awarded a Pulitzer Prize in 1966 for International Reporting for his 1965 coverage of the Vietnam War. He spent a significant amount of time in 1965 covering the Vietnamese Marine Brigade. He also made his mark in Baghdad, Iraq for CNN during the spectacular air war over that city in 1991 in *Operation Desert Storm* which kept TV viewers (myself included---MDK) spellbound with his reporting and visual accounts of war into the wee hours of the morning back in the United States. He returned to Baghdad in 2003 during the U.S.-led Coalition *Operation Iraqi Freedom*.

"When Arnett came to spend the day or up to 5 days with the Task Force, he never once failed to carry his own load. He was one correspondent that you could count on doing his share and taking care of himself. John Wheeler of the *AP* was the same type individual. In fact, Wheeler probably saved Capt. Paul S. Marcani, a 3d Battalion advisor's life. Arnett was a good reporter type in those days," recalled former Marine Maj. Bill Bond Jr., an advisor in the 4th Battalion, Vietnamese Marine Brigade in 1965.

(*AP*'s Pyle noted, "John Wheeler was among the best all-around war correspondents in Vietnam, fearless and a fine writer. He covered Khe Sanh among other stories and wrote by far the best stuff on the 77-day siege. He was in Vietnam as a member of the *AP*'s News Features staff, a stable of top-notch writers based in NYC. Wheeler was a very intense guy, who had been a SAC B-52 navigator...I don't recall the incident with Marcani but if Wheeler saved somebody's life, it would not surprise me.").

Lt.Col. Yen's departing comments had a huge impact on Bill as he was leaving Vietnam at the end of his tour. "Now you go back to your home. You have been in the field for a year. But how about me? I must stay in the field--this year, next year. What weel happen to me?" He recalled the colonel's melancholy appraisal of the plight of the Vietnamese professional soldier who, having fought an indecisive war for years, faced only the prospect of fighting on with little hope, until he is killed.[57]

"I will not soon forget Col. Yen or the Vietnamese Marines or Vietnam and there will be some rent consciences among old advisors if we cannot bring this war to a satisfactory conclusion and must leave the 'Yens' of this world to their Fate," noted Bill in a September 20, 1966 speech given before the Memphis Civitan Club.[58]

## Marine Warrior Returns Home, January 1966

Maj. Leftwich spent a well-deserved 30-day leave in Memphis during January 1966 and traveled quite often to the Memphis Naval Air Station Hospital at nearby Millington, Tennessee to undergo treatments to rid himself of amoebic dysentery. His wife recalled it taking 6 months to a year for him to get over the bugs he picked up in Vietnam.[59]

**Maj. Bill Leftwich poses with family, L-R, Scott, a future '82 USNA graduate, 7th in his class and retires a USN commander; wife Jane; Bill III, future '81 VMI graduate and retires a USMC major. (Photo courtesy of Bill Leftwich III)**

His 5-foot-11 frame was gaunt from disease brought on by bad water, a steady diet of suspect Vietnamese food and exotic Asian germs, which were thrilled to host on the healthy bodies of the American advisors. The following quotes from an article Maj. Leftwich wrote entitled, "COVAN MY, American Advisor," for *Shipmate*, USNA's alumni magazine (November 1966), explains where those germs came from in addition to replenishing the water in his empty canteens from streams in the field as a drinking source.

"The standard field diet is rice and fish in various forms, all of which are palatable, but more adjusted to the 1800 calorie Vietnamese requirement than to 200-lb. Americans. Some local delicacies are more trying. In the interest of good sportsmanship, most advisors at one time or another sample dog, squid, duck's blood, eel and inevitably the 19-day-old chicken egg, complete with the incomplete chicken inside.

"...There are some immediate favorites as well, *Café sua*, strong coffee with thick sweetened cream is an American staple and '33' or 'La Rue' Beer substitutes pleasantly for more familiar brands. The diet plus the exercise generally pares 20 lbs. or so off the fittest American."[60]

Although he never touched alcohol before Vietnam, Jane said once they were posted to Washington, D.C. for duty she found that Bill had acquired a taste for gin and tonic overseas and thought that was "a pretty good drink."

Bill Leftwich was an undeniable hero after his year's tour in Vietnam. He had been bloodied by war and not found wanting. He was in big demand and made himself readily available to talk to local Memphian civic groups about the Vietnam War and America's presence there.

He told them of how the U.S. Army's 1st Air Cavalry Division came ashore at Cam Ranh Bay in August 1965 fresh out of Fort Benning and looked so green. And yet in November they were plunged into a desperate battle against the cream of the North Vietnamese Army, the regulars that defeated the French, and under conditions in which they might have been destroyed, they defeated the enemy in the Ia Drang Valley and sent them scurrying across the border.[61]

Speaking before the Shelby County Young Republicans Club, he criticized American newsmen in Vietnam who say little when an operation is successful "but paint a bleak picture when an operation is unsuccessful."[62]

He noted that in some circles it seemed "unfashionable to be patriotic." He said young men should be aware that their service "was treasured and their sacrifice precious" and if they should be called they should serve "with great pride and confidence" as "the greatest privilege that can be offered us is the opportunity to serve God and Country."[63]

Having lived and broken bread and other less tasty "foods" with the VNMC Marines, Bill Leftwich was determined that Vietnam not fall to the Communists whom he had fought so hard against the previous year. I think the distant echo of war and the loss of fellow warriors in mortal combat beckoned to strong men such as Bill Leftwich like a destructive Siren's Song.

# Chapter 12

**2/1 Marines and 3rd Counterintelligence personnel captured enemy documents that revealed they had an unbridled fear of Cobras, Hueys and Sea Knights. The VC/NVA knew if they were caught in the open or with limited cover, they were as good as dead due to the aircrafts' massive and devastating onboard firepower. (VC/NVA troops cited the obvious--that they had nowhere to escape death from above. Helicopters, indeed, controlled the "high ground" in Vietnam---MDK).**

**1stLt. Thomas H. "Tom" Marino**
**CO, 3rd Counterintelligence**
**Camp Lauer**

## Passing on Combat Tips to Lieutenants at Quantico, 1966

While at Quantico in 1966 as a TBS tactics instructor, Maj. Bill Leftwich Jr. was instrumental in giving advice on constructing a realistic mock-up Vietnamese village. Lieutenants practiced cordoning off and screening its inhabitants to weed out the "VC" in the ville.

My C-69 TBS class ran an op in that ville in January 1969. The 3rd Platoon which I was a part of acted as the VC. We lost in our bid to escape the tightening cordon by the other four platoons. My VC partner and I were surrounded in a creek bed by a squad of "good guy" lieutenants and ordered to surrender. In response, I fired a long burst of M-14 blanks into a fellow officer's chest drawing "first blood." The "dead" officer was so upset and unnerved by my kamikaze attack he had to be restrained from slugging me. They, of course, "killed" me back. Who knew in the future the VC/NVA would react the same way rather than be taken prisoner?

Leftwich wrote many papers about Vietnam and leadership roles of Marine officers as part of a 36-week course at Quantico's Staff and Command College in 1967. He was also a systems analyst at HQMC 1967-68. He brought in a little extra money in those days writing articles for various publications including *Reader's Digest*, according to his son, Bill.

Between 1968-70 he was the Marine Corps Assistant/Aide to the Under Secretary of the Navy Charles F. Baird then his replacement John W. Warner, a WW II Naval officer and Korean War era Marine officer, who would go on to become Secretary of the Navy (1972-74) and later a U.S. senator from Virginia (1978-2008) and chairman of the Military Affairs Committee into 2007.

Perot's last visit with Leftwich was at a dinner honoring Bob Hope in the

Waldorf-Astoria Hotel in New York City at some point in 1970 where he showed up in his Marine dress uniform sporting an impressive chest full of medals including the distinctive Navy Cross from his first tour. Perot's recollection was that at some point when it came time for Bill to be reassigned to his next posting, Warner told him he could have any assignment he wanted and he had said, "I want to go back to Vietnam." He got his wish.

## Leftwich Begins His Second Tour in Vietnam

Bill returned to Vietnam for a second tour April 20, 1970 as a lieutenant colonel and assumed command of 2nd Battalion, 1st Marine Regiment on May 16. Little did we know at the time that this quiet, efficient colonel was one of the most highly decorated Marines of the Vietnam War after just one tour!

He began visiting the field on a regular basis getting an account of how our side was doing from the get-down-and-dirty grunts doing the actual fighting. He breathed life into 2/1, as did Maj. Grinalds when he arrived.

**Lt.Col. Bill Leftwich poses in front of 2/1's activity map for May-June 1970. (USMC Photo)**

2ndLt. David Siff, Fox 1 actual, said that Leftwich came to visit his platoon in the bush and asked to speak to the squad leaders. "They complained about patrol after patrol of only finding boobytraps but no VC. He asked me the last time I had a haircut. I didn't have a mirror and didn't check myself on a daily basis. I told him probably the last time we were in the rear about 3 months earlier. He had us at Stack Arms within the week and we all got haircuts by the gunny with a hand held clippers. Nobody complained."

I remember Lt.Col. Leftwich as a somewhat stoop-shouldered man with an athletic build who had a calm voice. I recall seeing the impressive rapier mark under his right eye and what I thought was a broken nose. My thinking at the time was that he had been in an automobile accident. He didn't brag or tell "sea stories" of his past accomplishments so we really had no clue as to his proven prowess from being in Vietnam in 1965. He never yelled or raised his voice, yet was still able to get things done and done quickly utilizing his quiet approach.

## 2/1's Intelligence "Makeover"

Lt.Col. Leftwich remade the Intelligence playbook at 2/1 with the help of Maj. Grinalds, S-3 chief (replaced Capt. Vincent O'Neill July 16 and would serve as the S-3 until December 15, 1970); 1stLt. Tom Marino, 3rd Counterintelligence (3rd CIT) chief (Marino's dates posted to 2/1 aren't included in the Operations Journal); 2ndLt. Gil Robinson, S-2 officer (replaced 1stLt. Alan MacDonald July 30 and would remain in that post until January 31, 1971); some village chiefs who worked both sides of the street; turned POWs into assets; and two pint-sized VC who chose to switch sides, Butch*, 14, and Sundance*, 16. (I decided to use fictional names for these two young Vietnamese boys in case the Socialist Republic of Vietnam--Communists--was still punishing its citizens and their relatives for fighting against them in the Vietnam War---MDK).

"The Viet Cong Infrastructure, VCI, had used the two boys since they had turned 12 years old for their liaison between units and village sympathizers," said retired Lt.Col. Robinson. "The VC had killed their parents. They knew the VCI in our part of the Quang Nam Province as to names, where they met, how often they met, how they moved, warning systems, escape routes, tunnels, where they hid their weapons and documents, etc. 1stLt. Marino was responsible for these two invaluable Vietnamese teenagers and exploited their information to our advantage.

"Marino's job was to turn VC operators and make them work for CIT by exposing their contacts. One way to coerce known VC into giving up information was to convince them if they didn't cooperate then the word would get out that they had provided valuable information. We would leak real information. If they did cooperate they would be classified as Civil Defendants, CDs, and spend 3-6 months in the Province Detention center and be released to their village. If not, they would be released and their VC superiors would have them killed to plug the intelligence leak. A couple of VCI tested Marino's threat and were not seen again," according to Robinson. Marino turned several VC in this manner.

Information the two boys passed along paid off one day near Hill 55. Lt.s Robinson and Marino drove over to Hill 55 in their jeep for a meeting with their counterparts there. Their driver parked next to a 6-by truck, which fortunately blew up after they safely entered a building. The jeep didn't fare so well. Apparently a VC had attached a bomb to the undercarriage of the truck with a timer hoping to kill a bunch of Americans on Hill 55.

Later as they were headed back to Camp Lauer in a replacement jeep on Highway 1, they passed through a ville that had culverts alongside the road filled with trash. On a hunch, they stopped and had SSgt. Tom Dunn take a whip antenna and lift the trash to see if the VC had hidden anything there as per the two VC boys' comments of documents and weapons in plain sight hiding places, especially under trash. Sure enough, the staff sergeant discovered an explosive cache of M-26 grenades, bouncing betties and claymores. A call was put into the U.S. Army's 80th Group, which sent an Explosive Ordnance Demolition, EOD, team to disarm the explosive devices.

A check of the serial numbers on the explosives revealed that they came from the Da Nang Barrier, a "friendly" minefield designed to stop the movement of enemy troops in an area north of Hill 55 (See Chapter 1). "It was basically a VC Explosives Resupply Depot. They would go into the minefield, disarm the mines and reset them in areas Marines frequented like trails or in pursuit of enemy troops sucking them into minefields of their own making. The ARVN should've been put in a position to watch over the minefield to stop that but they weren't and our Marines paid the consequences," said Robinson.

**1stLt. Thomas H. "Tom" Marino, (USMC Photo)**

He went on to say that Marino impressed him in a little psychological operation, Psyops, he ran on a VC cadre who was elusive and went by many names. The description they had of him sounded like the actor David Niven. This cocky, slippery VC had the brass balls audacity to put wanted posters up in the villes surrounding Camp Lauer setting a bounty on Lt.Col. Leftwich and 1stLt. Marino's heads for whomever killed them. Marino returned the favor by putting up wanted posters offering a nice chunk of piasters paid out to whomever brought them "David Niven" dead or alive.

"You have to understand the Vietnamese culture. They are a very proud people who survive on their ego. We had actually honored this guy by putting such a large amount of award money on him. This gave him bragging rights and a leg up on his contemporaries. So what Marino did, understanding the Vietnamese, was to periodically go back into the villes and replace those wanted posters citing a lesser amount of money on this guy each time. It was very insulting to him that we thought less and less of him by reducing the reward payout. That was just a small but effective Psyops Marino ran on this guy to throw him off stride," laughed Robinson.

The S-2 chief noted something Leftwich did that showed a certain respect and compassion for his enemy. When an NVA or VC soldier was killed by our 2/1 Marines, their personal effects were gone over with a fine tooth comb at 2/1 and CIT for any usable intelligence information. "Most of them had letters on them or kept diaries which contained some valuable intell information for us. We were supposed to pass their personal effects up the chain of command to 1st Marine Division. Instead, Leftwich directed me to take their personal effects to the Red Cross ship docked in Da Nang Harbor knowing they would make sure the enemy KIAs' personal belongings would be sent to their families so they would know what happened to them," recalled Robinson.

"Vietnamese Sgt.Maj. An was the Quang Nam Province interrogation chief. When the POWs heard that he was coming to interrogate them they would tremble and provide the S-2 section the information as they knew him by reputation. Today, he would be the guy the Obama people (in 2011) would go after for his interrogation techniques," noted Robinson.

Another twist to picking up POWs was that they were not immediately turned over to the ARVNs or sent to POW camps. Marino flipped them, had them classified as CDs and sent them back out to the bush to work for him. Robinson said he was called on the carpet at 1st Marine Division and threatened with a Letter of Reprimand for not following SOP directives to turn them over to Division. Leftwich allowed his CIT and S-2 chiefs to work and think outside the box and as a result kicked some serious ass in our area of operation.

"Every time Division or 2/1 went after anyone before we changed our tactics, we would hit a dry hole," recalled Robinson. We found out that after a VC cadre was caught or documents were captured it took only 6 hours for the entire cell to shut down or go to ground. We had to develop a faster method of striking a hard target without alerting the enemy at a time and place they didn't expect."

That "faster method" was composed of a quick striking platoon of Marines accompanied by what is today called a Human Exploitation Team sub-team combined with a 3rd Interrogation-Translation Team (ITT) and S-2 scouts. They were tweaking the Kingfisher operations covered in Chapter 1 as well as the similar Pacifier heliborne assault packages by including Vietnamese CIT/interpreters/interrogators for their language capabilities which was the key to the whole operation.

The 2/1 team was designed to hit a hard target without prepping the landing zone (to go without a prep took a major sales job by Col. P.X. Kelley, Leftwich, Grinalds and the MAG-16 S-3) like in the Pacifier operations, kill those who took them under fire, collect POWs, have the Vietnamese CIT/ITT troops interrogate those POWs in the bush in real time (whereas the Kingfisher was an all Marine operation), develop new targets/objectives within that 6 hour window and immediately move to attack the new targets before they had a chance to run for cover. The brain trust at 2/1 was nothing short of awesome in developing its quick turnaround tactics.

Robinson said that initially Division didn't like the concept since it had never been done before and had no track record. 2/1's XO Maj. N.E. Henry didn't like the concept either and the Marine Corps manuals didn't cover it thus it wasn't normal procedure. Leftwich wasn't one to march in lockstep with what was "normal" or standard operating procedure. The colonel was out on that proverbial limb depending on the success of the raid force to work or he'd pay the consequences for its failure.

## Cam Sa Raid, aka, "The August 4 Caper"

The fruit of those tactics at 2/1 occurred on Tuesday, August 4, 1970 when Leftwich and Maj. Grinalds meticulously worked out a daring daylight heliborne raid against an estimated 30 VC--cadre commanders and their small security detachment. The local enemy leaders gathered regularly in a large field just inside the ROKMC border below Cam Sa (1) between the villes of Phong Ha and Quang Ha (1) 7 clicks due south of Camp Lauer.[1A]

Division would officially tag the heliborne assault in its Operations Journals as the "Cam Sa Raid." A key architect of the "raid" 3rd CIT's 1stLt. Marino thought "The August 4 Caper" sounded more like it, according to the S-2 shop's Robinson. The brilliantly planned operation would earn Leftwich a Silver Star and reaffirm his reputation as "a water walker," someone who could do no wrong and everything he did, the mundane or innovative, eventually turned to gold.

2/1 was working off intelligence generated by CIT and the S-2 from a captured female member of the VC's District III Da Nang Headquarters Complex. The Marines assaulted the area by foot and tracked vehicles on three occasions after they received the information, a daylight raid and two nighttime sweeps, without success. Boobytraps and an excellent early warning system resulted in their leaving empty-handed each time, as the VC continued to meet in the same location defying the Marines to catch them. A bold plan was formulated over the next 2 weeks to kill or capture the brazen and elusive VC leadership.[2]

HML-167 CO Lt.Col. Douglas A. "Doug" McCaughey, 39, of Bellevue, Washington, was tasked with coordinating the air operation over the target area and would be aboard the Command and Control, C&C Huey. He said that he was surprised when 2/1's senior officers, Leftwich and Grinalds, came up to MMAF and sat down with all the flight participants, Comprise HML-167, Scarface HML-367 and The Purple Fox HMM-364, to plan everything down to the last minute detail. He was impressed at how well the daytime heliborne assault was organized and that everyone was able to provide input to the final operations order, ground and air.

On August 2, Sundance found out through his source in the vicinity of Cam Sa that the target area had minefields to the north and south but none to the east or west. The VCs' evasive tactics would be to try to lure any approaching Marines into the minefields, which they knew a path through either to the north or south. The Cobras were given the assignment to stop the enemy's escape in either of those directions. The Marines on the ground would pursue any VC trying to run out of the area to the east or west. The 16-year-old Sundance saved many Marines from serious injury or possibly death by that important piece of information.

Golf 3 led by 2ndLt. Michael R. "Mike" Greene, 23, of Harleysville, Pennsylvania, a '69 Holy Cross (Worcester, Massachusetts) graduate and former NROTC member and in TBS class A-70, would offload on top of and around the objective in the northeast corner of Dien Ban District by Sea Knights. Reinforcing Golf 3 was an S-2 Recon squad and 3rd CIT/ITT personnel. 2/1's S-2 chief 2ndLt. Robinson and Sgt. Wayne "Rock" Inouye were over the Recon squad, while 1stLt. Marino was in charge of the 3rd CIT detachment. Altogether, 63 Marines, Docs and a few CIT/ITT Vietnamese troops would be in the heliborne assault.

The pilots referred to the area on the border between 2/1 and the ROK Marines as the "Horseshoe." Due to the tight security veil over the entire mission, the bush Marines wouldn't be briefed on their target until one hour before lift-off. The innovative aerial envelopment didn't include the use of blocking forces that might give the plan away.

Another telltale sign of an approaching attack that was omitted to add to the element of surprise was avoiding overflights by helicopters or aircraft reconning the area and any preparatory fires on the LZ by Cobra gunships or artillery.[3] Robinson noted that the Marine Air Wing's S-3 was not happy his helicopters would not get preparatory fire on the LZs they were to land in as was the case in previous heliborne operations. Leftwich and Grinalds convinced him the main objective was the element of surprise and any prepping of the LZ would alert the VC to scatter to the winds.

**2ndLt. Michael R. "Mike" Greene (USMC Photo)**

Greene, a lieutenant colonel in 1993, recalled telling his 3rd Platoon from Golf Co., (1stLt. Lew Puller's old platoon in 1968) members after being briefed that it was another operation where helicopters would set them down about 500 to 1500 meters away from the suspected site. At that point they would hump in and basically conduct a "County Fair" after cordoning off the target area.

"We'll do what we always do. We'll arrest everybody and collect their ID cards and the guys from CIT will come down and decide who they want to talk to." Greene and his Marines were in for quite a surprise themselves.

The closely guarded "Top Secret" operation kicked off at 1415 Tuesday, August 4 as four CH-46D Sea Knights from HMM-364 Purple Fox squadron arrived at Camp Lauer's LZ to pick up the assault force. The transport helicopters headed north rather than directly towards the suspected enemy meeting site to the south.

At the same time the HML-167 Comprise C&C Huey gunship flown by 1stLt. L.M. "Larry" Thrasher and copiloted by Lt.Col. McCaughey (call sign Comprise 6) with 2/1's S-3 Maj. Grinalds as well as 3rd CIT's 1stLt. Marino aboard flew southwest towards Hill 55 from 2/1's LZ. The two Scarface Cobra gunships led by HML-367 CO Lt.Col. Harry E. Sexton of Laguna Beach, California also flew over Camp Lauer giving the Sea Knights overhead protection as 2/1's grunts ran aboard the transports. The Cobras broke off their gunship escorts of the Sea Knights near MMAF and went into a moving holding pattern.

The four HMM-364 pilots/copilots and the total combat troops aboard were 1stLt.s Stephen P. "Steve" Cook and James F. "Jim" Gillies (Gillies, 25, of Bardonia, New York, would die 3 days later when as copilot his helicopter was shot down by enemy fire during a medevac near Quang Loc Tay (1)),[4A] 17; 1stLt.s Walter R. "Worm" Wise, 26 of Town & Country, Missouri, and John Narney, 24 of Aurora, Illinois, 17; 1stLt.s Robert L. "Bob" Marshall (while piloting the Sea Knight with Gillies as his copilot he would be wounded in the crash at 2045 Friday, August 7) and Gary W. "Hammer" Benson, 14; and flight leader Maj. Duane S. Jensen, HMM-364 S-3 chief, and 1stLt. John Patrick "Pat" or call sign "Swift Chuck" Kenny of Overland, Missouri, 15. August 4 would be Jensen's last day as The Purple Fox's Operations chief having taken over the job in June. This day became part of the Corps' rich heliborne assault history.

(No After Action Reports exist for HML-367 in the Marine Corps Archives for this date. The flight of two Scarface Cobras, lead by Lt.Col. Sexton, whose logbook also failed to shed any specifics on the Cobras' participation, was pivotal to the success of this heliborne operation and should be given equal credit along with the Sea Knights and Huey---MDK).

Lt.Col. Greene explained that the VC knew where helicopters were headed by just the direction they left Camp Lauer so the diversionary tactic was to fool their rudimentary but effective early warning system that was in place. This involved hand signals and raising farm implements (i.e. a hoe) to indicate the Marine helicopters' general flight path, which they passed along village to village down the coast so the VC gatherings could disperse into tunnels and villes.

Robinson said there were enemy air guards on Marble Mountain who were also part of the VC's early warning system. The Marine units had gotten into the habit of running Kingfisher operations early in the morning looking to drop in on any unsuspecting VC so it was essential no operation kick off from Camp Lauer in the early morning as the air guards would sound the alert for their compatriots to scatter. The VC relaxed around midday to mid-afternoon as they knew the Marines never ran a heliborne operation in the heat of the day. That's why 1400 was chosen as the time of day to launch the mission.

Just north of Da Nang the unescorted Sea Knights took a heading due east out over the South China Sea at a 2500-foot altitude looking like a routine flight about to make its turn north towards Phu Bai. The helicopters disappeared over the horizon beyond Monkey Mountain leaving Da Nang Harbor behind before dropping down to below 800 feet in their turn south out over the South China Sea.

At a predesignated point, Maj. Jensen's flight of Sea Knights travelling at 120 knots turned back west towards the shoreline and at the same time passed along a code word for the Huey and Cobras to break off their holding patterns and head for the VC commanders' meeting site.

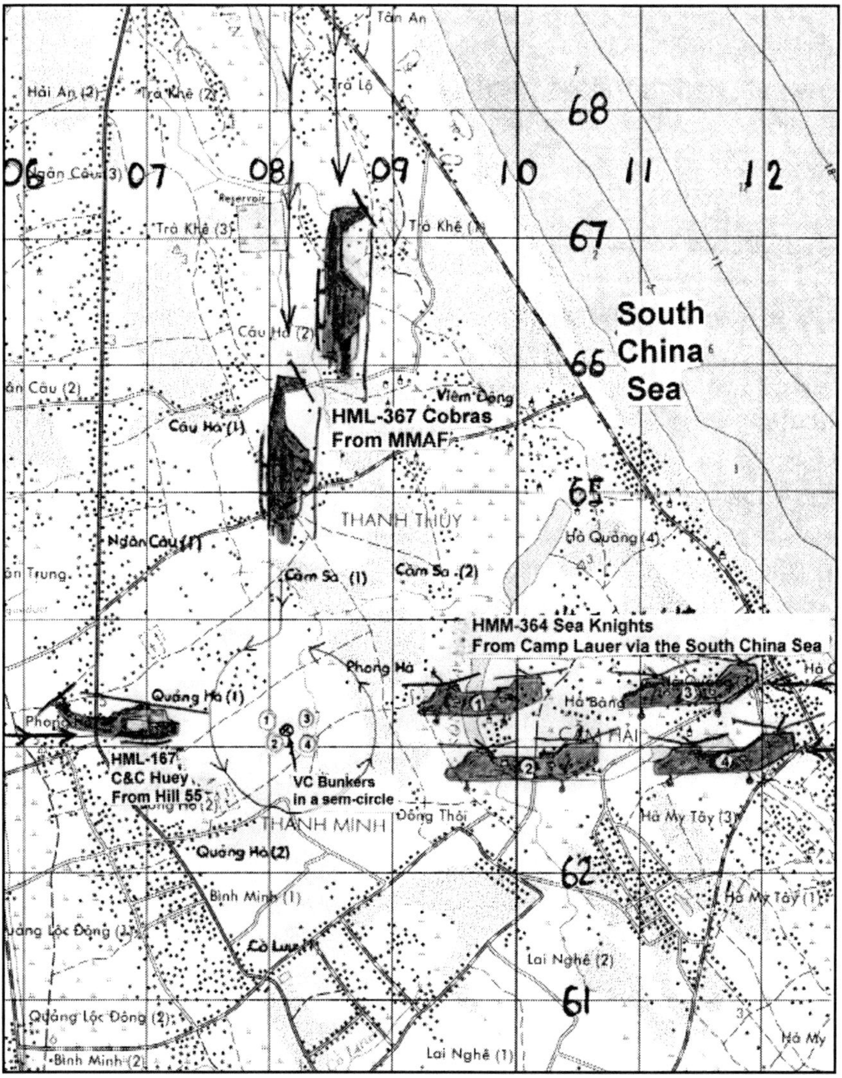


Lt.Col. Bill Leftwich Jr. and Maj. John Grinalds worked up a heliborne assault plan with three Marine Air Wing squadrons that was innovative in its execution. The HML-167 Huey C&C bird flew in from Hill 55 in the west, HML-367 Cobra gunships swooped down from MMAF in the north and the four HMM-364 Sea Knights delivered the ground troops from Golf 3, 2/1's S-2 Scouts and 3rd ITT/CIT coming off the South China Sea. The Viet Cong leaders meeting between Quang Ha (1) and Phong Ha was instantly surrounded by the simultaneous arrival of the Marines in the air and on the ground as shown in the illustration. After three previous attempts to catch these same VC ended in abysmal failure, the Marines had the last laugh as the result of their killing 12 and capturing 12. (Dai Loc map, Sheet 6640 IV, 1965, Overprinted by III MAF, G2, 1968, Illustration by Dan Kellum)

Upon receiving the code word, Lt.Col. McCaughey's C&C Huey orbiting over Hill 55 to the west headed back east and the two Cobras near MMAF swung around to fly back to the south at 130 knots (a slow speed for Cobras but necessary for the Huey and transports to arrive at the same time). The three flight paths had a time and distance calculation predetermined to make their turns towards the target area so that they would arrive simultaneously from the north, east and west.

"It was unorthodox but it worked superbly," enthused Jensen, who was 35 at the time from Pensacola, Florida.

"I remember we flew out to sea and couldn't see the land anymore. Then we flat-hatted so low we thought we were gonna get our feet wet! The idea was to stay out of sight (of shoreline pickets) as long as possible. The 46s turned until we were headed back due west towards shore and came in right over the sand dunes (4 clicks inland off the South China Sea) dropping us *right on the money!* I was amazed!" said Lt.Col. Greene.

## VC Commanders, Bodyguards Caught Flat-footed

Asked how far apart the four Sea Knights landed around the objective, Jensen's copilot 1stLt. Kenny, 26, of Overland, Missouri, had this to say, "Hell, I sure didn't know what those other guys were doing. I was too busy sucking my seat cushion up my ass when the pucker factor got real. I was fixated straight out in front of me and reading off engine, speed and altitude to Maj. Jensen. He was busy scanning from his 8x10 aerial photo on his kneeboard to the ground and back to the photo as he controlled his glide path to land dead center on the VC bunker layout!"

**Maj. Duane S. Jensen (Photo courtesy of Doug Orahood)**

"Our planned landing scheme was for me as Division flight leader to land forward and to the right in the LZ. My wingman (#2) would have landed to my left, perhaps 50 meters. The second section leader (#3) would have landed at my 6 o'clock and tailend Charlie (#4) would have landed at the section leader's left," recalled Jensen. "By design, we would have formed a square 50 meters on a side. Because there were buildings and paddy dikes in our LZ, each plane commander had to pick his own landing site and that may have skewed the actual landing pattern somewhat."

The HMM-364 helicopters carrying the three squads and attachments landed far enough apart to encircle the bunkers of the suspected VC cadre commanders meeting area. The bunkers were adjoining dugouts formed in what was a small semicircle so that they could stay hidden in bunkers and still hold a conference just as though they were sitting at a corporate conference table, according to 1stLt. Kenny.

The 63-man Marine/Vietnamese ground force had action from the get-go. The C&C bird with Maj. Grinalds aboard and Cobras arrived at the same time over the Phong Ha and Quang Ha (1) location5A from the west and north. The Cobras and Huey menacingly orbited the four insertion points over a 1,000-meter square area. 1stLt. Benson, 24 at the time from Sioux Falls, South Dakota said he thought more Cobras might have joined the fray, as the air seemed filled with attack aircraft looking for targets of opportunity.

"It was a classic assault. When we landed 20 yards from the main VC bunker, the shit hit the fan. We were ordered to not open fire so as not to hit friendly troops offloaded on the ground taking prisoners. As we hit the ground, we could see the VC in the bunker in front of us and to both sides of the helicopter," said 1stLt. Kenny.

He continued, "There was a VC who jumped up 10-20 yards in front of us and could have easily killed both Maj. Jensen and me. But he was so shocked, he decided to take off running and fired his AK-47 back at us over his shoulder without looking. The rounds kicked up all around the front of the aircraft as he was shooting low. If he had taken the time to aim, I wouldn't be here."

Greene enthusiastically recalled, "We ran off the ramps and could hear the *'Pop! Pop! Pop!'* of AK-47s taking us under fire! My guys aggressively started chasing the people who were firing at them. This was a first for them to have legitimate targets in broad daylight!"

"I ran off the second helicopter to land. We caught them in the middle of eating. The VC were just stunned that the helicopters came in so fast right on top of them! They were running around like gnats on speed. We weren't supposed to be operating that way," enthused Robinson, who disembarked with his S-2 Recon team and 3rd CIT/ITT troops.

Golf 3 and its reinforcements were chasing the VC all over the wide field that was sprinkled with bunkers used to protect them from H&I artillery fire. Cornered in a bunker, some VC threw chicom grenades out at the Marines who returned the favor by throwing in their own concussion grenades. Robinson noted that rather than trying to kill the VC in the bunkers with M-26 baseball grenades the idea was to use concussion grenades to stun them and take them prisoner.

"One guy jumped up and ran. I emptied a magazine from my M-16 at him and didn't even come close," chuckled Greene.

Sand kicked up by the Sea Knights inserting the ground forces and smoke from the gunfire gave the sun a reddish hue. 1stLt. Benson recalled it being very hot and there being a lot of smoke around the LZ. As he gazed to the west, he said Stephen Crane's famous simile from *The Red Badge of Courage* was his first thought for some odd reason, "The red sun was pasted in the sky like a wafer."[6]

"As we discharged the troops, Bob (Marshall) reached for his camera to document the scene. At that moment three men popped up over a shallow dune to our 1 o'clock about 50 yards away. One guy in a white shirt appeared unarmed but the other two had AK-47s and began to raise their weapons in our direction. Bob ordered our gunners to fire. At that point, I was yelling at them, 'Run! Run!' but I'm not sure if it was audible. Our aircraft, named *The Grateful Dead*, was armed with two .50 caliber machine guns and a minigun which fires about 6,000 rounds per minute.

"Our doorgunner (crew chief Sgt. Kenneth V. "Buzz" Sawyer) and gunners, Sgt.Maj. R.D. Brandt (Lt. Wise indicated that office personnel frequently served as gunners for the extra flight pay associated with it as well as the need to stay connected to the combat side of the war) and LCpl. D.J. Hyche opened up on them as they turned to flee. One of them was lifted off the sand and appeared to be undergoing multiple hits and amputations in midair while one of the others briefly appeared to accelerate from the impacts," recalled Benson. "I've always wondered who the guy in the white shirt was and if he might've been one of the principle objectives of the mission."

As part of the overall planning, two of The Purple Fox Sea Knights returned to MMAF while Jensen and his wingman orbited at a point east of the LZ over the beach as an on-scene medevac. These two helicopters would also serve in the capacity of moving troops around in the field ahead of the fleeing VC.

Lt.Col. Greene likened the heliborne raid to having kicked over an anthill. Most of the time he was in contact with the C&C bird overhead trying to figure out where the anthill had gotten off to beyond the target area. One of his squads rushed back to their LZ to be helilifted to a point in front of the fleeing VC.

"We spotted one male with an AK-47 who fired three or more bursts at our (Huey) aircraft. The crew chief (Cpl. Dwight R. Williams, 21, of Pensacola, Florida) returned fire and killed the shooter," reported Comprise pilot Thrasher in his After Action Report. "The doorgunner, John T. "J.T." Bouley, 21, (of Harrisville, Rhode Island,) laid fire in front of three men running to make them stop. One had a rifle and another a pistol. They split up as two of the men lay down in the grass while the third man with the pistol (officers carry pistols) kept running. The doorgunner shot the single man in the leg. He fell and immediately shot himself in the head."

The suicide of what turned out to be a VC lieutenant colonel upon seeing the hopelessness of the situation was a high compliment to the Marines' successful attack plan. Other high-ranking VC officers also followed their colonel's example and ended their lives inside the bunkers.

An Air Wing engagement rule for the helicopter pilots in 1970 involved a requirement that the bad guys fire first or run before the Huey, Cobras or Sea Knights could take them under fire. The AAR by Lt. Thrasher indicated the enemy fired first or ran each time before his gunners or aircraft turned them to Swiss cheese. Thrasher and McCaughey's Huey took one hit from ground fire in its "right transmission and cowling" and saw "one VC/NVA male firing at the aircraft and (green) tracers going by the windshield."

"I remember the bad guys were everywhere and running in all different directions. We were very low level, probably less than 50 feet above ground, and a bad guy pointed his rifle at us. Because of the gun mount lock, which prevented us from shooting our own chopper, I couldn't get my gun in the down position enough to shoot him. He shot right at us and missed," recalled Cpl. Bouley, Huey doorgunner.

Williams said the cowling was hit on his side of the aircraft. He had the same problem as Bouley and had to take his M-60 machine gun off its mount to fire it "Rambo-style" to eventually take out the VC.

Another VC bolted from one of the numerous bunkers scattered about the area and took several shots at Greene and his men before jumping down in a ditch for cover. The lieutenant ordered one of his men to go get him but he refused.

"I don't know if he'd decided it wasn't his job, that he was scared or that this guy was no danger to us and it'd be wrong to shoot him. I don't know what was going through his mind." Greene's right guide jumped into the ditch with a rifle and killed the enemy soldier.

Another VC fired off several wild shots at the Marines and began to run out of the field at a fast clip. Greene pulled out a green smoke pop flare and popped it. He reached for the radio handset from his radio operator at his side.

"The pilots were begging for us to give them something to shoot. At first I told them I couldn't give them a target to shoot at in this mess. So here was this guy running away straight outbound. I called (the helicopters) overhead and told them a guy 75 meters due east from that green smoke, running like hell had shot at me so you can shoot at him.

"Whereupon it was *'WA-A-A-A-A! WA-A-A-A-A!'* and their guns turned him to toast. As far as I know, we weren't shooting anybody that didn't need it. We didn't sustain one single casualty." Landing in the middle of a concentration of armed enemy troops in broad daylight and engaging them with fire without suffering one injury was truly an amazing feat.

Leftwich and Grinalds made excellent use of the gunship escort Cobras and Huey doorgunners as they prevented the VC from going north or south by firing into the ground just in front of them to make them stop so the Marines could catch up and take them prisoner. If the VC were foolish enough to turn their weapons on the helicopters or continue to run, the Cobras, Huey or Sea Knights (during the CH-46Ds limited time in the Horseshoe area) had the green light to shoot them.

The Comprise pilot gave credit to crew chief Cpl. Williams for two more VC KIA and WIA as one of the two men raised a rifle to take a shot at the bird. The Purple Fox CH-46Ds did one helluva job picking up and inserting the Golf Co. Marine squads to other parts of the battlefield to block the fleeing enemy soldiers' escape.

"The Cobras shot in front of this one guy to get him to stop but it didn't faze him as he kept walking. The Cobras went back to support the Marines at the insert area a few hundred yards away while we kept firing in front of him to try and get him to stop as he was headed south (in the direction of Co Luu (1)[7A])," recalled Cpl. Williams. "It was evident he wasn't going to stop so I suggested we pick up some Marines and airlift them in front of him. A Sea Knight was doing just that as we landed in an open spot about 50 feet from him.

"I jumped out and held an M-16 rifle on him until the squad came up. We then departed back to the insert area. The next time I saw the guy, he's a POW in the grunts landing zone back at Hill 55. The onboard commander passed along soon after his capture that he had a pistol and documents under his conical straw hat. This guy exhibited something that I saw on a number of occasions. It seemed he had nerves of steel. He didn't alter his actions when shots peppered all around him...just calmly continued to walk away. At other times, the response from those guys was to freeze, hoping that they weren't spotted. In the wide open or wading across a stream, it didn't matter. They froze! It took a lot of courage and I admired them for that. Sometimes it worked and other times it didn't."

Robinson said one VC made it into a tunnel near the river. The two boys, Sundance and Butch, had briefed the Marines on the tunnels coming out on the river embankment. The Marines ran for the river and shot the VC as he emerged from the tunnel to effect his escape on the river.

As the Huey ran low on fuel, Lt.Col. McCaughey informed Maj. Grinalds they were returning to MMAF to refuel. 2/1's S-3 major had them drop him, 1stLt. Marino, a Marine rifleman and their radioman not far from the original LZ and most likely where one of the Golf squads had been reinserted ahead of fleeing VC south towards Co Luu (1).

Lt. Robinson, one of the few black 1stMarDiv officers in 1970, was in the thick of the battle by that point trying to snatch some VC for later interrogation (a typical crazy Intelligence officer priority).

"The Intelligence officer, Gil Robinson, accompanied the raid and captured one of the Viet Cong as he ran out of a bunker into Robinson's arms," recalled Maj.Gen. Grinalds.

Robinson said one of his S-2 scouts, (spelled either Rienow or Reneau from Thibodaux, Louisiana), ran down the ramp of the Sea Knight and immediately tackled a man dressed as a woman taking him prisoner as he tried to run away. Robinson pounced on another VC taking him prisoner.

**1stLt.s John Starr, liaison with the ARVN and former Echo, 2/1 CO, left, and Gil Robinson, 2/1's S-2, check out a captured AK-47 rifle. (Photo courtesy of Gil Robinson)**

Sometime after they triumphantly returned to the Rear, I was incensed to hear the lieutenant's name besmirched with the racial term, "Super Nigger." A Golf Co. Marine said this didn't have anything to do with racial slamming but rather what he had done that day on the ground.

The Golf Co. troops were impressed with the strength and bravado of 2ndLt. Robinson's seizing the VC rather than killing or wounding him. Thus, what on the surface would appear to be an improper racial reference was instead a "politically incorrect" high compliment paid him by the bush Marines for a brave officer. (Lt.Col. Robinson said he had never heard the term "Super Nigger" applied to him at 2/1. If he had heard it, he said he would have let it roll off him like differentiating his being called "Duke" and his CO being a "Duke" as well serving with the 5th Marines and being renamed "Bwana Duke." I think at every command he joined there was probably some inappropriate name applied to Gil Robinson since he was an obvious minority but in the end he simply proved to his CO and his peers that he was the best damn officer regardless of color in that outfit---MDK).

Greene said his own men were seizing POWs rather than killing them as well on August 4th.

Collecting bodies from the bunkers later, Greene recalled that either 1stLt. Marino or 2ndLt. Robinson told him that a lot of the dead they found had not died by the Marines' or CIT/ITT/S-2 scouts' hands. Many of the VC sustained self-inflicted bullet wounds to the head rather than risk capture and breaking down during interrogation.

The final tally was 12 enemy troops KIA and 12 POWs (3 were WIAs), four AK-47s, two K54 pistols, one SKS rifle, 12 magazines, 12 M-26 grenades, two chicom grenades, 782 gear, clothing, foodstuffs, medical supplies and 2 lbs. of documents including Top Secret papers of the VC District III Da Nang (DIIID) personnel, organization and activities. Among the 12 KIAs was the much sought after Lt.Col. Bon Tsong, VC DIIID chief Da Nang; Ong Hai ("Ong" is typically the last name of a Cham tribal member belonging to Montagnards located in the south and central mountains of South Vietnam. Robinson points out that all these men's names might have been bogus as they generally went by three or four fake names---MDK), military affairs chief; Ong De, security chief; male unnamed, the artillery unit commander and one of his men from Group 44; Ong Lu and Ong Lien, both security section members; Ong Thang, a Recon scout for the DIIID; and two unnamed NVA soldiers.[8]

Also, three POWs who were WIA included Ong Cat, DIIID doctor; Ong Nga, tax collector for Region 606; and the (unnamed) Region 606 hamlet economic cadre leader.[9]

Later, during interrogation of the POWs, they said that if they had been given five more minutes the assault force wouldn't have caught them. The margin of success, in other words, was a matter of five minutes or less.[10]

The dead VC/NVA were stripped naked with notes attached to them and lined up on the ground in front of the bunkers, according to Kenny. Cpl. Williams in Thrasher's Huey shot some raw Super 8 footage of the body collection and their being lined up. Some of that footage appears in the video depicting Marine pilots, *Vietnam's Helicopter Heroes*, narrated by actor Martin Sheen.

Two of the dead VC leaders were delivered to the Tu Cau Hamlet and later to the Dien Ban District chief, who planned to display the corpses in the hamlets as gruesome but graphic evidence that the allies were winning the war. The lone headquarters survivor of the surprise heliborne attack Thi Sua, chief DIIID proselyte, managed to escape. Leaflets and Psyops broadcasts urged her to rally to the South Vietnamese side.[11]

The VC who surrendered turned over important documents to the Marines. Sundance and Butch showed the Marines how to look for other documents amongst the scattered trash piles around the bunkers. Important lists of VC cells, planned upcoming activities and enemy rosters were uncovered hidden in the trash piles. With the Vietnamese interpreters along from CIT/ITT as well as the two boys, the Marines were able to interrogate the POWs in the field and get crucial information to act on in real time. Robinson said the rich intell haul led to other successful operations in quick succession.

Marino and Robinson were sent down to Red Beach at one point to brief the MAF G-2 (Intelligence) at Lt.Gen. Keith B. McCutcheon's, commanding general of III MAF, Headquarters on their modus operandi of turning VC into double agents and killing or capturing the VCI leadership as a result. Robinson said that a Marine colonel was ripping them a new one outside McCutcheon's office when they showed up for the meeting straight from the bush, dirty, whitened jungle boots from trudging through the sand and rice paddies, ripe from working out in the hot sun all morning and wearing Vietnamese "troom uy," lieutenants' bars. "The colonel ran that place like a Doggie (Army) Headquarters all spit-shined boots and starched jungle utilities. We really upset him but it upset him even more when Gen. McCutcheon invited us to eat lunch with him to explain more of what we were doing in the bush," laughed Robinson.

"MAC-V's CG Gen. Creighton Abrams sent the MAC-V Counterintelligence officer up to Camp Lauer from Saigon 2 months later to interview me and Marino on how we were developing our targets and being so successful. We were the textbook source for these new type raids," commented Robinson.

## Maj. Jensen Receives Vietnamese Medal

After the August 4, 1970 raid, HMM-364's Maj. Jensen had the honor of transporting 9 VC POWs back to Camp Lauer for CIT to interrogate while the 3 WIA VC POWs were taken to the U.S. Army's 95th Evacuation Hospital to be treated for their gunshot wounds. The major and his wingman were also tasked with returning Greene's Golf 3 to the Battalion Rear. Jensen received the Vietnamese Cross of Gallantry with Palm for the day's activities.

1stLt. Kenny recalled that the flight that day was part of his "check ride for troop insert" to qualify him for helicopter aircraft commander. He had one helluva "check ride" with Maj. Jensen.

Another one of the keys to success for the midday heliborne raid was said to be Leftwich and Grinalds' decision to leave their Vietnamese counterparts out of the information loop.

"The major assumption the enemy made was that we would coordinate with Vietnamese authorities, where their spies were located, before we commenced an attack. We never did that, and as a consequence, they had no warning," stated Maj.Gen. Grinalds.

By not coordinating their raid with the local "friendly" Vietnamese hierarchy, the Marines caught the VC commanders completely unaware and so sure of their safety they didn't have the necessary armed escort had their spies tipped them off. Nor could they scurry down into their well-hidden tunnels or melt into nearby forests to await the Marines' departure, according to Grinalds.

The ever-humble Lt.Col. Leftwich indicated he was surprised to have fallen into such a rich booty of prisoners and dead important VC commanders after the raid. He said the intelligence report he was given led him to believe they might only be able to catch a few detainees.[12]

"The results were beyond my fondest hopes. We've played cat and mouse with them for a long time. We've had several unsuccessful efforts to kill or capture these people and we feel this will have a significant long term impact on the direction of Viet Cong and North Vietnamese activities in the Da Nang area," said Lt.Col. Leftwich.[13] The firefight and round-up of prisoners from start to finish lasted only 25 minutes![14]

It did, indeed, turn out to be a bonanza for 2/1. Golf 3, ITT and CIT with help from above (Cobras, Huey and Sea Knights) cut the legs out from under the VC command infrastructure in that part of the Quang Nam Province for quite some time.

Leftwich later received a Silver Star for engineering the bold heliborne attack and its star-studded outcome. Both the colonel and his S-3 chief also became the envy of many contemporaries and higher-ranking officers in and out of Vietnam for this innovative surgical operation.

Golf 3 was extracted from the area at 1720 with their prisoners. The 2/1 Recon squad, Spooky Trip, was left behind to ambush the enemy's' recovery of their comrades' bodies neatly laid out at the bunker complex. Three VC approached the bunker complex from the west at 1800 and opened fire from 200 meters away. The Recon team returned fire and the C&C Huey which was on the ground visiting the reaction force (Charlie-2, SSgt. Coleman, SNCOIC of a tank section of 2nd Platoon, Charlie Co., 1st Tank Battalion and 2ndLt. Wellington, in command of 1st Platoon, Bravo, 1/5) 1 kilometer away took to the air but was unable to locate the VC who had fled west.

The next day at 0800 Wednesday, August 5, 1st Engineer personnel were flown in to destroy the previous day's targeted 14 bunkers that were heavily reinforced with bricks, sandbags and timber. EOD Marines used 200 lbs. of TNT and 40 shaped charges to level the bunkers.

## 32 Bunkers Found in Same Vicinity, August 7, 1970

On Friday, August 7, a mere 200 meters away from the 14 bunkers that were destroyed on August 5, 32 more wooden bunkers were discovered and destroyed.[15A]

For the August 4 heliborne assault Lt. Greene received a Bronze Star and all of his men came away with the Vietnamese Cross of Gallantry which was equivalent to our Bronze Star. Individual medals were also written up for various Marines who earned special recognition but Greene said the men were probably civilians before the awards came through the Marine Corps bureaucracy.

The young second lieutenant had a strange problem to contend with sometime after the annihilation of the VC cadre leaders. "Lt.Col. Leftwich asked me how my men's morale was and I told him they were scared to death. I said, 'Sir, these guys are all upset. They're afraid the VC are going to come after us because we did such a good job (killing the VC/NVA leadership).'"

Lt.Col. Leftwich asked him if he thought the men wanted to be transferred to other platoons throughout the battalion. "I thought it over and said, 'Nah.'"

## Helicopter Firepower Threat Saves 2/1 Marines

And how important were the helicopters in the August 4 operation and all heliborne assaults? The captured documents Lt. Marino mentioned at the beginning of this chapter indicated that a VC company had been overtaken in tall grass on an open plain south of Camp Lauer sometime in December 1970 by two Marine Huskies and a few accompanying ground troops. They were close enough to see a Marine major directing the operation by radio on one of the Huskies. Maj. Grinalds was at 1st Marines at this point so I can only surmise it was his replacement.

The VC commander considered ambushing the major and his 2/1 Marines but thought better of it as Cobra gunships and Sea Knights were in the skies nearby. Any attack on their part would result in their own self-destruction by the aircraft from above. He chose to live to fight another day. The enemy unit remained hidden until the Marines departed. 2/1 Marines dodged a bullet thanks to the helicopters holding the "high ground," according to the 3rd CIT chief.

### Butch* and Sundance*

Robinson said that their teenage Chieu Hois were interesting individuals, scared of the dark when it came to going to sleep in the bush on an operation and wanting to be close to their American friends as a consequence, but fearless in the attack night or day accompanying the Marines.

"In different cultural settings, we decided that with their personalities, Butch would rise to be president while Sundance was decidedly more the dictator type," laughed Robinson. As 2/1's Marines were pulling out of Vietnam, Sundance was sent to work with the Vietnamese Sea Commandos where the 18-year-old would be killed as part of a Special Operations Group raid north of Ben Ha after the Easter Offensive in March 1972.

"At the same time, I received a letter from Butch telling me he was fed up working for the ARVN and was going to Da Nang to become a civilian." Robinson indicated that was the last he heard from Butch. The weary 16-year-old combat veteran had seen enough of war from both sides.

### Lt.Col. Leftwich Reassigned to 1st Recon

2/1 would lose Lt.Col. Leftwich when he was reassigned as CO of 1st Recon Battalion September 12 working out of Camp Reasoner north of Division Ridge. Our loss was the Recon unit's gain as the enthusiasm he had instilled in the ground troops at our battalion was repeated there.

He wrote Jane after being posted to 1st Recon Battalion to tell her how much he hated to leave 2/1. In his letter he indicated that he preferred to stay with 2/1 since he had been able to accomplish a lot in the short time he was the CO and there was still so much more he could do.

Maj.Gen. Grinalds, USMC (Ret.), noted that Maj.Gen. Charles F. Widdecke, Deputy CG (Ground) for III Marine Amphibious Force (MAF) Headquarters, ordered Leftwich's transfer to 1st Recon Battalion. He said he didn't know why he was transferred and assumed it was merely a case of the Recon unit needing a replacement CO.

Greene, who was a graduate of the U.S. Army Ranger School, accompanied Leftwich to 1st Recon Battalion in September. In joining the Marines, he was following in a family tradition in that his dad, Richard Greene, retired as a USMC major. The Marine Corps had always been in Mike's blood as he was born at the U.S. Naval Hospital, MCB Camp Lejeune, North Carolina.

Lt.Col. Greene said that career officers like himself, 1stLt. Mike Cross and 1stLt. Bob Fawcett, all from 2/1, didn't want to get stuck as XOs or find themselves rotated to Okinawa out of the action. Cross and Fawcett were also graduates of the U.S. Ranger School. 1st Recon Battalion represented action and a longer tour in-country. Greene stayed in Vietnam until March 1971.

Some irony existed for Lt.Col. Leftwich having to operate his Recon battalion out of Camp Reasoner. The base was named for 1stLt. Frank S. Reasoner, a '62 USMA graduate and prior to that an enlisted Marine from 1955-58. He was posthumously awarded the Medal of Honor the same year the colonel was in-country as an advisor to the Vietnamese Marine Brigade. Reasoner died getting his Medal...Leftwich lived and came away with the Navy Cross.

Reasoner's 3rd Recon Battalion patrol faced a force of 50-100 VC in a vicious firefight Monday, July 12, 1965. For exposing himself to fire to protect his men, holding off a superior force, recovering a wounded radioman and giving his life as the ultimate sacrifice while trying to save others, he was awarded The Medal. He was survived by his wife, Sally, son, Michael Lawrence, and parents, Mr. and Mrs. James C. Curry of Kellogg, Idaho, one brother and two sisters. He was buried with full military honors in Greenwood Cemetery, Kellogg, Idaho.

**Camp Reasoner: Home of 1st Recon Battalion**

I wondered if Lt.Col. Leftwich ever thought about how close he came to etching his name on that Medal of Honor roll each time he passed the hand-lettered sign near Camp Reasoner's front gate that read: "...First Lieutenant Reasoner sacrificed his life to save one of his wounded Marines. 'Greater Love Hath No Man.'"

SSgt. Bailey Newman Eames was a 19-year-old corporal from Martinsville, Virginia in 1970 serving as Echo Co.'s radioman to CO Capt. Hopgood. Eames said the captain, who would become a major general in the years ahead, made the statement around the time Lt.Col. Leftwich was leaving 2/1 for 1st Recon that he would no doubt be Commandant of the Marine Corps some day.

Echo 1's Lt. Fawcett remembered that as Lt.Col. Leftwich came around to the various 2/1 units to say goodbye he approached the colonel for that transfer to 1st Recon Battalion.

"He was so humble. He said he was taking over 1st Reconnaissance Battalion and, by golly, he couldn't even spell 'Reconnaissance.' Of course, he was kidding. He was a highly intelligent man."

"In cassette tapes to his family (back home in Virginia), Dad repeatedly expressed his appreciation of his Marines and fretted that he shared so little of their work and danger," noted his son, Bill Leftwich III.[16] At 1st Recon Lt.Col. Leftwich would have the opportunity to share a great deal of danger with his Marines and Navy Corpsmen...too much as it turned out.

# Chapter 13

**"The born leader is a fiction invented by 'born followers.' Leadership is not a gift at birth; it is an award for growing to full moral stature. It is the only award a man must earn every day. The prize is the respect of others, earned by the disciplines that generate self-respect." Marine Maj. Bill Leftwich III said his father kept this quote, which he lived by, attached to his dressing room mirror as a reminder of what leadership was all about.[1]**

**Lt.Col. William Groom "Bill" Leftwich Jr.**
**2/1 CO, 1st Recon Bn. CO, Vietnam, 1970**
**Navy Cross, 1965, Silver Star, 1970**

## Leftwich Loses Three Platoons to Redeployment

Lt.Col. Leftwich was reassigned to 1st Reconnaissance Battalion by the strict, mercurial Maj.Gen. Widdecke. The "permanent change of assignment" took Leftwich from 2/1 where he commanded 42 officers, 1,090 enlisted and 58 Navy medical personnel to 1st Recon, which was standing down piecemeal at this juncture.

Instead of five Recon companies that included 50 officers and 639 enlisted Marines, one U.S. Navy doctor and 53 Corpsmen and from 1st Force Recon, 12 officers, 143 Marines and 7 Navy Corpsmen, which Drumright oversaw from January 27 to August 10, Leftwich would command two companies that included 28 officers, 359 enlisted Marines and one U.S. Navy doctor and 28 Navy Corpsmen by October with an attachment of one officer and 31 enlisted Marines from 1st Force Recon Co. The outfit was so elite that Leftwich would bypass other command authorities and only be answerable to Gen. Widdecke.

Junior officers looked upon 1st Recon as the most prestigious, glamorous, medal-producing and dangerous job in Vietnam. Having lost three TBS platoon mates KIA in Recon units in Vietnam, I have to say that frequent fatalities and injuries were commonplace in Recon. Lieutenants and enlisted men could significantly enhance their careers with a successful stint with the Marines in the floppy camou bush hats and camouflage-painted faces inserted to "snoop and poop" far out in Indian Territory and days later extracted by helicopters. Our enemy spoke respectfully of the elite Recon Marines as "the painted faces," as Col. Drumright noted.

On November 20, 1970, Lt.Col. (Lt.Gen., Ret.) Bernard E. "Mick" Trainor would be reassigned to 1st Recon as CO following in Leftwich's footsteps. The general had this to say, "I did not see my reassignment to 1st Recon to be a 'step up' from 1/5. I was equally honored to serve in them both." Previously, he had been the CO of 1/5, (August 29-November 19, 1970). The general said he had been a company commander in that same 1/5 in 1950 at the outbreak of the Korean War. He served as an advisor with the Vietnamese Studies and Observations Group (SOG) in his first tour in 1965 when Leftwich was with the Vietnamese Marine Brigade.

He noted, "I do know that Gen. Widdecke rode Bill very hard but then he rode everybody hard. He was really a hard-nosed gent, but for whatever reason he apparently liked me and never hassled me. When I had 1/5, he frequently choppered in to visit me on operations and never had an unkind word."

## Maj.Gen. Widdecke Criticizes Quality of 1stMarDiv Marines

"We were often fragged to be the 'taxi' driver for 1stMarDiv," recalled retired Col. Les Williams, HMM-263 Peachbush pilot. "Benefits were a day off from flying and eating great chow in the general's mess. No one liked to have this mission because (Widdecke) was such an insufferable bore. The general was a sullen, seemingly depressed individual. He also never liked to fly in our choppers. He rarely went to the field and when he did he insisted we fly at or above 2500 feet (to avoid enemy ground fire).

"Once at LZ Baldy he was fearful of enemy fire and made us spiral down from 2500 feet. So we did, profoundly. He was nearly sick by the time we flared and landed. He asked if we had to do that? We took on the old 'But sir, you wanted us to spiral and that's what it takes!' We laughed as he walked towards the jeep on the verge of puking." Col. Williams was a 25-year-old first lieutenant from Lakewood, Colorado in 1970.

Brig.Gen. Simmons, Widdecke's Assistant Division Commander in Vietnam, described Widdecke as "a fine, fine officer." He went on to say that the general was a hard man, more interested in results than approval. "He was not a popular officer. Demanding, impatient and he made no particular effort to be pleasant...Very much a loner...not at all satisfied with the caliber of officer or (enlisted) man that he had in the 1st Marine Division at that time..."[2]

Leftwich, as the previous chapter attests, had spectacular "results" at 2/1 and his retention as CO would seem to have been good for 2/1, 1st Marine Regiment and 1stMarDiv. Since his arrival at 2/1, enemy rocket and mortar attacks in 2/1's AO ceased, according to Grinalds; he earned a Silver Star for the August 4th operation that severely damaged our enemy's command structure; the Human Exploitation Teams were changing the face of Intelligence work in our AO; Marine casualties took a nosedive thanks, in part, to his implementing life-saving tactics; and his efforts to instill a sky high morale in the battalion was right on track. The colonel was hitting on all cylinders May-September 1970 and the battalion was kicking some serious VC/NVA ass.

So the question that begs to be asked is, "Why would you want to reassign a battalion commander who is obviously spectacularly successful and implementing innovative tactics that are dismantling the VC infrastructure that even MAC-V in Saigon has taken notice of?"

### The Blame Game

On August 24, 1970 Maj.Gen. Widdecke, 51, responded to a series of friendly fire incidents in the Division by warning all commands that top units' leadership would be held accountable for future mishaps.[3]

"At G-3 (Division Operations) I would brief Widdecke who took over from Gen. Wheeler April 27 after he was injured in a helicopter crash April 18. Widdecke was distant to us compared to Wheeler. His big thing was intramural (friendly on friendly) firefights," recalled retired Lt.Col. Gil Robinson.

Was Leftwich "reassigned" on the basis of friendly on friendly accidents that may have forced Maj.Gen. Widdecke's hand? After the general issued his dire consequences warning, 2/1 had the misfortune of having three such incidences in less than 3 weeks.

2/1 recorded two friendly on friendly incidences prior to the edict from 1stMarDiv beginning on August 4. Seems 1st Platoon, Bravo Co., 1/5 while under operational control to 2/1, had three artillery rounds impact within 50 meters of its perimeter injuring one Marine. That was followed up on August 6 when two enemy soldiers opened fire between nighttime ambush teams from Hotel 2-4 and a Golf Recon squad resulting in the Marines firing each other up with a resultant 2 Marines KIA and 2 WIA.

The day after Maj.Gen. Widdecke's warning, 2/1's Fox 3 personnel in a watchtower fired three M-16 rounds into their Fox CP lightly injuring a civilian diving for cover. Hotel 1-5 lost a Marine WIA to an accidental M-16 discharge on September 1 followed by a September 11 Hotel 2 friendly fire incident involving the improper disposal of a boobytrap by a platoon sergeant that killed a Marine and wounded three others. Leftwich was coincidentally reassigned September 12.

Robinson noted in the previous chapter that Division didn't like 2/1's failure to turn over POWs for processing but rather flipped them into double agents. He also said he heard Division was upset that 2/1's Dr. R.D. Cox, Battalion Aid Station U.S. Navy physician, had checked out some women in Nui Kim Son for venereal disease after Marines had contracted venereal disease from dallying with the ladies there. The local Vietnamese authorities were upset they had not been consulted and filed a complaint.

In the Marine Corps, as in civilian corporations, there is only one CEO, which in our case is the Commandant. The competition is stiff to reach the pinnacle of a long, arduous climb to the top of the ladder. Learning to carefully balance the inevitable politics and deflecting jealous officers with tact along the way is very important to success as is having a well-placed "sponsor." Leftwich's "sponsors" most likely included anyone he had worked for or knew such as the "well-placed" Secretary of the Navy John H. Chafee (a Korean War and WW II era Marine officer who had seen action on Guadalcanal and Okinawa), Undersecretary of the Navy John Warner and Lt.Gen. Wieseman.

What you saw with Bill Leftwich was what you got...no facade, just an unassuming, extremely brave Marine officer who took his work seriously and cared about his men. He wasn't above bypassing red tape barriers to get the job done or to ultimately save Marine lives.

For instance, a MAG-16 colonel from 1970 indicated to me that if a crucial part or replacement aircraft was hung up in the Marine supply pipeline he knew to contact Leftwich who would make a direct call to someone in the Secretary of the Navy's office to solve the major malfunction and expedite its arrival. I don't think this sat well with some folks in his chain of command for him to be able to bypass the cumbersome Marine bureaucratic supply system and go way over their heads for a fast track solution.

He had a few detractors in his career that did not believe in his leadership and command abilities. I think they were in the infinitesimal minority as evidenced by the recognition that the colonel gained beyond Vietnam.

After he was reassigned from 2/1, the rumor mill shifted into high gear fed by officers who were in that "minority." I think the colonel's departure was as simple as Maj.Gen. Widdecke drawing a line in the sand that was not to be crossed...in front of a cattle stampede. Friendly on friendlies happen in a war zone...it's an unfortunate fact of life. To be fair I cannot know the pressure that may have been put on Maj.Gen. Widdecke to issue such an ultimatum by his superior, Lt.Gen. McCutcheon, CG III MAF.

"From my own experience with (Widdecke), he was a rather (unusual) personality. I could conceive of Widdecke, who was under tremendous pressure to reduce friendly casualties, relieving a lieutenant colonel of one battalion and then sending him to another, particularly 1st Recon," said Maj. Bill Bond Jr., 1st Force Recon CO in 1970, a close friend of Leftwich's and served under him with the VNMC in 1965. (In July 2003 Bond found his counterpart in the VNMC from 1965 living in Houston, Texas, after spending 16 years at hard labor in a POW re-education camp in North Vietnam near the Chinese border.

He was thrilled to discover his friend had made it out of Vietnam and was okay---MDK).

And I can understand the motivation behind unit commanders leaning towards reconfiguring their combat reports to 1stMarDiv if a career-ending out of their control friendly on friendly showed up there as a result. I'm sure some picayune incidences sometimes went unreported.

"...It doesn't sound right that Leftwich would have been given 1st Recon Battalion as punishment. That was a coveted command and there were plenty of eager officers without reprimands who could have taken it," opined Dr. Gary D. Solis, former Marine lieutenant colonel with two tours of duty in Vietnam, a former USMA law professor and author of *Son Thang, An American War Crime*.

## Recon Marines, Pilots Praise Lt.Col. Leftwich

Regardless of the reason why the colonel ended up at 1st Recon, he undertook his new job with the same spirit and enthusiasm he exhibited at all his previous command assignments. And as was typical for him, he showed a genuine concern for his men's welfare and was always there for them just like at 2/1.

"(Lt.Col. Leftwich) wouldn't just look at a map like some people and say, 'Uh, you go there and do this.' He would ask a corporal who had been on a piece of terrain exactly what it was like and what he thought," said 1stLt. Michael O. "Mike" Fallon, of Oceanside, California, 1st Recon's Bravo Co. commander who was serving an extended tour and was 22 when the colonel came aboard.

He added, "He checked out every angle. That's why the men respected him. Our morale was fantastic. Our battalion was like a bunch of athletic teams, each one outdoing the other. We hadn't lost a man to hostile fire since he took over. He planned everything."[4]

"I recall a worried executive officer pacing around a jeep with the motor running as the colonel was talking with a young lieutenant on his first (Recon) patrol. The general could wait, the lieutenant couldn't," recalled Lt.Cmdr. Lloyd Rupp, 1st Recon Battalion's Catholic chaplain. He said that Leftwich was the embodiment of the term "Christian officer and gentleman" and as a priest "he understood his compassion for people."[5]

Bravo Co. 1stSgt. Maurice Jacques, a Korean War-era Marine who joined in 1948, had positive things to say about Leftwich in his book, *Sergeant Major: The Biography of Sergeant Major Maurice J. Jacques, USMC,* (co-author, Maj. Bruce H. "Doc" Norton). "In my opinion, he was one of the better officers I had known, and he had a knack for being a good listener. As we had joined the battalion at the same time, I knew that he was spending a good deal of time getting to know the Marines in his battalion."[6]

As for 1stSgt. Jacques, former 1st Recon Cpl. Roland C. "Ron" Huegel had this memory of him when he first arrived in Vietnam. His office clerk greeted him to the unit using the familiar "Top" reference. Jacques bristled and set him straight by growling, "You can call me 'Top' if you can spin me around." Everyone from that day forward knew to call him 1stSgt. Jacques in his presence.

Former 1stLt. Raymond J. "Jay" Norton of Norfolk, Virginia, a HMM-263 Peachbush pilot in 1970, said that Leftwich came in as CO of 1st Recon Battalion and did something that no other CO had ever done. "He explained the big picture to the pilots as to what the Recon teams were doing. No one had ever done that before. Most the time our briefings were 'Take this Recon team there,' and 'Pick that Recon team up over there.' I was impressed with Lt.Col. Leftwich. He was a number one squared away guy."

**Lt.Col. William G. Leftwich Jr., right, CO, 1st Recon Battalion and LCpl. Jake A. Switzer Jr., a team radioman, examine the contents of an enemy supply bag following an emergency extract 13 miles southwest of An Hoa. The supplies were being carried by two enemy soldiers killed minutes before the Recon team was extracted by a HMM-263 Peachbush Sea Knight helicopter. (This photo was part of the display of the *Leftwich Trophy* at the National Museum of the Marine Corps at Quantico, Virginia in 2010---MDK) (USMC Photo by Gy.Sgt. D.L. Baird)**

Purple Fox pilot Maj. Earl Miyamoto, USMC (Ret.), indicated to me that Lt.Col. Leftwich never failed to talk to the crew to give them a briefing on the upcoming extract or insert. He seemed to have a genuine concern for all the men around him, he noted. "He was a real sharp guy. It was just unusual for someone of his rank to be aboard. He was sending in a hot extract and was always ready to go."[7]

Chatterbox Sea Knight pilot 1stLt. Hanner recalled the day he was about to make a Recon team insert when his map and classified insert info flew out the open window from between the glare screen and windshield of his aircraft's cockpit in the Que Son Mountains. He informed the team leader and returned them to their base dreading the chewing out Lt.Col. Leftwich would rightfully lay on him.

"When we got to the Recon LZ, he was there waiting. I knew the end was near. Preparing for my head to drop through my ass, he calmly said, 'Don't worry about it.' He said the Recon teams had already cleared their original inserts and they'd just pull one afternoon team's planned insert and do it tomorrow. His voice never got above normal conversational tone and he never had a word of condemnation although I probably deserved any one he might have reserved for me," said Hanner.

**Colonel Excites Recon Marines With Speech**

Lt. Greene came back to visit his good friend 2ndLt. Robinson at 2/1 after he had been at 1st Recon for a short period. I figure they must've bonded during the August 4th heliborne operation. Several of us were sitting around the BOQ as he enthusiastically spoke of his new experiences under Leftwich at 1st Recon.

He was impressed with the spirit and gung ho attitude of the Recon Marines. He said Leftwich had given a speech during one of the meals in the mess hall and the Marines pounded their silverware on the tables and gutturally yelled out loudly, "*AARUGHA*," when they agreed with something he said...which was often.

During a lull in the speech, he said they heard the mess hall staff in the kitchen clanging pots and pans as they, too, agreed with what they were hearing from the charismatic Lt.Col. Leftwich. Greene understated by saying Recon was a whole new world of Marines compared to 2/1.

1st Recon was not without its subtle humorous side as the battalion's designated recruiter demonstrated with a sign he had in front of his office not far off Camp Reasoner's LZ 401 which had constant helicopter traffic inserting and extracting Recon Marines out in Indian Territory. 1stLt. David L. Cross, HMM-364 Purple Fox Sea Knight pilot, recalled, "Funny, I do remember a standard red and yellow sign on the recruiter's hut around there somewhere that sported a slogan which read 'Free Helicopter Rides.' I still chuckle when I think of that."

## Body Counts Measure of Success

1stLt. Bill Valentino, 25 in 1970 of Albany, New York, Air Liaison Officer/ Forward Air Controller (ALO/FAC) with 1st Recon, recalled Lt.Col. Leftwich as having a run-in with Maj.Gen. Widdecke shortly after his arrival over his battalion's low enemy KIA totals compared to other 1stMarDiv battalions. A board at Division listed each battalion with their current body counts. Success, as dictated by the Secretary of Defense, was apparently being crudely measured by how high the mound of dead enemy bodies each unit stacked up.

"I know that Leftwich told Widdecke in no uncertain terms that 1st Recon couldn't be measured by that standard since an enemy KIA equated to a blown patrol." Valentino said Widdecke wasn't happy with the colonel's response. "When I would go to Division with him, I could sense jealousy as well as respect among his peers and admiration among his superiors and the Division staff."

# Chapter 14

**A bulletin board outside 1st Recon Battalion's headquarters building at Camp Reasoner in Da Nang in 1970 listed all the unit's KIAs during the Vietnam War. Prominently lettered above the names of those brave Marines and Navy Corpsmen who died was this poignant statement:**

**DEDICATED TO THOSE WHO BELIEVED IT WAS BETTER TO DIE ON THEIR FEET THAN TO LIVE ON THEIR KNEES[1]**

## Widdecke Orders "Senior Officers" on All Hot Extracts

At some point, Maj.Gen. Widdecke found another bone to pick with Lt.Col. Leftwich that would prove to have fatal consequences for the 1st Recon CO. The general got upset with the practice of non-Recon officers accompanying 1st Recon extract/insert teams aboard Sea Knights on combat missions.

It was felt by Widdecke and those officers immediately under him that Leftwich was making a serious mistake by allowing "inexperienced" officers to "get their (career) card punched" on board Recon extract/insert helicopters "during very known critical VC activity time," according to 1stMarDiv G-2 chief, Col. Albert C. Smith Jr. of Honolulu, Hawaii. (He was a Marine senior military advisor to the Vietnamese Navy in the Rung Sat Special Zone the same time Leftwich operated with the VNMC further north in 1965---MDK). This information was in a letter written in response to a request for his views of facts for the USMC publication, *U.S. Marines in Vietnam: Vietnamization and Redeployment, 1970-71*. Col. Smith disagreed with the laudatory statement that Leftwich "voluntarily" went on hot extracts.[2]

A left-chest full of air and combat medals was involved in flying on those extracts. And medals are an important part of an officer's career ladder in attaining higher rank like getting published is to college professors gaining tenure. Leftwich had his share of air and combat medals from his first tour having made at least 60 overflights into enemy territory and didn't mind aiding other officers along the career path that ribbons and medals helped bestow.

Widdecke told Leftwich that every emergency extract package must have "one senior extract officer aboard to prevent mismanagement faults by 1st Recon and 1st Marine Air Wing inexperienced personnel," according to Col. Smith. The G-2 honcho said he witnessed Maj.Gen. Widdecke ordering Leftwich or a "senior extract officer" to accompany future flights.[3]

This meant that Lt.Col. Leftwich, Maj. H.C. Cooper as the XO or Maj.

Ronald L. "Ron" Bub of Fairfax, Virginia as the S-3 officer and later XO was required to fly on all hot extract packages. They were expected to be in the "high" position in the chase/wing aircraft for command and control and safe from enemy fire versus the "low" aircraft that did the actual extract. Cooper rotated home November 12 leaving just Leftwich and Bub as 1st Recon's "senior officers."

Bill Leftwich was not a "high bird" personality and was more apt to be where the bullets were flying and his Marines were being shot at on the ground. He liked to share the risks with his Marines as he proved with the VNMC Task Force Alfa in 1965 when he was an advisor.

Since 828 crew members and passengers were ultimately lost on Marine helicopters in the Vietnam War (5,086 helicopters were destroyed out of 11,827 deployed and 4,906 pilots and crewmen were killed among all the services), common sense dictated that Maj.Gen. Widdecke's order made it a strong possibility that a "senior extract officer" risked eventually taking ground fire and/or faced the possibility of injury or worse.

## Increased Recon Patrols in Rainy Season

1st Recon's Echo Co. had deactivated in August prior to Leftwich's arrival while Charlie and Delta Co.'s left Vietnam in September a few days after he became CO. The available Recon teams dropped from a peak of 48 to 24. Twelve teams were required to be in the field at all times working closer to the Da Nang area during the drawdown of troops in the overall 1stMarDiv.

Inserts and extracts increased by October and November 1970 for the two remaining 1st Recon companies, Alpha and Bravo, and the attached 1st Force Recon Co. Serving as the eyes and ears of the 1stMarDiv, 1st Recon stepped up its operations even though it was now shorthanded.

1stSgt. Jacques explained the increased patrols in the winter rainy season as a need to have someone on the ground during the long periods of limited visibility denying aircraft aerial observation. He said the encroachment tactics of the NVA were sure to affect the TAOR surrounding Da Nang.[4]

The French Union Forces at Dien Bien Phu in 1954 were hammered when the monsoons and cloud cover prohibited their air cover from protecting them and limited resupply. The Viet Minh used the inclement weather to move men and equipment into position to launch their final attacks. Marines were aware of this history and sought to prevent the VC/NVA from gaining the same upper hand under the guise of bad weather.

"Because fewer battalion Recon teams were available and operations in the mountains were restricted by the fall-winter monsoon, we concentrated patrolling efforts in the Que Son Mountains west of Da Nang, sending out patrols from our company's small patrol bases," explained Jacques.[5]

## Cpl. John F. Stockman: Third Vietnam Tour

Cpl. John Frank Stockman, 27, of Marcus Hook, Pennsylvania was serving his third tour in Vietnam having seen more than his share of war with 3rd Recon on two previous tours of duty with them as well as 2nd Battalion, 4th Marines. In 1970 he was initially with Lima Co., 3rd Battalion, 7th Marines before transferring over to Bravo Co., 1st Recon in mid-July 1970 when 3/7 rotated home. Lt. Fallon had high praise for Stockman who was in his company saying he was an experienced patrol leader heading up Team Rush Act. His nickname was "Long John Silver".

**Cpl. John F. Stockman (Photo courtesy of John Ferguson)**

He was no rookie, according to Lt. Fallon. Cpl. Feldman, whose hometown was just across the state line from Stockman's back home, agreed. Feldman said that Stockman logged in an impressive 57 Recon patrols (5-7 days in duration) at 3rd Recon Battalion near the DMZ (and possibly 1st Recon in that total---MDK). Fallon had chosen him as the new team leader of Team Rush Act.

Stockman began his military career when he received his draft notice in September 1966 to report to a U.S. Army facility for a pre-induction physical. Afterwards he decided he'd rather go to war as a Marine and signed up for a 3 year hitch. After boot camp at Parris Island and advanced training at Camp Lejeune where he was regularly made a team leader, PFC Stockman, now an 0311 infantryman, arrived in Vietnam March 5, 1966. He and four other Marines were pulled from a large group of men headed for grunt outfits and sent to Delta Co., 3rd Reconnaissance Battalion, 3rd Marine Division. After a 2-week reconnaissance training course at Phu Bai, he was sent up to Dong Ha to join his company.[6]

The Pennsylvanian was assigned the radioman's job on his first mission and sent to Mutter Ridge just below the DMZ to see if the NVA had reoccupied the area. A major operation had been ongoing to stop the NVA from infiltrating south. On the third day of their patrol from their vantage point on the ridge, an NVA battalion-sized complex was spotted in the valley below them. The Recon Marines called in a 105mm artillery fire mission on the NVA and destroyed the enemy position. An NVA squad pursued them to their extract LZ firing on them as they were lifting off.[7] This was how John Stockman was introduced to the

Vietnam War on his first patrol in-country with 3rd Recon.

He and his Delta Co. Recon team would go on patrols out of their base at Dong Ha to areas in and around Con Thien, National Forest, Hai Lang Forest, Cam Lo and Khe Sanh...in other words historic Leatherneck Square and beyond. Their base was under constant enemy bombardment at Dong Ha with the ammo and fuel dumps being hit by rocket and artillery fire. Having completed 25 patrols by September 13, 1966 that included working the Phu Loc and Ba Long Valley, the now LCpl. Stockman was chosen to work with 2nd Battalion, 4th Marines in the Qua Viet and Jones River area.[8]

After he rotated home he got out of the Marines at some point and joined the Merchant Marines. He reenlisted in the Marines after his stint with the Merchant Marines and spent some time with the 2nd Recon Battalion at Camp Lejeune and went to Quantico with the School Demonstration Troops. After 7 months, he volunteered to return to Vietnam for another tour with Delta Co., 3rd Recon. His company commander, H.W. Courter, noted that Sgt. Stockman, representing his company, should be considered for something called One Millionth Participant. "(Sgt. Stockman) to date (March 12, 1969) has completed over 45 patrols and 30 operations. He is constantly helping others and with his sense of humor and pleasing personality, firm convictions of our presence in Vietnam, he is considered to be in keeping with the highest traditions of the Corps and country....," enthused Courter.[9]

During his third tour in Vietnam, Stockman was a squad leader in Lima 3/7 before his arrival at 1st Recon. He would write a letter home October 24, 1970 saying in part, "...I'm back in Recon again as the 7th Marine Regiment went home. I'm glad my transfer went through in time. It's the same old routine, 3 to 5 days on patrol then back for 3 or 4, however, we get a platoon-size patrol starting the 1st of November to the 14th.[10]

"I feel pretty good now. I've lost 15 lbs. and I'm back with my boys again. They all have different faces and names but inside they are all the same. Two guys were wounded today from another squad (Ski and Adams). They are okay, just a few minor things. They should be back in action in 3 or 4 weeks. I hate like hell to see these guys get hurt. I got my own team now. They are a nice bunch of guys." He goes on to say he is having trouble with one of the men who is challenging his leadership skills. He indicates in the letter home he was biding his time when he could catch him away from the battalion area for a physical corrective session.[11] (This Old Corps solution rather than some picayune UCMJ punitive action was typical of the era Stockman and I came from. Plus, it gave the other Marine the opportunity to either come out on top in a fistfight or at least get a few punches in without worrying about office hours and losing pay and rank---MDK).

"I have read his letters (sent home) and he spoke of everyone in 1st Recon as family. (Perhaps that was why he came back to the Marine Corps and 1st Recon after getting out...he was returning to his Marine "family"---MDK). His youngest sister, Diana Stockman Ferguson, is my mother and I am named after him. I wish I could have met him or seen more pictures of him," noted John Ferguson of Prairieville, Louisiana. Stockman had four living siblings when he left for Vietnam, George, Francis, Diana and Dorothy. Another brother, Frank, had died when John was 7 or 8 years old.[12]

Stockman wrote that he had a good chance to make sergeant again by December 1st. "I got the highest cutting score, 135, in the company. I'm about 10th senior man in the battalion for bush time (time on patrols in Nam)." He went on to write in the letter dated October 24, 1970, "We're supposed to have a typhoon hit sometime around 2 a.m. to 6 a.m. but it'll come and go and the sun will shine again..."[13]

"His paperwork was in for sergeant while he was on patrol in the Que Sons. Bottom line--he was the team leader all the others tried to copy," explained Lt. Fallon. (Unfortunately, Stockman wouldn't live to see that third stripe again that he so richly deserved---MDK).

**Rush Act Inserted at An Thanh (1), November 4**

Stockman would be proven wrong about spending time with Lt. Fallon running patrols with other Bravo Co. teams off a mountaintop in the Que Son Mountains November 1-14. Instead he and his 6-man team would be inserted by Sea Knight helicopter at the base of the Que Son Mountains at 0830 Wednesday, November 4. The team would spend until Saturday, November 7 reconning the low ground 1,000 meters southwest of An Thanh (1) in a rice/swamp area.[14A] One trail sighting of a pair of Ho Chi Minh sandal imprints was the sum total of the 72-hour patrol.

Stockman's team members, age and hometown, team responsibility and total patrols logged in parenthesis were: LCpl. David V. "Dave" Delozier, 23, Altoona, Pennsylvania, point man (20); Cpl. Fernando "Nano" Villasana, 24, El Paso, Texas, rear point man (19); LCpl. Gary D. "Lizard" Hudson, 20, Joplin, Missouri, 1st radioman (9); LCpl. John Somers, age unknown, of Winlock, Washington, M-79 grenadier (7); LCpl. Robert E. "Tuck" Tucker, 19, Abbyville, Kansas, 2nd radioman (22); and HM2 Russell G. "Russ" Daniels, 22, Phoenix, Arizona, Navy Corpsman, patrols unknown.

The upshot of the November 4-7 patrol was that the team had difficulty communicating with Observation Posts Mike and Gunsmoke on their lofty radio relay positions from the lowlands. It was recommended they make their next insert on higher ground around Hill 212 for better observation and communication. Rush Act's next patrol would be their last.

## Sources Queried About Rush Act, Aircraft Crash...15 KIAs

In order to tell the story surrounding a terrible accident involving Rush Act and a HMM-263 helicopter occurring Wednesday, November 18, 1970, I came to depend on various sources after an exhaustive search 1989-2009. This included eyewitnesses, three teletype messages by Peachbush's Air Safety Officer, ASO, notifying all command authorities of the mishap and a judgment call as to the cause as well as a 1st Recon Patrol Debrief from a Recon recovery team on the ground at the crash site November 19. This detailed report was invaluable to my research.

I contacted the Navy Safety Center (NSC); Judge Advocate Group (JAG), Norfolk, Virginia and Washington, D.C.; 1stMarDiv; Marine Corps Historical Center; National Archives and Research Administration (NARA); MAG-16; HMM-263; 1st and 3rd MAW; Camp Pendleton History and Museum and Public Affairs Office; Headquarters Marine Corps (HQMC)-Aviation; Gen. William L. "Spider" Nyland, (former USMC Assistant CMC, Ret.); Marine grunt and helicopter websites. I struck out in my attempt to turn up any official written investigation of what happened to the Recon team or the aircraft sent to extract them. NSC and HQMC provided the Peachbush ASO's reports.

Lt.Gen. Trainor also stated that no report crossed his desk on the November 18, 1970 incident following his taking over 1st Recon from Maj. Bub (interim CO)/Lt.Col. Leftwich. Lt.Col. Bob Guay, MAG-16 XO, indicated there was "no written MAG-16 report" he was aware of undertaken on the incident. Copies of Peachbush HMM-263's investigation by either 1stLt. J.C. McGarigle or his replacement, Capt. T. R. "Tom" Edmunds, could not be found. I'm sure there's a copy of an internal Informal Board of Investigation or similar type report filed away somewhere and may yet be pleasantly surprised someday to discover that one exists.

What I present here comes from Marines' memories 30-plus years after returning from Vietnam. If any inconsistencies in fact are off by any degree, it is due to the passage of time, memory lapses or my own fault due to a lack of information or eyewitnesses. When at all possible, I have backed up the ground troops--1st Recon Marines, and perspective from the air--HMM-263 Peachbush, HMM-262 Chatterbox, HML-167 Comprise and HML-367 Scarface pilots' remembrances with the facts contained in official reports including After Action Reports and Patrol Debriefs made in the timeframe that's covered.

Neither view, air nor land, in and of itself tells the whole story or presents all the facts. The truth of what happened to Team Rush Act and the aircraft attempting to extract them lies somewhere in between what other pilots' observed from the air November 18 and the 1st Recon Marines saw on the ground the next day. And even then there are still questions that may never be answered and only be known to God.

The last act of Lt.Col. Leftwich's life began innocuously enough with the insertion of the aptly named Team Rush Act in the Que Son Mountains November 10, 1970. An injury to a team member would result in a rush to extract the team to provide the injured man medical attention...and be one day too soon as inclement weather fatally affected the attempted extract.

## Rush Act Inserted at Nghi Son (1), November 10

After just 3 days rest, another patrol by Team Rush Act was scheduled for insertion at 0840 Tuesday, November 10 in the vicinity of Nghi Son (1).[15A]

Stockman would again lead the 7-man team with all the aforementioned patrol members except for LCpl. Somers, who was replaced by LCpl. Charles A. "Chuck" Pope Jr., 19, of Independence, Missouri, who had 22 patrols to his credit and was the designated M-79 man. Somers was attending Scuba School in place of Stockman and credited his team leader for saving his life as a result.

Projected extract was set for 8 days later at 1650 Wednesday, November 18. This Recon insert was scheduled to cover 200 hours and would change the lives of those touched by it forever.

Since the Marine Corps' birthday was November 10th, Stockman's Recon team missed the celebrations that night at Camp Reasoner due to their early morning insert. A large cake and an impressive meal back at the Recon base was consumed in honor of the Corps' 195 years of existence as of 1970 (the same ritual was taking place at 2/1's Camp Lauer and wherever Marines were stationed around the world). Tradition calls for the oldest and the youngest Marines in each of the Enlisted Men's, NCO, SNCO and Officers Clubs to cut the cake and take the first piece.

Elbows were most likely frequently bent that night at all Marine clubs toasting those Marines who came before them and those to come after. A sober toast is always made in honor of the comrades who have fallen in combat. Little did Team Rush Act, a 1st Recon extract team or a Peachbush Sea Knight crew know this toast would be made in their honor in the years ahead.

Four sightings were reported by Rush Act in the vicinity of Nghi Son (1) between November 10-13. The hilly terrain in this area was 100-200 meters high with rice paddies on the low plains. The team was only a click from their previous insert on the other side of the hill to their north. This hill may very well have been Hill 212, the recommended hill in the previous Patrol Debrief.

## Rush Act Extracted to Nui Da Ne After Ambush, November 13

Rush Act observed several civilians and enemy soldiers with AK-47 rifles ducking under trees each time a helicopter passed nearby on November 13. The soldiers eventually entered two hooches attached to four bunkers. The team crept up on the hooches and threw grenades inside as well as killed an enemy soldier carrying an SKS rifle walking around outside.

Team Rush Act called for an extract as their presence was now well known. The extract helicopter picked the team up and deposited them onto high ground 4 clicks to the west on the approximately 800 meter (2,625 feet) high Nui Da Ne at a radio relay position designated as Gunsmoke commanded by Lt. Fallon in the Que Son Mountains.[15B]

Fallon, who was born at the Camp Pendleton Naval Hospital in 1947 and would put in 33 years before retiring as a colonel, the same rank as his dad, in 1999, said he was fairly certain the team spent the night before climbing down the hill with their heavy loads the next morning. They trekked over 3 clicks over hazardous mountainous terrain southwest of Nui Da Ne to about 140 meters (459 feet) below precipitous Hill 848 (2,782 feet).[15C] An unforeseen problem cropped up that stopped their mission cold and resulted in their having to call for a routine extract that was later upgraded to a priority then an emergency.

## Kilo, 3/7 Patrols Hill 848 Area Late 1969

To get an idea of the lay of the land from someone who had spent time in that area, 1stLt. Michael Brennan, a 23-year-old Marine artillery Forward Observer in Nam from Corte Madera, California, explained what he observed in the vicinity of Hill 848. He was familiar with Hill 848 having been deployed to those mountains as a FO with Kilo Co., 3/7 beginning in November 1969. 3/7's companies swept the Que Son Mountains in the vicinity of Hills 953 (Hon Nui Tau)[15D] and 848 for 42 straight days looking for the enemy's base camps.

"If (Team Rush Act) humped 3 clicks from Nui Da Ne to Hill 848, they must've been exhausted," explained 1stLt. Brennan. "We had to extract our casualties on Stokes litter basket stretchers (a metal stretcher attached to a cable lowered from a CH-46D by cable hoist through the tall canopy) since there were no LZs. The visibility during the monsoons was often O/O (zero ceiling-zero visibility). We went days without resupply. As an old FO, I would rate the terrain as the most difficult I personally saw. The triple canopy, steep hills and poor visibility made for very tough going."

He went on to say the NVA had used the mountains for years and that base camps were scattered all over the area. C-4 plastique explosive had to be used to blow a LZ about 2 clicks away from Hill 848 when 3/7 roamed the mountains, according to Lt. Brennan. He recalled spending Christmas on top of Hill 848 in 1969.

The enemy dropped 14-16 82mm HE mortar rounds into Kilo Co.'s perimeter at 1845 Saturday, November 1, 1969 up the east slope of Nui Bao Deo, 2 clicks east of Hill 848.[15E] Lt.Col. R.G. Kimmerow, 3/7 CO, had his command post with Kilo. A boot Battalion Supply officer, 2ndLt. Oliver Evans Deal Jr., 23, of Lancaster, California, was killed by the mortar barrage, which also inflicted an additional KIA and 12 WIAs, according to Brennan. Lt. Deal had just stepped off the resupply helicopter onto the LZ atop the hill that day. He and Brennan took cover on either side of a large boulder during the mortar barrage...a round dropped on Deal's position killed him instantly, noted Brennan. The lieutenant indicated it just as easily could have been him killed if he had chosen the wrong side of the boulder.

### India, 3/7 Sweeps Hill 848 to Que Son Valley, June 9-12

As recently as Tuesday, June 9, 1970, India Co., 3/7 had been helilifted to the top of Hill 848 and worked its way south to Hill 953 (3,128 feet) a tough 2 clicks away. On June 11 an India-1 security patrol ran into two VC/NVA on the east side of Hill 953 in a bunker losing their point man KIA and another Marine WIA in the initial barrage of a firefight.[15F] They managed to kill one of the enemy soldiers.

India's 2nd Platoon quietly set up its night perimeter on June 12 at the base of Hill 953. Thick undergrowth prevented them from seeing an enemy base camp a mere 50 meters away occupied by about 50 VC/NVA. Three enemy soldiers blundered upon the Marine position and a firefight with supporting airstrikes followed scattering both sides.

An India Co. platoon commander noted at the time that the enemy felt bold enough to engage a Marine platoon but refrained from attacking anything larger than a company. This was the same type situation the 7-man Team Rush Act found itself in on November 14 as monsoon rains poured down on them in their arduous hump to Hill 848.

### Doc Daniels Injured in Fall, November 14

Treacherous terrain claimed Doc Daniels who broke his leg and possibly wrenched his back in a fall from a cliff on Saturday, November 14. Of all the men to get injured and be the most medically knowledgeable to go down, his becoming incapacitated must have been the worst possible scenario for the Marines of Team Rush Act. And worse still was that the team was on the side of a precipitous mountain deep in Indian Territory.

Docs as a rule don't get hurt. Marines watch after their Corpsmen like mother hens as a well Doc makes for healthy Marines. Docs are the healer and medical caretakers of small Recon units as well as combat platoons, CAPs and CUPPs in the bush. Daniels' injury meant the roles were reversed in their deteriorating weather situation. Doc Daniels was the one needing treatment...a rarity in the bush.

A Recon team's options in Charlie's backyard involves hiding to observe and avoid enemy contact, calling in air/artillery missions on them or running and evade like hell if detected. With their Corpsman's leg broken, they could not run thus limiting their choices in the middle of enemy territory to only one...hide and hope Charlie didn't find them. If the enemy discovered the team, they faced the unenviable situation of being outgunned, outnumbered, unable to run and with their backs to the wall their only alternative would be to stand and fight and call in supporting arms.

1stLt. Fallon, who coordinated sending several Recon teams out from his lofty outpost on Nui Da Ne in the Que Son Mountains, said that a "routine" extract for the team was called by Cpl. Stockman through him on November 14 but "for a lot of reasons it did not happen." After some discussion between Stockman and Fallon, the Bravo platoon commander/Gunsmoke 6, a "priority" extract was requested on November 15.

I asked the question of 1st Recon's ALO/FAC 1stLt. Valentino, a Peachbush pilot loaned out to 1st Recon, why a priority or emergency extract for just Doc Daniels couldn't have been made like we do in the grunt units when a man is injured rather than the whole team.

Valentino responded, "You never extract just one injured Recon team member. That team on the ground is too vulnerable to being discovered by the enemy who generally outguns them way out in Indian Territory. The team had to stay stationary because of their injured team member and the nights in those mountains were wet from the monsoon rains and cold...down to 50 degrees."

Lt. Fallon apparently offered good reasons for Team Rush Act to be upgraded to a "priority" extract to Lt. Valentino and Lt.Col. Leftwich as his request was approved for the November 15 extract package. Rush Act was competing with five other Recon teams for pick-up on November 15 but moved up the list for retrieval thanks to the increased priority designation.

(In the following pages Lt. Valentino tells of two pilots' attempts to extract Rush Act sometime between November 15-17. A Chatterbox pilot concurs with Lt. Valentino by citing his effort on November 16 while a Peachbush pilot's hairy extraction mission with Valentino, Leftwich and two Recon Marines aboard can only be guessed at being November 15 as that was the squadron's rotation day to support 1st Recon. Peachbush pilot 1stLt. Les "Easy" Williams states he made an attempt on November 17. Either Scarface or Comprise gunships served as escorts to attempt the extraction of Team Rush Act off Hill 848. Other pilots may well have been involved November 14-18 and, if so, I apologize for not recognizing them---MDK).

**Peachbush Pilot 1stLt. Peter F. Goetz, November 15**

Team Rush Act patrolled the area around them off Hill 848 Sunday, November 15 and found a set of "Ho Chi Minh" type sandal prints on a trail that were 3 days old. The direction of movement appeared to be to the east on a 2-foot wide trail.[15G] (Map coordinates given in the Teletype report must have been in error as they are almost 2 clicks back in the direction of Nui Da Ne---MDK).

Making an attempt to extract Team Rush Act later Sunday was a pair of CH-46Ds from Peachbush escorted by two Scarface Cobra gunships. The "low" aircraft was piloted by 1stLt. Peter F. "Pete" Goetz, 26, of Fort Lauderdale, Florida and copiloted by 1stLt. L.M. "Mike" Stewart, 25, a former North Carolina native, and three crewmen. They tried to overcome the socked in conditions with a heroic effort that almost resulted in their crashing into the steep hillside. Lt.Col. Leftwich accompanied the 1st Recon extract team consisting of 1stLt. Valentino, Sgt. Rodney H. "Rod" or "Pu" Pupuhi of Honolulu, Hawaii and Cpl. Randall "Randy" Paul Manela, 19, of Eugene, Oregon.

Goetz flew into Antenna Valley under cloud cover and up a draw to just below Team Rush Act on Hill 848. Then the tricky part came as Goetz tried to take his helicopter up the side of Hill 848 into the O/O conditions as he approached the team's position about 140 meters from the summit.

"Once the pilot flew sideways in the thick fog…moving slowly uphill. The rear rotors were chopping the treetops off causing the bird to shake so bad we almost crashed. He pulled the throttle up hard and the G force made all on board fall to the floor," recalled Pupuhi, a retired gunnery sergeant who was in 1st Recon's H&S Co. in 1970.

Rush Act's Marines were men Pupuhi said he knew well as he had been a patrol leader then platoon sergeant in Bravo Co. before being transferred to his present job. He had a personal stake in bringing those boys home. He knew each and every one of them.

From ALO/FAC pilot Valentino's perspective, he was well-acquainted with the Peachbush pilots and noted, "Goetz got in the clear in the valley and attempted to hover his way up Hill 848 to the Recon team's position. Tall canopy and heavy fog that was like being on the inside of a marshmallow thwarted our efforts and we came very close to crashing."

"The CH-46 pilot with the crew chief as his 'eyes and ears' at the back ramp will turn its rear end to the mountainside and its high canopy in the vicinity of the Recon team as the aft rotor blades will take more abuse than the forward blades," explained Col. Williams, who retired in 1999 after having left Marine helicopters to be the CO of Recon units. He attempted his own extract of Rush Act 2 days later. Trees with branches less than 3-inches in diameter could be chopped into without suffering serious blade damage but synchronization problems would be affected causing the helicopter to vibrate as if it were falling apart.

"The crew chief would tell me, 'Sir, we're chopping firewood,' then let me know how much further we could cut without ripping the blades apart. Maintenance officers would throw a fit upon our return to Marble Mountain," Williams noted. Each 30-foot blade on the transport helicopter runs about $12,000, according to Peachbush pilot 1stLt. James M. "Jim" Martin of Marysville, Washington, and to replace three blades and a rotor hub was an estimated $75,000 in 1970 prices. Maintenance crews were not happy when a pilot returned a CH-46D to MMAF needing such repairs.

"Sometimes we had 'blade strikes' then we had to pucker all the way home hoping the thing (helicopter blades) wouldn't fall apart. So when I would see the grunts climb aboard with a relieved look on their faces, I used to think to myself: 'You don't realize it, but your real problems have just started,'" commented SSgt. Barney Espinoza Jr., Peachbush's S-3 Staff NCO-In-Charge, who frequently moonlighted as an aerial gunner.

Goetz recalled a cascading waterfall between the mountain Team Rush Act was on and an adjacent one that created a pocket of clear air allowing him to hover up towards the team's position. Cpl. Stockman could hear but not see the large Sea Knight and, thus, directed it in by sound.

"They kept saying, 'Keep coming, keep coming,' until I flew up into the clouds and got vertigo. We just got socked in. I tried to do a 90 degree pedal turn to get away from the mountain and since I had vertigo I was flying right back into the mountain. Mike (Stewart) grabbed the stick and said, 'I've got it! I've got it!' I let go of the controls and he pointed us due west but lost all his air speed," said Goetz.

"We started to fall down the mountain. I grabbed the controls back from him and nosed it over to get some air speed. I just about bounced us off the mountain. We came out of the cloud cover at about 1,200 or 1,300 feet and almost damn near landed right on top of the chase helicopter! That was it after that. We went home and changed our underwear."

Goetz went on to say that it was "worth the risk" they took to try and extract the beleaguered Recon team. I chided him for having a reputation, as most good pilots did, as a "cowboy."

"Let's face it. You didn't get into helicopters to be conservative, you know? It was the nature of the beast," stated Goetz.

Pupuhi summed up the wild ride with Goetz thusly, "Cpl. Manela and the 46 crew wanted to be the guys to complete the mission. They were as determined as the colonel to get the team out."

Upon their return to Camp Reasoner that evening following Goetz's very brave, hair-raising effort, Valentino recounted this memory, "It was the closest I'd come to getting killed in Vietnam. Lt.Col. Leftwich told me to come with him. We went up to the Officers Club where he ordered a double gin and tonic (a drink his wife, Jane, had said he preferred). That's the only time I ever saw him take a drink."

"The Rush Act team was getting chilled by the cold, wet conditions. The situation was getting pretty desperate for them to be extracted. The weather and mountainous terrain was frustrating all our efforts to pull them out of there," Pupuhi said recalling the urgency all of them felt.

**Chatterbox Pilot 1stLt. John Arnold, November 16**

HMM-262 Chatterbox pilot, 1stLt. John "Chatterbox Juan or One" Arnold, 25, of San Antonio, Texas and his copilot 1stLt. Ted Fay of Milton, Florida made an attempt to extract Team Rush Act in the early afternoon of Monday, November 16. 1stLt. Valentino was aboard the Sea Knight that flew in and out of the clouds trying to find a way to get down to the beleaguered Recon patrol.

"The lead Scarface Cobra (gunship) was piloted by the best Cobra pilot in-country at the time. I think his name was Joe Gallo. Neither of us could find a hole into that team," noted Arnold. The Cobra pilot led the way as Arnold played an aerial version of follow the leader. (1stLt. Joe "Cobra Joe" Gallo flew over 1,000 hours in Vietnam and would die in October 1978 flying out of MCAS Yuma, Arizona "running into the ground" at the Chocolate Mountains test range while conducting low level bombing training in a Harrier, according to former Cobra pilots, 1stLt.s Patrick G. Owens and Herb Silva of Chesterfield, Missouri).

Valentino added, "Arnold was a masterful expert at finding holes in the cloud cover then he'd drop down into the scud going inadvertent IFR (Instrument Flight Rules--going by instruments only, due to the O/O cloudy white-out conditions) flying in and out of the mountains. We did this for what seemed like an hour and a half but were unable to get down (to the team). He managed to scare me to death!"

Arnold said his log book showed he and Gallo tried to find a way in for 30 minutes (.5) before giving up and diverting to other mission assignments over the course of the day for a total of 4.1 hours of flight time.

**Peachbush Pilot 1stLt. Les Williams, November 17**

On Tuesday, November 17 former Peachbush pilot 1stLt. Williams looked for an opening in the clouds to make an attempt at an extraction. He searched futilely as an opportunity to get down to the team did not occur this day.

He said the cloud ceiling kept rising and falling rapidly due to monsoon conditions. Since Hill 848 contained tall trees, both Recon Marines and pilots unanimously agreed the only way to extract Team Rush Act was by special patrol insertion/extraction (SPIE) rig (a 125-foot nylon strap with "D" rings sewn into it in pairs to accommodate two men snap linked to it every 8-feet for a total capacity of 16 Marines on it that hung below the Sea Knight).

Each Recon team member wore a special harness similar to a mountain climber's Swedish seat harness with a snap link attached that he could pull out and extend above and behind his head to snap onto the nylon strap's "D" rings.

"A concern the team had was movement in the area but up to that point had made no contact. The day I talked to them they were very nervous that their position had been detected by the NVA. We told them to move up the side of the mountain and report their new position via secure net. We also told them we would be back the next day to attempt another SPIE rig extract," noted Col. Williams.

Valentino indicated it was always best if the Recon teams sought lower ground as the tops of the mountains had a tendency to be socked in by clouds or fog while the lower elevations remained clear. "I always told the kids not to listen to pilots."

Time was running out for Rush Act. Fallon said he and Stockman discussed Daniels' worsening condition and the potential for discovery and inability to evade the enemy. They agreed to upgrade their request to an "emergency" extract to put them on first priority for extract on November 18. One newspaper report later indicated two of the Marines had come down with fevers as well in the cold altitudes.

"I approved the extract request to an 'emergency' extract, which, of course changes the sequence the helos would work it from last to first. It also changed the risk factor the pilots would take, which means they would fly under the weather for an emergency extract. This they did. I believe the ceiling was 400-500 feet (November 18) which put the helos below that and the mountains higher," explained Fallon. (His father, Col. Eugene Brady "Doc" Fallon, saw service in post WW II China and fought in every war up to and including Vietnam serving two tours there in '68 and '69).

"Lt.Col. Leftwich sent 1stLt. Jim Burns, the assistant S-3, to me to say he needed an emergency extract called on Team Rush Act. The colonel felt the team was exhausted and with an injury holding them in place needed to have the highest priority of extract," explained Lt. Valentino, who endorsed the extract upgrade to MAG-16.

## SSgt. Pupuhi's "Wet Down Party"

Sgt. Pupuhi was presented his "rocker" Tuesday night, November 17. He was officially anointed as a brand new staff sergeant at the Officers Club. He had begun the night drinking one last time in the NCO Club on the house. The promotion to E-6 meant a career altering move upwards for Pu. Lt.Col. Leftwich was on hand to present him with his new rank.

In the SNCO Club Gy.Sgt. Terry Moore pinned Pu's staff sergeant's chevrons on him as a "wet down party" roared into high gear for the well-deserving Marine.

Drinks flowed freely and the newly minted SSgt. Pupuhi celebrated his promotion into the night. One of the "drinks" he was poured at the SNCO Club was a shot of every whiskey behind the bar as well as urine from one of the Staff NCOs, according to Pu. He was given the next day off as part of his reward for his new promotion.

Alpha Co.'s 1stLt. Marvin Hubert "Marv" Floom, (Col., USMC, Ret.), 24, of Los Altos, California and a 1968 USNA graduate, was the scheduled extract officer for the Wednesday, November 18th missions. If the weather cleared in the Que Sons the next day, Floom would also be on board going after Rush Act. Cpl. Manela would again handle the 125-foot SPIE rig line, a relatively new piece of equipment to 1st Recon having been in use for only 9 months. 1st Force Recon had been utilizing and perfecting the SPIE rig since mid-June of 1969.

Mishaps were expected with the new equipment as a downside. Already a Peachbush pilot unfamiliar with "the string" apparently forgot the Recon team was snapped onto the SPIE strap underneath his aircraft hanging from the 125-foot line or misjudged his landing pattern. He set the team down short of Camp Reasoner's LZ 401 dragging seven Marines through the perimeter's razor sharp German concertina wire.

A Recon SNCO came aboard to physically confront the pilot who was still at the controls. The lacerated and bleeding team happily boarded the aircraft for their medevac to 1st Med and some time off, according to Peachbush's SSgt. Espinoza, 30 in 1970, from San Antonio, Texas (retired as a master sergeant in 1979). He was again volunteering as an aerial gunner.

On the upside, the strong nylon line allowed helicopters to get in and out of mountainous terrain and tall canopy jungle LZs with the Recon team dangling on the end.

Another attempt at extracting Rush Act could do without SSgt. Pupuhi for one day. Besides, the weather was still miserable and the same was forecast for Wednesday. The flight package carrying the Recon's extract team would probably just fly around above the clouds then break off to do other extractions beyond the mountains in clearer weather…or so it was thought.

Many of Peachbush's long-time experienced pilots rotated home en masse the first of November. 1stLt. Norton, as one of the departing pilots, indicated that the HMM-263's CO Lt.Col. Louis K. Keck had subtly requested some of them extend their tours so as to not lose so many experienced pilots at one time. No one opted to remain for another tour or extend their present tour a minute longer, according to Norton.

**Slight Break in Weather, Extract Scheduled, November 18**

Everyone was hoping for a break in the weather so a CH-46D could descend to a LZ or a place to hover on the mountainside to snap link the Marines and the injured Corpsman onto a SPIE strap. Late in the afternoon that window of opportunity occurred as the conditions improved just enough at the extract site that the helicopters could fly under the clouds at the Recon team's lofty altitude on Hill 848. The emergency extract for Team Rush Act was put back on the schedule as the last extract of the day.

HMM-263 Peachbush Operations chief Maj. T.J. "Ted" Toben Jr. of Springfield, Virginia was initially designated the flight commander this day and was thought to be in the "low" position for the extract due to his being more experienced…or so Recon Marines at Camp Reasoner believed. 1stLt. Paul E. Wilson, 23, a 1968 USNA graduate from Lawton, Oklahoma, was Toben's copilot.

Valentino understood that the "high" HMM-263 Peachbush helicopter flying wing/chase would be piloted by 1stLt. Orville Curtis "Curt" Rogers Jr., 25, of Dallas, Texas and his copilot, 1stLt. James Edward "Rusty" Stolz Jr., 24, of Hicksville, New York. Rogers had been in-country flying since June 9 and became a full time helicopter aircraft commander (HAC) beginning October 14. Stolz made his first in-country flight on September 15. Working with 1st Recon all day November 18, the two pilots along with Toben's crew had put in 10.6 hours of flight time before going after Rush Act.

Curt Rogers was a devoted husband and Christian, according to several pilots who knew him. Comprise pilot 1stLt. James L. "Jim" Hunt, 24 in 1970 from Lawton, Michigan, trained with Rogers in Pensacola, Florida. He indicated the Texan would make the long roughly 10-hour drive to Waco, Texas on weekends to be with his new bride while everyone else caroused in Florida. She was attending his alma mater, Baylor University. In Vietnam, he helped the chaplains on his off-duty time to provide Christian support to the troops, indicated close friend, retired Col. Les Williams.

The "low" Sea Knight was rigged with the SPIE gear and the Recon extract officer and NCO would be on that bird, said 1stLt. Fallon. The "high" aircraft didn't generally have an extract knowledgeable enlisted Recon Marine aboard and wasn't normally rigged as a result. A few pilots recalled that the "high" aircraft occasionally had a Recon Marine aboard to throw down a SPIE rig with a jungle penetrator disk on the end as an emergency backup.

When Toben and Rogers' aircrafts landed at Camp Reasoner's LZ 401 to offload a Recon team Rogers had just extracted November 18th, Leftwich pulled Maj. Bub, 1st Recon Battalion's XO, aside. He informed Bub he could stand down as "senior extract officer" that day for Team Rush Act's extraction. As Fate would have it, he made the decision to go after Rush Act in Bub's place.

"Ron, you go do the dog and pony show for Gen. Widdecke and I'll take this one," was Bub's recollection of the last time he spoke to Bill Leftwich. So while the colonel boarded the aircraft, Maj. Bub had the "honor" of giving Maj. Gen. Widdecke his daily briefing on 1st Recon Battalion's overnight Recon activities and active patrols.

"Cpl. Stockman and 1stLt. Cleveland Ray "Butch" Harvey (of Alexandria, Virginia) came to 1st Recon (about the same time in July). They were best friends and Stockman was probably the best team leader (when he was in) 3rd Recon (on his previous tours). Butch had heard Rush Act was requesting an emergency extract. He went down to LZ 401 and bumped the scheduled extract officer of the day to handle the extract himself," recalled Lt. Fallon, a close friend to Butch Harvey. (1stLt. Floom had been handling the extract team all day and had been dropped off at 5th Marines' LZ en route to Camp Reasoner's LZ thinking there would be no more extracts that late in the day. 1stLt. Charles Chipps "Chip" Morin was initially selected to take the extract attempt for Rush Act. Harvey took his place---MDK). Records show that Stockman arrived at 1st Recon from the 7th Marines (as they were redeploying stateside) July 12 and Harvey arrived July 13. (I believe Butch came from 3rd Recon to 1st Recon after 3rd Recon rotated out of Vietnam---MDK).

"As the extract chopper pilots were being briefed, the Recon extract team loaded up at Camp Reasoner's LZ. When Butch realized I was set to lead the rescue operation, he realized I was one of the junior lieutenants in the battalion. He ordered me off the chopper and took my place. His last words were: 'The boys are going to be thirsty after this one.' He then handed me all the cash in his pocket and told me to go to Freedom Hill's PX to buy all the beer I could get. By the time I got back 30 minutes later, I was told the chopper was down," recalled 1stLt. Morin of Menifee, California.[16] Catherine Harvey Nitti, noted that Butch had spent a week in Hawaii on R&R with her before returning to Vietnam approximately 5 days earlier.

Lt. Floom explained that he didn't even know about the emergency extract that went out later. Neither helicopter was rigged with the SPIE when he was dropped off at 5th Marines, according to Floom.

## Greene, Ames See Extract Team Leave on Mission

1stLt. Mike Greene, Team Donnybrook patrol leader, and his 5-man team exited 1stLt. Rogers' aircraft that November 18th day at Camp Reasoner after 78.5 hours in the bush. They had been running patrols out of the base camp north of Nui Da Ne in the Que Son Mountains. The team was picked up by Rogers at 1555, according to Greene's Patrol Debrief and Rogers' AAR. He greeted Lt.Col. Leftwich, 1stLt. Harvey and Cpl. Manela back at LZ 401 as they were walking up the ramp to Maj. Toben's aircraft at the same time his weary team was deplaning Rogers'. "I was wondering where the hell they were off to that late in the day." He recalled that he was probably the last Recon Marine to see those three men alive.

Before lifting off, Harvey M.J. "Harv" Ames Hoa Vang District's senior advisor, who had become good friends with Leftwich, stopped by to pay his respects. The CH-46D was revved up and was about to head out when he arrived and was told by the ground support radio team the colonel was already aboard and about to leave. They informed Lt.Col. Leftwich that Ames was on the LZ.

"Over 30 years later, I still remember that November day he was headed out. He hopped off and we visited for a few minutes before he rejoined his troops...and went off on that terrible mission gone awry. I treasure having had the opportunity to have seen him that last minute...something I've shared with all in my family, with those others important in my life," said Ames of Hancock, New Hampshire. He worked for the State Department/AID in Vietnam.

He went on to say that Leftwich wasn't at all nervous or uptight over the upcoming mission but rather seemed relaxed as they conversed on the ground in the late afternoon. "In our minute plus together he was 'matter-of-fact' and as professionally sociable as ever. I had no idea of the gravity of the mission nor, obviously, of the potential outcome.

"His demeanor was that of a senior officer going on a mission that needed to be done, that had been 'planned,' that was within their professional expertise...

he and his team were off to do what they were trained to do."

### LZ Baldy: Toben Defers to Rogers for Extract

A fluke in timing and circumstances changed the fates of Leftwich, Manela, Harvey, Pupuhi, Bub, Morin, Somers, Valentino, Floom, Team Rush Act, Toben's and Rogers' Sea Knight crews and possibly a Recon NCO coming in on Rogers' aircraft after picking up Greene's team. Leftwich, as 1st Recon Battalion's "senior extract officer," should have been on the high bird this day but that would not be the case. Cpl. Bob Morris, Team Cayenne patrol leader, said he also almost boarded one of the helicopters and wonders to this day why he was spared as well.

Lt. Valentino distinctly remembered briefing Toben on the mission and naturally assumed the major would be directly involved with the extraction in the low bird. Toben's copilot 1stLt. Wilson agreed they were initially rigged with the SPIE rig at LZ 401 and planned to make the extraction until mechanical problems with their aircraft forced a change of plans.

Lt.Col. Wilson, who retired in 1980, indicated that Rogers was on a section leader check flight this day to give him some experience in that flight position.

On the way to extract Team Rush Act in the Que Sons, Toben said he was having a collective pitch brake trigger malfunction (the collective is what increases or decreases the "collective pitch" on the rotorblades so that the pilots can increase or decrease speed to make the helicopter ascend or descend). Toben turned the controls over to Wilson to see if he was having the same problems with his stick.

"As I recall, my trigger wasn't working properly. I am not certain about his brake trigger. It probably didn't work but I cannot recall that for certain," stated Lt.Col. Wilson. Toben told his copilot that this was "totally unacceptable."

"This meant we couldn't safely hover above the Recon team in the mountains so we landed at LZ Baldy and passed the SPIE rig over to Rogers' aircraft changing the helicopters' missions. Ted told Curt to take it as it was time for him to do something as section leader as part of his check flight," said Wilson. Col. Williams, a first lieutenant HAC at the time, also noted he had been suggesting to Maj. Toben that pilots like Rogers should be given "low" helicopter responsibility more often so that they could gain experience.

"Leftwich was advised by somebody about not getting on Rogers' aircraft (since they would be making the extract)," recalled Wilson. "Toben and Leftwich talked at length on the ground at LZ Baldy. Toben's concern was the extra weight on Rogers' aircraft and too much supervision. The colonel basically said, 'These are my kids and I'm going to watch the extraction and I want to be there.'"

Recon 1stLt. Fallon explained, "For Rogers' aircraft to be rigged with the SPIE and have both the extract officer and NCO aboard tells me he was the designated extract helicopter from the last refueling point or last stop before going to pick up Rush Act. Lt.Col. Leftwich would normally have been on the opposite aircraft from the extract officer and NCO. This was from practice and weight distribution. It was not standard that all three would ride in the same aircraft." No Recon Marine was with Maj. Toben's aircraft once Leftwich and the extract team boarded Rogers' aircraft.

"I believe Lt.Col. Leftwich and Lt. Harvey knew it was going to be a SPIE extract and both intended by choice to be on Rogers' aircraft. It may have simply been that the colonel had never been on the 'low' SPIE bird and wanted to be part of it," surmised Floom.

Several officers I interviewed made the comment that Leftwich didn't have to be on that aircraft and take such chances while others (1stMarDiv. G-2's Col. Smith) have said he had no option due to Maj.Gen. Widdecke's order.

Bill Leftwich's choice to accompany the only SPIE-rigged helicopter on the extract package that included the extract officer and NCO indicated he had made a conscious decision to share the danger with his men...when he didn't have to be there. He could just as easily have gone aboard Maj. Toben's aircraft and remained safe in the "high" position. This would have been the logical place for him as Toben had final say as to whether to attempt an extract or not, since he was the package leader.

Col. Cross, USMC (Ret.), recalled that he and his team were extracted by SPIE extract Friday, November 13 and at that time Valentino ran the extract from the low bird and Leftwich was in the high bird. "In my recollection, Lt.Col. Leftwich was on board the high bird on many extracts. He spent a lot of time in the air."

At some point after 1600, Lt.Col. Leftwich, 1stLt. Harvey and Cpl. Manela took their places on Rogers' ill-fated CH-46D at LZ Baldy as it lifted off and went nose-down to gain speed and altitude heading towards the Que Son Mountains and their Destiny.

## Rogers Told to Keep FM Channel Switched On

HML-167 Comprise gunship escort pilot Capt. James B. "Jim" Barr, 29, of Pittsburgh, Pennsylvania (call sign Comprise 29) became the lead on the flight when Toben told him to take it. Barr said Toben chose him due to his experience from a previous tour and familiarity with Rush Act's location in the treacherous mountains. (In two Vietnam tours, Barr would receive a Distinguished Flying

Cross, a Silver Star, 66 Air Medals and two Single Mission Air Medals---MDK). His copilot was 1stLt. W.R. "Randy" Knapp, 24, of Dallas, Texas; crew chief, Sgt. Robert M. "Bob" Brust, 20, of Fishtail, Montana; and doorgunner, SSgt. J.J. Vareill. The captain recalled that Toben said he was having some type of engine trouble and that Rogers would make the extract. The SPIE strap was removed from Toben's Sea Knight and rigged aboard Rogers' aircraft at LZ Baldy where Toben also turned the flight lead over to Barr.

"Toben asked me to brief the extraction as I had experience with insertion/ extractions on my '66-'67 tour (in UH-34 Seahorses). I distinctly remember briefing the pilot and copilot (Rogers and Stolz) who would make the pickup to leave the FM (medium frequency) radios switched on so I could talk with them in the event that it was necessary. I explained that I would not transmit unless it was necessary," explained retired Lt.Col. Barr, who was still flying commercially in 2003 when interviewed.

The Comprise pilot said that many of the transport (CH-46D) drivers had taken to turning all their external radio channels off so they could hear internal communications only so he asked Rogers to at least keep that one FM channel open in case of an emergency.

Capt. Barr told Rogers his plan was to be in the draw with him and provide covering fire should he take enemy fire during the extract. The flight strategy formulated by Barr was for Toben's "high" CH-46D and the other Huey, piloted by 1stLt. R.L. Mason and copiloted by 1stLt. Peter C. Gleim of Polson, Montana, to maintain an orbit 6 clicks away over a lake north of the draw beyond the Que Son Mountains above the clouds.

The Huey gunship was to fly around from An Hoa along the Song Thu Bon between the mountains into Antenna Valley to pinpoint Team Rush Act's location in the draw running off the valley. Capt. Barr would also ascertain that the weather conditions in the vicinity of the team were good to go for the extract and that no enemy troops waited to ambush the lumbering Sea Knight. The Huey would then return to An Hoa to guide Rogers into the valley and back up the draw for the extract. It was a good plan.

"Weather prevented flying in that area until around 1700. The package (total weight) Rogers had on board was normal and not a problem for those conditions. It was cool that day and overcast...perfect for more helicopter power," recalled Williams.

Fallon remembered Toben, Rogers and their two Comprise Huey gunships doing a lot of flying around trying to get into Antenna Valley below the clouds in their approach to Team Rush Act on Hill 848. "I'm 100 percent sure of the route they flew. It was the long way around. It took a long time and the CH-46 extract package was talking about flying back around and past the Arizona to get into the big end of Antenna Valley, which is on the western end."

Toben later told his S-3 SNCOIC SSgt. Espinoza of trying to get to Rush Act for 30-45 minutes. It took awhile to re-rig Rogers' aircraft at LZ Baldy and then make the circuitous route to just reach the valley where the draw leading up to Hill 848 was located. The weather window of opportunity was closing down.

Que Son Pass enters Antenna Valley from the east not far from LZ Baldy but the 200 meter wide, 3-click long pass prohibitively constricted their flight path as they would have to fly under the clouds. Also, the road into the valley rose to over 100 meters above sea level, which was another problem. A threat of close proximity enemy gunners lying in wait at eye-level in some areas as close as 100 meters away in the mountain pass left the extract package birds with no room to maneuver thus made that approach into the valley too risky.

From LZ Baldy, the four aircraft flew around then parallel to the Que Sons along the Song Thu Bon west over scenic Marine battlegrounds in the Arizona Territory that included Go Noi Island, Liberty Bridge and Football Island before reaching the An Hoa Combat Base.

## Huey Gunship Escort Locates Rush Act

At An Hoa, Barr left the other three helicopters at the LZ while he continued on turning south following the Song Thu Bon for 7 clicks through 300-400 meter high mountains to the large entrance to Antenna Valley. He entered the valley from the west flying over Khuong Trung (1),[17A] which was a small ville on the river and flew east back towards Que Son Pass following the dirt road below.

Locating the draw where the team was marooned, he established radio contact with the beleaguered Rush Act with the help of the radio relay at Nui Da Ne. From the Song Thu Bon the entrance to the draw containing Team Rush Act was 7 clicks away at Tu Tan (2).[17B] It was roughly 5 clicks up that draw from the ville to the team below Hill 848.[17C]

Team Rush Act directed Barr to their position by the sweet *"WHOP-WHOP-WHOP"* sound of his rotorblades echoing in the mountains. He asked the patrol leader to fire off a flare so he would know precisely where his position beneath the thick canopy was on the mountainside. Stockman hesitated fearing an enemy unit might descend on the team once he marked their position. The last 3 days of aborted helicopter extracts were probably weighing on his mind. Barr convinced him that if he wanted his team to be extracted he had to fire off the flare. He complied.

"It darn near went through our rotorblades!" exclaimed crew chief Sgt. Brust.

The Comprise pilot returned to An Hoa and had Rogers follow him back in to the team. The other two aircraft proceeded to a lake near Phu Loc (3) outside the mountains and orbited above the clouds awaiting Rogers' extraction of Team Rush Act.[17D]

## Rogers Follows Barr Back to Hill 848 for Extraction

The captain informed Rogers that the weather was marginal for a pickup. The area had low-flying clouds in the passes as well as the zone and there were many physical features such as mountainous terrain.

"In the event that they came under fire, they were to stop the pickup if possible and depart. If not, then I would attempt to suppress the fire until the pickup was made," stated the Comprise Huey pilot. Once radio contact with Team Rush Act was passed along to Rogers, Barr explained that he would leave the immediate area so the Sea Knight could have an unrestricted zone to work in during the extraction.

According to the report for that day, the cloud ceiling was staying at about 400 meters above the extract location on Hill 848 and that a Sea Knight might possibly hover without going O/O, calling for IFR, instruments only, for an extraction. The problem was the same as the day before in that the cloud ceiling was rising and falling quickly in the mountains. The monsoon rains and cloud cover made conditions alternately treacherous then vaguely clearing at the lower levels.

"I handed Rush Act off to the extract package by radio. Harvey was running the extract because he had the most experience and had been in-country in Recon the longest. I had conversations with both Harvey on Rogers' aircraft and Rush Act prior to the extract," said Fallon who remained on Nui Da Ne. It would be his last transmission to them both.

Tall trees, trimmed somewhat by Goetz and Stewart on the November 15th attempt, prohibited 1stLt. Rogers from getting too close to the ground so the SPIE strap had to make up the difference in the distance from the hovering aircraft.

The map coordinates for Team Rush Act showed Hill 848 rising above the helicopter at the extract site while 800-900 meter mountains hemmed them into a horseshoe formation--north, east and west. Not only was the helicopter below the Que Son Mountain peaks but also Team Rush Act hanging an additional 125 feet on the SPIE strap.

Aboard Rogers' aircraft besides the pilots were crewmen, Sgt. Robert A. Donnell, 22, of Clymer, New York, crew chief, and the two gunners from H&MS-16, Cpl. Enver Bajin, 21, (Mongolian ancestry) of College Point, New York and LCpl. Richard "Rick" Buttry, 22, of Anaheim, California. The Recon extract team consisted of 1stLt. Harvey and Cpl. Manela with Lt.Col. Leftwich (call sign War Cloud 6) as an observer sharing the danger with his men.

Following Barr's lead, Rogers flew under the fast-moving clouds up the draw to increasing elevations to the east-northeast to a position at the base of Hill 848. The Texas pilot maneuvered his helicopter up steep Hill 848 to a hovering position above Rush Act.

At this point I can only guess which way Rogers' cockpit was facing in relation to Hill 848 as the Huey crew in the draw was unable to agree after such a long passage of time. Col. Williams and Lt.Col. Moore suggested Rogers was facing away from the mountain due to the beating the rear rotorblades could handle in topping the trees on the mountainside in poor visibility. In that case, Sgt. Donnell would have spent much of his time at the back ramp during the extract directing Rogers away from the triple canopy unseen from the cockpit.

On the other hand, Lt.Col. Wilson and former Sgt. John D. "J.D." Barber, of Weymouth, Massachusetts, Peachbush crew chief and Donnell's friend, made a better case scenario for Rogers' cockpit facing his biggest danger, Hill 848. The cloud ceiling was confirmed to be at 400 meters above the extract point thus visibility would not have been a problem as he approached his hovering position above the Recon team. Then again, there was always the dangerous possibility for the cloud cover to drop down to envelope Roger's aircraft as it hovered above Rush Act.

"If it were me in that situation (as crew chief), I would have been running around like a one-armed paper hanger going from side to side and the rear (to guide the pilot into a hover above the Recon team) but at some point I know Donnell would have had to get down on his belly and be looking out the hell hole at the team," said Sgt. Barber (board member of the USMC Combat Helicopter Association and past president in 2001-2007).

Wilson concurred, "While I'm not certain how he approached, my guess is that he approached and hovered in the same direction as he went in. Once he had the SPIE rig loaded, he probably simultaneously increased altitude while doing a wheel turn (a pivot turn around the aft rotor) and went back from whence he came. The biggest thing in a pickup like this for the pilot is having an external reference to the ground/tree line/mountain (to avoid vertigo). In this case, his reference point would be the mountain (Hill 848)."

SSgt. Espinoza points out that a hovering helicopter cannot be held totally stationary. "It is more like a boat in water, sort of bobbing, drifting and it is hell for the pilot to hold. He can't see the spot he is trying to hold the aircraft over and has to rely on the crew chief and gunners."

Without much imagination involved, it could be said Team Rush Act probably let out an exhausted whoop of joy to see that beautiful bird appear overhead like an angel of mercy. They must have anticipated the hot food, hot showers, warm racks and would now get Doc Daniels some much-needed medical attention in a clean hospital.

The crew chief would have informed Rogers that he had spotted the Recon team on the side of the steep granite hill below. Pilots familiar with this difficult extract maneuver felt that Rogers might have turned his radios off to concentrate on what Sgt. Donnell was telling him on the helicopter's intercom system, ICS. Stolz as copilot was responsible for monitoring the radios piped into his headset and observing the cockpit's instruments to avoid equilibrium problems should there suddenly be any cloud/fog white-out conditions or Rogers experienced vertigo.

## Radios On or Off a Major Issue During Extract

Five radio frequencies carrying possibly a dozen simultaneous transmissions are piped into the pilot's and copilot's headphones. This includes ultra high frequency, UHF, tuned to air-to-air and air-to-ground (tower); medium frequency, FM, air-to-air or air-to-ground (troops); air direction finding, ADF, aids to navigation radio such as local radio and other areas with their own beacons; FM/Crypto, going to or from ground with crypto gear engaged (grunts called using crypto "going up green"); and Intercommunications Control System, ICS, helicopter's internal comm connecting the pilots to their crew, according to Wilson. It was not uncommon for the pilot to avoid distractions in a tricky flying situation by turning his selector to ICS and instructing his copilot to "monitor the radios." When all the radio frequencies were piped in to the pilots' headphones, the pilot or copilot had to be able to decipher their call sign from the almost continuous incoming chatter and respond to the calls affecting them.

A pilot was generally consumed with concentrating on maneuvering his aircraft in gusting winds in the mountains, white-out conditions, monitor his control panel, maintain level flight as the Sea Knight entered clouds, take input from his copilot, avoid hitting trees and granite hills, maintain a steady hover above the extract point and listen to the instructions passed along by the crew chief. Also, not to be overlooked was the possibility of taking ground fire in the form of RPGs, automatic or small arms fire and take evasive actions accordingly. It takes a lot of training and skill to perform what Rogers' was doing this day. This was where the tremendous amount of training and money spent on producing a pilot paid its dividends.

"It was not unusual for the working bird to turn off their radios so that they would only hear communications from inside the aircraft (and the ground)," reaffirmed HML-367 Scarface Cobra AH-1G pilot, former 1stLt. David W. Causey, 23 at that time, of Bergenfield, New Jersey. The majority of CH-46D pilots agreed with Causey's statement in a limited straw poll taken by Col. Williams.

Other pilots though are insistent that a HAC never turns any of his radios off in case the other three aircraft or ground troops need to contact him in order to provide a life-saving radio transmission. So there are differing thoughts as to how a difficult extract is made in potential O/O conditions. It all depends on the individual pilot and how well he can handle the distractions of incoming radio traffic. Regardless, flight leader Capt. Barr had specifically asked Rogers to keep the FM channel open.

## Rogers Lifts Rush Act Off Hill 848

Securely anchored in three places inside the Sea Knight was the SPIE rig line, a stout 125-foot flexible nylon strap with a 10- to 20-lb. discus-like weight attached to the end of it. The weighted strap was dropped out the hell hole, which was midway of the aircraft beyond the gunners. The Recon team moved out of the way below to await its "thunking" to the ground.

Manela would be the logical choice as the Recon Marine in the hell hole to drop the 125-foot SPIE strap below as he had the most experience, according to Pu and Moore.

Lt. Harvey was not as experienced with the rigging and, as extract officer, was probably at the back ramp, surmised Moore. This was something that had to be done right the first time so someone, like Manela, who knew his stuff, had to be operating the SPIE rig in the hell hole.

After crew chief Sgt. Donnell directed Rogers into a safe hovering position above Rush Act's colored smoke, Manela dropped the weighted line to the team.

"A pilot would want to keep his eye on the mountain, especially in this case because the crew chief was wrapped up in supervising the SPIE rig hookup and informing the pilot of the team's progress," said Wilson.

The 7-man Team Rush Act attached snap links from their harnesses to the "D" ring on the SPIE nylon strap two-by-two and grabbed hold of the strap with their inside hand and interlocked inside legs to avoid twisting while flying through the air at speeds exceeding 100 mph.

HM2 Daniels most likely had to be helped with his hook-up and I suspect he was hooked up alone closest to the helicopter as the odd man out of the 7-man team so the others could help him unhook back at An Hoa as they would be set down on the ground first. Stockman and Hudson, first radioman, hooked up last at the very end of the SPIE strap. Sgt. Brust remembered the radioman (most likely LCpl. Hudson) hooking on last as being very happy and excited in his transmissions for finally being extracted.

When the entire team was secured to the SPIE strap just prior to 1650, Donnell notified Rogers that the team was good to go. Stolz should have heard the radioman's radio transmission that they were ready to be lifted out as well over the FM extract channel.

**1st Recon Marines practice SPIE rig extractions and insertions at Camp Reasoner. They are attached to the D-ring embedded in the 125-foot long nylon strap by the snap link on their harnesses. (Photo courtesy of Larry Feldman)**

Rogers took the Recon team straight up over 75 feet, which put them above the trees before he started forward flight. Once above the triple canopy at a safe distance, Donnell eyeballed the Recon team and informed the pilot, "Clear." This much we know happened as the aircraft made its wheel turn on ascending and began to take its heavy load down the draw in a west-southwesterly direction. Unfortunately, safety lay in a southwesterly heading.

In hindsight, if Rogers had taken his Sea Knight straight up clearing the mountainous terrain surrounding his aircraft, he could have avoided the mountain factor altogether. As bad luck would have it, he probably didn't see the dense clouds that awaited him until he gained altitude and did his wheel turn to face the daunting obstacle above and behind him in his blind spot. He elected to enter the draw's treacherous maze to effect his rescue of the Recon team dangling precariously on the end of the SPIE strap.

What happened next is figuratively and literally shrouded in mystery. Rogers' aircraft failed to notify Toben or the Comprise pilots of their pickup, lift or forward movement. Clouds began to close in around him causing O/O conditions, probably forcing him to go IFR (instruments only) and to depend on Stolz's help in monitoring the radios and reading the cockpit panel. He should have also reacquired contact with the accompanying Huey to help him find his way out of the scud down the draw.

1stLt. Wilson, Toben's copilot, on the other hand thought he heard a transmission from Rogers saying something to the effect "heavy cloud cover" either directly before or during the pickup. "Then a transmission, as I recall, that they were lifting off and 'in the clouds' or 'in the goo' or words to that effect. They got the last kid off the side of that mountain on the SPIE rig…then radio silence. Nothing." Then again, those transmissions could have come from Barr's aircraft.

"We were told that all the other aircraft had tried to contact them while they were picking up the team," said Causey. At least two other Comprise aircraft (one Huey contained Col. Paul X. Kelley, 1st Marine Regiment's CO and future USMC Commandant) happened upon the rescue attempt and were hovering above the clouds monitoring Barr and Rogers' radio traffic. They observed some of Rogers' flight pattern below in the draw through broken cloud cover and witnessed some of what happened next.

Rogers began to exit the draw the same way he had come in only at a greater speed while flying behind Barr's lead Huey. Mountains rose 800-900 meters to the east in the direction of the South China Sea as well as to the north and due west. Again, he was boxed in on three sides and had only one viable exit in those mountains.

In terms of feet, Rogers picked Team Rush Act up at the 2,323-foot height off the 2,792-foot mountain. And with the team at the very end of the 125-foot SPIE strap, the helicopter was hovering roughly 350 feet below the summit of Hill 848. When the extract helicopter pulled the Recon team straight up 75-plus feet to clear the canopy, it still lacked approximately 250 feet (in addition to the 125-foot SPIE strap full of Marines/Corpsman on the end and a clearance safety factor) from clearing that range of mountains to the southeast. To the west and north the mountains rose to 2,625 feet as another barrier.

Retired Maj. Miyamoto, a Purple Fox pilot, indicated the rule of thumb was to always head back out towards the ocean if socked in by O/O conditions. Unfortunately a mountain range blanketed in dense clouds stood in Rogers' direct path to reach the safety of the ocean in this case.

Looking at the Hiep Duc map and Rogers' pick-up point below Hill 848, he had only one shot to escape the Que Sons that November 18th day... southwest with a dogleg to the left en route to Antenna Valley on the way out. He would have to maneuver down the draw between Hill 848 and Hill 800 in precisely that direction to safely fly Team Rush Act home.

Aerodynamics played a part in Rogers' dilemma going from hover to transitional flight. In order to exit the elevated draw with his heavy load of human cargo on the SPIE rig, he first had to drop his nose down losing his safe cushion of valuable altitude and gain speed--between 70 and 150 mph--before he could attain enough transitional lift to get some altitude.

Former Peachbush pilot Norton, who rotated home earlier in November, said that a Recon team hanging off the end of a SPIE rig in the mountains while swinging side to side from the windy conditions or from the movement of the helicopter was difficult at best for the most experienced pilots.

As an example, he said just the weight alone of an extra 100 lbs. on the aircraft made it handle differently aerodynamically. Rogers had seven weighed-down Recon team members swinging below him drastically changing the flying dynamics of his aircraft. Turns and lift would come more sluggishly for the CH-46D handicapped by the men hanging off the SPIE strap.

Feldman indicated for a 5-day patrol, a team would carry M-16 rifles with 11 magazines per man, 10-12 canteens, assorted can and long range rations, two PRC-25s, four claymores, one M-79 with 80 rounds, a demolition kit, one gas mask per man, one Ka-Bar per man and 40 assorted grenades. Conservatively speaking, the total weight per Marine would run in the 300 lb. range based on 185 lb. Marines, approximately 2,100 lbs. altogether.

MAG-16 XO Lt.Col. Robert P. "Bob" Guay explained, "On a turn that SPIE strap with those seven men hooked on was going faster than the helicopter... kind of like skiing behind a boat when it makes a turn...the skier swinging out on the ski rope is going much faster than the boat." That drag would have to be taken into consideration on any sudden course corrections.

Also, Recon Marines say it's always hairy to be lifted out of a hot zone then have to drop back down so the helicopter can gain lift and speed to get them out of there. Hanging helplessly off the 125-foot SPIE rig, the team is dropped back into range of anyone taking potshots at them from the ground or triple canopy trees reaching up to pull them out of the sky.

Col. Williams indicated that a Sea Knight's cruise speed is 100 knots and only takes a few seconds to achieve in the cool weather experienced in the mountains.

### Three Views of Rogers' Extract

(Capt. Barr, 1stLt. Knapp and Sgt. Brust aboard the Comprise Huey helicopter each have a different take on what happened next. The inability to locate an investigation report or the statements taken immediately following the accident has resulted in diverse remembrances of the occurrence. What you are about to read is similar to what police officers go through at vehicular accident sites with several eyewitnesses telling what they saw...delayed by 30-plus years---MDK).

### HML-167 Huey Gunship Pilot Capt. James B. Barr

"The 46 gained some altitude to ensure that he wasn't dragging anyone and began a wheel turn to exit the valley. He had to come out the way he went in because of the physical and weather constraints. The clouds shifted somewhat so the 46 had visibility constraints as he came out. I believe at this point in the extraction he attempted to fly through a small low cloud and became disoriented and chose to climb," according to Capt. Jim Barr.

"We could see the end of the SPIE rig with the Marines on it begin to turn too far (towards the mountains). The bottom of the transport disappeared and both my copilot and I were on the radios telling the transport (Rogers) the heading he should take. We did not receive a response.

"The SPIE rig was still visible so I fired a rocket below and ahead of the direction (of the transport) I believed would get his attention. We still got no response from the transport. We queried Toben to see if he could see if Rogers had popped out on top of the clouds (he hadn't)." Barr took his gunship up the draw and did a quick 4-minute search and rescue (SAR), which failed to turn up anything.

"I told Toben that I believed they had crashed and to notify whoever was our control. We did not hear or see the crash. I remember thinking that this was the first Recon folks that I had lost in over 30 some operations including Army Long Range Patrols. I was in shock and disbelief!" indicated Capt. Barr. (Barr's November 18, 1970 AAR shows that either he or both he and the other Huey with pilots 1stLt.'s Mason/Gleim aboard fired three missiles in 6.1 hours of flying time encompassing three missions---MDK).

**HML-167 Huey Copilot 1stLt. W.R. Knapp**

"It was an overcast day with rain showers and low clouds in the mountains. We were to fly gunship support for a CH-46 that was to make the extract. The whole team had to be extracted because one man was injured and couldn't walk out," Lt. Randy Knapp recalled.

"When we went into the valley we were very low, just above the trees because of fog and cloud cover being so low. Gunships didn't mind flying low because most of us wanted to draw fire so we could have some action but the transport pilots' mindset was different and they always tried to stay at 1500 feet above ground out of range of small arms fire."

He remembered the team popping a smoke and the Sea Knight going in to extract them on a SPIE rig. Team Rush Act snapped onto the SPIE strap lowered to them. The transport helicopter began to lift and once the team cleared the trees Rogers began forward motion to exit the valley.

"We were following and giving directions but I don't remember any answers from the 46. I thought maybe they had turned their radios off to concentrate on the tricky flying in the bad weather. We saw them rise up into the clouds and told them they were going IFR and needed to drop down. They never answered.

"First the helicopter and then the men on the SPIE rig just disappeared into the clouds. Jim repeatedly called (Team Rush Act) and gave directions from the last point we saw them but we never heard a peep out of them. We later learned that they had plowed into the mountainside near the top at probably near 120 knots which was pretty much full speed.

"We speculated that they had gone IFR accidentally trying to keep clearance between the last guy on the SPIE rig and the trees. Once they got in the clouds, there was no turning back and they probably started climbing to what they thought was a safe altitude before turning toward Marble Mountain. Either they thought they had the mountains cleared and didn't or they got vertigo and crashed in their disorientation.

"It was a haunting, helpless feeling watching them slowly disappear without a sound out of them," said Lt. Knapp. He was shook up that 15 men could die so soundlessly.

The CH-46D disappeared never to be heard from again. Knapp couldn't recall any rockets being fired to warn Rogers of the mountain or suppressing fire at the extract site.

## HML-167 Huey Crew Chief Sgt. R.M. Brust

While extracting the team off Hill 848, Bob Brust remembered the doorgunner opening up with suppressing fire as did the pilot with rockets into the nearby steep terrain to keep any enemy troops' heads down to prevent them from attacking the Recon team or firing upon the helicopter.

"The CH-46 was 30-50 meters off our right side going down the valley (with the team hanging from the SPIE rig). We had to make a sort of 'L' turn on the way out. I was leaning out watching them when I saw people start popping off the rig. I saw the guys on the bottom of the SPIE rig get torn off by the trees first then the next two," said Brust.

Capt. Barr and copilot 1stLt. Knapp were both concentrating on forward flight and avoiding the trees while threading the labyrinth the draw presented. They didn't know what was happening below Rogers' aircraft until he yelled over the intercom, according to Brust.

"TELL THEM THEY NEED TO BANK LEFT TOWARDS US. THEY'RE DRAGGING THEM THROUGH THE TREES!" (1stLt. Jim Martin recalled a radio message back at MMAF's Ready Room he thought came from Rogers saying something to the effect Marines were being dragged through the trees. It might have been Sgt. Brust's excited comment to his pilots or them repeating his warning to Rogers' aircraft---MDK).

"Barr immediately shouted a warning to Rogers to 'BANK LEFT! BANK LEFT!'" said Brust. As if on command, Rogers banked...but hard to the right into the cloudbank covering Hill 800, said Brust. He didn't recall any rockets being fired to warn him.

"The helicopter disappeared into clouds without acknowledging communications," stated the Preliminary Report of Aircraft Accident on file with the Naval Safety Center in Norfolk, Virginia.

Sgt. Brust indicated the whole incident was pretty traumatic...losing so many Marines in those mountains. He made a point of saying that Capt. Barr had done an excellent job putting Rogers into a position to extract the team. The general belief at the time was that Rogers had flown into that cloudbank, became disoriented, i.e. vertigo, and banked right when he should have banked left as Barr had directed.

Brust said he heard that when the cockpit was later recovered it was found that "both pilot and copilot's radio switches were set to the internal ICS mode monitoring the air crew." In that case, they would have never heard Barr's shouted warning to "BANK LEFT! BANK LEFT!"

So there were three views from three different perspectives--Barr, Knapp and Brust--and the facts of what actually happened that day are sandwiched somewhere amongst those stories.

**Rogers' Aircraft Silently Vanishes into a Cloudbank**

"The Marines on the rig were knocked off one at a time until the aircraft hit. From the photos I saw taken a day or two later you could follow their trail through the treetops to final impact," recalled Sgt. James R. "Jim" Casey, 21, of Syracuse, New York, HMM-263 Peachbush S-3 NCO.

Nothing else was heard on the radio from Rogers' aircraft or Team Rush Act with its three radios as it disappeared into the dense clouds at 1650, according to Toben, Barr and the Marines in Col. Kelley's Huey. MAG-16, HMM-263 Peachbush and 1st Recon Battalion had to assume the worst as agonizing minutes went by without radio contact from Rogers to the aircraft above or the radio relay teams, Gunsmoke or Mike. Col. Kelley's aircraft did not get involved in a search and rescue.

Nor did the chase Huey or Toben circling to the north or the two Hueys overhead see Rogers' aircraft emerge from the thick clouds sweeping over the Que Son Mountains. No matter how much they wanted to see Rogers' Sea Knight break through the clouds, it was not to be.

"I don't know what happened in their cockpit but my guess is they got vertigo and just ran into the side of the mountain. They took off from a higher altitude with their SPIE rig load than where they crashed further down the draw, which generally indicates vertigo. We were just hoping they had a mechanical problem and had landed safely on the side of a mountain," said Wilson orbiting north of Rogers.

"The irony of the whole mission is that Curt (Rogers) completed the most difficult part. He took a fully loaded CH-46D into mountainous terrain with up and down drafts. He hovered long enough to hook up seven Recon Marines. For whatever reason, he flew into a mountain cliff face. It was impossible to go back into the Que Sons that late in the afternoon or night. We were not as sophisticated in body extraction back then," said 1stLt. Martin. His close friend was the copilot, Rusty Stolz.

Espinoza said he didn't think the weight of the Marines swinging on the SPIE rig strap was a factor in Rogers' helicopter crashing since the squadron had flown inserts, extracts and resupply missions in the Que Son Mountains working with similar weight issues just about every day. He surmised that all aboard must have been elated at the successful recovery of the Recon Marines and might have become distracted.

"Even if the (entire crew) had been able to look out the front of the windshield through the cockpit, they would have only seen white clouds and probably not given the mountain much thought since you can't see it. Surely the pilot knows where he's headed. I think this distraction caused the pilots to lose their concentration." S-3 SNCOIC SSgt. Espinoza said he prepared the Command Chronology at Maj. Toben's request for November '70 which included a brief summary of the accident.

"I remember when Maj. Toben returned to the S-3 after Rogers' crash. His face was ashen. He proceeded to tell me what had happened and was clearly upset," recalled Espinoza.

Bad weather closed in with a vengeance as the overhead choppers began to run low on fuel and returned to LZ Baldy rather than nearby An Hoa, as it was flat and secure, according to Wilson. He didn't recall refueling at LZ Baldy but said they very well could have. The sun began to sink below the mountains to the west.

**One Last SAR Attempt Made as Darkness Fell**

At LZ Baldy, Barr made the decision to make one last effort to locate Rogers in the mountains before heading back to MMAF. Barr, Mason and Toben's crews orbited north of the location where Rogers' aircraft was last seen straining for any radio distress call or telltale sign.

"We hung around the area as long as we could in hopes of finding any kind of clue about them but the weather was just so incredibly bad that we couldn't see anything anyway," said Wilson. Finding nothing during the second SAR attempt, they returned to MMAF.

1stLt. Valentino was notified at the 1st Recon COC by one of the gunships that the extract aircraft had probably crashed. "The gunship pilot also said that they were going back to MMAF with the chase aircraft because the weather was so bad and wasn't forecast to get any better in the near term. They said they would go back out the next day."

At LZ 401 Valentino had last seen Lt.Col. Leftwich board Maj. Toben's aircraft where the SPIE rig was situated so he thought the major had attempted the extract and crashed. "I told (the gunship pilot) that since my battalion commander was on the aircraft (that went down), one of the flight crews had better come back and give me a debrief. When Toben landed at Camp Reasoner's LZ, I thought Leftwich was all right since that was where I'd last seen him."

Maj. Toben flew in, jumped out and explained that Rogers with Leftwich aboard pulled the extract as his aircraft was experiencing mechanical problems. He told Valentino he was running low on fuel and didn't have time to talk to him, then departed.

## Fallon Sends Recon Team in Search of Missing Aircraft

1stLt. Fallon noted that none of the six to 10 Recon teams running patrols off his Gunsmoke PPB high up in the Que Sons heard Rogers' aircraft crash into the mountains. LZ Baldy notified him of Rogers' missing aircraft.

While there was still light, Fallon sent Team Lynch Law, commanded by 6-foot-5 1stLt. John Murphy, towards the area he thought the helicopter might have gone down. Gunsmoke previously had direct radio contact with Team Rush Act. Not really having a fix on Rogers' crash site, bad weather and darkness stopped the team cold.

## U.S. Army Loaches Offer SAR Assistance

Socked in at nearby LZ Baldy was Lt.Col. Trainor and one of his 1/5 Pacifier/ Quick Reaction Force teams. He monitored the radio traffic from the Comprise pilots that Rogers' 46 had not come back down the draw to Antenna Valley after he had gone up to retrieve Team Rush Act and turned into a cloudbank. It was presumed he had crashed.

"There was a detachment of Army (Hughes OH-6A) Loach helos there with us (grounded at LZ Baldy). When we heard of the missing chopper and Recon team casualties, the Army warrant officer helo pilots volunteered to do a search, despite the weather and darkening day…a gutsy offer. I transmitted this to Division and was told in no uncertain terms that there would be no Army attempt made," indicated retired Lt.Gen. Trainor.

Former 1st Recon Marine SSgt. John Hare said the U.S. Army Loaches had something the Marine helicopters didn't that could have pinpointed Rogers' position if any radio gear was still functioning. They have a sensitive directional locator device to hone in on radio transmissions or radio signals from the helicopter's distress box to lead them to downed helicopters or Recon Marines lost in the triple canopy, scud or mountains. Hare recalled September 2, 1970 when Team War Cloud Mission Impossible he, Gy.Sgt. Moore and two other Marines were lost and hiding from enemy forces high up in the mountains in dense jungle. It took a U.S. Army Loach to find them with its sensitive equipment honing in on their radio signals when the Marine helicopters didn't have a clue. (See Chapter 8).

Martin said the decision was made to ground all aircraft until the next morning due to deteriorating weather conditions. The sun was also rapidly setting at that late hour in the day leaving no time for a search in the mountainous terrain. No one wanted to lose more aircraft in those treacherous flying conditions as darkness approached.

### SecNav John H. Chafee Calls Inquiring About Leftwich

"The day Lt.Col. Leftwich was killed, I was there when we got a call from Secretary of the Navy (John) Chafee *in* the 1st Recon Battalion's command bunker wanting to confirm what had happened," recalled Lt.Col. Greene who was a first lieutenant at the time. He was impressed the SecNav took such an immediate interest in Leftwich's death.

Scarface pilot Causey said, "We were put on call as soon as the accident happened but the weather was too bad for us to do anything. We stayed up all night waiting for a break in the weather to go out (on a SAR mission). A C-130 flareship was on call all night as well so we would've gone out in the dark if we could have."

LCpl. Raymond J. "Ski" Kozakowski, 19, of Evergreen Park, Illinois (who would log in 34 patrols before December 20th) was a member of 1st Recon's Team Wage Earner when he heard the news of Team Rush Act's crash in the mountains. A call was put out for volunteers to undertake a recovery mission the next morning. "I had met Doc Daniels and Villasana. Daniels was a very friendly and outgoing type of guy. He seemed to know everyone and was very popular.

"My team leader Sgt. Adkins came into the hooch and asked for volunteers because the recovery operation was going to be dangerous. He said Wage Earner was asked to go because of our record but if anyone didn't want to go that was okay. I don't think anyone in that hooch stayed behind."

"It was real quiet in our Officers and Enlisted Clubs that night. All of us were thinking about those Marines still out there in the Que Sons on that mountainside," said Martin.

The heavy cloud cover blanketed the Que Son Mountains as rain fell in sheets all night. The Marines at 1st Recon Battalion and HMM-263 awaited the dawn and what it would bring.

# Chapter 15

**The first rule of war is that young men and women die. The second rule of war is that surgeons cannot change the first rule. I think the third rule of war should be that those who have given their all for our freedom are never forgotten, and they are always honored.[1]**

**Col. Brett Wyrick, USAF, surgeon**
**332 Expeditionary Medical Group**
**Balad, Iraq, May 30, 2005**

### Rogers' Crash Site Located on Hill 800, November 19, 1970

Next morning Capt. Barr was the copilot to Comprise CO Lt.Col. McCaughey (a good friend to Leftwich and previously involved with 2/1's successful August 4 heliborne assault) leading several aircraft including Peachbush Sea Knights into the Que Sons. Recon teams were aboard each of the two transport aircraft as they headed to the area where Rogers had most likely gone down. A search helicopter discovered the crash site on the side of Hill 800 at 0702 Thursday, November 19 approximately 1200 meters across the draw from Rush Act's extract point.[2A]

Lt.Col. Keck, Peachbush squadron CO, flew one of the CH-46Ds with 1stLt. Mike Stewart as copilot inserting a Recon team. He was very upset over the loss of the 15 men when he came to Camp Reasoner's LZ 401 November 19 to pick up the Recon teams, according to Valentino.

When the crash site was located, it was thought the only way the two Recon teams could reach it in the forbidding terrain was by rappelling down on 120-foot ropes from the Sea Knights. 1st Recon's Team Mission Impossible was to be the first team on the ground. The 10-man react team was made up of experienced H&S Co. personnel led by Capt. Frank S. Blair III of Albuquerque, New Mexico, H&S Co. CO, with Gy.Sgt. Moore as second-in-command.

"I had rigged an aircraft for rappelling from the hell hole and 1stSgt. Jacques rigged the same for the other with Team Wage Earner aboard. It was still cloudy and misty fog like, as we hovered over the crash site. I couldn't see the ground," explained Pupuhi, Mission Impossible's point man.

"I threw the end part of the rappelling rope down and it untwined itself from the 2x4 wood. I was breathing hard and was starry-eyed looking at the other team members. Before I could jump through the hell hole, the crew chief gave the signal to scratch the jump so I started to pull the rappelling line up. Seems the pilot wanted to get out fast so I cut the rope. Found out the

Cobras had found an LZ so we landed a few minutes later," Pu recalled.

At 0705 Mission Impossible was inserted in a clearing at the 400-meter level downhill from the crash site.[28] Rogers' Sea Knight was about 900 meters away from the insert point on a gradual drop-off from Hill 800's summit, according to Capt. Blair's Patrol Debrief. The second team, Team Wage Earner with eight Recon Marines, was inserted 30 minutes later at the same coordinates.

Capt. Blair's group consisted of two gunnys, Moore and P.L. Hensley; three staff sergeants, Pupuhi, David M. Goulde and Robert J. Petroff; Sgt. Milan J. Cop; Cpl. Lester R. Beedle; and two Navy Corpsmen HM3 D.W. Wager and HM3 G.F. West. The extra Doc was brought along just in case several injured men survived the crash and the long night on the mountainside.

Peachbush pilot Capt. Tom Edmunds with 1stLt. Gary R. "Zeek" Zilla (Zilla would die in a helicopter crash while flying for the Montana National Guard in 1978) as copilot inserted Team Wage Earner after Lt.Col. Keck departed the small clearing. Sgt. Adkins led Wage Earner, whose members were Cpl.s L.E. Sparks, Evans, Hill and Givens; and LCpl.s Kozakowski, Lujan and R.E. Browne Jr. Kozakowski recalled how apprehensive he was about the mission since SSgt. Pupuhi and so many officers and Staff NCOs seemed to be involved.

"Being in a Recon team your security is being part of a small team and the numbers (going) were unsettling to me," recalled Kozakowski thinking back on that day.

Walking point for the lead Recon team was a distraught SSgt. Pupuhi. He considered himself the best SPIE rig operator in the battalion and wondered how he could have made a difference if he had been in the hell hole instead of Manela on Rogers' aircraft.

The going was tough. Blair's Patrol Debrief told of steep terrain and areas of thick undergrowth impeding their quick progress in the climb upwards. Pupuhi said the slow going was partially due to their being tactical in their approach to the crash site.

Moore related that upon departing their LZ they came across many bunkers which had been recently occupied. He figured the enemy soldiers departed the area following the crash fearing all the activity that was about to drop in on them.

Still, the two Recon teams had to be prepared for an ambush and approached the crash site with caution. With 18 men they lacked the manpower to fight it out with any substantial numbers of enemy troops, especially if they were entrenched on the hillside.

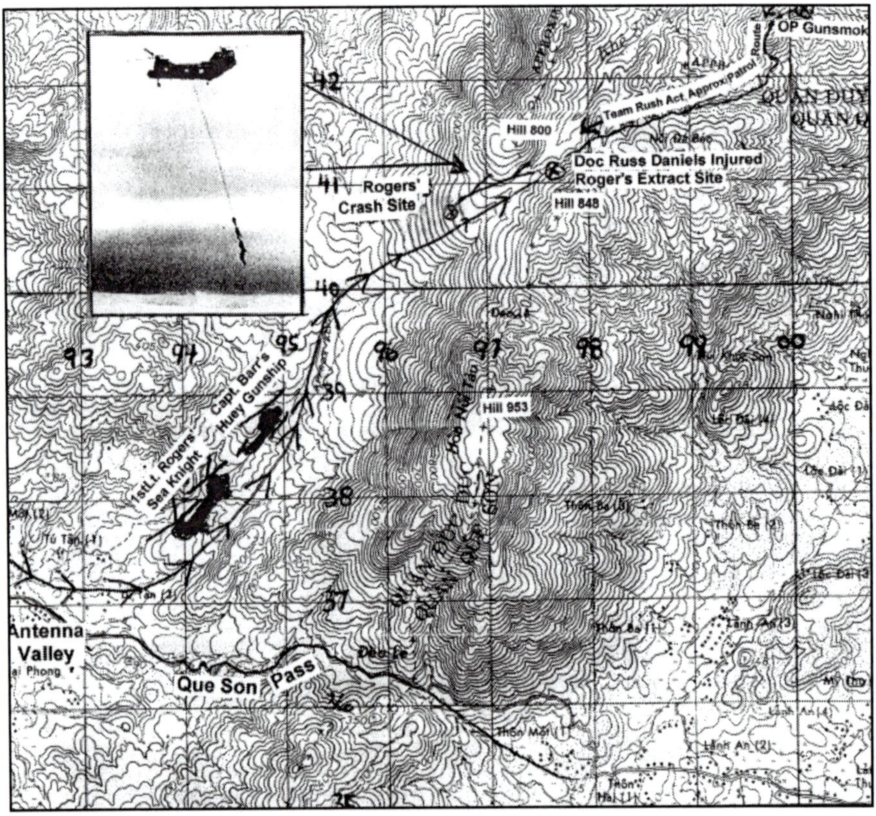


1stLt. Curt Rogers and Capt. Jim Barr's flight path up the draw off Antenna Valley is shown as well as Team Rush Act's hump from Nui De Ne (OP Gunsmoke), upper right, to just below Hill 848 where Doc Russ Daniels broke his ankle. The crash site is below Hill 800. Inset photo at top left shows a Marine Recon team being extracted by a SPIE rig. (Hiep Duc map, Sheet 6640 III, Map courtesy of the National Imagery and Mapping Agency, Inset photo courtesy of Terry Basham and the USMC Combat Helicopter Association, Illustration by Dan Kellum)

## SSgt. Pupuhi Spots Rush Act Team Member

Moving up the 70-degree incline to the 600 meter (1,968-foot) level near the crash site after a 2 hour climb, Pu parted some bushes and saw one of the Rush Act team members that he knew well just ahead staring at him. Pu put his finger to his lips to let the Marine know he should remain quiet. Circling the spot where he last saw the Marine, he came up on his flank and noted his gaze straight ahead was unchanged.

The Marine had died with his eyes open and unseeing. He was cut in half by either the nylon strap or as he was being pulled through the trees. What Pu was seeing was only the young man's upper torso.

"I remember as we got closer that I could smell fuel or gas," said Kozakowski. "As I was farther back towards the rear of the patrol, I could also feel a sense of urgency developing as we closed on the crash site. It was very steep and a bit slippery. The hump was getting more difficult and there were no breaks. As I looked up, I saw what was left of the helo up the incline and to my left. The ground and bush were black like there had been a fire, but I don't remember debris."

Moore noted that since there was not much of a burn area it would be logical to conclude the helicopter was low on fuel. Team Rush Act was found scattered about the mountain while most of those aboard Rogers' doomed Sea Knight were still either near or inside the aircraft.

Doc Daniels was found in a tree barely alive, according to Pupuhi. Moore disagreed by saying that Daniels died on impact the day before. Pu's recollection was the Docs worked on the Rush Act's Corpsman but he expired before they could medevac him.

Ski said he recognized Doc Daniels since he was fair skinned and had freckles. He became lightheaded when he saw the wound that had opened up his back and someone took pity on him by sending him to stand security watch further up the mountainside away from the body collection area. 1st Recon Cpl. Michael Schneider, 20, of Omaha, Nebraska, Daniels' hooch mate, recalled that a Marine later sent to identify him at 1st Med said he had died with a smile on his face. "That would have been characteristic of Doc."

Lt.Col. Leftwich had taken a solid hit to the head by a spare jungle penetrator aboard the helicopter, which killed him instantly. Pu said they based their identification of the colonel by the insignias on his collars. Feldman said he recognized Lt.Col. Leftwich in a photo of the crash site by his shined boots sticking out of the crushed fuselage. Of the seven Marines on the SPIE rig and eight Marines in the helicopter, all would die. (Records show that the most devastating Marine helicopter accident up to that date occurred on January 8, 1968 when a HMH-463 Sea Stallion CH-53 slammed into a mountain in the fog near Hue killing 40 Marines, three Navy Corpsmen and two Army personnel returning from R&R. Their bodies weren't recovered for several months as the helicopter was off-course and crashed into the Hai Lang Forest---MDK).

Capt. Blair noted in his report that "the SPIE strap was still attached to the forward section and stretched out 125 feet." He also reported that the "instrument panel indicated the fuel gauge was set at '4' and the radar altimeter indicated 25 feet."

Lt.Col. Wilson interpreted the "4" and the altimeter reading by saying, "That meant each fuel tank probably had 400 lbs. of gas (total 800) giving them approximately 40 minutes of flight time. Curt might have been light on purpose to maximize his hover power on the extraction. I recall the plan was to land at a secure site (after making the extraction) and put the Marine Recon team aboard. The radar altimeter reads directly under the cockpit so (its reading of 25 feet) makes sense as it is a relatively sensitive instrument."

The Patrol Debrief stated, "Teams arrived at the crash site and observed oil and hydraulic fuel throughout the crash site. The motor, tail section, stub wing and fuel tanks were sighted throughout the burnt area. Moving through this area 15-20 meters due east the teams found the 7-member Recon Team Rush Act thrown throughout an area covering 15-20 meters (49-65.6 feet).

"Three members were close together with the other four spread out. Three 'D' rings had been torn completely from the SPIE rig and all the team members had their SPIE (harness) equipment on. All the team members were accounted for in this area and all were dead."

The SPIE line was wrapped several times around a 7- to 10-inch in diameter tree beginning about 20 feet up in the tree. Either the nylon line or the helicopter had loped off about 10 or more feet from the top of the tree.

1stLt. Harvey, my old TBS classmate and fellow platoon member, was thrown clear of the aircraft suffering massive injuries that took his life. Pu said it looked as if Harvey had jumped and hit a tree on the way down ripping his shirt partially off. He felt he had died on impact.

But Moore said that if Harvey was standing at the rear ramp he was probably thrown rather than jumped to the location they found him on the side of the hill. He still had some color and rigor mortis hadn't quite set in like the others when they found him. It was reasoned from the condition of Harvey's body and other telltale signs that he was the only one to have lived through the night and had expired sometime that morning. The former Maj. Bub agreed with Moore's account from the stories he heard later from team members being debriefed on their return.

Col. Cross said he heard that Harvey survived the crash and was found away from the helicopter's wreckage with his utility blouse unbuttoned with his head on his crossed arms as if he had gone to sleep…and never woke up.

Kozakowski said it was thought that since Harvey didn't look as bad as the others and a radio was near him that perhaps he survived longer but he wasn't sure.

Maj. Bub concurred with the popular theory circulating around the battalion and MAG-16 at that time as to the cause of the accident. And that was the pilot probably suffered vertigo in the dense clouds and lost his sense of direction crashing into the mountain. Lt.s Goetz and Stewart's vertigo problems November 15 seemed to favor this version of why Rogers crashed.

Bub went on to say, "In an earlier operation on a mountain in the Charlie Ridge area, we were doing an extraction when we flew into low-flying clouds or a fog bank. I had my headset on listening to the pilot and copilot. One of them was having vertigo problems as was I standing at the back of the helicopter.

"The other voice was calmly reading off the instrument panel to get his sense of direction, up and down, etc. Vertigo was easy to suffer if you suddenly flew into a cloud bank or fog. This is what many people think happened."

**Stout Tree Theory**

What actually occurred that November 18, 1970 day might never be fully explained. Those who may have known died in that crash against Hill 800. The pilots I interviewed asked that I keep an open mind for the vertigo explanation. Naturally, there could have been any number of reasons why 1stLt. Curt Rogers pranged into the side of that Que Son Mountain peak killing all aboard and on the string.

Then again, if Sgt. Brust's eyewitness account was accurate, it could hold the key to what happened to 1stLt. Rogers' aircraft. Brust, Knapp and Barr agreed that the Huey pilot yelled at Rogers to "BANK LEFT" but, instead, he banked sharply right and flew into Hill 800 killing all aboard. If 1stLt. Rogers was already dragging Marines and the SPIE strap through the trees as the Huey crew looked on and the strap anchored itself to that stout 7- to 10-inch tree, maybe there is a reasonable explanation why the crew chief saw the CH-46D make a hard right bank into the mountain. It was the SPIE strap that pulled Rogers off-course and broke his aircraft in two against a boulder on the side of the tall granite hill.

Lt.Col. Moore explained that the tensile strength of the SPIE line (three or four nylon lines sewn together) was somewhere in the vicinity of 20,000 lbs. Then take into consideration the CH-46D weighs in at 26,000 lbs. and a SPIE strap wrapped around a tree could certainly present a serious problem for the aircraft. Moore pointed out that the 125-foot SPIE strap was still attached to three locations inside the crushed fuselage and back down to the tightly strap-wrapped tree.

Lt. Jim Martin recalled a story about an overlooked tie-down nylon strap still securing one side of a CH-46 to the deck of an aircraft carrier. That nylon strap had the strength to pull the helicopter down while it was lifting off and flip it.

## Capt. Blair's Crash Site Illustration[3]

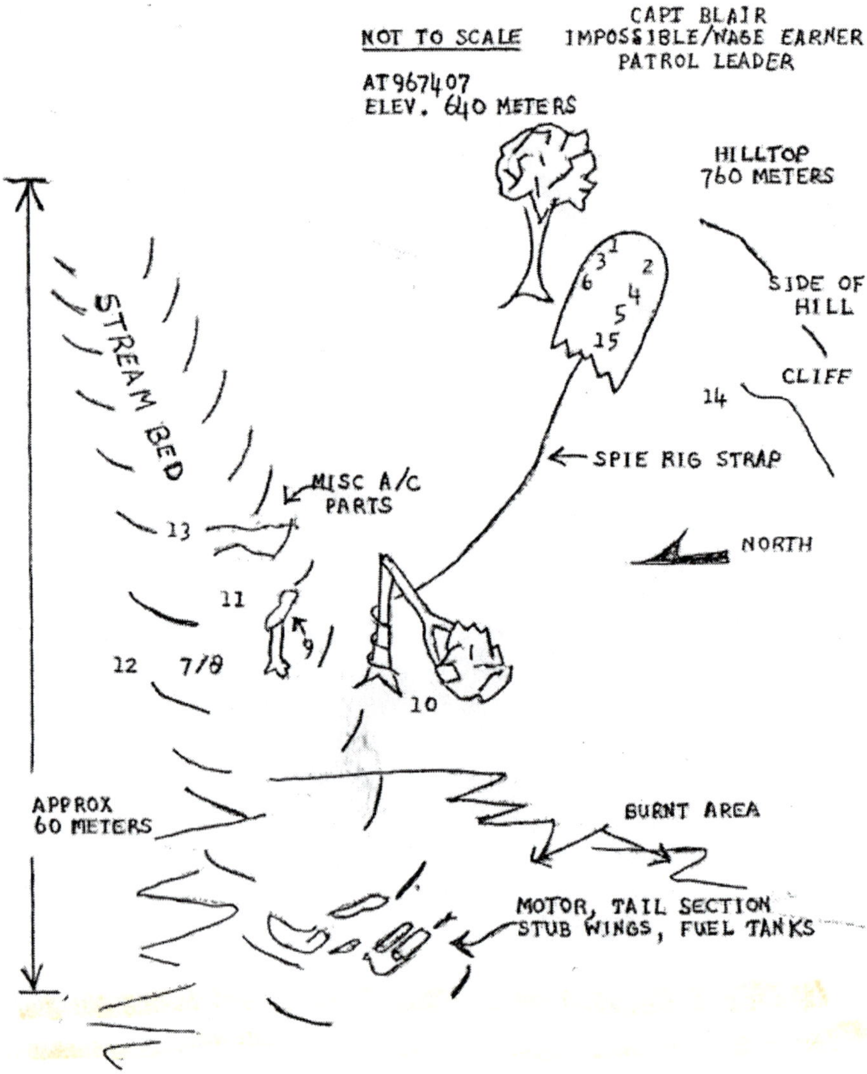


**Gy.Sgt. Rod Pupuhi's identification of Marines in illustration: 1. Rogers, 2. Stolz, 3. Gunner, 4. Donnell, 5. Gunner, 6. Lt.Col. Leftwich, 7. Tucker, 8. Doc Daniels, 9. Villasana, 10. Pope, 11. Stockman, 12. Hudson, 13. Delozier, 14. Harvey, 15. Manela. (Other eyewitnesses say 9. in the tree was Daniels---MDK).**

Moore stated that if the Sea Knight had hit Hill 800 head on it would have sent debris over the edge of the finger it crashed into rather than break up the way it did making a debris field below the fuselage. The gunny checked the area the Recon team was dragged through and indicated that very few trees were affected thus the team hit the trees about where they were and the SPIE line wrapped itself around that tree almost instantly.

He felt that Rogers never had a chance to react to his helicopter being pulled to the ground by the "rubber band effect" of the SPIE strap attached to the tree. The G-force of the sudden stop and the SPIE strap swinging the CH-46D into the side of the mountain gave neither pilot a chance to do anything to alter their predicament, according to Moore.

Pu agrees with Moore's assessment of the "rubber band effect" pulling the Sea Knight against the mountain. Blair estimated the canopy in the area to be 40-80 feet. Flying too close to those trees was a fatal mistake by Rogers but clouds obscured his view of them in his flight path.

Adding to the theory the Sea Knight's SPIE strap could possibly have become entangled in the tree, changing its flight direction and slamming it to the ground was that initially the aircraft was flying west-southwest but on its discovery at the crash site the front of the aircraft was pointed to the southeast. The aircraft was facing about 120 degrees away from its original flight direction.

The 35-meter (114.8 feet) long helicopter had broken into two parts. About 25 meters (82 feet) of the front of the aircraft had been compacted into an unrecognizable 10 meter (32.8 feet) tangle of metal about 30-40 meters above the SPIE strap-wrapped tree on the mountainside next to a ravine. Hydraulic fluid was all around this part of the aircraft...no fire broke out, according to Blair's report.

Moore recalled that very small pieces of the rotorblades were found scattered about the mountainside but no part of significance from that part of the aircraft.

The back 10 meters (32.8 feet) of the chopper broke off when it slammed into the steep mountainside and fell below the "anchor" tree to burn. The tail section, motor, stub wings and fuel tanks were located in a burned out area 25-35 meters below the "anchor" tree. Miscellaneous parts of the aircraft were found about 15 meters away in an area above the tree.

Giving cover for the recovery teams that November 19th day in shifts was Scarface Cobra pilot, 1stLt. Causey and his copilot 1stLt. Terry Crews of Clifton, Virginia. Causey said the crash site on the ground was very difficult to see from the air. The recovery team had to point out where the crash site was before he could recognize the crumpled parts of the CH-46D.

"The aircraft was pretty much accordianed into itself. It looked as though someone had thrown an egg against a wall and it stuck there," related Causey. He said there was actually two crash sites he could see—one where the aircraft hit the mountain and one where the team hit.

Causey went on to say that the mountain was a sheer cliff where the accident occurred. "There were corridors around the mountains but they couldn't be seen for the clouds most of the time."

Several Cobras took turns that day going to hot fuel back at either An Hoa or MMAF to keep their tanks topped off and relieving others orbiting the crash site. Bronco OV-10As were also alternating being on station for added security. Causey's Cobra alone logged 11 hours of flight time November 19 for the recovery operation.

**Who Wielded the Axe?**

The Recon Marines wondered who wielded the razor-sharp axe that was supposed to be used to cut the nylon SPIE line away when the helicopter became entangled with the tree. The axe was the responsibility of the Recon extract team aboard the helicopter and should have been in Manela's capable hands. The axe was found near Lt.Col. Leftwich's body at the crash site, according to Pu.

"The axe is supposed to be in the hands of whoever was looking down the hell hole. It has a leather strap to insert your wrist," said Moore. No one had it attached to their wrist when they recovered the bodies.

"Manela was qualified to handle the job. So I don't know who was at the hell hole giving guidance and instruction. You don't leave that position until the team is in the chopper or finally sets down in a safe area. You have to maintain visible eyeball contact at all times," said Pu. Manela was supposed to be belted in to prevent him from falling out the hell hole but Moore said this was not the case.

If the aircraft was flying in excess of 100 mph trying to gain transitional lift then neither Cpl. Manela at the hell hole nor Sgt. Donnell looking out the gunner's door or hell hole as well could have informed 1stLt. Rogers in time to prevent his plowing into the side of Hill 800 down the draw a mere 1200 meters away. And if the helicopter was flying in O/O visibility then they had no time to react to wield an axe much less warn the pilot.

Considering Rogers' aircraft was going an estimated 100-150 mph on impact and the evidence showed Team Rush Act was dragged roughly 60 feet through the trees then the men aboard may not have realized what was happening as the crash occurred so quickly. We are talking about split seconds before hitting the mountainside in the dense cloud cover.

And if the helicopter was jerked off course as violently and unexpectedly by its attachment to the tree as the scattered aircraft parts around it and the terrible impact of the fuselage indicates, then severing the SPIE line appears to have been absolutely impossible to accomplish regardless of whoever wielded the axe.

Moore noted that in helicopters today there's a "quick release" operated by the pilot to disengage the SPIE strap in case of emergencies. In 1970 the Sea Knight's pilot could only release the resupply net from the cockpit. By 2002 the pilot had the sole discretionary command decision to sacrifice a Recon team on "the string" if he felt his helicopter was in danger.

A strange coincidence was the timing of Rogers' slamming into Hill 800 November 18 and the projected pickup of Team Rush Act from its regularly scheduled return off patrol November 18…both 1650!

**Recon Teams Mission Completed by 1700, November 19, 1970**

All the bodies were accounted for by 1135 Thursday, November 19 except for Rogers and Stolz. A reexamination of the crushed fuselage/cockpit revealed their bodies were still trapped lifeless inside. An HMH-463 Dimmer CH-53D Sea Stallion was called in from MMAF to lift the fuselage so they could retrieve the pilots' bodies. Capt. Blair sadly radioed in that War Cloud 6 and his extract team, Team Rush Act and the Peachbush crew had all perished.

Once the crumpled metal was lifted, the men's bodies were pulled out of the wreckage. The fuselage was lifted back to MMAF by the CH-53D where it was examined and later buried in a large hole at the end of the runway. By 1700 the last two bodies were accounted for and extracted.

Gy.Sgt. Moore was injured during the lifting of the fuselage when a jagged piece of metal cut his arm. He was the only physical injury from Teams Mission Impossible and Wage Earner November 19th. The unseen "injury" or trauma from what they had seen that day would stay with the team members for the rest of their lives affecting some of them more than others.

All radios, crypto gear, equipment, maps and any other sensitive material that could be used by the enemy was rounded up to be carried back to Camp Reasoner by the Recon teams.

"There was not one piece of equipment, be it individual weapons or aviation gear, that was operational," Blair's report noted.

After the bodies were collected, a Peachbush CH-46D hovered over the accident site hoisting down body bags and rope in order to bring the bodies aboard.

"We hoisted the bodies up. It was a very long and stressful day," said Cpl. Jerry "Sandy" Sanders of Ozark, Alabama, Peachbush crew chief, aboard Capt. Edmunds' Sea Knight. "The pilots did a fantastic job of hovering on the side of that mountain while I hoisted the bodies aboard. The aircraft got heavier as I put more bodies on board and the hovering became more difficult. The crew chief (Donnell) was a friend of mine. We called him Rat. His initials were RAD and it just became Rat. One of the gunners, Buttry, had flown with me a couple of times. Good guy. I took a few pictures of the crash site with my little camera. I have never forgotten that day."

Crew chief Sgt. Donnell aboard Rogers' aircraft was the oldest boy and second oldest of 13 other brothers and sisters from Clymer, New York (three additional siblings were born after his death making 16 altogether). He had been drafted by the U.S. Army but didn't want to go to war as a soldier... instead he enlisted in the Marine Corps to go to war as a Marine, according to his sister Lisa (Donnell) Gruber. The sergeant met his Maker after he had done everything humanly possible to bring Team Rush Act home safely. Always surrounded by his many siblings growing up, he didn't die alone in Vietnam. Donnell departed this life in the company of 13 good Marines and a Navy Corpsman, his brothers.

## Gy.Sgt. Pupuhi Recalls Leaving Crash Site

At 1830 the two Recon teams were extracted from the crash site having completed their heart-breaking job of retrieving their dead comrades, aircraft crew and battalion CO. All the bodies were flown back to 1st Medical Battalion Hospital for identification.

Moore indicated that typically crash sites were napalmed by F-16s or F-15s as is standard procedure when they are unable to remove everything from a crash site. Pu said he thought he heard explosions come from an arc light carried off by a B-52 dropping 500 lb. bombs as they departed the area by air.

"Arc lights cost a lot of money. I'm 98 percent sure it was napalmed eventually," recalled Moore.

"We could hear them hitting the crash zone," indicated Pu. He said he recalled cheering, "Whoopie," when in the past an area was pasted by air after they'd been extracted. Not this time.

"But this drumming--*'BOOM! BOOM! BOOM!'*--I was crying for these guys," related Gy.Sgt. Pupuhi a little over 30 years later. He indicated that he still had problems from Vietnam that has allowed him to get professional help from the Veterans Administration.

Pu said he was on 100 percent disability. He noted he has had trouble coping with his traumatic combat experiences from Vietnam after having served in 1st Recon as well as Military Assistance Command-Studies and Observations Group (SOG). The effects of war still linger with Rod Pupuhi.

Scarface Cobra pilot Causey said he didn't think the site was napalmed or bombed November 19th as he and another Cobra escorted a Sea Knight to the location to give it a once over from the air November 20. He wasn't sure who was aboard the aircraft checking out the crash site.

**HMM-263 ASO's Preliminary Report, November 18**

The Preliminary Report of Aircraft Accident November 18, 1970 by Peachbush's Air Safety Officer (ASO), 1stLt. J.C. McGarigle noted: *"Aircraft lifted from zone with recon team on SPIE rig, was told to turn left when departing. Aircraft disappeared into clouds without acknowledging communications. No further communications received from aircraft. Aircraft lost. Condition unknown.*

*"Extract was an emergency tactical extract in mountainous terrain. Low cloud cover prevented search and rescue operations. Search and Rescue will be continued at the earliest possible time, weather permitting."*[4]

Lt. McGarigle marked in half-inch letters on this initial Teletype message, "UNK AAR (Unknown After Action Report." In the upper right hand corner of the page the following was scribbled in by an apparent higher authority, "DEA FMFPAC (Due to Enemy Action Fleet Marine Force Pacific)." This will be McGarigle's finding on the next message sent out November 19 that the air crash was "Due to Enemy Action."

**Supplemental AAR Notes Accident as "DEA," November 19**

Lt. McGarigle followed up with a cryptic Supplemental After Action Report released to 22 command authorities at 0934 Thursday, November 19, 1970 once the crash site was located, *"After disappearing in the clouds, aircraft crashed into mountainside and exploded from unknown causes. Aircraft wreckage was scattered over wide area of steep mountain slope, approximately 1900 feet above ground level. Aircraft wreckage discovered in known enemy territory."* Rubber-stamped on this report in half-inch high lettering is "DEA SUP AAR (Due to Enemy Action, Supported by After Action Report)."[5]

The ASO's finding or recommended finding as to the cause of the air crash was made less than 17 hours after the mishap and at the moment the 1st Recon teams reached the crash site. The last wording of the message is the catch phrase for a DEA finding.

**Supplementary Report of Aircraft Accident, November 22**

A second Supplementary Report of Aircraft Accident went out to 21 command authorities at 0449 Sunday, November 22, 1970 listing the Marine/ Navy Corpsman KIAs from both 1st Recon and HMM-263. Again, *"DEA SUPP AAR"* is rubber-stamped on the Teletype message. The message also states, *"Forward transmission and rotor head recovered."*[6]

**HMM-263 ASO Inquiry (1stLt. Paul Wilson assisted)**

Lt.Col. Wilson noted that he assisted Capt. Tom Edmunds, HMM-263's

ASO (he replaced 1stLt. McGarigle as ASO November 25, 1970) and doubled as the assistant Operations officer, in investigating the air crash for Peachbush. He said the "official finding" for the air crash was "Due to Enemy Action, DEA." (I was unable to locate a report other than the rubber-stamped "DEA SUP AAR" on the Supplemental AAR at any military command due to the passage of time---MDK).

Not knowing what occurred in the cockpit prior to the aircraft crashing into Hill 800, DEA was the only finding that could be reached. "Pilot error" may have been a contributing factor but the evidence for such a finding was not conclusive.

The monsoon conditions, the drag of the weight of the Recon Marines on the string, the emergency extract designation of the mission, towering mountains covered with tall trees, known enemy troops in the vicinity of the pickup point, the possibility of a mechanical problem or loss of power and a lack of radio response from Rogers' aircraft may have all or partially contributed to the crash.

Wilson said they were never made aware of the SPIE strap wrapping itself around a tree or the Marines being dragged through the trees. They just looked at the evidence from the aircraft's flight pattern and resultant crash. "The terrible tragedy was a topic of conversation for weeks in the squadron's Ready Room with the consensus being 'to fly the aircraft and don't worry about the enemy shooting them between the eyes because they ain't going to do it. Fly the friggin' aircraft.'"

As a postscript to the November 18, 1970 tragedy, 1stLt. Valentino noted that senior officers were no longer required to accompany emergency extracts at 1st Recon Battalion after Lt.Col. Leftwich's death. A single NCO or SNCO to handle the SPIE rig or ladder would accompany the "low" aircraft and an extract officer and NCO or SNCO were designated for the "high" bird thereafter to lighten the weight on the CH-46Ds, according to Valentino. It was a lesson learned too late.

### Irony of 1stLt. Harvey's Last Two Patrols

Some irony stands out from Teams Saddle Bag and Icebound's patrols led by Lt. Harvey on October 17 and 23. In all the length and breadth of I Corps where 1st Recon teams could have been inserted, Harvey's two teams patrolled near where he would lose his life on November 18.

Saddle Bag was inserted October 17 300 meters west of Hill 405,[7A] which is a mere 3 clicks away from where he would meet his fate one month and one day later on the side of Hill 800.[7B]

Icebound's insert on October 23 was 600 meters north of Hill 953 and just south of Deo Le.[7C] It was equidistant, roughly 1700 meters, from the helicopter crash site that would take his life and the extract point on the side of Hill 848.[7D] Oddly enough, a Navy Corpsman didn't accompany either of Harvey's teams.

"I was assigned only once to gather the personal effects of a KIA Marine and it was an honor to do that for Butch's wife and family. I will never forget the impact of that loss. Lt. Butch Harvey was on the same chopper with 13 other United States Marines and a U.S. Navy Corpsman that day. All gave their lives for their country and their fellow servicemen. All died as they lived... heroes," recalled Lt. Morin, whose place Harvey had taken on the doomed helicopter.[8]

**Marines Thoughts on Air Crash**

Lt.Col. Trainor, a '51 Holy Cross College (Worcester, Massachusetts) graduate, replaced interim CO Maj. Bub at 1st Recon Battalion on November 20, 1970. He would comment about that November 18th crash, "...a team normally did not ask for an emergency extract unless they really had an emergency. In truth, however, I did have to veto a few emergency extract requests where in my judgment the situation was not sufficiently threatening to warrant the risky rescue procedure. It's times like that when the responsibility of command takes on new meaning."[9]

Lt.Gen. Trainor indicated he accompanied every emergency extract of his own volition in the chase bird rather than the low bird for command and control. The general said a testosterone-driven battalion CO like Bill Drumright who enjoyed going in with the primary bird would distract the extract officer and SPIE team from doing their jobs. "Somebody had to make sure all the pieces fell into place. Many of the helo pilots were nuggets who were brave, but not battle smart...we had Cobras, OV-10s, A-4's and arty involved in all emergency extracts. A fire support coordinator was needed.

"Also, somebody had to bear the responsibility of aborting or modifying the mission if circumstances dictated. I strongly believe that was my job and I still do...I found that there were enough instances for the back-up bird to assume the primary duty to satisfy the gonad requirement," said Trainor, who would serve as a military consultant for *NBC News* during *Operation Desert Storm* in 1991 and *CNBC* for *Operation Iraqi Freedom* in 2003.[10]

(If Bill Drumright, and by inference Bill Leftwich Jr., were "testosterone-driven" for opting to go on the primary extraction bird during hot extractions on a too regular basis then I'd have to defend their actions by saying that such behavior is typical of many Marines. Those over-sized "gonads" were clearly in evidence as practiced by the bush units and pilots/crew day-in and day-out in Vietnam up and down the pay scale. I see the point Trainor is making about Command and Control but some notable individuals simply preferred to lead from the front "to share the work and danger with their men," i.e. Chesty Puller, Merritt Edson, Dan Daly, Smedley Butler, Mac McVey...Drumright and Leftwich, etc.---MDK).

"I think they could've waited one more day to be extracted," agreed Lt.Col. Moore.

Cross, who served under Leftwich at 1st Recon and went on to flight school after Vietnam retired a colonel in the Marine Air Wing, had this to say, "Most squadrons wrote off accidents to 'Due to Enemy Action.' It was much easier on the paperwork, not to mention reputations. It was also a time (it still is) when a CO would be relieved for a pilot error accident or maintenance foul up. 'DEA' saved careers. The problem is that a few design or parts problems that should have been fixed also probably escaped unnoticed." (See pages 191-194).

Col. Williams weighed in on the rescue attempt by saying, "My thoughts from the perspective of critical analysis is that we lacked patience on missions like this on more than one occasion and maybe should've waited for better conditions. But that is Monday morning quarterbacking now. Yes, this (Recon) team was hurting but there was not a life or death situation confronting them. They were in a bad tactical position with thoughts of being discovered by the enemy.

"The courage of the men who attempted this rescue is beyond question. Their heroism was in the finest traditions. The perplexing fact is that the next day we recovered the bodies and aircraft when the weather was clear with visibility unlimited!" Col. Williams, USMC (Ret.), retired as a Division Chief in the Lakewood, Colorado Police Department in June 2007 after 24 years on the police force.

Williams and 1stLt. Porto almost had a similar accident to Rogers' in bad weather and heavy cloud cover in the Que Sons while laden with troops on November 23...just 5 days later. Williams showed exemplary skill in flying his aircraft to keep it from falling off into a steep gorge. His CH-46D was damaged and the troops only suffered minor bruises and injuries.

"If Bill Leftwich had done anything contrary to exerting his every physical and mental action in saving his men, it would have been totally out of context with the way he lived his life. He was extremely competent, always well-prepared and to those who admired him he was the Corps' best example of a humble person," stated Bond.

Dr. Solis noted, "I recall the widespread questioning among we career officers about Leftwich being aboard the extract helicopter in which he was killed. What the hell was a battalion commander doing on a flight that was known to be headed for a hot extract? A company commander, okay, but not a battalion commander. Those with whom I traveled agreed that, yeah, it was a gutsy and inspirational thing for Leftwich to do, and he did it repeatedly, but that isn't the role of a battalion commander." Dr. Solis retired in 1989 after 26 years in the Marine Corps.[11]

Valentino said he had to laugh to think anyone would even entertain the notion that Leftwich was "demoted" to 1st Recon considering what happened after he turned up missing November 18. "The evening of the day Leftwich was lost but before the aircraft was found, the eligible lieutenant colonels were already lobbying to get the Recon job. The day he was lost I also met about everyone of a full bird's rank and above at Division who appeared to have both love and admiration for the man. His reputation was about as good as it gets with many of the colonels saying that Leftwich had been on track to becoming Commandant."

Gen. Widdecke presented the recovery teams, Mission Impossible and Wage Earner, with Certificates of Commendation. The certificates cite the Marines for "working for more than 11 hours at a fatiguing pace and under physical and emotional strain" to "recover the 14 Marines and one Corpsman deep in enemy-infested territory" and to "move 1,000 meters over treacherous terrain and evacuate the remains and equipment."

"(Gen. Widdecke) indicated to me that he was impressed with our report," recalled Moore.

Curt Rogers Sr., the deceased pilot's father, told Lt. Jim Martin that in the late 1990s Maj. Toben had talked to him about that November 18th day to try and explain to him what had happened. It must have been hard for Toben to tell the 80-plus-year-old man how his son had come to die on a mountainside in Vietnam. Toben passed away in 2005 and is buried in Arlington National Cemetery, according to Lt.Col. Geis, who attended his funeral.

Based on his need to talk to Curt Rogers' dad, I would imagine that Toben had survivor's guilt to some extent. Thousands of servicemen returned stateside having some form of it.

Most of the Marines I contacted for this story revealed they were still grieving and trying to come to terms with other men's deaths to some extent. All still had strong feelings for those long dead young men who gave their lives almost 4 decades ago in a war that divided this nation and seems but a footnote today in school books to their grandkids and great-grandkids.

In August 2002, the former Col. Williams sat down with Curt Rogers' family in Colorado and in an emotional retelling tried to piece together what occurred on November 18, 1970. Their wounds and Williams' were still fresh after all those intervening years. Lt.Col. Wilson met with Rogers' family in November 2004 to tell them what he remembered.

Bub was still dealing with the fact it could just as easily have been him crashing into that mountain November 18, 1970, rather than Lt.Col. Leftwich when I interviewed him. At the time of our conversation he was a highly successful lawyer in the Washington, D.C. area. He had ended his career in the Marines as an attorney in the Judge Advocate General's office.

That's what makes us higher up on the food chain...we care about one another. Plus, Marines never forget other Marines' sacrifices. And as November 10th rolls around each year, we hoist a cold one in their honor and remember, "But for the grace of God, that might have been me."

Hanging from the wall in the Recon Marines' briefing room at Camp Reasoner was this gentle reminder by Confederate Gen. Robert E. Lee, "Duty is the most sublime word in the English language."[12]

In the category of "it's a small world," Scott Leftwich said his dad regularly stopped for gas in Alexandria, Virginia near their home at the Harvey's family-owned filling station over the years. The colonel probably knew Butch predating his entry into the Marines. Who could have imagined that someday with their age disparity they would meet the same fate together on the other side of the world?

## 2/1's Heliborne Assault on November 18

Another ironic footnote to this fatal air crash comes from Lt.Col. Leftwich's old 2/1 Marines on that same November 18th day.

Roughly 4 hours before the colonel crashed into Hill 800 in the Que Sons, Golf Co. and a contingent of Echo Co., 2/1 Marines arrived unannounced in a successful daylight heliborne attack on another ville, Quang Dong (1) 2 clicks east-southeast of Hill 55.[13A] The attack resulted in four VC/NVA KIA as well as one NVA lieutenant, one NVA master sergeant WIA and being made POWs and seven people detained from 85 screened on Hill 55.

A daylight heliborne raid on unsuspecting VC/NVA soldiers netting at least two big fish again succeeded thanks to excellent intelligence gathering by 2/1's CIT, ITT and S-2. I credit 2/1's continuing success for intelligence gathering with Warrant Officer/1stLt. Tom Marino of CIT. I've always wondered how a warrant officer turned first lieutenant could depose the battalion XO, a major, from his quarters to be nearer his CIT interrogation area. He was also so highly thought of by the VC as to be ranked among the top 10 most wanted men dead in Quang Nam Province.

This came on Maj. John Grinalds' watch as 2/1's S-3 chief but also reminded everyone of Leftwich's Silver Star using the same tactics on August 4. Golf Co.

was the pivotal unit in both operations' successes as well. It was a fitting tribute and an unintended parting gift to the memory and indelible spirit Leftwich had stamped on "The Professionals" of 2/1.

"On that November 18th afternoon, Maj. Phil Monahan, the S-3 for the 1st Marine Regiment, called me over the radio to inform me that 'Bill was down,'" recalled Maj.Gen. Grinalds who was running 2/1's heliborne attack from Hill 55.

"(The major) started to cry when he heard that the colonel had died in an air crash. Then he went over to a sandbag and hit it," recalled Cpl. Bailey Eames who was serving as Maj. Grinalds' radioman on the November 18th operation.

"Lt.Col. Leftwich was my best friend in the Marine Corps and his death and loss to the rest of us was a real blow to me," indicated Maj.Gen. Grinalds.

Lt. Robinson noted that it seemed like the war stopped when the news got out that War Cloud 6, Leftwich, had been killed in that air crash. "I remember the troops were crying. I was in Da Nang with Maj. Grinalds, Maj. Monahan and Col. Kelley trying to eulogize Leftwich. They were trying to find one thing wrong with him. They couldn't. Finally, Grinalds said, 'He was the perfect leader.'"

**15 American Heroes**

The 14 Marines and the Navy Corpsman who died November 18, 1970 were the only Marines or Navy medical personnel to die in Vietnam on that date. Only Leftwich, Harvey and Rogers were listed as married. They gave the supreme sacrifice so that others might live. I honor them here:

**Sea Knight Crew, HMM-263**

| | | |
|---|---|---|
| 1stLt. Orville C. Rogers Jr. | 1stLt. James E. Stolz | Sgt. Robert A. Donnell II |
| Dallas, Texas | Hicksville, New York | Clymer, New York |
| 12Jun45-18Nov70 | 04Nov46-18Nov70 | 21Sept48-18Nov70 |
| (Pilot) | (Copilot) | (Crew Chief) |

**Sea Knight Crew, TAD from H&MS-16[15]**

| | |
|---|---|
| Cpl. Enver Bajin | LCpl. Richard R. Buttry |
| College Point, New York | Anaheim, California |
| 27Dec48-18Nov70 | 31Jan48-18Nov70 |
| (Gunner) | (Gunner) |

**Team Rush Act, Bravo Co., 1st Recon Bn.**

| | | |
|---|---|---|
| Cpl. John F. Stockman | Cpl. Fernando Villasana | LCpl. David V. Delozier |
| Marcus Hook, Pennsylvania | El Paso, Texas | Altoona, Pennsylvania |
| 13Oct43-18Nov70 | 22Nov50-18Nov70 | 16Mar50-18Nov70 |
| (Team Leader) | (Rear point) | (Point man) |
| | | |
| LCpl. Gary D. Hudson | LCpl. Charles A. Pope Jr. | LCpl. Robert E. Tucker |
| Joplin, Missouri | Independence, Missouri | Abbyville, Kansas |
| 13Mar50-18Nov70 | 14Feb51-18Nov70 | 12Nov48-18Nov70 |
| (1st Radioman) | (Grenadier-M-79) | (2nd Radioman) |

HM2 Russell G. Daniels
Phoenix, Arizona
23Sept48-18Nov70
(Navy Corpsman)

**Extract Team, 1st Recon Bn.**

Lt.Col. William G. Leftwich Jr.
Germantown, Tennessee
27Apr31-18Nov70
(CO, 1st Recon Battalion)

| | |
|---|---|
| 1stLt. Cleveland R. Harvey | Cpl. Randall P. Manela |
| Alexandria, Virginia | Eugene, Oregon |
| 16Jun47-18Nov70 | 14May51-18Nov70 |
| (B Co. XO, extract officer) | (Extract NCO) |

# Chapter 16

**"Leftwich lived---and as things turned out, died---by the soldier's principle: 'Never send a man where you won't go yourself.' As of the day Bill Leftwich died, 43,991 other American soldiers, sailors, Marines and airmen had been killed in Vietnam since 1961. On that grim and tragic roster, his name can only be a statistic. But it will be a statistic etched in gold on bright steel."[1] Col. Robert D. Heinl Jr.**
***The Detroit News***
**November 23, 1970**

### Gen. Van Ryzin, Navy Undersecretary John Warner Notify Family

Lt.Col. Leftwich's death at 39 impacted a wide range of people stateside. He left behind his wife, Jane, and their two boys, Scott, 9, and Bill, 11. Bill's mother Mattie Leftwich was still alive at the time. His father had died of a heart attack March 25, 1966 after his return from Vietnam.

The Leftwich family was notified at their Alexandria, Virginia residence that Bill was missing in an air crash Wednesday evening, November 18, 1970 (a 12-hour time difference exists between Vietnam and Virginia). The air crash occurred at approximately 0430 (4:30 a.m.) East Coast time. (I'm not sure if this holds true for all next-of-kin notifications but the one that I saw, Skibbe's, indicated the team was not to give a casualty notification to the family between 10 p.m. and 6 a.m.---MDK).

Jane said she was working on refinishing a piece of furniture downstairs in the afternoon when "Little Bill" informed her there were two men coming up the sidewalk.

"I was walking up the stairs when I looked out the door and saw Gen. William J. Van Ryzin and Undersecretary of the Navy John Warner coming to the front door. I told mother and she immediately understood the significance of such a visit. They reported that dad was missing," said Bill Leftwich III clearly recalling that tragic day.

There had been brief hope as it was thought an emergency beep from the helicopter's distress box had been heard and that someone on the ground was alive, but that proved to be a false rumor. On the other side of the world Capt. Blair made a KIA head count and identified 12 Marines and one Corpsman by 1100 (11 a.m.) Thursday, November 19, Vietnam time, 2300 (11 p.m.) Wednesday, November 18 in Alexandria. Still unaccounted for were the pilots inside the crushed fuselage.

The 1st Recon captain informed the circling CH-46Ds and Cobras who, in turn, passed the sad information onto MMAF. Before noon 1stMarDiv Headquarters in Da Nang sent a Teletype message stateside to the Navy Department to inform 15 notification teams to contact anxiously waiting families who had earlier been told of their loved ones' MIA situation that their Marines' status had been changed to KIA.

It was close to midnight Wednesday in Alexandria when Bill's mother, Mattie, came into the boys' room, woke them up and quietly told them the tragic news about their dad. Mattie had received information that her son was missing at 4 o'clock that afternoon and flew in from Memphis hours earlier to be with Jane and the boys.

Jane said that everyone who had come to the house when they were told Bill was missing stayed until she received the news of his being killed in the air crash.

**Lt.Col. Bill Leftwich Jr., CO, 1st Recon Bn. (Photo courtesy of Bill Leftwich III)**

"I got a call about 3 in the morning from John Warner who with tears in his voice said, 'We lost Bill,'" remembered Ross Perot.

The family flew to Memphis the next day in Perot's private jet to prepare for the funeral set for the day after Thanksgiving, Friday, November 27 followed by interment at Forest Hills Cemetery next to his dad. Memphis' *The Commercial Appeal* newspaper carried a front-page story Thursday, November 19 on the colonel with a photo under the headline, "Marine Hero Is Killed In Vietnam Action." The article quoted Jane as initially holding out hope Bill was okay until notified otherwise. The story referred to the worldwide photo of the then Maj. Leftwich wounded in the face in March 1965 en route to earning a Navy Cross.

## Maj. John Grinalds Brings Lt.Col. Leftwich Home for Burial

Maj. Grinalds accompanied his friend's body back home to Memphis, which was his parents' hometown now as well. They had accomplished so much together at 2/1 it only seemed fitting that he should be the one to bring the colonel back to his loved ones.

Young Bill remembered what a good job the major had done in putting the family at ease when they spoke with him. He was the right person to escort him home as his mother and Mattie were acquainted with one another.

**Maj. John S. Grinalds, XO, 2/1 (USMC Photo)**

Grinalds would eventually become a 2-star general before his retirement November 1, 1991. On August 1, 1997 he was named the 18th president of The Citadel in Charleston, South Carolina where young men and now, women are schooled to be military leaders. No better man could have been chosen for the job. He held that post until his retirement in August 2005.

To touch lightly on his many life-long accomplishments before and after Vietnam, Grinalds, in addition to graduating with honors from USMA in 1959 and being a Rhodes Scholar graduating with honors as well, was a White House Fellow in 1971; earned an MBA at the Harvard Business School with distinction in 1974; and was inducted into the Legion d' Honneur by French Pres. Francois Mitterrand for his work with the NATO and French military as a special assistant to the Supreme Allied Commander in Europe.[2]

Leftwich and Grinalds made up quite a brain trust at 2/1. Their strategies applied in 2/1's AO confounded our enemy and made "The Professionals" the Top Dog around Marble Mountain during their tenure. Upon his return to Vietnam in 1970 following the funeral, Maj. Grinalds became the Intelligence section chief for the 1st Marine Regiment under Col. Kelley December 15, 1970. He rotated home on April 1, 1971.

## Large Turn-out for Memphis Funeral, November 27, 1970

In Memphis the colonel's funeral was held in the Second Presbyterian Church where he and Jane had originally exchanged marriage vows 13 years earlier. The service drew upward to 1,000 people. A 7-man honor guard was on hand as well as 100 men from two Marine companies and a band playing "Semper Fidelis." The Navy and Marine Corps were well represented by various officers who had known Bill Leftwich through the years.

Warner presented Mrs. Leftwich with a letter from Pres. Nixon offering his condolences and news that U.S. Rep. Mendal Rivers of South Carolina, chairman of the House Armed Services Committee, would read a eulogy into the *Congressional Record* December 3, 1970, #39903.[3]

Congressman Rivers' "Tribute To A Fallen American" printed in the

*Congressional Record* concludes with the paragraph, "William Groom Leftwich Jr. was a splendid American. His record is one of honorable service and selfless sacrifice, and it is the collection of such records---the cumulative effect of them---that makes our country a force for peace and freedom throughout the world. We need remember this. We need honor those who so serve. As a nation, we are poorer for their loss."

Bill's Annapolis roommate, U.S. Navy Cmdr. Clyde R. Bell, CO of the nuclear submarine *USS Gurnard* (SSN-662), was also flown in for the funeral by one of Perot's private jets.[4]

Perot indicated that John Warner and Bill had long talks with him about playing a key role in getting involved with the POW/MIA issue. This resulted in his spending the next 4 years trying to bring the POWs held by the VC/NVA home. (USN Cmdr. William Porter "Bill" Lawrence of Nashville, Tennessee, a '51 USNA distinguished graduate and a close friend of Bill and Perot, was a POW in the "Hanoi Hilton" after being shot down over Haiphong, North Vietnam, in his F4B Phantom on June 28, 1967. He had flown 150 combat missions in Vietnam, 25 in the Korean War. He was finally repatriated March 4, 1973).

Perot put pressure on the Hanoi leadership to release the prisoners and had long talks with Secretary of State Henry Kissinger, Pres. Nixon and Gen. Alexander Haig as well. When the POWs all finally returned home, Perot received the Medal for Distinguished Public Service by the Defense Department for focusing the world's attention on their treatment by North Vietnam.

"All the TV stations (in Memphis) covered the burial service. Col. Harvey Spielman presented the American flag to mother," recalled Bill Leftwich III.

The honorary pallbearers (Marine privates actually carried the casket) were chosen from among Bill Leftwich's friends. They were Lt.Col.s Dwayne Gray, Richard C. Schulze, John A. Kinniburgh, Ronald J. Lynch, Don R. Christiensen, James J. "Joe" McMonagle and Maj.s Warren H. Wiedhahn Jr. and Curtis G. Arnold.[5] He was buried in Forest Hills Cemetery in Memphis.

**Memorial Services**

A memorial service was held for Lt.Col. Leftwich in Alexandria, Virginia, which the Secretary of the Navy John Chafee attended. Memorial services were also given for the colonel in Vietnam at 1st Recon and at 2/1. Maj.Gen. Widdecke read the eulogy at the service at Camp Reasoner for the nine Recon Marines and Navy Corpsman KIA. The general, a former Dallas, Texas resident and a graduate of the University of Texas (Austin, Texas) who was Phi Beta Kappa, would retire from the Marines on July 1, 1971 having earned the Navy Cross on Guam and a Silver Star in the Marshall Islands in World War II. He died not long after returning from Vietnam on May 13, 1973.

## Lt.Col. Bill Leftwich Jr. is Guaranteed a Place in Marine Corps History

***USS Leftwich***--With the passing of Bill Leftwich Jr., the honors and accolades came from all quarters of the country. The *USS Leftwich,* a 563-foot Spruance class multi-mission destroyer was christened in his honor at the Pascagoula, Mississippi Naval Yard on May 27, 1978. Jane did the honors by breaking a champagne bottle on the ship's bow as Mattie and Bill's sons, Bill and Scott, looked on.[6] Perot indicated that John Warner had a hand in getting the ship named for Bill Leftwich.

Sad to report that after 18 years on active duty the *USS Leftwich* was decommissioned on March 27, 1998 at Pearl Harbor, Hawaii. The ship was berthed at the Naval Inactive Ship Maintenance Facility until she was taken out to sea and sunk as a target on August 1, 2003 at longitude $022^{0}$ 48′ 47.0″ North, latitude $160^{0}$ 34′ 00.0″ West.[7]

**Leftwich College Scholarship**--Perot funded a competitive college scholarship program in Bill's name that went to the children of 1953 Annapolis graduates.

***Leftwich Trophy***--"Leftwich was the very best and Ross Perot pursued a fitting tribute to him by sponsoring the *Leftwich Trophy* for leadership and encouraging the Navy to name a destroyer after him," recalled Maj.Gen. Grinalds.

**Commandant of the Marine Corps Gen. James T. Conway presents the 2006 *Leftwich Trophy* to Maj. Matthew W. Tracy as Ross Perot looks on in the background. Perot's Foundation endows the trophy in honor of Lt.Col. Bill Leftwich Jr. (USMC Photo)**

Perot commissioned Dr. Felix Weihs de Weldon, the sculptor of the magnificent towering Marine Corps War Memorial, also called the Iwo Jima Memorial, adjacent to Arlington National Cemetery in Arlington, Virginia, to create the *Leftwich Trophy.* The 2x2-foot trophy was an extremely heavy bronze miniature of the colonel that commemorates the service and leadership of Marine captains in Lt.Col. Leftwich's tradition.

The trophy sculpted by Dr. de Weldon captured the essence of the colonel's leadership skills by showing him pointing his M-16 rifle at the enemy in mid-stride while looking back to beckon his Marines to "Follow me," with his other hand...in the forefront of his men leading the way. That's how the colonel should be remembered.

The *Leftwich Trophy* was first awarded to Capt. Clyde S. Brinkley Jr. on August 25, 1979 at the commissioning ceremony of the *USS Leftwich.* The trophy has been presented annually thereafter. The Marine Corps' 33rd Commandant, Gen. Michael W. Hagee presented the 25th *Leftwich Trophy* for 2003 to Maj. Farrell J. Sullivan of Huntington, New York (his brother Capt. Daniel M. Sullivan won in 1999).

The 27th trophy given in 2005 was, for the first time, awarded posthumously to Capt. John W. Maloney, 36, of Chicopee, Massachusetts, a former enlisted Marine. As CO of Charlie Co., 1/5, he was in the unit's lead Humvee south of Ramadi, Iraq, June 16, 2005 when a massive roadside bomb killed him and LCpl. Erik Heldt, 26, of Hermann, Missouri. Capt. Maloney's impressive leadership skills from March to June earned him not only the *Leftwich Trophy* but also a Bronze Star with Combat "V". (See *Leftwich Trophy* recipients from 1979-2009 at the back of the book).

"Ross Perot is a great and true friend of our family," indicated Bill Leftwich III.

**Leftwich statue**--Perot commissioned Dr. de Weldon to also sculpt the 9-foot-tall bronze statue (includes base) of Lt.Col. Leftwich that stands in front of Camp Barrett's TBS' Heywood Hall Administration Building at MCB Quantico, Virginia. The sculptor cast the statue as a copy of the *Leftwich Trophy* he had created. It was dedicated in a ceremony on November 28, 1985.

In 1993 I was shown the impressive Leftwich statue and *Leftwich Trophy* at Camp Barrett in Quantico by my old 2/1 Echo Co.'s 1st Platoon commander, Col. Bob Fawcett, at the time the TBS CO. He had more personal knowledge of Bill's heroism than most men having served under him at 2/1 and 1st Recon Battalion.

**TBS CO Col. Robert J. "Bob" Fawcett stands in front of the Leftwich Statue located at Camp Barrett's Heywood Hall at Marine Corps Base Quantico, Virginia. Dr. Felix Wiehs de Weldon sculpted the statue. (Photo by Dan Kellum in 1993)**

I was fortunate enough to meet that year's recipient of the *Leftwich Trophy* who I seem to recall was Capt. Michael L. Ettore, and was amazed I could barely budge the heavy bronze trophy, which was on display. USMC's 30th Commandant, Gen. Carl E. Mundy Jr., had been on hand to personally present the trophy to the captain 2 weeks before my arrival.

By the end of 1999, the *Leftwich Trophy* suggested a history of Marine heroism to a whole new generation of second lieutenants, according to Nathaniel C. "Nat" Fick, Dartmouth grad and author of the well-written book, *One Bullet Away, The Making of a Marine Officer*. Former 1st Recon Capt. Fick passed through TBS at Camp Barrett as a second lieutenant in November 1999 en route to joining Marine units fighting in Afghanistan and later Iraq.

**1st Recon's Headquarters**--On February 21, 1990, the 29th Commandant of the Marine Corps Gen. Alfred M. Gray Jr. approved the naming of the 1st Reconnaissance Battalion Headquarters at Camp Marguerita on the MCB Camp Pendleton military reservation in California in honor of Lt.Col. William G. Leftwich Jr.

**Leftwich MVP Trophy at Liberty Bowl**--"Twelve of us got together to get the MVP Trophy at the Liberty Bowl in Memphis named for Bill Leftwich," said

Memphian Chuck Bender. Between 1971-73 the trophy was given in Lt.Col. Leftwich's honor, according to his son, Bill Leftwich III.

I recall watching the bowl game on TV in 1972 not knowing about the trophy being presented in the colonel's name. I teared up when I heard that the Liberty Bowl MVP Trophy had been given in his honor. The trophy was a wonderful tribute to an outstanding Memphian and Marine.

"Bill shouldn't have died. He was a hard leader but he wouldn't ask you to do anything he wouldn't do himself," said Bender, Bill's friend from childhood until his death.

**Leftwich Tennis Courts**--Memphis also honored the colonel November 7, 1971 by building a new tennis center at Audubon Park and erecting a 5-foot high granite monument with a bronze bas relief photo of him with an inscription citing his achievements. Another of Bill's old friends and Marine legend Gen. Lewis W. Walt was on hand for the presentation ceremony, as were Jane, and Bill's mother, Mattie. Bill's childhood friend, Chuck Bender, served on the committee involved with the park.[8]

**DAV Certificate of Honor—**The Daughters of the American Revolution in Memphis presented Mrs. Mattie Howard Scrape Leftwich Sr. a Certificate of Honor in May of 1973 honoring her son. He was the highest-ranking Memphian to lose his life in Vietnam.

**USNA's Armel-Leftwich Visitor Center**--And not to be outdone, the U.S. Naval Academy has a building partially named in Lt.Col. Leftwich's honor on its campus at Annapolis, Maryland. The Armel-Leftwich Visitor Center was dedicated May 12, 1995. Mrs. Jane Leftwich Michael Jr. (she eventually remarried another outstanding Marine, Col. Richard L. Michael Jr., who served two tours in Vietnam and fought on Guadalcanal and Peleliu in WW II) attended the ceremony.

The facility is located on the harbor side of Halsey Field House just inside Gate 1. Bill Leftwich Jr. and Capt. Lyle Oliver Armel II, USN (Ret.) join many other notable USNA graduates to have buildings named in their honor…and rightfully so.

**USNA's Leftwich Tennis Courts**--New tennis courts on the academy grounds were also named in honor of the colonel.

**Marble Plaque from Marble Mountain Honors 15 Killed**--On August 16, 2002, former Cpl. Ron Huegel on behalf of the 1st Recon Association presented a plaque made from marble taken from Marble Mountain in Da Nang to the 1st Recon Battalion at Camp Pendleton. It was to memorialize all the Marines and Navy Corpsman killed in the November 18, 1970 helicopter crash in the Que Son Mountains.

Huegel was a 19-year-old in Bravo Co., 1st Recon Battalion in 1970 from Easton, Pennsylvania, and knew each of the Marines from Team Rush Act that were killed. Doc Russ Daniels, one of the 15 killed in the air crash, had been a hooch mate of his at Camp Reasoner.

The former Marine corporal takes war veterans and/or their families to World War II, Korean War and Vietnam War combat sites as part of a worldwide touring company.

He has made eight trips into Vietnam as of April 2008 walking over contested grounds with former Vietnam vets and sometimes their families seeking closure to their year-long experience there between 1955-1975.

"I've been trying to get close to the Leftwich crash site, but the (terrain in the) Que Sons kicked my butt rather quickly. I intend to try again, but earlier in the year when it is just a shade cooler and before the brush has started to grow." He hoped to overfly the site in a helicopter in the near future in order to find the best way into the remote area designated Hill 800.

Bill Leftwich Jr. wanted to be a Marine someday from the moment he learned to walk until he was able to draw the distinctive Eagle, Globe and Anchor on a piece of paper. He made his own permanent mark on the Marine Corps and the Navy. His "mark" is stamped on a ship, a yearly leadership trophy, a statue to inspire young Marine officers, an annual college scholarship award, sports facilities, a Recon building deep in the mountains at Camp Pendleton, a plaque, a USNA building and in the hearts of the Marines/Navy Corpsmen and loved ones who knew him.

### "He could've been a great man," Ames Tells Daughters at The Wall

Bill's friend, Harv Ames, recalled a May 1974 visit to Virginia with an Army major that had headed up the Quang Nam provincial liaison to the Phoenix Program in Vietnam. After telling the major of his last moments on LZ 401 at Camp Reasoner with Lt.Col. Leftwich, the major quietly told him Jane, Bill's wife, lived next door. They called and she graciously invited them over.

"I relayed to her those last moments I had with him and my admiration for the man he was--a Renaissance man, a soldier's soldier. I appreciated having had, serendipitously, the opportunity to bring her something 'positive' from that terrible time. Bill deserves to be remembered as a great man. He deserved to complete his life, to complete making his mark," said Ames.

After The Wall was erected in Washington, D.C., Ames took his three daughters there and pointed out Bill Leftwich's name among the over 58,000 Vietnam War dead listed and explained to them what a good person he was and what a great man he could have been.

## Robinson Remembers Leftwich

Lt.Col. Robinson said he, too, visited The Wall in Washington, D.C. when he was assigned to 8th and I Marine Barracks. He came to the panel that included Lt.Col. Bill Leftwich Jr.'s name and shed some tears upon seeing it and other Marines he knew personally from that time period scattered about that panel.

"We were blessed to have served under such an extraordinary leader as Leftwich. He was destined to have gone all the way to Commandant of the Marine Corps if he had lived. I met a Marine major in Memphis, Tennessee in 1975 and he asked me if I knew Lt.Col. Leftwich. Seldom are men produced in our society such as him. He was special…an amazing leader.

"Years after I came back from Vietnam I would run into old 2/1 Marines like Sgt.Maj. Houston Rogers at an evening parade and the conversation eventually got around to Leftwich. We were privileged to have served under him. Every command I had in the Marine Corps over my 22 years of service, the first thing I would do when I moved into my new office was to put the photo of Leftwich up that included me and the other officers from 2/1 who participated in the 'August 4 Caper.'"

## Quiet Leadership Qualities

Seventeen years before his death, the 1953 USNA yearbook, *Lucky Bag*, profiled the senior Midshipman Bill Leftwich Jr. thusly, "'Lefty,' modest almost to the point of denying all accomplishments…" So he was true to his personality and "quiet" leadership qualities at USNA to the day he died.

"(Leftwich and I) spent hours talking about the war. He was a student of Dr. Bernie Fall who authored such books as *Street Without Joy* and *Hell in A Very Small Place: The Siege of Dien Bien Phu*. Ironically, they were both killed in Vietnam. The colonel always understood the wider view of things military and political. He was noted as an officer who paid attention to details, to people, to being fit and to being ready. He was a 'Marine's Marine.' So all of us would follow him anywhere. That, it seems to me, is what leadership is all about," Lt.Cmdr. Rupp, Leftwich's 1st Recon Chaplain, wrote in "Leftwich Trophy Revisited," in the MCAS Beaufort, South Carolina publication, *Jet Stream*.[9]

"I wasn't surprised when he later came back to Vietnam as a lieutenant colonel. I had an opportunity to talk with him (in 1970). It was just a pity he was killed," said Arnett.

Former Chatterbox 1stLt. Hanner noted that when he retired from FedEx in 2003 after flying for 15 years out of Memphis that the city and county governments still remember Bill Leftwich and his sacrifice.

"He was a great man. His death is a big loss to the country. Look how he died. He went out to do something that a colonel doesn't have to do. He went out to get his men first. Well, that's my kind of guy," stated Perot.

The Texas businessman went on to say that he had commissioned Charlotte Robinson of Washington, D.C. to paint several oil paintings of Bill Leftwich. Two went to Scott and Bill and a third was hung in the stateroom of the *USS Leftwich*. The day we talked by telephone he said he had a photo sitting on his desk of Bill and the boys when they were young.

"Ross originally approached Norman Rockwell to do the paintings but he turned him down saying he only painted live subjects," Jane explained.

Col. Cross who had served under Lt.Col. Leftwich at 2/1 and 1st Recon in 1970 said he ended his career as chief of staff of 2nd Marine Air Wing. "At the change of command ceremony, I saw a major with 'Leftwich' on the name tag. I asked if he was related to THE Col. Leftwich and he said he was his son. I told him to come into my office after the ceremony. When he came in, I showed him a picture of his father promoting six young officers to first lieutenant (Cross among them) at 2/1 in 1970. Everyone always kept any pictures of Lt.Col. Leftwich."

The same road trip I took to visit the Milledgeville, Georgia gravesite of a Marine point man, PFC Charlie Fraley, whom I had known in Vietnam, I also drove up to Annandale, Virginia to interview Jane Leftwich Michael Jr. to better understand Bill Leftwich the man. She told me Bill wanted to serve his country and what better way than to go off to fight its wars.

"He was glad to be in Vietnam and doing what he was doing," said Jane. Before he left for his second tour, he sat her down and talked about his funeral arrangements should he die.

"I thought this was interesting. Billy said that before arranging the funeral I should check to see what sporting events were on for that day. He didn't want to be buried during an important sporting event and have people miss anything...he knew how that felt," she said remembering her husband as the avid, considerate sportsman and fan.

In the November 11, 1982 issue of Memphis' *Press Scimitar,* a reporter asked Mrs. Mattie Leftwich if she found it difficult to talk about her son after 12 years of his being gone.

"No, I love to talk about him. He meant so much to me. He was nothing but a joy to me and my husband from the day he was born till the day he died. He was always glad to serve his country. I've never been bitter. He chose this, you see," said the woman still proud of her son.[10]

Mattie Scrape Leftwich passed away in June 1992 at 88 in a nursing home in Aberdeen, Mississippi. She was laid to rest beside her husband and son in Memphis' Forest Hill Cemetery. Citing Lt.Col. Leftwich's heroism in the Vietnam War in 1965 and 1970, *The Commercial Appeal* staff writer William Thomas noted in the news article, "Only about 20 people were on hand when Mrs. Leftwich was buried Saturday in the family plot beside her hero son. But they were the people who knew the story best."[11]

## USNA Honed Bill Leftwich's Leadership Skills

On my research trip to the East Coast in April 1993, I walked the same sidewalks and into the buildings at the U.S. Naval Academy at Annapolis, Maryland that helped shape Bill Leftwich into the Marine officer that he eventually became. Pulling one of the huge metal doors open to Bancroft Hall where all the midshipmen stayed, I stood in awe of the enormity of the place.

Ironically, a biography of Ross Perot was highlighted in a display case on the way to the huge 4,100-plus seat mess hall. The rotating biographies were of successful midshipmen who made it big on the outside after graduating. It was to come down that very day, as Pres. Bill Clinton was arriving the next day for a visit. For Clinton to have seen a former rival presidential candidate's photo and biography prominently displayed at the USNA only a few months after his election would not have been good for the Naval Academy.

I sought permission and was approved to advance past a roped off wide stairway that led to the second floor Memorial Hall and to the residences of the midshipmen down hallways left and right of the shrine dedicated to America's fallen Naval heroes. Marble busts of famous naval captains and admirals as well as large paintings of sailing ships hung on the walls. The spacious second floor "art gallery" was reserved for a wedding reception that night.

All the Naval Academy graduates' names whose lives were lost in all wars through the years of America's conflicts were lit up in a long display case. Below a chalkboard at one end was an artist's rendition of two ships blasting away at one another with broadsides in the War of 1812.

Aptly enough, the painting showed the United State's ship *Chesapeake* in its epic battle against the British Royal Navy ship *Shannon*. As the American Capt. James Lawrence lay dying on his deck, he is said to have uttered words that reverberated throughout the U.S. Navy from that day forward, "Don't Give Up The Ship." And those words were prominently written on the chalkboard.

I double-checked to make sure Lt.Col. Leftwich's name and that of Lt. Vivilacqua's were on the USNA's Roll of Honor listing the graduates who gave their lives for their country.

Their names and 116 other USNA graduates also went up on a monument erected in front of Bancroft Hall on May 17, 1975 to honor their supreme sacrifices in Southeast Asia. By 1993 that figure had risen to 130 USNA graduates as having died in Vietnam.

I could see how Bill Leftwich would thrive in such an environment and draw energy from the patriotism and pride in serving one's country the Academy represented.

On the floor beneath the U.S. Naval Academy Chapel where the midshipmen attend services each Sunday was the crypt of John Paul Jones, father of the American Navy. His inspiring and impressive sarcophagus of black and white marble was surrounded by eight monolithic columns. Inscribed in a circle in the marble floor were the names of the seven ships commanded by Jones during the American Revolution: *Serapis, Alliance, Alfred, Bonhomme Richard, Ariel, Providence* and the *Ranger*.

Embedded in the floor in front of the sarcophagus was the inscription which read: "John Paul Jones, 1747-1792; U.S. Navy, 1775-1783. He gave our Navy its earliest traditions of heroism and victory. Erected by the Congress, AD 1912."

More tradition came in the form of a bronze bust of the famous Shawnee, Tecumseh, armed to the teeth with battle axes and a quiver of arrows that sits staring coldly at the midshipmen as they enter and exit Bancroft Hall. He and his brother, Tenskwatawa, sons of a Shawnee chief killed in battle with the Americans, tried to stage an uprising in 1811 to throw them out of their territory.

The pair failed and joined the British forces in Canada in 1812. Brig.Gen. Tecumseh was eventually killed while leading Indian forces against the United States' troops during the War of 1812 (Tecumseh would have been happy to know the United States lost in its bid to conquer the British in Canada---MDK).

Originally, the statue was that of a wooden figurehead off the *USS Delaware* of Tamanend, chief of the Delawares (his inscription is on the granite monument's base), but after it deteriorated the bronze bust of Tecumseh took its place.

Bill Leftwich had to have eaten this stuff up in huge gulps. Tradition, honor, duty, faith, discipline, respect, comradeship, the anticipation of combat, patriotism, fighting for the red, white and blue...all this came with attending the U.S. Naval Academy. I could now understand a little better about the man who became a Marine Corps legend and how it came to be.

The Academy oozed with history as I wandered the massive campus coming across various statues and words etched in bronze (many by the renowned Dr. Felix W. de Weldon) for generations yet to be born to read about America's rich naval traditions.

Two and a half decades earlier my fellow ECP from Camp Pendleton and best friend, Pineapple Miyamoto of Kaneohe, Hawaii and I had come to this same place. I wanted to rub it in to a former hometown buddy, Midshipman Charlie Bachtell, that what was to take him four arduous years to make second lieutenant/ensign would only take me 10 weeks as an equal rank in the Marine Corps.

As I silently observed the midshipmen proudly going about their business on that Saturday morning in April 1993, I realized my old hometown friend Charlie, Vivi Vivilacqua, Jim Webb and Bill Leftwich were the richer men for their experience. Those of us who entered the Marines from different venues came to share something after all…affection and pride for our Marine Corps.

**Both Sons Enter Military Service**

The colonel taught his two sons the same pride in their country--humbleness, athleticism and competitiveness--that his father instilled in him. He even made up a sign, which Scott kept and placed in his home where his children could see it, "Quitters never win, winners never quit," a quote from famous Notre Dame Coach Knute Rockne to motivate his football players.

Maj. (Maj.Gen., USMC, Ret.) Joe McMonagle, lived next door to the Leftwich family in Virginia when Bill was serving in Vietnam in 1965. He included the Leftwich boys, Scott and Bill, in his family's outings while their dad was away and looked after them for his good friend. Bill thanked him profusely upon his return from Vietnam for watching over his boys and including them in his family's activities. McMonagle recalled seeing the boys on many occasions preoccupied with playing in their backyard with little painted metal soldiers which very well could have been the same ones Bill had played with as a child and that Bender had talked about. The father and sons' childhoods seemed to be on a parallel course.

Like his father before him, who had brought his Springfield rifle home from the service, Bill was presented an AK-47 VC/NVA assault rifle by the Vietnamese Marine Brigade he had advised. Therefore, his sons also had a weapon involved in war around as they grew up.

And what of his sons who had played as Vietnamese peasants at Quantico at the ville Bill had helped construct true to life? Scott followed in his father's footsteps and attended the U.S. Naval Academy graduating 7th in his class in 1982 while older brother, Bill, won one of Perot's competitive scholarships and opted for the Virginia Military Institute in Lexington, Virginia. He joined the Marine Corps upon graduation in 1981. (Chesty Puller attended VMI briefly before the outbreak of World War I). Scott stuck with a Navy career.

Jane Leftwich Michael Jr. noted that her son, Bill III, was like his dad aiming for a life in the Marine Corps growing up. "Scott didn't like the idea of sleeping in the mud and stuck with the Navy," she chuckled.

Bill had been in Beirut, Lebanon as a grunt platoon commander with the 22nd Marine Amphibious Unit when a large car bomb exploded outside the U.S. Embassy April 18, 1983 killing 61 people, including one Marine Security Guard and 16 other Americans, and wounding more than 100. At one point, his unit ended up repelling attacks on the British Embassy with his platoon, according to Mrs. Michael.

He had rotated home to a duty station at Camp Pendleton but returned to Beirut when the Marine and French peacekeepers' barracks were both brought down by terrorist suicide attacks. The blast leveling the 24th Marine Amphibious Unit's barracks killed 220 Marines (the highest number of Marine casualties in a single day since WW II), 18 U.S. Navy men and 3 U.S. Army soldiers on October 23, 1983. Almost simultaneously a second suicide bomber drove a car into a building occupied by French paratroopers destroying the building and killing 58 Frenchmen.

Most the Marine officers in the unit were killed and replacement officers were direly needed. Capt. Leftwich flew in from Camp Pendleton and was tasked with the sad duty of identifying the dead and wounded, many of them he knew, as all the records had been destroyed in the horrendous blast.

A few years later he was involved in the Panama mission to bring the dictator, Manuel Noriega, to justice December 20, 1989. Bill also went ashore during *Operation Desert Storm's* overwhelming defeat of Saddam Hussein's troops February 24-26, 1991. He was under the overall command of Gen. Schwarzkopf who had the good fortune of meeting his dad, Bill Leftwich Jr., at Duc Co in August 1965. Like all good sons he had told his mom he wasn't part of the invasion force when he, in truth, spent 17 hours ashore in the mopping up of Iraqis in Kuwait.

Bill Leftwich III also managed to be a part of the Marine force to help the people of Bangladesh when floods ravaged their country. He served in Okinawa and Korea as part of his Far East tour. He did a stint at the U.S. Naval Academy for 3 years teaching English. He retired a major in June 2001 and began teaching English at the Hargrave Military Academy in Chatham, Virginia.

Scott stayed far above the "mud" by flying P-3Cs, anti-submarine aircraft, during the April 15, 1986 air raid on Tripoli, Libya to pay Moammar Gadhafi back for a terrorist attack against a West Berlin discotheque frequented by Americans April 5, 1986. As a lieutenant commander in 1995, he would receive an MBA with honors from the Harvard Business School.

He retired a Navy commander in September 1997. As of October 2005, he was chief operating officer for Anakam, Inc. He and wife, Wendy, have a fourth generation namesake son, William Groom Leftwich IV, and three daughters, Elizabeth, Caroline and Lindsey while Bill and his wife, Tate P., have two daughters, Tate G. and Jane.

Both Bill Leftwich's sons did quite well for themselves while on active military duty and as their mom proudly noted a few years ago, "They have lots of medals. Both of them."

It's interesting that after all his accomplishments and all the accolades heaped upon him, Bill Leftwich was laid to rest beneath the same simple Veterans Administration military-issued headstone as is common with military men and women buried in Arlington National Cemetery in Arlington, Virginia. And at 1st Recon's Memorial Service November 24, 1970 in Vietnam the same passage, *Ecclesiastes 3:1-8* from the *Holy Bible,* that I had read at a Memorial Weekend service in May 1970 for 11 2/1 Marines KIA in Vietnam the previous 3 months as Lt.Col. Leftwich looked on as our new CO, was also read for Rush Act and Lt.Col. Leftwich.

"He wanted a military marker. He didn't want anything but the normal headstone like those at Arlington Cemetery," recalled his wife. I thought that was just like the Bill Leftwich I had come to know through other peoples' eyes...to be seen as no better than the common Marine grunt...but we know better.

Bill Leftwich's indelible stamp on the Marine Corps disproves the description that he was "common." He was truly an "uncommon" man and a true "American Hero."

"I don't believe the simple gravestone was adopted consciously as a symbol of Bill's identification with enlisted men. That quality he always had; he looked after his Marines and enjoyed their company," stated Maj.Gen. Grinalds.

"There was only one Bill Leftwich. He never took on airs and was always the same person. We knew he was genuine. He got close to everyone—his Marines and his superiors—and always established a close relationship that made him very approachable. It gave him a great ability to communicate what he wanted you to do," Bill Leftwich III quoted a retired Maj.Gen. Grinalds as saying.[12]

"My father worked and led without ego, " added Bill Leftwich III.[13]

In an opinion piece written by Col. Heinl Jr. for *The Detroit News,* he wrote, "...Leftwich's bright reputation resulted from more than a montage of combat bravery and desirable assignments. He had brains as well as guts and personability. He was, like all the best soldiers, an assiduous student of his profession and the whole terrible necessary art of war.

"...Had he survived, he would assuredly have been one of the handful of devoted regulars who for love of service and for love of country, will perhaps even yet be able to rescue the armed services from the depths into which an ungrateful, divided, short-sighted, sick society has consigned its defenders."[14]

## An Immortality Reserved for Greek Gods and USMC Heroes

And the Greek tragedy reference I alluded to in Chapter 11 that suggested Lt.Col. Bill Leftwich Jr.'s growing fame angered the jealous Greek gods has an interesting comparable tragic ending to a well-known Greek story. In escaping the Labyrinth prison on Crete with wings composed of feathers and wax, Daedalus warned his son, Icarus, to not fly too low lest his wings touch the waves and get wet preventing him from staying aloft nor too high lest the sun melt the wax. Icarus, carried away with the thrill of flying, flew too near the sun whereas his wings melted and he fell to his death.

My belief is that Rogers, with Leftwich, 12 other young Marines and the injured Corpsman aboard or on the string, flew too low to the Que Sons' mountainous terrain, snagged trees below with the SPIE strap and met Icarus' fate in trying a "winged" escape down the "labyrinth" represented by the draw with all its fatal obstacles hidden by cloud cover.

And if the Greek gods exploited the colonel's "human flaw" to mete out its punishment for his star shining so bright it competed with theirs, it was that he loved his men so much that he would risk his own life to bring them to safety. Or as he told his family in the cassette tapes he sent home to them from Vietnam, he wanted to share more of the work and danger of his Marines. In the end he shared their ultimate adventure dying among the very men he cared so much about.

He may not have won a Medal of Honor while alive, but in dying Bill Leftwich Jr. gained immortality reserved for Greek gods and Marine Corps heroes. The Tennessee colonel joined the Marine Corps' long roll call of mystical warriors spoken of in reverent hushed tones with the respect he earned through his concern for his men and repeated display of heroism. He is the very definition of the word, MARINE.

# Epilogue

**It's difficult for someone who has experienced combat to lay down their "shield" and "sword" to return to normal civilian life after a year or more tour in a combat zone. The wife of a Navy SEAL told me her husband returned to our mutual hometown of Longview, Texas to sleep curled up in a ball on the floor next to their bed each night calling out dead men's names and crying the first few weeks upon his return. A 2/1 Marine tried to contact his buddy but the man's parents screened his calls and refused to let them talk because their son was having such a hard time letting go of the horror he had seen in Vietnam. They thought it best he not talk with anyone reminding him of his bloody combat action. As one inactive Marine put it upon returning from a combat tour in Iraq in Gulf War II, "It's hard to go from being the best, a Marine, to being just a civilian." War is tough on the warrior to put away and on his loved ones trying to understand why their son, brother, husband, wife, sister or daughter (as of the Gulf Wars), fiancé/fianceé or good friend came home changed...or not at all. Returning vets and their families from all wars have had the same trauma to cope with since the beginning of time. War is, indeed, Hell for all those affected by it. "Hard Men" undertake war only to become more hardened by the experience. And if it weren't for those "Hard Men," where would this country be today? MDK**

## Vietnam Tour Ends

I returned from Vietnam in January 1971 with deeply embedded crow's feet at the corners of my eyes and a hollow feeling inside that I had aged considerably beyond my 23 years. My heart ached for all those Marines I knew who would never come home and be forever young in my mind's eye.

In January 1970 when I stepped foot in Vietnam, the 1stMarDiv had 54,559 Marines in-country. By January 13, 1971 that number dwindled to a paltry 13,196 with the departure of most the helicopter, fixed wing, 7th and 26th Marine Regiments, 1stMarDiv headquarters and 1st MAW headquarters. CUPP and CAP operations would shut down in April and May, respectively. The 5th Marines would leave Vietnam in March 1971 with the last of my 1st Marines hard on their heels in May 1971. As was the case at the beginning of the conflict, 547 Marine Corps advisors were left behind along with 240,000 other U.S. Army troops. (The Army would complete the withdrawal November

30, 1972). Marines had come full circle.[1]

By the end of America's war in Vietnam in 1975, all U.S. military services sustained 58,277 hostile/nonhostile deaths and 153,303 WIA (Marines total deaths were 14,842 with 51,392 WIAE out of 391,000 Marines, or better put, roughly 1 in 5.9 Marines were KIA/WIAE, while serving in South Vietnam from November 1, 1955 to May 15, 1975).[2] The French Union Forces before us fought from the end of World War II to 1954 suffering 75,867 KIA and 65,125 WIA.[3]

As a footnote, following the fall of Dien Bien Phu and the massacre of Mobile Groupement 100 on Highway 19 in 1954, Vietnam was partitioned into North/Communist and South/non-Communist as per the cease-fire agreement. Dr. Bernard Fall pointed out in *Hell in a Very Small Place: The Siege of Dien Bien Phu* that a call-up for 120,000 young South Vietnamese to the colors of their own armed forces after the partition "had brought in only 7,000 draftees, of whom 5,000 were declared unfit for service."[4]

The writing had been on the wall since 1954!

## COC OD Duty: Marine Goes Berserk, January 9-10, 1971

My last night at 2/1, instead of a drunken celebration at the "O" Club with my brother officers, saw me standing Officer of the Day in the Camp Lauer COC bunker at the battalion XO's, the major's, insistence. As a senior lieutenant, I was taken off perimeter OD and assigned to the COC night watch by the end of June.

It only seemed right to complete my nearly 12 months in-country on a sour note by having to stand OD that last night. Besides, I think I was the kiss of death for any young officer to be seen with thanks to two hard-nosed 2/1 XOs/majors in a row. 1stLt. Tom Marino, 3rd CIT CO, and Capt. Don Johnson, S-1 chief, both bulletproof, were the only two officers I primarily socially conversed with by the end of my tour.

My OD duty that last time from 1900 Saturday, January 9 to daybreak, Sunday January 10, 1971 in the COC turned out to be a real cliffhanger and capped my tour off on a sad incident.

A CUPP Marine flipped out around 2130 Saturday on Hill 55 and ran to the main gate on the north side wearing his flak jacket, helmet and carrying his M-16 rifle. He made his way outside the wire and started firing his M-16 fully automatic in the air randomly without hitting anyone. The CUPPs sent a reaction team to look for him to no avail. He had disappeared into the darkness.

I don't recall hearing that he had been found until the next morning. The U.S. Army advisors for the 51st ARVN encountered the Marine at 0015 and held onto him until daybreak when they turned him over to the CUPPs for priority medevac at 0600. 2/1's Operations Journal states, "Marine appeared to have had a nervous breakdown." He was fortunate the VC didn't capture him.

I was told during the night that he had seen a lot of bloody gore and been under fire quite a bit with the CUPPs since I had sent him there a month or so before. Yes, he was one of the FNGs Echo Co. (we supplied them with manpower and carried their men on our rolls) posted to the CUPPs due to his high intelligence and ability to catch onto the Vietnamese language. I used my skill as the "psyche master" to talk him into "volunteering" for duty with the CUPPS. He was one of my Marines and I felt responsible for him.

I waited around the next morning as the CUPP unit left Hill 55 to bring him back at first light. How could I leave Vietnam not knowing if they medevacked him out or not? After they picked him up, he was flown up to 1st Med.

Relieved he had been located and feeling guilty that I had talked him into going to the oft-attacked CUPPs, I collected my gear and finished my checkout procedures to leave 2/1.

I have always wondered how that Marine made out upon his return home. Traumatic situations just affected Marines and Navy Corpsmen in so many different ways. Most could cope or compartmentalize the mayhem going on around them while others succumbed to the strain. I just hope and pray he got over his overwhelming mental shock and was able to get on with his life.

## Disobeying a Final Order

Echo Co.'s jeep driver came to my quarters where I loaded up my duffle bag and Val-Pac (a Navy grey fold over portable clothing bag with large zippered pockets) into the back of the jeep. He said the first sergeant had my orders and record book and wanted to talk to me about something one last time before I left so we stopped by the company office.

Turns out, by order of the battalion XO, I was directed to share my ride with a black Marine, PFC Short*, whom I had restricted to quarters allowing him to only go to the head and mess hall for the past week and a half. He had requested mast to get my restriction order rescinded so he could go up to Freedom Hill to partake in their civilian atmosphere. I was red-faced angry at having this Marine getting an undeserved trip to Freedom Hill.

A couple of weeks earlier he had been on point when his squad came across three or four VC trying to make their escape in a sampan on a river. He immediately shot them up and killed all but one of them...a prize catch, an NVA cryptologist, who was turned over to 1stMarDiv Counterintelligence boys. For his quick action, heroism and capture of a priceless POW, we had put him in for a Bronze Star medal and given him a couple of days off to spend in the Rear as a reward. That was our mistake.

In the Battalion Rear he had come under the influence of other black Marines spouting Black Power comments and convincing him he shouldn't be fighting the white man's war or accepting the white man's hero medals. As a consequence, he refused to go back to the bush and join his squad.

I called him into the company office and let him know he was being led down a treacherous path by someone in the Rear to forsake his bush comrades and refuse to go to the bush. I told him I wanted him to think about it by restricting him to quarters in order to consider his options: the Bronze Star and rejoining his platoon without punishment or office hours/court-martial that could very well result in his being incarcerated in the Da Nang Brig and a Bad Conduct Discharge. I honestly thought once he had time to think about it he would come to the right decision. I was wrong.

Shortly thereafter, his white platoon sergeant tried to walk point for his squad as no one had as much experience as PFC Short to take over the position. The sergeant tripped a boobytrap that ended his tour. Another sergeant, a black Marine, in the same platoon tried to walk point for Short's squad and was also injured by another boobytrap.

I called Short into the office and really laid into him that both sergeants tried to walk the point position he had held in his squad and had tripped boobytraps and were now injured. He asked if I thought it would have been better if it had been him setting off the boobytraps than them.

"Short, I'm just saying you know what you're doing on point. You're good at it and if you had been on point you probably would've picked up on there being boobytraps on those trails and I wouldn't have two sergeants laid up at 1st Med. seriously injured right now. Are you still refusing to go to the field?"

"Yes, sir." The guilt trip angle didn't work. I sent him back to the Echo Co. area. I decided to let the next Echo Co. XO or Echo 6 Capt. Charlie Morrison of Annapolis, Maryland decide what to do with Short as I was near my DEROS date. I left Short to stew in restricted to quarters limbo, that is, until he threatened request mast and convinced the Battalion XO I had mistreated him.

Short was grinning from ear-to-ear as I pulled the passenger seat up to let him climb in the backseat of the jeep. I was pretty much boiling mad by this point. He was ruining my excitement over going home at long last and was pretty cocky he had gotten his way by threatening to take his complaint to the 1stMarDiv level.

Headed out Camp Lauer's front gate in the jeep, Short started in on me asking if I was headed back to the states this day. I said I was. He said he might look me up. I thought I'd play it cool and laughed saying, "You do that, Short. And I'll buy the beer." He snorted and laughed. He was pulling the bolt back on his empty M-16 rifle and letting it go home over and over as he talked. I had turned my weapons in to the 2/1 Armory so only Short and the jeep driver were armed.

"Yeah, I'll come visit you in Longview, Texas, and you can buy me a beer. Sure that's what I'll do," he said menacingly still pulling that bolt back. I seem to recall he even mentioned my folks' street address as to where he would come looking for me. Somebody in my office had provided this angry Marine with my home address and that pretty much was the last straw. I caught the unmistakable drift of his veiled threat and decided that nobody was going to threaten me on my last day in Vietnam and get away with it.

I turned to the jeep driver and told him to pull over in front of the Green Beret POW Camp. When we came to a stop, I jumped out and pulled the seat up and yelled at Short.

"GET OUT! MY LAST DAY IN VIETNAM AND I DON'T HAVE TO PUT UP WITH THIS SHIT!" I said this through clenched teeth at Short. I think he was taken by surprise at how angry he'd made me.

"You can't do this, the major said you were supposed to take me up to Freedom Hill. You just can't..."

"GET THE F**K OUT OF MY F**KIN' JEEP, SHORT. NOW!" I yelled at him again. He was cradling his M-16 like I was going to take it away from him and beat him with it. About a nanosecond before I was going to yank him out of the jeep, he climbed out. As we pulled away, he was still yelling that I couldn't just leave him on the side of the road and that he was going to tell the major.

The jeep driver was looking at me like I had lost my mind as we headed off towards the Da Nang Airport. I think he must've thought I was joshing Short and would tell him to pull over and let him back in. I didn't. It wasn't a far walk back to Camp Lauer and vehicular traffic was busy along this road so he could catch a ride in either direction...the base or Freedom Hill. The driver said something to me about the major was going to be really pissed for leaving Short on the side of the road.

"And what's the major gonna do? Shave my head and send me to Vietnam? Too late!" I laughed at my own joke as we continued on up Highway 538 and the Freedom Bird that awaited me at the Da Nang Airport. By God, I was going home.

### Enlisted Men Cheer as Freedom Bird Clears Da Nang Airport

I remember the strange feeling of climbing aboard that commercial jet, the Freedom Bird, to return to The World after 11 months, 26 days of my life and most of 1970 in Vietnam. I was exhausted from the all-nighter OD duty and worrying about my CUPP Marine but at the same time exhilarated I was finally going home. I have to admit I was disappointed I had not accomplished more during my tour.

Hell, it appeared as if we not only failed to win the war like we had boasted about to one another while standing on the yellow footprints at enlisted boot camp in 1967 and later as cocky TBS C-69 officers, but now there was a massive pull-out indicating we had somehow lost the whole shooting match. I know it's cliché to say but, by golly, we *were* winning the war when I left Vietnam!

In Dorothy Fall's *Bernard Fall, Memories of a Soldier-Scholar*, she quotes her husband, "The immense influx of American manpower and firepower, and the ruthless use of the latter, have made the South Vietnam war, in the short run, militarily 'unlosable.'"[5] He was right, we didn't lose on the battlefield in the final analysis.

Flying out of Vietnam, officers were required to sit at the front of the aircraft while the enlisted sat in the back. When the jet rose into the sky, the enlisted guys whooped it up and yelled in relief. The officers were much more reserved...I wanted to go whoop along with the enlisted. Stewardesses came off as much happier on the return trip than when I first arrived a year earlier. Another reason to cheer came moments later as the pilot announced we had just cleared Vietnam's airspace.

**Sousa Marching Music Attempts To Lift Spirits, Camp Butler, Okinawa**

After a short flight, Marines disembarked on Okinawa where we spent a few days at Camp Butler to decompress from Vietnam.

I stood in a stall in the Bachelor Officers' Quarters head flushing water down the toilet over and over again amazed and awed by the simple minor modern convenience of water and human waste disappearing into a plumbing system. No more diesel burning halved 55-gallon barrels and that God-awful smell or digging cat holes in the bush! Also, rusty, suspicious smelling water didn't come out of the BOQ's showerheads like they did back at Camp Lauer. I was easily entertained by this point in time.

John Philip Sousa-like marching music blared from loudspeakers placed strategically throughout the base. I found myself unconsciously marching to the beat of the military music, get irritated I was being manipulated and slip out of step in defiance with whomever was trying to bolster my spirits. I preferred to have been sitting by a babbling brook in solitude coming to grips with my feelings about Vietnam and the death and injury of so many outstanding men like Lt.Col. Leftwich and my Echo Co., 2/1 Marines.

Okinawans were giving the military hell on the island while I was there as large stores of some type of anti-personnel gas (left over from World War II, I was told) was being removed from the U.S. bases in January 1971. They picketed and even threw rocks at military personnel at the front gate to show their displeasure for our having had stockpiles of the gas on their island. I couldn't understand why they were so upset if it was being taken off Okinawa like they wanted.

While on Okinawa, I started reading a paperback book, *Catch 22*, by Joseph Heller. On another commercial jet headed home a couple of days later, I finished it somewhere during the long flight over the Pacific Ocean racing to meet the sunrise back home. After concluding Heller's book, I chuckled at the similarity that all wars had their quota of quirky superior officers like Major Major Major and different versions of Catch 22s. Lord knows I had mine.

**Shocked to be Stateside and Alive, January 13, 1971**

We flew from Okinawa for what seemed like forever to get to Oakland, California, arriving to the welcome sight of a light snow. The jet sat on the tarmac for quite awhile before lifting off and taking us to MCAS El Toro south of LA where we were allowed to disembark the Freedom Bird. I walked outside the military air terminal still in shock that I was finally home. I asked myself, "What the hell do I do now?" You see, I never expected to come back from Vietnam, thus hadn't made any plans beyond it! A large number of taxis were on hand to take us to Los Angeles Airport (LAX).

Bedecked in my winter green Marine Corps uniform with Vietnam ribbons at LAX while waiting for my flight to Dallas, I encountered a bearded young man in a beat-up military field jacket covered in peace symbols and anti-war slogans seated nearby. He engaged me in an old-fashioned stare-down contest. We had been told war protestors liked to heckle newly-arrived Nam vets to get them to do something stupid…like attempt to kick their butt.

He and I never spoke but we knew where the lines were drawn by both our appearances. I gave him my best maniacal grin and tried to intimidate him by staring into his very soul through his eyes. I wondered how many Nam vets he provoked or made to feel unwelcome coming home their first day in the same manner. He finally blinked uncomfortably, looked away and moved to another part of the airport. Marines 1, War Protestor 0. Years later I found out MSgt. John Hare and I had the same philosophy about anyone being so foolish as to spit on our Marine uniforms…they would be sipping strained food through a straw for quite some time thereafter and be damned the consequences.

Back at Pendleton when I was an enlisted man, the story circulated that a couple of off-duty enlisted Marines had run across a long-haired hippy in downtown Oceanside, California wearing a Marine's dress blue jacket that he had purchased at an Army/Navy store that he had covered in sewn on anti-war patches and slogans. They told him to remove it and wear it no more...or else. He opted for the "or else" and a mismatched fight ensued as the Marines upheld the Marine Corps' honor with gusto. The Leathernecks beat the crap out of him. They were arrested by civilian authorities for instigating the fight (my thought it was the other fellow doing the instigating--MDK) and turned over to the Marine base for disposition. As the story goes, they were standing tall before either a colonel or general back at Pendleton in short order. They explained the situation and asked the officer if he wouldn't have done the same thing had he been there. He is said to have come from around his desk and shook both Marines' hands for a job well done. Whether true or not, the story made the rounds and we all had a good laugh over the possible veracity of it.

Col. Les Williams told me he stopped wearing his uniform off base in the '60s and '70s as it attracted spit and anti-war confrontations. It was a strange, hostile world we all returned to in 1971.

The Peachbush pilot said he carried around in his memory the medevac of a black Marine north of the Que Son Mountains in the spring of 1970 that had always made him wonder how this special casualty made out after he was dropped off at 1st Med. "I picked him up and he had lost a leg to a mine. He was brought on board on a stretcher and he yelled for me to hurry because 'he wanted to live.' If I could find that Marine, I would love to talk to him and perhaps both of us could put things behind us. Isn't it amazing how many of these stories there are? And how the 'mission' seemed to drive us to help these Marines then get onto the next one?"

### Determined to Get Home, Love Field, Dallas, Texas

Fixated on getting to Longview, Texas, that first night back, I flew into good old familiar Love Field in Dallas still in uniform sometime before midnight to discover all flights were through for the night. I hadn't told my parents I was coming home about a week early so there was no one waiting at the airport for me when I arrived. Like a good Marine, I had to improvise, adapt and overcome. Switching to Plan B, I caught a taxi to the Trailways Bus Terminal downtown and bought a ticket for a bus that ended up stopping at all the podunk towns between Dallas and Longview over the next 3 hours.

I only encountered blacks on my bus and many of them quietly welcomed me home from Vietnam when I told them I just finished a year's tour over there. I was surprised so many of them had family members or kinfolk who were Vietnam vets or still there.

### "Did you kill anybody?" Longview, Texas

When I finally rolled into Longview's Trailways station in the wee hours of the morning, I lugged my duffle bag and Val-Pac past the old 3-story Longview High School a block over to the Safeway Cab Co.'s dispatch location. LHS held a lot of fond memories for me as I thought how far, literally, I had come since 1966...West to East Coast, Cuba, Puerto Rico, Alaska, Japan, Okinawa, Vietnam, Australia, back to Vietnam and Okinawa again and now my starting point, Texas. I took a taxi to my folks' house. I woke them up around 3 a.m. ringing the back door doorbell after I used my key only to find that my dad had chained the door.

My mother prepared a big breakfast for me while my dad watched intently as I ate it in huge bites. Finally, he couldn't restrain himself any longer and had to ask.

"Did you kill anybody?" Dear old dad kept his record intact of always saying the wrong thing at the wrong time to me. There had been a news release to my hometown newspaper briefly touching on 1st squad, 1st Platoon of Echo Co., 2/1, (Echo 1-1) I was with killing a NVA courier April 6 in Nui Kim Son south of Da Nang in the vicinity of Marble Mountain. I really wasn't sure if it ever ran in *The Longview Daily News*. My mother suggested to my dad that maybe it wasn't something I wanted to talk about...God bless her good heart.

She told me later she recalled how messed up her nephew, 1stLt. Hugh Wood Jr. of Corsicana, Texas had been upon his return from WW II as a pilot flying B-17s over Germany. Anger and warring emotions seemed to be just below the surface upon his return from war and as he attended Texas A&M.

I suddenly lost my appetite and stared at my plate thinking about the NVA courier in Nui Kim Son and the enemy troops dressed as Marines I radioed Echo 1-1's squad leader LCpl. Don Youmans, 19 of Columbia, South Carolina to "kill" on another occasion. Or the first order I passed along from the Echo Co.'s Rear as CO in December that put 3rd Platoon in the vicinity of a boobytrap-infested area and cost a Marine his life and injured at least two others when he went to dispose of a boobytrap involving a grenade in a can. With that in mind, I turned and looked my dad in the eye.

"Yes, I did kill someone." And with that I told them I was really exhausted after travelling 15 hours or so and needed to hit the rack. And, of course, his question had to come within the first hour I was home. I probably should've added that the wide-eyed, innocent son they once knew was also killed in Vietnam.

My mother said she knew I needed time to deal with what I saw and did in my own way and in my own time. Women tend to be more sensitive in picking up on stuff like that. Poor old dad was clueless.

Despite our differences and his disappointment that I had joined the Marines as an enlisted man 3½ years earlier, I will concede that my dad evidently was proud of me for having been a Marine lieutenant. One of his morning coffee-drinking buddies said my dad had bragged about me being in Vietnam as a Marine Corps officer and had flown the Stars and Stripes out front of our house every day I was there. Too bad he could never tell me that.

My father passed away in August of 2000 before we could resolve the petty conflicts between us. Nor did we ever broach the subject of Vietnam again after my first night home.

**Recurring Nightmares and Enlightenment**

For the next few years after I returned home from Vietnam I suffered my nightmares from Nam in silence until I could face my own personal demons, rationalize their existence and lock them away. The dream that frustrated me the most and caused me to awaken in a cold sweat was hearing a Marine I had become acquainted with, Echo 2-3's point man PFC Charlie Fraley, screaming out of the darkness for me to help him. Heading for their nighttime April 7 ambush site, a boobytrap took his leg and next day his life. Slight variations to that dream always had me arriving too late to save the Georgia Marine.

In *Book I, American Heroes: Grunts, Pilots & "Docs,"* I told of my good friend from enlisted boot camp through the ECP program to become officers, Lt. Pineapple Miyamoto's enlightenment. This involved his Japanese ancestor, Miyamoto Musashi, taking lives as a ronin samurai warrior in the 1600s to Pineapple's saving Marines, civilians, RFs, PFs and ARVN soldiers as a helicopter pilot on medevac missions but capable of inflicting mass injuries on enemy troops taking them under fire by his onboard .50 caliber machine guns. I think back on my own maternal ancestors' sad legacy of owning slaves pre-Civil War then I remember how I sat down in my nighttime platoon patrol base perimeter in The Cemetery below Marble Mountain and cried over the death of 21-year-old Charlie Fraley, a black Marine. Maybe there has been some enlightenment in my family tree as well.

Remember this, my piddling experience in the bush was nothing compared to the enlisted bush Marines who spent their entire 13 months in harm's way, opted for multiple tours or served in a more active combat zone in the 1960s or early 1970s. I include Recon Marines, Navy Corpsmen and other Marines with varied military occupational specialties as well as fixed wing/helicopter pilots and their crews on that list. Think about the demons they had to live with for the rest of their lives? Vets from WW I, WW II and the Korean War in which America participated in had the same "violent issues" to contend with having served years in combat so we were in good company.

**"HEY, BABY KILLER!"**

I hooked up with my old childhood friend, Bob Starr, after a few days at home. For continuity's sake it was only right I would see him going to and coming from Vietnam. And besides, he always knew where there were young women and parties going on every weekend. Before heading off to just such a party, we stopped off at our old pizza hangout on Longview's Highway 80 main drag on a busy Saturday night to throw back some beers, eat pizza and catch up on each other's highly polar-opposite lives.

In the middle of our scarfing down a pizza and swilling cold beer, a strident voice in the busy pizza parlor rang out, "HEY! BABY KILLER!"

Bob and I exchanged glances upon hearing the loudmouth baiting me from across the room. I looked around at him thinking it might be someone I knew pulling my leg. It wasn't. I gave him my best drop-dead look. My short-cropped hair had given me away to this jerk.

"YEAH YOU, BABY KILLER. I'M TALKING TO YOU!"

I looked to the owner of the pizza parlor across the bar to shut this 18- or 19-year-old kid up before there was trouble. He stared at the kid a brief second then looked me in the eye and ignored the situation by going to the back to remove pizzas from the oven. I was on my own. I'm guessing that 90 percent of the enlisted Marines I knew in Nam would have cold-cocked this young man at the first challenge causing him grievous bodily injury.

"OH, BABY KILLER, HOW MANY BABIES DID YOU KILL TODAY?"

Okay, he was probably drunk and spoiling for a fight, which was at cross-purposes of what an "anti-war activist" purported to be. He had the attention of the young crowd in the packed restaurant focused not on him but me. Not one person rose to my defense. I was truly astonished crap like this went on back home...where we assumed we had support from our hometown people...not in 1971.

The vocal anti-war baiter was reminiscent of an airline stewardess who had pushed my buttons in 1969 at an Arlington, Virginia party calling me a "baby killer" then as well before I'd even gotten out of The Basic School at Quantico. Somehow inside that pizza parlor I was able to hold my tongue through sheer willpower but was quickly losing control of my temper. It seemed the right thing to do at the time to walk away. Making local news headlines as a Marine officer just back from Vietnam punching some young man's lights out just because he was exercising his right of free speech (albeit fighting words) would not have endeared me to the Commandant of the Marine Corps or my new CO at Marine Corps Air Station El Toro, my next duty station in California.

I turned to Bob and said quietly, "I'm less than one week out of Vietnam. If we don't leave now, I'm going to go over there and kill that kid." I think Bob was a little shook up by the icy conviction in my voice and suggested we leave. I never set foot in that pizza parlor again.

And I elected to return to California after a little over 2 weeks when I had a 30-day leave coming. Home was not as I remembered it in years' past. I needed to be around Marines who shared a common bond...Vietnam and the Corps.

And where do you think these young people got their prejudicial views on Vietnam and Vietnam vets? Longview, Texas was not exactly a hot bed of anti-war activity at that time so I guess they got their slant on the Vietnam War and the returning vets from TV, magazines and newspapers.

Rare instances like My Lai ended up painting us all in a broad paintbrush stroke disregarding the relatively good "clean war" (as if there is such a thing) the other 99-plus percent of us fought.

Atrocity for atrocity, the VC/NVA outdistanced us by a long shot. Enemy assassinations and terrorist sapper attacks against civilians were commonplace to keep the people in line...or else.

For the record, neither I nor anyone I knew ever killed a baby in Vietnam or entertained such a repulsive anti-social crime. Unfortunately, atrocities occurred on our side in the course of many years fighting in Vietnam but not without judicial consequences.

I don't think such constraints applied to the rules of war our enemy practiced...i.e. sending children ages 4-11 out to set boobytraps and getting blown up in the process, shooting a nurse in the head when she refused to accompany them, killing another woman in Nui Kim Son following an interrogation, beating up a woman suspected of collaborating with us or using the peasants as human shields when they ambushed us or for their getaways. (See *Book I*). And this wasn't even the tip of the iceberg. The massacre of approximately 3,000 civilians by the VC/NVA at Hue during the Tet Offensive in 1968 proved their ruthlessness.

## Foxtrot 2/1 Runs Last Patrol at Cam Ne, May 5, 1971

On Wednesday, May 5, 1971 Foxtrot Co., 2/1 had the "honor" of running the battalion's last combat op in Vietnam around the northern Cam Ne ville complex. 1st Marine Regiment, which included all of 2/1, rotated stateside to Camp Pendleton just down the road from where I was at MCAS El Toro. I started to visit them but thought better of it as I didn't want to find out some of my Marines had died or suffered serious injury after I had left.

## My Last Day in the Marines

I took an early exit from the Marine Corps as of June 1, 1971 in order to have plenty of time to enroll in college for the fall. Also, so I wouldn't be on the list for captain either that month or July and perhaps bump somebody from making that rank who intended to stay the full 20 years or so. I had had enough seeing as how there was no longer a war to be fought. Still, "Capt. Kellum" kind of rolls off your tongue nice and easy like.

With my car loaded up for the long trip back to Texas, I went through the process of checking out of the Marines my final day at MCAS El Toro. All I needed was an officer's signature from one last administrative office and I was out of there. A corporal took my paperwork and record book and put it all in his "In Box." He told me to take a seat and for the next 2 hours or so, I sat, alone. No one else was awaiting disposition of their paperwork so you'd think I would be next. My record book and paperwork didn't budge. The end of my Marine career as an officer was like the beginning as an enlisted man, "Hurry up and wait."

At some point I noticed the corporal's superior, a lieutenant sitting further back in the room at his desk, had Vietnam service ribbons either on his coat or khaki shirt. I waited for the corporal to go on break, walked over to his desk, recovered my record book and paperwork from his "In Box" and walked it back to the lieutenant. I told him this was my last day in the Marine Corps and I had a roughly 1,400 mile drive ahead of me to get back to my hometown on the other side of Texas and needed to get on the road. I explained to him that all I lacked in my checkout procedure was to turn in my record book and get an officer's signature and I was on my way. I even laid it on thick from one Vietnam vet to another. He immediately signed off on it after looking over my paperwork and record book. And just like that, I was a civilian again.

Before leaving, I thanked him profusely and pensively said, "You know, you'd think I'd at least get a brass band, balloons and streaming confetti send off for my 3½ years and a Vietnam tour. It just seems like something is missing from my last day in the Marines." He put his hand out and I shook it. His parting comment was, "I guess this will have to do." It did.

**Annie**

When I finally settled in back in Longview, I called my former girlfriend from high school, Annie, whom I thought had broken my immature teenager's heart when we split up prior to my joining the Marine Corps. (See Chapter 3, *Book I*). (In Vietnam I discovered losing Marines in combat hurt one's heart a whole lot worse than the insignificance of breaking up with a girlfriend---MDK).

I took her out but neither of us was the same as we were at 17 and 19. The magic we once had as teenagers was gone. We had both moved on with our lives and no longer shared anything in common except for a few selective pleasant memories. College and war will do that for you.

She was finishing her college degree that summer while I was trying to decompress from my Vietnam Class of '70 experience. She was 21 going on 22 and I was 23 going on what felt like 50. It was sad in a way but that's how Life is sometimes and you have to move on.

### 4 Years on the GI Bill, SFASU, Nacogdoches, Texas

I returned to college in East Texas to finish what I started at the University of Houston in 1966 before dropping out and joining the Marines. When I enrolled at Stephen F. Austin State University in good old Nacogdoches, Texas in the fall of 1971, I pointedly asked if Vietnam veterans were welcome.

A day earlier I was made to feel unwelcome at the University of Texas at Austin when an admissions counselor suggested Vietnam veterans needed to attend college elsewhere since too many of us were attempting to enroll there (and, most likely, screwing up the anti-war student demographics). SFASU turned out to be more veteran friendly than UT.

With the financial assistance of the GI Bill, I came away from SFASU with a Bachelor of Arts degree in communications (emphasis in journalism) and a secondary major in English in 1974. Besides maturity gained from 3½ years in the service, I credit the Marines for teaching me to make a strong effort to finish whatever I started.

Having said that, I will have to eat some crow as I fell a few hours and a thesis short of completing a master's degree in communications in 1975. I guess it could be said *Books I* and *II, American Heroes: Grunts, Pilots & "Docs"* constitute my much belated thesis and my "grade" will have to come from my peers in the general public...always the final judge in such matters.

### All My "American Heroes" Served in Vietnam

An anti-war, over-educated gentleman I encountered in the 1990s had the audacity to suggest that "not all American heroes of the Vietnam War went to Vietnam...some went to Canada." I told him I planned to write a book about all the Marine and Navy Corpsmen heroes I'd known who served in Vietnam. He insisted I'd be remiss if I didn't tell the draft dodgers' stories as well. I stand "remiss" as I leave it to others to tell their stories of avoiding military service to their country.

He just didn't have a clue as to what the roughly 2.6 million servicemen and approximately 7,465 servicewomen who served in Vietnam during the war went through. He didn't know the 535 Marines killed or 4,278 wounded[6] or the 30 Navy Corpsman (or roughly 688 "Docs" the entire war), who were killed in 1970.[7] Those of us Marines/Navy Corpsmen who survived will hoist a cold one in honor of them every November 10th (the Marine Corps' birthday) until the day we die.

All my heroes fought in Vietnam. Some came home zipped up in black plastic body bags placed in silver caskets or were left to rot unfound in the Vietnam countryside while others came back proudly on two feet or, in some cases, one foot or none at all having fought for their country to the best of their ability.

U.S. military volunteers and draftees returned to the states as the "messengers" to be spat upon and treated as if they had been fools for going off to an unpopular war. Never forget that at least four U.S. presidents and 19 years worth of senators and representatives of the U.S. Congress, plus the voters who put those elected officials into office, committed us to Vietnam for the duration of our participation.

News flash! All wars are unpopular to those who fight them, but they go all the same because someone has to go battle Don Quixote's proverbial "windmills" allowing others to remain at home to have the freedom to grouse about it.

I read once where those who most vigorously oppose war are the same ones who have been and know its fear, horror and heartbreak. Union Gen. Wm. Tecumseh Sherman did, indeed, hit the nail on the head when he said, "War is Hell."[8]

Maybe my Marine adventure began as an escape from a teenager's broken heart from a relationship gone south and a conviction I needed to validate my being a red-blooded American citizen worthy of walking around on land others have defended before me. The time I spent in the Marine Corps evolved into an experience I will always cherish as I matured and was blessed to meet some truly amazing people in and out of Vietnam.

They were all outstanding Marines and Navy Corpsmen as well as "American Heroes" who served the U.S. of A. with honor and pride. Those men and women live on in the echo of names from all the military services etched on a cold, dark granite slab slash in the earth in Washington, D.C., aptly named "The Wall."

Never forget the living and the dead who fought in Vietnam or their sacrifices. I haven't and won't. I will always be proud to have served in the United States Marine Corps and worn the Eagle, Globe and Anchor, 1967-1971. Semper Fi, Michael Dan Kellum, 2011.

# Postscript

**..."The tedious job of ferreting out the enemy from the proverbial sea of people requires both patience and sophistication. Countering the ever present threat of enemy rocket and mortar attacks demands ceaseless night patrolling, which turns the clock around for 2/1 Marines. The continuing hazard of boobytraps adds a frustrating dimension to all these endeavors. 2nd Battalion, 1st Marines has met and overcome all these challenges. Many Marines have passed through its ranks, the most recent are pictured in the (1970 Cruise Book). They represent the latest in a long line of brave men who have served Corps and Country under the colors of the 'Battalion Second to None.'"**

***2/1, Da Nang, Vietnam,1970***
**Cruise Book**

## Lt.Col. Bill Leftwich's Take on Future Wars

In an article "...and a few Marines" written for the *Proceedings of the U.S. Naval Institute* in August 1968, Lt.Col. Bill Leftwich Jr. noted with insight to future wars, "It is painfully obvious that we cannot maintain sufficient forces throughout the world to smother every smoldering insurgency, even if our presence was everywhere politically acceptable. The advisory structure provides us with the flexibility to maintain a 'front line' representation around the world, which is at once symbolic, contributory and relatively inexpensive. If properly employed and staffed to meet the pattern of aggression, the introduction of operational forces might be precluded altogether, or at least reduced in its proportions."[1]

## The Greatest Privilege is to Serve God and Country

Lt.Col. Leftwich held old traditional values about serving God and Country as most of us did back in the 1940s to 1960s before the Vietnam War seemed to drastically change things. A trust we had in our government and, particularly, the military took a severe beating that has unfortunately carried over into the present day.

I can think of no better Postscript to conclude *Book II, American Heroes: Grunts, Pilots & "Docs"* and our shared Vietnam experience than to take some insightful excerpts from a speech Bill Leftwich made to the Memphis Civitan Club in Memphis, Tennessee, on September 20, 1966. It was titled "Americanism Abroad 1966" following Bill Leftwich's first tour in 1965. Some of the same issues that Leftwich addressed then are still being debated today in new conflicts fought in the Middle East. Leftwich's laudatory remarks about our American boys fighting in Vietnam and our presence there could also be applied to our present generation which has fought in Iraq and Afghanistan.

"(As an advisor to the Vietnamese Marine Brigade), I came away from Vietnam with a great admiration for the individual Vietnamese. This little fellow averages 5-foot-2 and 110 lbs., yet can carry an American-sized load of about 40 lbs. 30 kilometers a day through the most difficult sort of terrain and still grin at you that night. They fought and died with the same sort of stoicism...

"...Anyone that spends a year amongst a foreign people inevitably returns with a profound pride in being an American. During my tour, I was often one of only three Americans with 1,400 Vietnamese Marines...The few inhabitants we'd encounter in the villes would cower in their doorways at our passing until they spotted an American (we stood a foot taller than the Vietnamese troops) then their faces would light up and they would surge forward unafraid to touch us and shout (the only English they seemed to know) 'Hello, okay.' That phrase had an unforgettable significance as in 'Thank you American for being here. All our hopes for the future rest with you.' Even after several thousand 'Hello, okays,' you never cease feeling a tug at the heart strings.

"Another major impression was a profound gratitude for the routine blessings that we so readily accepted at home. One of these is the opportunity for our children to go to school and church. We often spent the night amid the ruins of a deserted schoolhouse and in the course of operations walked past countless empty churches and pagodas. It took some reflection to realize that an entire generation of children would grow up without rudimentary religious or academic school. An entire stratum of Vietnamese society would be missing, incapable of fulfilling its obligation to its country...

"...Are we conscious of the incalculable blessing of physical security under which we live? Our children can grow up, learn and prosper free from the specter of violent death that haunts every Vietnamese child every day of his life. How quickly we slip back into our pattern of ingratitude.

"One year ago on September 20th, I was sitting alongside a road near Ban Me Thuot. One of the Vietnamese (Marines) was fixing our lunch cutting off slabs of a 300-gram rice ball, which he handed us along with a piece of dried fish. Today I have just finished a bounteous meal and am privileged to share this splendid occasion with you (the Memphis Civitan Club). I have to remind myself how fortunate I am and how, indeed, blessed all we Americans are.

"Well, why are we in Vietnam anyway? This was being debated when I went overseas, continued throughout my tour and was still being debated when I returned. Our nation's leadership in its wisdom has made and will make the decisions that determines our course. I would like to venture a modest unsophisticated opinion as to why we are there. Our presence in Viet Nam is perfectly consistent with our national heritage. The bedrock of Americans is freedom, individual liberties and Godliness. Today we are challenged in overt combat by a Godless tyranny. Is it not the traditional response of free men whose birthright is threatened? Our forefathers did not guarantee us a future free from sacrifice. They simply gave us a marvelous tradition to emulate. Today we ask a new generation to sacrifice and they are meeting their responsibilities admirably...

"...Unquestionably we are winning militarily (in Vietnam), but our challenge is more than a military one alone. Insurgency involves the systematic rupture of the social, economic and political structure of a country. Quite obviously counterinsurgency must entail the simultaneous rebuilding of these factors behind a screen of military protection. Today an American army is contending with these multiple problems--and successfully--a really remarkable undertaking.

"One of the problems for those of us here at home is the lack of a convenient yardstick by which to measure our progress. In World War II and Korea we could follow an advancing blue line on the map knowing that all behind it was secure and estimate the distance to Berlin or Seoul and guess at when it would all be over. Today we lack such a reassuring yardstick. Conditioned to expect dramatic victories, we cannot orient ourselves to seemingly sporadic indecisive action, but there is progress. It doesn't always lend itself to spectacular headlines.

"How can you paint in dramatic terms the fact that in the village in which a Marine platoon operates that today the women all came to market for the first time in weeks? Or that the farmers can harvest and sell their own crops? Or that you today got a shred of information from a man heretofore was silent? Yet these are tangible signs of progress. Not dramatic, but progress. The game is necessarily a long, hard one and the end is not in sight...

"...Through the haze and confusion, the debate and the uncertainty, one thing comes shining through--and in essence it is everything--the performance of our men. It has been and continues to be superb. Quite possibly this is the finest army that we have ever fielded. And this hasn't always been the case, as we know. With the traditional unpreparedness of a democracy, we have had our setbacks at the beginning of World War II and Korea. I had the occasion to see American servicemen throughout Viet Nam...

"...I was privileged to visit briefly with some Marine units in the north and I saw young 18- and 19-year-old squad leaders briefing their men who go on countless patrols that go out each night. They went into action with the same sort of people and élan that you see in a high school football game. It was most inspiring and while I lacked their fearlessness, I was proud to stand in their midst, however briefly. The same sort of attitude carried them through Con Thien.

"There's a great deal of hand-wringing these days about the present generation. I guess this is a ritual of sorts and the old service pros worry whether the present crop will ever amount to anything. Well I think we can put a lot of these fears to rest. There's nothing soft about the present generation and the Class of 1966 as represented by 500,000 crew cut young Americans who are meeting their responsibilities...The present edition of officers and men are worthy successors to those who have gone before them."

## The Final Curtain

Lt.Col. Bill Leftwich did not live to see the demise of the country he had tried so hard to save. I think it would have broken his heart to see South Vietnam fall to the Communists April 30, 1975 after losing good men--Marines, Navy Corpsmen and Vietnamese Marines--in his two tours there, 1965 and again in 1970.

I think back to 48-year-old French Col. Wainwright's comments to Dr. Bernard Fall (from Fall's *Street Without Joy*) in Chapter 1 of *Book I, American Heroes: Grunts, Pilots & "Docs."* Wracked by fever and still suffering the effects of an injury from a fall in a tank accident, he was temporarily pumped full of powerful antibiotics so he could be sent back into battle as a senior tank commander to fight alongside his men at the end of the French Indochina War...and probably didn't survive the conflict. The drift of his remarks to Dr. Fall was that there ought to be freedom-loving people willing to ride against windmills in this materialistic world.[2] Like the idealistic Don Quixote...and Col. Wainwright, Leftwich and 2.6 million other servicemen fought with a pure heart to keep South Vietnam from going over to the Communists.

In the end we failed in Vietnam through no fault of our own. At least we had the courage, the idealism and the love for our fellow man to take up arms and travel halfway around the world to fight to preserve South Vietnam's freedom as our forefathers had done in distant climes in World War I, World War II and Korea. That epitaph can one day be chiseled on all Vietnam veterans' tombstones, as well as maybe this passage from the *Holy Bible*:

I heard the voice of the Lord, saying, "Whom shall I send, and who will go for us?"

Then said I, "Here am I, send me." *Isaiah 6:8*

# Perspectives on the Vietnam War—Part II

Cpl. Robert G. "Bob" Morris, RTO, India Co., 3/5; team leader, 1st Recon

"What all (wars) come down to is fighting for each other. You depend on each other so much the initial reason why you're at war is forgotten...it gets personal. You get so close in combat situations that to a lot of guys their combat family becomes more important than their real family because they train, eat, sleep, live and die together. That's the by-product of combat.

"Col. Bill Drumright was the best CO 1st Recon ever had and I'm sure the guys before us will say the same thing about their colonel. He was tasked with getting a job done and passed that task on down to his men. He would physically get on a helicopter and go out to help pull his men out of hot extracts. And If one of them was killed in action, I bet he knew that man's name, the date, the time and how he was killed and where. The leadership position he was in I'm sure he couldn't help but think, 'My God, I have ordered these men to do that. I ordered men to their deaths.' That's another by-product of war...a feeling of guilt.

"I was a team leader and was fortunate to have brought all my men home from Vietnam. There were a lot of team leaders who didn't. If I had lost one of my team members, I would've carried that guilt to my grave.

"As for being scared in combat, I was scared every time. I used to be ashamed to admit that but not anymore. Anybody with half a sense is going to be scared. I was scared anytime we ran across a base camp because, 1. You knew you were going to be outnumbered and, 2. You knew you were going to have to hit it. I was afraid for my life and afraid for the lives of six other men in my patrol. Any leader whether over a small team like ours or a whole battalion, you knew you had a job to do and men behind you so you had to conquer that fear and most people did.

"Once you're in a firefight, the fear is gone. You do what you've been trained to do. If you don't, you don't survive. After it's all over with, I guess you become human again with human emotions and you see what you've done and the havoc you caused and the guilt begins to set in. You realize you took a human being's life. When I joined the Marine Corps, I wasn't going to take anybody's life. Death to me was a relation or someone involved in a car wreck in a funeral home setting.

"The men and women who came home from Iraq were said to be

'conquering heroes.' But if you ask them if they're 'heroes,' they'll tell you that the 'heroes' died in the sand over there. In our time the 'heroes' died in the jungle. In World War II their 'heroes' died everywhere. In Korea the 'heroes' froze in the bitter cold. A lot of us don't like the term 'hero.' I don't. There are too many 'heroes' nowadays.

"A fighting man is just a normal man who chose to fight for his country or his God or his service outfit. He chose to do it. He didn't run and he willingly went. After he got there, he and the men he bonded with fought for each other."[1] Cpl. Morris served in Vietnam in 1970-71 and was a 20-year-old squad radioman (RTO) with India Co., 3rd Battalion, 5th Marine Regiment; transferred to 1st Recon where he was a point man then Team Cayenne team leader, made 25 patrols, 1st Reconnaissance Battalion, 1st Marine Division (Bronze Star with Combat "V", 2 Navy Commendations with Combat "V", Purple Heart, Combat Action Ribbon).

Lt.Col. David A. "Dave" Marshall, USMC (Ret.), FAC, 1/9

"I had 197 combat missions as an A-4 Skyhawk fighter-bomber pilot when I volunteered to serve with the 1st Battalion, 9th Marines as their Forward Air Controller in January 1967. I thought that I knew something of war and leadership when I got there. I didn't.

"Due to the extreme number of casualties that 1/9 received, mostly in the Con Thien area, I ended up being designated an Infantry Officer---the distinction in which I take the most pride in my 31 years of active and reserve service. The leadership of Marines in combat is quite straightforward: You can't push a rope. Take a personal overriding interest in the welfare of your men and go first. They'll follow you anywhere."[2] Lt.Col. Marshall served in Vietnam from 1966-68. He was a 25-year-old first lieutenant, Forward Air Controller in 1967, 1st Battalion, 9th Marine Regiment, 3rd Marine Division; also, pilot flying A-4 Skyhawks with VMA-223 Bulldogs, Marine Air Group-12 before transferring to O-1 (Birddog) Detachment, H&MS-16, Marine Air Group-16, 1st Marine Air Wing (Distinguished Flying Cross, 22 Air Medals).

LCpl. Howard Ball, Forward Observer, 2/5

"I'm often asked what it was like being put in a position you may have to kill someone. In July of 1968 I was 18 and had completed one year of college and was enjoying the summer hanging out with my friends, drinking beer and dating. I was a typical teenager. Six months later I was 19 and in the jungles of Vietnam. I had to grow up fast but I was basically the same person. A kid trying to survive.

"The area 2nd Battalion, 5th Marines patrolled in was called the Arizona Territory. I came in-country January 1969 and left 11 months and 25 days later. The entire year of 1969. You can actually hear a round from an AK-47 rifle whiz by your head. You have been trained but the first sight of someone being put into a body bag is an experience you never forget. I was scared but I wanted to survive my tour so I listened and learned from those who were getting close to rotating out.

One day while I was checking out a hill to call a fire mission from on an adjacent hill, I stepped in a small hole that was covered by cardboard and dirt almost tripping a wire underneath it attached to a large bomb. As they defused the bomb, I remember my leg was shaking unstoppable and someone said, 'Ball, you are the luckiest person in Nam. There is no reason why this didn't go off.' By the end of 1969, I believe I was."[3] LCpl. Ball served in Vietnam in 1969 and was a 19-year-old Forward Observer for mortars attached to Fox Co. primarily, but also spent time with Golf, Hotel and Echo Companies, 2nd Battalion, 5th Marine Regiment, 1st Marine Division (Combat Action Ribbon).

Lt.Gen. Wallace C. "Chip" Gregson, USMC (Ret.), 1st Recon

"I arrived at 1st Reconnaissance Battalion, 1st Marine Division at Camp Reasoner in Vietnam on February 1, 1969. It was not an auspicious arrival. I sprained my ankle playing pick-up basketball in Okinawa the day before and was limping noticeably when I arrived at 'Recon.'

"In the next 18 months I would be a platoon commander, a patient at Naval Hospital Guam, a company executive officer, the assistant Operations officer and then finally the Operations officer. No doubt it was a junior leaders' war, as at least two of the billets called for officers more senior than my modest first lieutenant grade. More important than my experience, many of our missions were led by corporals and an occasional sergeant instead of the officers or staff non-commissioned officers called for in our standing operational procedures. Invariably these junior non-commissioned officers were on their initial enlistment and had proven to be well above average in savvy, ingenuity and initiative. They also served as platoon sergeants and other billets calling for far more senior Marines. They excelled in that most demanding leadership challenge, that of leading their peers. Many were serving on their 1st, 2d or even 3d voluntary extensions of their initial tour.

"The Marines in 1st Recon had few illusions about our situation. We knew we were an economy of force effort, that we were to prevent enemy pressure on what was called 'the Da Nang Vital Area,' and, later, that we were to train Vietnamese Marines to perform the same mission in preparation for our own withdrawal. This 'training' meant that we were sending out missions led by a corporal made up of eight Marines, four speaking English and four speaking Vietnamese.

"When they returned home they found an America beset with racial and narcotics problems entirely unappreciative of the contributions of these Marines and their comrades. The exemplary performance of our battalion was built on their shoulders. I don't think we'll ever be able to give them proper credit."[4] Lt.Gen. Gregson served in Vietnam in 1969-70 and was a 23-year-old first lieutenant platoon commander then executive officer in Delta Co.; Operations assistant (S-3A) then Operations officer (S-3) in 1st Reconnaissance Battalion, 1st Marine Division; a 1968 U.S. Naval Academy graduate (Bronze Star with Combat "V", Purple Heart).

Sgt. John D. "J.D." Barber, HMM-263 crew chief

"I had less than a year to serve on my enlistment when I volunteered to go to Vietnam. I was assigned to the Peachbush HMM-263 Sea Knight helicopter squadron on August 3, 1970 in Da Nang, South Vietnam flying out of the Marble Mountain Air Facility. I told the sergeant major I was a qualified crew chief and wanted to fly. I worked my way up from aerial gunner to crew chief by October 1st.

"From my first mission as an aerial gunner, it was apparent that the people I was flying with were all focused on one thing, doing whatever was necessary to support our Marine Brothers on the ground. Whether flying medevac, Recon inserts and extractions, troop insertions or resupply, our pilots and aircrews would do anything that was required to take care of our Marines in the bush...many times at great personal risk. Night medevac missions required flying sometimes many miles to landing zones located in dense jungle or in mountainous areas without the high tech navigational aids of today. It never ceased to amaze me that our pilots would find these landing zones in nights so black you couldn't see your hands held in front of your nose.

"When these Marines in the field were under fire from hostiles, we could see from a great distance what we were heading into. Once on scene the pilot would determine his best landing approach into the zone, often putting the aircraft between the enemy and the wounded. We would sit in the zone, under fire, until the wounded were loaded on board the aircraft. No matter how intense the fire, we would always make an attempt to land to evacuate the wounded. If the enemy fire was too great, we would wait until air or artillery support softened the area and then make another attempt.

"This daily heroism by the aircrews was commonplace. While on the ground our aerial gunners would lay down protective fire from their .50 caliber machine guns while the crew chief and Navy Corpsman would assist with the loading of the wounded Marines. Sometimes crew members and Corpsmen would leave the aircraft to bring the wounded on board. These forays from the aircraft resulted in many awards for heroism including the Medal of Honor and Navy Cross.

"If dense jungle or mountainous terrain prevented us from landing to medevac a wounded Marine, we would hover and lower a rescue hoist which took a tremendous amount of skill on the pilot's part in coordination with the crew chief. I would be remiss if I didn't mention the Marines who spent long hours repairing the aircraft sometimes through the night.

"Many of my friends that I grew up with joined the Marines. Most served in Vietnam long before I did. They, along with the Marines that I served alongside with in Vietnam, did this voluntarily for a couple of reasons: to be a part of the world's greatest fighting force and more importantly, because we all felt that we owed a debt to our country."[5] Sgt. Barber served in Vietnam in 1970-71 and was a 21-year-old crew chief, Peachbush HMM-263, Marine Air Group-16, 1st Marine Air Wing; board member of USMC Combat Helicopter Pilots Association and past president, 2001-2007 (21 Air Medals, Combat Aircraft Wings).

Susan Rogers Eveland, sister to 1stLt. Curt Rogers Jr., KIA, 1970

"1st Lt. Orville C. "Curt" Rogers Jr. was first and foremost my big brother. He left for college (Baylor University in Waco, Texas) when I was 9 years old, but he was already my hero. He rescued me from dangers---real and imagined---and he let me jump up and throw my legs around him, even after I was too big to do that.

"When I would put my small hand in his big one and then he would tease me by letting go, he taught me that holding hands has to be done by both people or it isn't holding hands.

"He was my big brother. It was hard for him to leave his family, but he was a Marine, willing to serve, and he went. (I just realized that my oldest daughter is the age now that Curtis was when he went to Vietnam. That puts things in a different light!).

"I was 16 when he died at age 25. Our family grieved, but we received comfort from God knowing that Curtis knew Him, too, and knowing we will be reunited with him. We relied on the Bible verse: *'And we know that God causes all things to work together for good to those who love God, to those who are called according to His purpose,'* from *Romans 8:28.*

"War and death are not part of God's design. But He can bring good from evil. He has blessed our family in countless ways since. The most recent way happened right after 9/11. I was looking on the Internet, for what, I'm not sure. I ended up on the USMC Combat Helicopter Association (Popasmoke.org) website and looked at pictures and read for hours. Then I fired off a letter to see if I could find anyone that might have known Curtis. I got a quick reply from the Popasmoke President J.D. Barber, who knew him!

"My query was published in the organization's magazine and it has been our great surprise and delight to become friends with many others, including Les Williams and Paul Wilson. Knowing them has been such a blessing to our family. Their memories of 'Curt,' as he was called, restored my brother to me and my family. We are so thankful for you Marines...not only for what you do for our country, but what you do for each other and their families. Semper Fi, Susan Rogers Eveland."[6] (1stLt. Curt Rogers Jr., a 25-year-old Dallas, Texas, Marine flying as a Peachbush HMM-263 Sea Knight pilot was killed in a helicopter crash while extracting 1st Recon's Team Rush Act in the Que Son Mountains of South Vietnam on November 18, 1970).

HMC Richard J. "Jim" or "Doc" Pearston, USN (Ret.), 1st Recon

"I was a 2nd Class Petty Officer (E-5) during my tour from October 1969-October 1970. I was Senior Corpsman of Charlie Co., 1st Recon Battalion, from October 1969-April 1970, and then held the same job in Bravo Co. from April-June 1970. As Senior Corpsman, I was responsible for all Corpsmen in the company. I made it my priority to speak personally with all the Corpsmen when they were initially assigned. I would give each of the new Corpsmen a lecture on 'this is why we are here, and the importance of the kind of Marine unit where we served.'

"I lost one Corpsman KIA the first month after I arrived and one WIA serving in my companies which is truly an unusual statistic. It struck home with me because my Field Medical Services Class had gone to Nam from 1968-69 where 85% came home in pine boxes.

"As Corpsmen, we knew we were serving with the most elite, skilled and deadly Marines in the field. I knew when 1st Recon was tasked with doing the forward reconnaissance of a proposed 'big push.' We put a lot of teams in harm's way resulting in the loss of some fine Marines and Corpsmen, and then no major offensive was mounted. We were the best at what we did, but it didn't make any sense to have Marines and Corpsmen lost, when all our efforts went for nothing.

"For those of us who were there and have seen the worst things that

Humanity can do to one another, I always come back to this simple truth. We were members of the finest military in the world, and did our mission exceptionally well, but we are the one's who hate what war does.

"I retired in 1995 as a Chief, Hospital Corpsmen, with 28½ years of service. Of those years, I served 10 with Marine units, including Bravo Co., (-), 4th Amphibious Assault Vehicles in Jacksonville, Florida, where I retired. My Meritorious Service Medal is signed by 'C.E. Mundy,' and is a source of pride. My former daughter-in-law asked why it had been signed by 'some Marine Corps General.' Only a Corpsman who has served with Marines can appreciate when their highest personal decoration has been signed by the (30th) Commandant of the Marine Corps, not a Fleet Admiral or CNO. I've always considered myself to be an original 50/50--blue on one side, and green on the other."[7] Hospital Corpsman Chief Petty Officer, HMC, Pearston served in Vietnam in 1969-70 and was a 23-year-old HM2 Senior Corpsman, made a total of 16 Recon patrols with Charlie and Bravo Co., 1st Reconnaissance Battalion, 1st Marine Division (Combat Action Ribbon).

Lt.Col. Norman F. "Pete" Hanner, USMC (Ret.), HMM-262 pilot

"My perspective of the war in Vietnam was framed by the generation in which I grew from childhood. All the adult males from both sides of my family were drawn into the military service in World War II after Pearl Harbor was attacked. As an adult, I fulfilled my military obligation in 1962 just as 'Vietnam' began to appear in news stories. I entered college in 1963 but when the Tonkin Gulf Accords were enacted by Congress and LBJ, I saw my opportunity to do 'my duty' in a real shooting war the same way all the men in my family had done and, full of patriotism, volunteered to go fight in this new war.

"After all my training, I arrived in Vietnam in November 1969 as a Sea Knight CH-46 helicopter pilot. Helo crewmen attrition was just below that of an infantryman. I was assigned to Chatterbox HMM-262 and flew in support of the 1stMarDiv in Quang Nam Province around Da Nang. Initially, we flew out of Phu Bai to the Marble Mountain Air Facility in Da Nang to begin our missions. Later the squadron moved to Da Nang when the U.S. Army took over Phu Bai. At this point, I think I should tell you that I was fearless and I was going to do my part to win the war. That jingoistic attitude changed during my tour when I, like any Marine with his eyes wide open, could see that there was no intention to WIN! Too many friends, too many memorial services, too many times annihilation of the enemy was forbidden by vague rules of engagement, convinced me and others that what we were doing was meaningless in the large scheme of U.S. strategic involvement. To be sure, I was dispirited. I reconciled my involvement to doing everything I could to save a Marine's life flying medevac missions that 'held meaning' rather than the senseless operations that put lives at risk and accomplished little. In the end, flying medevacs was the most gratifying contribution I made.

"During my tour, I can say that with the exception of a few senior officers, I have never seen such incompetence among field grade officers during 25 years of military service. Those few, whom I held in high regard, convinced me to stay in and help change the landscape of leadership. I'm proud to say that those of us who fought in that war were determined not to let anything like that happen again. U.S. Army General Norman Schwarzkopf and others saw to it."[8] Lt.Col. Hanner served in Vietnam in 1969-70 and was a 28-year-old first lieutenant pilot with Chatterbox HMM-262, Marine Air Group-16, 1st Marine Air Wing.

Georgine Tortorella Hembrough, fiancée to 2ndLt. Skibbe, MIA, 1970

"Few people realize that The Fighting Illini (football and basketball teams, etc.) from the University of Illinois are named after men and women from Illinois who gave their lives for the United States.

"The columns at Memorial Stadium symbolize University of Illinois graduates and men and women from Illinois who have died fighting for their country. Some people think The Fighting Illini are named after Indians that roamed the plains, hence, Illini from Illinois, but the association is really more patriotic.

"As I was working today, I found myself just west of Memorial Stadium at a stop light. The western sun was streaming into the columns granting some shadows, the shadows of those who associated themselves with the university over the course of many years. I looked over and the columns and the memorial inside just seemed to speak to me today to remind me that this great structure was built to commemorate the lives of soldiers who died in combat.

"The name of David W. Skibbe was added inside in 2002 when a new memorial was erected for wars subsequent to World War I. David and I graduated from this great university in 1968-69. He went on to graduate from Quantico as a Marine second lieutenant, shipped out and gave his life with dignity and respect within a very short time. David was very committed to his studies and his work here. He was extremely committed to the Marines and his country, his family and his faith. He was special. His name is forever here at the University, his alma mater, for all to see, to remember and to cherish.

"It took awhile for me to come up with a comment for my 'Perspective on the Vietnam War,' but the words finally came to me and it wasn't until today when I paused at the stadium and reflected on how David and I met here as students committed to our educations and then realized we had much more in common.

"I remember Mr. and Mrs. Skibbe coming to my apartment (in March of 1970) to tell me about David (being MIA, presumed dead). Death had not been much a part of my life at that point. Maybe these emotional moments are now resurfacing because they just got buried for a long time. Even when David left, I had never thought about his not coming back and then his parents said he wasn't. I guess the memorial service for him got us to go through all the motions, but it never helped us to cleanse our souls. I think I 'buried' what happened and just got back to living my life. The stages of something like this, they say, include anger and denial. Maybe those emotions, now that I am older, make me see this whole incident in a new fashion as well. (I contacted Georgine and gave her some specifics, according to official Marine Corps records, as to how David Skibbe ended up Missing-In-Action March 2, 1970 and his subsequent death at the hands of a VC soldier---MDK).

"After recently reading the explanations and facts (you presented to me) as to what exactly happened, I found myself in a much better position to deal with all of this. It was an explanation that never found its way to me (39 years ago). What I previously had were too many unanswered questions, so all I could do was try to put it all aside for all of this time. Now I have something concrete to deal with, something that makes better sense, not that I want to accept it either, but I have found a better peace."[9] The former Georgine Tortorella was 2ndLt. David W. Skibbe's 23-year-old fiancée when he was wounded by enemy fire while on his first 1st Recon patrol in the Que Son Mountains. He was accidentally left behind by his 1st Recon team after the wounded man's cable line snapped as he was being hoisted to a hovering Sea Knight helicopter as night fell resulting in his being declared MIA, presumed dead. He is one of 213 MIA Marines still not recovered from the Vietnam War.

Gy.Sgt. Rodney H. "Rod" or "Pu" Pupuhi, USMC (Ret.), 1st Recon, PRU

"I joined the Marine Corps Reserve in May 1953 under my older brother's name at 16 and was caught for being underage at boot camp and shipped home. A year later I rejoined legally and stayed for 6 years before going into the Reserves where we were redesignated the 6th Force Recon and became scuba and jump qualified.

"I went active again in 1965 with Bravo Co., 1st Platoon, 1st Recon Battalion and headed for Vietnam to link up with the 1st Force Recon and Navy SEAL and UDT teams. We worked farthest south then any units from a

U.S. destroyer just off the South China Sea.

"During my second tour in Vietnam, I was wounded twice, in February and May 1968, and got some hero medals. I was transferred to MAC-V as a PRU (Provisional Reconnaissance Unit) advisor for the Phoenix Program and joined 1st Force Recon. I returned for a third tour in 1970 as a platoon sergeant with Bravo Co., 1st Recon. I was medevacked once more just 2 days before 1st Recon was sent stateside in May 1971. I did a lot of tours and know a lot of Recon Marines. I was well-known by many.

"Late in April 1971 we ran our last Recon operation with the grunts somewhere in the Que Son Mountains. We were inserted to find a POW camp. We were making a last ditch effort to retrieve them as we were their last hope. We came across the POW compound but it was empty.

"We were sitting there waiting for the CH-46 birds to pick us up. A grunt lieutenant and his platoon were also nearby. He was really tired and it was a long walk back to An Hoa for them. They had humped all the way to our position and were going to hump back. When the birds were overhead and approaching my yellow smoke makeshift LZ, this lieutenant was begging for he and his men to come aboard. The ramp came down and my 5-man Recon team ran in. I spoke to the crew chief and he spoke to the pilot and it was thumbs up for them to come aboard.

"That lieutenant had a smile from ear to ear. Everyone had to sit on the floor. The seats had to be folded up and we looked like four rows of sardines. The bird was farting to lift off as the grunt Marines were hooting and hollering. The pilot let them off at An Hoa's LZ. I ran out to shake the smiling lieutenant's hand. I don't remember his name but we all felt good that day.

"A replica of The Wall was set up on my island (Oahu) in Hawaii. All sorts of higher-up officers from all the military branches attended. I didn't expect I would react (to seeing all those names on The Wall). I searched for Lt.Col. Leftwich's name. I began to search the row of lines. A full bird Col. Gray was there. I didn't notice. I found our colonel's name, then I choked up because everybody's name was there alongside his...Team Rush Act and the CH-46 crew (15 men altogether).

"I just busted out crying like a baby and couldn't control myself. I had a camouflage jacket on with all my ribbons and Recon badges. Col. Gray comforted me and asked if I knew Lt.Col. Leftwich. He was more surprised when I spoke of how he and the others died. He later became the (29th) Commandant of the Marine Corps, Gen. Alfred M. Gray Jr. (Pupuhi was granted 100 percent disability benefits by the Veterans Administration as a result of the trauma he incurred due to his tours of duty in Vietnam. Many Recon Marines are categorized the same as Pupuhi for the intensive combat they experienced in the Vietnam War---MDK)."[10] Gy.Sgt. Pupuhi served three tours in Vietnam, 1965-66, '67-'68, '70-'71, and was a 33-year-old sergeant promoted to staff sergeant in Bravo Co., then H&S Co., 1st Reconnaissance Battalion, 1st Marine Division in 1970 (Silver Star, Combat Action Ribbon and at least 2 Purple Hearts).

Nick Ut, *AP* Photographer

"I covered the Marines for *The Associated Press* taking pictures from 1968-71 in places along the DMZ, Khe Sanh and the Laotian border. I was able to take a lot of good pictures when I traveled with the Marines on their helicopters and C-130s (to the action). They put you in the right position to give you good combat pictures and even provided us with meals and helped us. I covered a lot of Marines fighting the North Vietnamese in Central Vietnam.

"I loved the Marines so much. They were the best. All you had to do was show them your press pass and camera and they'd let you go anywhere in Vietnam. I could get a ride in a helicopter anywhere in Vietnam within 20 minutes of arriving at a military airport. It's different in Iraq today.

"My friends who have been to Iraq tell me that I don't want to go to Iraq because it isn't like the Vietnam War. The military doesn't help us like they did in Vietnam. Iraq is much more dangerous than Vietnam. They kidnap people. In Vietnam nobody kidnapped you. You were free to go anywhere. Your media pass allowed you to go anywhere in Vietnam...but in Iraq they (al Qaida or Iraqi insurgents) see your media pass and that you are a U.S. citizen and they might kill you. They don't care who you are. I think I covered enough war in my life in Vietnam. I'm not young anymore. I'm an old man now.

"I go back to Vietnam often. I will go back next year. I always make stops in Hue and the DMZ. Sometimes I come across people selling old Marine clothing, dog tags, helmets...just all kinds of war souvenirs. A lot of the landmines are still everywhere. Along Highway 9 they're still finding unexploded 105mm, 155mm and 175mm artillery shells. Children die almost every week from the ordnance they find. I read a story just last week that a bomb explosion in Vietnam killed two kids.

"The Vietnamese welcome Americans to Vietnam today. They don't want to talk about the war. You go over there and tell them you were a former Marine serving in the Vietnam War and they'll welcome you, cook for you and hand you anything you want. I had some Marine friends who retired, moved to Vietnam and married Vietnamese women.

"A Navy Vietnam War veteran who's a good friend returned to Vietnam

10 years ago and was almost 60 when he married a girl 18 years old in Hue. They opened up a business and have made a lot of money while raising two daughters. Everything has changed in Vietnam (since the Vietnam War)."[11] Nick Ut began his *Associated Press* career as a 16-year-old Vietnamese photographer intern in 1966 under Horst Faas' tutelage. Ut would win the Pulitzer Prize for combat photography in 1973 for taking a photo the year before of a young Vietnamese girl running out of a ville naked having had her clothes burned off from a napalm bomb attack by South Vietnamese pilots. He would be seriously wounded three times in Vietnam while going about his job as an *AP* photographer.

# Maps

Vietnam maps were made available for this publication by the following mapping services: Dai Loc Map, Sheet 6640 IV,1965, Overprinted by III MAF, G2, 1968, and Thuong Duc Map, Sheet 6540 I, 1965, both maps courtesy of the U.S. Army Corps Engineers, U.S. Army Map Service; Da Nang Map, Sheet 6641 III, 1967, Overprinted by III MAF, G2, 1968, courtesy of the U.S. Army Corps of Engineers, 29th Engineers Battalion; Ben Giang Map, Sheet 6540 II, 1965, courtesy of the National Imagery and Mapping Agency, U.S. Army, 1966; Hai Lang Map, Sheet 6442 II, 1968, courtesy of the National Imagery and Mapping Agency, U.S. Army, 1968; Hiep Duc Map, Sheet 6640 III, 1965, courtesy of the U.S. Army, U.S. Army Map Service, 1965; Hoi An Map, Sheet 6640 I, 1984, courtesy of the National Imagery and Mapping Agency, Defense Mapping Agency Hydrographic/Topographic Center.

**The following pages contain Vietnam maps in this order:**

**Dai Loc map, Sheet 6640 IV, (Courtesy of National Geographic Service, Vietnam, and U.S. Army Corps of Engineers, U.S. Army Map Service, 1965)**

**Dai Loc map, Sheet 6640 IV, (Courtesy of National Geographic Service, Vietnam, and U.S. Army Corps of Engineers, U.S. Army Map Service, 1965)**

**Dai Loc map, Sheet 6640 IV, (Courtesy of National Geographic Service, Vietnam, and U.S. Army Corps of Engineers, U.S. Army Map Service, 1965)**

**Da Nang map, Sheet 6641 III, (Map Courtesy of National Geographic Service, Vietnam, 1967, and U.S. Army's 29th Engineer Battalion, 1967, with overlay by III MAF, December 1968)**

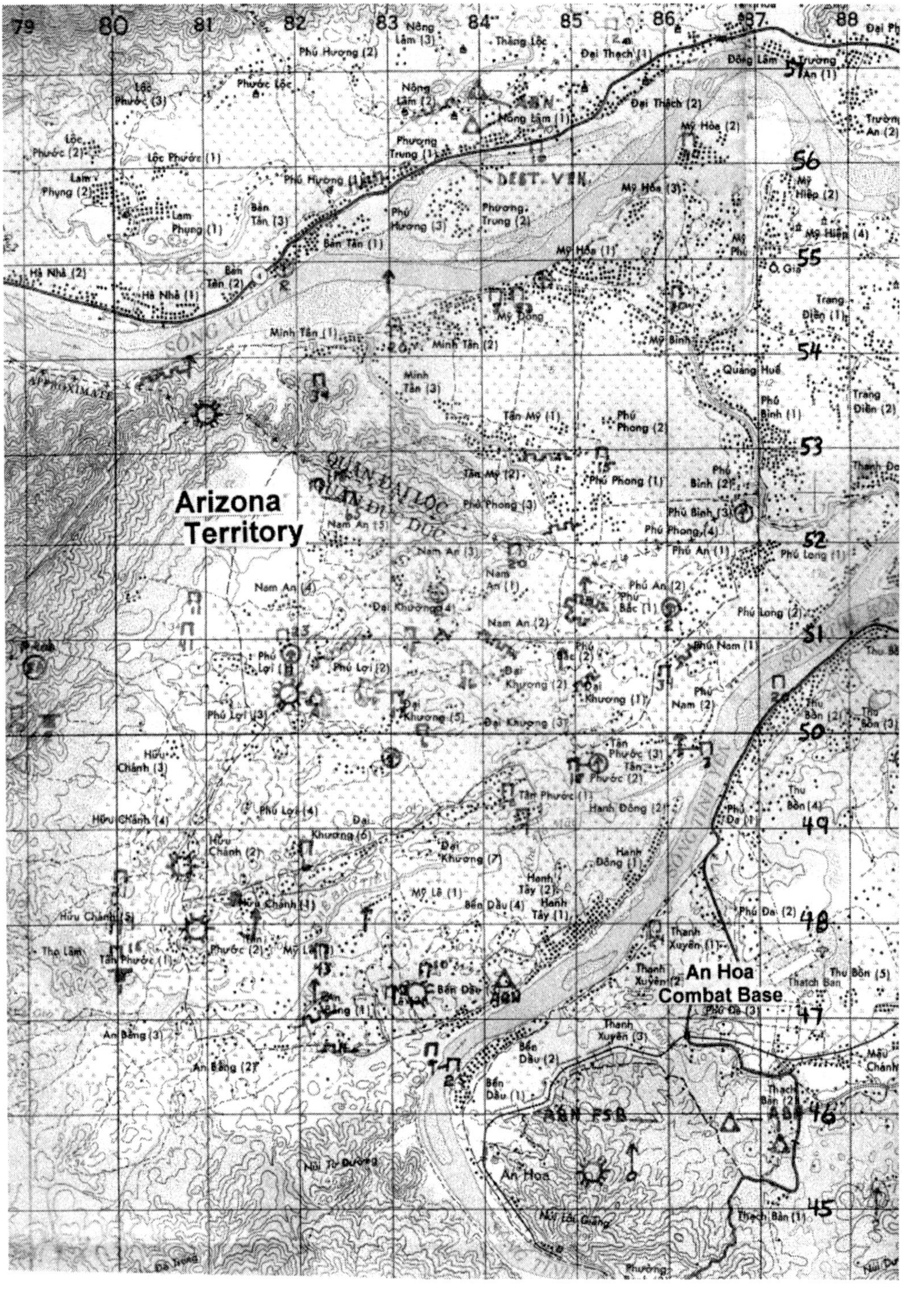

Arizona Territory
An Hoa Combat Base
AN HOA FSB
79
80
81
82
83
84
85
86
87
88
57
56
55
54
53
52
51
50
49
48
47
46
45

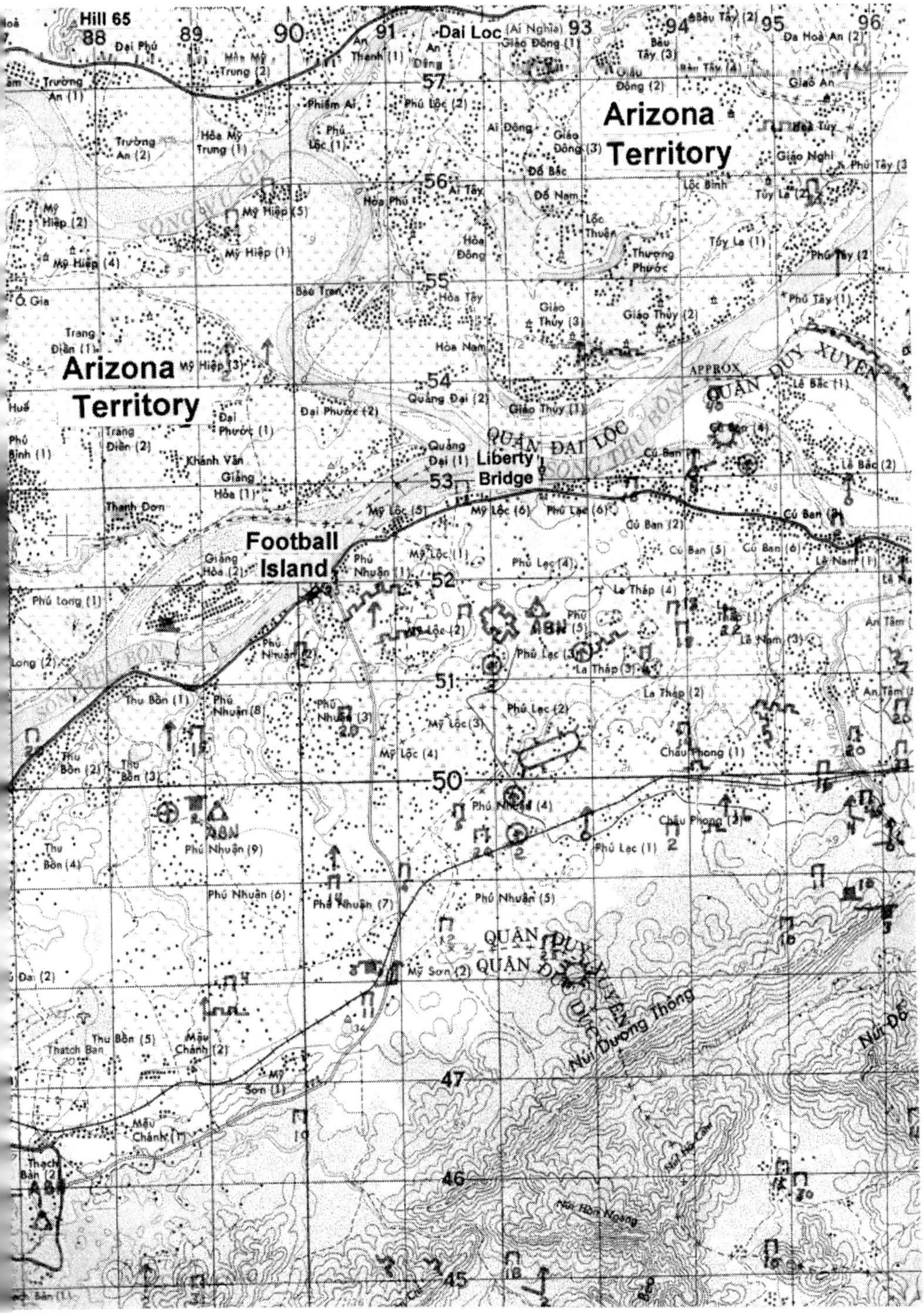

Hill 65
Dai Loc
Arizona Territory
Arizona Territory
Liberty Bridge
Football Island
QUẬN ĐẠI LỘC
QUẬN DUY XUYÊN

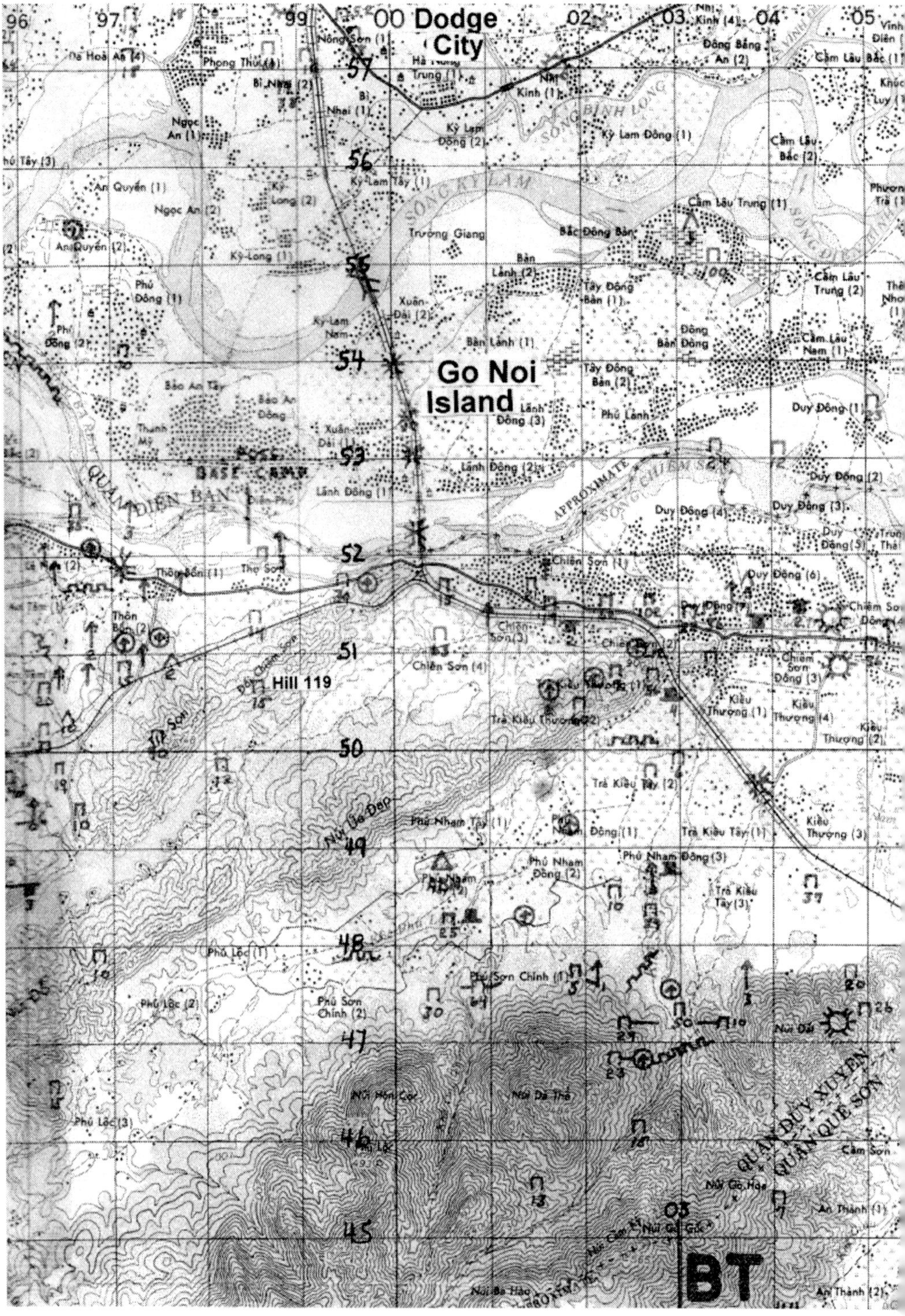

Dodge City
Go Noi Island
Hill 119
BT

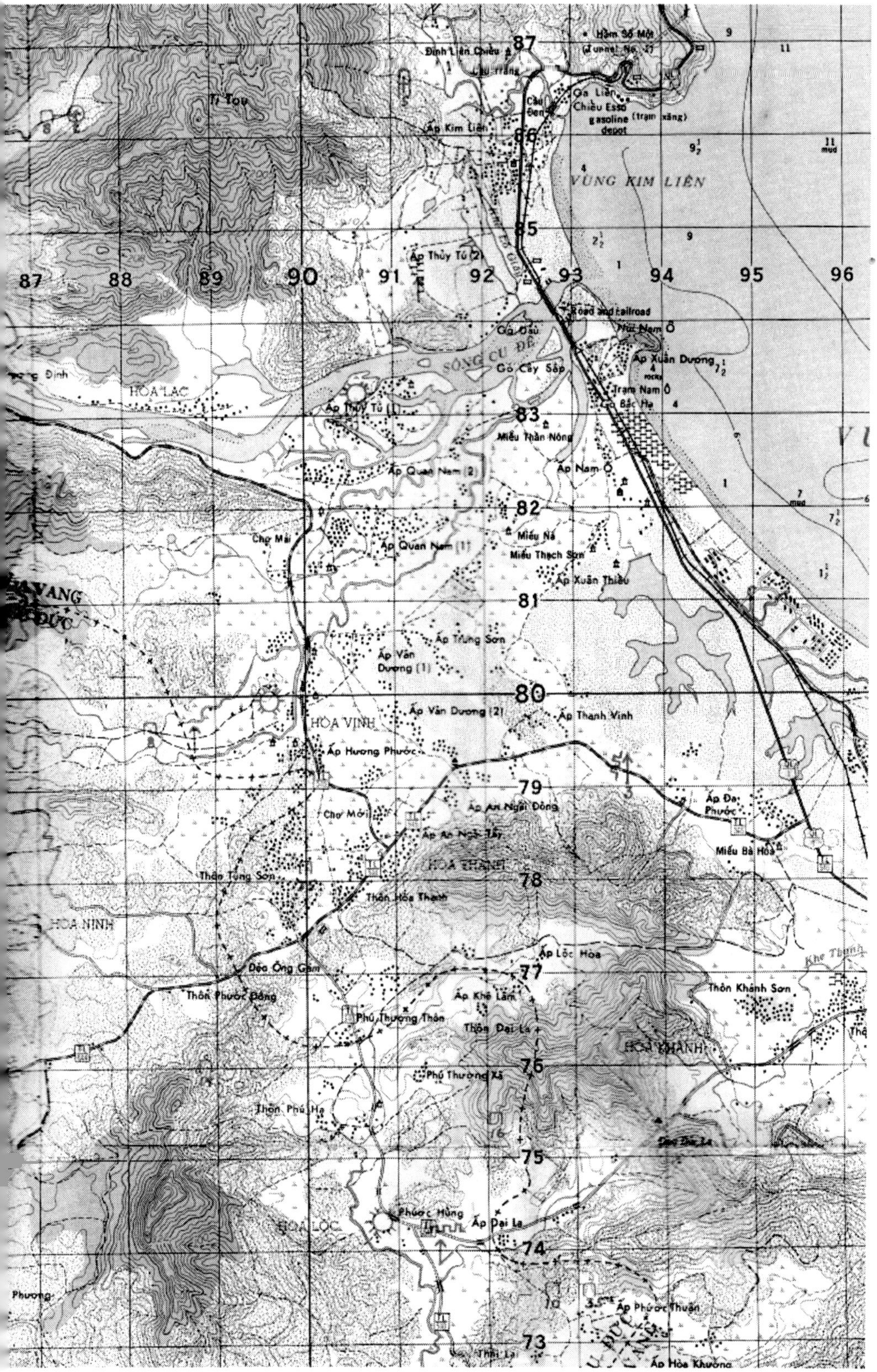

Định Liên Chiểu
Ga Liên Chiểu Esso gasoline depot (trạm xăng)
Ấp Kim Liên
VŨNG KIM LIÊN
Ấp Thủy Tú (2)
Road and railroad
Núi Nam Ô
Gò Đầu
SÔNG CU ĐÊ
Gò Cây Sắp
Ấp Xuân Dương
Trạm Nam Ô
HÒA LẠC
Ấp Thủy Tú (1)
Miếu Thần Nông
Ấp Quan Nam (2)
Ấp Nam Ô
Chợ Mai
Ấp Quan Nam (1)
Miếu Nà
Miếu Thạch Sơn
Ấp Xuân Thiều
Ấp Trung Sơn
Ấp Vân Dương (1)
HÒA VINH
Ấp Vân Dương (2)
Ấp Thanh Vinh
Ấp Hương Phước
Chợ Mới
Ấp An Ngãi Đông
Ấp An Ngãi Tây
Ấp Đa Phước
Miếu Bà Hỏa
HÒA THANH
Thôn Tùng Sơn
Thôn Hòa Thạnh
HÒA NINH
Ấp Lộc Hòa
Đèo Ông Găm
Thôn Phước Đông
Ấp Khê Lâm
Thôn Khánh Sơn
Phú Thượng Thôn
Thôn Đại La
HÒA KHÁNH
Phú Thượng Xã
Thôn Phú Hạ
HÒA LỘC
Phước Hưng
Ấp Đại La
Ấp Phước Thuận
Phương
Ấp Hòa Khương
87
88
89
90
91
92
93
94
95
96
86
85
83
82
81
80
79
78
77
76
75
74
73

# Leftwich Trophy Recipients 1979-2009

The Leftwich Trophy for Outstanding Leadership is an award presented annually in memory of Lt.Col. William Groom Leftwich Jr., USMC, killed-in-action in the Republic of Vietnam on November 18, 1970. Eligible nominees are Marine captains in the ground combat arms serving on active duty as company or battery commander with the ground forces of the Fleet Marine Forces at the time of the nomination. (The recipient of each year's award is for service performed in the previous year. The Commandant of the Marine Corps makes the annual presentation).

The trophy is provided to the Marine Corps through an endowment by the H. Ross Perot Foundation. Lt.Col. Leftwich and Mr. Perot were classmates at the U.S. Naval Academy, graduating in 1953. The trophy itself was designed by Dr. Felix Wiehs de Weldon, designer of the Marine Corps War Memorial (Iwo Jima Monument) in Arlington, Virginia near Arlington National Cemetery. (Asterisks show the officers I know to have been promoted to general as of March 2010. I do not have a complete list of those officers promoted to major, lieutenant colonel or colonel therefore I did not include that designation---MDK).

1979-Capt. Clyde S. Brinkley Jr., CO, Hotel Co., 2/2
1980-Capt. Charles R. Sherrill, CO, Bravo Co., 2d Tank Bn.
1981-Capt. John Caldwell, CO, Bravo Co., CO, Weapons Co., 1/6
1982-Capt Dirk R. Ahle, Weapons Co., 2/1, 1stMarDiv
1983-Capt. Ronald L. King, Battery I, 3/12, 3dMarDiv
1984-Maj. Robert K. Dobson Jr., CO, Golf Co., 2/8, 2dMarDiv
***1985-Capt. Dennis J. Hejlik, BLT, 3/8, 22d MAU
1986-Maj. David W. Mauldin, Echo Co., 2/8, 2dMarDiv
**1987-Capt. Paul E. Lefebvre, 2/9 ground forces, FMF
***1988-Maj. John R. Allen, S-3, 3/4, (2nd Nomination)
**1989-Capt. James B. Laster, Inspector-Instructor Operations Officer, 25th Marines
1990-Capt. Ronald F. Baczkowski, Kilo Co., 3/1 ground forces, FMF
1991-Capt. Dennis M. Greene, 2d Light Armored Infantry Bn.
1992-Capt. Michael L. Ettore, 1/8, 2dMarDiv ground forces, FMF
1993-Capt. Robert F. Castellvi, BLT, 2/9, 15 MEU, 1st MEF
1994-Maj. Steven M. Zotti, BLT, 1/6, 22d MEU, II MEF

1995-Maj. Jeffrey J. Sharrock, Recon, 3dMarDiv
1996-Capt. Jeffrey J. Kenney, 2/2, 2dMarDiv
1997-Maj. Julian Dale Alford, 3/8, 2dMarDiv
1998-Capt. Jason Q. Bohm, 2/1, 1stMarDiv
1999-Capt. Daniel M. Sullivan, CO, Weapons Co., 3/8, security operation, Albania and Kosovo
2000-Capt. Jason L. Morris, Bravo Co., BLT, 1/5, 31st MEU
2001-Capt. Michael D. Grice, Co. E, 2/11, 31st MEU on East Timor
2002-Maj. Farrell Sullivan, CO, Lima Co., 3/8, 4th MEB in Kabul, Afghanistan
2003-Capt. Christeon C. Griffin, 3/1, 1stMarDiv, I MEF
2004-Capt. Christopher J. Bronzi, CO Golf, Co., 2/4, 1stMarDiv, 31st MEU, *Operation Iraqi Freedom*, Ramadi, Iraq
2005-Capt. John W. Maloney, Charlie Co., 1/5, 2dMarDiv, II MEF, *Operation Iraqi Freedom*, Ramadi, Iraq, (posthumously awarded, first time in 27 years)
2006-Capt. Matthew W. Tracy, 2/3, 3rdMarDiv, III MEF, MARFORPAC
2007-Capt. Jonathan R. Smith, BLT 2/4, 31st MEU, III MEF
2008-Capt. Jonathan B. Hamilton, 1/9, 2dMarDiv, II MEF, MARFORCOM
2009-Capt. Christopher S. Conner, 2d Light Armored Reconnaissance Bn., 2dMarDiv, II MEF

**Active Duty, Maj.Gen. (as of March 2010).
***Active Duty, Lt.Gen. (as of March 2010).

# Acknowledgments

Marines, Docs, various individuals, archivists and librarians who took the time to provide me with invaluable resource material, contacts or advice on passages over the years were Harv Ames, John Arnold, Peter Arnett, Howard Ball, J.D. Barber, Alan Barbour, Jim Barr, Chuck Bender, Lynn Benson, Bill Bond Jr., Curt Bradley, Mike Brennan, Bob Brust, Ron Bub, Chuck Burin, David Causey, Roger Cleland, Bill Drumright, Bailey Eames, Barney Espinoza, Tom Evans, Dorothy Fall, Mike Fallon, Bob Fawcett, Larry Feldman, Dave Fuller, Joe Galloway, Royall Geis, Larry Gifford, Pete Goetz, Mike Greene, John Grinalds, Lisa Gruber, Jim Harvey, Ron Halvorsen, Pete Hanner, John Hare, Georgine Hembrough, Al Herlicka, Fred Hillmann, Allyn Hinton, Mildred (McVey) Holmes, Ron Huegel, Bob Hungate, Jim Hunt, Duane Jensen, Maclear Jacoby Jr., Bruce Judge, Pat Kenny, Knight Kiplinger, Randy Knapp, John Kosinski, Ray Kozakowski, John Lakin, Walt Ledbetter Jr., the staff at the Longview Public Library, archivist Frederick J. Graboske and his staff at the Marine Corps Archives, U.S. Library of Congress staff.

Also, Bill Leftwich III, Scott Leftwich, Jeff Lippincott, Tim Luhrs, Dave Marshall, Jerry Martin, Jim Martin, Ed Mason, Jack Maxwell, Jeff and Sally McVey, Jane (Leftwich) Michael, Terry Moore, Bob Morris, Sid Nanson, Al Nelson Sr., Catherine (Harvey) Nitti, Ray Norton, William Nyland, Tom O'Bryon II, Bob Ondrick, Tom Parry, Jim Pearston, Ross Perot, Steve Plunkett, Ed Powell, Janet (Skibbe) Preston, Rod Pupuhi, Richard Pyle, Jim Rider, David Rivard, Gil Robinson, Julie Samuelson, Sandy Sanders, Wiley Sellers, John Sherman, Joe Silvoso, Mike Simpson, Jeff Skibbe, Dick Smith, Bob Syler, Joan (Skibbe) Tomoff, Bernard Trainor, Bill Valentino, Bill Walsh, Mary Schanck Wasilewski, Jim Webb Jr., Ed West, Neil Whitehurst, Les Williams, Paul Wilson and Bill Woidyla. Actually, I'd like to thank and give credit to all those listed in the Interviews and Correspondence section for making this book possible.

A special thanks goes to Benjamin Franklin "Gentle Ben" Hobbs who did me the honor of proofing most of *Book II, American Heroes: Grunts, Pilots & "Docs"* and was my journalism instructor at Stephen F. Austin State University in Nacogdoches, Texas, 1971-74. Giving me the tools over the years to write this manuscript with confidence and without whose teaching or professional expertise I would never have embarked on this gargantuan research and writing project were (all newspapers mentioned are in Texas) Ben Hobbs; Dr. Francine Hoffman, former SFASU Journalism Department professor; Emmett H. and Marie Whitehead, owners/publishers of the weekly newspaper *The* (Rusk) *Cherokeean*; Bettye Craddock, SFASU journalism graduate assistant and teaching at Kilgore College in 2011.

Also, Carol Collyar then Jim Giametta, former managing editors of the daily newspaper *Longview Morning Journal*; Bill Turner, former owner/publisher of the bi-weekly newspaper (Atlanta) *Citizens-Journal;* Maris Fletcher, former editor of the *Jacksonville Daily Progress;* and Donnis Baggett, former East Texas editor of the *Longview Morning Journal,* assistant managing editor of *The Dallas Morning News,* former editor-in-chief of *The Bryan/College Station Eagle,* and as of 2011 the publisher of the *Waco Tribune-Herald.* Donnis, a fellow SFASU graduate, was my editor at the Longview newspaper and he later threw some string work on an East Texas story my way when he was at *The Dallas Morning News*. The experience allowed me to see how it was like to write for a statewide distributed daily newspaper and made me realize that I could write with the "big boys and girls."

Providing encouragement and/or offering constructive suggestions after reading portions of my book were my sisters, Barbara Haight, and Sandy Bolls and her husband Jack; Johnny Johnson, a World War II U.S. Navy PBY pilot; Evelyn Sibley, a retired teacher; Tom Cutler, Naval Institute Press senior editor; Jack McCubbin, a fellow writer; Steve Jackson and Gene McWhorter, computer technical help. Also, my mother, Evelyn Ruby (Wood) Kellum, provided me with a huge gift growing up by instilling in me the love of reading. As an example, it seemed she was never without a book in her hands and provided us kids with a large selection of *Reader's Digest Condensed Books* which I read cover-to-cover. I was whisked away to places I would never tread and vicariously had experiences I would never have but dreamed the dreams of an adventurer. The reading, while building up my vocabulary and writing skills, made me yearn to see the world outside my little East Texas burg and secure the first Kellum family college degree that turned out to be a no-brainer in communications/journalism and English, naturally. And to this, I owe all to my mother who set my course in life.

Vinnie Burdziuk, 2/1's website webmaster, gave invaluable computer advice and graciously offered "a Marine helping another Marine" by taking my raw data and worked his magic by putting *Book II's* impressive front and back covers together as well as my books' **www.MichaelDanKellum.com** website. And a special nod to Buford, an African-American a few years older than me from my hometown I knew as a young boy growing up, who taught me to be a better human being and to judge people by their heart and not their color.

My wife, Karen, has been my one constant in all this writing and my anchor when my ship seemed adrift. Yes dear, in answer to your question over the years, "Are we there, yet?" We're finally "there" at long last.

# Footnotes

### Perspectives on the Vietnam War—Part I

1. Col. William Covington "Wild Bill" Drumright, taped interview on May 24, 2003, Columbia, Tennessee.
2. Sgt. Larry K. "Giff" Gifford, telephone interview on February 7, 2003.
3. Richard Pyle, *AP* Bureau chief/correspondent, 1968-1973, Saigon, RVN, email dated August 27, 2002.
4. MCHC David L. "Doc" Snider, emails dated July 17, 19, 2009.
5. H. Ross Perot Sr., telephone interview on March 3, 1992.
6. MSgt. John F. Hare, reunion at Col. Bill Drumright's farm, Columbia, Tennessee, May 24, 2003.
7. Cpl. Larry M. Feldman, telephone interview on August 12, 2008.
8. 1stLt. John Patrick "Pat" Kenny, email dated May 8, 2008.
9. LCmdr. John H. "Doc" Erceg, USN (Ret.), email dated June 19, 2008.
10. Lt.Col. Gilford G. "Gil" Robinson, telephone interview, April 26, 2009.

### Chapter 1

1. Ed West, *Gopher Broke: A Tribute to the Crew of 'Blood, Sweat & Tears' and the Marines of 3rd Platoon, Alpha Company, 1st Battalion, 1st Marine Regiment 1st Marine Division.*
2. Graham A. Cosmas and Lt.Col. Terrence P. Murray, USMC, Chapter 2, The War Continues, *U.S. MARINES IN VIETNAM, Vietnamization and Redeployment, 1970-71*, (Washington, D.C.: History and Museums Division, Headquarters, U.S. Marine Corps), p. 34.
3. *Ibid.*
4. Dai Loc map, Sheet 6640 IV: IV: A. AT970620.
5. Cosmas and Murray, *op. cit.*
6. *Ibid.*, p. 35.
7. *Ibid.*
8. Dai Loc map, Sheet 6640 IV: A. AT951558, B. Grid square BT0565, C. Grid square AT9564, D. AT965655, E. Grid square AT9766.
9. Cpl. Ed West, email October 15, 2008.
10. West, *Gopher Broke*, *op. cit.*
11. West, *Ibid.*, p. 1.
12. Lori Yount, *Beaufort* (S.C.) *Gazette*, January 30, 2007.
13. Dai Loc map, Sheet 6640 IV: A. AT963654.
14. West, *op. cit.*, p. 1.
15. West, *Ibid.*

16-18. West, *Ibid.*, p. 2.

19. Dai Loc map, Sheet 6640 IV: A. AT962654, B. AT960654.

20-23. West, *op. cit.*, p. 2.

24. West, *Ibid.*, pp. 2-3.

25-32. West, *Ibid.*, p. 3.

33-37. West, *Ibid.*, p. 4.

38. West, *Ibid.*, pp. 4-5.

39-40. West, *Ibid.*, p. 5.

41. West, *Ibid.*, pp. 5-6.

42-46. West, *Ibid.*, p. 6.

47. West, *Ibid.*, pp. 6-7.
48. Dai Loc map, Sheet 6640 IV: A. AT959651, B. AT959652.

49-53. West, *op. cit.*, p. 7.

54-56. West, *Ibid.*, p. 8.

57. "Monument to war hero unveiled...Late Medal of Honor recipient's feats remembered," (PFC Mike Clausen), by Debra Lemoine, *The Advocate*, Sunday, January 28, 2007, Main Metro

Edition, Section B, page 01, Dateline Ponchatoula, LA. Mike Clausen Memorial: http://www.mikeclausen.com/

58. Roger Herman, USMC/Combat Helicopter Association founder and past president, email posting May 31, 2004 on popasmoke.org website.
59. Trista Talton, "A tribute to courage: Medal of Honor recipient to get headstone; rescue helo restored," *Marine Corps Times*, November 13, 2006, Jacksonville, North Carolina.
60. *Times Report*, "Ponchatoula hero finally properly honored"; also, *Advocate*, Mike Clausen Memoriall: http://www.mikeclausen.com/
61. *Times Report, op. cit.*
62-63. Talton, *Marine Corps Times, op. cit.*
64. Talton, *Marine Corps Times, Ibid.*
65. David Permutt, "Above and Beyond the Call: Museum Shows Off Restored Helicopter, Veterans Pay Tribute to Marine Who Helped Rescue Platoon Trapped in a Vietnam Minefield," *The Charlotte Observer*, p. 1B, Metro, October 21, 2007.
66. LCpl. Jeffrey A. Cosola, "Angels, legends walk among us," *Marine Corps News*, MCAS New River, December 6, 2005.
67. *Advocate*, Mike Clausen Memorial: http://www.mikeclausen.com/
68. Lori Yount, *Beaufort* (S.C.) *Gazette*
69. Permutt, *op. cit.*

## Chapter 2

1. James H. Webb Jr., "Heroes of the Vietnam Generation," *American Enterprise Institute,* (AEI), August 2000. *Reprinted with the permission of The American Enterprise Institute for Public Policy Research, Washington, D.C.
2. Knight Kiplinger's address upon receiving the Landon School's Anthony Edward Kupka Distinguished Alumnus Award, December 1998, website: landon.net/home/content.asp?id=1187
3. *Ibid.*
4. *Ibid.*
5. "Marine Lieut. Kupka Dies In Viet Fighting," *Falmouth Enterprise*, Falmouth, Massachusetts, Tuesday, April 29, 1969, p. 1.
6. Kiplinger, *op. cit.*
7. "Marine Lieut. Kupka Dies in Viet Fighting," *op. cit.*
8. Dai Loc map, Sheet 6640 IV: A. AT824453, B. AT825458.
9. Kiplinger, *op. cit.*
10. *Ibid.*
11. *Ibid.*
12. "Theodore Vivilacqua, Scholar, Grid Star, Dies In Vietnam War," *Huntington Park Daily Signal*, Huntington Park, California, May 23, 1969, p. B-1.
13. Donna Hurley, Reference Department, U.S. Naval Academy, Nimitz Library, Annapolis, Maryland, email dated July 26, 2007.
14. Dai Loc map, Sheet 6640 IV: A. AT871533, B. AT827503, C. AT829507, D. AT831507 E. AT822492, F. AT822495, G. AT870515, H. AT870517, I. AT873514, J. AT837471, K. AT832470, L. AT822472, M. AT850498, N. AT848507, O. AT864544, P. AT863543, Q. AT867544, R. AT878544, S. AT877542, T. AT873542.
15. John O. Walling, tribute to 2ndLt. Ted Vivilacqua, February 21, 2000, Vietnam Veterans Memorial Fund website: vvmf.org
16. "Theodore Vivilacqua, Scholar, Grid Star, Dies In Vietnam War," *op. cit.*
17. 1stLt. Ed Mattingly Jr.'s tribute to 2ndLt. Al Nelson, July 19, 2000, Vietnam Veterans Memorial Fund website, vvmf.org
18. Dai Loc map, Sheet 6640 IV: A. AT895495, B. AT898490 C. AT899507, D. AT898499, E. AT898498, F. AT877505, G. AT888513, H. AT894484, I. AT897488, J. AT841445, K. AT850447, L. AT887503 M. AT884498, N. AT888489, O. AT886497, P. AT903506.
19. Capt. Robert A. Beeler, CO, India, 3/5, letter to Col. and Mrs. Albert O. Nelson Sr., May 31, 1969.
20. CMC Gen. Leonard F. Chapman Jr., letter to Col. and Mrs. Albert O. Nelson Sr. awarding their

son the Bronze Star posthumously, April 1, 1970.

21. "Street Named for 2nd Lt.," by Mark Herberger, Staff Writer, *The Scout*, MCB Camp Pendleton, Wednesday, November 26, 1986.
22. *Ibid.*
23. *Ibid.*
24. Col. John W. Lakin, USAF (Ret.), tribute to his son, 2ndLt. John Lakin, October 29, 2000, Vietnam Veterans Memorial Fund website: vvmf.org
25. Dai Loc map, Sheet 6640 IV: A. AT825457, B. AT827774, C. AT998463, D. AT999463.
26. Dai Loc map, Sheet 6640 IV:: A. AT979503, B. AT988508.
27. Bach Ma map, Sheet 6541 II: A. ZC157713, B. ZC033864, C. ZC042857.
28. John Dullighan, Boeing tech representative comments, "Brothers Killed in Action in USMC Helicopters or While Assigned to USMC Helicopter Squadrons in Vietnam," 690621, HMM-165, USMC/Combat Helicopter Association website: popasmoke.com/kid/incidents.php?incident_id=218
29. 1stLt. Stan Jorgensen, HMM-165 copilot, personal narrative on hostile fire, crash June 21, 1969, "Brothers Killed in Action in USMC Helicopters or While Assigned to USMC Helicopter Squadrons in Vietnam," 690621, HMM-165, USMC/Combat Helicopter Association website: popasmoke.com/kid/incidents.php?incident_id=218
30. John Lane research of injuries sustained by HMM-165 Sea Knight crew shot down June 21, 1969, "Brothers Killed in Action in USMC Helicopters or While Assigned to USMC Helicopter Squadrons in Vietnam," 690621, HMM-165, USMC/Combat Helicopter Association website: popasmoke.com/kid/incidents.php?incident_id=218 .
31. Jorgensen, *op. cit.*
32. Dai Loc map, Sheet 6640 IV: A. AT841495, B. AT852513), C. AT864511, D. AT844504, E. AT933520, F. AT915547, G. AT938525.
33. *The Impossible Dream* (The Quest), lyrics by Joe Darion, from the *Man of LaMancha*, sung at 2ndLt. Al Benson's funeral.
34. Dai Loc map, Sheet 6640 IV: A. AT825496, B. AT818484, C. AT819487, D. AT822484, E. AT814485, F. AT854495, G. AT835495, H. AT834484, I. AT846494, J. AT846484, K. AT830475, L. AT835475, M. AT826473, N. AT918514, O. AT882503, P. AT920516, Q. AT904508.
35. 2ndLt. Nick Huth's obituary, *The Corpus Christi Caller*, Corpus Christi, Texas, July 1969.
36. Hiep Duc map, Sheet 6640 III: A. AT947287, B. AT934395. C. AT971393.
37. Dorothy Fall, *Bernard Fall, Memories of a Soldier-Scholar,* (Washington, D.C.: Potomac Books, Inc., 2006), p. 214.
38. Catherine Harvey Nitti, email Re: Butch Harvey, May 30, 2005.
39. Khu Pho Nam Tho map, Sheet 6641 II: A. BT091733.
40. 1stLt. Walt Pinkerton, Cobra copilot, HML-367 Scarface, commenting on aircraft being shot down, December 4, 1970, and KIA of 1stLt. John Irving Lassitter, Vietnam Helicopter Pilots Association, website: http://www.vhpa.org/ Lassitter.
41. *Ibid.*
42. Lt.Col. Royall "Goose" Geis, email response of January 11, 2006 to Cobra pilot Lassitter's crash in the South China Sea on December 4, 1970.
43. Scarface HML-367, "Memorial," website: scarface-usmc.org/memorial.htm
44. 1st Marine Division Command Information Notebook, p. 8, Marine Corps History and Museum Division, Vietnam War CD #16.
45. "AARUGHA!" *Wikipedia*, 1953 or 1954, 1st Amphibious Recon Marines used this term as part of their cadence on a conditioning run imitating the 'Dive' horn sound of a submarine from WW II. Marines at Camp San Onofre made this sound upon being dismissed from formation in 1968, also carried over to the Marines in Vietnam.

## Chapter 3

1. Dai Loc map, Sheet 6640 IV, A. AT980664.
2. Hoi An map, Sheet 6640 I, A. BT078694, B. BT077691.
3. Dai Loc map, Sheet 6640 IV, A. AT982682, B. AT975660.

4. Hoi An map, Sheet 6640 I, A. BT067698.
5. *The Mourning Bride* (1697), Act III, Scene 8, William Congreve (1670-1729).
6. Dai Loc map, Sheet 6640 IV, A. AT993684.
7. Cosmas and Murray, *op. cit.*, p. 109.
8. *Ibid.*, p 110.
9. Dai Loc map, Sheet 6640 IV, A. AT98608, B. AT970620.
10. Hoi An map, Sheet 6640 I, A. BT0706 70, B. BT07680, C. BT096677, D. BT089691.

## Chapter 4

1. Jeff Skibbe, University of Illinois (Urbana, Illinois), confirmed statements made about 2ndLt. David Skibbe previously on the UI Alumni Association website, January 28, 2008 email.
2. David Mott and Rick Obermeyer, "Face Painting," *Native Tech: Native American Technology and Art,* December 1990, from Louis Capron's "Florida's 'Wild' Indians, the *Seminole*," website: http://nativetech.org/seminole/facepainting/index.php
3. Thuong Duc map, Sheet 6640 I: A. Vicinity of ZC030440, B. ZC031436, C. Sea Knight helicopters have the extraction point at ZC034436, while Homecoming II Project, September 1, 1990 and the P.O.W. NETWORK, 1998, list the loss coordinates at 154501N 1075001E or ZC036432, and Team Thin Man's Patrol Debrief lists vicinity of ZC031436, D. ZC030442.
4. Richard Pyle, *AP* Bureau chief, email September. 1, 2006, explains that in Asian culture the last name comes first, i.e. Zo Rum Au, but in proper reference to the person in question he is "Mr. Au."
5. Thuong Duc map, Sheet 6640 I: A. ZC036432.
6. Joint Task Force-Full Accounting, Hickam AFB, Hawaii, report, August 26, 1998, Maj. Kenneth M. Royalty, Team Leader.
7. Thuong Duc map, Sheet 6640 I: A. Grid Coordinates 48P ZC 03128 43504 determined by the Trimble Trimpack Receiver using the Global Positioning System tracking six satellites.

## Chapter 5

1. "Soldier--His Prayer," *Poems from the Desert,* (a poem found on a scrap of paper in a slit trench in Tunisia during the battle of El Agheila was published by members of the British Eighth Army in 1944).
2. Dai Loc map, Sheet 6640 IV, A. AT812448.

## Chapter 6

1. Publilius Syrus, *Maxim,* 1st Century, BC.
2. Thuong Duc map, Sheet 6640 I: A. ZC034445, B. ZC034446.
3. Michael C. Hodgins, *Reluctant Warrior, A Marine's True Story of Duty and Heroism in Vietnam*, (New York: Ballantine Books, 1996), p. 26, 32.
4. Thuong Duc map, Sheet 6640 I: A. ZC036447, B. Vicinity of ZC034446, C. ZC037438, D. ZC048543, E. ZC050450, F. ZC048477.

## Chapter 7

1. Thucydides, "Funeral Oration of Pericles," *The History of the Peloponnesian War* (431- 413 B.C.), p. 40.
2. Defense POW/Missing Personnel Office (DPMO), Personnel Missing-Southeast Asia (PMSEA) as of January 10, 2010 listed on website: dtic.mil/dpmo/
3. *Ibid.*
4. *Ibid.*
5. Thuong Duc map, Sheet 6640 I: A. Grid Coordinates 48P ZC03128 43504, Trimble Trimpack Receiver using Global Positioning System, B. ZC036435, C. ZC030442.

## Chapter 8

1. MSgt. John Hare, telephone interview on October 26, 2008.
2. Dai Loc map, Sheet 6640 IV: A. AT822704, B. AT838707, C. AT839708.
3. Da Nang map, 6641 III: A. vicinity of AT816782, B. AT816782.
4. LCpl. Tim Luhrs postings on Vietnam Veterans Memorial website, vvmf.org on March 28, 2007.
5. Da Nang map, 6641 III: A. vicinity of AT829772.

6. Dai Loc map, Sheet 6640 IV: A. AT987508.
7. Bach Ma map, Sheet 6541 II: A. ZC070760 or a previous location denoted in the AAR, ZC070800.

## Chapter 9

1. Cosmas and Murray, Chapter 17: Artillery and Reconnaissance, *op. cit.*, pp. 310-311.
2. *Ibid*, p. 311.
3. *Ibid.*
4. *Ibid.*
5. Da Nang map, Sheet 6641 III:: A. AT835976.
6. Cosmas and Murray, *op. cit.*, pp. 309-310.
7. Gary Wayne Ragsdale's Silver Star, Internet website: http://www.homeofheroes.com/valor/08_WOT/SS_GWO

## Chapter 10

1. Dorothy Fall, *Bernard Fall, Memories of a Soldier-Scholar,* (Washington, D.C.: Potomac Books, Inc., 2006), pp. 57, 112, 205-206, 209,
2. American National Biography Online, February 2000, James Friguglietti, "Fall, Bernard B.," biographical service to the U.S. Library of Congress.
3. Dorothy Fall, *op. cit.*, pp. 24-25.
4. *Ibid.*, pp. 15-17, 23-24.
5. *John Roth, Editor, The Holocaust Chronicle, A History in Words and Pictures,* (Lincolnwood, Illinois: Publications Limited, Ltd., 2000), pp. 699-702.
6. American National Biography Online, *op. cit.*
7. *Ibid.*
8. *Ibid.*
9. Colin L. Powell with Joseph E. Persico, *My American Journey*, (New York: Random House, Inc., 1995), pp. 147-148.
10. John Simon Guggenheim Memorial Foundation, "1965 and 1966 Reports of the President and of the Treasurer," New York, p. 141, primary contact G. Thomas Tanselle, senior vice president.
11. *Ibid.*
12. Leftwich Jr., "An Afternoon With Bernard Fall," *op. cit.*, p. 25.
13. *Ibid.*, pp. 25-26.
14. *Ibid.*, p. 27.
15. *Ibid.*
16. *Ibid.*
17. Dr. Bernard B. Fall, *Viet-Nam Witness 1953-66*, (New York: Frederick A. Praeger, Publishers, 1966), p. 291.
18. Dr. Fall, *Street Without Joy*, *op. cit.*, p. 172.
19. Leftwich Jr., "An Afternoon With Bernard Fall," *op. cit.*, pp. 25-26.
20. Leftwich Jr., "...and a few Marines," *op. cit.*, p. 41.
21. Dorothy Fall, *op. cit.*, pp. 184-185, 205-206, 210.
22. *Ibid.*, p. 255.
23. Hai Lang map, Sheet 6442 II: A. YD528438, B. YD562431, C. YD570424, D. YD591400, E. YD600395, F. YD536436, G. YD565410, H. YD541427
24. Dr. Fall, *Last Reflections on a War, Bernard B. Fall on Viet-Nam,* (New York: Schocken Books, 1964), p. 266.
25. Hai Lang map, Sheet 6442 II: A. YD553436
26. Dr. Fall, *Last Reflections on a War, Bernard B. Fall on Viet-Nam, op. cit.*, pp. 267-268.
27. Hai Lang map, Sheet 6442 II: A. YD559427, B. YD578428, C.YD578428, D. YD579424, E. YD590498.
28. Thomas P. Evans, *Home From the War: Memoir of a "Walking Dead" Survivor*, (New York: Writer's Club, later called iUniverse, Inc. September 2000), p. 46, also, quote appeared in "Vietnam War: Death on 'The Street Without Joy,'" *Leatherneck* magazine, Quantico, Virginia, July 1996.

29. Dorothy Fall, *op. cit.*, p. 255.
30. Hai Lang map, Sheet 6442 II: A. YD596398
31. Dr. Fall, *Last Reflections on a War, Bernard B. Fall on Viet-Nam, op. cit.*, p. 271.
32. Leftwich Jr., "An Afternoon With Bernard Fall," *op. cit.*, p. 26.
33. Hai Lang map, Sheet 6442 II: A. YD593393, B. YD594395, C. YD592415, D. YD532318, E. YD594398
34. Thomas P. Evans, *A Poverty of Thoughts*, (New York: iUniverse, Inc., July 2007), p. 170; also, quote appeared in "Vietnam War: Death on 'The Street Without Joy,'" *Leatherneck, op. cit.*
35. Leftwich Jr., "An Afternoon With Bernard Fall," *op. cit.*, p. 26.
36. *Ibid.*
37. Safer, *Flashbacks: On Returning to Vietnam, op. cit.*, p. 117.
38. Safer, *Ibid.*, pp. 117, 118.
39. Richard Pyle and Horst Faas, *Lost Over Laos*, (Cambridge, Massachusetts: De Capo Press, 2003), pp. 43-44.
40. Dorothy Fall, *op. cit.*, pp., 69, 88, 89, 204, 215-220, 230.
41. Dorothy Fall, *op. cit.*, p. 253.
42. "Interment in Arlington Cemetery is Denied to Bernard Fall by U.S.," *New York Times*, February 24, 1967, p. 2.
43. *Ibid.*
44. "Service Set Monday For Bernard B. Fall," *The Washington Post*, Washington, D.C., March 4, 1967, p. B4.
45. *Ibid.*
46. Dr. Fall, *Last Reflections on a War, Bernard B. Fall on Viet-Nam, op. cit.*, Dedication.

## Chapter 11

1. Gen. William C. Westmoreland, *A Soldier Reports,* (Garden City, NY: Doubleday, 1976), p. 136; also MGySgt. Mel Jones, "Major Leftwich Called Best Advisor In Vietnam," *Quantico Sentry*, Quantico, Virginia, May 6, 1966; also Maj. W.G. Leftwich Jr., "Bong Son Operation," *Marine Corps Gazette*, June 1966, p. 29 (Quotes and information reprinted with permission and copyright by the *Marine Corps Gazette); also* Maj. W.G. Leftwich Jr., "COVAN MY, American Advisor," *Shipmate: Magazine of USNA Alumni Association*, November 1966, p. 7.
2. Thomas BeVier, "Boyhood Dreams Of Military Glory Led Straight And True To Destiny," *The Commercial Appeal,* Memphis, Tennessee, November 20, 1970.
3. Nathan Bedford Forrest, (1806-1872).
4. Maj. William G. Leftwich III's notes of Lt.Gen. Frederick L. Wieseman's comments, dated March 27-28, 1993.
5. Jack Shulimson and Major Charles M. Johnson, USMC, *U.S. MARINES IN VIETNAM, The Landing and the Buildup,1965*, (Washington, D.C.: History and Museums Division Headquarters, U.S. Marine Corps, 1974), pp. Introduction xiii, 206.
6. Gen. H Norman Schwarzkopf with Peter Petre, *It Doesn't Take A Hero: The Autobiography of General H. Norman Schwarzkopf*, (New York: Bantam Books, October 1992), p. 107.
7. Brig.Gen. Edwin H. Simmons, "Marine Corps Operations in Vietnam, 1965-1966," *THE MARINES IN VIETNAM, 1954-1973, An Anthology and Annotated Bibliography*, (Washington, D.C.: History and Museums Division Headquarters, U.S. Marine Corps, 1974), p. 60.
8. Maj. W.G. Leftwich Jr., "Bong Son Operation," *Marine Corps Gazette*, June 1966, p. 29, (Quotes and information reprinted with permission and copyright by the *Marine Corps Gazette.); also,* Leftwich's Completion of Tour Report, "History of Task Force Alfa," p. 1, to the Office of the Senior Marine Advisor, Naval Advisory Group, MACV, Jan. 10, 1966.
9. Leftwich's Completion of Tour Report, "History of Task Force Alfa," *op. cit.*
10. Leftwich Jr., "Bong Son Operation," *op. cit.*, p. 29.
11. *Ibid.*
12. Navy Cross citation awarded to Maj. W. G. Leftwich Jr., January 24, 1966 by SecNav Paul H. Nitze for the battle at Hoai An.
13. *Ibid.*

14. *Ibid.*
15. MGySgt. Mel Jones, "Major Leftwich Called Best Advisor In Vietnam," *Quantico Sentry*, Quantico, Virginia, May 6, 1966.
16. "Leftwich Gets Navy Cross For Heroic Action In War," *The Commercial Appeal*, Memphis, Tennessee, May 1, 1965.
17. Leftwich Jr., "History of Task Force Alfa," *op. cit.*, Enclosure (1).
18. Leftwich Jr., "Bong Son Operation," *Marine Corps Gazette*, *op. cit.*, pp. 30-31.
19. *Ibid.*, p. 31.
20. Division of Information, Headquarters, U.S. Marine Corps, Washington, D.C. in Service Information Release No. CGD-107-65, dated April 19, 1965.
21. "Picture Comforts Family—He Won't Be Disfigured," William J. Miles, *The Commercial Appeal*, Memphis, Tennessee, March 12, 1965, p. 1.
22. Leftwich Jr., "Bong Son Operation," *Marine Corps Gazette*, *op. cit.*, p. 31.
23. Jane Leftwich Michael Jr., interview, March 31, 1993, Annandale, Virginia.
24. Leftwich Jr., "History of Task Force Alfa," *op. cit.*
25. Shulimson and Johnson, *op. cit.*, p. 206.
26. Leftwich, "Bong Son Operation," *Marine Corps Gazette*, *op. cit.*, p. 31.
27. Maj. William G. Leftwich Jr., "Americanism Abroad 1966," p. 1, speech given before the Memphis Civitan Club, Memphis, Tennessee, September 20, 1966.
28. *Ibid.*, p. 4.
29. Maj. William G. Leftwich Jr., "Decision at Duc Co," *Marine Corps Gazette*, (Quantico, Virginia: Marine Corps Association, January 1967), p. 36, Quotes and information reprinted with permission and copyright by the *Marine Corps Gazette)*.
30. Schwarzkopf with Petre, *op. cit.*, pp. 110, 119.
31. *Ibid.*, p. 110,
32. *Ibid.*, photo section between pp. 114-115 photos Arnett took of Schwarzkopf at Duc Co, pp. 117-118.

33-38. Leftwich Jr., "Decision at Duc Co," *Marine Corps Gazette*, *op. cit.*, p. 36.

39. *Ibid.*, pp. 36-37.
40. *Western Times*, Sharon Springs, Kansas, "Lt. Richard Goudy Shot Down in Viet Nam," August 13, 1965, p. 1; "No Word From Missing Flier," August 19, 1965, p. 1; "Capt. Richard Goudy Viet Nam Casualty," November 18, 1965, p. 1.
41. Leftwich Jr., "Decision at Duc Co," *op. cit.*, p. 37.

42-46. *Ibid.*, p. 38.

47-48. Department of the Army, Headquarters 173d Airborne Brigade, Command Report for Period 1 August 1965 to 31 October 1965, dated 28 November 1965, "173d Airborne Brigade at THANH BINH PASS, PLEIKU and KONTUM, 10 August 1965-7 September 1965, Combat Operations After Action Report," p. 5.

49. Schwarzkopf with Petre, *op. cit.*, pp.112-113, 119, 122.
50. Westmoreland, *A Soldier Reports, op. cit.*; also MGySgt. Jones, *Quantico Sentry, op. cit.*; also Maj. W.G. Leftwich Jr., *Marine Corps Gazette, op. cit.*; also Maj. W.G. Leftwich Jr., *Shipmate: Magazine of USNA Alumni Association*, *op. cit.*
51. Schwarzkopf with Petre, *op. cit.*, p. 118.
52. Lt.Col. William G. Leftwich Jr., "...and a few Marines," *Naval Proceedings,* (Annapolis: U.S. Naval Institute, August 1968), p. 38, "Reprinted from Proceedings with permission; Copyright © 1968 U.S. Naval Institute/www.navalinstitute.org."

53-54. Charlie Black, "U.S. Advisors Still Important," *The Columbus Enquirer*, Columbus, Ohio, January 13, 1967, p. 4.

55-56. Jones, *Quantico Sentry, op. cit.*

57-58. Leftwich Jr., "Americanism Abroad 1966," *op. cit.*, p. 4.

59. Jack Martin, "Memory Of War Invades Lazy Afternoon," *The Commercial Appeal, op. cit.*, February 22, 1966, p. 2.
60. Leftwich Jr., "Americanism Abroad 1966," *op. cit.*, p. 3.
61. *Ibid.*, p. 7.

62. Barton Fruhman, "War Will 'Just Peter Out'--We'll Win, Says Memphian," *The Commercial Appeal, op. cit.*, February 24, 1966, p. 1.
63. Leftwich Jr., "Americanism Abroad 1966," *op. cit.*, p. 8.

## Chapter 12

1. Hoi An map, Sheet 6640 I: A. BT071631.
2. Cpl. Ed Burriss, "2/1 Marines Led To VC Headquarters," *SEA TIGER*, Vol. VI, No. 35, August 28, 1970, p. 8, publication of the Public Affairs Officer of III Marine Amphibious Force, RVN.
3. Cosmas and Murray, *op. cit.*, pp. 79-80.
4. Dai Loc map, Sheet 6640 IV: A. BT045595.
5. Hoi An map, Sheet 6640 I: A. BT072632.
6. Stephen Crane, *The Red Badge of Courage*, (New York: Pocket Books, 1894), p. 71.
7. Hoi An map, Sheet 6640 I: A. BT084615.
8. 2/1's After Action Report for August 4, 1970, dated, August 5, 1970, pp. 3-4.
9. *Ibid.*, p. 3.
10. *Ibid.*, pp. 1-2.
11. *Ibid.* , p. 3.
12. *SEA TIGER, op. cit.*
13. *Ibid.*
14. *Ibid.;* also 2/1's S-3 Operations Journal for August 4, 1970.
15. Hoi An map Sheet 6640 I: A. BT073632.
16. Capt. William G. "Bill" Leftwich III, "Lt.Col. Bill Leftwich: Remembering the Man Behind the Trophy," paper submitted as fulfillment of requirements for the Publishable Paper Program and the Writing Program at the Amphibious Warfare School, Quantico, Virginia, March 22, 1989.

## Chapter 13

1. Capt. Leftwich III, *Ibid.,* quote sometimes attributed to Lt.Col. William G. Leftwich Jr. p. 2-3.
2. Gary D. Solis, *Son Thang*, (Annapolis, Maryland: Naval Institute Press, 1997), p. 264.
3. Cosmas and Murray, *op. cit.*, p. 351.
4. Don Tate, staff writer for *Scripps Howard*, "Lt.Col. Leftwich Died Against Cloud-Shrouded Hill 864," *Memphis Press-Scimitar,* Memphis, Tennessee, December 3, 1970, p. 1.
5. Chaplain Lloyd Rupp, "Leftwich trophy revisited," *Jet Stream*, Marine Corps Air Station, Beaufort, South Carolina, VOL. XXII, No. 37, September 1980, p. 2.
6. Maj. Bruce H. "Doc" Norton, USMC (Ret.), and Sgt.Maj. Maurice Jacques, USMC (Ret.), *Sergeant Major: The Biography of Sergeant Major Maurice J. Jacques, USMC*, (New York: Ballantine Books, 1995), p. 275.
7. Earl Masaji "Pineapple" Miyamoto, telephone interview, March 22, 1993.

## Chapter 14

1. Attributed to Emiliano Zapata as a slogan during 1910 in the Mexican Revolution and earlier to Jose Julian Marti y Perez (1853-1895) during the Cuban Revolution, original quote, "It is better to die on your feet than to live on your knees!" Reference: Internet, Wikiquote, Wikipedia.
2. Col. Albert C. Smith Jr., USMC (Ret.), letter to Gen. Edwin H. Simmons, USMC (Ret.), director of Marine Corps History and Museum Headquarters, USMC, commenting on statements made by Maj.Gen. Charles F. Widdecke concerning Lt.Col. William G. Leftwich Jr. to be considered for use in the U.S. MARINES IN VIETNAM, Vietnamization and Redeployment, 1970-1971, dtd. May 1, 1983.
3. *Ibid.*, p 114.
4. Norton and Jacques, *op. cit.*, p. 276.
5. *Ibid.*
6. H.W. Courter, CO, Delta Co., 3rd Reconnaissance Battalion, Subject: One Millionth Participant; Nomination of Sgt. John F. Stockman, letter dated March 12, 1969.
7. *Ibid.*

8. *Ibid.*
9. *Ibid.*
10. Cpl. John F. Stockman's letter home to his sister, Diana Lynn Stockman, dated October 24, 1970.
11. *Ibid.*
12. John Ferguson, nephew to John Stockman, emails dated December 31, 2009, January 8, 2010.
13. Stockman's letter to sister, *op. cit.*
14. Dai Loc map, 6640 IV: A. BT042432.
15. Hiep Duc map, Sheet 6640 III: A. BT045426, B. BT002427, C. AT976411, D. AT969389 E. vicinity of AT998412 and AT999428, F. AT970382, G. AT994420.
16. Vietnam Veterans Memorial website: http://thewall-usa.com/guest.asp?recid=50031, 1stLt. Butch Cleveland Harvey, posting by Chip Morin, October 5, 2003.
17. Hiep Duc map, Sheet 6640 III: A. AT857406, B. AT935375, C. AT976411, D. AT975465.

## Chapter 15

1. Col. Brett Wyrick, USAF surgeon with the 332nd Expeditionary Medical Group in Balad, Iraq.
2. Hiep Duc map, Sheet 6640 III: A. AT967407, B. AT961402.
3. Patrol Debrief, Teams War Cloud Mission Impossible and Wage Earner, Capt. Frank S. Blair III's crash site illustration, p. 5, 1630-H November 22, 1970, Da Nang, RVN.
4. Preliminary Report of Aircraft Accident, OPNAVIST 3750.6, November 18, 1970, 1stLt. J.C. McGarigle, Aircraft Safety Officer (ASO) for HMM-263.
5. Supplementary Report of Aircraft Accident, OPNAVIST 3750.6, November 19, 1970, 1stLt. J.C. McGarigle, ASO for HMM- 263.
6. Supplementary Report of Aircraft Accident, OPNAVIST 3750.6, November 22, 1970, 1stLt. J.C. McGarigle, ASO for HMM-263.
7. Hiep Duc map, Sheet 6640 III: A. AT934395, B. AT967407, C. AT979394, D. AT976411.
8. Vietnam Veterans Memorial website: http://thewall-usa.com/guest.asp?recid=50031, 1stLt. Butch Cleveland Harvey, posting by Chip Morin, October 5, 2003.
9. Cosmas and Murray, *op. cit.*, p. 312.
10. Lt.Gen. Bernard E. Trainor, emails "Re: Leftwich," March 1, 2003, and "Re: Appreciate the comments," March 2, 2003.
11. Dr. Gary Solis, Lt.Col. USMC, (Ret.), emails RE: Widdecke II, March 27, 2006.
12. Confederate Gen. Robert E. Lee, (not an exact quote), Letter to his son G.W. Custis Lee (April 5, 1852), published in *The New York Sun* on November 26, 1864; also inscribed beneath his bust in the Hall of Fame on the former New York University campus, New York City, New York, Reference: Internet, Wikiquote, Wikipedia.
13. Dai Loc map, Sheet 6640 IV: A. AT990610.

## Chapter 16

1. Col. Robert D. Heinl Jr., "Marine was heroic in life---and death," *The Detroit News*, Detroit, Michigan, November 23, 1970.
2. Biography of Maj. Gen. John S. Grinalds, (USMC, Ret.), The Citadel (Charleston, South Carolina), website: http://citadel.edu/pao/president/bio.shtml
3. *Press Scimitar,* Memphis, Tennessee, "Perot, Military Officials Pay Tribute to Leftwich," November 27, 1970; also, U.S. Rep. Mendal Rivers' eulogy to Lt.Col. William Groom Leftwich Jr. titled, "Tribute To A Fallen American," in the *Congressional Record*, December 3, 1970, #39903.
4. *The Commercial Appeal,* Memphis, Tennessee, photo caption, "Shared Loss," and interview in Annandale, Virginia with Mrs. Jane (Leftwich) Michael Jr., March 31, 1993.
5. Thomas DeVier, "'Taps' Marks Fallen Marine Hero; 'Always Faithful' Describes Him," *The Commercial Appeal*, Memphis, Tennessee, November 28, 1970.
6. *The Commercial Appeal*, Memphis, Tennessee, "Christening Of Destroyer Honors Memphis Marine," May 28, 1978.
7. NavSource Online: Destroyer Photo Archive, *DD-984 U.S.S. Leftwich* website: navsource.org/archives/05/984

8. *The Commercial Appeal*, Memphis, Tennessee, "City Park Will Be Dedicated To Marine Hero of Vietnam," November 21, 1970, and "Monument to Marine Hero To Be Dedicated Sunday," November 5, 1971.
9. Chaplain Lloyd Rupp, "Leftwich trophy revisited, *Jet Stream*, Marine Corps Air Station, Beaufort, South Carolina, VOL. XXII, No. 37, September 1980.
10. Lt.Col. William G. Leftwich Jr., biography, *Press Scimitar,* Memphis, Tennessee, November 11, 1982, p. 5, located in Special Archives Section of Memphis/Shelby County Public Library and Information Center.
11. William Thomas, "Death of war hero's mother recalls bravery," *The Commercial Appeal*, Memphis, Tennessee, June 16, 1992, pp. B1-2.
12. Leftwich III, "Remembering the Man Behind the Trophy," *op. cit.*, p. 3.
13. Leftwich III, *Ibid.*
14. Heinl Jr., *op. cit.*
15. Buttry and Bajin were from Headquarters and Maintenance Squadron, H&MS-16, for Marine Air Group 16, MAG-16. H&MS-16 had a few helicopters and primarily flew administrative and logistical missions. Marines from H&MS-16 went to the various Sea Knight and Huey squadrons to accrue "strike" credits for combat mission, 20 combat missions, as aerial gunners to earn an Air Medal, according to Alan H. Barbour, Historian, USMC/Combat Helicopter Association, who had 660-plus combat missions as a UH-1E Huey pilot.

## Epilogue

1. Col. Jon T. Hoffman, USMCR, editor, *USMC A Complete History*, Marine Corps Association, (Hong Kong: Hugh Lauter Levin Associates, Inc., 2002), 1970 and 1971, p. 582, 590-593.
2. Records with Unit Information on Military Personnel Who Died During the Vietnam Conflict (COFFELT), *op. cit.*, also "Vietnam Conflict-Casualty Summary" as of June 15, 2004 prepared by Washington Headquarters Services, Directorate for Information Operations Reports.
3. Dr. Fall, *Viet-Nam Witness 1953-66, op. cit.*, p. 309.
4. Dr. Fall, *Hell in a Very Small Place: The Siege of Dien Bien Phu, op. cit.*, p. 416.
5. Dorothy Fall, *op. cit.*, p. 216.
6. Hoffman, *op. cit.*, p. 590.
7. All U.S. Navy raw casualty statistics provided by Vietnam Veterans Memorial Fund website: vvmf.org, Advance Search for Navy Corpsmen personnel KIA in Vietnam.
8. Union Gen. Wm. Tecumseh Sherman's quote, "War is Hell," graduation address at Michigan Military Academy, June 19, 1979, from the *National Tribune*, Washington, D.C., November 26, 1914.

## Postscript

1. Leftwich, "...a few good Marines." *op. cit.*, p. 43.
2. Dr. Bernard B. Fall, Chapter 10, "Diary: The Men," *Street Without Joy,* (Harrisburg, Pennsylvania: The Stackpole Company, 1967), pp., 258-259.

## Perspectives on the Vietnam War—Part II

1. Cpl. Robert G. "Bob" Morris, Nashville, Tennessee , television crew interview at 1st Recon reunion at Col. Bill Drumright's farm, Columbia, Tennessee, May 24, 2003; also, email, October 27, 2009.
2. Lt.Col. David A. "Dave" Marshall, email dated June 20, 2008.
3. LCpl. Howard Ball, emails dated September 10, 11, 2008.
4. Lt.Gen. Wallace C. "Chip" Gregson, USMC (Ret.), emails dated July 6, 7, 2008.
5. Cpl. John D. "J.D." Barber, emails dated July 14, 15, 2008.
6. Susan Rogers Eveland, email dated August 12, 2008
7. HMC Richard J. "Jim" or "Doc" Pearston, USN (Ret.), emails dated July 17, 19, 20; also, October 6, 2009.
8. Lt.Col. Norman Frederick "Pete" Hanner, USMC (Ret.), emails dated July 18, 19, 20, 2008.

9. Georgine Tortorello Hembrough, email dated March 14, 2009.
10. Gy.Sgt. Rodney H. "Rod or Pu" Pupuhi, USMC (Ret.), emails dated February 26 and March 1, 2002.
11. Nick Ut, telephone interview, September 9, 2008.

# Interviews and Correspondence

*Denotes multiple interviews and/or correspondence

Ackman, Dean "Slick," 1st Recon Bn.
Allison, Fred, USMC, MCB Quantico, Virginia.
*Ames, Harvey M.J. "Harv," U.S. State Department's senior advisor to Hoa Vang District, RVN.
*Andrus, Lt.Col. Kermit W. "Andy," (MAG-16 S-3, pilot),
Annis, Claudia Gary, senior editor, *Vietnam Magazine*.
*Aquilina, Robert V., Assistant Head, Reference Branch, USMC History Division, Quantico, Virginia.
*Arick, John C., HML-367 pilot.
Armstrong, Sgt.Maj. Joe.
Arnett, Peter, *Associated Press* war correspondent, Saigon, RVN.
*Arnold, 1stLt. John "Chatterbox Juan or One," HMM-262 pilot.

Bailey, Sgt. Philip, 1st Recon Bn.
*Ball, LCpl. Howard, Forward Observer with 3/5 in 1969.
*Barber, Cpl. John D. "J.D.," HMM-263 crew chief, board member of USMC Combat Helicopter Association and past president, 2001-2007.
*Barbour, Alan H., VMO-2 pilot, Research Historian, History and Archives Division, USMC Combat Helicopter Association.
*Barr, Capt. James B. "Jim," HML 167 pilot.
Barrett, USN Steve "Doc," Navy Corpsman, HMM-364.
Bender, Chuck, childhood friend of Lt.Col. Bill Leftwich Jr., Memphis, Tennessee.
Benson, 1stLt. Gary W. "Hammer," HMM-364 pilot.
*Benson, Lynn, 2ndLt. A.D. Benson's brother.
*Besley, Richard W., U.S. Air Force veteran, childhood friend of 2ndLt. Tony Kupka.
*Bond Jr., Maj. William H. "Bill," VNMC advisor; CO, 1st Force Recon.
*Bouley, Cpl. John T., HML-167 doorgunner.
*Boyd, Cpl. Roger L., HMM-263 crew chief.
*Boyer, Lynn L., HML-167 pilot.
*Bradley, 2ndLt. John Curtis "Curt," Landon School '64 graduate, close friend to 2ndLt. Tony Kupka.
*Brennan, 1stLt. Michael, artillery Forward Observer, Kilo Co., 3/7.
*Brust, Sgt. Robert M. "Bob," HML-167 crew chief.
*Bub, Maj. Ronald L. "Ron," S-3/XO, 1st Recon Bn.
*Burin, Capt. Charles E. "Chuck," "Hostage Igor," VMO-2, OV-10 Bronco pilot.
*Bushnell, USN Lt. Scott, U.S. Naval Academy website: webmaster@usna64.org

*Casey, Sgt. James R. "Jim," S-3 Operations NCO, HMM-263.
*Causey, 1stLt. David W., HML-367 pilot.
*Ciccarelli, PFC Ciro "Chick," 1/9's S-3 radio operator (1967).
Cleland, Sgt. Roger, patrol leader, Echo Co., 1st Recon Bn.
Connolly Jr., 1stLt. John P., (Plt. Cmdr., Alpha 2, 1st Engineers),
Cornetta, 1stLt. Ron, HMM-263 pilot.
Craig, 1stLt. Larry, Hotel Plt. Cmdr./XO, 2/1.
*Cross, 1stLt. David L., HMM-364 pilot.
*Cross, Col. Mike, USMC (Ret.), Golf 2, 2/1; 1st Recon Bn.
*Curtis, MSgt. George T., USMC (Ret.), HMM-364 flight line.

Dalton, Debra R., West Point Parents Club Coordinator and Directorate of Communications.

(USMA Rhode's Scholar information).
*Delfarno, Maureen, 2ndLt. Garry Schanck's family friend.
DeSantis, Maj. Brian, Joint POW/MIA Accounting Command (JPAC) Public Affairs.
*Doerr, Doug, USMC Museum.
Donohoe, HM2 "Doc," Navy Corpsman.
*Drumright, Col. William C. "Wild Bill," CO, 2/26; CO, 1st Recon Bn.

*Eames, SSgt. Bailey Newman "Atom Ant," H&S Co. radioman, with Echo 2/1.
*Erckman, USAF Capt. Paul N., (MD, flight surgeon).
*Espinoza Jr., MSgt. Barney, SNCOIC, S-3, HMM-263.
Evans, Mark, Naval Aviation History, HQMC, (Aircraft Accident, November 18, 1970).
*Evans, Sgt. Thomas P. "Tom," mortar team, Alpha, Co., 1/9.
*Eveland, Susan (Rogers), sister of 1stLt. Curt Rogers.

*Fall, Dorothy, wife of Dr. Bernard B. Fall, author of *Bernard Fall, Memories of a Soldier-Scholar* and *Last Reflections on a War: Bernard B. Fall on Viet-Nam.*
*Fallon, 1stLt. Michael O. "Mike," Bravo Co. Plt. Cmdr., 1st Recon Bn.
Falmouth, Town of, George Trudeau, webmaster, population for Falmouth, Massachusetts in 1969 and 2006, website: gtrudeau@town.falmouth.ma.us
Falmouth Public Library, Adrienne Latimer, Reference Department, *Falmouth* (Massachusetts) *Enterprise* article on 2ndLt. Tony Kupka, dated April 29, 1969, p. 1. Information received February 22, 2006, website: falmouthreference@mail.publiclibrary.org
*Ferrante, Cpl. Joe, 1/9 field radio operator (1967).
*Fawcett, Col. Robert J. "Bob," USMC (Ret.), Plt. Cmdr, Echo 1, 2/1; Plt. Cmdr., Alpha Co., 1st Recon Bn.
*Feldman, Sgt. Larry M., Echo Co., S-3 radioman, 1st Recon Bn.
*Ferguson, John, Cpl. John F. Stockman's nephew.
Fick, Capt. Nathaniel C. "Nat," 1st Recon Bn.
*Floom, 1stLt. Marvin Hubert "Marv," (Col., USMC, Ret.), 1st Recon Bn.
Flying Leatherneck Historical Foundation, MCAS Miramar, Robin Daubert, office manager.
Foos, Deb, Sharon Springs, Kansas.
Foxx, Sara Michelle, office manager, Vietnam Veterans Memorial Fund, website: vvmf.org.
*Forbush, 1stLt. Wayne, HMM-364 pilot.
*Ford, Col. Walter G., USMC (Ret.), Publisher/Editor, *Leatherneck* Magazine, Quantico, Virginia.
Fraley, Gladys, mother of PFC Charlie Fraley.
*Fuller, Dave, Fox 3 RTO, 2/5.

*Galloway, Joseph L. "Joe," *United Press International* war correspondent, Vietnam, 1965-66, '71, '73, '75; Saigon bureau chief, 1965-66; co-author with Lt.Gen. H.G. 'Hal' Moore, U.S. Army (Ret.), of *We Were Soldiers Once…and Young* as well as *We Are Soldiers Still: A Journey Back to the Battlefields of Vietnam.*
Garcia, 1stLt. Anthony J. "Tony," HMM-364 pilot.
Gedra, M.A., Reference Section, Textural Archives Services Division, National Archives and Records Administration.
*Geis, Lt.Col. Royall "Goose," HMM-263 pilot.
*Gifford, Sgt. Larry K. "Giff," Team Thin Man team leader, Charlie Co., 1st Recon Bn.
Gladwin, Lee A., archivist, Electronic and Special Media Records Services Division, National Archives (USA).
Gleim, 1stLt. Pete, HML-167 pilot.
Godwin, Lt.Col. Robert E. "Bob," HMM-164 pilot.
Goetz, 1stLt. Peter F. "Pete," HMM-263 pilot.
*Goudy, USN MM2 Mark S., USAF Capt. Richard Goudy's son.
*Gray, Rosanna, U.S. Naval Academy, Nimitz Library, Reference Technician.
Green, Jack A., Naval Historical Center, Public Affairs Officer.

Greene, Lt.Col. Michael R. "Mike," Plt. Cmdr, Bravo Co., 1st Recon Bn.; Plt. Cmdr., Golf 3, 2/1.
Gregory, Gary, Naval Safety Center.
*Gregson, Lt.Gen. Wallace C. "Chip," USMC (Ret.). Delta Co., also S-3A lieutenant in 1st Recon Bn., 1969-70.
*Grinalds, Maj.Gen. John Southy, S-3 Operations officer, 2/1; S-2 Intelligence officer, 1st Marine Regiment.
*Gruber, Lisa, Sgt. Robert Donnell II's sister.
*Guay, Lt.Col. Robert P. "Bob," MAG-16.

Hall, Jerry, HMM-262 crew chief.
*Halvorsen, LCpl. Ron "Gap," Team Nail Brush, 1st Recon Bn.
Hammers, Ann, head of Casualty Section, HQMC.
*Hanley, John J. "Doc," Navy Corpsman, 1st Medical Bn.
*Hanner, 1stLt. Norman Frederick "Pete," HMM-262 pilot.
*Hare, MSgt. John F., Team Mission Impossible, 1st Recon Bn.
Harris, Frank P., Reference Services, County of Los Angeles, Public Library, Norwalk, California.
*Harvey, James Richard "Jim," 1stLt. Butch Harvey's brother.
*Harvey, Thomas James "Tom," 1stLt. Butch Harvey's brother.
*Hawkins, Col. "Hawk."
*Helweg, Lt.Col. Paul, USA, University of Rhode Island ROTC Alumni Association president.
*Hembrough, Georgine (Tortorella), 2ndLt. David Skibbe's fiancée in 1970.
*Herlicka, PFC Albert Udo "Al," Team Grade Level, Delta Co., 1st Recon Bn.
*Hillmann, PFC Fred, FAC radioman with 1/9.
*Hinton, 1stLt. Allyn, HML-167 pilot.
*Holmes, Mildred (McVey), Capt. LaVoy Don McVey's mother.
*Huegel, Cpl. Roland C. " Ron," Bravo Co., 1st Recon Bn.
*Hungate, PFC Robert "Bob," Echo Co., 1st Recon Bn.
*Hunt, 1stLt. James L. "Jim," HML-167 pilot.
*Hurley, Donna, U.S. Naval Academy, Nimitz Library, Reference Department.
Hyson, Maj. T.C., Aircraft Mishap Investigations Instructor, School of Aviation Safety, NPS Monterey, California.

*Jacoby Jr., Maclear "Mac," Landon Middle School principal/teacher.
Jenson, Maj. Duane, S-3 chief and HMM-364 pilot.
*Johnson, Ed, (3rd Amtracs).
Johnson, Lt.Col. Gregory J. "Greg," Penn State.
*Joint POW/MIA Accounting Command, (JPAC), Maj. Rumi Nielson-Green, OPA, Camp Smith, Hawaii.
*Joint Task Force-Full Accounting, 1stLt. Ken Hall, USAF, PAO, Camp Smith, Hawaii.
Jorgensen, Janis, U.S. Naval Institute Photo Archivist.
Judge Advocate General Office, Department of the Navy, Washington Navy Yard, D.C., USN Lt.Cmdr. E. A. Miller, JAGC, Deputy Director, Claims, Investigations and Tort Litigation.
*Judge, Lt.Col. Bruce, assistant Chief of Staff G-1, Training and Education Command.

Keen, 1stSgt. Lawrence E. "Larry," 1st Recon Bn.
*Keenan, Col. John A., USMC (Ret.), Editor, *Marine Corps Gazette,* Quantico, Virginia.
Kelley, Gen. Paul X., CO, 1st Marine Regiment, 28th CMC.
Kemp, Barbara E., U.S. Naval Academy, Nimitz Library, Head, Reference & Instruction Department, Annapolis, Maryland.
*Kenny, 1stLt. John Patrick "Pat" or call sign "Swift Chuck," HMM-364 pilot.
*Keys, Lt.Gen. William C. "Bill," CO, Delta Co., 1/9.
*King, 1stLt. Patrick, HML-167 pilot.
*Klimp, Lt.Gen. Jack W., USMC (Ret.), Plt. Cmdr./CO Golf Co., 2/1.
*Knapp, 1stLt. W.R. "Randy," HML-167 pilot.

*Kosinski, 1stLt. John L., HMM-262 pilot.
*Kozakowski, LCpl. Raymond J. "Ski," Team Wage Earner, 1st Recon Bn.
Kratz, GS-15 J.J., Deputy AC/S G5 Plans and Policy, Marine Forces Pacific, Camp Smith, Hawaii.

*Laba, Christine, Records Service Section, Code MMSB-10, Unit Diaries, Headquarters, USMC.
Lakin, USAF Col. (Ret.) John W., father of 2ndLt. John Lakin.
Landon School Alumni, Kupka Distinguished Alumnus Award website: landon.net/page.cfm?p=1156
*LaRue, Roger "The Walrus," team leader, Delta Co., 1st Recon Bn.
*Larson, Larry, Marine at Khe Sanh 1967, provided USMC photo of Dr. Bernard B. Fall with Charlie Co., 1/9, February 21, 1967.
*Ledbetter Jr., Col. Walter R. "Walt," USMC (Ret.), CO, HMM-263; S-3 chief, MAG-16.
*Leftwich III, Maj. William G. "Bill," son of Lt.Col. Bill Leftwich Jr.
Leftwich, USN Cmdr. Scott Ferrer, son of Lt.Col. Bill Leftwich Jr.
*Lippincott, USN Jeff "Doc," Navy Corpsman, Golf 3, 2/5.
*Lokey, Candace, The National League of Families of POWs and MIAs in Southeast Asia.
*Los Angeles Public Library, County of, Norwalk, California, Kathy Nieser and Frank P Harris, Reference Services.
*Luhrs, LCpl. Timothy James "Tim," Team Chili Pepper, 1st Recon Bn.
*Lyall, Beverly, Archives Technician, U.S. Naval Academy, Annapolis, Maryland.

*Marine Corps Heritage Foundation, Washington Navy Yard, Vietnam War CDs.
*Marine Corps Historical Center, Frederick J. Graboske, Head Archives Section, Navy Yard, Washington, D.C.
*Marshall, 1stLt. David A. "Dave," FAC, 1/9; H&MS-16, pilot; VMA-223, pilot.
*Martin, 1stLt. Gerald W. "Jerry," HMM-263 pilot.
*Martin, 1stLt. James M. "Jim," HMM-263 pilot.
*Mason, PFC Edward A. "Ed," radioman, India 1, 3/5.
*Maxwell, Capt. Jack C., S-2 chief, HMM-164, pilot.
McCaughey Jr., Lt.Col. Douglas A. "Doug," CO, HML-167.
McMonagle, Maj.Gen. James J. "Joe," close friend to Lt.Col. Bill Leftwich Jr.
*McVey, Jeff, son of Capt. LaVoy Don McVey.
*McVey, Sally, Jeff McVey's wife.
McVey, Shawn, son of Capt. LaVoy Don McVey.
Mehalic, Leo S., USNA Public Information/Webmaster, Public Affairs Office.
*Michael Jr., Jane (Leftwich), Lt.Col. Bill Leftwich Jr.'s wife.
*Mitchell, LeeAnn, Director of Marketing and Communications, Marine Corps Association, Quantico, Virginia.
*Moore, Lt.Col. Terrence L. "Terry," Team Mission Impossible, 1st Recon Bn.
Morin, 1stLt. Charles Chipps "Chip," Plt. Cmdr, Bravo 3, 1st Recon Bn.
*Morris, Cpl. Robert G. "Bob," RTO, India Co., 3/5; Team Cayenne patrol leader, 1st Recon Bn.
*Morschauser, 1stLt. Michael "Mike," HML-167 pilot.
*Mullins, USN HM3 Thurman G. "Doc," Navy Corpsmen, 1st Recon Bn.
Murphy, Cpl. John, HMM-165.

*Nanson, Sid, aircraft historian, Thirsk, England.
National Archives & Records Administration (NARA), Clifford Snyder, Archivist.
*Navy Safety Center, Department of the Navy, Rear Admiral S.A. Turcotte, USN, Norfolk, Virginia.
Neimeyer, Dr. Charles P., Head, USMC History Division and Chief Historian, Quantico, Virginia.
*Nelson Sr., Col. Albert Oscar, father of 2ndLt. Al Nelson Jr.
Nitti, Catherine (Harvey), 1stLt. Butch Harvey's widow.
Nixon Presidential Material, Charles M. Sutton, archivist, Nixon condolence letter to 2ndLt. Ted. Vivilacqua's family, burial location., Website: Project.Nixon@nara.gov.
Norman, Tom, HMM-263.

North Carolina Wesleyan College, Rocky Mount, North Carolina, Tom Maze, Alumni/Development Office, Subject: Butch Harvey.
*Norton, 1stLt. Raymond J. "Ray," HMM-263 pilot.
Nyland, Gen. William L. "Spider," Assistant CMC.

O'Bryon II, Tom W., Landon School '64 graduate and close friend to 2ndLt. Tony Kupka.
*Ondrick, Maj. Robert M. "Bob," S-3 chief, HML-167 pilot.
*Orahood, 1stLt. Douglas R. "Doug," HMM-364 pilot.
*Owens, Lt.Col. Patrick G. "Pat," HML-367 pilot.

Parry, Thomas Victor "Tom," (Lt., USN, Ret.), '68 USNA graduate and 2ndLt. Vivi Vivilacqua's friend.
Pate, Lt.Col. Gerald, CO, HMM-262.
*Pearston, USN HM2 Richard J. "Jim" or "Doc," Navy Corpsman, 1st Recon Bn.
Pendleton, MCB Camp, History and Museums.
Pendleton, MCB Camp, Public Affairs Office.
Perot Sr., H. Ross, '53 USNA graduate and close friend to Lt.Col. Bill Leftwich Jr.
*Plunkett, Cpl. Michael S. "Steve," Team Thin Man point man, Charlie Co., 1st Recon Bn.
Porcaro, Patty, Head of Readers Services, Dinand Library, College of the Holy Cross in Worcester, Massachusetts.
*Porpotage II, 1stLt. Frank M., XO, Echo Co., 1st Recon Bn.
*Post, 1stLt. Barry, 11th Regiment, Artillery FO.
Powell Jr., Edward Bennett "Ed," (Lt., USN, Ret.), '68 USNA graduate and 2ndLt. Vivi Vivilacqua's friend.
Powell, Sgt. Dave, HMM-262.
*Preston, Janet R. (Skibbe), sister to MIA 2ndLt. David Skibbe.
*Pupuhi, Gy.Sgt. Rodney H. "Rod" or "Pu," Team Mission Impossible, 1st Recon Bn.
*Pyle, Richard, *Associated Press* war correspondent in Vietnam from 1968-73; Saigon *AP* bureau chief, 1970-73, co-author with Horst Faas of *Lost Over Laos*.

*Resmondo, John W., Summerdale, Alabama, background information on 1stLt. John Lassitter.
*Rider, Maj. James W. "Rifle," HML-367 pilot.
*Rivard, PFC David A. "Bozo," Echo 2 RTO, 1st Recon Bn.
*Roberts, 1stLt. George "Skip," VMO-2, OV-10 pilot.
*Robinson, Lt.Col. Gilford G. "Gil," G-3, 1stMarDiv; S-2, 2/1.
Roush, Gary, Vietnam Helicopter Pilots Assn.
Royce, 1stLt. Doug, HMM-364 pilot.
*Rudd, PFC Thomas M. "Tom," (1st Recon).

*Saal, 1stLt. Tom, TBS Plt. Cmdr.; 5th Marines, RVN.
Sage, MSgt. Robert, U.S. Army, A/15, 9th Infantry Division, 1968-70.
Samuelson, Julie K., editor/publisher, *Western Times*, Sharon Springs, Kansas, background information on Capt. Richard Lee Goudy, USAF.
Sanders, Cpl. Jerry "Sandy," HMM-263 crew chief.
*Schanck-Wasilewski, Mary Arvaline, 2ndLt. Garry Schanck's sister.
Schmitz, USN "Doc Lurch," Navy Corpsman, Golf Co., 2/26.
Schneider, Cpl. Michael J., Bravo Co., 1st Recon Bn.
Scholten, Michael J., '68 USNA graduate.
*Schwartz, Eric "Doc," Navy Corpsman, Team Wage Earner, 1st Recon Bn.
*Sellers, Maj. Wiley J., S-3 chief, HMM-262 pilot.
Sharr, Maj. Dan, HML-167 pilot.
*Sherman Jr., USN Lt. John, Landon School '64 graduate and 2ndLt. Tony Kupka's friend.
*Silva, Capt. Herb, HML-367 pilot.
*Silvoso II, 2ndLt. Joseph A. "Joe," Plt. Cmdr., Alpha 3, 1/1.
*Simpson, Doug, S-3 NCO, HML-367.

*Simpson, LCpl. J.H. "Mike," Team Turf Club, Charlie Co., 1st Recon Bn.
*Skibbe, Jeff, first cousin to 2ndLt. David Skibbe.
*Slack, Brig.Gen. Paul D., 3rd Bn., VNMC.
Smith Jr., Col. Albert C., G-2, 1stMarDiv.
*Smith, U.S. Army Spec. 4 Richard "Dick."
*Snider, USN HM3 (Master Chief Hospital Corpsman, Ret.) David L. "Doc," Navy Corpsman, Delta Co, 1st Recon Bn.
Stathis, Tom, *Associated Press* Regional Picture Editor, Los Angeles Bureau.
*Stith, Capt. Fred, HMM-164 pilot.
*Strausbaugh, Gy.Sgt. Joseph "Joe," Echo 1 platoon sergeant, 2/1.
*Syler, USN Bob "Doc Bob," Navy Corpsman, Alpha Co., 1/9.

*Tanselle, G. Thomas, senior vice president, John Simon Guggenheim Memorial Foundation, New York City, New York.
*Tomoff, Joan M. (Skibbe), sister to MIA 2ndLt. David Skibbe.
Tornga, 1stLt. John.
*Trainor, Lt.Gen. Bernard E. "Mick," CO, 1/5; CO, 1st Recon Bn.
*Tripp, 2ndLt.Raymond W. "Ray," (actually Tripicchio), (Plt. Cmdr., Alpha 1, 1/1),
Turner, Gary, U.S. Army, Vietnam 1967-68; honoring Capt. Richard Goudy at Kansas State University.

Ut, Nick, *Associated Press* photographer in Vietnam.

*Valentino, 1stLt. Bill, HMM-263 pilot, 1st Recon Bn.'s ALO/FAC.
*Van Nortwick, Lt.Col. John, CO, HMM-263.
*Vernier, 1stLt. Darcy A., HMM-263 pilot.

*Walker, Sarah Goudy, widow of USAF Capt. Richard Goudy.
Wally, Robert "Bob," Assistant Director for Alumni Career Services, College of the Holy Cross in Worcester, Massachusetts
*Walsh Jr., William Bertalan "Bill," Landon School '64 graduate and 2ndLt. Tony Kupka's friend.
Warner, Maj. Gilbert A., *Leftwich Trophy* recipients information, Marine Corps University, Quantico, Virginia.
Warren, Capt. Bill, CO, Bravo Co., 1st Recon Bn.
*Webb Jr., 1stLt. (SecNav, U.S. Sen.) James H. "Jim," Plt. Cmdr.,/CO, Delta Co., 1/5, author of *Fields of Fire, A Sense of Honor, Lost Soldiers, Something to Die For, The Emperor's General.*
*Weidenbacher, PFC William J. "Weid," Alpha Co., 1/9 field clerk.
*West, LCpl. Ed, FAC radioman with Alpha 3, 1/1, author of *Gopher Broke: The Story of 'Blood, Sweat & Tears' And the Marines of 3rd Platoon, Alpha Co., 1/1.*
*Whitaker, Jeff, *The Tennessean.*
*Whitehurst, 1stLt. Neil, HML-367 pilot.
Wiedhahn, Col. Warren, close friend to Lt.Col. Bill Leftwich Jr.
*Williams, LCpl. Dwight R., HML-167, crew chief.
*Williams, Col. L.K. "Les," HMM-263 pilot.
*Wilson, Lt.Col. Paul E., HMM-263 pilot.
*Wise, 1stLt. Walter R. "Walt' or "Worm," HMM-364 pilot/ASO.
*Woidyla, Capt. Bill, HMM-371 pilot.
*Woods, Cpl. Doug, USMC combat correspondent/photographer.

*Yoder, Sgt. Bill Joder, City of Long Beach, California webmaster.
*York, Don, MMAF.

*Zeller, 1stLt. Don, HMM-263 pilot, 1/1 ALO/FAC.
*Zoeller, Chuck. *Associated Press* Photo Archives, Buffalo, New York.
Zuppke, 1stLt. Thomas S. "Hooper," HMM-263 pilot.

# Bibliography

*AP Wirephoto* of a wounded and under fire VNMC advisor Maj. Bill Leftwich Jr. taken by Huynh Cong La, also known as Huynh Thanh My, *AP* staff photographer, dated March 9, 1965.

"Armel-Leftwich Visitor Center Exhibits…Opens May 1995," USNA, news release, March 1995.

Arnett, Peter, *Live From the Battlefield, From Vietnam to Baghdad, 35 Years in the World's War Zones*, (New York: Simon & Schuster, 1994).

Baldwin, Hanson W., Military Editor, *New York Times*, "We Are Not Alone in Vietnam," reprinted in the *Reader's Digest*, May 1968, p. 125.

*Baltimore Sun, The,* "Hero of War Dies in Crash," November 20, 1970.

Basic School, The, MCB Quantico, Camp Barnett, Charlie Co. 1969, Mess Night, January 14, 1969 publication/platoon group and snapshot photos of graduating officers, teaching staff, tradition cited, schedule of the night's celebration/guest speakers and listing of superior officers.

Beeler, Capt. Robert A., CO, India Co., 3/7, condolence letter to Al Nelson's family dated May 31, 1969.

BeVier, Thomas, "Boyhood Dreams Of Military Glory Led Straight And True To Destiny," *The Commercial Appeal,* November 20, 1970.

BeVier, Thomas, "'Taps' Marks Fallen Marine Hero; 'Always Faithful' Describes Him," *The Commercial Appeal*, November 28, 1970.

Black, Charles, "U.S. Advisors Still Important," *The Columbus Enquirer*, Columbus, Ohio, January 13, 1967, p. 4.

Blair III, Capt. Frank S., (H&S Co. CO), and Moore, Gy.Sgt. Terry (Mission Impossible patrol leader), 5-page 1st Recon Patrol Debrief, November 22, 1970 with accompanying crash site illustration.

Burriss, Cpl. Ed, "2/1 Marines Led To VC Headquarters," *SEA TIGER*, Vol. VI, No. 35, August 28, 1970, p. 8, publication of the Public Affairs Office, III Marine Amphibious Force.

Cash, John A.; Albright, John; and Sandstrum, Allan W., *Seven Firefights in Vietnam*, (New York: Bantam Books, 1985).

Chapman Jr., CMC Gen. Leonard F., letter to Al Nelson Sr. family dated April 1, 1970 awarding son Bronze Star posthumously.

Chastain, Wayne, staff writer, *Memphis Press-Scimitar,* "On Way to Front for Second Tour, Col. Leftwich Confident of Our Policy In Vietnam, April 13, 1970.

Chong, Denise, *The Girl in the Picture, The Story of Kim Phuc, the Photograph, and the Vietnam War*, (New York: Viking Penguin, 2000).

Citadel, The, Maj.Gen. John Grinalds biography and awards, website: http://citadel.edu/pao/president/bio.html

*Commercial Appeal, The*, Memphis, Tennessee, "Christening Of Destroyer Honors Memphis Marine," May 28, 1978.

*Commercial Appeal, The*, Memphis Tennessee, "City Park Will Be Dedicated To Marine Hero Of Vietnam," November 21, 1970, and "Monument to Marine Hero To Be Dedicated Sunday," November 5, 1971.

*Commercial Appeal, The*, Memphis Tennessee, "Leftwich Gets Navy Cross For Heroic Action In War," May 1, 1965.

*Commercial Appeal, The*, Memphis, Tennessee, "Leftwich Honored," August 26, 1978, caption and photo of Mattie Leftwich with Adm. Thomas B. Hayward at the commissioning of the *USS Leftwich.*

*Commercial Appeal, The*. Memphis, Tennessee, "Death Strikes Groom Leftwich," March 26, 1966, and "Rites Are Planned Today For W. Groom Leftwich," March 27, 1966.

*Commercial Appeal, The,* Memphis, Tennessee, "Top Figures To Attend Leftwich Services Friday," November 25, 1970.

*Congressional Medal of Honor Library, Vietnam, The Names, The Deeds, The*, The Complete and Authoritative Record of the Men Who Received America's Supreme Honor For Heroism

Under Fire, (New York: The Dell Publishing Co, Inc., 1983).

*Congressional Record,* December 3, 1970, #39903, U.S. Rep. Mendal Rivers of South Carolina, eulogy to Lt.Col. William G. Leftwich Jr., titled, "Tribute To A Fallen American."

*Corpus Christi Caller,* Corpus Christi, Texas, obituary for "2ndLt. P.N. Huth," July 1969.

Cosmas, Graham A. and Murray, Terrence P., USMC, *U.S. Marines in Vietnam, Vietnamization and Redeployment, 1970-1971,* (Washington, D.C.: History and Museums Division, Headquarters, U.S. Marine Corps, 1986).

*Daily News, The,* "Memphis Marine Is Decorated For Vietnamese Action In Directing Troops While Wounded," Photo/Caption, Memphis, Tennessee, April 1, 1965, p. 1.

Davis, Walter B., *MARINE!: The Life of Lt.Gen. Lewis B. Puller, USMC (Ret.),* (Boston: Little, Brown and Co., 1962).

Drumright, Lt.Col. Wm. C. "Wild Bill," Personal Letter to Capt. "Mac" McVey's mother, Mildred (McVey) Holmes, March 26, 1970; follow-up letter in response to Mrs. Holmes query letter of April 13, dated April 17, 1970.

Evans, Thomas P., *A Poverty of Thoughts,* (New York: iUniverse, Inc., July 2007).

Evans, Thomas P., *Home From the War: Memoir of a "Walking Dead" Survivor,* (New York: Writer's Club, later called iUniverse, Inc., September 2000).

Evans, Thomas P., "Vietnam War: Death on 'The Street Without Joy,'" *Leatherneck,* Quantico, Virginia, July 1996.

Fall, Dr. Bernard B., biographical information, Library of Congress, The, Digital Reference Team, Washington, D.C.

Fall, Dr. Bernard B., *Hell in a Very Small Place: The Siege of Dien Bien Phu.* (Philadelphia: J.B. Lippincott Company, 1967).

Fall, Dr. Bernard B., Inventory of His Personal Papers, John F. Kennedy National Archives and Records Administration, Washington, D.C.

Fall, Dr. Bernard B., *Street Without Joy,* (Harrisburg, Pennsylvania: The Stackpole Company, 1967).

Fall, Dr. Bernard B., "Street Without Joy: Operation Camargue," *Marine Corps Gazette,* January, 1962, pp. 34-42.

Fall, Dr. Bernard B., *Viet-Nam Witness,* 1953-66, (New York: Frederick A. Praeger, Inc., Publishers, 1966).

Fall, Dorothy, *Bernard Fall, Memories of a Soldier-Scholar,* (Washington, D.C.: Potomac Books, Inc., 2006).

Fall, Dorothy, from the notes of Dr. Bernard B. Fall, *Last Reflections on a War,* (New York: Schocken Books, 1964).

Fall, Dorothy, Lt.Col. William G. Leftwich Jr.'s letter sent to Dr. Bernard B. Fall's widow in either January or February 1968 requesting permission and annotation of an article prepared for publication to the *Marine Corps Gazette* in March 1968 titled, "An Afternoon With Bernard Fall."

Fall, Dorothy, return letter from Dorothy Fall to Lt.Col. Leftwich, February 6, 1968.

*Falmouth Enterprise,* "Marine Lieut. Kupka Dies in Viet Fighting," Vol. LXXIV No. 104, April 29, 1969, Pg. 1, microfiche information provided by Falmouth Public Library, Reference Dept., Falmouth, Massachusetts.

Ford, Col. Walt, USMC (Ret.), Publisher/Editor, *Leatherneck* Magazine, Quantico, Virginia.

Friguglietti, James, "Fall, Bernard B.," American National Biography Online, February 2000.

Fruhman, Barton, "War Will 'Just Peter Out'—We'll Win, Says Memphian," *The Commercial Appeal,* February 24, 1966.

Fruhman, Barton, "War Veteran Says US Is Winning," *The Commercial Appeal,*" September 21, 1966.

Fulbright, Alice, "Mother to attend ship honors," *The Commercial Appeal,* August 27, 1978.

Gedra, M.A., Reference Section, Textural Archives Services Division, National Archives and Records Administration, Subj.: U.S. Army's Vietnam Combat Activities for 173rd Airborne Brigade, July 28-September 7, 1965.

Godwin, Lt.Col. Robert E. "Bob," provided Vietnam War CD #82, HMM-164.

*Handbook for U.S. Forces in Vietnam*, Foreword by U.S. Army Gen. William C. Westmoreland, MAC-V commander, Armed Forces Information and Education Department of Defense, DoD Gen-25/DA, Pam, 360-521/NAVPERS, 15222/AFP, 190-1-2/NAVMC 2612.

Heinl Jr., Col. R.D., News Military Analyst, "Marine was heroic in life—and death," Opinion, *The Detroit News*, November 23, 1970.

Hodgins, 1stLt. Michael, *Reluctant Warrior, A Marine's True Story of Duty and Heroism in Vietnam*, (New York: Ivy Books, 1996).

Hoffman, Col. Jon T., USMCR, editor, *USMC A Complete History*, Marine Corps Association, (Hong Kong: Hugh Lauter Levin Associates, Inc., 2002).

*Huntington Park Daily Sentinel*, Huntington Beach, California, "Theodore Vivilacqua Rosary Wednesday," May 27, 1969, A-3.

*Huntington Park Daily Sentinel*, Huntington Park, California, "Theodore Vivilacqua, Scholar, Grid Star, Dies In Vietnam War," May 23, 1969, p. B-1.

Joint Task Force-Full Accounting, Camp Smith, Honolulu, Hawaii.

Jones, MGy.Sgt. Mel, "Maj. Leftwich Called Best Advisor In Vietnam," *Quantico Sentry*, May 6, 1966.

Jones, Lt.Gen. William K., CO Fleet Marine Force, Pacific, Silver Star citation for Lt.Col. William G. Leftwich Jr. for the August 4, 1970 innovative heliborne operation around Phong Ha and Quang Ha (1) that killed 12 VC commanders/security forces and captured another 12.

Judge, PFC T.J., "Navy Cross, Bronze Stars And Air Medals Bestowed On Ten During Ceremonies Here," *Quantico Sentry*, Quantico, Virginia, April 29, 1966, p. 1.

Landon Alumni: Anthony Edward Kupka '64 Distinguished Alumnus Award, history, eligibility, past award winners, website: landon.net/alumnia/kupka.htm

Lawless, Chuck, *The Marine Book*, (New York: Thames and Hudson, 1988).

"Leftwich Trophy for Outstanding Leadership," Marine Corps Order 1650.32C, Dec. 14, 1988.

Leftwich Jr., Maj. William G., USMC, "Americanism Abroad 1966," speech given before the *Memphis Civitan Club* in Memphis, Tennessee, on September 20, 1966.

Leftwich Jr., Maj. William G., USMC, "An Afternoon With Bernard Fall," *Marine Corps Gazette*, March 1968, pp. 25-27.

Leftwich Jr., Lt.Col. William G., USMC, "...and a few Marines," *Naval Proceedings*, the U.S. Naval Institute, August 1968, pp. 34-45, Leftwich Jr., Maj. W.G., USMC, "Bong Son Operation," *Marine Corps Gazette*, June 1966, pp. 29-31.

Leftwich Jr., Maj. William G., USMC, "Completion of Tour Report," 25 pages, report from Maj. Leftwich as Senior Marine Advisor, Naval Advisory Group, MACV to Chief, Naval Advisory Group, MACV, includes History of Task Force Alfa, 11Feb-28Dec1965; Statistical Analysis; and Campaign Map.

Leftwich Jr., Maj. W.G., USMC, "COVAN MY, American Advisor," *Shipmate: USNA Alumni Association Magazine*, November 1966.

Leftwich Jr., Maj. William G., USMC, "Decision at Duc Co," *Marine Corps Gazette*, (Quantico, Virginia: Marine Corps Association, January 1967), p. 35-38.

Leftwich Jr., Maj., William G., USMC, "Freedom, My Heritage, My Responsibility," entry into the Valley Forge Historical Society Essay Contest, 1967.

Leftwich Jr., Lt.Col. W.G., USMC, "Management By Suggestion," Scrapbook, *Marine Corps Gazette*, November, 1968, pp. 25-25.

Leftwich Jr., Lt.Col. W.G., USMC, "The Newest Breed," *Shipmate: USNA Alumni Association Magazine*, November 1968, pp. 7-9, 13.

Leftwich Jr., Lt.Col. William G., USMC, "Vietnamization Marine Corps Style," *Shipmate: USNA Alumni Association Magazine*, November 1970.

Leftwich III, Capt. W.G., USMC, "Remembering the Man Behind the Trophy," paper submitted as fulfillment of requirements for the Publishable Paper Program and the Writing Program at the Amphibious Warfare School, Quantico, Virginia, March 22, 1989.

Leftwich III, Maj. W.G., USMC (Ret), research notes including 12 legal-sized pages, photos, newspaper clippings, magazine articles, copies of Marine Corps awards certificates, March 27-28, 1993.

Library of Congress, The U.S., Digital Reference Team, "Dr. Bernard B. Fall."

Long Beach, City of, California, website, Bill Joder, Webmaster@longbeach.gov, Vivilacqua information and Maywood statistics.

*Lucky Bag, 1953*, June 6, 1953, 109 Academic Year, United States Naval Academy yearbook, Annapolis, Maryland, (Washington: United States Government Printing Office, 1953).

*Marine Guide To The Republic of Vietnam,* September 20, 1968.

Marine Corps Historical Center, Danny Crawford, head, Reference Section, History and Museums Division provided Lt.Col. Leftwich's biography, Navy Cross and Silver Star citations, *Leftwich Trophy* information, extracts from Command Chronology, 2/1, August 4, 1970 and 1st Recon Battalion, November 18, 1970, in letter dated November 18, 1992.

Marine Corps History and Museum Division, Archives Section, (Frederick J. Graboske, section head), 1254 Charles Morris St. SE, Washington Navy Yard, Washington, D.C. 20374-5040, (Air Wing After Action Reports, Ground Units Operations Journals): 3rd Marine Division, G-3 Operations, July 1966-March 67, Vietnam War CD # 27.

1st Battalion, 9th Marine Regiment, S-3 Operations Journal, February 1967, Vietnam War CD # 56.

3rd Battalion, 26th Marine Regiment, S-3 Operations Journal, October 1966-January 1970, CD # 61.

1st Marine Division, G-3 Operations, May 1969-April 1971, Vietnam War CD # 16.

1st Marine Regiment, Regimental Operations, February 1968-April 1971, Vietnam War CD# 19.

2nd Battalion, 1st Marine Regiment, S-3 Operations Journal, November 1968-April 1971, Vietnam War CD # 21.

1st Reconnaissance Battalion, July 1968-January 1970, Vietnam War CD # 11.

1st Reconnaissance Battalion, February 1970-April 1975, Vietnam War CD # 12.

2nd Battalion, 26th Marine Regiment, March 1968-February 1970, Vietnam War CD # 61.

Major Operations, 1965-1967, Vietnam CD # 64.

Marine Air Group 13, August 1965-October 1970, Vietnam War CD # 77.

Marine Air Group 16, Vietnam War CD # 77.

1st Marine Air Wing, May 1966-July 1971.

HML-167 (Comprise), November 1968-March 1970, Vietnam War CD # 84.

HML-167 (Comprise), April 1970-June 1971, Vietnam War CD # 85.

HMM-262 (Chatterbox), July 1969-September 1970, Vietnam War CD # 93.

HMM-262 (Chatterbox), October 1970-May 1971, Vietnam War CD # 94.

HMM-263 (Peachbush), August 1966-October 1969, Vietnam War CD # 94.

HMM-263 (Peachbush), October 1969-December 1970, Vietnam War CD # 95.

HMM-364 (Purple Fox), May 1970-March 1971, Vietnam War CD # 103.

HML-367 (Scarface), March 1968-April 1975, Vietnam War CD # 104.

Marine Corps Order 1650.32C, CMC establishing Leftwich Trophy for Outstanding Leadership, Biographical Sketch, dated Dec 14, 1988.

Marshall, S.L.A., *The Fields of Bamboo, The True Story of Dong Tre, Trung Luong and Hoa Hoi--Three Battles Just Beyond the South China Sea*, (New York: Dell Publishing, 1971).

Martin, Jack, "Hero Sneezes At Draft Protesters," *The Commercial Appeal*, January 23, 1966, p. 10.

Martin, Jack, "Memory Of War Invades Lazy Afternoon," *The Commercial Appeal*, February 27, 1966, p. 14.

Mason, Robert, *Chickenhawk*, (New York: The Viking Press, 1983).

McGarigle, 1stLt. J.C., HMM-263 Peachbush, Aircraft Safety Officer (ASO), Preliminary Report of Aircraft Accident occurring 18Nov70 at 1650 involving CH-46D, 154837, HMM-263, names withheld pending investigation, teletype message sent to 22 command authorities on November 18, 1970, "UNK AAR" (Notation on page "DEA, FMFPAC").

McGarigle, 1stLt. J.C., HMM-263 Peachbush, Aircraft Safety Officer (ASO), Supplemental After Action Report, 19Nov70, at 0934Z indicates crash site found, helicopter crashed and exploded from unknown causes at 1900 feet above ground level, "DEA SUPP AAR" appears on teletype message sent to 22 command authorities.

McGarigle, 1stLt. J.C., HMM-263 Peachbush, Aircraft Safety Officer (ASO), Supplemental After Action Report of 22Nov 70 air crash, teletype message listing 10 1st Recon Battalion Marines KIA and 5 Peachbush crewmen KIA, "DEA SUPP ARR" appears on page, was sent out to 21 command authorities at 0449 November 22, 1970.

McVey, Capt. LaVoy Don, "Recon Marine Records 100th Parachute Jump," *Scout*, Camp Pendleton newspaper.

McVey, Capt. LaVoy Don, letter from USMC, 3/24, 4th Marine Division, Topeka, Kansas, reporting McVey's MIA status as of 8:30 p.m. March 2, 1970, dated March 5, 1970.

McVey, Capt. LaVoy Don, letter from USMC, 3/24, 4th Division, Topeka, Kansas, 1stSgt B.R. Armer informing Mildred McVey Holmes her son's status change, MIA to deceased, March 12, 1970.

McVey, Capt. LaVoy Don, Memorial Service program, service at Smokey Point, Washington, March 1, 2003.

*Memphis Press-Scimitar,* Memphis, Tennessee, "A Hero Is Laid Respectfully to Rest," November 28, 1970.

*Memphis Press-Scimitar,* Memphis, Tennessee, "DAV to Honor Marine Colonel," May 18,1973.

*Memphis Press-Scimitar*, Memphis, Tennessee, "Lt.Col. Leftwich Dies in Vietnam," November 19, 1970.

*Memphis Press-Scimitar,* Memphis, Tennessee, "Monument to Marine Hero To Be Dedicated Sunday," November 5, 1971.

*Memphis Press-Scimitar,* Memphis, Tennessee, "Park Will Be Named For Lt.Col. Leftwich," November 21, 1970.

*Memphis Press-Scimitar,* Memphis, Tennessee, "Perot, Military Officials Pay Tribute to Leftwich," November 27, 1970.

*Memphis Press-Scimitar*, Memphis, Tennessee, "Ship Commission Honors Memphian," August 25, 1978.

*Memphis Press-Scimitar*, Memphis, Tennessee, "Ship Is Named For Memphian," May 26, 1978.

Miles, William J., "Picture Comforts Family--He Won't Be Disfigured," *The Commercial Appeal,* March 12, 1965, p. 1, 2.

Mitchell, LeeAnn, Director of Marketing and Communications, Marine Corps Association, Quantico, Virginia.

Moore, Lt.Gen. Harold G., USA (Ret.) and Galloway, Joseph L., *We Were Soldiers Once...And Young, Ia Drang--The Battle That Changed the War in Vietnam,* (New York: HarperTorch, 1992).

Morgan, Kay and Robbins, Jerry L., Perot, Military Officials Pay Tribute to Leftwich," *Memphis Press-Scimitar*, November 27, 1970, pp 1, 4.

Murphy, Jeremiah, "Colonel killed...a day in Da Nang Recalled," newspaper unknown, published sometime in November, 1970, clipping provided by Bill Leftwich III.

National Personnel Records Center, Military Personnel Records, 9700 Page Avenue, St. Louis, Missouri 63132-5100.

Naval Aviation History Department, CH-46D, MIR, 18Nov1970, Mark Evans gathered information on helicopter crash requested by Fred Allison, Gen. William L. "Spider" Nyland, Assistant CMC, (Ret.).

Naval Aviation Training & Operations Procedures Standardization, (NATOPS), manual.

NavSource Online: Destroyer Photo Archive, *DD-984 USS Leftwich* website: http://www.navsource.org/archives/05/984

Navy, Department of, USN Lt.Cmdr. E. A. Miller, Judge Advocate General's Corps, Washington D.C., letter dated April 25, 2002 indicating no JAG investigation on CH-46D, Bureau Number 154837, which occurred on November 18, 1970.

Navy, Department of, Headquarters USMC, Washington Navy Yard, re. Lt.Col. Wm. G. Leftwich Jr.: biography, Navy Cross citation, Silver Star citation, press release for Vietnamese Cross of Gallantry with Palm for March 9, 1965. Information provided in an information packet, November 18, 1992.

*NAVY TIMES*, "New Spruance-Class Destroyer To Honor Leftwich," May 8, 1978.

Nitze, Secretary of the Navy Paul H., Navy Cross citation for "extraordinary heroism" exhibited on March 9, 1965 at Hoai An in leading his Vietnamese Marine Brigade in an assault on a hill above the ville and calling in airstrikes after being wounded by a VC machine gun, citation dated January 24, 1966.

Nolan, Lewis, "Marine Hero Is Killed In Vietnam Action," *The Commercial Appeal*, November 19, 1970.

Norton, Maj. Bruce H., USMC (Ret) and Jacques, Sgt.Maj. Maurice, USMC (Ret.*), Sergeant Major: The Biography of Sergeant Major Maurice J. Jacques, USMC*, (New York: Ivy Books, 1995).

Page, Tim and John Pimlott, *Nam, The Vietnam Experience 1965-75*, (London, England: Orbis Publishing Ltd., 1988).

Porteous, Clark, staff writer, "Boys Learn Daddy's a Hero: Leftwich Kept Going Despite a Hit in Face," *Memphis Press-Scimitar*, November 1965.

*Post and Courier, The,* Charleston, South Carolina, "Grinalds to lead Citadel," Sybil Fix, staff writer, January 6, 1997.

*Professional Knowledge, Gained From Operational Experience in Vietnam*, NAVMC 2614, 1965-1966, Department of the Navy, Headquarters USMC, Washington, D.C. 20380, February 24, 1967.

Pyle, Richard and Faas, Horst, *Lost Over Laos, A True Story of Tragedy, Mystery, and Friendship*, Foreword by David Halberstam, (Cambridge, Massachusetts: Da Capo Press, 2003).

Records Service Section, MMSB-10, "Unit Diaries," Headquarters, USMC, 2008 Elliot Road, Suite 202, Quantico, Virginia 22134-6001.

Rupp, Chaplain Lloyd, "Leftwich trophy revisited, *Jet Stream*, Marine Corps Air Station, Beaufort, South Carolina, VOL. XXII, No. 37, September 12, 1980.

Schwarzkopf, Gen. H. Norman and written with Peter Petre, *General H. Norman Schwarzkopf, The Autobiography, It Doesn't Take A Hero*, (New York: Bantam Book, October 1992).

*The Scout,* MCB Camp Pendleton newspaper, "Street Named for 2nd Lt.," (photos) for Al Nelson at Camp Los Flores, November 26, 1986.

*2nd Battalion, 1st Marines, DANANG VIETNAM 1970*, Cruise Book, Camp Lauer, RVN, published in August 1970, picturing 2/1's officers and enlisted, billets held, history of 2/1 and Lt.Col. Leftwich in front of May-June 4, 1970 VC/NVA versus Marines AO statistic's board.

Shulimson, Jack and Johnson, Major Charles M., USMC, *U.S. MARINES IN VIETNAM, The Landing and the Buildup,1965*, (Washington, D.C.: History and Museums Division Headquarters, U.S. Marine Corps, 1974).

*The Sidney Argus-Herald*, Sidney, Iowa, "Lt. A.D. Benson Was Killed In Vietnam Battle July 6," July 10, 1969, p. 1. News clipping provided by Ellen Longman.

*The Sidney Argus-Herald*, Sidney, Iowa, "Military Rites Here Tuesday For Marine Lt. A.D. Benson," July 24, 1969, p. 1. News clipping provided by Lynn Benson.

Simmons, Brig.Gen. Edwin H., "Marine Corps Operations in Vietnam, 1965-1966," *THE MARINES IN VIETNAM, 1954-1973, An Anthology and Annotated Bibliography*, (Washington, D.C.: History and Museums Division Headquarters, U.S. Marine Corps, 1974).

Skibbe, 2ndLt. David W., "Marine's Parents Accept Award," (Des Plaines, Illinois) *Herald, The,* October 8, 1970, p. 1.

Skibbe, Jeff, comment about his cousin, David Skibbe, KIA, Vietnam, March 2, 1970, University of Illinois Alumni Association website, uiaa.org/urbana/illinoisalumni/utx0204b.html

Skibbe, Mr. & Mrs. Wm. C., letter to Mrs. Mildred (McVey) Holmes, May 17, 1970.

Skibbe, Mr. & Mrs. Wm. C., a copy of a laminated photo of their son 2ndLt. David W. Skibbe with his fiancée held by a Viet Cong deputy commander that was turned over to the Joint Task Force-Full Accounting in 1991 looking for his remains in the Que Son Mountains of Vietnam after he was declared MIA in 1970.

Solis, Gary D., *Son Thang, An American War Crime*, (Annapolis, Maryland: Naval Institute Press, 1997).

Steverson, William, "USS Leftwich Will Honor Hero," *The Commercial Appeal*, May 14, 1978.

Summers Jr., Col. Harry G., *Vietnam War Almanac*, (Novato, California: Presidio Press, 1985).

*Sun Tzu's Art of War, The Modern Chinese Interpretation*, by Gen. Tao Hanzhang, translated by Yuan Shibing, (New York: Sterling Publishing Company, Inc., 1990),

Tate, Don, Scripps-Howard staff writer, "Lt.Col. Leftwich Died Against Cloud-Shrouded Hill 864," *Memphis Press-Scimitar*, December 3, 1970.

*Tennessean, The*, obituary for Colonel William Covington Drumright, December 7, 2003, Jeff Whitaker, E-Commerce Specialist.

Thomas, Gen. Gerald C., USMC (Ret.), Heinl Jr., Col. Robert D., USMC (Ret.), Ageton, Rear Admiral Arthur A., U.S. Navy (Ret.), *The Marine Officer's Guide*, (Annapolis, Maryland: United States Naval Institute, 1967 3rd Edition).

Thomas, William, "Death of war hero's mother recalls bravery," *The Commercial Appeal*, June 16, 1992.

*TIME* magazine, "The Heroes," October 22, 1965, p. 39A.

*TIME* magazine, "On the Street Without Joy," March 3, 1967, p. 31.

Trujillo, U.S. Army Capt. Ben, made available his research into the death of his cousin 1stLt. Joe Montoya, Hotel Co., 2/1, September 20, 1970, that included background information and photo, Record of Service, general information from the National Personnel Records Center in St. Louis, Missouri and correspondence from Doc Ron Neff of Hotel, 2/1 about the boobytrap that took the officer's life.

Tsouras, Peter G., *Warrior's Words, A Quotation Book*, (London, England: Arms and Armour Press, 1992).

Tuohy, William, "The Relief of Duc Co," *Newsweek*, August 23, 1965.

*Unit Leaders Personal Response Handbook*, NAVMC 2616, Department of the Navy, Headquarters U.S. Marine Corps, Washington, D.C. 20380, October 12, 1967.

U.S. Library of Congress, Charmisa Redmond Nash, Photoduplication Service, Reference Section, 101 Independence Ave., SE, Washington, D.C. 20540-4570. JTF-FA, POW/MIA database, microfiche archives, 2ndLt. David Skibbe--Case #2051/Capt. LaVoy Don McVey--Case #1565.

USMC ISO photo by SSgt. Ed Grantham of Capt. James Curd with Dr. Bernard B. Fall, dated February 21, 1967, photo provided by Khe Sanh Marine Larry Larsen.

USMC/Combat Helicopter Association, John D. "J.D." Barber, president, Popasmoke, website: popasmoke.org

United States Naval Academy, Jane H. Price, Assistant Archives, William W. Jeffries Memorial Archives, 589 McNair Road, Annapolis, Maryland 21402-5033. Enclosures in information packet dated March 11, 1993 on Lt.Col. (Midshipman) Wm. G. Leftwich Jr.: *'53 Lucky Bag*, annual pages; Registrar's records; page from the Annual Register of the USNA; Public Information release and two newspaper articles; three biographical sketches; *Shipmate* articles written by Lt.Col. Leftwich, November 1966, November 1968 and November 1970; *Shipmate* article July-August, 1975 regarding memorial to the memory of those killed or missing-in-action in Vietnam.

United States Naval Academy, Vice Admiral C.T. Joy, USN, USNA superintendent, Special Order No. 70-53, letters of commendation to 15 1953 USNA graduates that includes William Groom Leftwich, Jr., June 1, 1953.

United States Naval Academy, Vice Admiral C.T. Joy, USN, USNA superintendent, Special Order No. 128-52, letters of commendation to six USNA midshipmen including William Groom Leftwich Jr., who, at the end of the academic year contributed most by their officer-like qualities and positive character to the development of military spirit and loyalty within the Regiment, October 6, 1952.

*USS Leftwich, DD-984,* United States Ship Commissioning Ceremony book, contains vital ship statistics and information on the ship's crew, Pascagoula, Mississippi, August 25, 1979.

Vietnam Helicopter Pilots Association, website: http://www.vhpa.org/

*Vietnam Veterans Memorial Directory of Names*, Vietnam Veterans Memorial Fund Inc., Washington, D.C., Ninth printing, May 1991.

*Washington Post, The,* Washington, D.C., "Crash Fatal To Officer In Vietnam," November 24, 1970.

Wayne State College (Wayne, Nebraska) Hall of Fame Inductions, October 11, 1980, news release, A.D. Benson.

West, LCpl. Ed, author of *Gopher Broke: The Story of 'Blood, Sweat & Tears' And the Marines of 3rd Platoon, Alpha Co., 1/1.*

*Western Times*, Sharon Springs, Kansas, "Lt. Richard Goudy Shot Down in Viet Nam," August 13, 1965, p. 1.

*Western Times*, Sharon Springs, Kansas, "No Word From Missing Flier," August 19, 1965, p. 1.

*Western Times*, Sharon Springs, Kansas, "Capt. Richard Goudy Viet Nam Casualty," November 18, 1965, p. 1.

Westmoreland, Gen. William C., *A Soldier Reports*. (New York: Doubleday, 1976).

Wilcox, Col. E.A., 1st Marine Regiment CO, upon being replaced by Col. Paul X. Kelley as new CO submitted an "Interim Letter" to be included in Lt.Col. William G. Leftwich Jr.'s Fitness Report recommending an end of tour award for all his accomplishments and immediate impact on 2/1 between May 16-June 28 while under Col. Wilcox's command, letter dated, June 29, 1970.

# Glossary

**AAR:** After Action Report, Marine Air Wing's squadrons' forms filled out by pilots listing the day's activities, i.e., time out, time in, flight time, map coordinates, crew members, medevac, supply, troop transport, Recon extract or insert, ammo expended, highlights, etc.

**AARUGHA!:** typically the guttural sound of approval or enthusiasm a WW II or Vietnam-era Marine made. Marine Raiders (forerunner of Recon Marines) picked the word up from the sound a submarine horn made following the order to "DIVE! DIVE!" in WW II as they were being taken to and from attacks on Japanese-held islands in the Pacific

**AK-47:** VC/NVA rifle, with a curved magazine holding 30 7.62mm rounds, made by the Russian Mikhail Timofeevich Kalashnikov and is named in his honor, the Kalashnikov AK-47 can be fired as an automatic rifle with an effective range of 400 meters

**AO:** double meaning, area of observation as well as aerial observer assigned to the backseat of an OV-10A fixed wing Bronco

**arc light:** B-52 mission out of Thailand or Guam involving the dropping of up to 96 500-lb. high explosive bombs on enemy troops

**Arizona Territory:** enemy badlands hostile to Marines southwest of Da Nang

**ARVN:** Army of the Republic of Vietnam soldier

**autorotate:** helicopters that lose power in flight, the pilot has some control over the still turning rotorblades to land and "autorotate" to the ground for an abrupt, bruising landing

**AWOL:** Absent Without Leave.

**Battalion Rear:** any battalion's rear area, i.e., 2/1's compound also known as Camp Lauer

**boobytrap:** any explosive or injury-causing contraption set by the enemy

**boot:** new guy to a duty station, comes from a Marine's initial beginnings at boot camp

**boot camp:** recruit training facility that in 1970 was 8 weeks of physical and mental preparation for war Marine Corps style at San Diego, California or Parris Island, South Carolina

**bouncing betty mine:** boobytrap that is boosted up to waist level before primary charge explodes

**"bullet bouncer":** ceramic vest worn by pilots in cockpit as upper body armor

**bush, the; also boondocks and boonies:** located outside the safety of any base surrounded by concertina wire in Vietnam

**C-4:** plastique explosives, would only explode if set off with a blasting cap or other explosive, also small amounts could be pinched off to be used as a heat tab and lit with a match to warm up water or food in the bush

**C-rats:** canned food rations provided to the bush Marines in the field

**CG:** commanding general

**Charlie:** one of many nom de plumes for the South Vietnam Communist guerrillas opposing the Republic of Vietnam government, also known as Mr. Charles, Victor Charlie, VC, Viet Cong, dink and gook

**chicom:** Chinese Communist grenade

**Chieu Hoi (Open Arms Program):** South Vietnamese amnesty program designed to get enemy troops to defect for a cash money bonus, better living conditions, salary and track down and capture or kill their former comrades

**"chopping the collective":** helicopter term for changing the angle of the rotorblades and dropping to the deck posthaste

**"chopping firewood":** what a crew chief tells his helicopter pilot when the rotorblades begin chopping the tops off trees to get into a landing zone (LZ)

**CIDG:** Civilian Irregular Defense Group, Montagnard, Chinese Nungs and multi-national mercenaries working with U.S. Army Special Forces in Vietnam

**CIT:** Counterintelligence Team, interrogated prisoners

**click:** taken from the 1,000 meter "click" on the range adjustment of an artillery piece, also "klick" for kilometer

**CO:** commanding officer

**Cobra:** sleek Marine escort gunship AH-1G helicopter, Scarface HML-367 Squadron
**COC:** Command Operations Center, typically an underground bunker where all combat operations in respective AOs are conducted by means of large banks of radios on various frequencies to all units in those commands and the nerve center enemy forces try to destroy
**Da Nang Anti-Infiltration Barrier:** a seismic detection and partial minefield barrier primarily above Hill 55 in the western AO from the Song Yen to near where the Ha Dong railroad bridge crosses the Song Bau Xau, 3 clicks east to west and about 100-200 meters wide. Parts of the barrier were partially constructed around Da Nang to stop enemy infiltration
**DASC:** Direct Air Support Center
**deck:** ground
**Doc:** See Navy Corpsman
**Dodge City:** notoriously bad area below Hill 55 southwest of Da Nang to An Hoa
**DOA:** died on arrival
**DOW:** died of wounds
**dung lai:** to halt, to come to a halt
**ECP:** Enlisted Commissioning Program, enlisted Marines selected to become Marine officers
**EOD:** Explosive Ordnance Device team
**1st Med:** trauma casualties were medevacked to 1st Medical Battalion Hospital in Da Nang, also called Charley Med by helicopter pilots
**golf ball grenade:** a V40 golf ball-sized mini-fragmentation grenade, the grenade was lethal up 5 meters and dangerous up to 300 meters, weighed 4.8 oz. with a 4 second delay
**grease gun:** Swedish-K submachine gun fires .45 caliber bullets and looks like a "grease gun"
**HE:** high explosives
**hell hole:** a 34-inch square hatch in the middle of the CH-46 Sea Knight for emergency exit or extracts of Marines by cable hoist or rappelling down ropes
**high speed trail:** well-traveled enemy path wide enough for men to pass or for carts
**Highway 1:** the major highway artery running from Saigon to Hanoi, also called Route 1, National Highway 1
**Hill:** topographical high points in Vietnam designated in meters on maps, i. e. Hill 800
**Hill 55:** Nui Dat Son, was a large complex of various ARVN and American military units southwest of Da Nang running operations in the Arizona Territory and nearby mountains
**Ho Chi Minh:** a fervent nationalist who was the founding father of North Vietnam as a Communist nation, died in 1969 before he could see his vision of two Vietnams become one in 1975
**hot LZ:** helicopter term to indicate a landing zone for medevac or troop removal is under fire by the enemy, flipside is cold LZ, no enemy fire
**Huey:** Bell UH-1E helicopter utilized as gunship escorts, command and control and medevacs in a pinch. Marine HML-167 Comprise and occasional U.S. Army or Vietnamese Hueys assisted us
**Huskie:** tracked vehicle for transporting troops
**I Corps:** the northernmost combat zone in Vietnam that ran from the DMZ to just below Da Nang, 10,000 square miles where Intelligence estimated 78,000 enemy troops operated, borders Laos to the west and North Vietnam to the north
**II Corps:** Central Highlands combat zone, borders Laos to the west
**III Corps:** Lowlands combat zone in and around Saigon, borders Cambodia to the west
**IV Corps:** Mekong Delta combat zone below Saigon, borders Cambodia to the west
**ICU:** Intensive Care Unit, trauma center at 1st Medical Battalion Hospital in Da Nang
**illume:** illumination fired by individual pop flare, mortars, artillery or dropped from aircraft
**ITT:** 3rd Interrogation/Translator Team, worked closely with CIT
**JTF-FA:** Joint Task Force-Full Accounting locates and identifies bodies of fallen American fighting men on distant shores from all wars
**JPAC:** Joint POW/MIA Accounting Command, replaces JTF-FA and is headquartered at Hickam Air Force Base in Honolulu, Hawaii
**KIA:** killed-in-action
**Kingfisher:** a quick-reaction heliborne assault team consisting of three Sea Knights containing three Marine squads, four Cobra gunships, an OV-10 Bronco, a Huey command and control

lead aircraft and sometimes a Loach to flush out targets of opportunity on the ground (enemy troops in the open)

**Kit Carson Scout:** former Viet Cong crossing over to South Vietnamese side to work with the Marines as scouts, interpreters and intelligence agents

**ladder:** flexible 120-foot long wire and aluminum ladder rolled up inside a Sea Knight helicopter at the back ramp and attached underneath the helicopter, thrown out to be thrown out to waiting Recon team in the bush for quick snap link extraction

**loach:** Hughes OH-6A, light helicopter

**M-14:** Marine rifle used in Vietnam until around 1968, fires 7.62 round

**M-16:** Marine rifle replaced the M-14 around March 1967, lightweight model, fires 5.62 round

**M-60:** machine gun fires 7.62 rounds linked together

**M-79, also called blooper:** 40mm grenade launcher

**malaria pill (chloroquine pill, M11):** taken once a month to prevent malaria carried by mosquitoes, caused severe cases of short term diarrhea immediately after taking

**Marble Mountain:** 105 meter marble monolith rising out of the flat coastal plain, four smaller rock formations are to the west and southwest

**MMAF:** Marble Mountain Air Facility, air support for the 1st Marine Division and other allied forces flew out of MMAF

**Marine:** an American warrior who is feared by United States' enemies around the globe because a Marine is only called into action when this country means to accomplish a military solution, endowed with the fighting spirit of past Marine legends, he strives to make his own notable history in his time (also, Leatherneck, grunt, Jarhead, Gyrene, infantryman)

**medevacs:** the rapid removal of injured Marines from the field by helicopters. Categories of urgency included permanent routine (KIA), routine, priority and emergency

**MSF:** Mike Strike Force, Montagnard, Chinese Nungs and multi-national mercenaries working with U.S. Special Forces in Vietnam

**mortars:** varying sizes fire high explosive rounds and illumination in support of their respective units

**MOS:** military occupational specialty, what field of endeavor Marines were trained to have expertise in

**NATOPS:** Naval Aviation Training & Operations Procedures Standardization manual

**Navy Corpsman:** medical personnel attached to Marine bush units, stabilizes wounded Marines for medevac and was responsible for saving untold Marine lives

**NCO:** non-commissioned officer, enlisted Marine sergeant or corporal

**95th Evac:** U.S. Army's 95th Medical Evacuation Hospital in Da Nang handled the less serious casualties in I Corps

**Nui:** a Vietnamese word for "mountain," as in Nui Kim Son

**NVA:** North Vietnamese Army soldier, also referred to as dink and gook

**0311:** Marine enlisted infantry military occupation specialty (MOS)

**0301 (boot officer)/0302 (anointed as experienced infantry officer):** the numeral codes for the infantry-designated officers' MOS

**Old Battalion Rear:** also called Cau Ha Combat Base, near ROK border, 2/1's Battalion Rear until January 1970

**"painted faces":** term used by VC/NVA to describe the camouflaged face-painted Recon Marines

**rappelling rope:** Recon teams used the 120-foot rope to rappel out of a Sea Knight from the back ramp, side door and hell hole to the ground for a quick insert in Indian Territory as the aircraft hovered

**Patrol Debrief:** 1st Recon report filled out after a Recon team returns from a patrol in the boonies

**Patrol Leader: a** Recon Marine, either a bush-savvy enlisted man or an officer, who is in charge of a patrol sent to the bush to gather intelligence, call in supporting arms and/or ambush enemy troops

**PAVN:** People's Army of Vietnam, another term for North Vietnamese Army

**platoon commander, also platoon leader or actual:** a lieutenant in most cases but can be a staff sergeant who is in command of a bush platoon, a key leadership position and is expected to coordinate the actions of the men under his command as well as direct supporting arms--artillery, mortars, tanks, aircraft, etc.

**PPB:** Platoon Patrol Base is the perimeter each platoon sets up in the bush to operate ambushes and patrols out of to search for and destroy the enemy

**platoon sergeant:** second-in-command in a bush platoon, usually a staff sergeant with bush experience working on his second tour

**"plumber, a":** Air Wing term for a pilot who knew how to technically fly his aircraft but had difficulty improvising in stressful situations

**Punji sticks:** sharpened sticks in a hole, boobytrap

**R&R:** rest and recuperation, each Marine in-country earns a trip to a vacation area in the South China Sea or Pacific area after 6 months for enlisted and 3 months for officers (officers generally rotated to Okinawa after 6 months thus 3 months was the midway point of their tour)

**Ready Room:** Sea Knight helicopter pilots on-call at MMAF's Ready Room wait for medevac or Recon emergency extract requests from bush Marines being overwhelmed by superior enemy forces or due to dire injuries needing immediate medical attention

**"Redeye":** a surveillance plane with nighttime infrared capabilities

**Rockpile, The:** 10 clicks south of the DMZ, 750-foot mountain that dominated the surrounding terrain where three river valleys converged, Marine units rotated holding this ground to prevent NVA infiltration into I Corps

**ROKMC:** Republic of Korea Marine Corps

**RPG:** rocket-propelled grenade, enemy shoulder held rocket launcher, fires B-40 rocket

**SAR:** search and rescue, helicopters fly SARs looking for individuals or downed aircraft

**Seahorse:** UH-34 transport helicopter used in the early part of the Vietnam War, looked like a large banana

**Sea Knight:** CH-46D helicopter used as transportation, resupply, medevacs and inserts and extracts of Recon units, had three 30-foot rotorblades fore and aft, 114 feet in length, that was the workhorse helicopter in Vietnam

**Sea Stallion:** CH-53D, large transport helicopter with a much higher capacity load limit than CH-46D

**search and destroy:** a term deemed "politically incorrect" to search out and kill or capture the enemy

**short:** refers to the amount of time a Marine has left in-country closing in on the end of his 13-month tour

**60mm:** Marine mortar tube or round

**61mm:** enemy mortar tube or round

**SNCO:** staff non-commissioned officer, enlisted Marines staff sergeant and above

**SOG:** Vietnamese Studies and Observations Group, also known as Special Operations Group, worked with the South Vietnamese to kill the enemy no matter where they were located

**Song:** Vietnamese for "river"

**South China Sea:** the ocean lapping the eastern shores of North and South Vietnam

**SPIE:** 125-foot Special Patrol Insertion/Extraction strap with D-rings sewn into it 8 feet apart dropped by a hovering helicopter to a Recon team to snap onto in areas helicopters cannot land

**squad leader:** ideally a corporal in command of three fire teams, a Navy Corpsman and a radioman in a bush platoon, a competent NCO responsible for his squad in a bush platoon

**Street Without Joy (French, la rue sans joie):** a French reference to Highway 1 in French Indochina War, generally denotes the coastal area from above Hue to the DMZ, also title of Dr. Bernard B. Fall's book, *Street Without Joy*

**Starlight Scope:** the AN/TVS-2 was an expensive night vision scope that pulls light from the stars to turn night into day

**survival radio:** a small handheld radio favored by pilots in case they were shot down they had a means to communicate with overhead aircraft to effect a rescue

**TBS:** The Basic School, Marine officer training facility at Camp Barrett on the MCB Quantico, Virginia base

**TAOR:** Tactical Area of Responsibility, same as AO

**Toepopper:** a pressure boobytrap containing a shotgun shell, rifle or pistol round or a small amount of C-4 explosive that once stepped on takes off the front of a foot

**USMA:** United States Military Academy at West Point, New York

**USNA:** United States Military Academy at Annapolis, Maryland

**VC:** Viet Cong, means Vietnamese Communist, South Vietnamese guerrillas working against the South Vietnamese government and SEATO allies

**VC/NVA:** enemy soldier cannot be identified as either Viet Cong or North Vietnamese so both references are used to identify him or her

**ville:** village containing Vietnamese peasants

**XO:** executive officer of a Marine unit, the second Marine officer in command

**WestPac:** Western Pacific, generally the word on newly issued orders meant "Vietnam"

**WIA:** wounded-in-action

**WIAE:** wounded-in-action, evacuated

**WIANE:** wounded-in-action, not evacuated

**willie peter:** artillery white phosphorous spotter round

**0/0:** Marine Air Wing term meaning zero visibility, zero ceiling due to cloud cover or fog, also called scud, goo, "being inside a marshmallow"

# Index

Some of the combat medals awarded to the Marines and Navy personnel are listed in parenthesis below. Not all the decorations earned are cited since every individual's medals could not be found due to the lack of access to the records of everyone named in *American Heroes: Grunts, Pilots & "Docs."* Abbreviations for the medals are: Medal of Honor, MOH; Navy Cross, NC; Distinguished Flying Cross, DFC; Silver Star, SS; Bronze Star, BS; Navy Commendation Medal, NCM; Navy & Marine Commendation Medal, N&MCM; Legion of Merit, LM; Purple Heart, PH; Vietnamese Cross of Gallantry, VCG; Vietnamese Honor Medal, VHM; Air Medals, AM; Distinguished Service Medal, DSM; Distinguished Service Cross, DSC; Single Mission Air Medal, SMAM; Combat Air Crew Wings, CACW; Combat Action Ribbon, CAR; Presidential Unit Citation, PUC; Meritorious Unit Citation, MUC; Navy Unit Citation, NUC; Civic Action Unit Citation, CAUC; Vietnamese MUC Civic Action Color w/Palm and Frame, VMUCCAC w/Palm and Frame; Naval Achievement Medal, NAM; Navy and Marine Corps Commendation Medal, NMCM; Army Presidential Unit Citation, APUC; Vietnam Service Medal, VSM; Defense Distinguished Service Medal, DDSM; Marine Corps Distinguished Service Medal, MCDSM; Defense Superior Service Medal, DSSM; and Medal for Distinguished Public Service, MDPS.

# Books I & II Ordering Information

To purchase extra copies of this book for yourself or to send as a gift to someone else by mail, copy the following information accompanied by a check or money order and fill in the address for whom the book is intended below and send to the address at the bottom of the page.

☐ Yes, I want ___ paperback copies of ***Book I, American Heroes: Grunts, Pilots & "Docs,"*** subtitle: ***Building "Hard Men"...U.S. Marines, Vietnam War Stories, 1966-71*** at $26.95 plus $3.95 shipping & handling per book. Total: $30.95.*
*Texas residents add sales tax of $2.22.

☐ Yes, I want ___ hardback copies of ***Book I, American Heroes: Grunts, Pilots & "Docs,"*** subtitle: ***Building "Hard Men"...U.S. Marines, Vietnam War Stories, 1966-71*** at $39.95 plus $3.95 shipping and handling per book. Total: $43.90.*
*Texas residents add sales tax of $3.30.

☐ Yes, I want ___ paperback copies of ***Book II, American Heroes: Grunts, Pilots & "Docs,"*** subtitle: ***Leathernecks Find 'em, Fix 'em, Kill 'em, Vietnam Combat Stories, 1965, '69-'70*** at $25.95 plus $3.95 shipping and handling per book. Total: $29.90.*
*Texas residents add sales tax $2.14

☐ Yes, I want ___ hardback copies of ***Book II, American Heroes: Grunts, Pilots & "Docs,"*** subtitle: ***Leathernecks Find 'em, Fix 'em, Kill 'em, Vietnam Combat Stories, 1965, '69-'70*** at $38.95 plus $3.95 shipping and handling per book. Total: $42.90.*
*Texas residents add sales tax $3.21

My check or money order for $________ is enclosed.

NAME____________________________________________
ADDRESS_________________________________________
CITY/STATE/ZIP___________________________________
PHONE (______)________________ EMAIL________________________

Please make checks or money orders payable to: **Navarro-Hill Publishing Group**

Send to: **Navarro-Hill Publishing Group**
**P.O. Box 1088**
**Longview, TX 75606**

For credit card orders go to **www.MichaelDanKellum.com**

# Author

Michael Dan Kellum served in the U.S. Marine Corps for 3½ years with a tour of duty as an infantry officer in Vietnam in 1970. He attended Stephen F. Austin State University in Nacogdoches, Texas receiving a BA degree in communications with a secondary degree in English. He has worked at Texas newspapers in Jacksonville, Longview, Rusk and Atlanta, the latter two publications, a weekly and a bi-weekly, he was managing editor and associate publisher, respectively. He has also done limited string work for *The Dallas Morning News*. He is presently a self-employed contractor which gives him time to indulge his first passion…writing and research on his favorite subject… the Marines. This is his second book. His first book in a 2-part series is titled *Book I, American Heroes: Grunts, Pilots & "Docs"* with the subtitle of *Building "Hard Men"...U.S. Marines, Vietnam War Stories, 1966-71*. His next writing project is a fictional work entitled *Cherokee Springs' Chronicles*.

CPSIA information can be obtained at www.ICGtesting.com
Printed in the USA
LVOW082212160911

246655LV00001B/2/P

9 780984 513222